Take Hold Upon the Future

Letters on Writers and Writing 1938 - 1946

William Everson and
Lawrence Clark Powell

Edited by William R. Eshelman

The Scarecrow Press, Inc.
Metuchen, N. J., & London
1994

British Library Cataloguing-in-Publication data available

Library of Congress Cataloging-in-Publication Data

Everson, William, 1912–
Take hold upon the future : letters on writers and writing by William Everson and Lawrence Clark Powell, 1938–1946 ; edited by Wm. R. Eshelman.
p. cm.
Includes index.
ISBN 0-8108-2878-2 (alk. paper)
1. Everson, William, 1912– —Correspondence. 2. Poets, American—20th century—Correspondence. 3. Powell, Lawrence Clark, 1906– —Correspondence. 4. Authors, American—20th century—Correspondence. 5. Poetry—Authorship. 6. Authorship. I. Powell, Lawrence Clark, 1906– . II. Eshelman, Wm. R., 1921– . III. Title.
PS3509.V65Z493 1994
811'.52—dc20 94-6471

Manufactured in the United States of America

Printed on acid-free paper

The title of this book is drawn from
the poem "Vices" in the volume *Roan Stallion*
by Robinson Jeffers

Powell, as a fellow at the Center for Advanced Studies at Wesleyan University, arranged for Everson to give a poetry reading in the Spring of 1968. Their close ties had been loosened when Everson became Brother Antonius in 1951, and they had not met since 1960. Powell recalled, "We must have made a sight walking across campus to the Honors College, he in a white robe and black surplice, a head taller than I and so long legged that I had to trot to keep up with him." The reading was recorded by Caedmon records. Photo by Fay Powell.

CONTENTS

FOREWORD

William Everson and I met first in 1938 at a point in our lives, he at 26, I at 32, when each needed what the other had to give. That was *Encouragement*. He was a laborer and poet, I a librarian and writer. I had received recognition for my biocritical book on Jeffers—the first to be written. Because of that and my seniority of six years, he deferred to me, at least at first until it became evident that we were coequals in our perceptions and judgments of literature.

From its tentative beginning our correspondence took off and remained aloft for a decade, until his conversion to Roman Catholicism ended an uninhibited exchange of personal confidences. There was never a lasting break, although the fire had gone out. When we met at Wesleyan in 1968, where I had booked a poetry reading for him, it was our first meeting in eight years. I saw him off on a commuter flight from the New Haven airport. We sat in the sun awaiting his plane to New York and agreed it was good to be in touch again.

During my first six years at UCLA, when I had a worm's eye view of the university library I knew in my bones I was destined eventually to head, his belief was central to my creative survival. I intended to be more than a housekeeping librarian, more than a critic and reviewer. Not until the late 1940s did I find my true voice as an essayist, and in 1944 I became the head librarian. My vision was of a great library of and for a great city. By the time I retired from UCLA in 1966, the vision had been realized.

In this later age when electronics have relieved librarians of housekeeping routines, those potentially bookish servants are no longer seen as guides to culture, urban or academic. They can be vital links between scholars, writers, and readers. In their first visits to me at the UCLA library, Everson and Henry Miller were seeking unusual literary material. I proved as helpful to them as they were later to me. In writing what was not published until 1977 as *The Blue Train,* those two were great encouragers.

The correspondence published here reveals Everson's reaction to my public and private lives, while my response was to find publication for his now classic volume, *San Joaquin*. Both Everson and Miller recognized my conflicting needs as librarian and writer. They were not alone. Ward Ritchie, Gordon Newell, Hal Bieler, and M.F.K. Fisher also perceived my twin selves, a controlled schizophrenia.

My hope is that these letters will offer encouragement to young artists whatever their medium of work. Now that Everson and I are old men, let what we wrote as young men to each other speak to those who are now as once we were.

Such are my thoughts in old age upon reading these letters of long ago. Even though distance separates Everson and me, the passage of time does not. To him who inhabits the Californian coast, I send heartfelt greetings from the Sonoran desert.

—Lawrence Clark Powell
Tucson
Bajada of the
Santa Catalinas

INTRODUCTION

For the aged poet, confrontation with his correspondence of fifty years back does not betoken an occasion of euphoric retrospection. After all, it was his verse that he perfected. Discounting his juvenilia and allowing for the faults tolerable in all creativity, he fiercely defends the substance of his achievement, defying the imputation of any critic to the contrary. In his view, a poet is defined by the unmistakable signature of God: the touch of genius, and very little else. Approaching his demise, in his mind's eye he sees himself ensconced in his setting, his home and his region, surrounded by his books, his faithful wife and grown children by his bedside, with his true friends gathered at its foot. Sustained by Yeats' observation that as the saint perfects his life so does the poet perfect his art, he awaits with folded hands the recognition of his Maker.

But correspondence is a riddle. In his poetry he sought a conversion from the lower to the upper octaves of consciousness, evoking a vision of an Absolute beyond the reaches of the mind. But the words he tossed off in letters were gauged to no such purpose. The letter is primarily an agent of communication, it serves an immediacy no poetry can be expected to match. But by the same token, its tendency is toward facile trivialization. The care a poem requires would daunt the resourcefulness of the most gung-ho correspondent, for whom language is provisional, and revision is forgone, or at least minimized.

There are rare exceptions like D.H. Lawrence, a virtuoso of immediacy, whose first drafts and published correspondence seem to presuppose a common denominator, eliminating the gross distinction in genre. The blaze, the vibration of immediacy, breaks out of the naked language, envelops the syntax and, in effect, dissolves the differences in mode. But the more universal practice emphasizes the formal divergence in aesthetic strategy, and the perfectionist poet remains restive under the handicap of epistolary discourse.

I am no exception. Although I value immediacy in verse as much as anyone, I confess that when I see my correspondence reproduced in print, which cannot approximate the facility of the pen, much less the tonalization of the spoken word, it sets my teeth on edge. Then I can understand why Robinson Jeffers is said to have taken the trouble to rewrite his correspondence at least once. But in practice this makes for a certain stiffness, a rather stilted epistolary style, as if one were to say only how one ought to feel, rather than how one does in fact feel.

I was pleasantly surprised, then, upon undertaking this publication of my early correspondence with Lawrence Clark Powell. I expected the inevitable youthful gaucheries would be there and I braced myself for them, but they proved not to be as painful as I feared. I had discovered my vocation as a poet of mood in the fall of 1934, but soon found it incumbent upon me to become a poet of ideas as well, which, since I had none of my own, I acquired from Jeffers, my fabled hero. It was my espousal of him that led to my contact with Powell, who, for his doctorate at the University of Dijon in France, had written the first full-length study of the California poet. Soon we branched out into other interests, but we always returned to the abiding focus—the exigency of the vocation of the writer, and the factors that prejudice it, not the least of which is the abnormal prolongation of adolescence.

For the poet's bent is founded on an Oedipal fixation that binds him ineluctably to the maternal image buried in his soul, as protectress and nurturer as well as, later on, queen of the libido; a prolongation that drenches and steeps his psyche in the charismatic efflux of the eternal feminine, the profound psychic chemistry that combusts into genius through a kind of blazing entelechy. We see it in the ecstatic faces of mothers beholding the first son to open the womb: it is revelation, beatitude incarnate. The only other event to rival it in the life of a woman is the orgasmic night of defloration, the ecstasy that ushers in conception, the joy for which she was made. Defloration and parturition, twin flaming angelic acts, defining the mystery of the life of the womb. The conceptive moment is intense but brief, whereas the birth night lives on in the son, thrusting its weight through childhood and adolescence, to arrive at the threshold of adulthood, when he finds his mate and severs at last the psychic umbilical cord, to embrace his patriarchal heritage and in responsibility gain his freedom.

But not the poet. For him responsibility (response-ability) surges through the umbilical cord, feeds his soul. His radical adhesion to the maternal imago renders him out of phase with his time and his culture, his creative angle of vision enabling him to see what others cannot, but by virtue of his eccentricity he is pronounced effeminate, disdained and dismissed: a pariah. Thus, all too often, in spite of his gifts, he stands in jeopardy of his native masculine equipoise and drifts into wretchedness: alcoholism, drug addiction, as well as sexual malaise, and aesthetically into uncouth gaucheries and stultifying banality.

But I digress. Powell and I did not attempt to unlock the Pandora's box of the unconscious with the key of depth psychology. That would come later. I bring it up now because that's what I was going through. And Powell's letters were helping me hold to the course. For even banality can be freshly employed, as every comedian knows, and Powell was good at it. In his letters, enthusiasm elevates cliché to aphoristic jocularity, an unforced gaiety, whereas in mine it limps like a gimp. In his own wild youth, Powell acquired an ambient worldliness that was more a survivor's gambit than an innate disposition. But this has stood him in good stead socially throughout his distinguished career, as his gently nudging me into a semblance of literary sophistication herein attests.

But beneath his gaiety and my gimp a current of invigorating energy was taking shape, making for a sinuous dialogue between two minds that swam and sustained each other through the troubled waters of literary creation. Moreover, this became a rite of passage to the mystery of vocation, the night sea journey whose only light is the promise of the dawn, as the heart's travail foreshadows the morning of the mind in the hemisphere of the soul.

For despite the presence of superficial small talk there is obviously in play here an element that cuts beneath the surface dialogue and gives pause: a certitude that fosters an eagerness and disposes the energies in a continuity of quest. It veils the unconscious earnestness that denotes a true relationship. Powell recognized it from the beginning and coaxed it into being, but I had to do some growing up before I could grasp its truth. Then came the War with its fearful toll of lost love and marital disintegration. Through those terrible four years Powell sustained me, and at war's end I emerged a changed man.

What, then, do we have here? In the most sanguinary surmise I hardly dare spell it out. But reading these letters from so long ago, after the distancing of multiple decades has cast them in a tempering light, I suggest, in all humility, that Powell and I, without conscious plan and all unbeknownst to our normative awareness, through fidelity and candor, have touched the nerve of an American archetype. I am left feeling a little like Lewis and Clark, who set out to discover a trade route to China, but instead achieved the opening of the American West. In any case, however one chooses to weigh the odds, candor and faith are the saving graces of this story—making fifty years as one.

—William Everson
Autumn Equinox, 1990
Kingfisher Flat
Davenport, California

EDITOR'S NOTE

This publication is an intimate document that records the interaction between two very different writers who shared tastes in both poetry and prose. A high regard for the work of Robinson Jeffers drew them together at the outset—Everson's early poetry shows the influence of the master in attitude and outlook; Powell's doctoral dissertation was written on Jeffers and his poetry. But there were other shared enthusiasms: Baudelaire, Rilke, Whitman, Archibald MacLeish, D.H. Lawrence, Joyce, Henry Miller, and B. Traven, to name a few. Each man served as literary mentor to the other as they strove to perfect "the craft so long to lerne."

The fertile San Joaquin valley sustained them both. Everson worked its farms and fields, its vineyards and canneries; Powell made it the centerpiece of many of his essays and columns. Music, too, soothed and invigorated them. Powell had childhood music lessons and played in dance bands; Everson's introduction to music was via the school orchestra and his father's professional concert band. Both soon came to classical music, and this series of letters is replete with their shared insights and discoveries. Those who had concluded that Bill was too solemn were due for a revelation when the record on the phonograph was by Muggsy Spanier, Bessie Smith, or Bunk Johnson. The tall, Lincolnesque Everson sat punctuating the air with a forefinger, transformed into a full participant in the jazz. And when Powell was at the piano, one forgot his diminutive stature as the music rolled.

And then there was printing. Everson avoided his father's job-printing shop when a youth, but took it up while interned in a camp for conscientious objectors at Waldport, Oregon. He was a founding member of The Untide Press there, one of the activities of The Fine Arts group which he directed. After World War II he bought a handpress in order to produce his poetry. Much later, after leaving the Dominican Order, where he had been a lay brother, he established the Lime Kiln Press at the University of California at Santa Cruz.

Powell, active in the printing circles of southern California, was an early member of the Rounce and Coffin Club, made up of printers, booksellers, and librarians, which sponsored the annual Western Books exhibitions. In 1941 he was tapped for the Zamorano Club, an exclusive group of book lovers. Most notably, he directed UCLA's William Andrews Clark Memorial Library for more than two decades, building its good collection of fine printing into an outstanding one by his nurture and knowledge.

The two met in 1938, when this correspondence begins. In December 1943 I joined Everson at the Civilian Public Service Camp #56 in Waldport, Oregon, and helped to set type, impose, and feed the press on almost all Untide Press publications. In late 1945 on furlough, I met Powell at UCLA to ask his advice about moving the Untide Press from Cascade Locks (where it had been located after the closing of the Waldport camp) to Pasadena at war's end. In 1950 Powell adroitly diverted me from my graduate studies in the English Department at UCLA, first into the University library, which he headed, and then into the library school at Berkeley. This volume, then, is a joint effort by three friends, making common cause yet again, after almost half a century.

The "Chronology" that precedes the correspondence ends in 1946, as does this volume. That year was a watershed time: for Everson, who was closing out phase one of his career; for Powell, having recruited his cadre of assistants, who was ready to launch the UCLA library on its astonishing trajectory into the front ranks of academic libraries. Although the file continues through 1984 with letters from Everson, Powell's letters dwindle and cease in 1949. Their friendship, however, blossomed again in 1968, and continues to this day. The originals of the letters are in the library at Occidental College, Powell's alma mater (and Jeffers').

Everson was demobilized from the Minersville camp, located in the Trinity Alps in northern California, in July, 1946. He immediately began to establish himself in the Bay Area literary scene, along with Kenneth Rexroth and Robert Duncan. In 1948, with Powell's help, he applied for a Guggenheim

Fellowship, and was among the winners in 1949. (Later, Powell received Guggenheim Fellowships in 1950–51 and 1966–67.) During this period Everson was increasingly drawn to Catholicism, due in large part to the influence of Mary Fabilli, a short-story writer and artist who became his second wife.

The next phase of Everson's life may be said to begin in 1950, with his move to the Maurin "House of Hospitality" in the Skid Row section of Oakland, one of a number of such establishments founded by the Catholic socialist, Dorothy Day, paving his way into the Dominican Order. As Brother Antoninus, he soon became the premier Catholic poet of the U.S. His many confessional volumes of poetry describe his struggles to achieve a religious faith through depth psychology and self-analysis. He was in demand as a reader of his own works, and developed a charismatic platform style. He wrote, but did not publish, a 500-page autobiography. In 1960, he became emotionally involved with a woman who had come to him for counseling, resulting in the poetic sequence, *The Rose of Solitude.*

During the decade of the 'sixties Antoninus made many nationwide tours, giving poetry readings to college groups and lay audiences. At the close of the decade he gave a reading at Wesleyan University, where Powell was a resident fellow at the Center for Advanced Studies. This was the first time the two had met in many years.

Everson's life began a third phase at the close of 1969. In a dramatic ending to a poetry reading at the University of California, Davis, he dropped his robes and announced his impending marriage. A week later he married Susanna Rickson, who had an infant son, and the marriage endured until 1992.

In 1971 Everson was invited to become a lecturer at the University of California, Santa Cruz. In addition to his duties as a lecturer, he volunteered to oversee the working of a handpress recently given to the University, named the Lime Kiln Press. A number of students each term showed an interest in printing. Under Everson's direction, they produced the monumental *Granite & Cypress,* a selection of Jeffers' poems.

Everson learned in 1977 that he was a victim of Parkinson's disease, which soon meant that he could no longer work on the press. He continues to write and publish, however, adding to his more than two score books of poetry and a half-dozen prose works.

Powell, in 1947, was beginning his fourth year as director of the Clark Library and as university librarian at UCLA. Although deprecating administrators, he developed a highly personalized management style based on his motto, "Getting things done through people." He recruited some of the most able librarians in the country to help him realize his vision: to make the UCLA library an equal partner with the UC/Berkeley library.

During the next fourteen years he added a million volumes to the library, partly through the purchase of such large collections as those of Michael Sadleir, C.K. Ogden, and Isaac Foot. The Clark Library was transformed from a mausoleum into a vibrant research library, with seminars and a publication program. He encouraged his staff to establish intellectual camaraderie with the faculty, thereby demonstrating that the profession of librarianship was on par with that of teaching and research.

From his own disappointing experience in library school, Powell never lost sight of the need for a new emphasis in education for librarianship. His dream of establishing a School of Library Service at UCLA was not approved by the Regents of the University until 1958, and then only after Powell mounted an intense lobbying effort. The first class was admitted to the library school in 1960; Powell had recruited an outstanding faculty to greet them. Most of that first class was admitted only if a background of significant library experience had been achieved. That prerequisite, Powell believed, was vital to prepare them for the humanistic, bookish, and service-oriented goals of the school. The coursework was brightened by a galaxy of visiting scholars, authors, booksellers, and librarians. Assistant Dean Andrew Horn established a printer's chapel so that students could have hands-on experience in printing.

As Dean of the School, Powell had to relinquish the post of university librarian. For the next six years he watched the new research library building he had planned become a reality. His successor, Robert Vosper, began a drive that added another two million volumes to the UCLA library, an effort he was prepared for by his years as Powell's taciturn but able assistant. Coinciding with his retirement in 1966, the Regents named the original library building the "Powell Library." It now houses the undergraduate library as well as the library school.

The voluminous writing and steady speechmaking that Powell began in the 'forties never flagged. Columns were published in such periodicals as *Westways* and *Arizona Highways,* not to mention scores of book reviews in the *Los Angeles Times* and the *New York Times.* Many of his essays were gathered into books and found a large audience.

Powell retired in 1966 in order to travel and write. Then in 1971 he began a third career as consultant to two presidents of the University of Arizona. He reinvigorated the library there by recommending a new librarian, David Laird; he helped the University of Arizona library school gain accreditation. Two of his four novels, called "Quintet" in these letters, were translated and published in France. The four were gathered and published in one volume, *The Evening Redness,* in 1991.

In 1993 Powell celebrated his 87th birthday. Everson, who was 81, is at work on his autobiography in verse. The first canto, *In Medias Res,* was printed and published in a limited edition by Adrian Wilson in 1984, and is included in the first volume of *The Engendering Flood* (1991). A festschrift appeared late in 1992, *Perspectives on William Everson.*

* * *

The editorial arrangement of the book is straightforward. There are no footnotes and few headnotes; the spelling and punctuation have been corrected as necessary. There are few deletions, except for directional maps drawn for visiting purposes, texts of poems and prose writings exchanged for comments and suggestions, and the like. Deletions are marked by three asterisks spaced on one line. Proper names other than those of well-known persons are given a brief identification in the Index.

The legends at the head of each letter describe the letters:

ALS: autograph letter signed
TLS: typed letter signed
APS: autograph post card signed
TPS: typed post card signed
AL: autograph letter unsigned
TL: typed letter unsigned
AP: autograph post card unsigned
TP: typed post card unsigned

To begin, the reader may want to scan the "Chronology" and "The Small Circle of Friends," both of which follow this Note. Readers who want to learn more about the principals are referred to the following:

Bartlett, Lee, *William Everson: The Life of Brother Antoninus.* New York: New Directions, 1988.

———, and Allan Campo, *William Everson: A Descriptive Bibliography, 1934–1976.* Metuchen: Scarecrow Press, 1977.

Powell, Lawrence Clark, *Fortune & Friendship: An Autobiography.* New York: R.R. Bowker, 1968.

———, *Life Goes On: Twenty More Years of Fortune and Friendship.* Metuchen: Scarecrow Press, 1986. Includes a Checklist of Publications, 1919–1986, by Robert Mitchell and Betty Rosenberg.

ALA World Encyclopedia of Library and Information Services. 2nd edition. Chicago: American Library Association, 1986. Biographical sketch of Powell by Wm. R. Eshelman.

Perspectives on William Everson, edited by James B. Hall, Bill Hotchkiss, and Judith Shears. Grants Pass, Oregon: Castle Peak Editions, November 1992.

A special word of thanks is due Tyrus G. Harmsen, long-time librarian of Occidental College and later the Director of the Book Arts Program there. He went through the files of the letters, making photocopies of pages that were indistinct or faulty, found missing pages, and answered the Editor's questions promptly and faithfully. Carolyn Rahnema was indispensable to this project, deciphering the handwriting and carefully correcting the many errors that are inevitable in converting hundreds of pages of autograph manuscript into machine-readable form. Thanks are also due to David Lewellen, who transcribed the early years, before becoming a staff writer for the local newspaper.

Although her only credit is on the Table of Contents page

for constructing the Index, Pat Rom's contribution is far greater than that. She read through the entire manuscript several times, noting where editorial explanations were needed, and marking errors of spelling and grammar. At the end, words fail me. They cannot convey the worth of one who meets every need with insight, understanding, and humor.

—Wm. R. Eshelman
Portland, Oregon

CHRONOLOGY

WILLIAM EVERSON		*LAWRENCE CLARK POWELL*
	1906	Born, September 3, Washington, D.C.
	1911	Family moves to South Pasadena, Calif.
Born, September 10, in Sacramento, Calif.	*1912*	
Family moves to Selma, Calif.	*1914*	
	1922	Father dies.
	1923	Friendship with Ward Ritchie, known since kindergarten, is strengthened when Ward lives for a time with the Powell family.
Beginning in the summer, works at the Libby's cannery.	*1924*	With Ritchie, enrolls at Occidental College; meets Gordon Newell.
Works summer at cannery	*1926*	Occidental professor Carlyle MacIntyre influences the three friends; takes a term off to play in dance bands.
In high school; works summer at cannery.	*1927*	Mother ill, restored to health by Dr. Hal Bieler.
In high school; works summer at cannery.	*1929*	Meets Fay Ellen Shoemaker, a first-year student at Oxy; graduates, joins Ritchie working

		at Vroman's bookstore in Pasadena.
Now a high-school senior, meets Edwa Poulson, a junior; works at cannery.	*1930*	Sails to Paris, where Ritchie had apprenticed himself to F.L. Schmeid, master printer.
Graduates, works at cannery; enrolls at Fresno State College in the fall.	*1931*	At Dijon to write Ph.D. thesis on Robinson Jeffers; lives with fellow doctoral student Alfred Young Fisher, who had married Fay's old friend, Mary Frances Kennedy; Ritchie returns to Pasadena.
Drops out of F.S.C. after one term; works at cannery; to New Mexico to harvest piñon nuts; project fails, returns home.	*1932*	Defends thesis on Jeffers; Ph.D. awarded *mention très honorable;* tours Europe with mother.
No job; in summer advances at cannery from laborer to syrup-maker; in November enlists in Civilian Conservation Corps.	*1933*	Finishes tour in London; returns to California; meets Jeffers. Fay had married, had son Norman, later divorced.
Reups in C.C.C.; Edwa, feeling abandoned, takes up with another man; quits C.C.C. to reclaim Edwa; discovers Jeffers' poetry in library; decides to become a poet.	*1934*	Hired by Jake Zeitlin to work in Jake's bookstore; marries Fay; his *Robinson Jeffers* published.

After two semesters, drops out of F.S.C., heads home determined to work the land and be poet of the San Joaquin; Selma cannery closed; to Sunnyvale as syrup-maker; pilgrimage to Jeffers' tower; published first collection, *These Are the Ravens.*	*1935*	Continues at Jake's bookstore; son Wilkie born; with half-brother, Norman, brings the family to four.
Selma cannery still closed, hired as laborer to build new post office; Edwa graduates, begins teaching in Tranquillity, a distant hamlet; both begin to save up for marriage.	*1936*	Recruited to librarianship; enrolls at U.C. Berkeley; assigned to a desk behind Fay Porter, who was a friend of Everson's.
Gets job laying cement irrigation pipe; this job plus summer syrup-making allows time to write in spring and fall; Fay Porter sends his poems to Powell; Edwa begins teaching at nearby Dinuba.	*1937*	Finishes library school; applies to UCLA, is ignored; gets temporary job at L.A. Public Library thanks to director Althea Warren, who had recruited him to be a librarian.
Begins correspondence with Powell; still pipe-laying and syrup-making; Edwa continues at Dinuba; marries Edwa; on honeymoon, they visit Carmel and the Powells in L.A.	*1938*	Appointed junior librarian at UCLA; begins correspondence with Everson; begins editing and typing Al Fisher's "The Ghost in the Underblows."

San Joaquin printed by Ritchie at Powell's suggestion; Edwa begins sculpting; friendship with Lee Watkins; syrup-making and pipe-laying continue.	*1939*	Continues efforts to improve library procedures at UCLA; mounts many exhibits and has catalogues printed; makes many faculty friends.
Still laying pipe; Edwa continues teaching at Dinuba; corresponds with Robert Duncan; registers for draft as a conscientious objector; Edwa improves rapidly as a sculptor; mother dies; submits poems to *Poetry* magazine, has contretemps with editor.	*1940*	Revised edition of *Jeffers* book published; head librarian denies promotion despite outstanding performance and publication record; *Ghost in the Underblows* published with his introduction; mounts exhibit of Jean Hersholt's Andersen collection; M.F.K. Fisher's second husband, D. Parrish, dies.
Publisher Decker accepts "The Masculine Dead"; friend Carothers underwrites $85 subsidy required; Henry Miller visits him in Selma.	*1941*	Continues to publish essays, book reviews, columns; gets travel grant to read paper at Harvard; mounts more exhibits.
The Masculine Dead published replete with errors; insists Decker include an errata slip; classified IV-E (conscientious objector) by draft board; bought vineyard, planted more vines; syrup-making	*1942*	*Philosopher Pickett* published by Univ. of Calif. Press; friends begin to recommend him for chief librarian at major universities; exhibits program continues; publishes columns, book reviews.

and pipe-laying continue; Duncan visits; they visit Powell, Miller; protests father's re-marriage.		
Drafted and sent to Civilian Public Service Camp #56 at Waldport, Ore., to do "work of national importance" for no pay; camp publications printed his poems; co-founds The Untide Press, and publishes his *X War Elegies* by mimeograph; Edwa continues teaching, sculpting, and working the vineyard; Edwa begins seeing Carothers; she twice visits Waldport in effort to save marriage; goes to Selma to harvest grapes and help Edwa when she lost her job and was evicted from their rented ranch-house; they auction possessions, sell vineyard, and leave Selma forever; returns to Waldport; Edwa joins Carothers in San Francisco.	*1943*	Invited to interview for head librarian at Northwestern Univ.; resigns UCLA job on way to train station; offered post, but UCLA faculty urges Pres. Sproul to counter-offer; Pres. appoints review committee; Pres. appoints him director of UCLA's William Andrews Clark library (rare books) and university librarian as well; works in arctic sleeping bag factory until beginning new jobs.

Organizes a "special interest school" called the Fine Arts at Waldport; painters, writers, musicians and theater people transferred from other camps; Edwa visits three times; visits Edwa in Berkeley; marriage in jeopardy; designs the first printed Untide Press chapbook, Glen Coffield's *The Horned Moon,* which new camper Eshelman helped to print; Untide Press publishes his *Waldport Poems* and a new, printed edition of his *War Elegies* with an added poem.

1944 Appointed university librarian and director of the Clark Library beginning Jan. 1 at Clark, university librarian July 1; to report to Pres. Sproul, not to UCLA chancellor; recruits H. Richard Archer; makes peace with Academic Senate library committee, which had not been consulted; begins planning branch libraries—law, medicine, engineering; along with Don Coney of UC/Berkeley, becomes a key member of the newly formed statewide Library Council, which was to develop policies for all UC campuses.

Father dies, attends funeral; visits Powell in L.A. and the CPS camp at Glendora, where *Pacifica Views* was published; in July, announces he would no longer appear for work; *The Residual Years,* done on the mimeograph, distributed by the Untide Press; he alone prints his *poems mcmxlii* for private distribution; on trip to Bay Area meets Ken-

1945 Acquires large Percival collection of children's books by persuading Pres. Sproul to fund one-half the cost; recruits Neal Harlow, Betty Rosenberg, Johanna Tallman, Louise Darling; visits Henry Miller, C.F. MacIntyre, and Jeffers (whose *Medea* was about to open on Broadway); proposes a European bookbuying neth Rexroth; begins hunt for a handpress; asks advice of Wilder Bentley, noted hand-press printer; Waldport camp closed; internees transferred to CPS #21, Cascade Locks, Oregon.

Returns to Waldport to help pack the press for carting to the Locks; buys handpress in San Francisco to be picked up when demobilized; assigned to nightwatch duty, has more time to write; with Eshelman completes printing of Kenneth Patchen's *An Astonished Eye Looks Out of the Air*; joins in work-strike; releases are held up for strikers; Cascade Locks camp closed; with Eshelman and four other strikers, is sent to Minersville, Calif., camp; finally released on July 24; settles in Berkeley; uses trailer made at Waldport to move his handpress from San Francisco to Sebastopol, where Mary and Hamilton Tyler were farming and forming an artist colony; there meets Duncan's artist

tour to Pres. Sproul, which was approved; in December, Eshelman visits Powell and Vosper at the UCLA library.

1946 Recruits Everett Moore; library begins to take primary responsibility for book selection; Library council persuades Pres. Sproul to conduct pay study for librarians and a survey of quality of book collections on all campuses; continues development of branch library system, which ultimately numbered nineteen; continues to write columns, book reviews, essays, and to give talks to library groups, at conferences, and to library school students; visits Everson at Sebastopol.

friend Mary Fabilli; before year's end follows her to Berkeley to take up life with her, write poems, and print.

THE SMALL CIRCLE OF FRIENDS

Hal Bieler	surgeon and friend of LCP
Hubert Buel	long-time friend of WE; artist
Kenneth Carothers	friend of the Eversons; music lover, patron
Edwa Everson	high-school sweetheart; wife of WE; sculptor
Alfred Young Fisher	fast friend of LCP; poet; professor; first husband of Mary Frances Kennedy
Mary Frances Kennedy	early friend of Fay & LCP; divorced A.Y. Fisher to marry D. Parrish; prolific author known as M.F.K. Fisher
Carlyle MacIntyre	LCP's influential college professor; poet; translator; known as C.F. MacIntyre
Stuart McKelvy	college friend of WE
Henry Miller	author; friend of LCP, who introduced him to WE
Gordon Newell	friend of LCP from college days; sculptor
Dillwyn Parrish	painter; friend of Fay & LCP; second husband of M.F.K. Fisher
Fay Powell	wife of LCP; "sail and anchor"
Ward Ritchie	LCP's friend from school days; renowned book designer; printer; publisher; poet
Lee Watkins	long-time friend of WE; "the only intellectual in Selma"
Jake Zeitlin	friend of LCP; poet; bookseller; publisher; mover & shaker in the burgeoning culture of Los Angeles

1938: FIRST MEETING

On October 5, 1937, Everson's friend Fay Porter wrote to him from Fresno State College:

> Just received a letter from my friend Powell, much interested in what I said concerning you and asking whether I could send him some of your poems. How about it? *Please.*

Everson agreed, and Powell responded with the letter that begins this correspondence, which Porter forwarded to Everson. Porter and Powell had been classmates at the University of California's School of Librarianship, 1936–37, where the students were assigned seats alphabetically. Based on his liveliness and keen appreciation of literature, Porter identified Powell as someone who might advance Everson's career. Powell returned the sixteen poems with detailed comments in the margins, some of which are summarized in the letter. Right at the start Powell perceived Everson's talent and suggested that he gather a group of poems for publication in a book. As a title for the collection he recommended the inevitable—"San Joaquin."

Edwa Poulson, Everson's sweetheart since high school, graduated from Fresno State College in 1936. She was in her second year of teaching when this correspondence begins. Everson had done two six-month hitches in C.C.C. camps while Edwa was at F.S.C. He joined her there for a term, but dropped out and was working around Selma as a pipe-layer in the vineyards.

Fay and Larry Powell were married in 1934 and Powell, with his Ph.D. from Dijon, began work for Jake Zeitlin in his bookstore. After almost three years, Powell was recruited to librarianship and enrolled in the UC/Berkeley school. As the correspondence begins, he sought and won appointment as a junior librarian at UCLA on February 1, 1938.

Jan. 2, 1938
Lawrence Clark Powell
Eagle Rock
AL, 2 p., 1 sheet

Dear Porter—

I am glad you sent me Everson's poems. I have read so many poets in ms. that now when someone new comes along, I am naturally prejudiced at the start just by the sight of the stuff. For 99% of all that comes along is worthless. As editor for Primavera Press for 3 years I suffered agony in reading amateur poets.

You may tell Bill Everson for me that I believe in him as a poet. He's got the stuff. Herewith are the poems. I re-read them a last time this noon, while listening to the N.Y. concert, and made a few notes on each. I haven't re-read my notes yet, but I'm afraid they'll sound pompous; I hope not.

Jeffers' spirit is throughout nearly all the verses; only occasionally his diction. E. seems to owe most in diction to MacLeish. Both are damned healthy influences, and it is a very fine thing that Bill Everson had been influenced only enough to give him the punch to transcend his debt. What I mean is, he has not imitated, and that is a hard thing *not* to do.

It's all very good, & you tell him that he should set to work (if he has not already done so) and shape his poems into a book to be called "San Joaquin." I don't know how much more he's done, nor if he means to be a poet for once and for all, nor at which point in his development he is now. I think though that he has been writing for quite a while. Only in the most exceptional cases do poets attain such sureness of expression without lots of practice.

I hope to God the boy has a burning ambition to be a poet & the strength to keep the vision coming through onto paper, & still keep alive—make a living. Jeffers was fortunate in inheriting enough money to keep him out of the city. To my knowledge the San Joaquin valley has never had a poet. There's a great life there crying to be expressed in poetry which will be special yet universal.

Make up a book, then get it published. Macmillan is always looking for new poets who are real poets. I might be able to help.

Jan. 18, 1938
2844 A St.
Selma, Calif.
ALS, 2 p.

Dear Professor Powell,

Fay Porter sent me your letter and notes. I'm not adept enough in the world's ways to give an adequate thanks, but what I mean is a good deal more than words and paper, though I can't make it show through.

There was no reason for me to expect so favorable a verdict as yours. For the most part, only immediate friends have seen those poems, and the prejudice of friendship can be misleading. You do not know me, and have no reason to say other than what you think, and since it came as it did, it's brought that lift necessary occasionally to keep going. After all, when a man puts his heart and guts in a work, appreciation helps, and you've given me enough to last awhile. I'm probably jumping away ahead of your conclusions, but the fact that your impression was favorable is enough for me. I read your work on Jeffers two or three years ago, and considered it then well written, detailed research. I think you got to the heart of things, though I differed once or twice ("Tower beyond Tragedy," if I remember you correctly). But the important thing to me is I thought it was good, and it is only by knowing a man's opinion of another's work that I can understand his reaction to my own.

I'm twenty-five and a manual laborer. I intend to keep writing until I'm convinced I'm lousy, do my labor for money and for health, and live as rich a life as I can. I have about thirty-five poems toward a volume. If I can do a few more by spring I'll enter the Yale Younger Poets Contest. Failing there I'll hound publishers.

There's not much more I can say, except that I'm deeply obliged—and that—well—you've made this writing business taste better.

Sincerely,
Bill Everson

Feb. 14, 1938
14052 Davana Terrace
Sherman Oaks—Los Angeles
APS, 1 side

Dear Bill Everson—

Thanks for your letter—am glad you got some good from my notes. Good idea Yale Younger Poets contest. If you have copies I'd like to read the things you're doing now. Note new address. Skip the "Professor" handle.

yrs.
Lawrence Clark Powell

Feb. 18, 38
Selma, Calif.
ALS, 1 p.

Dear Powell:

These are new poems, except the gold town piece, which is two years old and included here because it is my favorite. The rest are since Nov. I think, and perhaps not finished; not clear finished. I rework sometimes for months, so anything I send at one time may be altered drastically soon. A fault, I think sometimes. Who was it said Tate's "Ode to the Confederate Dead" smelled heavily of embalming fluid? But how can a man with any conscience regard happily an old work that seems bad? Sometimes I get moods in which everything I write seems bad and banal—ridiculous even, and then go over the old stuff pruning and weeding. I'm in that mood now. Most of these new poems are today different from what they were last night, but now I feel better, whether it'll stay or not. They seem vigorous and sure, but that I have found can be merely the rosy glow of after-birth sensation.

Bill Everson

Pardon the lousy typing, the spelling, and the not-as-yet-complete punctuation [a reference to the poems enclosed].

May 5, 1938
Van Nuys
ALS, 2 p., 1 sheet

Dear Bill Everson—

I'm a long time answering your letter of February 18th. I've been breaking in on a new job at UCLA library and swamped with reading, & a bit of work of my own. Here are the poems back. They don't affect me the way the other group did, except in one or two instances. You must reject the easy MacLeish-isms that you fall into: wind running, grain waving, blood burning, nerves blazing, spades leaping. It's too glib. Do it the hard way. Write more personal poems, love poems. Leave the racial meditations to Jeffers; leave him to brood on his big eggs. Get hold of that San Joaquin valley; be consciously local, regional; grapple with that region. Fix it once & for all, so that no other poet dare write of it after you. I said this before, but it's worth repeating. Don't stop writing.

Did you send a ms. to Yale contest? I see it closed May first. Have you ever sent poems to *Poetry* in Chicago? My friend Carlyle MacIntyre got a Guggenheim fellowship for poetry. I did a piece on him which the *Sat. Rev.* has, but I doubt they print it. Have you read his *Poems* (Macmillan 1936)? If not, you should. It's only $1.25. Worth owning. He's an honest to god poet; one of the few we have. I want you to know his stuff. Tell me when you do.

Do you see Fay Porter? Tell her to write to me. I sent her a little book last December, but haven't heard if she got it. She's the only good memory I have of Library school.

Did you read Bezzerides' *Long Haul?*

There are some fine short poems in Jeffers' last book.

I'd like to hear from you again. And some more poems. How old are you anyway? I'm 31.

yours etc.
LC Powell

May 17, 1938
Selma, Calif.
ALS, 3 p.

Dear Powell:

Working for months on smoothness, fashioning as diligently as I was able the clean lines, sounds, I find now that fruit sours under the hands; what I took for smoothness in reality is glibness. It took me a week of hard physical labor to come to the truth of your letter. (Sweat, body-movement, energy expended through the flesh, while the mind wallows in its hard bed unhindered: so I arrive at my conclusions!) I hated to believe it. Wouldn't at first. Now out of a cleared mind I see how right you are: the very syllables flip along—vulgarly. Well, what's behind is behind. Let it lie. There's work ahead toughening that language into muscle. I rarely get criticism like that. My friends are far now, and seldom write, and I was never a one to see my own faults. The import of your letter was huge, and will stay with me long. I needed it badly.

Answers: My ms. is with Yale now—sent off in great haste, with barely enough poems to qualify—some of which I am beginning to regret.

In *Poetry* for June 1937 I had two poems. H. Monroe accepted them in 1936. Both Zabel and Dillon have refused work that I believe is superior to those published ones.

I have not read Bezzerides: read almost no fiction; have not even completed my favorite: D.H. Lawrence.

What poems of MacIntyre's I've seen (*Poetry* Feb. '38) I did not like. Word-arranging so characteristic of modern verse—too skillfully contrived:

I write you as we drift. . . . perhaps myself
shall beat the delivery of a post too late — the one solid line [Everson's comment]

and I shall glide, a-swirl in phospher-light
to your pelagic urn on the coral shelf.

* * *

. . . . unplotted tombs
await the dossils of these suppurate souls. . . . .

* * *

Grip hands and dedicate to him this work:
red hecatombs before the whirlwind strewn.

* * *

Where the last Indian rots by the stone quern
and on raptorial compass-arcs for flaws
wide vultures scan, or still as urns on cairns,
solicitously regard the starving calves
and whet beaks sharp as a committees greed.

I get none of the—intensity? what is it lacking? Mood? Big language? Something structurally to do with what your book on Jeffers speaks of as "quantity"?

Oh but we lived splendidly
In the brief light of day
Who now twist in our graves.

This quotation may not embody what you referred to in your study—that specific constructional phenomena—I'm not learnéd enough to know, but something blows out—there's a spiritual wind—a dead earnestness—the packed and ringing language of something said out of an urgency pounding in the blood. That's what I look for and can't find in most modern poetry.

I do not see much of Fay Porter. Fifteen miles away, and I'm a laborer at 40 cents—9 to ten hours a day, and thus do not go into Fresno often.

I'm twenty-five, will get married the end of the month. Trip to the coast I suppose, and stare at Tor House.

I'll send some poems later

Bill Everson

P.S. If someone stops [to introduce himself] you using my name for it, it's Hubert Buel, a young artist, graduating from U.C.L.A. this year, and one of the best. He won a $250 award in a S.F. show this spring for a small piece of sculpture, the award means nothing, no awards do; they can't; but Hugh has what it takes and I hope you like him—if he finds you in this last-of-the-season rush.

B.E.

Did you see an article on Jeffers and Faulkner in the old *American Spectator*? Bob Linn wrote it; lives in Lindsay, near here, and my friend. A story of his is in *O'Brien's Best Short Stories* of '37. Probably has a good future in literature if he can learn control.

Memorial Day, 1938
Highlands Inn
Carmel, California
ALS, 3 p., 2 sheets

Dear Powell:

I am sitting in a cottage overlooking a bay so beautiful it is impossible, facing the woman who within these sixty hours is my wife, and the sight of Jeffers not an hour old. We circled the House: a window open: the pigeons flying: the late sun on the tower: the scene not changed from my 1935 one. There was no one: there had been no one in the morning: some say he can at times be seen gazing from the yard. This time we cut over toward the River, found that last road running back toward town, skirting pastures, fields; the Mission dome showing over trees. We were watching nothing; there were people in the road ahead; coming on them as they walked, their backs to us, we saw them actually as woman and man—then the dog: bulldog, white, on a heavy leash; they were any woman and any man until the sudden illuminating, devastating sight of that renowned dog: and Jeffers stooped, walking quickly, a bit bent-kneed, his wife quickly agile. Jeffers following that dog on the taut leash as active as it: energy: the dog quickly from bush to bush, pissing. There was something similar in all their manners—the sense that every bush, rock, weed, stump, fence post, tree, corner, and stick was of importance.

All Jeffers' pictures show a young man, clean-featured,

eagle-featured. This man old, grayed, the features, in the quick explosive quality of those sudden seconds, seemed almost passion ridden. Dark corduroy trousers—no boots—no pipe—light brown coat—the wide-collared Lord Byron shirt—evidently his only affectation. We were on them, and the woman turning to cross the road, waited our passing, looking up suspiciously, wary of intrusion. Jeffers not looking. Una [Jeffers] hatted, hip-long full cape—a cane moving actively. Our eyes met—she was any woman you'd meet on a street. I nodded instinctively, and we were by, guilty to the heart's core for having stared, for intruding, for—whatever it is in a man that hungers, and does not wish the hunger to show. (Remember how Ashenbach hounded the boy in *Death in Venice?*) Through the mirror I watched. A block ahead we stopped, hating ourselves, waited, watched mirror. They knew our intent—suspected us of worse than we dared, turned up toward their home. The dog did not wish it, stood in the road envious of pasture, snuffling river-ward, and Jeffers poised to turn—the active legs planted, giving the dog time. It would not—it stood strained toward the open, so he dragged it, and went from our sight.

There is out of this window Venus like a huge lamp these days following the new moon into the sea. My wife is looking at me—it is bedtime—this is a honeymoon—I shall use this last empty half page for curtain, and tend to a husband's duties.

Bill Everson.

June 7, 1938
Selma, Calif.
ALS, 1 p.

Dear Powell:

The rapid-fire barrage of experiences last week threw at me left me with little solidity to hang to. My visit with you exists in my mind as though seen through some screwy false-light. Too much preceded it: it came on the end of a week that was the most magnificent of my life—and magnificence blinds me.

However, what I remember is very pleasant. You accorded

me an interest I do not deserve, and I and my wife thank you for the attention you showed us. The night at the Ritchies' was fine, and we beg forgiveness for appearing so late. It is difficult for me to meet people, and to do justice to all the social graces. I invariably leave under the impression that I have unpardonably sinned. Forgive us our transgressions!

The separate letter was written and sealed in Carmel, and I hardly know what it contains, but since ignorance of your address was the only thing that prevented your receiving it earlier, I'll send it on, and trust to the validity of the intense emotion that produced it.

I think I told you everything about the pamphlet [*These Are the Ravens*]; most important of which is my present attitude toward it. It is only three years old, but such is the nature of our tastes, that today I regard it with humiliation and chagrin, and send it only because you have asked.

We are quite comfortably installed now. I have worked like a horse these two days: the heat has been almost intolerable in the windless vineyards, and I am exhausted. It is amazing how a hard man can soften in one week of luxury. My work has shown it, and left me open to the well-meant obscenity of my fellows, and they have not spared me.

There is more I should like to say, but cannot, and will close, wishing you good luck, and inviting you if you are ever this way.

Bill Everson.

If there are MacLeishisms in the verse, it is a coincidence, for I was unaware of the man until a year after these were published.

June 29, 1938
Van Nuys
ALS, 4 p., 2 sheets

Dear Bill,

Please excuse the delay in acknowledging your two letters & the pamphlet. Truth is I've gotten increasingly swamped in work; the past week I've been nearly helpless with flu. Now I feel better, but have not yet gotten back enough strength to wade into the pile of papers on my desk. I observe it with disgust, that it is so high & that I enthusiastically called it into being.

Your letter from Carmel just after seeing the Jeffers is good stuff. I do wish you could meet him personally & write me an impression that I could incorporate in the next edition of my book. Since you were here, I have arranged for its publication by the University of California Press. They will cut the type sizes all down a point, reduce the margins, & produce a book to sell for $2—which pleases me immensely. But the revision & bringing up to date are not pleasant to contemplate. While in bed I reread *Solstice* & the last volume. "Birth of an Age" is a very fine poem. "Such Counsels" is almost too clinical. But the two marvelous figures: impregnation of womb, & the boy's dreaming mind as he drops off to sleep.

It seems years ago that you were down here. That evening at Ritchies' was a bit scrambled, but it was better than none at all. I'm sorry you missed both MacIntyre & Gordon Newell. I told the latter about Buel, & N. is prepared to meet B. if & when he drops by. I wish that we might have had a quiet evening here at our house. We will next time you come south. Gin makes a very noisy party & that's all there was at Ritchies'.

You are right in preferring your later work to the *Ravens* book. But it is nothing to look down your nose at. It's the good earth stuff. Perhaps you will now write a companion piece to "Tor House." I hope you do.

You won't want to, but I want you to send me a batch of the pamphlet. You said you had several hundred. Will you send me 25 of them? I do not want them to scatter indiscriminately, but want only to send them now & then to a few friends who will appreciate them for what they are. Both Ritchie & Newell want copies. They were here the other night & we read them aloud. I have friends in Europe I want to send copies to. Please don't refuse me.

Separately I'm mailing you a copy of the Lawrence catalog I did. Am working on a paper to be printed by Ritchie to commemorate the presentation of Lawrence's Biblical drama "David" at Occidental last month—to be on the subject of Lawrence & the Far West.

Our plan is to park the children, when my vacation comes 1st two weeks or so of September, & drive north, up the coast to Carmel & SF, Sacramento to Tahoe, back way to Yosemite, & out via Merced etc. If this works out we will surely see you wherever you are in the Valley. I want to get away from books for awhile. I work with them every day, & then at night go on a busman's holiday.

You think I'm unfair in J. book to his "Tower beyond Tragedy"? I'd like to know how you feel about it.

There's a great deal we failed to talk about!

I enjoyed meeting your wife. There seemed to be something good between you, understanding. I wish you all the good things marriage can mean.

Any word from Yale contest?

Best wishes!
LC Powell

July 9, 1938
Selma, Calif.
ALS, 8 p.

Dear Powell:

You are right: I do not want to send these pamphlets: I want them to be safely out of sight and mind until what work I have to do is finished, and then it won't matter. I resent this work because it is in print, and stuff I like better is not in print—that's the story. I send it because in view of your interest and kindness I can do nothing else. But distribute it cautiously—make no claims, I mean. Its value lies in the future and you're taking a mighty long chance. There are so many things about it that are distasteful—the unfortunate title, the ridiculous foreword by a man of such poor taste, the very nature of the publishing itself. No one admires private editions more than I. In the light of modern publishing they have about them a reserve that is really admirable, but when a private edition attempts to assert itself beyond what natural dignity it may have and adopts the very pressure-policy it should shun with horror, it becomes merely contemptible. If I had gone to some printer and had this pamphlet done without ostentation I should not be half so reluctant about showing it as I am. But it seems so long ago, and I was walking with all the extravagance of adolescence. I was working at a fruit cannery in Sunnyvale, lonely for my girl and my few friends and when Hoffman wrote that foreword I literally swooned with delight and vanity. Well, I've got it now—the bed I made!

Your Lawrence catalog is very good. Chock full of all sorts of interesting material. You must have put in a terrific amount of preparation on it. Your own writing is very good. Clean and sure and right—the way it should be. No letting of emotion color the language—admiration dealt with reserve and restraint. I like it all. Format too. That cover is fine.

I take back most of the things I said about MacIntyre. Take back all I *inferred* about him. His book came through the library and I started it with little interest, but before I had gone far the particular spell of that intellect began to come over me. He puts all romantics, all classicists to shame. He puts them to shame because they all assume they have something serious to write about, and he knows better. He is not interested in emotions, but in the source of emotions, and none can stand up against him. His fundamental concepts are just about impregnable—"The thin smile of the mind" he says and can never be duped as most poets are duped. I had to partake of violent and thunderous verse, and lose myself completely in torrents of language before I could recapture my own standards, or do anything but smile that sterile smile sadly at my own beloved illusions! I am more sorry than ever I missed him, for curiosity has turned to respect.

About Jeffers' "Tower Beyond Tragedy." I cannot remember exactly what you said in the book, and it has been borrowed from the Fresno library so that I cannot check my conclusions against yours. At any rate, when we talked at UCLA, I quoted Zabel as saying the piece was Jeffers' masterpiece, and did not mean it as my own opinion. I think part I is bad—in spite of intense and moving *incidents,* very dynamic and gripping action, but the language seems so orotund and bombastic that the thing loses all its force. Part II picks up, I feel, but still Clytemnestra bogs it with her mouthing and it is not till the last that the piece shakes free and burns with the fire that only

Jeffers can kindle. Don't you think that last final speech of Orestes' is about as vividly as Jeffers has ever stated his concepts? I think it is unfortunate that the piece should drag as it does. A finale cannot compensate for a whole work, and I suppose that if that work in its entirety were placed against most of his others it would come away the loser.

It is interesting though, how successful Jeffers has been in that pageant medium. "Dear Judas," "At the Fall of an Age," and "At the Birth of an Age" seem to me to hold much of his best work. He gets out of the modern setting, and all the language that seems unreal in contemporary staging becomes true and fine in the stories of those other ages. Maybe his rhythms are not modern rhythms. Maybe it is only the pathetic imagination that likes to think of the past as more romantic. But certainly the violence, the speech of characters, the exaltation and spiritual force seem much more in place in these pageants. "At The Birth of an Age" is, I think as you do, a magnificent poem, and "At The Fall of an Age" another, although New York is seemingly unaware of its existence. When Jeffers dies men will see his true worth, while he lives they cannot keep from carping.

I have received no word from Yale, but if I had been chosen I think I should have heard. Surely by this time a winner has been selected. When I get the manuscript back, I'm going to revise it, but not send it East, as I told you. To hell with them. There is something repelling about New York publishing—the blurbs on the jacket, the pretense, the emphasis on wrong points. I'll save my money and bring out another pamphlet. If the stuff is any good it'll get around to a few people like you anyway and that's all I want. Besides, I'm scared to death of those Eastern critics and their continual howling about social consciousness. You'd think a poem had to be written in the end pages of the Manifesto before it could be considered.

These manuscripts I'm sending are done with an apology—you're too busy with your own work. Lay these aside till you're free. They are all new—two since marriage, and I have hoped to eradicate the ghost of A. MacLeish. Your criticism has straightened me out I hope—at any rate this verse will show it. I'm glad you read that verse aloud—the way it was written—every word mouthed to fit in a sound-pattern that dictates the shape of the whole poem. Expecting you this fall. Turn off the highway on Second St—the main drag—south for 6 blocks across from the school house. Thanks for that book on the Lawrence manuscripts. Please forgive my flat statements about Jeffers to you who know his work better than any man in the country.

Sincerely,
Bill Everson

Buel suddenly got a job in S.F. and has gone north.

July 31, 1938
Route 1, Box 25
Selma, Calif.
ALS, 1 p.

Dear Powell:

My ms. has finally returned from Yale, with a little note from Stephen Benét. No criticism; consolation, rather. He liked my feeling for my particular locale, and hoped I'd not quit writing etc. etc. It's not hard, in view of what you told me about publishers wanting a unified whole in a book, to see why I lost. In that respect the work is uneven. My emphasis is poem to poem; hell, it's all I can do to shape one poem much less a whole volume! There were some bad poems too that I have since discarded. You tipped me off to them, and I'm well rid of them, but they undoubtedly hindered me at Yale. This winter I'll try to bring the poems out myself. I have in mind a very small edition, with a format modeled on *Poetry* magazine. The cover is of course the big draw-back, but the way your Lawrence was handled seems to me to be fine. Although the poems I have discarded were long ones, new poems and expected poems will build it physically back up to 35 or so—ensuring a volume just about the size of the monthly *Poetry*. Of course I know nothing of production costs, and it all hinges on that item.

We've moved, and are out in a vineyard, very satisfied and contented. I have a vacation between summer and winter jobs and am soaking in reading. Horton's *Hart Crane* is damn good. Crane's theories in the back are also good. It's good to lie here day after day and soak up ease, as indolent as can be after so much heavy labor. Out here in the country no traffic bothers; that Second Street was a race track. We love it: it's new: in spite of the contents of the *Ravens* sheaf, I was reared in town: that was wishing mostly. The nights are so wide—no street lights: you don't have to hunt Antares between two houses and the Wain between two more. The cannery will start soon: long hours, from seven a.m. till midnight or later, but Sundays free. Late season. We'll work up till Oct. I think.

The note is for the new volume. It's probably silly, in view of my immaturity and obscurity. But technical problems have really interested me. And I want it known how I feel. There are also a new poem and a revision. I hesitate to send these, in view of your heavy work, and I don't want to grow to be a pest. Don't look at the stuff till you feel you have the time. *Please.* I know how it is, and really don't want you to bother until you feel like it. I'll draw a map to our place. Our phone is 12 F13 in case you want to phone from town.

Bill Everson.

Aug. 3, 1938
Van Nuys, California
TLS, 2 p.

Dear Bill:
Your letter here today. An earlier one to answer. Thanks for the pamphlets. You may be sure that I will "distribute them cautiously and make no claims for them." Ward Ritchie and Gordon Newell have each received one; so far that's all I've given away; oh yes, one to Jake Zeitlin. I'm sorry to hear of the Yale rejection; their loss however. Your idea for your own pamphlet sounds good. Why not let Ward Ritchie figure on it? I know that he will give you a break on the cost; and thus you will get a cheap job that doesn't look cheap. His imprint on the thing would be a help. Why not send me your ms. when ready and I'll go over it with Ward?

For that new edition of my Jeffers book I should like a statement from you as to what his poetry means to you; will you do this for me? My last chapter is called "Critical Conclusions"; I quote other people's opinions of him. I'm writing Steinbeck and Millay tonight; Jeffers means a lot to them, and I know he does to you too. So knock me off a page or so, will you? Believe me when I say that it will mean a great deal to me to have such a statement from you to include.

Seven-and-a-half hours a day at the library is too much; here at home tonight I'm hot and sweating and my desk groans under its burden of things crying to be done. I'm not going to try now to write about the poems you sent in your last two letters; let me keep them a little longer. Newell was here Saturday and I read him "we moved south where the streets turn" and it sounded good to both of us.

And now you've moved again. MacIntyre used to live in a vineyard. Goddam it, man, why isn't there more time? There's a great sheaf of things you and I have got to hash over before our time comes. Mac for instance. Your remarks after reading his book pleased me because I was sure his book would affect you strongly. Before it he had published only a single pamphlet, back in 1930, which incidentally was the first book Ward Ritchie ever printed.

My piece about Mac has been rejected by the *Saturday Review of Literature, Atlantic, Harper's, American Mercury;* now it's gone to *Virginia Quarterly.* The postage is breaking me! I will send it to you before long.

Right now I'm mailing you the last *New Masses;* in it is a piece I wrote about B. Traven. If you haven't read *The Death Ship; The Treasure of the Sierra Madre,* and *The Bridge in the Jungle;* you must. I've been four years gathering the material for the one article. Your county library will either have the books or get them from Sacramento; I mean I hope they will! I first sent the Traven piece to *New Republic;* Cowley replied he had already assigned the new book for review. Did you read what their reviewer perpetrated? The bastard; the impudent bastard. I shall demolish him if I can get around to it.

Thanks for the map. It will be a little after the middle of September when we come through. Will try to hit you on Sunday.

Please return the enclosed photo. It's Frieda Lawrence with Jeffers. J. and L. never met. J. sent one of his books to L. It arrived in France 3 days after L. had died.

Please excuse this wretched potpourri. Don't be chary of writing because I holler about being busy. The more I am swamped the more I get done. The truth is, when I have any long leisure, I accomplish exactly nothing.

Yours,
LC Powell

Aug. 7, 1938
Selma
ALS, 5 p.

Dear Powell:
Your invitation to write for your volume floors me—lays me out cold. Surely you are letting your generosity get the better of your judgement. Even if I were able to formulate a cogent opinion, my obscurity, in so brilliant a company, would render my remarks valueless. And the truth is I am incapable of bringing off a decent piece of prose. It's simply not my medium. In order to keep from sounding absurd in that volume I should have to write as well as the big-timers, to say something really new, and I can't do it. I should have to speak of something very personal, and, again in view of my obscurity, that would be presumptuous, or if I dealt in generalities, the same condition would render it merely as platitudes. I love Jeffers, surely, and I know why, and I think I have as deep a feeling for his particular virtues as any one. But I love him for pretty much the same reasons as you do—in fact I was not able to find out exactly the seat of my liking until I read your book. That chapter on Jeffersian prosody, and especially that discourse on what the Greeks called "quantity" let me into the whole examination of the field of technique. I had never read before a study of technique that I felt I could understand, that dealt in matters I felt were truly at the roots of poetry. It's what I had been unconsciously trying to do myself; I never even understood the fundamental motives behind my intuitive

search for poetic effect until I read your book. Therefore anything I could say would merely echo you—you've covered the man too fully for anyone to come along and do more than repeat. I hate to refuse you anything; you've been too Goddam good to me, but I'm scared; really scared. Millay and Steinbeck! I'd be ridiculous in that company!

Ever since I've thought about a second booklet I've thought about Ward Ritchie; but I didn't know the nature of his business, and didn't know how to broach the subject. I'd as soon have him do it as Grabhorn or Nash—I think he does excellent work. He seems to have an intuitive ability to achieve a fine typographic effect. All the work of his I've seen I've liked. I've been interested in the subject for a long time, dug up Nash books, and Grabhorn, and attempted to form some criteria for typographic taste. My father's a job printer. Except for temperamental differences between us I'd probably be a printer too. Certainly I've hungered for a hand press. I'd like to talk with Ritchie sometime, and try to learn a little. I think he's got the real stuff. So you can see how I'll jump at your offer. The ms. is still in bad shape. It came back from Yale looking as if every railroad clerk that handled it between New Haven and my door had jumped on it, thrown it at walls, laid it under the wheels, and God knows whatall. I've discarded poems, so the numbers are changed, and the erasures are messy. It should be retyped, but that's drudgery for me; so if you can possibly get by with it I'll send it in its present disreputable condition. Half is typed in elite type and half in pica! I won't have it ready for a while, which will probably be better for you too. Besides, the financial situation will not permit me to go ahead for some months, and in spite of my wanting to get it off and behind me so that I feel I have escaped a bond with an old technique, I still must wait.

I send you poems too fast. Every one you've received recently has been altered, so disregard the whole batch. Don't waste time on them. You can see them in their final stages when I send the ms.

Thanks for the *New Masses.* You've done a good work. I'll try to get *The Bridge in the Jungle* and read it. I had never heard of the man until your letter, and will read the book with interest. But Rabelais, Cervantes, Breughel, Hogarth,

Whitman, and Thoreau—them's mighty big words, podner! Did you see the review of *The Bridge in the Jungle* in the last *Saturday Review?*

Steinbeck's pamphlet is interesting and at times overwhelming. I work with these Oklahomans the year around. Our ranches locally are all small, though, and no camps are near here. Neither is the country fitted for the squatter's camps he speaks of. West of here my wife taught school in the real cotton country, and is also reading the pamphlet. That problem is one of the big problems in California. I can think of those poor bastards with nothing but pity, chiefly because more than once I've been down to their wage scale and except for a good middle class home to fall back on would have been down to their living scale. But among the populace all you can find is scorn and contempt. The word Oklahoman, or "Okie" has become almost a synonym of contempt. The natives scorn the Okies and the Okies scorn the negroes and they all scorn the Armenians. And none is better than the other. It's cutthroat. Dog eat dog. The Okies come through here destitute, hungry. Will work for nothing. I've lost jobs on ranches because they would do the work for fifteen and twenty cents an hour. I understand, but some of these 12th-century minds do not; just as the Okies themselves hate the guts of every nigger that walks and recount with relish the race-riots in their own state. So where are you? This question of sociology has me completely bewildered. I know we workers must organize, but for personal reasons I hate organizations with all my strength. I hate them the way Lawrence hated them, and just as hard, just as fervently. I hate them the way Jeffers does, though not as devastatingly. I'm in the good old romanticist's tradition! But I also see they are necessary. Everything we got came through organization, applied force, inch by inch. My dad's been a union man many years, and hasn't forgotten the bitter strikes of the 90's for adequate hours and even ventilation. And I work in a lighted cannery because some poor devil sometime or other had his head broken getting it. I'm pulled apart. Every day I'm faced in one way or another with resolving that problem. The workers themselves have little in common with me. They jeer what I worship, they jeer my ideals, they call me fool, they sneer at my back if I let them know my mind.

I don't. Given the slightest chance they'd abuse Capital as capital has abused them. The bad lies in men's natures. And I can see no reason for thinking the proletariat have the intelligence or the benevolence to save the world. Yet I love them. They're good workers, good fellows, they can move at their jobs splendidly, and are happy with little. They make me write stuff like

> "Humanity, the bond of the blood, the narrow brotherhood of
> the seeking nerve"

Where's the way out. What can the compassionate man do? Oh God for an ivory tower!

Well, I've wandered. I'd like to talk about Steinbeck sometime. It seems to me that he and Saroyan have one thing at least in common. They both write great stuff and they both write sheer junk. You'll probably hit me for this, most people do, but *Mice and Men* I think is bad, bad writing. Van Doren had it down in his review in the *Nation.* How a man could write *Tortilla Flat* and the *Red Pony,* and yet have done *Mice and Men* is beyond me. Just as I can't see how *Roan Stallion* could follow *Tamar.*

Thanks for letting me see these photos. Your whole letter made me feel as if I were moving in the select circle!

The cannery situation is very bad this year. Record carry-over of stock from last. The fools last year went hog wild. Control! control!—where's the way out? The way things look we might not be working when you come by, so we can really talk.

I broke down and sent six poems to *Poetry.* Why? I don't know.

"Oh why will you climb up the turrets of another folly?"

Yours,
Bill Everson.

Sept. 6, 1938
Van Nuys
ALS, 1 p.

Dear Bill—

I shan't be able to give a decent answer to your last letter. All you said about the problems Steinbeck's pamphlet raises are interesting to me. We shall talk of them. I am trying to get the hatches battened down before we start on our trip. Finishing the Jeffers' revision to take north with me. Putting in an exhibition at the library—"Printers of Los Angeles"—I have assembled & annotated 65 items by a dozen printers all of whom are flourishing today. Great fun. It is the first time it had ever been done. I wish you could see it.

We are leaving sometime this weekend, going first to Carmel, thence the Bay Region—& home down the valley. I'll drop you a card from Berkeley a day or two before we leave. I have your map & phone number. Perhaps you'll have your ms. ready?

Hastily!
LC Powell

Sept. 21, 1938
Van Nuys
ALS, 2 p., 1 sheet

Dear Bill—

I am sorry to report that we were unable to call on you as planned. We went up the coast, stopped over in Carmel & saw the Jeffers, spent nearly a week in Berkeley, then were called home hurriedly by a telegram. I had looked forward to seeing you, even brought a little book to give you. So now I mail it to you: an example of not too bad regional verse & Ritchie's handling of an inexpensive job.

I don't go back to work until the 27th. Came home to some family matters to settle, & a flock of mail, & a host of unfinished work. Before going north I put in an exhibit at the

University library which would interest you: "Printers of Los Angeles"—75 items by about 8 or 10 printers. The Public Library has asked to have it during their Book Fair in November, but my real joy in that occasion will be in putting in an exhibit of my own Steinbeck collection & giving a talk about it. I am doing a background map of Monterey County, annotating the books, etc. I like such things. They lead people to read.

Tomorrow night Ritchie & Newell are coming out for a session—to sit & talk & read & reconsolidate our forces. We shall eat smoked fish, celery, & olives, & drink beer, with maybe an occasional "boilermaker" thrown in to combat any unlikely inertia. I wish you were to be present.

I feel very sorry about not having seen you. The University printer has my revised Jeffers ms.—we'll see what happens.

What does your ms. do?

Regards!
LC Powell

Sept. 24, 1938
Selma
ALS, 4 p., 2 sheets

Dear Powell: If ever deflation thoroughly floored a person behold him! He is here! The smoke isn't out from the pear trees after the mailman's passing—and of all possibilities I had considered this one never occurred to me—sooner or later I thought you'd come. You've no idea of the significance this household had placed upon your visit. It had become the premier expectation-point, with all others gathering up to and falling away before the day you would come. I'm not just making words. The surprise is beginning to seep off, but the disappointment is just seeping in. I'll not answer fully because the book you mentioned hasn't arrived—a hell of a lot hinged on your visit—well, now the real disappointment is gathering in as the last traces of surprise wear off, and I'll quit till tomorrow, for right now I could swear down the rest of the god damned bastardly page.

Sept. 25, 1938

Your little book came and many thanks. It's a nice little booklet, feminine, a bit prosy, but fresh and smooth, not cluttered up with the usual woman's-verse crap. I seemed to hear a Jeffersian rhythm in it now and then. In spite of the prosy touch it reads right along—holding the interest very well I think. I read right through it, and every verse I rather looked forward to the next. Thanks very much.

As for the printing I don't like it nearly as well as your Lawrence work. At first sight the smallness of the type discourages you, though as you read you are aware of a finely-wrought chiseled beauty, and the spacious margins, and the excellent paper. You are certainly aware of the fact that it was handled with great care; as I consider further it seems appropriate to the spirit and the essence of the verse. But for me—well, suppose I say what I would like, and find out what it'll come to; then we can always cut down later if it can't be done. I've been stewing about this for some time, and hardly have known how to get into it since I know nothing of costs, and don't like to make a fool of myself discussing something over my head.

What I like is that Lawrence catalogue; type-size, page size, cover, sewing, everything. I think that's a dandy. Ward has handled that thing as neatly and ably as I could wish, and if I could get something like that for myself I'd be clicking my heels all over this vineyard. It's fine. There wouldn't have to be any color work, but I would prefer section sewing, because my wife and I are learning book-binding and would like to do up a few of them as we get time, rather than the sewing of today's little booklet. Would the paper of *Sondelius* make it too expensive? The edition will be small—I think a hundred copies is enough; twenty people are all I can think of to give to, and that'll leave a good reserve. Maybe fifty copies will do—what do you think?

Well, I hope I haven't sounded too independent or something. Remember as I said I know nothing of costs, and this vision of mine may stagger me. If so, we can perhaps consider something much smaller, etc. Anyhow, I'll leave it up to you, hoping it won't force you too much for time.

Here's my ms. Just finished. Newly titled. The Invocation or sermon or what-not at the front is pretty new, also. All in all it's greatly changed from the one I sent to Yale. If you see any glaring mistakes let me know, but for the most I'm pretty near through with it. Fact is, I'm tired of it, want it behind me. I wish I were as rich as Croesus so I could throw that thing on the press, off the press, and get started on something new. My ms. reads 44 pgs, but I suppose it'll print up smaller than that??

If I offended you about that Jeffers' comment you asked of me, please forgive. I was so flattered to have you ask me my wife couldn't stand me around her for a couple of days. I wrote up a couple of pages in my best prose style, but it was no good. If I'd sent it, it would only have embarrassed us both, and much as I wanted to appear in your book, and much as I hated to refuse what you'd asked of me (you've practically picked me off the streets, haven't you?) my better judgement couldn't see it. Thanks many times for considering me.

Discard that note I sent you some time ago. You can see what I would have done for your book! My new one may be superfluous, but remembering what you told me of publishers wanting a well-developed whole in a book, I had to remark.

I think I'll quit now. This is a lousy letter, I know, and I haven't got very far, I feel. I had depended an awful lot on being able to discuss these things with you, and getting your advice; it would have been a lot better that way—but since it can't be done this will have to do. Edwa (my wife) and I will try to get down sometime this fall. What week is the book fair? I'm not working myself, and the raisin market is shot to hell, but she's teaching now and we'll be able to make out. Forgive this bad writing; consider the extent of my confusion and disappointment, and judge me not too harshly!

Bill

P.S. The snap was taken in the winter of 1935 about the time of the writing of the *Ravens* ms. It's the only decent snap we've ever had!

Oct. 4, 1938
Van Nuys
ALS, 2 p., 1 sheet

Dear Bill—

Ms. arrived okay. I am sorry about missing you; you may be sure that I would have made it if it had been at all possible; I was helpless, with no choice. I note what you say about coming south. Why not? The Book Fair is mid-November, 14th to 19th. But there won't be much to see. Any excuse though to get you away! I'd plan one evening here for you with Ritchie & Newell present; it would be fine. You'll let me know in advance.

Regarding the manuscript & your comments on it: I object first of all to the title. Did it come to you in a vision? I don't believe you could have invented it in a waking moment. "Blue Wind of September." Ye gods, man, isn't that what we're trying to leave behind us?

My suggestion is this. Title all the poems. Some already are. Call no. XII "San Joaquin"; and then title the volume simply "San Joaquin and other poems"; that is simple & true; "Blue wind etc." is neither.

I'd favor scrapping the forenote, which chiefly states what the book is *not*. Make the acknowledgements & let it go at that. The "San Joaquin" title will point the book in the right direction.

I don't know about your present invocation. Perhaps there's too much ecstasy & not enough toughness. I'd like to see you try an Invocation to the Valley, rather than just to the sun & the seasons. Do one to the Valley. Put all you have into it, like you were leaving it the next day, perhaps forever. We could call it simply, "Invocation"; let it head the book; and everything would be better.

Ritchie comes out to lunch with me one day this week, & I will go over your letter with him, & the ms. Except for the three points I've made (Title, Titles, Invocation) I think it is *right*; & will make a fine book.

Thanks for the snapshot. I am glad to have it of both of you.

Work piled up as usual. For a week I've been putting in spare hours arranging the books in a new 40 room mansion near Beverly Hills. They have 3000 volumes and need 1000 more to fill their shelves. People with no taste.

Am trying to start a piece for *New Masses*—on Steinbeck. Reading Yeats' and J.C. Powys' autobiographies. Have you read the *Death Ship* yet?

I'll write you when I've seen Ritchie—you must lay your plans to come south for a pow wow.

Sketchy letter. It is late; I am tired. So much to do; So little time & strength.

yours,
Larry Powell

On the back of the envelope, Powell added:
Agree with you about *Mice & Men.* I read it once when it appeared & have never opened it since. Same goes for *Roan Stallion,* & yet Selden Rodman included it in his anthology—Too bad.

Oct. 12, 1938
Selma, Calif.
ALS, 2 p.

[no salutation]

And over my left to the slant of my jaw his fist striking (forenote) and with his other, hard, straight sudden and hard, to the chin, his weight with it, (invocation) and as my arms lifted, his fists into the soft open utterly defenseless portion of my belly, plunged driving—(title! title!) Yeah, ever'ting went black. Not only you—McKelvy—an old standby—took one look, covered his face, and groaned.

You win. But not San Joaquin. You'd have to live here to understand. Every female poet in every town in this Valley entitles her first virginal, hesitant, O so fragile sheaf of po-ems "San Joaquin." The restaurants' menus carry quatrains with that title, quoted from leading local songstress:

> The beautiful San Joaquin
> The beautiful San Joaquin

The noble hills beyond us
The lovely fields so green.

You get so you can't see the name on the letter-head of a commercial firm without gritting your teeth. A good name gone bad—soulfully chanted into oblivion—a good name, but Jesus!

Funny about that title—I thought I had a pip—even now, in the face of the most convincing ridicule I mouth the words and fail to detect the overtones of lushness, of ecstatic gasping, of drooling sentimentality, so evident to the more critical sensibility. "The Blue Wind of September." Perhaps it lies in the connotative effect of the word Blue. Because I have liked it in sound and actuality, I suppose I have refused to admit the increasing overtones of triteness.

So I guess it's "Poems"; no footnote, no invocation (I can't write another, Larry, I've gone all flabby inside recently)—and if I tried to title those poems I'd only blunder further. Spender in his *Poems* avoids them and gets by nicely. You see. The two titles I've left are necessary.

One thing remember: if it's necessary, pour it on. Living here without critical advice I build up habits and viewpoints, unable to see them in their true character, pursuing some romantic notion that becomes merely foolish. Of all artists, the Romanticist is most likely to blunder, and his blunders are all on the side of excess. If a Classicist fails, he merely becomes dull, uninteresting, but if a Romanticist fails he becomes unbalanced, and ludicrous. He needs at all times an atmosphere of critical pressure. But he must also refuse to become too pliable. He treads a hard path between the dictates of his sensibility and the dictates of intelligence—usually of his friends since he himself has little. So don't be afraid of jumping down my throat. I need it. I may not carry out all you tell me—but I need pressure. I want to know when I'm headed right and when I'm headed wrong.

I can't get Traven. Silly library rule orders no fiction. Someplace I'll get it.

Halfway finished with Joyce's *Ulysses.* One of the most—oh hell—the most magnificent work I have ever read.

Bill

Oct. 12, 1938
Van Nuys
ALS, 3 p., 2 sheets

Dear Bill—

Today I met with Ward Ritchie, & he figured on your ms. Providing the book will come out at 48 pages, including title, etc., he will print it in format similar to the Lawrence catalog, one color throughout, on a better grade of paper, and sewn in heavy paper wrappers (He would leave as many unbound as you wanted)—100 copies at a total cost of $110.00. Fifty copies would cost nearly as much—only a few dollars less; so a printing of 100 copies is the best bargain.

I have no idea of what you have figured it would run, or whether you want to put $110 into the book—but I will say that the price is very fair in view of what the finished product will be. There would be a *small* sale for the book, at, say, $1.50 a copy. I'd suggest sending out a dozen or 15 review copies—for which I should like to write a little informative insert, which Ward would print up as a gesture.

What I mean to say is, if you go through with it, I'd like to help you launch the book & see that it gets to a few of the "proper" people.

Ward agreed with me about the change of title. Also titling all of the poems.

Let me hear from you.

yours,
LC Powell

P.S. I hope you will come next month. I want to shape up a Saturday night session here for you & Newell & Ritchie. They will leave their wives home, & your wife & mine will go to a movie together. You will find N. & R. very fine men, both strong & sensitive, & both poets. The three of us are lifelong friends, have grown all these years together, & I want very much for you to sit in with us on an evening.

There is a fourth one of us, Al Fisher, who is in exile, teaching at Smith College. Several years ago he wrote a

500-page poem—& I am just mad enough to be engaged now in preparing it for publication; retyping it all from his typescript. It will cost about $1500 to print; & we propose to do it by subscription—150 copies at $10.

It is a poem which attains greatness. I have believed in it for 8 years. Fisher doesn't believe in it—& won't have it appear under his name—He's finally given me the ms. & allowed me to edit it & proceed.

I want to send you a couple sections of it to read. It is in 12 books, each about 40 typed pages.

I type; Ritchie will donate a printed prospectus; Newell will try to mail it out. We all believe in the poem.

Newell was speaking of your book & offered an idea. There is a group of painters, sculptors, architects, etc., called "The Club," which meets weekly at Ritchie's for a sketch class—about 30 members. Newell will sign them all up to buy a copy of your book, if published; this money would all go to you & would help reduce your expense.

We've all got to help each other, man, before we go under.

When will you be down? Why wait till November? Come for Hallowe'en!

We don't have any extra sleeping quarters, but we are just south of Ventura Blvd.—101—which has many auto camps all along here. But of course you may have other connections down here.

Please excuse my innate planning instinct!

Regards!
LC Powell

Oct. 16, '38
Selma
ALS, 6 p., 3 sheets

Dear Powell:

One hundred and ten dollars is O.K. and we shall set ourselves about amassing that sum as quickly as we can. This is certain: it cannot be done before Spring: there's old business behind us that we feel must be cleared up. Attempting it now would be gambling upon our luck a little too heavily (the first duty to ourselves is to be good animals and other proverbs pertaining to the point). We think we can do it then, but we like to feel free to either advance or postpone as our affairs dictate.

About the selling we hope it shall not be required. The chief reason for our desiring private publication was that by so doing we should let the thing into the hands of only those we knew to be genuinely interested—and those people we are quite willing to present it to without any charge. If things work as we hope they will we shall be able to do this thing correctly, and although it may be necessary to resort to that, we'll try it first without. Newell's very generous offer on the part of "The Club" comes as a surprise. Patronage has maintained the arts for ages: it is I suppose the classic, the traditional way for an artist to exist: certainly enough big men have been obliged to use it, to save it from the disdain of a fly-by-night hack like me: but we'd like to try to get along without: thirty people of even that type couldn't all want to smack down a buck and a half for a flimsy little pamphlet they couldn't put on a shelf.

There's a favor I've been considering asking you for some time; since you've volunteered an insert perhaps it will not be too presumptuous to suggest your doing an introduction for the entire edition. I haven't mentioned it until now because it seems to me to be nothing but sheer guts for one man to ask another to introduce his work. He's presuming any number of things when he does it, and I've come to you now principally because I feel that anything to be said in an insert might more adequately, and to my greater advantage, be said in an introduction. Would you do this for me? It's bad I know, but I feel that a few words by you would add much to the book.

About issuing for review: I'm not so sure. My aims have never, since adolescence, been toward the acclaim of the masses. If I can get the respect and admiration of only a few of the good men of the country, I'll die happy. I wouldn't have the popular reputation of, say, Jeffers for anything: they must drive him crazy. What I want is the good will of men like yourself, who look at a poem for the poetic substance that's in it, and are not put off by the artist's irrelevant concepts. I don't want to be known as a regionalist: I want to be known as a writer of good poems: that's the start and the end of my ambition.

I am looking forward to seeing you and Ritchie and Newell, and sitting in on a pow wow. I'm not much of a pow wower, issuing, I feel, my best blooms in the privacy of my natural habitat. But there's a hell of a lot to talk about—Jeffers (I've changed my mind again about the "Tower Beyond Tragedy"—and am a little ashamed of that extravagant speech I wrote you). However, I doubt if we can make it down very soon. We're pinching to catch up—it's that book that's important—but I'll let you know before we do. One thing though: my wife and I are pretty close together, and she'd like to sit in rather than attend a movie. Stags are fine, but she's been looking forward to being with you as keenly as I. Would it be too great a violation of the male tradition?

God man, I've never seen anyone so deeply immersed in projects as you are. How do you keep your strings straight? Every new letter I get you've something else on the hook. And you're always right in there where the inner wheels are working—right now it's the publication of a long poem. Jesus, you seem to thrive on work.

Interesting development: a couple of weeks ago I got a card from a fellow named Tom Boggs, of N.Y., requesting that I submit poems for consideration for an anthology he's editing. He seemed on the level, not like these "vanity press" announcements that keep coming in. Said he'd be glad to give the names of contributors and/or any facts. His work (two poems) is in the current *Poetry* issue and I remembered that sometime back his anthology *51 Neglected Lyrics* was favorably commented on by the editors of that magazine. Still I was hesitant. As I told him, it seems that an anthology including birds as obscure as I am, would be much too large, and I don't think it does anybody any good to come out jammed with 1500 others. But I've received another card denying any claim to the "mammoth" anthology, listing these as contributers: Kimball Flaccus, Marshall Schacht, Amanda Hall, Lloyd Frankenberg, Boris Todrin, Rose O'Neill, Wallace Stevens, Oscar Williams, Edward Weismiller. Schacht, Stevens, and Weismiller I know to be good men, and all in all the work seems to be on the level. My book will appear first however (he'll publish next Aug.) and uncollected poems are required. That lets me out there. I really can't see why he asked me. The book is to consist of short lyrics, and caters to the rhymed. I've only appeared 3 times in the East, where he must have seen it. This line from his card I can't quite get next to: "Your work is modern, but it has an 18th-century quality—a bit like my esteemed Johnson." I don't know 18th-century verse from 15th-century. I know I never stemmed out of them or Johnson either. I thought Johnson was a critic. But the incident shows what might turn up; I'm a bit flattered!

Bill Everson

Oct. 17, 1938

P.S. Interesting development No. 2.—About the time you and I started writing one another, I set to work and produced a fairly long (for me) poem based upon the sexual experience. In this poem I tried to relate sex and ordinary natural phenomena, by talking first about the general topography of the earth, then switching to a particular sexual incident, then back again to the forces under the earth, then back to the incident, and finally merging incident and astronomical phenomena in a grand finale. This sounds pretty simple; but the thing has as much intensity as anything I've done. I did not enclose it in the ms. because it is very loose, and I am not at all sure of it. Artistically it has faults, I think structurally and rhythmically it has serious faults. Enough to keep it from my collection. But last spring I read notices of a magazine called *The Phoenix*, supposed to be based upon the principles of D. H. Lawrence, and being interested sent this poem, and a letter explaining my intentions (I also pointed out your Lawrence work). The editor, J. P. Cooney, replied with a friendly letter, asking to keep the poem for further consideration, and remarking that you were a subscriber, and he had your work, that he had written you, but that you had not replied. Well, we exchanged letters, and finally today he wrote me that he would use the poem in the next issue, with a few minor changes if I would permit. I see now that the changes are much for the better, and today am writing my agreement. So you shall see it in the coming autumn issue. I'm writing this to prepare you—I don't know about the work myself, I think it has enough intensity to justify its appearing somewhere, if not in book form. Cooney likes it, though about his judgement I don't know—look for it. I don't send the poem now because I've written many versions and can't remember which one *The Phoenix* has!

B.E.

I've just about come around to your view on the "San Joaquin" title. My reasons are various. It has been pointed out that only local people would, if any, be aware of the overtones I declared were implicit in the name, also it comes to me that one work cannot corrupt another no matter how much of a bastardization it tends to become: it corrupts only itself. A work stands separate, in one sense of the word, though of course all work is in another sense related. I mean, to use the first example that comes to mind, that Joyce's *Dubliners* cannot possibly be affected by all the Irishwomen who are undoubtedly chanting odes to that city, another reason is that the title has a typographical presentation that is very fine, and the last reason is that I'm scared to move one way or another since my critical faculties in this regard seem to be strangely childish, and, having written the stuff (that's really the end of it!) I had better put the matter in abler hands than my own! Give me a few days to stew.

B.

Oct. 21, 1938
Selma
ALS, 3 p.

Dear Powell:—
Rope's End—a good title for this letter. Friday night, and I'm restless, and haven't got myself settled for days. I got out

your letters tonight and reread them, and saw that a great many things were brought up and never finished. 1. What happened to the paper on MacIntyre? Was it ever published? If it is will you let me know so that I can check it up, and read it? Am I right in comparing him, more or less, with Wallace Stevens? Stevens a better technician, a better craftsman, but neither as wise nor as interesting as MacIntyre. MacIntyre is one of the most *interesting* poets I've read (speaking of subject matter) and infinitely wise. When I finish reading him I feel like a school boy. 2. When is the publication date of your Jeffers work, and will it be available direct through the University Press? I've been trying to locate the first edition, but have been unsuccessful. I want it because of Ritchie's printing and to have as a first. I want to go over it again, but some bastard snitched the copy from the county library, and I can't get another. I'll keep after them, though. I saw a copy in Santa Barbara—now sold, and two in S.F. last year, but could not buy then. I've not reread it since we began writing, and would like to check it back against what I now know of you. If you know of any stores yet having the book let me know. 3. Did you get comments from Steinbeck and Millay? Millay especially I'm interested in. She's a real poet, and some of her stuff will go down as the cream of this period. *Epitaph for the Race of Man* is some of the best poetry I've ever read. It's solid: I read it and know inside of me that it's the real stuff. Porter told me of your interest in Steinbeck, and then your mention of the talk, and the paper you're writing. I think some of his work is very good, but I believe that as a *stylist*, from a strictly literary standpoint, he's greatly overrated. You hear so much about his ability to handle words, and yet it seems to me that that is his greatest defect. His drive, yes, his guts, yes, his themes, interpretations, moods, yes, but his style—only when he's hot is it good. No real stylist could have written as badly as that "Their Blood Is Strong" that you sent—again, thanks!—and even in his creative work—I'm thinking of the "Ears of Johnny Bear"—it was his theme and his intensity and his terrific climax that got him over a beginning that was simply rotten. Actually, I think any slick-paper hack in the country could have made that first material solider, tighter. But then, he's California: that Coast country comes out golden and brown and hazy in his stuff—I think of him and Erskine Caldwell together—I've read only *God's Little Acre*—both write terrific stuff, but both can write badly. 4. Last, though I didn't mention it, I'm really interested in the long poem you are bringing out—how the hell do you get into the middle of things the way you do? Now, being the benefactor of a future great poem—an episode to last an ordinary man a lifetime, but for you, just more work. And being in on the rare Lawrence material, and the Jeffers acquaintanceship and treatise. Right in there where the wheels are working. I feel like a hermit. Actually, you awe me.

And again my own frustration coming over me in a wave. Since June I have completed nothing (Invocation excepted). I'm loose, up in the air. I have ideas for poems, and I've poetic moods, but not the coalescing. I can't get that inevitable combination from which the satisfaction of this business springs. If there is any more sterile feeling than that flat one after a mood and a theme won't jibe, when you feel your chest flushed with exhilaration and power and creation and exaltation and then feel it wear off, voiceless, futile and sour, till you're left cold and flat and nervous as a cat. I've started at least six different poems and dropped them. I'm tied to the chain of my own sensibilities, and right now the chain won't move. And technique. My rhythms are getting stale. The last sound like the first: I'm repeating my figures, I lean so heavily on Nature and the interest of natural phenomena that I can't write any other themes without bolstering them up with lines about the wind. There's no progress in that. If I'm to get anywhere I've got to deal with the fundamental problems of human existence, the problems that have loomed over man for ages. And to do that you've got to have a technique that can deal dynamically with intangible subjects, or abstract ones.

In a week or so I'll be back in the harness, and maybe I can work myself into some condition of spiritual health.

This autumn. The fellow that works this vineyard and I have gone back to the bartering stage: The nights are getting cold, and we had no stove, but his was available, an old squat wood-stove. We carried it in from the barn and set it up, dusty, unused for three years. To square things I help harvest the crop. The year has been bad for storms, and much of the raisins have been ruined, but several days now we've been out under a coming cloud, stooping and bending, stacking the trays into safe piles. Last two days we've dumped the raisins into "sweat boxes" and hauled them in. It's good work, the vineyard on all sides of you yellowing, heavy with foliage yet but the year's mark on it (good figure for future poem!). The team and wagon swim through it like a boat through water—(another figure I've worn out, the vineyard-ocean one). It's later than hell. I've tried to wear out my unrest, frustration, by writing, but I can't. I could write for another hour, and do no good. I've had longer spells than this one though before. I don't like being tied to the fickle impulses. I envy these men who can turn out good stuff, day after day—Joyce, Proust—12 hours a day. And Lawrence, who never ran dry.

I've thrown a lot of presumptuous questions—mainly to let you know I really didn't drop them for lack of interest but for concentration on other points. You're worked to death, barely the time to write when you do, and I pop questions. Well, hell, I'm sour. God I feel flat. So long.

Bill

These titles, I've clipped them to mere handles, to avoid blunders by attempting more striking ones. If you don't like any, sing out, they're nothing to me—if you have better ideas, I'd certainly like to hear. "San Joaquin" it is. One thing important—that foreword—please don't think it presumptuous, my asking you.

October 29, 1938
Van Nuys
ALS, 6 p., 3 sheets

Dear Bill—

According to this evening's paper a big storm is coming toward us from Alaska. It will be welcome. All about here is parched.

I shall try to catch up with your recent letters. Be assured that I am always glad to hear from you, even though I don't answer immediately. I think back on some of the great idle periods I've known, & wonder if they're gone for good. Times when I did nothing but dream and write letters. I guess I've written a million letters all told.

By arguing yourself into "San J." as title & naming the individual poems, you saved me the trouble—thanks! Our arguments were identical. I'll compare the titles with the poems—this weekend, I hope—& they'll probably match. They read well.

I don't know about writing a foreword, though it's not in the least presumptuous of you to ask me; in fact it's darn nice of you. I don't think it would do the book any good—but if it can be done without doing the book any *harm*, I'll do it. Which means I'll try one & see what happens. I to be the judge! I've never done a foreword in my life, but I'm willing to try.

Of course *Ulysses* is magnificent. I envy you reading it for the first time. Mine was in Florence, in the spring of 1933, my studies all over, a few dollars left, and a wonderful sense of life unknown ahead of me—mornings in my sunny room looking over a sea of tile roofs, an hour or two of reading & then out for long walks through the city; it took me three months to encompass the book. Since then I have read in it frequently. At the University next month I am putting in a show of "The Moderns," & am getting all the Joyce I can lay hands on. I'd like you to see my India paper *Ulysses,*—slips in coat pocket! Continental edition; printed in Leipzig—no longer obtainable.

Bless your wife! of course she may sit in with us all when you come south. We'll not be in the least inhibited, & if she will enjoy hearing a lot of lofty nonsense, well and good.

So you're coming out in Cooney's *Phoenix!* Good stuff. I'll look eagerly for the long poem you speak of. Cooney's a bit of a nut, but I'm for *him* if not for his ideas. He seems to have inherited Lawrence's vain wish to get a small band & hike off together over the horizon to the Green Pastures & way points. I've had the two issues that have appeared & he's appealed to me to contribute something about Lawrence. Perhaps. But I'm doubtful if I can go the whole hog to satisfy Cooney. I love Lawrence, in my fashion. You will be interested to hear that

Frieda Lawrence made me a gift of the manuscript which is #58 in the catalog. I shall treasure it.

Your anthology invitation appears to be a good thing. Why don't you write new poems for it?

Which brings me to your last letter. Don't worry about being empty. Take it as an autumnal manifestation. The intensity of a love marriage honeymoon is bound to drain the creative energy; let it be so. Let it work naturally. Come spring and you'll be filled up again. If work won't fuse now, let it go; read. Keep a journal. Write letters, such as your last one to me. Mull things over. Bend over & let frustration maul you, but mind you give it a good kick in the butt as it creeps away. Come down as soon as you can. I have some other people for you to meet—good people who will do you good.

You're right in what you say about Steinbeck's style. He's worked very hard to learn how to write. He's not a stylist at all. Did you see Whipple's review of *Long Valley* in *New Republic?* Last week I sent *Masses* a piece on Steinbeck—a sort of answer to a point in Whipple, & to Eda Lou Walton's piece in *Nation.* I'll send you a copy if it appears.

You ask about some other things. The MacIntyre piece has been rejected 5 times. I've sent it off a last time. If it bounces I'll send you the typescript to read. This last time I had to keep from gagging when I retyped it; it's so stale it stinks in God's own nostrils.

Mac's subjects *are* interesting; you're right. I hadn't thought about him & Stevens. Mac has a poem in the new *Atlantic Monthly*. He's somewhere in Europe.

I don't know when the new book on J. will be out. Everything's fearfully slow at the Univ. press. The Primrose edition is rather scarce. I have only my own copy left. Jake & Ritchie have single copies. Gelber, Lilienthal Inc., 336 Sutter St., S.F. & John Howell, 434 Post St., S.F., had copies last year. Might try them.

I have some things to mail you as soon as pay day comes around: for you & your wife to read & send back. Also some sheets for you to bind—soiled sheets, not too bad, which I plucked for you from the burning.

Two books I'm just finishing. *The Illusion of Immortality* by

Corliss Lamont; & his *Man Answers Death, an Anthology of Poetry*. See if you can get them at or through your county lib.

I'm always reading a book or two in French. Makes me homesick, damn it. The Fascist grab makes me sick at heart. Jeffers once had a line about the gathering drops of a rainstorm—The whole show seems foredoomed. My desire to be a man of goodwill seems pitifully microscopic.

Later in the month (November) I'll send you a book or two of the long poem I've engaged upon. I'm curious to know what it will mean to you.

Cheerio for this time—
Larry

Will send sheets in this letter. Books next week.
Mac used to live in a vineyard. They're wonderful in autumn.

> The mist arises, the leaves fall,
> Pour wine of seasons olden.
> And we will turn the gloomy days
> To golden days, aye, golden!

Stanza from Mac's translation of Storm's *Oktoberlied*.

Hallowe'en
Selma
TL, 6 p.

Dear Powell:

Having put in so much time recently upon the Jeffers work, you probably want to concentrate on something else for awhile, and having just received two letters straight from me, you probably won't welcome a third. However, I've been doing a little independent research, and since I cannot remember having read any similar material, I'm taking the liberty of sending it on to you; if you have already covered this aspect put me down as some kind of blunderer, harmless but annoying. Also forgive my use of this bastardly, impersonal, machine; the special nature of this business seems to require it.

If I can remember correctly, the passage in your work

treating Jeffers from a technical standpoint concerns itself in the main with a discussion of metrics. At any rate, it is developed that his line can be scanned to fall into lengths determined by the number of accented syllables. Jeffers, I think, has acknowledged this point, even voicing appreciation that someone has discovered that his verse is not as "loose" as it had been considered. Doubting the structural importance of this scanning, in spite of Jeffers' endorsement, I'll open my argument.

A short time ago, in order to simplify confused passages in my own work, I broke up the line construction, and isolated the phrases. Working from a strictly phonetic viewpoint, I would arrange such lines as "Musty, floors fallen, the smell of dead time on it," to this:

> Musty,
> floors fallen,
> the smell of dead time on it.

my attempt being to approximate *visually* the fundamental *vocal* basis of the poem. The beginning word of each line I left capitalized to show where the line actually started. Sentences beginning in the middle of lines I left capitalized, but bracketed the cap. Thus these three lines:

> They ran down singing. And I who hold the poor dream as
>   passionately as any,
> Expect it never. We have sprung from the loins
> Of that mother, the past.

were broken up to this:

> They ran down singing
> (A)nd I who hold the poor dream as passionately as any
> Expect it never.
> (W)e have sprung from the loins Of that mother
> the past.

So much for the method. I hope I'm not being presumptuous in reverting to my own work here. I use it because it was in this work that I started this business, and I know what I'm doing, whereas putting it on Jeffers is merely a theory. I applied it to him out of curiosity, believing my structure to be copied from his, though my diction, as you pointed out, is probably from elsewhere. The validity of this argument rests on the assumption that mine is a direct utilization of his, for it presupposes a likeness of structure. The validity also rests on the assumption that in Jeffers it is the phonetic that is important rather than the visual. As this verse is presented, it has a very unsightly appearance, and would never do to be finished thus. Of course I don't mean that. But I believe it is the phonetics that count, and to get away from the distraction (for the purpose of this argument) that is visual, it is necessary to put ear and eye on the same basis before we can get down to fundamentals. For an example of a Jeffers lyric, I quote a passage from "To the Rock that Will Be a Cornerstone of the House," from the *Roan Stallion* volume, on page 247:—

> Old garden of grayish and ochre lichen,
> How long a time since the brown people who have vanished
>   from here Built   fires
> beside you
> and nestled by you out of the ranging sea-wind?

*   *   *

For an example of the narratives I quote from *Cawdor,* pg. 68.

> Jesus Acanna Saw something like a jewel gleam in the rays on
>   the heap of   surface
> earth at his feet;
> he stooped And picked it up:
> a knife-edged flake of wrought Chalcedony,
> the smooth fracture was pleasant to feel.

*   *   *

These quotes are enough: nothing to gain going on: see how those phrases are the rhythmic structure of the verse? Of course I know that in some places my interpretation may be wrong: places I pause, might better have been read without a pause. But it really doesn't affect the question. I broke them as I would read them, mindful of my own use of phrase-rhythms. Neither does my system provide for the difference in weight of each pause: to read all those pauses with the same weight would be stupid. What that difference in interpretation does show is the necessity for phonograph recordings made of the poet's reading. (Has any been made of Jeffers, by the way?) If my argument is right this point is very important. It's those pauses that count, and punctuation cannot always be made to serve, for punctuation was designed to clarify the meaning, and often a comma put in where the poet wants a pause would disrupt the "thought." Somebody ought to get Jeffers' readings. I believe the ideal way to present poetry (all practical considerations aside) would be through phonograph records used along with the book. This need not be the poet's rendering, though that is of course preferable but it must be done under his supervision.

Therefore to sum up, my thesis is this: the structure of Jeffers' poems is based upon the rhythmic juxtaposition of spoken phrases; it may be an ascension, or a balance, or a regression, (I'm using these in the musical sense, though they're not the right terms) but the relation, one to another, and to the whole, is the phonetic basis of the work. It seems to me that Jeffers adopted a method of line-length-by-syllables to give order to his page, to avoid what must have appeared to him with his classical training, as looseness, to give his material a sense of form and restraint. I think its weakness lies in that it is not an integral part of the work, in that it seems to have been *imposed* upon the poem after it was written. I think you state in your book that he doesn't always stick to his pattern, that he drops it at will—almost proof enough in itself. I do not mean to say that intersyllabic phonetics is not important. Certainly it is; but as used as a basis for structural analysis of Jeffers, I think it is secondary. It is meat rather than bone. Look how much meter plays a part in the line:

> When to the sessions of sweet silent thought

but how little meter has to do here:

> Steep up in Lubitavish townland stands A ring of great stones
> like fangs.

If you *listen* to Jeffers being read by another, you have no sense of that scan-pattern at all. It exists only on paper. What you do get is a harmonic rising and falling of intonation, a majestic and somber music, varied in its tones, and building beautifully an orchestral structure that is of the very highest verse. [This interest in prosody and scansion held the seeds of Everson's much later insight into Walt Whitman's Preface to *Leaves of Grass*. In 1981 the fruit of this plant was the "restoration" of Whitman's prose "to its native verse rhythms and presented as a living poem." The monumental volume, *American Bard*, was produced at the Lime Kiln Press, with Everson's woodcuts and under his direction.—W.R.E.]

However, I'm no critic, nor aspire to be. On no one else would I have spent so much time, and I really wasn't interested in Jeffers so much as myself. If this stuff is all wet, and certainly it is soggy writing, then I've only wasted a little time—no, not wasted, for if it doesn't hold true for his it does for my own. At any rate, don't feel obliged to reply with a detailed critical discussion—this is merely an angle, and of little importance—Jeffers will burn in the blood as long as men read English, no matter on what basis his structure rests. All of which you were already aware. . . . .so goodnight.

Bill

P.S.: I've figured out how to answer those birds who say Jeffers will not last because of his negation. The secret is his utterance is affirmative. He is affirmatively negative. Not that his philosophy does not have value to us—tremendous value if we weren't such fools—but he won't live because of it. He will live because he has the voice, the affirmative view that *declares* its negation. . . . . and the truly negative is inherently passive. Jesus I sound stuffy.

Bill

Nov. 1, 1938
Selma
ALS, 6 p., 3 sheets

Dear Powell:—

Not an hour ago, the mailman, some minutes late, lashing his V-8 into a lather, snapped up my letter and snapped down yours; out of the white froth of my enthusiasm I'll dump out my gibberish and try to get it on the same mail.

You've no idea the boost these letters give me. Hermit by inclination and necessity though I am, these fresh gusts from the horrid metropolis get under my wings and whoof me up. There's only my wife and one other here that I can really get down into the guts of reality with, and when your letters breeze in sprouting talk of men and letters and giants, well, I walk around off the floor, my bare feet sort of paddling the air. Christ I feel good.

A lot of good advice in that letter: I wore off my dearth a time back and drove into production—produced all over the place, as Saroyan would say. Nothing finished yet: pages that will have to be dropped, and others I'll have to hammer till I wear out the anvil—that's good though. Work's good—sweat's good, come up out of the ditch with your face streaming sweat: grinning for work: get down into the bones of your matter and start pounding. Work's good.

Cooney's a squirrel all right—rushing off down to the jungles someplace with a handfull of nudo-romantics! When he gets there he'll have the same problems he left. He swears he's not an escapist, but Lawrence's "shining words" can be a will-o-the-wisp on the boys. If you're going to follow Lawrence's shining words you've got to follow them within you—within and up. He is in many ways the greatest writer of our time—there's something vibrating behind those words that absolutely flames. Christ but I love it. And I see by the reviews he was a fascist! Because fascism exploits frenzy and emotionalism some of these birds think every man who feels a slight coloring of inspiration is immediately going to start running around shouting heil Hitler! in everyone's face. Jeffers a fascist! And Lawrence! Stupid.

You speak of a fascist grab. We take no paper, and have no radio, and it's only through conversation with my friend Watkins that I pick up the world's rumblings. Too bad if it happened. Too damn bad. There's a hell of a lot of work to be done in the world, and I'm one of the shirkers. A Communist friend in Fresno—"You and your damned Ivory Tower. If there's a contemptible symbol in the world today, it's that one. At a time when we're hanging in the balance between dawn and dark, and need all our strength for the push into the light: you play with triolets in the privacy of your home! Sing grapevines! The glory of the larks! At a time when men and women are suffering, when the very civilization that makes your precious little art possible, and that justifies it, is hanging in the balance you dally your hours in a pink-sheeted bed, gently coupling with a Muse in violet lingerie! When the Fascists have us, and saddle you with a straight-jacket and gag that singing mouth of yours with a horse-dung, you'll sing your grapevines—through your bum!"

What can I say? It's true enough. As far as it goes. But Larry, I can't help but feel the real problems are deeper. No—that's nonsense too. If the real problems are deeper, we yet have to master this one before we can get into the real problems. But devoid of argument, with nothing to say, I still can't come running out scribbling manifestos and swinging the scythe! Whatever I've got to do lies elsewhere within me somehow, lies something that concerns itself with esthetics. It's my work. My whole being seems shaped toward it. And Ivory Tower I need and hang to, though I see it invaded tomorrow. Well—I feel depleted after that one. I'll sign off for a while. Gather my thoughts. Come back later.

* * *

The storm you mentioned came over us too—strange to think of the same storm drenching us both, though miles apart—

> words in the wind, and over the face some girl's song and the
> breathing of toilers—

Saturday went down fair: but that night the clouds came over, and we got out in the dark to stack the trays of raisins that were left. Fumbling and swearing in the dark—Not many trays left now—it's the equinoctial storms that hit the vineyards full of soggy, heavy trays, and labor scarce, and those sudden storms blow up.

> The year through September and the veils of light
> Broke equinox under: west darkened:
> The-wind-of-no-rain northwest and steady all day running the
> valley
> Swung with the dusk, came west, and the cloud gathered,
> Raiding the plain of the open sky.
> Under the whisper we watched it come over,
> The raisins heavy yet in the fields, half-dried, and rain a ruin,

> And we watched it: perceiving outside the borders of pain
> Disaster draw over: the march of the pinch of the coming months,
> The clouds deadly, and being deadly, beautiful:
> Incredible curtain sliding above us:
> Destruction a splendor for the dreading eyes:
> The untouchable beauty loosed, seen suddenly, caught in the implication of fear,
> And it rode us, blown in on the back of the hugging wind;
> Above and beyond; the east closed under;
> It let down the ruin of rain.

Man, it seems as if you've sent us fifty dollars worth of reading material! We don't deserve it, and we can't decently return the favors, and we can't decently thank you—I mean we don't know how—these last sheaves are beauties. Tell Ward that that is a typographic achievement to make Grabhorn green, and to make Nash, with his slap-dash sick. Those pages have a beauty that is so superior to the blowing of Van Wyck that it seems sacrilegious. They're superb! You read that stuff aware of handling something infinitely rich—beautifully done! Jesus I envy a man that can appear in such a format!

I don't disagree with Van Wyck. There's too much talk now-a-days about Jeffers being o.k. except for his philosophy. We need the cauterizing effect of the Jeffersian spirit—and Van Wyck points this need. But why couldn't he have written it decently? That's a school-boy's fumbling. Such lines as this:

> In fact the average person is so stupid that he or she regards anyone with a cosmic quality as a "crack-pot" and lets it go at that, entirely content to be like the next person.

That's simply crude, that writing. He does it more than once. And although Jeffers is tops you can't laugh off Joyce and Proust and Lawrence as thumb-twiddlers. Any of them is right up there panting at Jeffers' heels, and only the future will pick the winner. Also, man doesn't love to destroy rather than construct. It's action he's after. Watkins has sat here over his wine more than once and, after drawing up the whole sad story, finished off with: "If you study man over the last ten-twenty thousand years, he doesn't show much. Our only hope lies in looking at the last half-million. Surely there's *some* hope for us or we'd still be swinging by our tails." I say a breed that can produce a being like Jeffers has done something.

But even so, bad writing or not, I'm glad to see someone besides yourself pointing the good in Jeffers. We're so obsessed in this social struggle we can't look over the dust we raise. Thanks for these sheaves, Larry, I mean it—one of my hopes is to collect fine typography, and it would have to go some to beat these. We're slowed up on our binding—can't get material anyplace in Fresno, and the wholesalers deal only through the trade. But when we're a little better we'll bind these sheaves up. They're beauties.

Interesting note on Eliot—thanks.

No dealer in town handles the *New Republic*. The lib. does the *Nation*. The *Nation* is gradually concentrating more and more on the social, and devotes less to the esthetic. *New Republic* is better for this. I want to subscribe. They're the only two I ever see (except *Poetry*) that take a hard clean look at literature: the rest (*Saturday Review, Harper's*, etc) are too busy collecting dough from the book-ads. We'll try to get down. Let you know. This has exhausted me. I haven't even the guts to reread it!

Bill

Nov. 2, 1938
Van Nuys, Calif.
APS

Dear Bill—
Regret to inform you that we will be out of town from Thanksgiving eve through Sunday. Hope you will be able to postpone trip. Will write you later this week.

LC Powell

Nov. 4, 1938
Los Angeles, Calif.
APS

Dear Bill—

Sending you two books. Keep one. Return other when read. New rate on (1-1/2¢ per lb.) is a wonderful thing. Two letters from you yesterday; both read with great interest. Will write later.

yrs.
LC Powell

Nov. 16, 1938
Selma, Calif.
ALS, 1 p.

Dear Powell:—

The books arrived: were gratefully received and read. You are going to too much trouble, time, and expense. I have as yet read only snatches of the gift, but so far it proves interesting. *The Death Ship* [B. Traven] is a fine work, easily, and on the whole, excellently written. Up to about the middle it builds beautifully, incidents and social-criticism gathering the theme up to a powerful climax: the death ship. Right there is some splendid work, and I hated to see him wander into other incidents: patrol dodging, shanghai-ing, ship-wrecks. When only he and his companion escaped the crash, I thought, Robinson Crusoe! But the finish lifts again. The book ends on a very high pitch and my quibbling is really unwarranted. The aim of the book is social criticism: I don't suppose Traven gives a hoot about my aesthetic mewing: and as social criticism is a splendid achievement: the best of this type I have read, done with authority and conviction, and literacy, and excellent humor. Thanks ever so much for showing it to us, and for the trouble you've taken. We shall return it when we go down, which will be the weekend after Thanksgiving. This may be a bad time for you, considering the holiday, and if it is too much so we can postpone. But Edwa has a vacation, the first of which is taken up with teachers' institute, and it seems to be our best bet. Therefore, unless my own work butts in, and unless a note from you directs otherwise, we shall be down on Friday, and shall be glad to accept any plans you desire to make. I have a brother in Burbank, who has not one ounce of literature in him, and who gives himself consummately to the construction of airplanes: but who can provide diversion in case any plans you have previously made require you. Feel free to suggest, advise, direct, or explain.

My last letter was written out of terrific heat, and I fear for some of its matter. Perhaps I was too abusive toward Van Wyck. In spite of admiring his passion for Jeffersian philosophy, which I, too, feel to be very valuable as a steadying factor, I simply cannot feel that this last volume reveals "the greatest Jeffers of them all." "At the Birth of an Age" I think is his last *great* achievement to date—one of the most magnificent things he has done—those last pages of the poem [are] really tremendous verse. Also, consider (reverting to Van Wyck) the construction of this line:

> He tears down all the accumulated superstitions of the world with a few wonder-words tipped with flame which he flings as darts to penetrate the hard steel of our armor of life escape, by which most of us follow a nefarious path unmindful of that system of ethics which the earlier schoolmen called the psyche.

!!!! Bill E.

December 6, 1938
Van Nuys
ALS, 2 p., 1 sheet

Dear Bill—

Excuse my delay in writing. Nearly every night that I've been home since Thanksgiving weekend I have been working on the long poem by my friend Fisher. I am mailing you the last three of the twelve books—his typescript, done in 1934 from his manuscript written 1929–31. From this typescript I am making another for a printer's copy. I am very anxious to have your reaction to the books I am sending you. Could you let me have them back in a week from the time you get them?

I believe I wrote something of Fisher & of how he has become indifferent to the long poem—"Notes for poem" he calls it. I kept him from destroying the whole thing; since 1934 I have been after him to let me have the work—& just got my way! Newell & Ritchie & I plan to publish it privately, by subscription—to make cost is all we want.

Fisher's only condition is anonymous or pseudonymous publication.

I think you will be interested in Mrs Jeffers' letter, referring to your letter about his & your metrics. Please return it.

I got some good rest on our vacation over Thanksgiving. Took no work, no books. Merely sat & looked at the ocean—& paddled a canoe & played with my boys.

Last night we heard Millay read. Disappointing. She puts on a false act. Huxley's introduction of her was superb.

But tell me, have you new plans for coming south? I'm so sorry we were away this last time. Let me hear from you soon.

Do you & your wife like "classical" music? i.e. Beethoven, Bach, Haydn, Mozart, etc. Strange that Jeffers doesn't.

Regards!
Larry Powell

Dec. 8, 1938
Selma, Calif.
ALS, 2 p., 1 sheet

Dear Powell—

I am amazed that you sent the "article" to the Jeffers'. Frantically looking over my penned draught of that letter I see that my slang (employed willfully in an effort to avoid a pedantic tone) merely coarsens and nullifies much of my effect. At the most, I was concerned with an angle, which I attempted more or less as a diversion, and which I sent you timidly (under my brass-front of colloquialism) afraid I was overstepping. And you put it to a test for which it was never designed. No wonder Jeffers was bored!

It was evidently misconstrued. Mrs. Jeffers writes: "He stands by his line, long though it may be," and "long lines with lots of pauses seem natural enough to me." Never did I intend to suggest that his line should be shortened. I believe in long lines, in the sense of body and dignity they give to a poem. I tried to make it clear that it would be absurd to break up the line as I had in my experiment, and that I realized those pauses were infinitely varied in their weights and would never do to be emphasized by being separated. I did not intend a discussion of line length at all—it was merely the method for determining line length that I was regarding. Surely a metrical, or rather, a "physical" arrangement so unessential to the verse that four years elapsed before its basis was even discovered could logically be called to question.

His example of the sea I think was very apt and very true, to such an extent that I feel it justifies my contention (though this is impudence in the face of Jeffers' personal denial). The major movement of the sea is a long swell, and the minor movement is the wave, which exists within the swell, or upon it, and is part of it, as the swell is part of the ocean, and is in direct relation to the swell as the swell is in relation to the ocean. So in the verse of Jeffers the major movement is the long phrase, and the minor movement the stressed syllable, which exists within and upon the phrase and gives it pace and rhythm and beauty, but is always secondary to the long majestic running of the phrase beneath it. As I see it, it is as futile to attempt to measure and adjust the fundamental movement of his verse by counting the ten stresses as it would be to determine the length of a swell of the ocean by counting ten waves. This whole discussion, however, is itself futile, for the basis of the verse is phonetic: it exists outside and beyond any typographical arrangement. You read it, and it comes over you in long magnificent rhythms, lifting and falling, gathering up into some final consummation from which line lengths and metrics dwindle to nothing. The verse is there. It exists. All my quibbling cannot touch it, nor can Jeffers by the lengths of his lines. He can break where he wishes without fundamentally altering: only the eye is affected. The ear knows nothing of all that pattern: change and change, the ear knows nothing: it is listening for phrase-lengths, not line-lengths, it is waiting to be awakened, stirred, shaken: and it cannot be fooled.

Sincerely
Bill E.

P.S. Will read Fisher this weekend, and reply. Thanks very much for allowing me to see this material. Our visit a long way off, I suppose. Working hard. Am returning Traven, thanks again ever so much. And for letting me see this letter from Mrs. Jeffers, which I have copied. Incidentally, what do you think of all this discussion?

Sunday, Dec. 11 '38
Selma
ALS, 4 p., 2 sheets

Larry:—

It is remarkable how our conceptions of literature widen as new work drives into our experience: MacIntyre made me shove back my borders to include him, and now this "Ghost in the Underblows" thing rolls in and surrounds me and when the fog lifts I see my borders pushed back again and the "Ghost" staring me in the face. It is a remarkable piece of work; and a hard one to place; you read on and on carried by a readability that is amazing. The lines running one onto the tail of the other, the verses one on another, and the sections, and the books, like water flowing, mobile and fluid and wide, running and running and curling back over and upon itself in channels and currents. It is so loose that at first sight you think it cannot be poetic, but after you read awhile, you know better, you think these are not poetic rhythms, but after awhile there rises up out of the river a mist and spreads over and around you and you know you have the real thing: you read on and come to a passage that gathers you up higher than a kite and after awhile you glide down and run along level, effortless and smooth, and then are picked up again, easily, and lifted. Never was I either soaring or falling, but always lifting or settling;

and never was I really sure what it was all about. I was listening to water and the water was trying to tell me something of immense import if I could only understand; but the water, although speaking in words that I knew, was talking about something I never had known myself, something that was beyond me, was farther than I had ever gone. I listened and listened: and after so long a time it began to come over me: something I could not place, could not describe, but the water had talked so long and so earnestly, and had spoken with such utter conviction, that gradually I began to feel that I knew what it meant. This sounds phony but I mean it; I cannot tell whether Fisher has written a *Waste Land* or an *Inferno,* but he has written humanity that much I know. I believe in this work: it is no looser than Whitman and five times as readable: you get the conception of an infinitely sensitive and intelligent man laying his ear to the earth and writing verbatim every delicate response and flux that twitches his being. It's great. It's great because it's so goddamned big and so goddamned sensitive: beautifully sensitive: and yet so big you've got to take it in its books to get it. It is the first thing I have ever read that has struck me as being so sensitive, and so wide. I don't mean bigness in the way I feel it in Shakespeare: that's profundity, or something solid: I connected that somehow with weight—but this isn't heavy. I don't know how to say it, I'm straining to grasp in this moment how this work hits me—it's like water, but thin: like a level thin stretch of water—a thousand miles wide and half an inch deep and as sensitive and delicate as light. It's remarkable; it's beyond me in a way that I never will be able to grasp, because it's a temperament that is opposite to mine literally etched on paper. It's beyond me because it is so *intellectual* and I am so *sensual* and never will I be able to encompass it. But it encompasses me it's all around me. It's wide!—

I'm talking gibberish. Please forgive:—I've come hot from the thing and have been writing this almost subconsciously trying to place my feeling. I'll leave it, because it probably comes as close as I can come, though it may be absurd, my figures are so mixed!

Dec. 13—Tuesday

This "Ghost in the Underblows" will stand as one of the achievements of American Literature. I've read it to my wife and we both rise to it. Only my skimping to get out my own prevents me from subscribing. It seems intolerable that this first edition of such an amazing poem should lie so close and we not in on it. Perhaps we can yet. Sitting here, the poem before me, I reflect on it that I am privileged to read it before it appears. That's something. I'll remember these nights.

I talk too much. Sometimes I forget I'm a poet. However much Robinson has lost since his death, for one thing must he be admired. He never forgot he was a poet. Asceticism. Never did he forget it. Close lipped. Whatever he gave off was in a poem. I talk too much.

Jeffers forgets. Quit poetry for prophecy. Remember what he wrote in Van Doren's review about the poet's war with himself? It looks as if the man Jeffers has finally conquered the poet. "The Birth of an Age" his last great achievement—and a really great one.

I've had your Jeffers book from the state library. This second reading leaves me thinking better of it than the first. You've done a fine bit of work, detailed, clear-headed. A warm work. And what you've done is proved every point with a magnificent quotation. Every claim you've made you've backed up with a quotation—it's almost an anthology of splendid lines. So is the Lawrence work. By your selection in that work you make what would have been a musty, dry, uninteresting catalogue burn with life. In the Traven piece (though it does not come up to these purely because Traven is not artist enough) your selections show the essence of the man. I was much more capable of "getting" Traven after reading your piece. Also I've found your piece on Ritchie in an old *Reading and Collecting.* Had no idea Ward had been so far and accomplished so much, and feel silly to have passed judgement on such an artist. It floors me to think of his doing my work—pleases me to learn Jeffers and MacLeish are favorites of his. Looking forward to meeting him again—and to meeting Newell and the people you speak of. You're all so damned learnéd and experienced, what with your speaking French, and your European backgrounds, and your university trainings! I've had three miserable semesters in a miserable college, and am so provincial.—Shit!

In this same *Reading and Collecting* you've written what I consider to be a perfect review: you're right in the essence of your material and the piece really comes off. Warm, spontaneous, lively, close to the subject. It couldn't be better done. M.F.K. Fisher. The dedication to the "Ghost" is to M.F.K.F., which makes both the Fishers writers, and apparently, both excellent ones.

I talk too much. Shit. It is needful for a poet to remember his poetry and, in everything else, shut up.

Bill Everson.

I'm terribly sorry about keeping Traven for so long. I get up before daylight and don't get back from work till after dark, and the days slide. Please forgive me. If there's anything I value it's other people's books, and am terribly sorry.

Do not care for classical music. Only emotional, sensuous music, and then, not objectively. I won't have a radio (or newspaper, incidentally) and have tried to narrow my tastes into the one field of poetry. My father is one of this part of the country's most active musicians, and has written some military marches that are really superb in this, of course, inferior field, and I have been subjected to music all my life. I'm even a fair tuba player (of all things!) but on maturity I shoved it all and left it entirely. It's not in my blood.

Long Haul is junk. I couldn't get over two chapters. Stinks. Many poems and many stories are now being written in a San Joaquin locale, but nobody seems to get the spirit of the Valley. They run characters about it as if it were anyplace. There's something here bigger than those fellows, deeper than they go, something infinitely rich that I feel and want to grasp. I once spoke against regionalism, but as I see now it is by becoming steeped in the mood of the locale that the universal is attained. This valley is waiting for a spokesman. You quote in the Jeffers work a remarkable paragraph by L.C. Eiseley. Ambition enough for any poet, the gist of that paragraph.

Dec. 16, 1938
Van Nuys
ALS, 6 p., 3 sheets

Dear Bill—

First of all, the *Death Ship* made port. I knew you'd like it. Second, I'm sorry I vexed you by sending your letter to the Jeffers. You're right, they didn't understand it. But that was not because of the way it is written. I think you've got a hold of something. I really know little of prosody. You are a poet; I am not. And I think you're better fitted for getting inside of Jeffers' metrics than I, or anyone else I know. Have you read Chard Powers Smith's *Pattern & Variation in Poetry* (1932)? If not, ask for it from the State Library. I will try later to come to honest grips with your paper.

Today you called on me twice. First at the University, in *Phoenix;* & second, at home tonight by letter. Here in my quiet room I've just read aloud the poem. It's good; it's very good. It speaks to me so clearly. It speaks to me out of my own past. And it expresses that solemn insane prophetic sad sweetness we feel when we stand naked in the window & look out on the earth & heaven that dwarf us, & then turn away, back to the naked beauty that awaits us in the still, roofed room. And we go to meet it, with all our senses increasingly heightened by our knowledge of transiency, and there is truly a "shining of plasm"—and then, as truly, we sleep.

You have written a fine poem. I'm sending a copy of it to a few people I know who will like it. Should "serria" be "sierra"?

Strange that the following poem, by Brewster Ghiselin, is by a man I knew 5 years ago, for the space of a few weeks, when we were living south of Laguna—& since lost complete track of. I remember him as being very jealous of his pretty wife. He knew Lawrence in France, just before L's death.

I've written one or two things about love, in prose, that I'd like you to read some day. Is there a chance of your coming down the New Year's weekend?

Please don't think of yourself as provincial. You are a poet & you embrace the wide world in your imagination. It's that quality of wide sympathy I like & respond to, & people do not acquire it either by schooling or travel. One of my close friends is a middle-aged bachelor who teaches high school in Dijon—& I don't believe he's ever been out of the province of Burgundy. Yet his curiosity & sympathy reach around the world & we keep closely linked these nearly 6 years gone by.

I have the finest friends a man ever had, Bill, and now I like to think of the way you've been growing to be one. I don't care much what I write. I've proved myself no poet, no novelist (I wrote three to complete the proof); and I have no frustration because of it. I want to work with all my heart & soul for my friends' work. Not that they need me to gain recognition. No; simply because I love to do this. I have something in me that brings me together with those who are speaking deeply & truly for this our time. I have no time for dilettantes or fashionables or popularizers. Give me that artist who writes from the very crying need of his guts.

Which, I guess, brings me to your letter about Fisher. God, man, it's a magnificent tribute you've written! I've been so close to the "Ghost" for nearly 10 years & have come slowly to have a very high opinion of it; & have worked like a sonofabitch to get Fisher to let me take it over; & these past 3 months been typing my tail off to get it ready to print—& then to have your eloquent justification. It's just what I needed. I hoped so it would sweep over you. It has, & how I am delighted!

Publication will be a big job. None of us have money. Will you help us? I mean with your enthusiasm & advice & moral support. The prospectus must be carefully considered. I have an idea for a group of opinions of the "Ghost"—not by "names"; I'm not going around kissing anyone's arse nor am I going to send the poem the round of N.Y. publishers—opinions by a few who have been deeply moved by the poem. Yourself, myself, Newell, Ritchie—& maybe a few others yet unknown. When I get the 3 books back from you I am going to send them to Jeffers—and see what happens! I'd give a nut if I could get him to write a foreword to the poem. I'm very selfishly thinking of the sales value it would have!

Yes, Mary Frances Kennedy was Al's wife. They married in 1929 & went to France. In the peace she gave him, he wrote the "Ghost." I went over a year later, & for a year & a half I lived in the same *pension* with them. I saw the poem being written. I grew to love the two. We were & are very close. But they have separated. It's a strange tragic story. They went to Switzerland in 1936 with a man who came into a lot of money. The brother of Anne Parrish. A fine man. She fell & was driven into love with him. Fisher returned to this country a year & a half ago & has been teaching at Smith. A few months ago, in Switzerland, Parrish was instantly stricken with a nearly fatal embolism. They have removed one leg at the hip, & the other probably will go too. He will never walk again. She is nursing him now at a sanitarium in the Bernese Oberlander, up in the "Magic Mountain" district. I had a sad brave letter from her last week.

It's all a fine brave dignified tragedy, Bill, acted by strong people. Jesus, it tears my heart.

I have told you this because it helps explain Fisher's present attitude toward the "Ghost." You see it was all for M.F. He wrote it to her & she's in it. So if it's published he insists it can't be under his name.

See if you can get her book from the library. If not, I'll send you mine.

Fay says that if you can come down the New Year's weekend she will fix our double studio couch for you to sleep on. This would save you a little—& we would all eat here together. Consider this well, & if you can, let me know soon so that I can book N. & R. for Sunday night. No use trying to get them for New Year's Eve. We always stay home that night—& we the four of us could sit very snugly—

Am reading Whicher's *This Was a Poet—a Critical Biography of Emily Dickinson*—quite good. And Edmund Wilson's *Triple Thinkers*—& Mumford's *Culture of Cities.* That's a lot for me these days.

God bless us all!
Larry

Dec. 20 '38
Selma, Calif.
ALS, 2 p., 1 sheet

Dear Larry:—

What you say of my poem leaves me prouder than anything could have. It is strange even to me, for some parts I feel are bad, but I am almost afraid to touch it, for fear of smothering it under form. Words like yours once in a while are all I want: there are a few real men in the world, and what I want so much to do is to identify myself with them. To be one of the real men, accepted by them, honest to the core of my being, earnest as the earth is, in some way living deeper and cleaner than my vanities and conceits that press so close about me. To walk with the real men—if I can only do it. Words like those from you hit me where it means something to be hit. I want more than ever now to do real work. Sierra is right. You've seen my letters enough to know my trouble. Poor Cooney must have wondered about that word, it was my error, not his!!

The "Ghost in the Underblows" stays with me—I cannot forget it. It is in me now, part of me, I can never forget it now. But my letter was wrong—it's not like water—aliver than water, much more alive—like plasm it is. That sensitive, that quick. It is gradually resolving itself in my mind. It is somehow like plasm and nerves. Advice and enthusiasm and moral support you ask. My advice would be worthless, and moral support dubious, but enthusiasm I have, and whatever I can do, in any way at all, will be a privilege—one of the luckiest things that happened to me. To be near this thing before the world gets it gives me a feeling of intensity—as if I were right on the inside of the big events of the day. That thing will go down in the language. I feel it. Whatever I can do, or whatever you'll *let* me do, I shall be glad. The story of his personal life, and hers, is indeed tragic. There are dark inscrutable forces shoving us around, toying with our sensibilities, tricking us shamefully. Spitting in our faces. A tale like this one beats me. Scares me to death to consider it personally.

In looking over some old material I found two of these pamphlets [*Ravens*]. When I came back from Sunnyvale in '35, jobless, I moved in again on the family, and kept shop at the Printery while my father kept Justice Court. The pamphlet was too flimsy to satisfy me, and I thought of covering it. My father had taught me to set type when I was a boy, and I got this out secretly, knowing he'd either be pleased immensely or angry as hell for meddling with his stuff. He's never seen this. Twice he almost caught me, and I smudged two copies! I was limited in types and stocks, but at that it's probably the best I can do. You're born with or without the sense for plastic design, I guess. I don't even have enough friends to exhaust an edition of fifteen copies! I haven't any good reason for sending you this. The other goes to Fay Porter, who told me she had never seen the pamphlet at all.

For a time I consciously resisted any tendency to give myself over to regionalism *per se* and I think my feeling was a sound one, for it is only by interpreting regionalism in a firm and sound art that it has any value. I have not, of course, any reason to assume that my structure is such that I can blithely forget about it, but it seems that I am come to the point where I must begin to shape myself toward some larger more definite end, to gather my sensibilities toward some sustaining purpose. This is high talk, and a little over my head, but anyway, just for the sake of making the declaration, I'm going to start doing purposefully what I must have been doing anyway for a long time: using the San Joaquin as the supreme foundation for all I hear rushing around me. I am now in love with the title "San Joaquin," so much so that I think of it as a large general heading, under which separate volumes fall and into which they also grow, as Whitman used *Leaves of Grass*.

Poetry magazine makes me sick—it's now so sterile, so lifeless, so absolutely devoid of anything that looks like flesh and bone, so insistent upon treating literature as an abstract technique. When it does forget technique it gives $100 to something like H. H. Lewis' "Farmhand's Refrain." Those bastards turned down everything good I've written. *Nation* and *New Republic* cutting down on literature, focusing on sociology, "the one deadly direction." I stand by *Phoenix*. I love that little magazine for everything it stands for. D.H. Lawrence on Democracy crystalized all my vague longings and leanings and gropings. And this New Mexico article and religion. Lawrence has beaten me to everything I want to say, and has said it better than I could ever even hope to, some of the most alive writing ever done, but I'm going to build poems out of this stuff, my own poems. I believe it too deeply to let it go by.

You speak of failing in poetry and novels, but in appreciative criticism you have the quality of closeness to subject that is so rare today. To read it is to know you *feel* your literature, you're in there living with it, and never showing off dogmas or what not, you're writing to get across to the world what you feel the world will enjoy and use, and in this day of suspicion and hedging and regarding reputation first and the work under consideration last, your stuff has a warmth that is courageous. I believe in that. To hell with scientific criticism. The only kind of criticism is appreciative criticism—holding it up to the sensibilities and being honest about what it shows. It's a good work you're doing—a live, warm blooded work. It shows in the type of men you treat. That Jeffers work was fine work; your first chapters dealing with Jeffers personally and your visit was hard work well done, mighty hard to "get" a man the way you got Jeffers. It had interest and warmth and set the book off to a fine start.

New Year's is best for us too, but because of the usual rush we didn't suggest it. We'll leave after my work Saturday evening, and so probably won't get down till late. We have enough now so as not to crowd in on you and will take an auto court. I don't know how to find you, but we will call from the highway and you can straighten us out. Is this O.K.? It takes four or five hours to go down. If I do not work we can, of course, arrive sooner.

Bill

Christmas Eve—1938
Van Nuys
ALS, 2 p., 1 sheet

Dear Bill—

I am pleased to know that you will be down the New Year's weekend. Do try to fix it so you won't have to work Saturday afternoon & can leave so as to bring you here by evening. You will be more comfortable in an auto court, & I am glad to know that your finances will permit you to put up in one.

* * *

We will be up that New Year's Eve till midnight, right here at home. (We have a standing custom of never going out that night); so phone us any time up till then. If you arrive after midnight, I suggest you proceed eastward on 101 about 1/2 mile, & look at the couple of auto courts you will encounter on the south side of the street. Then phone us in the morning.

I hope though that you will arrive early so that we may spend the evening together.

I am mailing you another book of Fisher's "Ghost"; one of my favorites. Bring it down with you.

The specially covered *Ravens* is very welcome. I read the poems over last night. They are very sharp in sight & sound—Perhaps I got something from them that I would get from looking at a portfolio of Japanese prints.

We will have a good session with Ritchie, talking about your next book. I have him & Newell booked for Sunday, New Year's night.

yours,
Larry

1939: EVERSON'S SAN JOAQUIN

Jan. 24, 1939
Selma, Calif.
ALS, 1 p.

Dear Powell:—

When we were down Newell said that if I could find out from Buel how he could be contacted in S.F., and would let him (Newell) know through you, that he (Newell) would look Buel up in February. I shall quote from today's letter from Buel:—

"Newell can reach me by phoning me at the *Chronicle* (Douglas 1414, c/o This World Dept.) any day from Monday thru Thursday, 10 A.M. to 9 P.M. Friday, Saturday, and Sunday he could leave word at my girl's house (phone Tuxedo 6109) as to where I could contact him. On weekends I am seldom home, and besides, my landlady speaks very bad English and Newell might get discouraged but I always see my girl sometime on those three days. Here's hoping you can make sense of the directions, am anxious to see Newell."

This poem ["The Dancer"]—it would take a better man than I to derive an art from the preceding work of two superlative artists, so that I was doomed to failure before I had begun. But this was not bred of a phony mood, as was my Tor House—done because I felt obliged to create something in memory of my trip. All the way home from L.A. the photo of the sculpture, and Newell's gestures of description as he told us his source, and that Jeffersian image from *Point Sur* moved in my mind, so that when we arrived home, jittery from traffic, and I went out to the vineyard to quiet myself, the wind in blowing a storm from the west, bred also this; you can show it to Newell if you wish; and if it is any good.

Sincerely
B. Everson

P.S. When I was gathering autographs I did not realize that you also were a contributor to the Founders Day Exhibition Catalogue. Next time! Also many thanks from Edwa and me for a magnificent weekend. Perhaps, if Newell is not too rushed, he could stop by on his trip. We're home weekends and Sundays. Phone 13F12 Selma.

Another P.S. Ward said the book ("San Joaquin") could be bound for 25¢ per copy. This makes only $25.00, and since we are going as far as we are, we feel we should take this one more step and make the book permanent. Tell Ward to count on binding also.

Jan. 28, 1939
Selma, Calif.
ALS, 3 p., 2 sheets

Dear Powell:—

The problems and the aesthetic attitude of a minor artist are identical with those of a major one—it is only in the degree of achievement that they differ. But because even the word *artist* denotes distinction, its self-applied use by one who is unsuccessful has come to be looked upon as presumptuous. An "arrived" artist can quite safely refer to his "artistic duty," yet an unknown, faced with identical problems, pursuing identical ends, filled with as high a purpose, cannot apply that phrase, nor any similar one, without fear of provoking ridicule.

Such a preamble is unneccessary with you I know, but I have an exaggerated, hypersensitive fear of appearing ridiculous (my father once scoffed me out of the house for speaking of my "artistic purposes"—the quotes are his!) and I should never have broached this subject at all were it not for a point that has come up between us. In order to fully explain my reasons for not wanting to send "San Joaquin" out for review, I must do so in terms of my "artistic attitude" (the quotes are *not* mine) and I trust that you will appreciate my distinction in the use of these terms as denoting *attitudes of endeavor* rather than references to achievement. I must, of course, admit my belief in the validity of that endeavor—to such presumption I will admit—if you will grant me that much perhaps I can make it clear how I stand, regardless of whether or not I am able to change your opinion.

My artistic attitude, then, is concerned with the creation of a solid, moving, beautiful poetry, to be formed under a personal criterion that has been shaped by natural sensibilities, and can have little to do with the temporal conceptions of any period. To define in my mind my attitude towards permanency in poetry, and then apply myself towards attaining it, is clearly my basic duty; and the only way that contemporary opinion should affect me, if it must, is in regard to my fundamental beliefs as to the true nature of poetry. To do this it is not necessary to judge my personal achievement. The prevalent artistic conceptions make themselves felt in enough quarters for any conscientious and alert poet to judge whether or not they have any value for him. And having made such a decision, there is nothing for him to do but go on working in the solitude of his integrity, and construct, in his own way, what he is able to. When he has attained his stature, when he has trained himself and tempered his medium to the point where he knows it, and can use it to purpose, and when he has matured enough to transfuse his personal problems into the universality of his art, then is the time to offer at large what he is doing. To measure him before that time is not only useless, but dangerous.

I have not arrived at such a point. This book is obviously a step—even if I never do better than its best it is yet a step—for it reveals plainly those qualities of transition that mark most works of growth. As a step I do not wish it to pass for public and professional appraisal. Outside its faultiness it contains attitudes I do not now believe, and whatever is publicly said of it in literary journals I feel will only tend to divert me from the important purposes which are for me and none other to resolve.

Then why print at all? To get it down in the clarity and permanence of type: to get it actually behind me: to get it together good and bad, as a portion of my development, as an interval of my life: to get it behind me so that I can look ahead to what there is for me, and develop and mature beyond this book and its problems. "Then," you'll ask, "why did you ask me to write a foreword to this book?"

Not to use your considerable influence as a California critic to gain me a public, though that I think would be a legitimate reason were it true: not in the hope you'd say nice things about me and flatter my vanity—vanity I have but by being savage toward it can sometimes keep it in hand. I asked you because there has grown between us a friendship that I value. Your interest has been constant in a way I had no reason to expect, your discernment has helped me to shape my work: you have influenced others in my behalf, and brought me friends I could not have had. Through you alone is it possible that I can bring out this book in a format better than it deserves. I asked you as a declaration of friendship and faith, to solidify in this permanent way the relation between us.

In fact, the reasons for which I asked you are all personal ones, and that's as it should be, for they are the only reasons in which I am now interested. However, I see that, as you suggested on our evening together, by entering into this project you are entitled to a voice in the ends of its disposal, and so I have gone into detail here in a manner I should rather not have done in order to let you see that my motives are not bred of a pose, and to try to persuade you that perhaps the restricted disposal that I had planned might be best. To submit for review would be to nullify my chief reason for not hunting a publisher: were it publicity I wanted I should have tried all New York—though at that were I successful I would not have a Ward Ritchie book!

Sincerely
Bill Everson

Feb. 23, '39
Selma
ALS, 1 p.

This letter was written a month ago, and the lapse of time has strengthened, not softened, my belief. McKelvy, a close friend and a good critic believes as you do, but I cannot see it. The farther I get away from "San Joaquin," the more dissatisfied I become with it. And though you and McKelvy and Curtin [college chum] and Buel swear by it, I who am very proud of that swearing-by, feel the gnawing within that I cannot ignore.

It has to be in print, but beyond that, I cannot agree. It seems so transitory, almost gawkish, adolescent, so damned young. I think of *Point Sur* and *The Waste Land* and my daring to write becomes mere impudence.

The other day a friend came up and said: "Say, did you hear how Jeffers' wife tried to kill him in Taos last summer?" So you see how tales travel.

Question: Is Una Jeffers jealous of his preoccupation with sex, and of his use of it in his themes? Do you know anything about this?

How are things with you now? It seems a decade since we were there. A great weekend, though we must have been a burden coming on such a malicious sequence of trials. That Jeffers work of yours has been drained clear off the market. I can see why, for our county library copy has been loaned 10 times in the last two months.

Is the "Ghost" coming along?

Would like to hear from you again.

Sincerely,
Bill E.

In the F.S.C. library I ran across an article on Jeffers in the *Drake University English Quarterly*. He referred, of course, a number of times to your work, but his point was one that I thought everyone who knew Jeffers had seen. Certainly not important enough to justify such a heavily footnoted document. When I first read Krutch [*The Modern Temper*] in 1936 I was immediately struck with the similarity of the two men's attitudes.

Feb. 26, 1939
Van Nuys
TLS, 1 p.

Dear Bill:

Sorry to be so long in acknowledging the fine poem to Newell. I gave it to him and he was mighty tickled. I note what you say about binding the book; I told Ritchie. I have delayed turning over the ms to him, waiting on my getting the forenotice written. This I will do very soon now, and you should be receiving a dummy from him before long. This will tie in with your schedule, will it not?

Enclosed is a good notice of Saroyan which I've been saving for months to send you. Needn't return.

Just up from a week with the flu. For a week I did nothing except read a couple of books: about and by Rabelais—in English. Do you know this great writer?

What are you doing these days?

Yours was an excellent visit. Have you completed that ode to southern California stucco?

Regards.
Larry

March 12, 1939
Van Nuys
ALS, 2 p., 1 sheet

Dear Bill—

At last I can write you with untroubled mind. At last, after months of shrinking from the task, I have done the notice for your book. Hurrah! A damned hard thing to do, my lad—& that's why I kept from tackling it. I feel pretty good about the result right now—but I won't later. So I guess for both our sakes we'd better get the book printed as fast as we can! Tomorrow evening I shall deliver the ms. to Ritchie.

And now I can answer your letter of a couple weeks ago, about sending out review copies. You make out a good case for yourself. I would warn you against taking it all too seriously. I still think it would be good to send out a few copies—to *Poetry*, *N.Y. Times*, *N.Y. Herald-Tribune* "Books," & *Saturday Review of Literature*. However, I shall not press the point. You decide.

You'll want to copyright the book. Ritchie will acquaint you with the procedure, & probably has a stock of the necessary forms on hand. When copies are ready to distribute, I should like to give you the names of some libraries that ought to have them.

I have been as busy as usual. Prospectus for the "Ghost" got a lot of work out of me. I've done it over six times, until now I think it's ready to print. The typescript I made is being gone over by Fisher.

You'll know some potential subscribers. Suppose I send you a batch of the prospectus for you to send out? An accompanying note will help. It's going to be worth scrimping to have a copy of the "Ghost," but you are well aware of that. We've got to spread the enthusiastic infection to many people. Right now we figure on 300 copies of which 275 will be on sale at $6—.

The deal on my book with the University Press fell through; I got a bad deal. But all's well that etc. A new press in Pasadena, sponsored by a wealthy banker, is going to do it, on a royalty basis. They have no editor, so I had to write my own prospectus. I'm really in trim for that sort of business, & did it without a blush!

Soon as I can get it back from a friend, I'll loan you a copy of the *Colophon* which contains a piece I did on Steinbeck. Or maybe your library has got that quarterly. In the autumn 1938 number.

Let's hear from you. Regards,

Larry Powell

Mar. 14, 1939
Selma, Calif.
ALS, 3 p., 3 sheets

Dear Powell.

Today your very welcome letter arrived and I'm glad to hear that you have the piece done to your satisfaction and ready for the press. As things stand now, the first of the month will see us ready with the money for the printing—barring accidents—and then Ritchie can complete this business and all our chests will be clear! About Buel: I don't know what to think. Ritchie asked for some sketches merely to show technique in order to know what style he should have to work with, and I told Hubert, but he has the idea & thinks that even this preliminary work should be essentially a draught of the final product, and in trying to do his best is giving the business more attention than it merits. I've written again, and hope for a response shortly, but I can't tell about Hubert. For myself, time in this matter means nothing. This year or next is all the same. What worries me about Hubert's slowness is that Ritchie won't feel like spending much time on so small a job, quite naturally, with other work pressing, and I'd hate to have any reason of mine holding him up. I told Hubert we plan to be ready by the first, so surely I shall hear from him soon.

I'm glad the Jeffers reprinting is coming through, and hope this source will prove more advantageous to you. The work deserves the best, and I'm looking forward to its appearance. That first printing is scarcer—to quote you—than type-lice! And the "Ghost" also. All my friends are so poor I doubt even if my gifts of persuasion can break them loose from $6, but send down the prospectus and I'll put my best eloquence into the business. You can, of course, count on us for a copy.

Am looking forward to seeing your article on Steinbeck. The *Colophon* I've seen only twice in my life, and know what it means to appear there. Good going! The *New Masses* and the *Colophon!* "I am large. I contain multitudes." I envy you that printing.

Today also came a very complimentary card from a man named Franklin Patterson, who has received "from a friend" *These Are the Ravens.* Did you send it him? That's about the only fan mail I ever received.

Speaking of *The Ravens,* I'm enclosing a clipping of the only review it received, from a quarterly called *Literature* (of all titles) in Akron, Ohio (of all places). This review was printed shortly after the pamphlet appeared, and will, I believe, go down in history as the most touching and exquisite example of this particular literary art. In those few lines is crammed everything—absolutely everything. Hoffman (my publisher) must have done something awfully nice for that editor to get them to publish this. Please return. "Well worth ten cents." That beats me.

I'm not getting much done. My company is undergoing the spring rush and we're swamped with work. I come home at night completely exhausted and can only sit by the stove and gasp through the evening. It's really brutal labor I do, and my back is troubling me for the first time in my life. Sometimes I feel those vertebrae grate together under a heavy load and it scares the pants off me. Piles showed up last fall and now this. I've got to get a ranch before this business makes an old man of me.

This has been my most unproductive winter in four. Next letter I'll send what I have to show. I am creating less, but reworking more, a practice that will lead to the better, I hope. At any rate, it seems that's the direction my future activity will move. It is sure that one sound poem is better than a dozen glib ones.

I am finally beginning to "see" Hart Crane. Some of those passages in *The Bridge* I think are magnificent. And as a poem I'll probably have to move over *Point Sur* and *The Waste Land* to let it up. Marianne Moore I can't see. Excellent prose. Really some splendid writing, but poetry? No No. Even Eliot in his introduction to her *Selected Poems* seems careful not to come right out and call her a poet. Phillip Horton's biography of Crane is good stuff.

Rebecca West's *Strange Necessity* contains the best criticism of *Ulysses,* as an artistic whole, I've seen. Besides being a good materialistic definition of art.

Watkins and McKelvy are philosophy sharks, and we've been working the subject over all winter. This business of metaphysics is the most important problem in a man's life, and I'm not quite mature enough yet to resolve my intuitional leanings with the dictates of my logic. One thing is certain. Even if we have to make the most colossal assumptions to do it we've got to get out of this materialism into which science has led us. When I think, I can't see a way. It seems to me even Beauty can be explained materialistically. But intuitively I know better. Like Lawrence in the paper, "New Mexico," I can *feel* that tremendous something blowing in the wind. To hell with the mind. It probably evolved to keep us from running into trees and things, or getting our fingers caught in mousetraps, and not designed for ultimate speculation at all. Monism suits me, but the smart boys say it can't be so. Maybe in ten years I'll have it all straight in my head.

I guess my relation with the *Phoenix* is all off now. When Cooney saw I didn't intend to sell all my stuff and shuffle off to Mexico he cooled toward me. Rejected also the poem to

Newell. Well, he's got a fine magazine there. I believe in the necessity of someone making the stand he's making, someone resisting the too-heavy drift toward socialization. It's such a blind drift, almost fanatical, with all we've learned in these thousand years about the human spirit, suddenly ignored. *Poetry* magazine the high point of American verse, giving its 100 dollars to H.H. Lewis's "Farmhand's Refrain"! Oh god! Oh god!

Getting back to your letter: I shall be the first to admit that perhaps I am "taking it all too seriously" and I was careful to include the little preamble for just such a reason. What I said there does not justify my heroics, for the simple reason that heroics are unjustifiable. I still believe everything I said, because it is necessary for me to believe it; where I erred was in talking about it. There is something embarrassing about a man's attempting to defend his own egotism, and the reason I did it was because I thought it better to be honestly egotistical than to try to explain my stand by some gracefuller subterfuge. This does not, I know, excuse the self-centeredness explicit or implicit in all my letters. This very snatch I am writing exhibits the tendency as plainly as any, and I shall try to make it the last of the sort. At the root lies the fact that I cannot help taking myself seriously, however it appears. I am quite willing to make myself a bore, a dupe, a fool, or all three, on very meager chance that some later result may be of sufficient attainment to explain it, for I cannot hope to justify it.

But perhaps even this is a trick. I learned from my work among laborers, who have more pride than any type I know, and who will defend themselves to the bone's breaking against any personal derogation, that to declare yourself at the outset to be a bastard, a son of a bitch, and a goddamned shitheel will disarm and mystify them completely. You have reduced all their standards to nothing and they cannot place you. But such tactics will not work with you, for all my gesturing and sparring, so I shall have to resort to my second and last trick:

"You're goddamn right I'm a poet. Wanna make something of it?"

Bill Everson.

P.S. What in hell is a dummy, what is its purpose, and what am I supposed to do with it when I get it?

Like a fool I forgot to thank you for the fine photo. It is very good, and we are glad to have it.

3–31-39
Van Nuys
ALS, 1 p.

Dear Bill,

Can't answer your last letter in the detail it deserves. Guess you've heard from Ritchie. Will go by his place tomorrow & hope to see specimen pages.

Here's a piece on Mac for you to keep. It's cut way down; probably just as well.

Just finished Steinbeck's new book—*The Grapes of Wrath. Look out for it. It's going to land on you like a ton of bricks.* I'm warning you! It's published in about 2 weeks.

Mailing you a *Colophon* [Steinbeck, Autumn 1938] because I want you to read my piece. Please return at your leisure.

I'm eager to have your book finished.

Regards,
Larry

April 3, 1939
Selma
ALS, 4 p., 2 sheets

Dear Powell:

Your note arrived today, and I read the paper on MacIntyre with much interest. A very good note, telling much about the man, which is more important than the usual literary-personage gossip because this is one case where knowledge of the author is necessary to fully realize the poems. It is too bad the piece could not have had a wider publication, for MacIntyre seems to be a mystery, and the note in *Atlantic* was not enough. Another thing that struck me was the photograph—I had envisioned an entirely different man: this hard face I see is very forceful; cold, severe; and shows none of the sensuousness of his poems. Anyway, the piece stimulated me, and because I had really never fully realized in my mind MacIntyre's "place," I made tonight the attempt to do so, and dug back in what magazines I have to find his poems and reread them. And coming part way to the answer I stewed and stumbled and tried to put it down, with much hemming and hawing, but suddenly I remembered that the *Poems* had been reviewed in *Poetry* and I dug that out, and there it was, all I had been trying to say, in an excellent review by Winfield Townley Scott (*Poetry* Aug. 1937, pg. 289). If I could be sure of that kind of clear-headed balanced scrutiny even I should submit my book to *Poetry!* Incidentally, your paper should be sent to Scott personally: good might come of it. Scott is one of *Poetry*'s fair haired boys, and may turn out to be one of the future "guns." The important thing about MacIntyre, and the thing hardest to locate, and to describe when you have located it, is his, as Scott says "curiously combined gifts of the ironic and the sensuous." It is that subtle blend of purpose that lies at the root of his appeal. These last two poems in *Poetry,* "The Old Woman Waits Spring," and "The Ex-Senator," are perfect examples of this quality, and as poems are really excellent. There is something about them that completely takes you in: You look at the things on the surface and you think you shouldn't be: you think nothing good can come out of two such subjects: those subjects have been the use of so goddamned many bad poems: but these click: beautifully they click, and you get through them wondering how he did it. Two other excellent poems are in the four previously published in *Poetry*: "By a Patriot's Grave," and "Revenge Is Not a Food to Be Eaten Hot." The first one is not typical of MacIntyre because it has neither irony nor sensuousness. Look at it closely and you see that it is diamond-hard and written out of a cold and vital purpose: every word in its place and every word deadly: look at MacIntyre's picture when you read it and you shiver a bit. There's hate in that poem. And there's hate in the "Revenge" poem too, but of a different kind. There is a playfulness about that poem that is misleading, and when you get through and you see that you were misled and that here is no playfulness at all but only hate, sheer hate, like a savage chuckling a little to himself as he goes about getting ready to stick darts under your finger-nails; or like a child, with a child's insensitiveness to another's agony, seeing only its own pleasure in it. There's something horrible behind that poem. That playful: "Let us chop some of the heads off" with a total disregard for the human implications of the act. That poem is not of a civilized mind. And look—what it is saying is: revenge for its own sake only. "Before our anger starves and dies of mold" in other words, there's no more need for anger, its causes are past, it is no longer alive—but Revenge! Revenge is the thing! That was written out of a communist ideal, probably, but by god this is fascism! And in the night letter poem: "garrote traitors with a halyard-rope." My dictionary says garrote means strangle—that's terrible. And in the Patriot's poem: "red hecatombs before the whirlwind strewn" and hecatombs means generally a slaughter of victims. Jesus Christ!

But excellent poems, except the "Night Letter" one, and the "Sincerely Not Artesian," which is downright lousy. MacIntyre has one trick that I think is a bad one and which is probably taken from the modern American classicism of which Tate is a good example: the trick of using erudite words in unusual places, done I think, with the intention of introducing intellectual material into a general sensuous subject for the purpose of hardening, or for shearing the poem out of the way of possible sentimentality. In "Sincerely Not Artesian" it shows itself at its very worst. This group of poems has ten words I had to check to understand: dossils, suppurate, garrote, pelagic, assoil, hecatombs, chines, meniscus, quern, and gravidly. That's no good. But when the poems succeed, when there is no pulling of smart words out of the intellectual sleeve, when the mood and the purpose are one, and purpose is to show how really significant much insignificant material really is; they are beautiful and fine, and we know them for the real thing.

I think Scott has got his finger also on the reasons for Mac's occasional failure—the playing the "red and the black." Rarely is there a bad poem like "Artesian"—mostly it is revealed as ineffectuality, and you say, "that's no subject for a poem" until you remember his successes were of those same subjects. So you say, he lacks discipline, but remember his best poems are extremely well disciplined. Perhaps it resolved itself into the fact that his failures are such because on these particular poems he has not exerted that discipline. It is as if he quit too easily, and finished a poem like something out of childhood—"SAL" very dissatisfied, or even "Stag Party," which in spite of its heartiness doesn't quite come off—the colloquial quality being a little too evident, a little too dependent upon itself alone.

April 7, 1939

So the *Colophon* came, and we read with interest your Steinbeck article. You have a way of making an account that would normally be dry as dust very readable and very interesting—it's partly your own enthusiasm, partly your complete lack of affectation, and partly your supply of anecdotes and personal experiences with which you salt the thing down. I've noticed that in all the work you've done that I have seen, with the possible exception of the Jeffers work, which is more studious and detached, though also, of course, lacking in affectation. It's that touch of the personal and the intimate, the *closeness* to the subject, which most critics attempt to break with entirely. You've got something there. When all the pompous and ponderous accumulation of rationalistic literature has been stacked and classified, we'll still have these readable, intimate, very personal accounts of yours which will help us to get really next to these men. I'd like to see you treat Jeffers in this fashion sometime. It would make a good article: the human side of this High Priest whom everybody either worships or execrates. I guess you know him as well as most, and you could write it better than any.

Those metal corner-covers are o.k. My limited *Solstice* came from Dawson's with the top corner bent. Could I have done anything about that? Oh yes, just letting you know that pg. 560 of the *Colophon* was already wrinkled when it came!

I am waiting to begin trampling out the vintage where the Grapes of Wrath are stored.

We have finally mustered the admission price to "San Joaquin," a feat we thought with our combined income would be fairly easy, but the truth is in spite of the fact we have more money than either of us had ever had before, the nature of our debts and the effort to meet this book have kept us right in there grinding. But now we've done it we are taking great gulps of fresh air and are beginning to eye all the books we've both wanted to buy for so long!

I received a beauty of a specimen page from Ward—the poem "August" which shines a new glamor in its dress. It was in print once before: *The Carmel Pine Cone:* but with a typographical omission that was appalling. Now in this fine type and beautiful arrangement it makes my heart feel good to know it was an off-spring of mine! God, but I'll be a proud papa when that "San Joaquin" is born!

Every once in a while I let off some crack about socialization which must seem to you pretty naive—that last one about the too-rapid drift. When I go down to my job every morning and see Reed and think of his half-dozen half-starved children, and Hastin in the same fix, and the rest of them living in huts and shacks with no plumbing etc.—it makes a remark like that absurd. And the goddamned Supreme Court back there smugly knifing every attempt to help matters. What is back of my fear is the unholy dread of the love of the State: that abstract something that grips men's minds and makes them shoot down any sort of criticism, any sort of individuality. But reading Randolph Bourne's essay on the State, and seeing how our whole past and tradition is simply the glorification of the State itself, it seems hard how any form of socialization, even in war-time, could go much further; I suppose ideally my feeling narrows down to the desire for a distinction in the aspects of life that are to be socialized. All the economics, all the petty and mundane ways in which man gets food from the earth to the mouth are it seems to me in imperative need of socialization. What I fear is the carry-over the emphasis *might* have into the forms of spiritual life by which we are individuals: There are more Trotskys and Stalins in this life than there are Lenins, unfortunately, and they're the birds that take the supreme delight in getting at the head of something or other while the men who count see how much more important other aspects of life are, and won't waste time on it. At the bottom I am potentially a socialist—any concept of justice must arrive there finally—but never will I believe in revolution: not while society has some claim to excellence as ours has. That way I think lies only destruction. But this is all old stuff to you, and I say it here only to resolve all the half-cracks I've been making from time to time.

What is the name, incidentally, of the sculpture of Newell's I wrote that poem to?

Sincerely
B. Everson.

April 13 '39
Selma
ALS, 1 p.

Dear Powell:—

Well, the proofs have come and gone back—great long sheets of things like medieval scrolls—and I took the liberty of changing a few punctuation marks. I got an immense lift reading the poems for the first time in print, hard as it was to isolate them in the mind in that proof-sheet form: but they gain tremendously by type. They gain a semblance of chiseled and clean-cut clarity that typescript or ms. never had, and I feel proud of most of them. There are bad poems there however, that the best deluxe treatment in the world couldn't justify, and I suppose now that they are down in print they will gall me forever. But still I am anxious to have this book out, to see it before me rounded out to completion, three years of my life as good as I could make it. Buel contributed a sketch that Ward seems very pleased with, so I suppose everything will be dandy. I noticed you changed some titles, which was perfectly all right except for one: "Sierra Nevada." Together with the title page it seemed to me to offer a too-obvious leaning toward regional patriotism, the manner as it were of a chamber of commerce ad, so I restored the original title "Walls," which is simple, if somewhat bald. Is this OK with you?

I had been looking forward to reading your forenote which I

had thought would be here, but which was not, so I shall have to wait for the book.

I wonder how soon it will be completed, Ward has not said, and I'm not going to ask, but I'm nervous as a new bride when the wedding day sun is setting. When it does come out, keep a number of copies for your own use, which will save express running them back from here.

Bill Everson

4-15-39
Van Nuys
ALS, 2 p., 1 sheet

Dear Bill—

A couple of letters from you to answer. I had a set of proofs too, & sent them back today. Neither did I get a proof of my squib. Maybe it smelled too bad to set! Did I change "Walls" to "Sierra Nevada"? I don't remember doing it. But I do like it better. Don't be too sensitive about regionalism. Call things by their names. It's not important though.

I note what you say about my keeping some copies. I'd like to see the following libraries receive copies: U.C.L.A., L. A. Public L., L.A. County L., Occidental, Claremont colleges, Scripps College, Mills College, Stanford, State Library, U.C., and some individuals such as Jeffers, Fisher, Newell, Dr. Hal Bieler, M.F.K. Fisher, MacIntyre, Carey McWilliams, Pres. Sproul (U.C.), B. F. Stelter (Oxy), Ewing (UCLA), my mother, my mother-in-law, two uncles, Georges Connes (Dijon), Jean Matruchet (Dijon), Charles Cestre (Paris), Clinton Williams (Berkeley), Steinbeck, Albert Bender (S.F.). Does that stagger you? How many are being printed? These are all good people, & good libraries too. But if you'll be needing the copies, I'll cut down somewhere on the list. The book ought to be completed in another month at the most. I'm trying hard to get the "Ghost" prospectus out of Ritchie. He is very busy.

Corrected "Ghost" back from Fisher—& 8 different starts on a preface. He wants me to use his notes & write the preface myself. They are wonderfully interesting. We hope to see that project completed a year from this autumn.

I don't know if & when & what *re* my Jeffers book. Perhaps a Pasadena press. In the meantime, if you still want a copy of the Primavera edition & are still flush, Jake Zeitlin has one cataloged at $5.00 (624 S. Carondolet, L.A.) I do wish I had one to send you.

Colophon arrived. Glad you enjoyed the Steinbeck piece.

I like all that you write about Mac. You're right about that review in *Poetry*—it's a good one. Don't know name of Newell sculpture. Am eager to see what Ritchie-Buel combination produces.

yrs.
Larry Powell

April 16, 1939
Van Nuys
ALS, 2 p., 1 sheet

Dear Bill—

I send you herewith a manuscript to read [revised and published in 1977 as *The Blue Train*]. I don't know just why I send it. I haven't looked at it for six years. Suddenly the thought came to me to send it to you to read. In Europe I wrote a couple of novels in the conventional mold: plot, counterplot, etc. Back home in 1933 I determined to attempt a straightforward, colloquial narrative in the form of a novelette. This is what I typed out from my original draft. I intended to write it once again—refine the style, point up the individual sections, expand parts, add details—in short, put the raw material in the best possible shape.

But I never did it. My life changed. I was caught up in a whirlwind of new life, spun fearfully for a few years—then deposited on the great highlands of my 30's—thank God!

I feel a bit reluctant to send this to you; it is so crude in places. I should like some day to do the European years—I got all I went for & much, much more—& then a final third part, the return to America. Then the story will be complete. All of this of course not something to be published—but a few copies made for my friends. This first part that I send you herewith has been read only by Dr. Hal Bieler, Ritchie, Newell, & my wife Fay. Keep it as long as you like, & after you two have read it, send it back to me. I think maybe a trip out in the world will do it good; it's been cramped away so long. I know you will be tolerant of it.

yours,
Larry

P.S. I am including a copy of Paul Landacre's "Anna," printed from the original block. I remember you admired it—& I just got an extra one, which I intend to frame—So here's one for you. It's very beautiful, isn't it.

[April 19 (?), 1939]
[Selma]
ALS, 2 p., 1 sheet

Dear Powell—

Your typescript arrived, and though I am no critic I shall try to come to grips with it in my next letter; honesty is all I have to offer in a business like this, but it does please me to be trusted with your account. And the Landacre woodcut is superb: thanks very much.

Well, Steinbeck I see has shaken the world to its roots. He brings out an epic impassioned with the injustice and the shame that abounds in this valley the San Joaquin: and the same year I bring out a slight sheaf, faintly adolescent, extolling the region's scenic pretties. Dandy, isn't it? Lust, violence, depravity, injustice, intolerance, disease, destitution, starvation, poverty—all the condemnatory evils of humanity rife in the place, and a humane and mature artist takes it, and jars the country awake, dealing one of those terrific blows to evil that may well rival the "Jungle" situation, and the same year and a month later only, I bastard and shit-heel and double bastard—I sing sweet lays to grape vines. Of all the years to bring out my book this is the worst. What can I say? The material was here. I've known it for years. Hell, man, I *work* with that material; every day of my labor I rub shoulders with the very Okies Steinbeck deals with. It was thrown in my face; and what do I do? Sing sweetly modulated chants to grape-vines. There is nothing for me but to shrug with prurient evasion and say with MacLeish—

We are whores, Fräulein; poets Fräulein are persons of known vocation following troops.

Is it just to demand of us also to bear arms?

* * *

You are quite welcome to copies of *San Joaquin*, though you shouldn't have to bear the expense and trouble of sending to the libraries, which should be my worry. Maybe you could give me their addresses, and I could relieve you of that burden.

Some of the individuals on your list scare the pants off me—imagine what Steinbeck will think, for instance!—but since you're in on this too you've got me tied! Who the hell incidentally is Carey McWilliams? And Jeffers—"The pallid pursuit of the world's beauty on paper, unless a tall angel comes to require it, is a pitiful pastime."—where's my tall angel? But do what you like. There are a hundred copies, of which I won't immediately need much over a dozen, though I'll give a batch to Buel for his friends, since he was good enough to help me: All I want is some for future acquaintances.

I'm glad to hear you're doing the "Ghost" foreword rather than Jeffers. It's your job, not his. I'm glad to hear that; it's right.

I've ordered from Jake Zeitlin; it'll be good to see that book of yours come in: after so much searching.

Is your Pasadena contract [with] the San Pasqual Press? I got a notice from them of their venture. A woman who used to work at Dawson's and would answer my queries, is editor—I guess it was through Dawson's mailing list that I got the notice.

Maybe I sent that title in to you as "Sierra Nevada"—if so, apologies; there were a couple of titles I thought you changed that I must have done myself, and forgot to make the change on the list I kept. I'm very sorry. The changes were for the better, with this one exception, I think. That was stupid of me!

Sincerely,
Bill E.

Apr. 25, 1939
Los Angeles
APS

Bill,

If you've got an extra $1.50, get a copy of Harry T. Moore's *The Novels of John Steinbeck, a First Critical Study*. Chicago, 1939. Lots of good stuff in it. I want Moore to have a copy of your book.

LCP

May 3, 1939
Los Angeles
APS

Dear Bill—

Ritchie is holding up the book for the drawing from Buel—He has received only a preliminary sketch. I suggest you tell Buel to send final drawing without further delay.

LCP

May 30, 1939 [i.e., May 3]
Selma, Calif.
ALS, 2 p., 1 sheet

Dear Powell—

After I read the first section of the narrative [Personal Record] I took notes, jotting down for future revision my impressions, and trying to formulate how I would begin this answer. The two motives implicit behind the writing of a personal narrative are "the illustration of variety of experience, and/or the illustration of quality of appearance." But after reading the second section, I saw that that was no go. It is harder than hell to talk about a paper like this because it is so personal that it is almost untouchable, and because it is written out of a man's past, and it means to him what the past means, something unutterably private. To read it is almost comparable to watching two people coupling; yourself outside; yourself absolutely estranged from the fierce intensity of what those two are doing; and there is between only the tenuousness of writing to take you into the action.

I am enclosing the bald and crude notes I took when I had finished section one; and which I have not revised because it is in section two that the true validity of this narrative resides. It starts out in much the same vein as part one, and I think the same notes can be applied, but as it grows it gathers a richness of awareness that part one does not have, as if you were writing from something deeper inside you, rather than the simple wish to set down events. From about the desert scene onward the narration begins to take on significance; it means more: and the Paris scenes come through with intensity and richness. But all along there are aspects of the style that will need revision: matters of sequence and variation: rhythms; there is need of expansion and contraction; the ecstatic element I think should go—"O unforgettable etc." More time must be spent on it. Chapter titles I think are also unnecessary. If you go on with this I think you should put upon it the work you put upon the Jeffers treatise, which shows that you were writing under control, watching your words. I do not mean a thing like this should be written cold—that makes for dead writing—but after you have poured yourself out I think you must go back, and analyze and study. I think the writing of a personal narrative is the hardest writing a man can attempt—I found that out wryly—for he tends to be so close he cannot see what he otherwise would see—he cannot tell when he strays because he is seeing what was important to him without making it important to the reader. The best writing of yours I have seen I think is the introduction of the Lawrence Catalogue; but that is perhaps not a method, or rather style, you could apply to a passionate work like this. I think probably the European Years will be the best section when you are finished. I feel that it will be sounder, more integrated as experience and as experience transferred to writing. Look again at the sections of your Jeffers work that deal with your time spent with him. That's in this vein, and well handled I think. Soundly written. I'll wager you went over and over that work.

Well, this is wandering. Looking back I see that I have crabbed more than anything else, which I didn't mean to do, for there is much more credit coming to this narrative than I have given it; and I am no one to fidget at any man's writing, least of all yours, who have produced more work in your time than I ever will. But I have crabbed in the hope that you will go back and sweat over this thing; the worst thing I think can happen is to be too satisfied, to quit too easily. The tireless perfectionist stuff does have something, if a man knows when to quit. And this is the kind of thing you want to be sure of—dead sure—before you let it out.

May 4

Your card today, about Buel's drawing. I detect an undercurrent of testiness for which I cannot blame you. I won't attempt to apologize for Buel: I was aware of his procrastination long before this; but thought that over so long a time surely he could manage a little sketch. Well, I'll try to jack him up—have already sent off my letter in fact—but it's harder than hell to keep prodding a man when it's a favor you're asking.

Your Jeffers book finally came in—in pristine condition. Dust jacket, beautifully clean. The day that book came out you must have been walking on air! There's something exhilarating about a new clean well-printed book, and I prize this one. It will not stay that way long, alas! Even my scarce Jeffersiana bear the marks of so much handling. I noticed among the ads on the dust-jacket, that Laura Riding book sold for $2.50. I can't imagine so magnificent a thing going for so little. Jake Zeitlin's catalogue is the best bookseller's catalogue I have ever seen—bar none. The only bookseller I ever heard of putting emphasis on poetry. Fine runs of Eliot, MacLeish, Jeffers. I had never even seen MacLeish catalogued before. And I don't go in for first editions, but that first appearance of "The Waste Land" in the *Dial* makes my mouth water. I see you do not have Zeitlin's name on your list of copies. Would it be all right to give him one? You also mention Harry T. Moore. I'll tell you—you hold out forty or so copies when they are done, for people you have forgotten or haven't met yet—that'll leave you eight or ten to go on. There are plenty. I also noticed in Zeitlin's catalogue those Ritchie "incunabula" which you described as scarcer than type lice. The hell of it is we're broke. My work has shut down and the uncertain summer ahead. This always happens; but we have to tone down our expenses after the spending orgy of "San Joaquin," and get a grip on things!

Bill

5-8-39
Van Nuys
ALS, 2 p., 1 sheet

Dear Bill—

I am sending back corrected page proof to Ritchie & am puzzled by a line in "Abrasive": *In Fall resent winter, in Winter Spring*. It seems to be thus in your typescript. What does it mean? Write direct to Ritchie.

I trust Buel has come through by now. Strangely enough it's the illustrator who's holding up the "Ghost" prospectus. Damn their eyes!

Glad to hear that you got the book from Zeitlin's catalog. Get those early Ritchie items if you possibly can. Of course Jake must have "San Joaquin." I note your suggestion that I keep about 40 copies to distribute down here, & from down here.

I know just how you felt after reading Steinbeck's new book. No help for it though. You're 10 years younger than he. You cannot get ahead of yourself. There is a place for both books. You must take my word for it. There is no single answer to the world.

Thank you for writing me in detail about the "Personal Record." I know that I made no mistake in sending it to you. Above all I wanted an emotional understanding. You did not fail me there. And just behind it in value to me are your critical remarks. I know what it needs. As I wrote you, I was shaping it critically (the ms. corrections were written back in '34) and then my life changed in a way that made it impossible to go on with the work. I thought I had a finished story to chronicle. I was mistaken.

I don't see myself doing anything more with it. I don't even know when the next chapters will be written—the European ones—My life is so full, so busy, so happy, the nostalgic backward yearning desire to tie up the loose ends of the past almost never comes over me.

Isn't it strange that one wants to write these intimate things down? That one must do it? I am haunted, this moment, by Fisher's lines from the "Ghost" quoted as epigraph—"There might be peace for me. . . . "

Only for my friends; the desire for deeper understanding. God bless you, Bill.

Larry

May 9, 1939
Selma
AL, 3 p.

Dear Powell—

Tonight, laying aside the Goncourts, trying to break the spell of French literature that is in this house now—Proust, Flaubert, Gautier, with that faint reek of *indoor*ness, of perfume, of urbanity, closed air, over-refined emotions, over-sensitized introversion,—I picked up *The Return of the Native,* and thought to go out into the raw air of England. I failed. After all I've read and heard about Hardy and his Egdon Heath to find it out at last . . .

> To do things musingly, and by small degrees, seemed, indeed, to be a duty in the Egdon Valleys, at this transitional hour, for there was that in the condition of the heath itself which resembled protracted and halting dubiousness. It was the quality of the repose appertaining to the scene. This was not the repose of actual stagnation, but the apparent repose of incredible slowness. A condition of healthy life so nearly resembling the torpor of death is a noticeable thing of its sort; to exhibit the inertness of the desert, and at the same time to be exercising powers akin to those of the meadow and even of the forest, awakened in those who thought of it the attentiveness usually engendered by understatement and reserve.

There, in those few lines, Hardy gives himself away. Words. Nothing but words, words, words. Vague, wandering, meaningless dead, vitiated: the pall and clammy chill of lethargic words. You are supposed to find in Hardy the mood of the heath as no one has ever done it; you hear of Hardy as one of the top examples of the man welded, fused to the region. Havelock Ellis himself swears by him, and Lawrence, who could grasp the meaning of region as none other I've read, finds this man excellent. This doddering, fumbling, verbose word-monger! Shit! He wasn't writing for country, for mood, for sensation, for quality of experience. He was writing to hear the stupid and mumbling elaborations of his stupid and mumbling mouth, and I'm sick to death. Lawrence, who had the grasp, the feeling, that beautiful awareness that lets landscape literally run in through the eyes, and pervade the entire being, till the inner quickness goes out of it in a vast wave of expansion, Lawrence, we have Lawrence, and they talk about Hardy yet. To identify the inner self with region is one of the paramount necessities of a man's spiritual life: as Jeffers has done, and by God as I am doing—and then we have this blubber-mouthed faker held up for light!

Response after part 1.

The first chapters are sketchy and diffused. Many leads are picked up and then dropped without development. Looking back one cannot remember all the incidents because the incidents have only a very tenuous relation to one another and do not have any seemingly cumulative process, it is only in the large aspect that any cumulative process comes through. The main impression is one of speed, incidents come click click click, but they do not come evenly, with each incident its logical build-up and transfer-process into the next incident. And because of this lack of expansion, of development, you never get inside these characters. You never really know what this girl Laura looks like; you are only slightly aware of any depth of feeling in this young man. There is not enough of personal reverie here, not enough of pausing to explore feeling or sensation. As I take it, this section is to show youthful conflict between opposed personalities that yet have points of attraction, and if this is so there is too much speed to gain the point. On the surface, this is the running narrative of a modern youth, interested only in action, in living life actively to the core, driving from experience to experience, with never a pause to test experience; but there is interposed intellectual material that is in direct opposition to this idea. We get snatches of poems, references to symphonies, which for all we can learn about this young man are distinctly not his line. The style is slangy and modern, and as the narrative of a modern youth that is good. But I do not think that is the total point meant: it is quite true that such a youth could exist who, caught in the stream of modern life could yet have leanings and urges toward a richer meaning: I think in fact most imaginative mature men go through such a phase: but in this narrative, that richer side is merely referred to: indicated but not illustrated. If this first section is to be a psychological study of the conflict of young love it must be slowed down, widely developed, much extraneous material must be removed. The grasp on the action and conversation must be surer. If on the other hand this section is to be merely preparative for experiences yet to come: an interval of a life that will later gain richness and fullness, but yet shown here in all its speed and intensity, then the details must be compressed: many incidents which cannot be removed because this is, I almost forgot, a personal narrative, must be merely touched on, with the emphasis on significant material; and yet more reverie, more psychology, more indication that this youth is poignantly aware, and shows emotionally the richness his love and knowledge of literature reveals him to possess.

There are, however, attributes: evidence of sincerity running under the events, though that is sometimes almost lost by emphasis placed upon insignificant material. Whenever the narrator turns to describe the natural setting he is on ground he can handle. And the ship-board chapter is sure and valid: these events move firmly and quickly: the whole temper is surer and stronger: the part has tension and awareness and communication, and is, as structure and as writing, the best portion of the section.

Two justifications for a personal narrative: one to show the variety of experience: one to show quality of experience.

May 10, 39
Selma
ALS, 1 p.

Dear Powell—

Your letter today. The line in "Abrasive" is right, though it is obscure, as you point out. What I mean is "When I'm adjusted to one season I hate to have to re-adjust to another." But obscure as it is I'll have to let it go. I can't touch those poems. They're cold now. Dead.

I do not think my criticism of your narrative did it complete justice. I was a bit uncertain as to how I should proceed, and my response in that letter was almost entirely technical—which was a mistake. Let me say that the events of that record live in my mind very vividly. I know you from it far better than you will ever know me, and the urgency of that narrative has a compulsion that makes those events stick. I get the sense of desperation, almost, from the stream of those happenings, the plunge outward to meet experience, and the experience going over like a wave, breaking over, and the narrator never fully satisfied by that wave, but hungering the next, and rushing to meet it. There is much of that record that is my own—it is strange how a personal narrative touches a person in his own past: the shape of written events, touching and urgent, into all that lying behind the reader. Your narrative does that; and my rather pretentious note-taking did not get to its center, though I do not mean what I am saying now greatly alters what I said there—only extends it, enlarges upon it. It meant much to me to be able to read, to be trusted with that account.

I am enclosing a letter which I started last night—a violent one I see now.

Contrary to my previous letter I haven't read *The Grapes of Wrath*. But the thing's in the air. Wherever books are discussed the title comes up. *The Grapes of Wrath! The Grapes of Wrath!* It was that influence of which I was speaking.

B. Everson

June 3, 1939
Van Nuys
ALS, 2 p.
Buel's vignette is a beauty.

Dear Bill—

I never have thanked you for your last letter. The semester's end caught us up in a social whirl, which in addition to my regular curricular & extra curricular work, has left me a bit dizzy.

We're all getting excited along with you over your book. I am increasingly fond of the title page—have a black & white proof pinned up in my study—& when it's run in all the colors it's going to be stunning. I was by the press today & saw the first two forms completed.

I'm mailing you separately an item to go with your "Lines for the Last of a Gold Town"—I think it will also interest you as a Ritchie imprint.

Have you read Jesse Stuart's "Man with a Bull-Tongue Plow"?

I am in the midst of a talk to be given later this month in San Francisco at the American Library Assn. national convention—"The Function of Rare Books"—Gosh!

We're going to & fro on the train so will miss seeing you. I'm hoping to pay you a visit in September—but that's far far away. Who knows?

You'll be interested to know that Ritchie is getting unusual pleasure from doing your book. He enjoys all his work, of course, but this book had affected him more than anything he's done for a long time. The result is going to be something beautiful & alive. It does me good to know that I brought you two into collaboration.

God bless us all, my lad.

Larry

June 12, 1939
Selma, Calif.
ALS, 3 p., 2 sheets

Dear Powell—

We returned from a short vacation to find your letter and the Millerton number waiting. We started out on what was supposed to be a two weeks' stay—the purpose of which was to be a change of scene for Edwa, and an attempt on my part to see if the urban life of S.F. could perhaps get some material out of me. It never got the chance. We cut into the mountains at Modesto and took in that Mother Lode country from Sonora to Jackson: quaint small towns on the hills, narrow-streeted and dreaming 70 yrs. back. In Sacramento I looked up my birth-place, and stood outside for the first time since 1912 (when I was breaking into the world Jeffers was breaking into print: and the whole country was breaking out with that *vers libre* rash!). I tried to sound myself for reverberations of that return to the womb complex without success—it might make a good poem if handled rightly. The best thing in Sacramento was the State Library. Quiet, half-dozen people, large, fine service—if I had research work to do I'd head for there. I suppose the University Library is just as good, but I've still got a freshman rating scholastically, and I couldn't get in the door. (I'll never forget your taking me into the stacks of UCLA that first day we met. Fairyland.)

After that we took in the vineyard country above S.F. (Napa, St. Helena). Beautiful country in its way. The vines smaller, the valley smaller, the vineyards smaller—but the wine! All along we looked up our friends and by the time we reached S.F. we were homesick, exhausted, and rattled by the crowds. One day's prowling among old book shops and we came home—right by the Fair without turning our heads!

So you like the book. So do I except that I can't visualize it as a book yet. The time is getting very close now. Crack the Maidenhead of the Muse. I'm also quite moved to hear that Ritchie is especially interested in my book—anything he'd do would be more than I could expect, so it isn't the job I'm referring to—it's the remembrance that in your narrative Ritchie possessed a great store of quotable poems, was in fact a true verse-lover—and to have my work quicken in him more than the everyday job I regard as a very deep tribute. That kind of thing helps a man along in the world. You feel sort of justified, somehow.

The Millerton item is quite unusual, and I've learned from it. My own information about the place was very scanty, and I should have done more research work—that Fresno Historical Society scares me out, though: I can't knock on doors, damn it, scared to death—so I picked up what smattering I could and dealt in generalities. You see how information about Murrietta's head being preserved in a barrel of whisky instead of alcohol affects my poem. I could have got much more color had I known that. The place is interesting, and these photos are excellent. It is the oldest thing around and it quickened my imagination. Ritchie puts his touch on everything he does, doesn't he?

Too bad you can't stop by on the way through. Too damn bad. You can't see this country from that railroad or highway either. Billboards. The intestinal tract of the valley; hell, I'm pulling my punches, I mean the asshole of the San Joaquin! I'd like to hear that lecture of yours.

I've read Stuart, but there's nothing there. Flabby. No control. Good poetry comes out of control. Stuart has the feel for poetic expression—the color, the life, the rhythm, the images. But he lacks that imperative discipline that pulls a line into the tension of firm verse. Our poets run in opposites. All the young poets of the thirties—the intellectuals so fondly presented by *Poetry* magazine—have a surfeit of tension: sparse rhythms, exact words, tight verse, controlled, firm and colorless, lifeless. Yet we have Jesse Stuart and Paul Engle, wealthy in the *life* of poetry and not an iota of the discipline that whips that wealth into shape. A job for me there. Combine 'em. Make poems that burn but keep 'em in hand. Tight verse and alive. A job ahead of me.

"How you digress!" When my book comes out I shall take a copy of it into some still silent corner, and hold it close to my belly, and glance furtively over my shoulder in intense jealousy of any who would share with me that first sweet moment of triumph.

Bill E.

P.S. One man to watch is Robert Linn ("Robinson Jeffers and Wm. Faulkner"—*American Spectator*). He's teaching in Napa now, and steadily writing. He'll never do real work, I don't think—I mean the real work, the real aesthetics, but he will do as well as most of our writers—he's got power, and imagination and guts—what he lacks, what all our writers lack, is style. Style. And because of its style, James Joyce's *Ulysses* will go down as the great book of our time. Another man to watch is John Moodey, a friend also, and a poet. He is beginning to develop, and his tendency is to the compressed lyric—metaphysical. I'm enclosing his best poem, which I think is really fine.

The Edge of Death

Up to the very quiet edge of death
Along fine highways of converging air
The senses come like evening cattle home
And they meet there.

They are the sum of the last shuddered breath
Become alike the hail and the farewell,
But what they hail, forever afterward,
They cannot tell.

For Lethe runs just there, the edge of death
The silent swirls where all the dead have been
They wait upon the last shuddered breath
And then plunge in.

John S. Moodey

June 22, '39
Selma
ALS, 3 p.

Dear Powell:—

Thanks very much for this first issue of *Black and White*. I liked your paper. Speaking technically, it is, as expository prose, I think one of your best articles. You pay Steinbeck a fine tribute, and you pay it well.

There is, however, an implicit problem behind your piece that has been troubling me for some time, and it had better be rationalized now while I'm young and plastic enough to be molded. It is a problem that Steinbeck hints at when he scores those writers who are concerned with technique and definitions "the precious tricks that have separated art from life," and it is the motive behind your paper because you felt it necessary to defend Steinbeck against charges of having no objective humanitarian purpose. Those implications point one direction—and all our thought is slowly grooving toward the one direction: the belief that there is only one contemporary battle worth the fighting.

I am a socialist. Though I remain non-political all my life, nevertheless those aspects of my nature that are touched by politics are definitely in favor of social reform. My father struck time and again in the early printers' strikes of the nineties and is a union printer to this day, though he has owned his own shop for twenty years and kept his card that time purely for principle's sake. As for myself I am a proletarian—actually more one than many so-called proletarian devotees I know—and I have experienced enough in my own life to justify my socialist sympathies. Suffice it to say that now when I work my employer gets a dollar an hour for my labor and gives me forty cents of it. It's a fight—it's a worthwhile fight and in some aspects even a noble one—but mulling this thing over I have about decided it isn't the only one—sometimes (though this is heresy) I think it isn't the most important one.

Sometimes I think the most important fight started away back 15,000 years ago when those men of the later Paleolithic Age squatted in the filth and shit of their caves, and reaching out of it formed those beautiful bison on the wall. It was the start of the fight of humanity to overcome the inertia of human sloth. It was the war of aesthetics to break through the barriers that are our own sluggish natures and touch that quick and vital something that makes all this business of existence really valid. It has been a winning fight at times: the Greeks were winning: the Renaissance Italians were winning: the Elizabethans. Beyond that it has been lone champions: artists, musicians, poets: they have gone into it with all their beings—and they weren't taken in by the surface movements of their time, not really taken in—they knew in them that the real fight was old, and would last beyond their time, but that what was important was that they should break a hole: with a poem, with a picture: a hole that would let all humanity look through and see what lay beyond in the upper realms. Across the room from me now is a good-sized color reproduction of a painting called "Portrait of a Youth," by Bellini. I know nothing of art nor of Bellini, but the thing speaks to me in a way I wouldn't have missed for anything. It is bigger than I—much bigger—when you feel a thing like that it sort of justifies everything. All the great discords and stripped-gears of your life sort of resolve themselves before that indescribable work of art, and you know you've touched home. You know that also whoever Bellini was he probably suffered over the injustices of his time, and hated them, and felt the cross-purposes of his life urging him against them. And whatever you feel of pity and anger for those same aspects of his time, you nevertheless in your inner being know that this is right—that Bellini was right—that actually, in humanitarian terms, the race has been benefited infinitely more than if he had followed some lesser voice, regardless of the actual good he had done in his time. I suppose Goya was a great artist who saw the horror and caught it so that the men of all time could know it for what it was. But even so, we wouldn't have wanted all the art of the past to have been socially revolutionary art. Man against outer reality—man trying to touch through the grossness and sloth to the infinite—is somehow more valid in its implications than trying to straighten his domestic affairs. More valid and more important—the basic problems are still before us, and now in our times of material abundance, they need more than ever to be touched and held up. For the life of me, I think one poem like MacLeish's "Immortal Autumn" is more valuable to the race—again speaking in actual humanitarian terms—than the whole of Dialectic Materialism. That is something we need to remember—for all the shaping of our economic structure we must keep in mind it is only secondary, only an important byplay to the great pageant. When all are well-fed, when there is neither injustice nor pity nor poverty to plead for us, and we stand naked in our own beings, in the light or the darkness of our inner selves—then will it be seen, and we will wonder how we could have forgotten it, so important will it be to us then. And if there has been a man of our time who understood, who knew his real purpose—a big man I mean—and knowing his purpose drove toward it, refusing to be sucked down and into the boiling of his time—then will that man—we have him in the earlier Jeffers—be known for what he was and his name will be praised in the halls.

So Larry, if I write no "workers arise" poems forgive me. I have to use this small and puny tool for what I think best. I shall soak myself in technique, in, if you will, definitions, conscious that it is only through form (form is the line drawn between meaning and chaos) that I can get to the light. And I don't think it is either mean or spiteful or small of me to suggest that Steinbeck (though I haven't read *The Grapes* and am basing this on the earlier work) would himself be better able to really help humanity if he paid a bit more attention to technique and a bit more attention to definitions.

Sincerely
Bill

P.S. I sent a letter to the *Nation* protesting the Jeffers review. I didn't like to do it. I don't want to get mixed up in any literary squabble, or make any literary enemies, but I couldn't sit back and let this sort of thing go on. They probably won't publish it, to hell with them. They have one of the best review departments in the country, though. It's just that everyone's against Jeffers. Every day I expect the book. Every day I'm set back. The suspense is terrible. I can't write, I can't work, I don't know what I'll have to think about after the great event.

Watkins and I are both broke, but were going halves on a subscription to *Black and White,* on the belief that California needs this kind of paper and needs it badly. The article on the prorate is very revealing. It hits us hard here. The ranches are mostly small ranches, and can't stand it. This ranch I'm on almost went under on that account last year.

June 26, 1939
Van Nuys
ALS, 4 p., 2 sheets

Dear Bill—

We're just back from that week in San Francisco. I had a letter from you just before I left, & was glad to hear of your trip. We travelled both ways the coast route by train; up by day, down by night. I hadn't been on a train since 1933. A wonderfully active week. Porter came to hear my paper—& afterwards we had only a few seconds to chat. Tells me she is going to Honolulu. Told her I'd like to see her when I come your way in September. I plan to come alone.

Thanks for the poem by Moodey—good. Talked with Ward on the phone. Your book is printed & awaits a turn in the bindery. I am as keen as you are to see it. Do you still have list of people I wanted to send copies to? Will you send me those names? Was it 40 copies you wanted to leave down here? Please instruct Ritchie.

Your letter today about *Black & White.* I'm glad to hear you've subscribed. Do you want to write something for them? Your remarks about Art are good. I shall never expect you to write "workers arise" poems. And I too love a poem like "Immortal Autumn"; I wouldn't trade it for all of Upton Sinclair. You'd better read *Grapes of Wrath* before you say anything more about Steinbeck. It has plenty of technique. That article of mine was written last year when *Long Valley* was published. I gave it to *Black & White* with the condition that Wilbur Needham bring it up to date. The opening paragraphs are his—& they're not so good. Tain't my language. Needham's end piece is well done. He is stone deaf. Reads your lips. Big, shaggy, hard-drinking guy.

T.K. Whipple died just after my article appeared. Abdominal cancer. Only 49. English prof at Berkeley. A good liberal. Do you know his "Spokesman" volume? I am having a tribute written to him for *Black & White.*

As usual I'm up to my ears in a dozen things. The latest is we've bought a house, in Beverly Glen canyon over the hills in back of us. Enlarging it to give us more room. Having a study built with great bookcases. Move in a couple of weeks. Brings me 3 miles from UCLA instead of 8. We're a bit excited.

Back to art: I like your writing because it is just the way it is. All I want is that the writer be himself, be what he has to be. The writers to whom I'm drawn are a motley crew, but they all have in common an intense seriousness of purpose—I seek the writer who writes because he has to write. I have no time for the amusing, the dilettantish. I want that facing of the great issues, that abundance of life; and I find it in writers of such differences as Jeffers & Traven; Steinbeck & Lawrence; Auden & Everson; MacIntyre & Fisher. Etc.

At the same time in the library that I am writing a paper on the function of rare books, I am helping organize a staff association; & writing a constitution for it, which will help improve the position of librarians as writers. I read *New Masses* & the *Transactions* [i.e., *Papers*] of the Bibliographical Society. I love everything about books: their contents & their format. It is my ambition to become the head of a large library & make it a great vital center of culture. I want to increase knowledge, sympathy, & tolerance, at least in a little circle around me. The way of the world is unchangeable. All I want to be remembered for is that I was a man who loved life in many of its manifestations & who wanted to enjoy & promote friendships & loyalties. The nomination of Archibald MacLeish as Librarian of Congress is immensely encouraging. I hope the Senate confirms it. What increased pride I can take in my profession with such a man at its head!

I saw Jeffers recently down here. Called *Grapes of Wrath* a "great book." Said his favorite character is—the turtle!!

This letter is a hotch-potch. It is night. Today was my first day at the library. I came home with the same Bellini print you got & found your letter about it! I put it up in our boys' room. I'm sorry you missed the fine arts exhibit at the fair—& the fountains & sculpture.

Did your copy of *Phoenix* arrive today too? Cooney's headed for South America. Are you going to join him?

yours ever,
Larry

July 13, 1939
Selma, Calif.
ALS, 1 p.

Dear Larry:—

It has come, and is here before us—I have just scribbled a note to Ward, and have enough good clean exuberance to write a dozen notes to everybody in this goddamned country. This is the most magnificent book ever offered to the eyes of man—Ritchie, Powell, Buel, and Everson! This is—hell, I'm supposed to be a poet, and poets are supposed to be the slick users of words, but I'm speechless—stopped cold—but before I am I want to thank you for the fine and sure and earnest foreword, and to say it makes me feel fine and strong enough to whip the world with my bare hands, let alone this pen, and to sing and yell and run this room till the walls and the sky and the sun itself cave right in upon me!

Bill

P.S. Did you ever, really, see a book more tastefully done, in all departments? That title and the binding and the typography with a sureness that is amazing! I don't deserve it. I simply haven't done enough good to life to deserve so fine and terrifically clean a monument as this!

July 14, 1939
Selma, Calif.
ALS, 3 p., 2 sheets

Dear Powell—

I have cooled off a little in these twenty-four hours, but not much. I maintain that that is the finest book of poems ever printed—the printing, of course, the poems stink. You look through those pages and every one of them begs you to read. I don't know what it is but the type size, and the typeface and the body as a whole combine with the paper in a way to make you want to dive in. And the funny part of it is, that when we had planned to bind a few of our own, we had selected just this cover: brown paper and a white spine. Buel's cut, which in the black proof I got looked a little like an eighteenth-century engraving for a book of garden verse, and seemed a bit out of place in a book of California impetuosity, is now resolved in that brown tone into something subdued and right. That title page has what it takes, there is a harmony there that gets you; you know you're before the real thing when you pick up that book, and I'm stopped. I can't understand how it happened to me. I can't understand how any printer would take the trouble to do this. I've dreamed about my stuff in fine editions all my writing life, but I've never expected to see it, and when I did extravagantly imagine it, I never conceived of anything so perfect as this. There have been fine books, yes, but by god and by Jesus I'll defy any printer to show me a book more harmonious from cover to cover than this one. It rests in your hands in *one piece,* not a series of spectacular units as so many books are, but *one.* I can't get over it. It gets me inside, and when I think that it was you that made this possible, and that it was you that spoke in that foreword, why I realize I've a debt ahead of me I never can work off. You spoke in your last letter of loyalties and friendships. Whatever happens you have one here you can be sure of.

Because this book has closed the past, it's time for me to open the future, so I am sending on all my completed work since the last poem in *San Joaquin,* "Clouds." Looking at *San Joaquin* now "in the clarity and permanence of type" I can see that what it was mostly was a struggle with form. I had not yet thoroughly resolved my conception of this poetic structure: I was intuitively working with phrase-rhythms, but I was not yet sure what was right and what wasn't (I'm not sure of that yet, nor ever will be, but I'm beginning to know what I want). And I see that what is important for me now is not only to make poems that are structurally satisfactory, but to weld into those phrases the tonal depth and quantity and soundness that is the root of true poetry. In *San Joaquin* I sometimes was contented to leave a poem because its phrase-structure satisfied me, and I know now that that's no more the criterion for a true poem than getting all the syllables in a sonnet. I've got to get the *right* syllables. I've got to make poems that have solidity of tone, and depth of feeling, and are deep and alive and full.

I offer these mss. as first trends in that direction. They are, I think, the soundest poems I have written, and I hope they have a formality and a unity that is recognizable in all the good stuff. They are a winter's work, and most of them are the result of revision after revision, a long and laborious struggle with syllables and intonations and quantity. I might have fallen over backward and in gaining control lost life, or spontaneity, or feeling. I hope not. I hope like hell not, for if that's so I'm doomed from now on to write stuffy nothings. But if I can only keep the drive that is in the stronger poems in *San Joaquin* and yet wrap it into some unity of form, then I shall do what I want to do. At any rate, here is my winter's work, I offer it with considerable apprehension.

I liked your last letter. You have an aesthetic there that will permit you to live in the drive and flood of this age as a sensitive man ought to, whereas my own is tending to shut me in more and more. Yours is bigger and honester and on the whole better than mine. I think as a worker in stubborn stuff I ought to specialize, and go in deep through the little narrow opening: that's why I won't let myself be put off from formal considerations. I've seen too many poets with drive lose their effect by sprawling all over the page. (Lindsay, for one, Lawrence in his verse for another. Even Whitman. God what a man Whitman would have been with a sense of form. Even Jeffers' lyrics are time and again turned away from that final irresistible magnificent plunge by diffuseness of his rhythms. Looking at it now I think that ten or fifteen of MacLeish's very best poems are the lyric highspots of modern poetry—the form! the form!—but the rest are trash.) But still yours is the best aesthetic. When our times come to die you'll go under with a deeper satisfaction than I for you'll have breathed the age in. In your looking for the gist of what a man says you'll have tasted this time in all its sourness and fineness, and by God I admire you. It's the men with your aesthetic who live life and know it.

* * *

MacIntyre will hold his nose when he reads the book, but by God there are three or four poems in that collection I can hold my head up for

What the hell.

Bill.

17 July '39
Los Angeles
ALS, 3 p.

Dear Bill—

Am I to gather from your letter that you like the book? Ritchie seemed to get the same impression from a communication you sent to him. I hope we are not mistaken.

Did I tell you we were moving? We have. A dream come true. We own this place. It is due south from Van Nuys, across the hill range, in a canyon, about 2 miles north of the plain on which the University stands. We have lost much & gained more. I shall miss the wonderful San Fernando valley. But here I shall be happy & productive. We bought a place & spent as much again in enlarging & remodelling; made two stories out of one. I have a room all my own, lined with ceiling-high bookshelves. The whole house panelled in knotty pine. I want you to see it. We are pretty tired from the sheer labor of moving & the attendant disarrangement.

Copies sent out by me

1. UCLA archives
2. Goodwin, head lib. UCLA
3. Los Angeles Public Lib.
4. Occidental Public Lib.
5. Stanford Public Lib.
6. Albert N. Bender, San Francisco bibliophile
7. B.F. Stelter, head of Eng. Dept. Oxy
8. U.C. library, Berkeley
9. Calif. state library, Sacramento
10. Sydney Mitchell, head library school, U.C.
11. MFK Parrish
12. Carey McWilliams (read his life of Bierce)
13. Pres. Sproul, Univ. of Calif.
14. Dr. Hal Bieler
15. Jeffers
16. Steinbeck
17. Georges Connes (Dijon)
18. Jean Matruchet
19. Clinton Williams, Berkeley friend
20. Joseph Henry Jackson, SF
21. Jens Nyholm, Danish writer, UCLA
22. Wm. Rose Benét
23. Jake Zeitlin
24. Edward L. Tinker, NY Times, friend
25. J.M. Lilienthal, SF bookseller, friend
26. S.S. Alberts, Jeffers bibliographer, Yonkers, N. Y.
27. Huntington library
28. New York Public Lib.
29. Dorothy Bevis, San Pasqual Press, Pasadena
30. Majl Ewing, UCLA
31. Mother Powell
32. Mother-in-law Shoemaker

33. Dr. Elmer Belt, L.A.
34. Frank J. Hogan, Wash. D.C.
35. Marian Cooch, aunt, SF
36. Newell
37. Fisher

Do you know that Archibald MacLeish is the new Librarian of Congress? Will you send him a copy? I think you should send one to *Poetry* magazine. The copies I sent to Benét & Jackson were not to them as reviewers, but as corresponding acquaintances of mine. Do send one to *Poetry*. Skip all the other periodicals if you will, but not *Poetry*. Will you concede me this wish?

I have read the finished book through several times. The poems sound to me better than they ever have before. This pleases me.

Keep working & growing, lad.

Larry.

P.S. Let me know when you come down to earth.

7-22-39
Los Angeles
ALS, 3 p., 2 sheets

Dear Bill—

Sunday night, the end of a day and a half all my own, working at home, settling our new place, making it ours. Except for a bookcase full upstairs, here in my study are all the books I own; the first time they've ever been all together in one room.

I used to think some special setting was necessary for a writer. When I landed in Paris 9 years ago next month, I began a novel. The only place I could work at it was in the Luxembourg Gardens. Every afternoon I walked there with my notebook, & worked at the great American novel. Later I found that if the necessity was strong enough, one could work anywhere—& I did. Now I have an ideal work room, which is the more wonderful to me in that I know I don't need it to get done what I have to get done. But I *do* have it, & I am a bit exultant, because I just can't be stopped in a place like this. Even have a new (second-hand) desk.

Your new poems are here before me. I have read them several times during the past several days. You are right; they are the best you've done. They show the hard work you've given to them. They are more measured, surer, & inevitable. All that you say about form is true. "Art in its intensest raptures, in its most truly natural moments, desires & obtains the strictest & most formal laws. It is, I suppose, immaterial what these laws are . . . all testify to the important & essential rule that freedom is chiefly free when it is most bound, & bounded by restrictions which we should call artificial, which are in truth, in the highest sense, natural." (Arthur Machen)

It is your preoccupation with form which pleases me most of all that you are doing.

As to your subject matter in these new poems, I am disappointed that you are not writing more of specific local places & incidents. The feast day, yes. The Forms, yes. But not strong enough in sharp detail.

Bill my lad, you must watch your tendency to play the philosopher & write of equinoxes & eras & all the vast cyclic things. It can become a bad habit. And remember, there's your westward neighbor Jeffers. Even when he's at his vastest, he keeps his eye on his immediate surroundings. "November Surf."

Put more detail into your poems. And I don't mean "local color." Although I recall you preferred to read the Millerton poem of all your poems. Put in more of your Valley—of your day, & your labor.

I don't find enough of this in your new poems to suit me. What do you think about it?

You're giving a copy of your book to Porter?

And so to bed.

Larry

P.S. If *S.J.* isn't one of the 50 books I'll eat it.

On the back of the envelope:

1. Cooney is an amazing creature. I admire his spunk.
2. I recommend to you Somerset Maugham's autobiography, *The Summing Up*.

Monday, July 24, '39
Selma, Calif.
ALS, 4 p., 2 sheets

Dear Larry:—

On July 29, 1935, from Sunnyvale, California, I sent to *Poetry* magazine a group of five poems: "Martin's Homestead," "To an Indian-Hunting Posse," "Over the Roads," "Muscat Pruning," and "Who Lives Here Harbors Sorrow." They were rejected a month later with a very pleasant and encouraging note from Harriet Monroe. I did not submit again until Mar. 16, 1936, and this time the good woman accepted "Dust and the Glory" and "We in the Fields," and rejected "The Flesh and the Bone" ["Fisheaters"] and "Nothing Was Moved" ("Fog"). The acceptance, and similar ones, must have caused the office underlings no end of annoyance. The senile old woman, long past her prime, was continuing to stuff the magazine with pompous and wordy romanticism, while the voices of the future were crying for recognition from all corners of the land. At any rate, the old witch died before those poems were printed (I can imagine the relieved sighs from the home office when the South American news came in) and from then on the stout little mag that had opened its doors to every kind of literature capable of being anywhere near scanned, closed its doors to all but the chosen. On May 21, 1937 I sent in "Millerton," "Song for the Winter Solstice," and "The Rain on that Morning." Editor Zabel declared them too diffuse. (I'd rowed with him about printing my name "Bill"—shades of Walt Whitman!) and the situation became closed. On Nov. 8, 1937 I sent "Notes on the Year's End," "She Goes More Delicate" (The Knives) and "Noon." The new editor, Dillon, liked them but not enough to print, nor did he like, later (July '38) "House on Second Street," "Wind West," "Spade," "Elegy for a Ruined School House," "Thunder," or "Trifles"; and this spring he turned back all the mss. I have just sent you—"These Have the Future"—"The Roots of Compulsion," "The Forms," "The Dancer" (Gordon Newell) and "Equinox." So you see that aside from the unfortunate aberrations of childish old Harriet, *Poetry* magazine has managed to keep itself clean of that particular kind of dirt classified among soil experts as Fresno Sandy Loam. That, briefly, is the dreamy history of my extended campaign against the fortified walls of that journal. I say briefly, because I could have extended the account by listing the gradual psychological buildup before each determination to submit, occasioned by the amount of shit that magazine published in the name of the Muse, through all the processes of confidence and anticipation and self satisfaction, through subsequent violent letdowns with their subsequent violent indignation, until, as psychologists have noted in sensitive persons the numbing of the sensibilities, I have myself been numbed into a sort of calloused contempt that will take many years of the most brilliant success to soften. Not only that, but I have followed closely the fate of verse-volumes reviewed within the rear pages, and if statistics could be gathered, I'm sure earth-lovers of my particular breed would be found to have in most cases undergone the axe. For the most part we are ignored: occasionally one comes along that has attracted enough attention to demand study, or one comes along that is so goddamned bad in a fairly good way that it is used as the illustration of the defects of us all. We hear the echo through all this stuff—"is this the modern poet's answer to the urgent need for adjusting his art to the new social consciousness?" It reverberates and resounds through intellectual preening of these boys in every issue. They are classicists, by god, and they jockey the poor mule of Romanticism into the dust. Imagine how I should fare at the hands of some smart son-of-a-bitch who had had his learning at the hands of guys like Allen Tate or Yvor Winters. Add to all this the fact that certain of these poems were included because I was sure in my mind the book would not be reviewed—poems that I now see as so bad I writhe to think of them, included to allow the volume to act as a sort of guide to any development I might make, included further because although I now dislike the poems I once thought they were real stuff (that's as good a poetic license as any) and you can see how your plea puts me on the spot.

For on the spot I am. After all, I owe you a hell of a lot more than the refusal of this small request would justify. Not only are you also a contributor to this book (and I want now to definitely state my appreciation and my admiration of the handling of that foreword. It was a tough job, and you handled it on all points with complete success—an admission that reveals me bragging on myself, though you know I cannot agree with your final statement!) but were it not for you I should never have had this particular book out at all. You helped in the development of its matter with your criticism, and you almost single-handedly pointed the direction of its publication: so that the thing is in good part yours. Looking back, I see that in spite of all the encouragement and the backing you have given me I have been forever snarling at every slight request you have made, and as I consider it now I am beginning to feel very sheepish indeed. After all, the sons of bitches can't hurt me, I'm big enough spiritually and mentally too to take the petty stuff they pass out. Besides, the book could very well be reviewed by some sane and intelligent individual (there are a few) who could overlook my obvious immaturities and really help me, really see the real dangers of my direction and point them out sympathetically. I'll welcome any kind of serious criticism from anyone. It's the bastards that take you to town simply because they don't like the smell of earth that I hate. So I'll send one off. I shan't expect anything at first, because I know that the fact I'm a romanticist, and the fact that my book wasn't published in N.Y. are prime reasons for overlooking anyone these days. I know what to expect—which is nothing—or if something, what to expect there too.

That is a terrific list you've sent out. Jesus Christ, man aren't you afraid? What if I'm a dud, and leave you high and dry? You're playing mighty long odds.

Your house sounds very fine, and I envy you very much in having a place of your own. A man needs his own house, to come to and know and feel time gather behind him. Lawrence could keep his life integrated traveling all over the world. I could not do that. Our five-day vacation ruined us for a week. A man needs a permanent place. Edwa wants to come down and sit under those ceiling-high shelves and read and read.

The Heart of Darkness is a superb work. Conrad had the

sense of reality. He had the style to resolve that sense into magnificent prose. *The Heart* and *The Nigger* are all I've read, but they are very fine.

Also, the snatches I've read of *Look Homeward Angel* are fine. Another man that had the sense of reality. And the style too except where he was careless. Much of it right out of Joyce—I'm looking forward to reading it after the cannery season. *Ulysses* is still tops though. I received a letter from Ward today. Among other things he says the book seems to be one of the best he's done. He's modest. It's one of the best things any man has done!

Bill.

I sent a copy to MacLeish and one to Eda Lou Walton. There incidentally is a critic I'd trust my book to in any journal. Also I sent one to Porter in Reedley, applied two on copyright: altogether I've sent out about 10 or 12 books to friends but only one has bothered to reply. Did I tell you I was working on a critical study of *Point Sur*?

Tues. July 25, 1939
Selma, Calif.
ALS, 2 p., 1 sheet

Dear Larry:—

Your letter has just arrived, and I am very glad that you think those poems a step forward. I was afraid that you would find them stiff and stuffy and stilted. "Measured and sure and inevitable" that is a criterion that any poem should come up to and it does me much good. I have tried very hard to curb them down into the deep tension of restraint. Also your quotation from Machen is very fine and very true: I intend to copy it into my notes. The most subtle and penetrating treatise on the nature of form I have ever read is Kenneth Burke's *Counter-Statement*, and so well do I like it that I shall probably keep it at my side as the official creative Bible. In what reading of critical theories of aesthetics that I've done, I've wanted and not found so fundamental an application as Burke's. I have been digging up all his work from periodicals at the library and find the same keen insight. Here is a passage from the general summing up at the last of the book (pg. 257) that is as good a poetic creed as any I've seen. After quoting Wordsworth on the future use of science in poetry he continues:

> But insofar as the poet 'looks before and after' or 'binds together by passion and knowledge the vast empire of human society' he cannot at this time be concerned with the new alone. He will, if he is sensitive to the entire situation, retreat slowly (or advance slowly, as one prefers) relinquishing only what must be relinquished, retaining the vocabulary of past beauty so long as he can bring himself to feel its validity, yet never closing his eyes in the interests of comfort and respite, but continually testing the valves and wheels of his poetic mechanism, and not for a moment attempting to conceal from himself the fact that some part or other is outworn.

What you said about subject matter puzzled me a bit. I winced also at your good-natured allusion to my "playing the philosopher"—as I winced before at your admonition "not to take it all too seriously." However, it is very important criticism, and I should far rather have you point it out than someone less sympathetic—or more important, I should rather have it pointed out before I go on and devote hours of work on what might be a fatuous direction. I suppose I do tend to the grandiose in my conceptions of the nature of things—it's a hangover and a poor imitation of the Jeffers tendency. My feeling is however that the evil lies not in the direction but in my execution. It seems to me a rather dubious way of attaining any universality by focusing too sharply on the local. I should have thought that it was the universal seen through and beyond the surfaces of the local that was what was important: and I tried in those poems to get the pervasion of local regionalism in such terms as to naturally carry beyond into the greater significances. I have related all these except "The Dancer" in some way to the Valley. By reading "November Surf" I see clearly what you mean—the reference to specific detail—orange peel, papers, condoms, and dung. And I know that there is a valuable sharpness there that gives the poem a cutting edge. It is a good point you have and I shall watch it. I rather doubt, however, that I can escape the "philosophical." I shall try to harden my view-point, but I feel that it is only by dealing with the human generalities, even if I lead up to them through specific detail, that I can attain any poetry worthy of the name. What I have to do is keep it from sounding phony, but that is a matter of craft rather than direction. It worries me, what you've said—of all the hypersensitive fears I have, the deepest one is the fear of appearing ridiculous.

Bill

I'm sending a letter I wrote yesterday in answer to your last.

Aug. 7, 1939
Los Angeles
ALS, 2 p., 1 sheet

Dear Bill—

I have been unable to get around to your letter of July 25, & even now I don't think I can answer it the way it deserves. We're still getting settled. And I've been turning out several little things, all of which I want you to see if & when they are in print. Your study of *Point Sur* interests me. No one has ever given it the study it merits: A book could be written about it. Let me see what you've done, when it's finished.

Do you want to write a critique of MacIntyre's poetry for possible publication in *Black & White?* Along the line of what you've written me in letters. Mac was just here, on his way home from Europe, to Berkeley where he will teach from now on. We had a couple of wonderful sessions—he & Ritchie & I. He has a book of poems in proof with Oxford Univ. Press—to be published this autumn—"Cafés and Cathedrals"—poems written on this last trip to Europe. He is pretty cocky about the Oxford imprint.

Thanks for sending the copy to *Poetry.* I know how you feel toward them. But you are tough, & resilient; you have to be.

Nothing anyone says or writes can affect you really. If we hold to our inner belief & integrity, nothing else matters.

I enclose some acknowledgements of the book—a mixed lot—some will make you smile. The only one I want back is Una Jeffers'.

* * *

Tor House
Carmel
Aug. 1, 1939

Dear Larry—Robin & I are both enthusiastic about Everson's poems—they are truly unusually arresting! I think he will go far. Thanks so much. The book is beautifully printed! I hope you like your new house.

Cordially U.J.

Carey McWilliams
900 Spring Arcade Building
Los Angeles, California

August 8th
TLS, 1 p.

Dear Larry:

Thanks for sending me the book by William Everson. I agree with you about his work: it shows very great promise. I'm going to write a notice about it for *Westways*. You will get a copy of my book in the next day or two. I haven't had time to mail your copy yet.

Hastily,
Carey McWilliams

[autograph postscript addendum]

Dear Bill—

As part of his job as State Commissioner of Immigration & Housing, McWilliams is interested in talking to farm workers all over the state. He wants to see you next time he's through the Valley. I gave him your address. I want you to know him. He's one of the finest men I know.

LCP

* * *

Life is very full these days. "The Ghost" prospectus is being folded & stapled. I shall send you one soon. The bulk of them goes out in mid-September.

Read Carey McWilliams' *Factories in the Field, the Story of Migratory Labor in California*—just published. I'm introducing him tomorrow night at a talk at Zeitlin's.

I've started an entirely new project—a work in California history—a monograph on an unusual pamphleteer, who was active from 1850–1883. He died up your way, in Mariposa. I plan to go north in Sept. to complete my work on him at the Bancroft Library. Travel by Santa Fé bus & streamliner. Could you meet me at Fresno on my way south, keep me overnight & put me aboard the next day? I'm sure the train makes no stop at Selma. This will be about 6 weeks from now.

Glad you like the foreword. So do I!

Larry

Aug. 14, 1939
Selma
ALS, 1 p.

Dear Larry:—

I am scribbling a very hasty note in reply to your last letters and this booklet. I should certainly have done this sooner, but we are working shifts that run from 12 to 14 hrs, and I simply haven't had the time. I liked all the "returns" on the book: Most of all Carey McWilliams. I felt he meant it; which somehow I did not feel about Una Jeffers' card, congratulatory as it is. I am looking forward very much to seeing McWilliams if and when he comes through. I don't deserve such a visit and will probably be speechless, but I'm still looking forward to it. Also to your own. The Santa Fé does not run through Selma, so we will be glad to pick you up in Fresno and carry you down. We have only the one bedroom, but we can make arrangements in town at one of the hotels, and that will be fine. Let us know which day you will arrive.

I'm sending on a letter I received from MacLeish (please return) and am returning U. Jeffers card: I shall try to write again soon.

Hastily,
Bill

8-14-39
L.A.
ALS, 2 p., 1 sheet

Dear Bill—

I am as proud as you are of the MacLeish letter. It's great stuff! The finest thing that's happened.

Enclosed are a couple more. Please return both. Sproul is the President of the University—all its branches. Has been a good friend to MacIntyre.

I've been cleaned out of every last copy of *San Joaquin*—have refused copies to a number of people—have been very calculating in disposing of them. Don't even have a copy for myself. Can you spare me 2 or 3 copies to stow away for the future? You were so generous with them that I hate to ask for more. In any case send me one—& please inscribe it to me.

Now we must point to your next book with Harcourt Brace!

yours,
Larry

P.S. It'll be just a month from now that I'll go north.

P.S. I enclose also what is certainly the strangest of all the acknowledgements we'll ever get on *San Joaquin.*—from William M. Cheney, a local eccentric, young, prints for a hobby. I am eventually getting you a copy of a book he just did all himself—wrote & printed & bound. Perhaps I showed you his *Voyage to Trolland* when you were down.

Please return.

Aug 25, 1939
Selma
ALS, 2 p., 1 sheet

Dear Larry:—

A moment grasped in this hell of production. I'm returning the acknowledgements and sending the books, and I want to say that that letter from Newell is the kind of thing that makes a man go on working. You feel you can speak to somebody, with some assurance that what you say will at least be listened to. Most people read poems like they read a newspaper—it takes more than that. It takes the whole being focussed in an act of complete intellectual absorption on the realities and the overtones of words. I feel Newell does that. I feel by God I can write when he says what he does. It makes me proud. The best poem I ever wrote was one written over a portion of that spirit of creation of his, and I'm proud of that too. By God I am.

Somehow it makes the frittering of your aesthete with his perfumed paper and his phony script and his shades of Oscar Wildeism stink (to use a phrase of yours) in God's own nostrils. Forgive me. Sproul's letter is nice. I suppose it's good politics.

I received one of those abominations from the Cal. State library. You mentioned an article on MacIntyre. I'm pleased and flattered and was all a-tingle, but I can't do it. Mac's really not my man. Every word I wrote about him was a groping, a blind attempt to grasp an intangible quality of the intellect that is simply an atmosphere I don't really breathe. I'm impressed by him: I admire very much the strength of his craft: the sureness of it: the confidence of his writing, the supreme subtlety of his awareness—I think really that he is one of the subtlest and finest craftsmen that I have read of all the living poets. But he's not my man. I'm outside, looking on. At the last he escapes me, and I regard him with wonder and a little awe. Not only that. I can't write; I cannot order prose into a structure.

I've quit my *Point Sur*, as I've quit every formal paper I've ever tried to write. It's one reason I like to write letters: I can let myself babble on and on without the rigid discipline I feel so necessary in verse or presentable prose.

I must leave now. I have tried to read *The Grapes* but have given it up. I cannot surmount the abrupt and over-simplification of the rhythms of that style. I think at heart he's a sentimentalist. I think he has a strong and compassionate sense of humanity: a remarkable sense of observation: a flaming sense of the injustices of life. I believe he is a fine and splendid man. I believe he is no artist: at heart, not an artist: the true artist. You will never forgive me this but I had to say it. No true artist would use shock for his effect and shock alone. I think it was Kenneth Burke said that a club was much better for that purpose. Anyway, we'll talk it over when you come. Regards to your wife. Mine sends hers.

So long
Bill

Nevertheless I want to thank you for the interesting item on Steinbeck. And that was a neat little foreword of yours. My friends all think you did a real job on the *San Joaquin* foreword. Myself, I'm proud of it.

9–9-39
L.A.
ALS, 1 p.

Dear Bill—

In yours of the 25th August, you mentioned you were going to send books. I haven't received any. I do hope it's that you've been too busy & not that a package has been lost.

Present plans call for northern trip the 18th—& return late that same week, via Fresno, Selma, etc. I'll warn you from Berkeley when I'm coming through.

Question: how far is the town of Mariposa from Selma? It is where the man I'm working on died (1883), & I'd like to visit there & see if I can find his grave, etc. Also, do you have a kodak?

Busy as hell at the library—

Please return the MacLeish letter.

Hastily,
Larry

Sept. 12, 1939
Selma
ALS, 2 p., 1 sheet

Dear Powell—:

Sorry about those books. Things piled up on me and I never got to it. Sending them down now.

Mariposa is within nice driving distance. Edwa uses the car during the week but the weekend would be fine for us to go. We can do that nicely, and it will be great fun poking around that place. I've been there only once—a wedding, sort of an elopement. Best friend. The oldest courthouse still in use in the state, or something. Those old mining towns have something about them.

For birthday I received *Finnegans Wake; Exagmination Round His Factification for Incamination of Work in Progress* (New Directions) an excellent little book but wretchedly proofread. You can't tell whether quotations from Finnegan are authentic or typographical errors! Also received Conrad Aiken's *Selected Poems*. All in all a beautiful haul. The family finally got around to giving me books. Usually Edwa gives books and the rest haberdashery! Finnegan, once you have amassed enough critical estimates to understand its attempt (which I haven't, of course) will be interesting. You get the general meaning of a given section through outside reading and then tackle it. Reading it aloud you get the great sound and torment of it, usually meaningless, but every so often, just enough to keep you going, a word or a segment kind of pops up to the surface and you wade on. Rhythmically it is right. Tonally it is right. I believe in ten or fifteen years, when enough smart men have given their eyes and their sanity to the thing, we can begin to get next to it. Joyce has influenced everybody—even Jeffers! It's a fact. Read from page 82 to 88 in that magnificent incantatory after death scene of Gudrun's in "At the Birth of an Age" (incidently in my opinion, this poem and *Point Sur*, or rather, reversely, are Jeffers' poetically highest). This scene seems to me directly from Joyce. I couldn't think of seeing it in pre-Joyceian literature.

These are nice notices. Thanks for sending

Bill

Come any time you want: we can always arrange to have the car to pick you up in Fresno. I'm no longer working.

Sep. 20, 1939
Berkeley, Calif.
APS

Dear Bill—

I leave here *Sat.* 8 a.m., arrive Fresno 12:15 noon, via Santa Fé. Can we make Mariposa Sunday? I must leave Fresno Monday, 12:17 noon. Gives us 48 hours.

Larry

Sep. 27, 1939
Los Angeles
APS

Dear Bill—

Home safely. No letter from Mac. Am mailing you the Miller book. Many thanks to you & Edwa for matchless hospitality. A fine session.

Larry

10-1-39
Los Angeles
ALS, 1 p.

Dear Bill—

Seeing the date reminded me to send you the enclosed! Mac must have been dreaming, for I have had no letter from him about your book or anything else.

Am taking family to Balboa this week.

Trust you received the Henry Miller book.

Don't forget to send me names & addresses for "Ghost" announcement.

Larry

Oct 2, '39
Selma
ALS, 1 p.

Dear Larry:—

Miller is one of the best things I've run across in a long time: really good. It's a goddamned shame that this book is censored. Utterly stupid. *The Tropic of Cancer* is a real book. Are they at all available? Here's my list [for the "Ghost" prospectus]. I'll write to most of these people personally.

Bill

Miss Frances M. Wilson
825 Yale—Fresno Calif.

Dr. Earl D. Lyon
Fresno State College
Fresno, California

Mr. John S. Moodey
Jackson High School
Jackson, Calif.

Mr. Stuart McKelvy
Yosemite Nat'l Park
California

Mr. Robert Linn
Napa High School
Napa, California

Mr. Walter Fitzpatrick
Yosemite Nat'l Park
California

Sorry I can't make it longer than this, but it would just waste the prospectus. I don't expect much as it is.

Poems back from the *Wheel*—criticism identical with yours.

Oct. 9, 1939
L.A.
ALS, 1 p.

Dear Bill—

Just back from an idyllic week at Balboa to find your letter & the enclosed one from Mac. He had neglected to mail it. We're certainly coming at you from all points of the compass! And the *Wheel* turneth. Please make yourself a copy of Mac's & return his to me. You must follow it up by correspondence with him & a trip to Berkeley.

Thanks for the names for "Ghost" list. I have not yet sent out the prospectus. Before the end of the month, I hope.

Glad you are enjoying Miller's book. Perhaps someday I'll be able to get you one. If you wanted to risk $2.50, I might send the money in advance to a friend of mine over there. Your risk would be that it wouldn't clear customs.

Please return both enclosures as soon as possible; I have yet to answer them.

yours,
Larry

Oct. 11, 1939
Selma
ALS, 1 p.

Dear Larry:—

MacIntyre criticism came in, and your letter and the other. Quite all right about the Connecticut Prison request to publish. Odd. I wish Mac had had the time to particularize, even to give one or two examples. I don't understand about the weak verbs—or about the indefinite endings. We'll try to see him this fall. I'm writing him today.

I've been reading Stuart Gilbert's *Ulysses*. It could be better as a critical work, it's not unified and cohesive, and you have to follow him down too many loose ends. But some of the material has literally revolutionized *Ulysses* in my mind. Example:—For a long time I had regarded the Homeric parallel behind *Ulysses* with distaste. I thought of it as a pedantic trick, born of a love of past literature, and a phony attempt to give a modern narrative classical dimensions by imposing brutally a classical structure without regard for the aesthetic problems such a work would entail. I read *Ulysses* in spite of the parallel and tried to forget it. But reading Gilbert's study and seeing Joyce's theory of reincarnation, of all things repeating, of the past constantly being reshaped in new material but the spirit and the relations eternal, this Homeric parallel suddenly became to me enormously alive—the *enormity* of that conception!—all the intricacies of the Odyssey carried over, readjusted into modern terms, its circumstances relived, the whole scope and detail of the past literally swept up over centuries and repatterned in the lives of these Dubliners, and the motif elaborated through the work by the same sort of reference to other actions of the past not Homeric, both preceding and antedating the Odyssey, and by references repeating themselves within the very course of the day—all this vast system of cross-reference revealed as the river of time reshaping itself by the minute and by the century, recurring and recurring—Christ! Philosophically, it's overwhelming! It has never been creatively conceived before—and so beautifully realized in this form. All the dead wood turns green, all the dead blossoms of an antique tree revive and give odor. God Almighty. *Ulysses* was great to me before this, for stylistic and literary reasons, but now—I simply haven't the adjectives!

I am returning the letters. Thanks for sending them down. We're short now, but we'll get our "Ghost" subscription in next month—also the attempt for the Miller book.

So long.
Bill.

I really expected harsher treatment from Mac. I thought he would blast me. From the tone of this thing I rather think that underneath he sort of likes some of those poems. It makes me feel good that he didn't blast them—it's like receiving eulogies from some one else!

10-24-39
[Los Angeles]
ALS, 2 p., 1 sheet

Dear Bill—

I am in the midst of getting out the "Ghost" announcements, so will just dash a note to accompany the enclosed. As you will see, the wheels are turning. I know you will cooperate & not take any rash actions without consulting me!!

Write the [Phelan] award people right away for your application blank. I don't know how many references they'll want, but give C.F. MacIntyre & Archibald MacLeish and Robinson Jeffers. Mac is very willing; I have corresponded with him about it. As you see by this letter, President Sproul has already recommended you for the award, in addition to myself.

With regard to Jeffers as sponsor, I enclose a card from Una. Return it & letter. Give his name in any case. You can't lose either way.

I feel hopeful that you'll get the $900. It will enable you to devote all of your strength to writing for a good period. It will not obligate you to anyone but your muse, God bless her! When you receive your "Ghost" announcement in the mail, you'll know your friends have theirs too. So let 'em have the letters.

Let's pull together, lad.
Larry

P.S. Chretien is a professor of Public Speaking at U.C. Berkeley & has a good literary background.

P.S. Newell reported that Jeffers spoke spontaneously & warmly of *San Joaquin,* when Gordon was at Tor House last.

Oct. 26, 1939
Selma
ALS, 5 p., 3 sheets

Dear Larry:—

It must seem like outright ingratitude that I haven't thanked you for that interesting and pleasant little book, or answered your cards, or given some kind of an account of myself. But to speak truthfully, I haven't been able to focus objectively on anything but my latest obsession for two or three weeks. Distractions! Distractions! I was hot, riding the wave of a good creative burst when I was undermined and spilled down, and goddamned near drowned in it. Jesus. I think the seeds were sown when you were here: I cautiously betrayed myself then. At any rate, a local friend had been pestering me to at least give music a chance, listen to it once, I didn't know what I was missing, etc. I told him I couldn't be bothered, but finally out of sheer desperation I consented and bam! I went under. Tchaikovsky's No. 6 started it. Cesar Franck's Symphony in D minor set it under way (the way that strain lifts out of the orchestra really gets me!)

and Beethoven's Fate rapping at the door finished it off.

Since then I have literally been unable to do anything but eat music, sleep music, breathe music, dream music. I have read constantly musical criticism and musical treatment: my brain is swarming with allegros, andantes, scherzos, fugues. We went into Fresno and put our last five dollars down on a console radio-phonograph with a 12 in. speaker that really brings these symphonies in, and that is our pride and joy—I, who not a month ago got red in the face and swore and stamped at the mere thought of bringing a radio into the house—I, poor fool, spend my evenings leaning over the thing, doing my damndest to segregate the thin strain of a classic from the ocean of swing. Nothing like this has happened to me since I got the tennis craze in post-adolescence. Suddenly my life has become broader, wider, deeper, fuller, richer, bigger, grander. All I had been trying to do through the thin trumpet of the muse I see lifted before my ears in the voice of this symphonic ocean. To sit there entranced, and hear the first theme resolve itself, and blend into the second, and be resolved there, and mingle, and grow through statement after statement, through all the organic growth and development and expansion, lifting, resolving itself, like a tree growing, like some vast embryonic life unfolding and shaping itself up to some enormous and magnificent thing of beauty. O god, my poor muse whimpering in the corner, my poor whimpering female muse how she shivers when this male, this broad chested, male-throated, golden bearded giant shouts at the door, sings thunder! Poor puny soul, I wonder if I can ever look her in the face again. Odd how our lives unfold behind us. For the last five years I've considered all the time I put in playing music had been wasted. Now suddenly I see that it was not wasted. All the hours I have behind me making thunder through that tuba in the "Poet and Peasant" and "William Tell" are not wasted at all. I have had an unconscious foundation there to step from to meet this new expansion. I remember in my first semester at Fresno State I took orchestra and we presented a symphonic program. I didn't know what it was all about and I didn't much care. I wasn't interested, I'd been brought up on marches mostly and slip-horn cakewalks, with an occasional overture that I hadn't found interesting. I had forgotten what we played on that symphonic program. I knew I was bored because I'd have to rest for forty or fifty measures and then hit one note—on the nose, too—and then rest again. And when I did get a chance to blow a little it was so goddamned fast and hard and high that I couldn't touch it: I forgot the incident easily. But the other day I heard grow out of the speaker

and it all came back like a wave, immense, like one of these roadside seeds that sleeps too deep for a dozen years till one winter the farmer sets his plow too deep and up it comes for the sun to take. Last night I heard Schnabel play Beethoven's fifth concerto, and then later came in Mozart's fourth symphony, the first time I had heard it, and it was very good, and later, Dvořák's 4th also, and it too was very good. Last Sunday we listened to the Wagner program: which moved me immensely, but I don't know why: it seems fundamentally so simple: so un-complex: the effect seems to be gained by manipulations of volumes rather than by manipulation of notation: the texture while not being soft, neither is it tough and wiry and resilient as is Beethoven or Tchaikovsky. They sneer at Tchaikovsky now, these moderns, but he'll outlive them: there's something behind that music, as B.H. Haggin (critic for the *Nation,* and the best I've read) puts it: Tchaikovsky's interpreters have given him his bad name. Well, I'm beginning to ramble. I'm trying to get back to poetry: it's scared me a little, this music. When I get through it and get it behind me I hope I will be a better poet for it—I know I'll be a better man.

I got a letter from Mac—which I'm almost ashamed to answer now I've put it off so long. Also I don't quite know what approach to take: he suggested I read his poems in *Poetry* and *Black and White* for reference to what he meant by weak verbs. I don't know whether he wants my opinion—I surely can't ignore the poems, yet anything I say could be presumptuous or groveling. I don't think much of the ones in *Black and White*. I don't think the ideology behind them is sufficient to merit first rate verse—that's a shitty statement and I don't mean it—I don't know what I mean. I can't really talk with the man—we don't see eye to eye, and I'll say the wrong thing sure. I'll write something. Also the note from Fisher you forwarded: thanked me for the Prospectus quotation and complimented—with caution, naturally—*San Joaquin*.

Well—I'll quit now Larry for a time. We enjoyed your visit with us very much. We are looking forward to seeing you again—any place. Odd how we change: after *San Joaquin* came out and my friends liked it, I began to like it myself—that's when I sent those copies off—now it's cold again: stinks: no guts in it, no body: nothing said. Hell.

Flanner never has replied. Smart girl. My poems are all coming back from *Saturday Review*, *Atlantic*, *Harper's* etc. It's the first thing in years I've submitted, and I'm cured again! Oh, god.

Sincerely,
Bill

No sooner signed my name than received your letter. Christ man; things are picking up. My muse is now out of the corner and patting my cheek, my hand is under her skirt and as soon as I can get this down we will retire to a known place and commit one of those major indecencies by which poets populate the world with irresponsible bastards. She's a good wench, and Beethoven has lost his bid: not that I'll close him out cold; but he's a rival of mine again, and if I can use any of his tricks to make the eyes stick out of the heads of these Phelan men: so be it. Beethoven, he's a good start, and if I could write a symphonic poem to end all symphonic poems using his tricks, I'm sure he'd be all in favor. He knows I'm a disciple. Anyway, Hallelujah!

We'll have the Miller book bound very shortly.

Bill

I'll return these things next letter, and I'll write Mac a fine round and decent one too, and shape things up. All is well. Peace reigns. It's great about Jeffers and *San Joaquin:* It's great about everything!—and, incidentally, you're dead wrong about those poems I showed you—dead wrong!

10-29-39
L.A.
ALS, 2 p., 1 sheet

Dear Bill—

Writing the above date reminded me that it is just 7 years ago today that I passed my final oral exam at Dijon, & so completed a cycle in my life. Left at once on a circular tour of Switzerland & found that country in all the glory of autumn colors.

Your letter here yesterday. It tickles me immensely! A belated response to my inquiry of over a year ago as to your feeling for music. I know just what you have been through, for I have experienced it in my time. I had an early musical education, & played the classics in recital at the age of 10. Then I abandoned it all for jazz, & lived for nothing else all through my teens. And then all of a sudden, on the verge of my 20's, I went positively crazy in my response to classical music. Ever since then, I have given a good deal of myself to music. The most exalted times in Europe were in connection with music heard—everything from the Ring Festival at Bayreuth to a Haydn quartet in Rome's Santa Cecilia Hall.

I have been through all the grand styles. Tchaikovsky I know well—you can't have had intercourse with the finale of his 5th symphony & ever forget him! Or Wagner—having made love throughout the 4 hours of Tristan & Isolde. Jesus Xist.

I think the apotheosis of the symphonic form is reached in

Brahms' First. I wore out a recording of it. I can whistle it backwards.

As I think I told you, I have reached the stage where the string quartet speaks to me most profoundly of all the forms of music—Haydn, Mozart, & Beethoven.

I am very pleased by your letter. It gives us a great deal more in common. All of my close friends are intensely musical—no exceptions.

It will help your poetry.

Play ball with Mac. Don't say everything. Remember he is 50 years old & intensely egotistical. Learn what you can from him. He is anxious to help you. Be smart. I know you will.

I wish I had time to write you my musical autobiography, which your letter calls for—but Pickett pickets me. More another time.

Larry

Nov. 10, 1939
Selma
ALS, 2 p., 1 sheet

Dear Larry—

I'm almost ashamed to write, because of *Tropic of Cancer*. Edwa bound it long ago, but I haven't printed the plate. Truly I'm sorry. It's a damned lousy trick to keep a book so long.

The accompanying letter to Fisher is in reply to the note he wrote me, thanking me for the quotation in the prospectus and paying me a fine and sincere (I felt) compliment on *San Joaquin*. I was very pleased.

Today I received a letter from your friend Watkins [not Lee] asking to reprint your foreword and some poems. I almost fell over! I'd peddled those things to cold doors all over the east and now come *offers!* It's magnificent! And your foreword, smearing me up all over the place!

I have received application blanks from Phelan. The award requires I think devoting the year to writing, which is right. It would be good to change locations and intensify for a year. Staying here I would do no more than I would otherwise, but to go elsewhere, with the definite intention of writing, and feeling the justification, even the obligation, of living purely in creation for a year, might stimulate me to better, or at any rate, more work. It is a problem, however, for Edwa's teaching position would be sacrificed, and it is hard for married teachers to get positions.

I'm applying however, but one thing worries me: the application in asking for references definitely states—"three persons competent in your field of study and well acquainted with you personally." Can I, in any honesty—even with any respect to these men, give their names? I'm doing it, of course, because you've advised me, and you know best. But what will the men think when questions about me reach them? It's my conscience.

I'm beginning finally to get back on an even keel. String quartets don't appeal to me—though persons of discrimination assure me as you do that nothing quite touches it as a medium. My feeling, if I could objectify what is purely a feeling, would indicate that the quartet lacks the complete tonal resource, that it, physically isn't the complete thing that a symphony orchestra is, that of necessity it operates in the upper register of tones, and even admitting the marvelous complexity and texture capable of performing, there are fundamental seats of emotion left untouched. I am not a speaker for sheer sound, volume for itself, but I am a speaker for dimension, for depth and for breath, tonally, in order to get an equivalent emotionally or aesthetically. I have no favorites, because I have not heard enough to know. I have not heard Brahms' first. What I have heard has been one time, and not enough to get next to. The "Pathetique" is marvelous. The "Eroica" is marvelous. The "Unfinished" is marvelous. Sibelius is marvelous. Franck's symphony is marvelous. I'm at the magnificent stage, the new innocent stage of any art where anything in it is marvelous, and that's how I feel about symphonies. I would never have believed this could have happened to me. Life has more riches than ever I suspected, and the creative attainments of man are far in excess of his merits.

Bill

I think I've forgotten something, but I don't know what it would be.

I know—

I thought of attaching a note to the application explaining exactly my relations with these men. I am listing your name also as a sponsor, and that at least will be one person competent in my field who *knows me personally*. That's a hell of a condition. What good is it? If I write the best poems in the history of the language and everybody says so, and yet I don't have any *personal* friends—I'm cut off. It's a stinking trick. They are scared to death they are going to have to make a responsible decision on one thing—the merit of the work. To avoid such uncomfortables they rope in all this extraneous—

A good defense of Jeffers in last *Poetry*, and one that lays the opposing article low. All the abuse against him is based on a misunderstanding of his beliefs. See the Miller review in the *Nation*?

11-20-39
LA
ALS, 1 p.

Dear Bill—

Don't worry about the Phelan requirements—the personal acquaintances. It is only a form. Qualify your names, as you suggest.

I sent the letter on to Fisher.

The "Ghost" prospectus has evoked a small but enthusiastic response. Orders are mounting toward 50. Are you still going to be able to come in? I hope so. I am driving for every last penny.

Been writing a fearful number of letters. And in between, trying to get the Pickett written. Ritchie wants to bring it out in the spring.

Keep the enclosed. Do you remember Gloria Swanson? The tables are turned. Movie star *writes* fan mail!

You have given okay to Watkins at Connecticut State Prison?

Can you send the *Tropic* book soon? Good notice in *Nation*, but not quite good enough. I am hurried. Larry

Nov. 27, 39
Selma
ALS, 2 p.

Dear Larry—

A friend just brought out the Beethoven 3rd (Eroica) and we played it twice in close succession, and if there was ever music that spoke to me, that spoke deep, got through all the shells, the crusts, the sloth, the waste scum of humdrum existence it was this symphony. It is a greater symphony than the Fifth—against all opposition I maintain this. In the fifth I am not completely taken in, its triumph is too easy—a little too easy, and the pomp of the finale a little too self assured. It's martial music, the music of triumph, of conquest, there are drums beating somehow and horns blaring, and we're all feeling very good as after a high school football game and you've beaten the other guys and you're hot stuff. Life simply isn't that way. There isn't that kind of triumph. It doesn't exist, and there's no reason for it. In the third there is a touch of that same self satisfaction, that Beethoven egotism, in the finale, but not much, it's more dignified, it has had a harder fight, the difficulties were much greater, (that "funeral march" andante is I think the most profound and touching music I've heard anywhere), and all in all the belief, the achievement, is much more aware of the tragedy and the true nobility of struggle than in the other. I felt it very profoundly. Speaking of beliefs, one type of belief I can accept, and feel consolation, is the affirmation in the Tchaikovsky 6th. There is terrible struggle, but there is no triumph—no pomp I mean, none of that self congratulation trampling and banner unfurling. There is affirmation—terrific affirmation, but it is made in *spite* of the tragedy and not as a conquest. It is aware always of the forces of negation, and it never really masters them, but it breaks up to them in a passionate blind magnificent refusal to be duped, refusal to be cajoled by all the forces of logic into believing what logic requires. It is spiritual affirmation, and as such, as *belief* (I'm not talking about music) is superior to the belief of Beethoven.

I'm sending along the Miller book. Really we're sorry about the delay. I hate to give it up though. Also a check for the "Ghost." Also a letter—one of the best I've received. Send it back. Stuff like this is the supreme justification for writing. I o.k. Watkins at Conn. of course. It's very fine. He said in his letter the associate editor of *Travel* wanted a copy of *S.J.* I'm hanging on to the few I have. That Ritchie printing will be valuable soon. Good old Gloria—thanks a lot.

Bill.

12-5-39
LA
ALS, 2 p., 1 sheet

Dear Bill—

I only have time for a note to acknowledge your "Ghost" order, & the Miller book. Edwa did a beautiful job. And your label's in the fine Aldine tradition, lad. I am so pleased by its new dress. Thank you both very much.

"Ghost" subscriptions keep coming in. Now over 50. Must get an angel to put it over. Did you see the notice in *Saturday Review* this week? The bastard got the price wrong ($3.00), but it'll give us another mention in the correction which I rushed airmail.

Tomorrow night I am talking about the project to a joint meeting of USC & UCLA literary groups.

The Eroica is an old favorite of mine. The funeral march is one of the saddest pieces of music ever written. It never fails to bring my heart up into my throat. Its simplicity & restraint put Tchaikovsky's "Pathetic" purple sorrow to shame. But I am willing to admit that the latter has the power to move me also.

At Newell's first marriage (to Gloria Stuart) for a wedding march I adapted the central theme of the Eroica *marche funèbre,* where it goes rather cheerfully into the major! It served splendidly.

And then toward the close, when it swells in sort of a brave protest to grief, but is overwhelmed, choked, broken, & sinks back to simple heartbroken utterance—then is one of the high marks of musical art.

Mac's Oxford book (*Cafés & Cathedrals*) is due any time now. Keep your eye [open] for it. I tried to get to review it for *Poetry* or *Saturday Review*—no luck.

Have you sent all Phelan data in?

Halfway through writing Pickett book. It goes well.

Greet Edwa—yrs.
Larry

12-23-39
L.A.
ALS, 2 p., 1 sheet

Dear Bill—

Merry Christmas!

I should like very much for a copy of *S.J.* to get to Harry Thornton Moore, who did the little book on Steinbeck & who has a Lawrence piece coming out in the *SRL* & is a former student of Mac's at UCLA—a Californian now living in Illinois. He has made a valuable contact for me with James Laughlin, owner of New Directions, in my attempt to get N.D. to take over the "Ghost" & make up what we lack. It would be printed just the same at Ward's. It seems to be our only hope. Subscriptions have bogged at 50.

Moore is a fine chap & will be friendly & helpful to you in the best sort of way. I have only my inscribed copy. May I ask you to squeeze out a copy & send him, with a note that you do so at my request? *It will be a very good thing for you.* Please hark to my judgement.

His address is 607 Provident Ave., Winnetka, Illinois.

Ward placed 2 among the 50 books of '39. Unfortunately privately printed books are not eligible. He & I think *S.J.* one of his best of all time.

Am enjoying a 9-day vacation. Too broke to go anywhere. How about your paying us a visit?

Working on "Ghost" & good old Pickett.

Noël!
Larry

Day after Xmas, 1939
Selma
ALS, 3 p., 2 sheets

Dear Larry:—

There is no worse news to receive in so joyous a season than the fate of our project with the "Ghost." I had wanted so much for this thing to go through. I wanted to see those 350 copies make literary history—Two of my people were on the verge of coming through, but indolence and Christmas caught them and that ended it—it takes a religious zeal to put poetry over, and both these people are particularly inactive Wastelanders. Well, perhaps New Directions can see the light. Jesus I hope so.

I'll of course send Moore a book. It sounds very good. I have determined to hang closely to what copies I have left; since I'm sure from Ritchie's record that this particular printing will be very valuable. This sounds good though.

Too bad about the ineligibility—we'd have taken them though—eh?

How is the "Philosopher" coming out? I can already see that irascible old bastard howling Gantian rhetoric up and down pages of superb Ritchian typography. I think you have something in that old man. Most "early" literature fails because it has nothing but its earliness to hang to. This old coot, now, seems to have the essential flavor of a rare but important frontier element—the semi-cultured, fairly-well-educated man who has plunged himself into a society crude and coarse, where his eloquence clangs out of entire tune with his fellows. They are the most tragic element of the frontier, for they belong to and love another way of life.

For Christmas we received Handel's Overture in B minor

"Freely transcribed" by Leopold Stokowski. "Freely transcribed" is right, he uses full orchestra and zooms around over those progressions like a plane in a whirlwind. We like it, though, like it a lot—it has much power. Then also Toscanini playing Preludes to Act 1 and 3 of "Traviata." Prelude to 3 is astonishingly beautiful. We treated ourselves to the "Pathetic" symphony—Edwa's favorite. Haggin says that most criticism leveled at Tsch. is the fault of his interpreters. He says Stokowski's handling of the 6th is strained, hysterical, feverish, almost intolerable. Also Koussevitzky. Whereas, says he, Eugene Ormandy produces something firm, restrained, and remarkably beautiful. We bought the latter, and Larry, if you have not heard this recording by all means do. The last movement by Stokowski is so wild it is like a drunken lunatic masturbating in a blazing tabernacle; but this last movement by Ormandy is so beautiful you can hardly believe your ears. There is not a purple patch in the symphony. "Eroica" is still my favorite: there are other symphonies too I like better than this one, but I never expect to hear anything more touching, or deeply troubling than this final movement of the "Pathetic."

I haven't gone all music, though. And this autumn has been an especially fertile one. The most sustained and in some ways the richest creative gust I have ever experienced came in late October and early November just after my immersion in music and as a direct result of it. I wrote a series of lyrics ["The Sides of a Mind"] on a theme—a sort of elaboration around the ego—all personal, even autobiographical, in that they deal with incidents of my life, and explorations of my moral attitude. Whether they will work out I do not know. Winter usually finds me in a classical frame of mind, cold and severe, demanding the utmost of every syllable, as it were, while this series was written out of a terrific gust and urgency. I hope I can complete it however. If I can, I shall have upwards to twenty five poems towards a new book!

And I'm back to work in the fields. I used to need work, I used to get in a high nervous tension and my physique would cry for labor. No more. I hated to get back to it. I can write, or re-work, persistently now with no sterilizing effects, and I need time. It's such a damned waste of good time to have to work. I am banking much on this Phelan that you are trying to get for me. Not that I really in my heart expect to win it (someone is probably writing the biography of Phelan himself this time!!) but the possibility hangs so alluringly before me, and try as I will not to place trust in it—I cannot escape absorption in the thought. If won, Edwa would stop teaching and we would move to a new locale. If we stayed here it would be little better than a vacation, and I would have all the local obligations to confront, but moving for the express purpose of writing, I feel would whet and stimulate my consciousness and my imagination, and I think I could do good work. We shall see. And so long. And a healthy productive fully complete new year.

Bill.

My stuff is all in for the contest. Also a fine letter from Watkins (whom I gave permission to quote from *S.J.*) asking if he could not help me. He claims friendship with Sandburg's and L. Adamic's lit. agent. He seems to be a real chap.

I'm sending 2.50 to risk on *Tropic of Cancer*. O.K.?

1940: POWELL'S ROBINSON JEFFERS

January 1, 1940
Los Angeles
ALS, 2 p.

Dear Bill—

A nine-day vacation draws to an end. My last evening I devote to some intensive loafing, & at last a letter to you. MacIntyre was here all afternoon. He feels sanguine about your Phelan chances, having just come down from a meeting with the administrator, Chretien. There will be plenty of other applicants, however, and a few deserving ones. Don't count it in the bag, although you have a pretty powerful gang pushing you. Don't know who the judges are. Hope it's Jeffers again.

Mac was in good form; sober as a judge, although he had been drinking at a big party at Ritchie's till 3. Talked a lot of his Guggenheim trip. I have great affection for Mac, the crazy son-of-a-bitch. We sit on the edge of things awaiting his Oxford book & the Rilke.

We stayed home last night, as usual on N.Y. Eve. Had a log fire & popcorn. Tabulated our N.Y. Eves for the 30's. Never in the same home twice, together or apart. The 40's should find us more stable. A year ago you two were here.

The end of a decade. I am really impressed. A magnificent span of years it's been for me—the grandeurs & miseries of love & separation & return, marriage; study, travel, & work. Never more than a dollar or two ahead of the wolves. If my life should close now, I'd not feel cheated.

Will you write a poem to the 30's? I hope you are bringing off the group you speak of, & will let me in on them.

Where would you move to in case you won out? The ocean? The mountains? The desert? The city?

Check received for *T. of C.* Let's hope it clears customs.

A very dry season here; only 2 small rains.

And so to bed.

Happy New Year to us all!

Larry

Jan. 7, 1940
[L.A.]
ALS, 1 p.

Dear Bill—

Please give me some information about *Phoenix,* Cooney's quarterly. He stopped sending it to me. The last issue I received was vol. 2, n. 1, spring 1939. I saw the issue following that when I was at your home. Has there been another since then? If it is still flourishing, I'll send Cooney 2 bucks for a subscription: I sought to do so in the first place, but he wouldn't take it.

When I didn't receive the issue I saw at your place, I wrote Cooney, but never had an answer. I told him I was anxious to keep my file unbroken.

Phelan asked for my report on you. I sent it. Here's hoping!

The rain is falling. A quiet Sunday in my study.

Larry

Jan. 11, 1940
Selma
ALS, 1 p.

(Time: Jan. 3, after receiving your letter)

Everson: Well, Lee, I guess I popped off too quick about the Phelan.

Watkins: Yeah? What's up?

Everson: Letter here from Powell, he's been talking with MacIntyre and it doesn't look so hot.

Watkins: Jesus Christ, that's tough. What's he say?

Everson: (quoting) MacIntyre was here all afternoon. He feels sanguine about your Phelan chances—etc.

Watkins: Well, Goddamn it, what's wrong?

Everson: Why—what it says, here:

Watkins: What the hell do you think sanguine means?

Everson: Why, bloody, bad, terrible, used in connection with exceptionally fierce battles.

Watkins: Oh for god's sake, here's your dictionary, look it up.

Everson: (scanning pages) blurb, bluhuhummmm—well I'll be God—*whoopie!*

* * *

Dear Larry:

I have received no further copy from Cooney, nor any further letters. My last letter was in August, and at that time he was thinking of farmland in Maine. He has a poem of mine sent last June and never definitely accepted.

I have started a poem on the decade, but nothing has come of it.

If we won out we both had in mind the hills behind Berkeley.

Bill

Jan. 18, 1940
Selma
ALS, 2 p.

Dear Larry:

Can you tell me who Roger Watkins is? What do you know about him? Is he the real thing or some nut? I don't know what to believe, and I hate to get sucked into a situation that I'd later regret. I've another letter from him offering help on any hand. "Six months from now I shall be in a better position to aid you than I am now; then I shall be free and I am not the connectionless being my position may indicate." What the hell is it all about?

Also a good letter from Mac. He said he had written to the Phelan Secretary, even sending along that refutation of his criticism that I had sent. I was floored. Also he said he'd talked to Chretien, and if the Phelan falls through there might be a scholarship at Cal. MacIntyre thinks I should get more training. He told the Phelan secretary I needed discipline. He told me (if I didn't mind) that I needed a change and more contact with the urban mind. My needing a change is right, but the rest isn't. Every time I've had too much contact with the urban mind it has scattered and diffused my poetic energy, taken up my time with nonessentials such as the social problem, left me nervous and agitated and brooding over trifling social errors. I write my poetry best when I'm alone, and I think I keep fairly well up with aesthetic interests through magazines. The needing discipline is absolutely not right. I can show ms. on a single poem over two hundred pages and a three years' interval, intense revision. Practically every poem I write runs to twenty or thirty drafts and covers months of time. Just because my letters straggle and bulge and run over the edges is no sign that my poems do. Maybe they do, but it's not for lack of discipline. I don't want a scholarship to Cal. That would involve concentration on work that is of no interest to me at all; it would project me again into a kind of discipline that I do not like—the discipline of meeting a situation that I have no interest in. Not only that, friends of mine that have been through the place come back with stories of educational corruption into mass industry that are appalling. The premium of kiss-assing because the papers can't be read properly; the tricks and subtleties used to get grades, the way "A" students frequently get "C's" in some new course because the reader didn't know them. All down the line the emphasis placed upon the wrong aspects. I'd once dallied with the idea of auditing a couple of courses, sitting in on lectures and getting the benefit without the intolerable crap. But no scholarships, no grinding to meet finals. To hell with it, I'm a poet and I know my ways of working, and I know intuitively what my creative energy needs, and Edwa too, would like to get a house back of the campus in one of those canyons they tell about, near enough to the place to benefit from the library, near enough to the concert halls and the galleries and the bookshops. But living essentially by ourselves, preserving the integrity that has been built up between us and which tends to dissolve under too much social life.—Maybe I'd better wait till the award is made before I get so worked up!

Sincerely,
Bill

1–27-40
L.A.
ALS, 2 p., 1 sheet

Dear Bill—

A poor week due to a heavy cold. I read in the paper that elementary schools are closed up your way. Perhaps Edwa is having a vacation. I hope you are both well.

About your last letter: I wouldn't get involved with Roger Watkins. I know no more about him than you do. About Mac's idea for a U.C. fellowship—I agree entirely with you—it's not the thing for you. When Mac gets the bit between his teeth, he goes stone blind. But don't have any showdown with him. It's all very hazy. Just string along with him. Phelan or nothing!

Laughlin [publisher/owner of New Directions] is interested. Fisher has sent him Book 7 to read. Now it's up to him.

If you have not read Enid Starkie's *Arthur Rimbaud*, go after it. If you can't obtain it through your county library, let me know & I'll mail you our library's copy. It's a very fine critical biography.

The Jeffers book is in proof. I almost wish it weren't! It's really wretchedly written. The drawings are fine though, & put Kent to shame. Here is a notice of the book, & also a paper I read last summer to a group of college librarians. You'll appreciate the Fresno reference!

"Pickett's" only 4 years short of the grave, thank God!

(I like your plan to go to Berkeley, if——. An excellent plan.)

Where's that poem about the Mariposa trip, the graveyard? I need it for my closing pages. To your quill, Mr. Journalist-Poet! There's a dead-line to meet.

Wait until you see the beautiful job Ritchie did on my Lawrence-*Colophon* piece! Be greeted.

Larry

Urology
Elmer Belt, M.D.
1893 Wilshire Boulevard Los Angeles, California Drexel 3285
January 31, 1940

TLS

My dear Lawrence:
From time to time I have thumbed over and admired your beautiful little book, *San Joaquin,* which you sent me a very long time ago and which I have been ungracious enough not to thank you for before this time.
Everson has reached great heights and the little book has brought me many moments of real enjoyment, and I want you to know that although silent until now I have been and am deeply grateful to you for thinking of me and presenting me with this beautiful gem.

Yours very sincerely,
Elmer

Feb. 12, '40.
Selma.
ALS, 5 p., 3 sheets

Dear Larry:—
For Christ sake get hold of the new issue of *Poetry* and read the article called "Poetry in the Making" by Charles David Abbott. It's very much in the vein of your article on Rare Books and I think you'll be very interested. I'm interested because I thought of this business long ago and took steps toward following it. It was back I think in '36, Buel came through one day and in talking jovially told me to hang onto my mss. Jeffers' have become very valuable, etc., etc. I was stopped cold. It had never dawned on me—in all my egotistical mooning over my future those mss. had never occurred to me. I remember every letter I used to send I'd wonder thrillingly if so and so would save this for Posterity—but drafts of those early poems I innocently threw away. I made up for lost time though. Every glimmer, every fragment and snatch that I put on paper I hoarded away, well-fondled, well-gloated over. I had lost the

first draft of "Millerton," on which I was then working, but I kept the following drafts, and except where rare moments of carelessness allowed a draft to disappear, I have fully complete mss. of all subsequent poems. After a while, as the thing went on, and more and more poems grew behind me, it finally came to me that this sort of thing had more value than the sentimentality with which it was begun. I could look back and see the processes by which my mind had worked, how, most amazing of all, the texture of a poem would so change that it was not even finished on the same subject as it was begun; how images conceived in inspiration would so alter the context of the thought that the poem would gather around the new nucleus and expand from there. Most of those changes I soon forgot—I got to remember the poem by its completed draught, and the roots from which it had sprung were gone. But rereading the draughts I can get back to what I had done and see how it had grown. Sometimes the rereading of first drafts is entirely meaningless to one, and it is only through second, third or tenth draughts that I could finally find the red herring that altered the course of that problem. I've never said much about this, because I've been ashamed. I've been ashamed of the sentimentality that permitted me to start the business and that undoubtedly permits me to continue it. In more violent moments of self-condemnation I've come close to chucking the whole works into the stove.

This article, however, redeems me. Somehow I feel sort of justified, as if whether the poems become important doesn't matter, regardless if that one type of creative development is illustrated. It's a point the man has made, and an interesting one. The analysis of Spender's poem shows that. Incidentally, in regard to completeness, whatever became of the typescript to *San Joaquin?*

I should have written when your last letter and the circulars arrived, because I was quite excited about the new book and could have written with more spontaneity and enthusiasm than now when other matters are uppermost in my mind. But I really am glad. We had thought the project had fallen, and this announcement came as a very, very happy surprise. You're wrong when you say it is badly written—the book, I mean. It is not. There has been no analysis as thorough and cogent as this one. This is your biggest work, and you will be remembered for it. We're sending our order soon.

I liked the article on Rare Books. Lively and sound and to the point. I hope it makes some effect. I remember getting a rare Grabhorn from the State College library and, turning with relish toward the title page as one turns to a picture (as of course it is) I found stamps and ciphers and other mundane material smack under the title: like stamping classification signs in the middle of a Van Gogh. Insufferable!

Odd, isn't it, how our tastes change? Ever since I first listened to music my tastes have been altering, and I think this is the last I will say in this line: there's no use giving you any more jokes to throw up at me later like that "Dear Professor Powell" episode. Go to hell, goddamn you; I am however, beginning to see what you fellers mean when you all hunch forward to hear a string quartet. And somehow, Mozart means more to me now than frilled ladies and wigged men capering under candle chandeliers. As for Bach—ah, Bach.

I've just read *Point Counter Point*—(the first novel I've read in years) and think it amazingly good, lacking only the total exploitation of the resources of language, the measured inevitability of Joyce or Proust to bring it up among the big ones.

This war, this goddamned bastardly hideous war! We're locking our front door resolutely to stay out of Europe—and just aching to walk into a scrap with Japan. To hell with it. To hell with everything. I'm creatively stuck, the spring's dry. I can't revise. Music emotionally drains me so that I don't write.

Read the poem by William Herber [Everson's pseudonym, used to prove editor of *Poetry* prejudiced] and the note about him in the back of the issue. Odd. The poem is crap, except for a couple good lines. *Poetry* will swallow anything you send them if you make it "left" and "proletarian." I speak from experience.

Sincerely
Bill

I can't do you a poem. Honest to God I've tried, but everything I felt about it had been said in "Millerton." I'm really sorry to fail you. No word from the *Cancer*? Are you sending for *Capricorn*?

2-15-40
Los Angeles
ALS, 2 p., 1 sheet

Dear William Herber—

An excellent hoax; a most excellent hoax! One after my own heart. Keep it up & become the great proletarian poet of the '40's.

yrs.
LC Powell

Dear Bill Everson—

Abbott was out here recently, but I missed him. He called on Mac in Berkeley. He has a good plan. You are right to keep your work in all its stages. I have a great deal of Mac's stuff in early drafts he's sent me.

I hear that his Oxford book has been withdrawn, because of libel threats by the old maid professor [Lily Bess Campbell] to whom he dedicated the Phallus poem! About 50 copies only had been distributed, all of them here in L.A. Thank God I got one! I suppose they'll cancel the leaves & turn the book loose again. I hope so, for it contains some magnificent poems. Later I'll copy you the two that caused the trouble. Most of the 50 copies were bought by his former colleagues at UCLA (where the old maid is) so he did get his revenge in the locale where it meant the most.

Buel called on me at the library about two weeks ago. He's a fine lad. I liked him instantly.

I send you a belated letter about *S.J.* (As far as I know, Ritchie has the typescript you ask about: write him)—Belt is one of the finest men on earth—much like Hal Bieler—an artist-physician. Belt is internationally famous surgeon—kidney, etc. Please return letter.

I sent for *Capricorn* at same time as *Cancer* for you. No

word yet. Mail is very slow. Some letters from France have taken 2 months.

Late, & I must sleep

yours ever,
Larry

Feb. 19, '40
Selma
ALS, 1 p.

Dear Larry:—

Last summer after my poems had again been rejected by *Poetry* I sat down in a rage and after an hour wrote this "Sign" thing, the letter, scrawled out in my illiterate longhand with a blunt pencil on smudged paper. I posted it that night on the S.P. mailcar to avoid local postmark. Having forgotten all about it I was very surprised when this issue arrived. The simpletons. The simple tits. Stupid sons of bitches. It was an underhanded trick, though, and in many ways I don't like it. Please don't say anything about it. I'm not proud of it, but filled with a kind of unholy glee.

Forgive my effulgence over my hoard of mss. In my enthusiasm with Abbott's article I had forgotten that literary quality is prime factor in this business.

Enjoyed hearing of the MacIntyre–Campbell episode, and am looking forward to the offending poems. Thanks for this letter from Belt. He wrote Ritchie for another copy, Ritchie sent it on to me, I answered Belt, and have just received a courteous note from him.

So long
Bill

Mar. 6, 1940
Los Angeles
APS

Dear Bill—

Am half under with flu, but want you to know that the "Ghost" battle *has been won*. Laughlin failed me; I got a local backer: Elmer Belt, a great man. Ritchie has started setting. Will take him till autumn to finish it. Rejoice!

Larry

Mar. 17, 1940
Selma
ALS, 1 p.

Dear Larry:—

Nothing has pleased me more than the success of the "Ghost" in seeing the light. Totally unexpected at this late day and a magnificent surprise. Congratulations on that bit of management. Belt must be a real man.

I am working like hell in the fields, and have just completed a trying week. My father-in-law was down from the Masonic Home in Decoto, Calif. and the situation was bad all the way around. We're moving from this place this summer, Phelan or no Phelan. There are too many people here who we are bound to be respectful to merely because we've known them all our lives.

I sent the book to De La Welch [Phelan Award judge] via McWilliams, but the slut hasn't thanked me. Who the hell does she think she is? She has a fairly good grasp of language, some of her lyrics are sure and taut, but her conception is limited and her social muse is prose.

Buel writes that he is living in Newell's old studio. He invites us down, and since we haven't been away all winter I think we can make it next weekend. So plan to see us. Can you send us a map of your place? I mean, how to get there?

I have written, of all things, a long poem for radio called "The Masculine Dead," but it will need much much work.

However I'm sending under separate cover another long poem, nameless, which I have worked on for a couple of years. Its conception is one of two years ago, but it has in it places of the best I have done. See what you think.

Bill

3–19-40
W.L.A. 30971
ALS, 2 p., 1 sheet

Dear Bill—
Glad to hear you're coming down. You don't say how long you'll be here. We have to be away Saturday afternoon & evening. Will be home Sunday all day & evening. Do you have to go back that day? I hope not, for we'd like you two & Buel to come out that evening. Or if you have to go back that day, you could come out on your way & through the hills & across the SF valley to 99. I'll be at the Library Sat. a.m. until 11:30. Call me there, if you are arrived.

* * *

Will save talk until your arrival.

Larry

Sunday, April 7
[Selma]
ALS, 2 p., 1 sheet

Dear Larry:—
Work has been so heavy this past week I have only now got time to thank you for *The Colophon.* A totally unexpected gift. We knew you had an article appearing, and we hoped to see it, but we certainly had not expected to be presented with the issue. It is a very beautiful periodical, and thanks from us both.

I read your article with interest, and found it a good supplement to the Catalogue which came earlier. I like the tone of all your Lawrence work, the admiration and reserve with which you come before it. I think it very likely that you yourself will turn out to be the energetic person you ask for, and that your book when it comes will be the work of love and necessity.

The Rebecca West item you mention as having been first printed in *New Adelphi* I read in *The Bookman* for April and May 1930.

Also (incidentally) have you seen the Lawrence criticism in C.E.M. Joad's *Under the Fifth Rib*. I haven't read it, but Edwa and L. Watkins both have. Joad is an important English philosopher. Wm. Troy had a good article on Lawrence in *The Partisan Review* for Jan. 1938 which you might have missed. I don't regard Joad's criticism as either valid or important, but I wanted you to know about it.

Did you receive the *Phoenix*? Another issue is out you know. More hysterical than ever—Jesus Christ the man has some kind of complex. AntiWar, mostly. The War Resisters League of America with entry blanks. Certainly there has to be some kind of organization, some kind of united movement if War is to be resisted—but this. The language is couched in such mystical terms and the whole tone shouts so morally that I doubt if few people are impressed. Certainly I'm not.

Also I'm sending you a letter from George Dillon [editor of *Poetry*] which I want you to return. What a mess. What an unspeakable mess. I regard myself only with contempt for ever getting into it, and I have written to Dillon showing up the whole affair before he publishes this last "poem."

It is the seventh, and no word of the Phelan. As soon as you hear who won it, let me know. The suspense.

I trust you received my long poem.

Bill

April 15, 1940
University of California
ALS, 2 p., 1 sheet

Dear Bill—

They've got me on the run, as per the enclosed announcement. Leave tomorrow for Long Beach. Taking family to Balboa & will commute from there. The old house on the bay front. I plan to get back down there by mid-afternoon each day of the week, for canoeing & swimming.

Glad you like the *Colophon.* Shame on you for weakening & exposing Wm. Herber! I'll bet you came near giving Dillon a stroke! Yes, I got the last issue of *Phoenix,* but not the one before it. I must get that one out of Peter Cooney before he explodes.

Won't you buckle down & write that study of *Women at Point Sur?*

Thanks for the bound copy of your long poem. I am glad to see you trying something new. It is a strange poem, throbbing & urgent. I like the way it starts out, & then the sowing interludes. But I don't care for the girl Minerva or the boy Joseph. These little vignettes are not satisfying. Why don't you write a real narrative poem? What are you waiting for? Tackle something really big.

But it is an interesting poem.

I have heard nothing about the Phelan award.

Hope I can settle down for a real letter after this convention is over.

Enjoyed your visit very much. Wish we lived nearer one another.

Taking Thoreau's *Journals* to the beach, for night reading.

Faithfully,
Larry

Apr. 25, 1940
Los Angeles
APS

Dear Bill—

Have you heard anything about the Phelan award? I have not. A bit of good news from this front: the Pickett book has been accepted by the University of California Press. Won't be out for 6 or 8 months because of the number of mss. ahead of it. Cheers!

LCP

May 6, Monday 1940
Selma, Calif.
ALS, 2 p.

Dear Larry—

I have just received in the mail this letter:—

> Dear Mr. Everson:—
>
> The trustees of the Phelan Estate, upon the recommendation of a jury composed of
>
> Mrs. Sara Bard Field
> Oscar Lewis Esq. and
> Professor George R. Stewart
>
> have conferred upon Mr. Sidney Meller of San Francisco the James D. Phelan Award in Literature for 1940–41. It is a matter of regret to the Trustees that so many meritorious competitors could not be rewarded for the work which they submitted. We trust however, that you will not be discouraged from competing again.
>
> Faithfully yours
> (signed)
> C. Douglas Chretien
> Director.

And I do now solemnly swear that I shall never again submit work of mine, or apply in any way, for any literature award, fellowship, or fund. It is not worth the weeks of suspense and worry, the loss of your mental equilibrium and the balance of your temperament to goad yourself on with these businesses. It is not worth it. *It is not worth it.* I could be heroic, stick my hand in my vest, assume a mock attitude and say: "Fate has decreed. This is a Sign for me to continue my Way unknown and unheralded: I must fashion my obscure Destiny in the darkness of Oblivion." I could say it but I'm not going to—I'm going to finish the "Masculine Dead," and when I finish it, I'm going to write another, and when I finish that I am going to write another.

Congratulations upon your placing of the "Pickett" ms. You deserve the best that can come your way, Larry. You work and sweat and grind for others as few men ever do. It makes me feel very glad and good to know that you can fashion your own successes.

The best of luck
Bill

May 10, 1940
Los Angeles
ALS, 1 p.

Dear Bill—

I am keenly disappointed that you didn't get the Phelan award. We certainly did all we could to get it for you. It is not unconsoling to know that they turned down Steinbeck when he applied, on the strength of his *Pastures of Heaven.* God knows who they gave it to instead—I don't know of anyone who's had it that's amounted to anything!

You can get along without it. You will get along without it. The experience has been good for you. I know what it is to agonize. I have been turned down. It doesn't really matter.

Enclosed is a New Directions project. Do you want to take part? I think it's a fine idea & am going to subscribe. Laughlin is due out here soon. He wants Ritchie to be one of his printers. Why don't you get ready with 32 pages of work?

Cheerio!
Larry

May 16, 40
[Selma]
ALS, 2 p.

Dear Larry:—

This is a very fine little catalogue [Western Books, 1939], and I feel very proud. I feel even famous to see my name presented under such auspices. Have you seen this exhibit? The foreword said the judges unanimously agreed only on nos 31 and 14. What the hell is wrong with the judges this year?

Excerpt from Joseph Henry Jackson in *S.F. Chronicle* Sun. May 12, 40:

> While we are on the subject of prizes and such it should be noted that this week's award of the Phelan fellowship to Sidney L. Meller is an intelligent one. Meller, as you may remember, is the author of "Roots In The Sky," published a year or so ago by Macmillan. He wrote this book partly on a Phelan Award—the one for 1937–38. This 1940–41 fellowship will enable him to finish his forthcoming novel, which should interest San Franciscans since it is set on and about Telegraph Hill. It isn't one of those pseudo-bohemian affairs, however, so don't get all prepared for the wrong thing. Alternate, with honorable mention, is Ritchie Lovejoy of Pacific Grove; and other Phelan honorable mentions go to Miss Joyce Campion of S.F., William Hoy of S.F., Jack Mail of S.F., and Miss Rosalie Moore of Berkeley.

Hell, Larry, six men ahead of us. Didn't even come *close!* Didn't have a chance. Is it unsportsman-like of me to gaze suspiciously at the geographical location of these people? Five in the Bay region, all six in Northern Calif. No L.A. men mentioned. This looks like a case of *You Know Me Al.* Have you read *Roots in the Sky?* Maybe the man is all right. I hope so. I really hope he is. It is infuriating to think of all that money going to someone who isn't worth the shit he drops of a morning.—Fine to be superior isn't it? There's nothing like the ego to save your vanity! God, I'm a miserable bastard!

Have you seen my *blitzkrieg* in *Poetry?* I never dreamed he would publish that letter. God I feel like an ass. O Jesus, will I never learn? The editor of *Ritual* advertised in *Phoenix,* wants some of my poems—wrote me a good long letter. Robert

Symmes [later, Robert Duncan]. His poem "We Have Forgotten Venus" is a superb poem. He is with Cooney now in Woodstock, and will print *Ritual* there. It sounds like a good thing. He asked for a lot of my stuff.

Thanks for the catalogue!

Bill

When I first saw *Poetry* I was sick, but I feel better now. To hell with it. To hell with it all. Be like Saroyan—don't give a Goddamn for any of them!!

May 20, 1940
Los Angeles
ALS, 2 p., 1 sheet

Dear Bill—

Thank you for your poem to the decade. I see you did not forget my commission! It's a beautiful poem, & speaks for us both. God, how time is rushing by! I feel it so poignantly, and wish that certain exalted states might be prolonged for ever. Nay, not so. I have been in a perfect welter of work—papers, lectures, & then wonderful quiet evenings in front of the fireplace, gathering my forces. Each Tuesday we go to the Beethoven quartet cycle at Occidental. It's marvelous to hear his style mature. Have just sent off two "scholarly" papers, one to the *Oregon Historical Quarterly,* & the other to the Bibliographical Society of America, both on particular aspects of Pickett's career. It will be 6 or 8 months before the Pickett book appears, worse luck.

Have you seen the new edition of my Jeffers book? I hope you have it requested at the county library. They made a damned handsome book out of it—& it's selling very well, they tell me. I still like my new preface, but not the rest!

I feel *very sad* about the invasion of France. A lousy business.

I am glad you like the little R. & C. catalog [Rounce & Coffin Club, Western Books]. We have the collection on exhibit, until June 15th. It travels until the end of the year.

Will be at Mills & U.C. Berkeley in the autumn. Let me know if you'd like a couple more copies of the catalog. I have a quantity, which are being given out at the library.

Indeed I saw your "blitzkrieg" in *Poetry!* What a letter! You carried it off magnificently! I thought Dillon was very fair in printing it all & with the mild comment. I believe you have won his admiration. (Don't blast me for that one!)

Cheerio!
Larry

May 22, 1940
Selma, Calif.
ALS, 5 p., 3 sheets

No, Larry, I'll not blast you. I blast too much as it is, and blasting is never constructive. There is so much blasting, so much pushing forward, elbowing, pointing the finger and bellowing, blasting, blasting! The easiest thing in the world is to blast, to let the ancient tides of hate and prejudice and meanness come welling up out of the heart and cover the eyes, cover the thinking mind, cover everything but the blind sensorium of the plexus. "Those Goddamned bastardly Jews, the money-grubbing tight-fisted sons of bitches! We oughta *run em out.*" or: "Those Germans are not human: there will never be a Christian peace until every German on the face of the earth is wiped out."

Christ but it's so easy to blast! It's so easy to write ranting letters to *Poetry*—and so hard to write a clear, rising and immediate poem.

I, as you do, admire Dillon for publishing the whole of that letter. I wrote to him in apology; told him I admired his stand, admitted that he came off better than I by his honesty and frankness, and told him I was sorry I tried to make trouble. What troubles me most is that my charge is perhaps not true. The out-and-out proletarian poems have not dominated the magazine—though those that have appeared have been for the most part bad. It manifests itself I believe more in allusions within poems themselves, and that is certainly legitimate. I use it myself. The stuff generally printed is certainly sterile, however meticulously done, and needs blasting, or strong rebuke, to vitalize it; but my specific charge of domination by a proletarian attitude does not appear to be true. My stand should have rested, as it partly does, on the fact that proletarianism is accepted uncritically when it comes in, whereas a non-proletarian must conform to the very narrow limits of the editor's poetic criterion. I simply do not believe that those poems last summer should have been rejected and these socialism poems taken. And Dillon is really wrong in maintaining that in my case "l'indignation fait les vers." The second poem he accepted was an old poem, conceived seriously a couple of years ago, and discarded for artistic and other reasons. I'm enclosing it, so that you will have the story complete.

I think I was rather small in quibbling about the Phelan in my last letter. It comes to me that it was really the natural thing for the judges to award the prize to a novelist. The money was to go to a writer to enable him to fulfill a definite project. I had none. No lyricist has one. The attempt to outline future work in the lyrical medium is foolish, and I'm afraid my letter trying to make my projected lyricism seem in the nature of a plan to be carried out was a bit lame. A prose writer can submit an outline. He can show the skeleton of a plan that obviously needs time and *consistent* application to master. It is something for a judge to get his teeth in and bank upon. He can partially determine the validity of the work by its scope and its intention, and it gives him some security that the applicant is serious and capable and intelligent. All a lyricist can say is, "Well, I mean to write some poems. What about? Well—that is, I mean:—I really didn't have anything definite—I—" and he can't go on; the project is formulated only in the instantaneous moment of conception, when all the heretofore inarticulate meanderings of his mind around the general concepts of Life and Existence and Agony and Survival are fused into the substance of a chance mood—only then do his structure and his plan and the validity of conception manifest themselves. The lyric poet is one of the most important individuals in the texture of humanity, and the least dependable. You just can't trust him. And he, poor fool, cannot even trust himself. So it isn't really to be wondered at—though some of the honorable mentions were poets. Rosalie Moore was a $100 runner-up in the World's Fair poem contest in N.Y. last year. I guess they're all good people. I hope they are—but I should like to have had that year of work.

It really pleases me that you liked the decade poem. I was beginning to think I could no longer do that—-I mean write a poem that you thought was good. I sensed a rift in our poetic ideals—a widening in that natural and un-crossable gulf that keeps two people from seeing eye to eye on anything. I was quite disappointed that the "Seed" poem didn't impress you more. I still think the poems I showed you last Fall are among the best I have done—it was for many months bewildering to me that you didn't feel that too. It was, in fact, only after a sufficient period had elapsed for me to realize that in poetic matters I am essentially unchangeable that I could find any stability following the triple offensive of Mac, *The Wheel*, and Powell.

I realize fundamentally that you are probably right. You see elements in this later work that you cannot approve of, and you have to tell me, and that is right. And even knowing this, and rather dimly sensing those elements you object to, it yet seems to me that those objectionable features are bred out of the only source of validity that my poems, or my personality, really has. I am no classicist. I simply cannot create the way Mac can. He has it over me in the matter of creation. He knows language, and how to use it, and bend it to his eye, and twist it, as a worker in iron shapes the outline of his concept. I am helpless before that. As I think I have probably too insistently maintained in the past, I am a little helpless before the blind pit of my poetic consciousness. It is a sort of hungry spot in me, that will be satisfied with only a certain kind of food—and I must admit it might very well, in seeking to satisfy that hunger, suck in a good deal of objectionable matter, like a whale in a school of herring. But at the bottom I have a supreme confidence in it. Bad as it is to say, and open as it is to violent attack—this admission I mean—even so I have a supreme confidence in it. In my moments of creation I feel I am a great man. I feel within the source of an emotional power that puts the artifice of a classicist to shame. In my sane moments I know how absurd I can be—that my poems have only a sort of surface stimulation, a deficiency of depth and allows me to rest on the surface urgency of the word (*San Joaquin* is only a long testimonial to that reliance on the surface aspects of emotional language). But down at bottom I know that in risking more than Mac, risking more that is in naïvete, in pathos, in sentimentality, I yet in the long run stand to gain more. I think the great work is an open, honest and essentially spontaneous thing (not spontaneous on its surface, which may be the result of much work, but spontaneous at its core, pure at its core). That is why I am willing to persist in this direction. And my only hope is that maturity will so harmonize and fuse and alleviate within me the dissimilar elements of these emotional utterances that I can speak once or twice a clear sound and moving speech. Bear with me, Larry. I don't want you ever to regret that foreword to *San Joaquin* (I fear you have done that already). I have in me the elements of something I have not yet been able to control, and I am shaping all that I am to the time that I can control it.

Bill.

P.S. I'll send the social poem I mentioned later. It doesn't seem the thing to do after this outburst. And please send a couple of those catalogues if you can; I shall enjoy giving them.

Am looking forward to the new edition—and congratulations on its immediate success.—

so long!

June 4, 1940
Beverly Glen
ALS, 3 p., 2 sheets

Dear Bill—

I am just now answering your fine letter of about two weeks ago. You must not fear that I might someday regret that *San Joaquin* foreword. I wrote it with the utmost deliberation, & I stand back of it today surer than ever. Your last letter convinces me that you know what you are doing, are being honest with yourself, & not trying to be something you cannot be. That is all that matters—that, and unceasing work. It does not matter that I may feel about your recent poems that you have gotten a bit drunken on the idea that you are a poet & have immense cosmic feelings; or that I miss the insistence on the immediate in preference to the distant. All that you are doing is necessary, & I share the faith expressed in your letter that you will eventually utter the clearest sound & movingest speech of any writing in our time. That we do not see eye to eye along the entire route is not important.

I have just read the *Southern Review*'s "Thomas Hardy centennial issue"—Don't miss it. Auden's personal reminiscence of what Hardy meant to him pleased me, because I loved Hardy at the same period. Mac gave Hardy to us—Ritchie & Newell & I—when we were freshmen at college, in 1924. I read him all through the 20's, & in Europe carried his *Collected Poems* with me. In fact, if I had not been able to get my thesis on a living writer approved, I intended to work on Hardy—a study of the fine arts in his prose & poetry.

Have you written that study of "Point Sur"?

The cycle of Beethoven quartets is ended. I realize anew the profundity of his saying, "He who attains an understanding of my music is uplifted above all the sorrows of the world."

I read W. J. Turner's life of Mozart, which I've been after since it appeared in 1938.

Am girding my loins to tackle the "Ghost" introduction. Am waiting for proofs before I commence the actual writing, although I have been making notes these many months.

The situation in Europe troubles me. Jeffers wrote a poem in '36 about the Spanish war, in which he called it the first drops of a gathering rainstorm. Here it is on us. How the French love their homes & families—& they are being smashed. Shit.

But we carry on, in spite of this heartache. A busy time at the University. Plans for vacation in August: to the Colorado Rockies, where my wife's people have a ranch, thence to northern New Mexico to visit Frieda Lawrence.

I have taken up a study of another early Californian—the

one for whom Kern river & county are named. He was artist & typographer with Fremont. I do not anticipate a book; merely a paper of some sort.

Damn it, I can't keep my mind on the track long enough to make a letter out of this.

Send me your work. Be greeted!

Larry

June 15, 1940
Selma
TLS, 2 p.

Dear Larry:

Let me thank you first for your candid letter, which was more tolerant and hopeful than I could ever deserve. I am very sorry that I keep thrashing about in these letters, wallowing about in my own emotionality, striking heroic postures and ranting egocentric mouthings. Please forgive me. I shall mend, if I can, my ways.

We have returned from four days on the coast, Aptos, below Santa Cruz, where my sister-in-law has a beach house. Her husband is a retired business man, well-off, but sickly, and the two days we spent there were dull stuff. Except the food. Tablesfull of beautiful, lavish, and magnificent food. I tell you we ate like swine. Leaving there we went down the coast to Carmel, perceived that a fire was in the Jeffers' fireplace, and thence down to Big Sur and Newell. We arrived at dusk, took a cabin at a resort, and after supper drove down until we located his place. Took them completely by surprise, inasmuch as MacIntyre had left not an hour before we came. Seeing them there in that magnificent locale, with that lean-to house built of sweat and hope and ingenuity, made our fat days at Aptos shameful. We spent a superb evening, Newell crouched over a lantern chanting page after page of the "Ghost," his wife beside him close in that matrimonial kinship, and the fire in that enormous and magnificent fire-place. The next day we came back and Newell took me up into the hills over the sea where we discussed every phase of reality that came to our minds. We like the same things, and that makes it right. All in all it was one of those periods you don't forget. Edwa and Emelia talked sculpture, while we were away, but they are both close-lipped and reticent; I don't think there was much thawing. We came home through King City and Coalinga, rather than Gilroy, a long tortuous mountain pass, but it was new country and we enjoyed it. This is artificial as hell, writing a letter on this thing. I can't get any spontaneity out of it, it's too damned remote. I don't like it at all. This poem that I am sending is no indication that I am becoming defeatist or neurotic. It's simply something I had to get out of my system, and is not supposed to show pessimism so much as bewilderment. I will make slight changes, I suppose, but this is about what it will be. I think I told you last fall that I had a long series of poems shortly after I got interested in music. This is all I salvaged. My next poems will be toward reaffirming a faith in existence. It is harder to write out of faith than it is out of despair. Out of despair the words pour out in a kind of torrential stream of abuse and condemnation. Out of faith it takes a shining palpitant vibrant and clear utterance, much harder to do. I think literary criticism has overlooked the fact that most writers' philosophy as exemplified in their work is conditioned very much by the limitations of the craft they naturally take to. I feel hopeful about reality but I can write more powerfully about despair. Therefore what is really the slighter element of my personality gets most expression.

Bill

June 30, 1940
Beverly Glen
ALS, 1 p.

Dear Bill—

Because I have been 2 weeks answering your last letter does not mean that I did not like the poem you sent. On the contrary, I think it is one of the most moving you have written. I like it immensely, & I have read it many times over. No reservations; it is a powerful thing. It has roundness, unity; it starts, it runs, it stops. None of these things I found in the last long one you sent me—the "Seeds" poem. There was no compulsion about it; it did not seem to have the necessity this last one has. This is a poem that Lawrence would have responded to. It is the utterance of one who *has* to write poetry, not merely *wants* to—poet & poetaster. Great stuff, Bill. It is what I have been waiting for ever since *San Joaquin.* Now go ahead & build a book on it. Certain fine lines—"the fragile torsos of weeds"—

Glad to hear of your visit to Newell. On the other side is what Mac wrote after his visit ["Man by the Big Sur"]. Sent you a "Pickett" piece. End of fiscal year at library has me pooped. Anxious for vacation in August.

affectionately,
Larry

Bill, for you alone. Regarding section V in the poem—Bieler told me recently that *it did not matter* when a vasectomy had been performed, he could right it by a simple operation. Remember this if & when you change your mind. I want you to know it.

L.

July 5, 1940
Selma
ALS, 5 p.

Dear Larry:—

You have no idea how your response to "I Am Your Son" ["The Sides of a Mind"] tickled me. I had expected condemnation—a veritable blasting, really. Then to find myself received with open arms—it staggers me! I'm really glad you like it. I feel proud, too. Hurrah for our side!

Our local library received a copy of your new Jeffers edition for permanent keeping—I hope—and I'm going through it. The new foreword is swell—rich and good, like it very much. And I think that what must have been a difficult job of bringing up to date has been well accomplished. To us who know the old edition any new material seems obvious—sort of sticks out at you where you expected something else—but I think a new reader will find everything sound and in unison. I liked best tempering of the thesis-hangover: I mean the little preambles and closings of chapters. They are better this way: the general reader, I don't think, likes too much formality whatever our professors demand.

Some places, inevitably, I suppose, you slipped—such as on page 23 you say—"in his *latest* poem"—and then quote from "Give Your Heart to the Hawks"! I noticed another but can't find now. Very minor: forgive me. More important: in both editions you say Barclay, Armstrong, and Hestor Clark are the only folk not of the coast people, but you overlook two of the protagonists of "Resurrection": you overlook this poem again in cataloguing instances of burning off the hills, and also "Solstice" and "Give Your Heart"—probably other instances. This last is petty, too: but I don't think you should have so thoroughly neglected "Resurrection." Some of his best writing is there—the dead man returning to life. I'd thought you'd have liked it particularly well, and the woman going up to look at the earthquake cracks. Too many people have overlooked this poem. But all in all I think the new edition is fine. I agree that "At the Birth of an Age" is the best "Classical" poem of Jeffers. The final pages are some of the best I've ever read. I prefer the poem to "Cawdor." (Did you notice in Benét's new anthology the statement that "Roan Stallion" and "Tower Beyond Tragedy" are considered best? His worst poems! This has to be resisted.) As to format, binding, and illustration, I prefer the earlier edition in every case. Seems better made, better designed, and Kent's illustrations I always thought were fine. Your new foreword in my copy wasn't sewed in, and I have trouble with it. Am I a wet blanket? Forgive: you have every reason to be proud. How are sales?

Received also your "Pickett" sheaf. What a man! This material will be incorporated in the book, I suppose. How do you get this stuff out?

Your book and your recent queries have turned my mind to a Jeffers examination myself, but I doubt if I do it. I've been sterile these last few days and in such cases I always seek out some new source. Most of the time my own poems grip my mind too much. Speaking of sterility—thanks for the tip from Bieler. I don't understand what my doctor meant—he's a specialist. Good to know, but I don't expect to use it. I meant that poem when I wrote it.

I didn't like MacIntyre's poem to Newell. Seems forced. Flat. Didn't like very well.

Incidentally did you see *Poetry*'s review of Mac? When I read it I chortled to myself: by God it's true, and smiled at Mac's rage for a couple of days. The old eagle. However, it slowly came back to me that you can't laugh him off so easily. And not on such grounds. Generally, I should agree with the tenets of that review. I like solid poetry: meat: rich sound full level measured poetry that starts one place and makes a circle, and leaves you with that rich satisfaction of a real orgasm. But MacIntyre is different, and if you condemn him for such reasons you have also to condemn Ezra Pound and W.C. Williams—and that, I fear, Mr. Haya would hesitate to do. There is a strange bond between those three. Pound and Mac are much alike. Irascible, biting, classicists. Their poems all have that fragmentary quality: that quality of genius, of starts, and flashes, and quick insights, and extreme mobility. Read Williams' "To Waken an Old Lady" and compare with Mac's "An Old Woman Waits for Spring." You can't laugh them off. They know their craft too well.

Also, when you consider that Mr. H. recently in *Poetry* published a detailed defense of E.E. Cummings, of all people, you begin to wonder when he gets on and how long he rides before he gets off—I mean is thrown off.

This poem I send as I sent the last—holding my breath. For myself—it is my best poem: most mature, most sustained, and soundest.

So long,
Bill

This is title poem for next volume—which incidentally is about ready.

Is Newell in L.A.; did he see the "Seed" poem? Did he like? Is Mac in L.A.? I'm going to print "Seed" in spite of all. Some parts are among my best.

Williams' collected poems is a beautiful book and has some fine things. Did you see the Lawrence elegy on p. 272?

I have been reading Keats's letters. He, too, poor fool, suffered under the delusion that he was a poet. A strange breed, these people. You would think they would learn to keep their place.

July 21, 1940
Eureka, Calif.
ALS, 3 p.

Dear Larry:

Eastward there are hills, partially burned or logged so that great dead skeletons show through the stubby stuff of the green. Westward lies the town, residences, then stores, then the water front with lumberjacks, sailors, C.C.C.'s, whores, and loafers. The high morning fog is breaking. It is Sunday.

* * *

We came up last Tuesday night, and stayed at an auto camp north of Berkeley on the bay. The next day was spent at the Arts of the fair—what little we saw beside that was godawful. But that was fine, the arts, I mean. A fine day. We found Hubert that night, and Jack and Kay Moodey (poet and story writer) and the next day Buel and Tyler and we went to S.F. to see Picasso. I came away shocked to the last thread of my sensibilities, revolted, horrified, in a way, by the attitude of a genius who somehow never was endowed with the blessed perception of seeing things whole.—Then that night the French film—*The Baker's Wife*—one of the best films I have seen. Thursday we came here through the redwoods. Since then I have spent my time contriving little escapisms. At the library here, a bound file of *Poetry* was available, and I learned these facts:

That Carlyle F. MacIntyre published in May, 1920 a group of poems. In the notes he is credited with a volume entitled *In Conclusion.*

That his book *The Brimming Cup* was reviewed in an omnibus review in the early thirties and dismissed with a single sentence.

That Daly's review of Jeffers' *Tamar* pointed out his ten- and five-stress line four years before Klein.

Somebody told me Mac was away, so I did not look him up. Too late I learned he was at Berkeley. We go back tomorrow. Tomorrow night we will try to see him. Tuesday we go home. Wednesday the cannery starts. Did you like the "Masculine Dead"? And did you see the review in *Poetry?* It was far better than I expected. I expected to be ignored; if unignored I expected to be blasted. I think my letter must have had something to do with its review. Odd.

Bill.

July 22, 1940
[L.A.]
ALS, 4 p., 2 sheets

Dear Bill—

I like your "Masculine Dead," though not as well as the "Father & Son" work. The weakest parts are those in which the deaths are chronicled. The other sections are much superior. The one on page 13 is superb, particularly the first paragraph—the cruising moles & the breeding worms. A wonderful vision of life underground & the inevitable words to set it forth. You've done nothing better—& if you can hoist all your work up to such a level—.

Jeffers still works on you, the opening in particular. I took your advice & reread "Resurrection." I like Mac's poem on Newell. What can you do with that theme? Yes, Newell is here. We dine with them tomorrow, & I shall leave your last 3 opuses with him. He was here last week, & I read him "Father & Son." He liked it, and wants to pore it over.

For the past 2 weeks I have been at *work* (every day & night) on the introduction to the "Ghost." Now it is finished. I am anxious for you to read it, but I'll restrain myself from sending it to you. I want the finished book to have its effect on you, undiluted by any advance notices. And these two weeks I have been reading proof on the poem—80 galleys of it. Fisher is also reading it. It fills my heart very full to know that it will soon be fixed between the covers of a book. And I am very happy that you have a copy coming to you.

The notice of *San Joaquin* in *Poetry* was tantalizing & inadequate. Really unfair to group it with those others & then regret that he had, still without doing anything to correct his error. Mac is in a rage about the Hayakawa notice. Wrote a reply to Dillon, but I am sure it was not printable. I am meditating a sort of introduction to Mac's poetry—a survey of his accomplishments—just a paper, not a book. As soon as the "Ghost" is put to press, I'll tackle it. It will be on the press in a week or so. Probably Nov. 1st before it is bound & issued.

Thanks for your remarks about the Jeffers book. I differ from you in preferring the San Pasqual format to the Primavera. I like the crisp paper in the former, & the binding. Don't care much for Hawkins—and they failed to print them black enough. Needed a separate run—but they printed them off along with the text. I was lucky to get the book out at all, for the Press folded—& is now the old job printing house & nothing more.

Do you have Mac's Rilke book? A little gem in format. Auden scolded him in the *New Republic*.

Back to the "Masculine Dead." Although I don't think it a complete success, I am delighted by the way you are striking out & essaying new things. You are growing, lad. It is *not* a backward step—& it is way ahead of "Seed," in my opinion.

Yesterday I overhauled my study; for the first time in the year we have lived here, I took down each book & dusted it & the shelves. Took me 3 hours! I am a confirmed & unrepentant bookworm.

Reading Frazer's edition of Pausania's *Description of*

Greece. Jeffers' note in "Fall of an Age" turned me to it. Also André Gide's *Journal,* in French. And *Walden,* again. And a memoir of an English musician, Philip Heseltine (Peter Warlock, pseudonym). Lawrence caricatured him in *W. in L.* I'll lend you the book. I'm sure it won't be available in your library. I want you to read it.

No word about the Henry Miller, worse luck.

We set out on Saturday August 3rd for Colorado. A bee line via Las Vegas, Nevada & Salt Lake—Return via New Mexico, so afraid will miss you each way. I am looking forward eagerly to the Rockies & long rides on horseback. Something good will come out of it. Write me before I leave.

Have ordered the W.C. Williams collected *Poems* at the library. Thanks for the note on the Lawrence elegy.

Be greeted!
Larry

Jul. 26, 1940
Los Angeles
APS

Dear Bill—

A good letter from Eureka. I hope you saw Mac on the way back. Today I mailed you the Peter Warlock. No hurry with it—When you do return it, please send to me at university.

yours
Larry

July 31, 1940
Selma
ALS, 1 p.

Dear Larry:

I have just got off a 12-hr. shift and it is 11.00 o'clock at night. I have been doing this for a week now, and will do it for another five. We came down from North via the coast (Fort Bragg etc.) if Jeffers ever sees that country he'll quit Carmel. God! and no stucco.

"—creatures going about their business among the equally
Earnest elements of nature."

Incredible country: Came down in one day (broke) 692 miles—15 hours. Missed Mac.

Your letter, book and card. Very deflated because of your coolness to "The Dead." Can't understand that, Larry. I think it is—oh well, not now. Book I am reading and will return. Have a great trip.

"Where the tall Rockies pasture with their heads down,
white spotted and streaked like piebald horses, sharp withers
And thunder scarred shoulders against the sky—"

Bill

August 7, 1940
Buford, Colorado
ALS, 1 p.

Dear Bill—

I got your letter just before we left, but didn't bring it along so can't answer it here. This bookworm is having a wonderful vacation; 1100 miles from his home tomes. I brought a few with me, I must confess, & this first rainy afternoon finds me reading & writing. We have a log-cabin to ourselves no plumbing—but a luxurious stone fireplace, which at this moment is stuffed with fiery logs. We are on the bank of a rushing foamy river, 7500 feet up, in a grove of quaking aspens, with peaks on both sides rising to 11,000 feet. Fay's uncle, Alphonzo Bell, is both rich & good. We enjoy everything here, including meals by a Chinese cook in the "big house"—We pick our mounts from a herd of 120 horses. I love to ride, & with enough practice could become a good horseman. I have hunted the local pest, ground hogs, with a 22 rifle, & killed a pack rat in the cabin. Utmost virility in all departments! A good and great change for me.

At the end of this week we drive to Kansas City, where Fay's ma & pa live. Home via Frieda Lawrence's, north of Taos.

Greetings!
Larry

Aug 17, 1940
Kiowa Ranch, N. Mexico
APS

Dear Bill—We are spending a few days with Frieda Lawrence. Sort of the end of a trail for me. Beautiful place—Lawrence described it in "St. Mawr."

L.

Aug. 23, 1940
Los Angeles
APS

Dear Bill—
Home again. Back to work Monday. What have you to report? Newell has had the three poems. I asked him to write you about them. 4,000 miles covered, without accident or untoward incident.

Larry

Aug. 25, 1940
Selma
ALS, 6 p., 3 sheets

Dear Larry—I wrote this a week ago. Still have my mss. And really sending your book. Letter today at last from Moore in Winettka. Sometime ago Ward forwarded Chicago order; I asked for Prokosch's *The Carnival* in exchange. Today it arrived, with the note that the order (via a bookseller) had been for the Harriet Monroe Memorial Library!

No, Larry, I have nothing to report. The summer has raced; our season at the cannery has been brief but intense and is now drawing to a close. Already the peach season is over, about the earliest conclusion in the history of the plant. Figs, which we can this year for the first time, are still in progress. I suppose I'll work only another week. Beyond that, I'm looking to the Autumn. Usually a sterile time with me, but this year I hope to put it to purpose. With maturity I find that my ability to create is expanding its bounds. Seasons no longer affect me so much. All I need is time, time, time. It is such a damnable curse to have to work, to waste energy, to feel yourself held down. But I should not complain. Last summer the cannery shut off about the first of September—I had three solid months of absolute leisure. My winter's work was late and held off to December. It stopped the latter part of April this Spring. I had May, June, and most of July. Six months. And then I cry about work. But I did not waste that time. Hours and hours of creative work. Revision after revision. Even when not actually writing my mind is filled with the problems of writing. My life is as full as I can pack it. My marriage is such a magnificent success that we seem more like one person than two. One of the most incredible and enchanting things that has happened to me is the way that the blue-blaze of adolescent love has resolved into the level, full, almost unbelievably rich love of maturity. It is a love of such complete understanding, as if all the facts of inter-sexual relation that before had been intense and bewildering and intoxicating are now seen with that wide and all-comprehending eye of spiritual perfection that lifts beyond the nerve, the blood, the phallus, into the upper level of an attitude that no man, least of all I, who am centered and selfish, deserve. I raise my head and regard my wife, and the contours of her head, the shape of her face, the stance and posture of her figure, come into my mind as the living reality of what I know and possess and include, and I am suddenly aware of what an incredible thing this is. Out of this kind of stability (if stability is what it takes) I can write a richness that no other state of being could produce. It goes beyond ourselves. It colors my entire attitude. When I feel it and relate it to the world I feel almost Christ-like—the all-forgiving omniscience that sees in the vast relation how all things reside. Forgive me my incantation, but truly, Larry, I am inspired.

Beyond that, the outstanding incident of the summer has been a correspondence with one Robert Symmes [Duncan]. He is a poet, originally from Bakersfield, then U.C., who went east and started a magazine, *Ritual,* in Philadelphia. He has now moved in with Cooney and this paper will continue on the *Phoenix* press. Our correspondence started when he wrote asking to use a poem Cooney had half-way accepted and never used. ("Feast Day"). Cooney said he wanted to use it and was sending it to Savage for confirmation; I heard no more. What happened I believe is that Savage, a rare bird with very definite ideas about verse composition, squelched it. Anyway; Symmes found it in Cooney's material and snatched it from him (probably much to Cooney's relief!). He wrote me about it, and sent a copy of *Ritual,* mimeographed. My comments on the paper must have socked him for here came a fifteen-cent-air-mail-postage reply. An incredible letter, really. I replied as best I could, and here came another. The man is seized by a Lawrence-like vision of individual salvation that lifts him into some astounding writing. His poetry has so far been negative—I mean, an attitude of negation, a rejection of the modern world. (You can see it in *Phoenix.*) You will not like it—an Eliot-like, or Crane-like, jamming together of images and associations. It suffers from formlessness, both in the structure and within the line itself. But my enthusiasm is based on some of the speeches in a *Hamlet* thing he is doing in *Ritual.* After a fake opening the speeches of the Ghost exhorting Hamlet are as fine almost as anything I have recently read. He likes my work somewhat, but will say nothing specific. He wants to use "Feast Day," my revision of the *Phoenix* poems, and possibly the "Illusion" poem. All in all, it has been an exceedingly stimulating contact. What he will do I cannot say. His stuff may never attain beyond a sort of jumbled intensity. But intensity is something lacking in most modern poetry, and I am watching with interest. He is concerned with a vision, not with technique, and his letters are vast clarifications of an inspired attitude like nothing I ever read. I sent him the "Masculine Dead," but he has not replied and it has been long. Something may have happened.

My book has been typed and ready to mail for a long time. I keep it by me for some obscure reason that I can't quite formulate. I know that once it is out in the world I cannot recall it. It will be gone, and gone forever—out of the heavy tyranny of Bill Everson into the really active persecution of the world. It will probably fizzle. Most assuredly it will fizzle. Likely as not it cannot find publication. But still I keep it as if it were some potential force, as if it were high-explosive, and must be released with caution. My attitude is unconsciously colored by the expectation that as soon as it sees light it will be the immediate focal point of all literary interest of the world. Fool. Still, it's a good attitude to have. We should treat all our stuff so, hold it as potential masterworks. Keep it until every point has resolved and we are willing to let it stand for what it is. If I had done so about that *Poetry* business I should be better off now. Did you read the comments? Saroyanism! I made an incredible blunder when I sent that letter.

So tomorrow I send my book to Harcourt, Brace, MacLeish's letter inclosed. It includes *San Joaquin* and the recent poems, concluding with "The Masculine Dead." 119 pages.

I liked this Peter Warlock book. An odd man, but an interesting one. The more I read of Lawrence's personal life the less I like it. I can see absolutely no excuse for this business of *Women In Love.* Return book tomorrow. Sorry for delay. *Poetry* has a Heseltine this month. His age is given as 23, just old enough to be Warlock's semi-illegitimate son. Your letters and cards from "abroad" sounded fine, and we envied you. What kind of person is Frieda?

Bill

Edwa's father, 79, passed this morning in the Masonic Home at Decoto.

Sept. 15, 1940
[L.A.]
ALS, 2 p., 1 sheet

Bought the Mozart G minor viola quintet. New record prices are fine. Reading Van W. B[rook]'s new book.
Dear Bill,

I am slow in answering your letter of a couple weeks ago. Did you get the book sent off? Let me know what you hear. Harry Moore said that he had written you. I have never met him, but I like him from our correspondence. He is interested in helping others. Through him Fisher has placed 50 pages of prose in the next New Directions annual.

Been busy as hell driving the "Ghost" to conclusion. Our designer, Alvin Lustig, is terribly slow—& I am having to see him every day to keep him moving. He is doing a full page design for each of the 10 chapters. The ones he has completed are superb.

Paul Landacre has been in bad straits—& Ward has been selling his prints for $3 & $5—I have sold a number at the Library. If interested in getting an original Landacre, it is a real opportunity. Write to Ritchie for details.

The most interesting thing that has happened is a growing friendship with Szukalski, the Polish sculptor. I met him in '33 in Hollywood, when he was Newell's "master." Then he returned to Poland, to execute some national monuments. He was triumphing, when the Germans moved on Warsaw. He & his wife (an American) went through the bombing & destruction of the city. What work of his was not destroyed, the Germans looted, as well as all their money & possessions.

Finally back to Hollywood, all his life work gone, broke & nearly starving. They are living here in the Village. Newell & I are hustling for him, & trying to get portrait commissions & students. Did I show you the photograph of the drawing he made of Fisher? (The original was lost in Warsaw.) I am using it for a publicity photo on the Ghost. Szukalski is doing a portrait of Fay & me together—very thrilling to sit for a master!

A very great & fine man, with warm human qualities. I wish

you could come down & meet him . . . Nyholm the Dane was here last weekend—We went worldly—shows & suppers!

"Ghost" goes to press this week. How anxious I am for you to see the finished book! . . . *Poetry*'s comment was unfair. You have learned a lot from the incident. Warlock received . . . yours,

Larry

Sept. 29, '40
Selma
ALS, 7 p.

A man named Cotter wrote me, mentioning you.
Dear Larry:—

I don't know of anyone who manages to keep themselves so embroiled in work as you do. Every letter that comes in is loaded with details of projects, campaigns, enterprises etc. You certainly don't let one job tie you up.

In answer to your letter of the 15th—

1. I sent my book to Harcourt, Brace [on] the tenth—my 28th birthday—to bring me luck. They are more than likely using it now to wipe their feet on—the bastards. How long does it usually take them to make up their minds? Not more than a month, surely.

2. I have, indeed, received a letter from Moore, after almost a year! He says he liked the poems, which amazes me. Also he is sending me his Steinbeck book. His letter was good—and he speaks of working with phonograph records of poetry—a field I am immensely interested in, although I have never heard such a record. Take it back—heard some Shakespearian records over the radio once by this new Shakespearian actor what's his name. Phonograph records will probably play a considerable part in the future of poetry, and I am shaping my verse to that possibility. What I mean is—I have reconciled myself to the decline of the lyric, the lyric will always be the only thing for that small group of poetry lovers to which we

both belong and upon which the art depends for its survival. But to get beyond that, to reach that larger group of bourgeois cultivated potential art lovers (the goers-to-concerts; the attenders-of-exhibitions) who do not now read poetry but upon whom the culture of the age actually rests, the poet must expand his medium. That is why I wrote "The Masculine Dead," and why I call it a radio poem. It is my first attempt to get beyond the book. I don't mean I'm forsaking the book. The book is finally the only medium poetry can really have—as proof there is Shakespeare, who has to be *read* to be got at. But there is no harm in combining those elements. Not only that but the radio will have a terrifically wholesome effect upon modern poetry. The great mass of poetry of the last decade (as exemplified in *Poetry* magazine, was written to be *seen*). Dry, thin, intellectual, wispish, paltry—it lacks that sonorous full measured round-mouth quality that is the bone and wind of the art. And it is just those verbal qualities that my poetry is peculiarly adapted to exploit. The "Masculine Dead" literally sounds its way into the listener's pulse. It would be swell produced over the air. Not with the Dead as a chorus. I experimented with that and it diffuses the intensity of those speeches—but with a series of four or five, or only three male voices interrupting themselves—speaking dreamily at first, each with fairly long speeches, and the voices not intense—and then as the poem gains, the Dead waking again to the realization of their plight, interrupting themselves more frequently until in those final passages they literally shout out their anger and despair and intensity—I think it would go very well. All this leads up to the fact that on the 24th I started another long poem—"for radio"—which will be a very important one in my development also. "The Sleepers" it is called, and takes a different departure than what I have been doing—I think it is not of speaking characters, as was the "Dead," but is a monologue—no, that's wrong too, it's just a *poem,* but one that will endeavor to exploit also those verbal qualities and adapt itself for radio reading. Even if these poems are too "strong" to be used in modern radio censored programs, the subtitle "for radio" will force the reader to consider it as a speaking voice, with the continuity of uttered speech rather than the more arid *visual* technique of the "Waste Land."

Well, I rather got off your letter didn't I? What you say of the concluding work of the "Ghost" is very exciting. Christ, to see a thing like that shape up after years of waiting, to encounter its resistances, and to see them finally surmounted, and then to see those wet leaves flick off the press—I can imagine your feelings. I can feel it also. God Speed it!

Landacre is bad news, but we're flat. Szukalski is very bad news, and the story you tell is appalling. What the hell have we to cling to? I remember the book of his sculpture, and the drive I got out of it. And then the pitiful circumstances they find themselves in now. We should very much like to see him, and may come down this winter. Edwa especially wants to meet him.—I haven't said anything about it before because I didn't know how to say it and make it right, but this wife of mine has amazed me. I met her in 1930. I was a senior in high school and she a junior, a couple of raw naïve kids. We fell in love and that started it. What lies between that day and this is too big for a letter. Trial and error. Clash and readjustment. Separation and reunion. But the separations were short and savage like any lovers' quarrels, and the reunions were long. We got to be one of the local institutions. It wasn't Bill Everson and Edwa Poulson, but Bill and Edwa, and it still is. My poetry began to develop and with it my hopes. I began to take her for granted. I felt the solid spirituality back of her and I loved that—I loved the long past we had together—it gave me mind to think of poetry. It gave me the woman my being needed without all the surface fluctuation most relationships with new women would require. I have never had another woman, never loved or wanted or needed another. I suppose that fact speaks worlds about me, but it is true. And I don't use it for sentimental purposes like the rural swain who marries his childhood sweetheart. I did that, but with me it was right. Well, when we married I just about had life figured out. I'd go on and do my work, create, make my name—I'd have her with me—that deep source of spirituality I knew so well and could rely on. I knew it would be there and I wouldn't have to worry about it. Edwa was the one thing I *knew* absolutely. She was my Rock. Swell for me, but not for her. She wasn't satisfied being Bill Everson's wife, even if she did think he was the coming thing in poetry. What about her? She couldn't sit around all day and watch me scribble. I couldn't see why not. After all the man was the creative center of the family and any normal female should adapt herself to that center. Females were supposed to be passive. No go. She tried book binding, but somehow it wasn't right. She read interminably, classic after classic. Not right. One day we went into a shop in Fresno and got some clay, and that started it. I'm writing in the kitchen now, and beside me is a square plaque of clay, upon which are evolving the figures of a man and woman that are the essence of the creative power of the race. Out of my wife's hands is flowing an interpretive strength that amazes me. Above me on a shelf repose figure after figure that tell how it happened—the first attempts and the surprisingly swift development. She started a year ago. I can hardly believe that this woman, this wife whom I have loved and abused and fucked and fondled for ten years was carrying this around in her all that time. It's immense, Buel saw it about Christmas. It opened his eyes. By spring he was raving. Now he just throws up his hands and stares. I do too. This sounds like blather. I want it to sound strong because if I don't, if I just casually say Edwa's doing sculpture, you'd take it quite naturally as the equivalent of needle-work or bridge—another hobby. It's not a hobby, I've slept with her and I know. She's got what it takes, that inner intensity that burns your guts out till it gets itself expressed. She's gone through book after book of sculpture, drinking it down, trying to get the trends and the styles in her mind. There are no museums here, and no galleries. But there is clay. She's had no schooling and knows no theory which isn't so good. I suppose her composition shows grave faults. But the vision she has, of that I am convinced, and there is no one happier, prouder, or more amazed than I. Forgive this infliction. I suppose a man can't be excused for running off about the woman he loves, but this has got me, Larry, it really has. You wait till you see.

Bill

Oct. 6, 1940
L.A.
ALS, 2 p.

Dear Bill—

Enjoyed your long letter. Regarding what you say about poetry for radio & to be read aloud, John Cotter who wrote to you is interested in just this thing. He has adapted Jeffers' "Shepherdess" to the stage & is making recordings of some parts of it. I referred him to the copy of your book in our library, & he liked it very much. He'd like to work up radio readings of some of your poems. He is a student at UCLA, works part time in the library, lives here in the Glen. Keep in touch with him. He's a "Ghost" subscriber.

Harry Moore had an article on Shakespeare on records in the June *Theatre Arts*—says he is going to write on the subject for *Poetry*—

Good for Edwa. I want to see her work. Bring some down & we'll meet Szukalski. It would be good if she could take some lessons from him. He is a marvelous teacher. Wants particularly students who have had no other training, & are free from preconceptions.

He has made a powerful lithographic portrait of Lincoln which Newell & I are peddling to raise him some cash. They are living hand to mouth on whatever we scrape in. If you can possibly spare $5.00 you would get a wonderful work and be a real help in this time of need. Better times are ahead. We are trying to line him up to give courses at Occidental. I am paying him a little every month for a portrait he has drawn of me.

It's likely that we'll be away the Armistice Day weekend.

Have you read Miller's *Cosmological Eye* collection? Some real stuff in it—several pieces collected from the *Phoenix*.

Jeffers goes to N.Y. On Armistice Day he gives an hour's talk & reading from his poetry at Columbia Univ.

A sketchy letter. This is Sunday afternoon. Soon go for a walk in the hills with the boys. Marvellous dull autumn colors. Halcyon days.

No word from my correspondents in France.

Keep me posted on your book ms.

Larry

Oct. 23, 1940
Selma, Calif.
APS

Dear Larry:—Writing from Post Office—have a letter at home but forgot to bring it. Har. Brace today rejected ms.

Bill

Somehow I'm not stunned!

HARCOURT, BRACE AND COMPANY, INC.
393 Madison Avenue, New York

October 21, 1940

Dear Mr. Everson:

We have all read your book of poems, "The Masculine Dead." I agree with Mr. MacLeish and Mr. Engle that your work has an original and authentic quality of its own, but these are dog days for the presentation of work of new poets, and we find it very hard to raise a number of the flags we should like to raise. There may come a time a little later on when, if you do not find a publisher, we should be in a position to launch this work, but alas we can't do it now.

I salute the manuscript, and I wish you every luck with it elsewhere. Thank you very much for giving us this chance at it, and please do not hesitate to show us your future work.

Sincerely yours,
(signed)
Stanley Young

P.S. I am returning the manuscript under separate cover, and I am enclosing Mr. MacLeish's letter.

Oct. 24 1940
Selma, Calif.
ALS, 4 p., 2 sheets

Dear Larry:—I'm afraid I haven't been a good correspondent, so I've dug out your last couple of letters to catch up on loose ends. I've been worried. Worried and scared. Ever since this draft talk started last spring it has preyed on my mind. Since Edwa is an earner my marriage will not exempt me, and I'm afraid that if my number is drawn I'll have to make a stand. I don't want to do it. I want to stick in this ivory tower and be let alone. I'm beginning to get my grip now. My mind is maturing and I see things clearer. My nature is being enriched by this kind of life and I love it. Of course no man was ever granted the certainty of peace, and I cannot hope to be an exception, so what I have been doing is trying to steel myself for the inevitable consequence. I don't mean to sound heroic, for I'm not. Physically I'm a coward, and though I'm ashamed of it there are too many instances in my past life that prove it to me. This one most certainly does. And yet, such is the situation that I am prepared to make the most outrageous act of my life. I intend to object. What I'm most afraid of is being lynched. I think I could stand their jails or their concentration camps if they do not actually torture one (in which case I could stand almost none), neither does being hooted, spat at, scorned really shake me although it could be a terrible source of agony—but dying young—I mean, dying before I have had a chance to resolve all the elements that are thrashing around inside me—that is what I really am afraid of. Sometimes I get brooding about it and am almost afraid to drive up the highway to Fresno. When I first wrote "The Masculine Dead" I considered it as a poetic attempt to avoid any direct exposition. But I know now that I wrote more into it than I suspected. I had, and I hope I'm not heroic again, but I had, figuratively, to die to write it. It worries me very much. To get cut off before you could mature. It's not a matter of my being a poet. That's incidental. It's me, my nature, my life that I love. When I'm old I think I should go down into darkness with vast love. But not now. That would be ghastly. I think of what happened to those wretched religious fanatics back East who refused to salute the flag, and I know how close fascism lurks to the surface of men's hearts. At my grocer's the other day some lout was saying: "All I know is if I had to do something like that there's nothing I'd like better than to cut down on one of these God damned Japs." The grocer chuckled obscenely: "Yeah. We talk about going out and getting us a couple doves. Maybe fore long we can go out and get a couple of Japs." His fat face shook as he laughed, and all my insides, my nerves, my brains shriveled as I heard those two. When I told my father he said: "Well, I don't blame them. I feel that way myself." I stood in a shooting gallery in Fresno not too long ago. A big man entered, picked up a gun and aimed. The smallest targets were small metal disks, about the size of dimes, hanging in pairs from a rod. The man shot five times and every time the disks whirled. He put down the .22 and turned, grinning. "Well, I can still hit a Jap. I just think them two little disks is a Jap's eyes"—he held out two spread fingers in a terrible gesture. "Two squinting eyes," he said "and I never miss." O god lord of hosts! When their towns are down and their homes leveled and their children slaughtered and themselves lie in their streets with bomb splinters in their entrails they will have only themselves to blame. They brought it most certainly upon themselves. I will kill no man. I will not degrade everything fine within me. For twenty-eight years our culture has shown, pointed, insisted, that war is crime and the winner loses. Do they think they can annul that in a month? What do they take us for? What do they think we are?

I received a letter from Moore, which I enjoyed. He sent me his work on Steinbeck, and I thought it fairly good—I mean that complimentarily. I would have preferred a more general opening, establishing his position, and orientating one into the body of the work. But he kept himself very well detached which is hard to do about a living man whom you like well and want to propagandize. There was more adverse criticism than favorable criticism, which was most astonishing for this type of thing. He seemed to accept Steinbeck's virtues as self-evident without need of emphasis. In a way this was bad. I, who agree with practically all the adverse criticism (and who would add more) had a twinge of something like this—"If Steinbeck is as defective as all this—why this book?" Moore could have had plenty to say of course about Steinbeck's good qualities, but I think it a defect in the work in that [it] fails to justify its attempt to the reader. I thought his writing was good, sober and sound, and not suffering from that razor-edged intellectuality that afflicts our modern smart boy critics.

Today it's six weeks since I mailed my ms. and no word. This is criminal.

You say *Poetry*'s comment was unfair. It is that, because it puts me slap with the conservatives on the one hand and the exhibitionists on the other. The last is particularly bad because my letter of contrition to Dillon showed quite clearly that I was not rejoicing in what publicity I got. Most of all the comment was hasty—I mean in absolving itself. The situation will not have become resolved until my status as a poet has been decided, until the worth of the poems they rejected has been decided, and until the worth of the poems rejected has been decided in comparison to those accepted. Until these matters have been ascertained the "repercussions" will not have all died away.

I sent Cotter a book. I hope he enjoys it. I was rushed when I wrote him, and didn't have much to say, so I hope he doesn't feel slighted. It would be swell if he read my stuff on the air (incidentally, does he read well, or has he all the mannerisms of most of these professionals?) but I couldn't tell him so—I mean, it wouldn't look right.

How goes the "Ghost"? Time drags, and it seems it will never come. I can hardly remember it. Only Newell at Sur crouching before his immense fireplace chanting "*Come down! Come down!*" and his wife sitting by quietly, and my wife, quietly, and Newell chanting on and on, and the Pacific Ocean down there rubbing its belly on the rock.

I should like so much to help Szukalski by buying something but simply cannot. God knows where our money goes.

I possess the *Cosmological Eye* and like it, but it is not the book that *Cancer* was, or is.

Nothing finer could happen to Edwa than instruction from Szukalski, and now is certainly the time since he needs everything he can get—perhaps if we can save for next summer? We must come down and talk this over. To Edwa and of course to me this is extremely important.

Jeffers speaking at Columbia! Incredible! One thing I have wanted to ask. Did MacIntyre ever mention what really happened behind the coattails of Old Man Phelan? I mean, why it was that everything seemed so rosy, and then failed so miserably? Could it possibly hinge on MacIntyre himself, such as academic persecution of him manifested by cutting me, whom he sponsored? Have you scented anything? Friends of mine at U.C. say he is bucking the usual resistances.

Buel is now teaching at Long Beach high. Twenty-seven hundred dollars per annum!!

Sincerely,
Bill

The past eight months have witnessed within me a growing love for Mozart that supersedes everything. Our collection owned jointly with a friend now includes Sym. 40 (G-Minor) Toscanini—Eb Sym. Walter, C major concerto Schnabel (incredible 2nd movement) G major concerto (Fisher) Beethoven 4th concerto (Schnabel) Beethoven quartet Opus 132, Beethoven Appassionata Sonata, Schubert C major Symphony Beethoven Symphony no. 5 (this now palls me) Schubert symphony no. 8, Tchaikovsky symphony no. 6. Edwa is a Bach lover but no records as yet.

October 29, 1940
[L.A.]
ALS, 4 p., 3 sheets

Dear Bill—

I have been wanting to write you & send you this letter of Henry Miller. Please return. He is mistaken, however; it was Fisher he met, the winter before I arrived in Dijon. Odd the way we're all coming together again. Slocum, mentioned in the letter, is with a New York literary agency—they represent Miller. S. has asked me to get him new authors. Suppose you send him the ms. of your book. Never mind about Harcourt. Thanks for the copy of their rather insensitive letter. Have you sent your work to Laughlin? Am in the midst of the 4 years of New Directions. Last year's has stuff in about poetry for the radio. Have you seen it? Laughlin is much interested in this.

The 1940 Annual is due next month. Fisher has prose in it—Laughlin was to review the "Ghost." At the last minute he wrote me that he was holding 3 pages open, & for me to fill it. I prevailed upon the eminent critic, Robin Meredith, to do the review, & away it went. Did you get Laughlin's recent catalog?

I got the *Phoenix* from the new Georgia nest. Still trying to get the missing number from Cooney.

The "Ghost"? They called me today that Lustig's forms finally were put on. The text has been printed for several weeks; it was done on a cylinder press. The designs have had to wait for a small hand-fed press to be free. If they can keep them on, they will be finished in 3 days. Then binding! I'll get the ordered copies out as fast as they are bound. Xist, but I'm anxious for that Ghost to start walking!

Am in the midst of preparing for an exhibit at the library of Hans Christian Andersen material—mss, letters, & 1st editions belonging to the Danish actor, Jean Hersholt. I have induced him to loan the collection to us. It is the finest outside of the Andersen museum in Denmark. Hersholt is a charming man, & an expert bibliophile. You will recall his essay in the *Colophon* I sent you.

Before doing my exhibits, I soak myself in the subject; & so have been reading biographies of Hans—& rereading his immortal tales. Shades of my childhood! Friday we have a luncheon for Hersholt. Pres. Sproul is our guest & bringing as his guest the President of Stanford. By such devices L. Powell goes up the ladder.

Reading aloud Rouse's translation of the *Odyssey* (Modern Age, 1937). Ezra Pound led me to it. How good it is.

Your letter here today. I can't hope to answer it all the way it deserves. Your letters are a joy to me. I depend on you, Bill; and always feel good when I think that we are friends. It gives me a good inner warmth to think about it. We need ones to whom we can turn without reserve or qualifications or explanations. You have proved such a one to me.

I know how you must feel about the draft. Don't martyr yourself, though. Insist on non-combatant service, if called. Don't go to jail. I am a Quaker, from both parents. & I will not kill anyone, unless it were someone screwing my wife without her permission! But I would work, or nurse, or whatever.

I was going to ask you about Mozart, & now you have answered my query. In 1932 in Europe I heard his G minor quintet (2nd viola) & read Sacheverell Sitwell's monograph on Mozart & its remarks on that Quintet—& since then have been on its trail. Finally I succeeded in buying it—our first album in too many years. Now I play it nearly every night. You must come down, if only to hear it!

Reading Mozart's letters, in the Anderson 3 v. edition, published a couple of years ago. First time they've been wholly translated—Fine correspondence. Rare letter writer. I recommend Sitwell's book to you. If you can't get it from library, I'll mail you a copy.

Love of Beethoven leads back to Mozart & Haydn, thence to Bach.

What do you write these days?

When do you come south?

Yours ever,
Larry

Nov. 7, 1940
Selma
TLS, 7 p., plus APS, 1-1/2 p.

Dear Larry:

It must be a week since I received your letter, and much national history has been made. The draft has been inaugurated and the third presidential term established. The war in Europe has spread. The Far East is seething. The political situation of the world is very tense. Try as I do I cannot help but watch.

I doubt whether any other moral problem of my life imposes upon me such a difficult choice as does the military service one. My number is very low, 2141, and I have only about a year in which to conduct myself as I have done now for so long. I had hoped for a high number but evidently the gods wanted to see what stuff I was made of. I am sure it will be as much a revelation to me as to them. There is force and resistance in the world and you cannot live without killing. We have to accept that. "Sad sons of the stormy fall you have to inflict and endure." There are also the concepts of right and of wrong. We know these concepts. We believe in them. Our life is based upon them. There is not a day passes but what we apply them. We have come to believe that life would be meaningless without their existence. We know absolutely that civilization as it is today cannot continue if these concepts are violated. They are being violated, and those who violated them are gaining power. The people among whom we live are arming themselves to defend those concepts which we admittedly accept. They are willing to sweat, to go hungry, to suffer, to die, in order that those concepts may be continued. They only ask that we do the same. I think that one of the hardest things in life to do would be to sever your connection with those among whom you live, to renounce your own people and live among them as an outcast. The pressure in this matter is tremendous. Ever since babyhood the importance of social conformity has been hammered upon us. And there is no greater, no more heinous, no more abominable a crime than treason. The emotionality of the thing is terrific. A conscientious objector must be prepared to face it. He must be prepared to remain passive year after year, to sit idle through every invasion, to sit there, while his people whom he knows and loves are bombed and blasted and slaughtered; while his home is being burned and his very region laid waste, to sit, moreover, while others die protecting *him* from the common enemy he refuses to face. Surely to the multitude there is no cowardice like this, nor no treason like this, and you can see how clear it must be to them that this creature be done away with, and the sooner the better. A conscientious objector must be prepared to face all this, for it can certainly happen, and he, if he has any honesty, must be able to consider all possible alternatives before he accepts his final stand.

I have given the defenders their best, because I have to grant them all in order that my choice take its final meaning. I haven't referred to the more obvious objections: That this is just another imperialistic war; that the big boys of Germany are locked in a struggle for markets of the world with the big boys of England and America, and that the common man is being used as a cat's paw. These things are probably true, as they appear to have been true in the teens, and they form ample ground for objection. But an objector against war must be able to maintain his beliefs against *any* kind of war, and when mulling this thing through within myself, I have given the opposition the very best I could. Having given it, I am still prepared to resist it.

For what I have been trying to do these last years is arrive at some system of values that lies beyond the fluctuation of social concepts. I have tried to make the prime purpose of my life refer not to my relation with the persons among whom I live, but to the forces above and beyond those persons. When your highest values are those of your people there is nothing to do but fight when they fight, defend what they defend. But those values are what I have been trying not so much to escape, since in their practical application I believe them, but to supersede, to out-distance, to arrive finally at some reference to which I can go in these extreme moments with a secure inner knowledge that I am doing what is for me inevitably right. I declare therefore that in my search for that quality, and in my finding and exploration of it, the social structure within which I exist takes on a secondary importance; that I can live richly and harmoniously under any of the modern systems of government, and that the difference between them is not worth the complete abnegation of my search that would most surely result if I went to War. This credo demands that I accept slavery in preference to resisting slavery, which I do. Certainly I should rather be in Denmark now than in England. I am not thinking in terms of states, of nations. If I thought in terms of those all my stand would be meaningless. I refuse to think in such terms. I refuse to acknowledge the importance of such conceptions. I say only that there are greater things than the social structure of a people, and that however obnoxious it would be for me to do so, in a final choice I would forgo absolutely one that I had come to love, and accept one I should detest, rather than die or shatter my life for the difference. I do not reject humanity. I do not say I could live alone. I know I am a part of humanity, and of its traditions, and its misery is my misery and its love my love. I say that I want to live beyond the surface *forms* of humanity, to see the German and the Jew and the Italian and the Greek as they exist under the sun, driven by their hopes and terrors and inner agonies, as I am driven, and suffering as I suffer in a world that will not conform to the beautiful and desirable picture of what we seek.

I will not tell the draft board these things. I will tell them only that I can kill no man, that I refuse to kill. I do that, but my stand rests on far deeper grounds than that, though I could not tell them. In the light of the above I do not see how I can accept the non-military activity. I would be still participating in the ghastly blind herdy [*sic.*] individual-subjugation of it all. I would be neither having my cake nor eating it. The only times I waver are when I am afraid, afraid to resist them, afraid to stand on what I believe, want to sink passively into that great current of human conformity that speaks so loudly to us. It would be so much easier to do that. Perhaps, my mind says, we won't go to war, then it would mean only a year and they would let you go, you could come back with honor and not be molested, you could do your work then and live among these people quietly. For they will surely not understand. Even if you convince the board and they release you how can you face the grocer and the laundry man and the hardware man when you meet on the street? What can you say to them that would make them see how seriously you feel this? What will your family do going about among their friends with the common knowledge that this son of theirs is a coward and a slacker and most of all that he has rejected the people whom he has known? They will have to endure that. I cannot let the short-sightedness of others seduce me into a short-sightedness of my own. I am prepared, quite unheroically, to face what I have to face. If there are ways to avoid it, I shall take any honorable one that offers, but at the last I shall not betray myself.

* * *

This is very good news, this letter from Miller. He can help much.

I had already made up my mind to submit next to New Directions, though I was unaware that Laughlin was interested in radio, as I have never seen one of the annuals. I am retyping the ms., and rearranging the typography. I doubt whether you will approve, but it seems to me that I must shorten my line somewhat. Much of the formlessness of free verse is due I think to the straggling typographical look of it, and I am trying to correct this by being sure no line will have to be broken back on itself. I do have trouble, because one of my most definite beliefs was that lines should be broken only at those places where the voice pauses, thereby forming a relation between eye and tongue. It is hard to get eye and tongue to agree and yet not have any lines running over. Some cases I am very successful and vastly improve the look of the verse, but some times I have to contort a little. I think I will persist however, as so far I feel I have been successful. Also in this matter, much of my comparison with Jeffers has been induced by a merely typographical similarity; the poems do not seem nearly so Jeffersian when the line has been moderated. I do not care for a short line, but a moderate one now seems about right and I shall write thus in the future.

I have been reading much Marlowe, and have just finished reading *Tamburlaine* aloud to Edwa. It is packed with magnificent imagery and he is one of my favorites, but his line lacks sensuousness, his prosody lacks music, often his rhythms tramp and stumble, buck, kick. I should like to approximate the musicality of Coleridge (I read Burke's article in the October *Poetry*—I have been trying for such effects for years, and am glad to see them reemphasized in this age of hard, brittle and intellectual poetry). Reading Marlowe I have been toying with the idea of a poetic drama myself, and feel confident that I can master the technical problems it presents. What keeps me back is that I do not think much in terms of plots, of continuous action. I think in terms rather of incidents, of dynamic situations that can be caught richly in a lyric-like treatment. I think I shall have to mature awhile, until my personality or rather character becomes more concerned with human problems. It is only I think when a man has matured that he can make the bone of a drama, the mood, the implication, the *idea* that makes it have a great significance above and beyond its poetic effect. That was the trouble with *Tamburlaine.* It probes nothing. The plot is only a sort of tour de force enabling the author to utilize his love of splendor. You are appalled by the blood, by the ruthlessness, but you are not moved to the quick of compassion by the overtones the writer makes aware to the reader. I do not think a drama should be just another form to exploit a man's poetic equipment. I think the aim must always be upon the situation, and enhanced, literally made by the language, but never dominated by it. Maybe something will come to me later. I think it is a great medium.

Reconsider the women in "The Masculine Dead." See them as contrasting elements to the luxurious passionate speech of the men, see them as dealing flatly in vivid situations, rather than, as do the men, eloquently in vague situations. They offer an element of contrast that gives the thing variety I think, and yet are poetic in their way. Compare them with "Spoon River." I think they will stand it. Ezra Pound's "The River Merchant's Wife" is done in a very flat and subdued manner, but it is famous, though undeservedly I think, and no more poetic than my women. I have rewritten three of them: the first Woman with her three recurrent speeches, the Gangster's moll, and the last drowning scene. I want them to be vivid and flat.

I start to work, and I shall hate it. More and more I resent any inroads upon my time. Curse it all! There is always over our heads the shadow of moneylessness, though we make enough to live well. Somehow we cannot get ahead. If you received the last Dawson's cat. look up the Shakespeare by Tauchnitz in the Poet's Corner. We have it now and it is a beauty. Some time ago Carothers got vol 7 for a nickel on a bargain stand, and our eye has been peeled ever since. It is very good and a joy to read. We had no collected Shakespeare heretofore. Dawson's were very good. I had no money, but they sent me the set immediately and gave me to December to pay. All I had hoped for was getting the set held until I could make it, and when the stuff came in a couple days later I was very surprised and pleased.

God Speed "The Ghost."

Can't make this *Tropic* now. Thanks for showing me these letters.

Bill.

Don't know when we shall be down.

Excuse this typewriter, but it slows me down and makes me more coherent. I think ahead of my pen and it just scribbles along trying to keep up. I don't think I ever did in my life a good piece of writing upon a first try. It takes revision after revision, and that is why my letters are so bad. For a literary man, they are appalling I know, but try to bear up. Maybe the typewriter will help me. Did you read Conrad Aiken's article in the August *Atlantic?* I was overjoyed to read it. These dry-ball poets have had their say, but they have influenced me too. It was only after reading Aiken's letter that I dared use an exclamation point for its own sake. Now I feel I can exploit some of the verbal richness without feeling guilty. Maybe I can even help create the new poetry revival.

I love Mozart. The slow movement of the C major (K 467) concerto is breathtaking. Record side after record side of all the music of his we have holds unbelievable revelations. And there is so much more to get. Edwa's favorite is Bach—I suppose it is the sculptor in her—and verily, I myself can listen to the architechtonics of the music hour after hour. We heard the other night "A Musical Offering," and it was very good. A friend has the "Well Tempered Clavier" which has some superb things in it. Beethoven is the man I have not heard enough of. It takes records for me to really appreciate a music—or constant hearing on the air. One time is not enough. But I have heard Beethoven's 7th symphony enough to know that it is a superlative work, far ahead of the Fifth, ahead of the sixth too; a more unified and sustained work even than the 3rd it seems to me, though the 3rd plumbs deeper depth, the slow movement of which is—well, you know! I think I told you we have the Schubert C major. This is, I think, one of the greatest symphonies I have heard. From start to finish it pulses along at a very high level. I love this symphony. The passion for Tchaikovsky has largely subsided, but I still think the 6th is a remarkable and moving work. It speaks to me something no other music has ever done. But Mozart! Mozart! My God, the man had music in him! And he never doubts, he never fumbles as Beethoven fumbles. We have Beethoven's 4th concerto, a magnificent thing, but some of the cadenzas are simply not right, mere twaddle—Mozart wouldn't do that—every note, every measure. I cannot get enough of him. Christ how music has expanded my soul—but not Brahms—oh God no, not Brahms—drab, muddy, uninspired, sequence on mathematical sequence. Chord piled on intellectual chord—no poetry, no lyricism, he never saw God, that man. Christ save me from Brahms. Give me rather the unregenerate splendor of Wagner, whom I love at times and lament at others—but certainly he soared whereas Brahms—! I never have thanked you for the *Horizons.* The article on Mozart I thought very good and true.

November 21, 1940
[L.A.]
ALS, 3 p., 2 sheets

Dear Bill—

Your long letter of two weeks ago has had me stumped for an answer. I can't agree with your uncompromising stand on the draft. Why put your neck on the world's chopping block? And I am ignorant of any standards of conduct which are beyond humanity. What can such ideals weigh alongside what you owe the woman you have married? You are not single any longer. You must keep the happiness for the two of you.

In other words, I think you would be colossally selfish to sacrifice those who love you to a super-human ideal.

And in still other words: a damned fool.

Then again—do what you have to do. And whatever you do, you can always count on me.

I think you are a sublime jackass. God bless you & keep you.

I've been meaning to write you about a conversation I had regarding you with President Sproul. We sat together at a luncheon for Jean Hersholt, & the first thing Sproul said was

"How is Everson?" The short of it is that he asked for your address so that he can call on you one time when he is in the Valley. He will write in advance.

He has no *arrière pensée* that I know of. Simply wants to bull with you. I am sold on Bob Sproul.

I haven't heard anything about the Phelan award. Haven't seen Mac since last New Year.

We spent the weekend with MF & Tim Parrish at Hemet. I wish you could see his paintings. Another Van Gogh. The death sentence is on him. He paints desperately. In the year since he painted the 2 pictures we have, he has grown immensely. Now his work brings tears to your eyes. I hope to arrange an exhibit at UCLA. If I am successful, you & Edwa must come, if only to see it.

Just finished W.J. Turner's *Mozart,* & still reading in the 3 v. Anderson translation of the Mozart family letters. I am glad his music means so much to you.

That pesky "Ghost"! This week finds it being bound. The Lustig illustrations were slow & painstaking to print. But what a book! You should have your copy in another week or ten days.

yours ever
Larry

Dec. 3, 1940
Selma, Calif.
ALS, 3 p., 2 sheets

Dear Larry:

Yesterday, at about 3:18 P.M., my mother died. Since she was a girl she had been troubled with a cough. Before she was married she went for a while to Arizona, thinking her trouble to be T.B. My earliest memories of her include those in which she coughed. A sudden fit would seize her; she would rush for the bathroom, coughing deeply, and painfully work up great pieces of phlegm. Every so often a violent hemorrhage would come upon her, and those times were bad. Nothing seemed able to be done. Then, in Fall 1937, a particularly bad attack struck her. She spent a week in the local hospital, and finally was sent to the tubercular hospital at Wishiah (Fresno County). She stayed several months, and the rest worked wonders, but no traces of active T.B. were ever found, only the old scars common to us all. She came home in 1938 and has never been active since. Last summer, my father went to the U.C. hospital in San Francisco, was operated on for a couple of things including, I believe, the prostate gland. The findings there were so contradictory to what local doctors had analyzed, and the results so successful, that he persuaded my mother to go there for an examination. This Fall she went up, and an x-ray from the side (this, incredibly, had never before been done, and she has had many) revealed a lung full of matter. Examination disclosed that one tube had never developed so that the lung wasted, became diseased, and slowed down her system all her life. The surgeons believed they could operate and cure. She believed so too, or would never have risked it. We took her up the weekend before Thanksgiving, and waited during the operation. It was a difficult and unusual one, and I think the entire staff watched the case. The surgeon, a superb doctor, did an excellent job, and mother came through, although once she was so near death her pulse could not be detected and the action of her heart barely visible through the fluoroscope. She gained rapidly, both Edwa and I gave her blood, and we left confident that she would recover. Dad and my sister saw her this weekend and she was in excellent condition; we expected her home within a fortnight. Suddenly, yesterday, she died. The doctors did not know the cause of death and asked for permission to conduct an autopsy. We have learned nothing yet. The funeral, which I dread, will be tomorrow.

There is no time in my memory that I can recall an intense mother-love. I say this mournfully, because I know from what I know of the spiritual condition of any love, that a great experience was lacking. When I was a child I was of course very fond of her, but it must have been the sensuous fondness of being held, caressed, loved. With adolescence she became a sort of symbol of restriction. I never confided in her. I hid my sexual development from her like poison. I went back into myself, and kept alone there till I met Edwa and fell in love outwardly for the first time. Yet I owe her many, many lovely and beautiful thoughts, and though I did not really love her, though this passing shocks me into the realization that the *home* that has been behind securely all these years is no more, our family life gone, my father seventy years now and little left—though as I say I am shocked but not numbed with any great agonizing sense of spiritual loss—even so I admire many traits of her character, and only wish that more of them were passed on to me. Where I am close-natured and rather grasping, she was the most generous person I ever knew. Tramps, stray dogs, invalids, abandoned wives, widows, all knew her attention and kindness. A sort of anxiety would grip her and she could not rest until she had aided. This is the thing I remember most about her, and it fills me with a sense of loneliness to realize that so utterly good a person was so near to me, and yet I was unable to offer any deep affection of my own. She was convinced of my greatness. I think of all us children she expected most of me, and conceded me most, and gave me a subtle partiality in any family dealing. That I was not nearer to her hurt her I know. These last years it has been only my own guilt and her insistence that I have kept as close to her as I have. The family is shattered now. My father, an egotist at the core, but an honest and sensitive man really, is stunned. Last night he said suddenly with a kind of pitiable loneliness—"I lived alone till I was thirty-eight and now I am alone again." My sister, who loved mother more than us all, is very hurt. I sit here and know that this is one of the great moments of my life. The bridges are burned. It is past, gone, gone by God—like that! It is bewildering, and terrifying, and there is nothing to be said.

Bill

I sent my MS., minus "Seed" and many others, to New Directions on the 26th Nov. Lee Watkins has a friend interested in Jeffers who might warm to the "Ghost," if you have any prospectus left—Miss Marion Powell 2597 Channing Way Berkeley, Calif.

Where the hell is it?—the "Ghost"?

I have never thanked you for the really fine little booklet of your mother. It is really well written—none of this professional slickness so many amateurs aspire to—but the fine, exceedingly sensitive writing of an acute personality stimulated by a particular journey. Far above the usual travel book class. I was very pleased with the richness of the description and what it revealed about the character of the writer. The whole thing a fine little item.

I think it was my own mother's complete lack of literary or aesthetic sense that formed the gulf between us. That is wrong, but a young man is blind, and does not realize the true virtues until he matures. That was perhaps my trouble.

December 7, 1940
[L.A.]
ALS, 1 p.

Dear Bill—

I am sorry that you've lost your mother. I hate to think that sooner or later I will lose mine. Remember what Lawrence went through, in *Sons & Lovers*. I've not had that kind of relationship. In fact, my relationship with my mother has been & is ideal.

From what you say, you'll miss your father more when he goes.

All of this is a sorry business at best.

I've gotten great consolation from Fisher's "Ghost." It's been a sort of Bible for me.

And where is the book? Bogged in the bindery, but due next week. I guess I've said a dozen times how anxious I am for you to see the finished book. You can imagine how Fisher is fretting.

Just a note. I hope the book will be my next message to you. Carry on, lad!

Larry

Dec. 10, 1940
Selma, Calif.
TLS, 5 p.

Dear Larry:

With your letter came *Poetry,* and I was amazed to see Jeffers' name on the cover so soon after his last contribution. Before that he appeared only in '27 or '28 I believe. But what surprised and pleased me most was the comparative excellence of these poems over other recent work. The "Come, Little Birds" was a fiasco, not because of its subject, but because he never organized his experience into solid enough material to give his poem the level fullness of direct expression. It was loose and sloppy and altogether poor. (Have you considered it? What do you make of it? Do you think it a true experience? If it is, the poem is important in any consideration of Jeffers' development.) But these new poems, with the exception of the prosy lines of the opening of the first one (9/19/1939) are all built around a much closer core of language and rhythm. The poem "The Stars Go Over the Lonely Ocean" is unique in Jeffers' work for the particular quality of its mood. Certainly a good poem. As is also "The Bloody Sire." Lines like this in "Great Men" are the blight that has ruined his verse from the very first:

> A great man must have a following, whether he gain it
> Like Roosevelt by good intentions, cajolery and bribes, or
> Hitler by fanatic
> Patriotism, frank lies, brutality and terror . . . etc.

What seems incredible is that a man who has written so very much fine work can year after year let that go by. Whitman was different. In only a very few poems did he ever strike an actually sound poetic core, and you can ascribe his success to luck. But Jeffers has written too much that is superb poetry, the mood, the level, the sustenance, the wholeness, to ever believe he doesn't know what is his good and what is his bad. It makes him hard to defend, so many lapses. It leaves him wide open to his critics. I suspect that much of it springs from his philosophy: in rejecting human values he rejects the terms of human merit, literally doesn't give a shit. It is a core that strains and distorts his work time after time, for he cannot reject humanity no matter how much he tries, no more than a fish can reject his fishiness. Jeffers is like the self-hanged god in "At the Birth of an Age." Magnificent, and terrible, and not to be helped. Heautontimerounimous. I hope to God these new poems indicate a finer new volume and a finer narrative than the last one.

I think if I had waited a few days before I wrote you last my letter would have been of a different temper. As the days went by it came to me in a hundred subtle and minute ways how much I had depended upon my mother's existence—and all taken for granted. I am back to my old self-sufficiency again, which is as it should be, but I know now a good deal more of what she really was, and as I reflect, Proust-like, upon what has gone by, those formative years when you were dependent tooth and claw on your parent, sudden waves of a kind of nostalgia run through me. Maybe it is just the emotionality and drama of the actual death working upon me, it will take time to tell, but right now I think about it more than I ever thought I would.

But my father? No. If my attitude toward my mother could have been called indifference, my attitude toward my father was direct antagonism. I can remember as a very small boy lolling happily in his arms one Sunday beside the old house on Logan Street, and also running down B Street to meet him as he came across the school yard from work. But that's about the last. He was gone too much. He worked in the print shops all day and played orchestra for dances all night, and became practically a stranger. When he was home he was tired, and being a musician and irritable he would go off in explosions at the noises any children make. At such times his pale blue eyes get a sort of wide unseeing stare, intense and really terrifying to behold, like a madman, or rather like pictures of Wotan and those old berserk rages, which is exactly what they were, the old Viking, uncrossable fury that enslaved him to it and carried him away beyond the softer side of his nature. He rarely punished us: a spanking maybe, once a year, never a beating, and no punishment undeserved. He stands clear there. But no sensitive child can live year after year in an atmosphere in which he never knows from one moment to the next whether his unconscious humming as he goes about his play will be taken with complete good will as it often was or whether it would release upon him a burst of temperament that in abruptness and intensity would scare the very shit from his bum. A moment after that, perfect peace, perfect equanimity. My whole attitude toward him was and still is: fear. It is ingrown. It was driven in over too long a time and through too sensitive and formative a period of my life to ever completely escape it. I cannot cross him, even today; I avoid issues, give in, say nothing. Then when I got out of high school in thirty-one, and there was no work, and I was too timid to ask for work, and he felt I should be out earning (he who was thrown an orphan and a foreigner, a waif, on the streets of New York at age twelve, no English, no money, destitute and bewildered, and who survived by tooth and claw, and made his way absolutely alone till he was 38 when he married), what compassion could he have for me, big strapping soft hulk of a six-foot-four incher, who hung around home afraid even to enter a store and buy when I had the money? The private agonies from 1931 to 1936 were deep and searching, and I went about every day through my own personal little hell. Not that it was entirely his fault, or even mostly his fault. Looking back I guess considering his past and his nature he did about the best he could. I was strung hair-trigger, adolescent, bewildered by the depression, not knowing even what I wanted to do, aware only that the outer world of men was a terrifying place for a fellow like me to have to go. All my emotions were exaggerated. I actually came close to suicide once. Without mother I doubt very much if I could have held out. She understood me fairly well, believed in me, and suffered many times as buffer between the inevitable temperamental clashes. It must have been very trying. When I finally broke away you would think the matter would have resolved, but instead intellectual differences manifested themselves as I matured and arrived at my own mind so that what contacts we had, Sundays, visits, etc., were characterized by a kind of smouldering opposition, and beneath the differences of ideas lay all those years of latent antagonisms. God Almighty this must make sordid reading! Looking back it all seems like one grand exaggeration, every year of it. He's old now, over seventy. Lost, too, since mother's gone. Meek. The Viking kicked clear out of him. He's just any other old man with his life behind him waiting for death. I've been down with the flu the past three days (longest time I've been sick in my life) and he came out to visit me. Sat here very quietly, and gently talked about this and that. He is not a really intelligent man—not, I mean, a man of ideas. His liberalism was wound up in the Bob Ingersoll days and got little farther. But one time he burned with an inner intensity that must have been a wonder and bewilderment to the men he knew. I know it was hell on wheels for the family. I'm a lot like him. The Irish and German of my mother blended that down a bit, but I hope it gave it greater scope and depth and a richness, but that remains to be seen. The sad part is that even now in reverie my mind concerns itself with opposing him, and that's only a useless waste, but I cannot help it much.

Reading Cleanth Brooks' *Modern Poetry and the Tradition.* An indictment of all I'm trying for, but the best of its kind. Best interpretation of the "Waste Land" yet. A thoughtful and soundly construed book.

This sounds odd coming from me, high priest of seriousness that I am, but may I commend your attention to the righteous jazz of one Muggsy Spanier? The only jazz I really like.

Somehow I always manage to write letters that are too long, too personal, too overburdened with my private griefs and miseries and petty scabs and puny deformities. Where is the amplitude of soul to which I aspire? I drag the withered legs of my spirit up to your door and whimper for entrance. When are you going to puke and shut the door in my face?

Bill

December 31, 1940
[L.A.]
ALS, 3 p.

Dear Bill—

This is the last day of the year. I near the end of a 9-day vacation. How happy I have been! Living out the days in simple acts—sitting in the sun, walking in the hills with my boys, chopping wood, perusing manuscripts in the Huntington library, & in the evenings working in my study on John Fiske—a paper which I hope will take us to Boston next June. I have petitioned the university for expenses. For Christmas I got Fay an album of cowboy songs & for myself an album of 11 sonatas by Domenico Scarlatti; played by Robert Casadesus. When do you come south?

Your letter about the *Ghost* came this morning. [*Everson's letter is missing from the file.*] How good it makes me feel. I've worked really alone on the project for years & now it belongs to everyone. I am glad you believe the introduction to be well done. A lot of work went into it. It was much longer. But I whittled at it. Now I see how it could be different in this way & that—amplified here & there—& yet that sort of thing could go on indefinitely. It's irrevocably in print!!

The poem itself has lost none of its magic for me. Upon receiving my first bound copy I devoted two evenings to a thorough reading of the poem—& now hardly a day goes by that I don't read in it. I know what a marvelous companion it's going to be for you. Write me what you get from it, whenever you feel like it.

Yes, a number of review copies were sent out. The obvious places. Keep me posted as to any notices you see. Fisher always said that people would either like or dislike the poem to an extreme degree—that there would be few if any middle-grounders. I am eagerly curious to see what reviewers say about it.

Perhaps the Lustig designs will grow on you. I like them immensely—

Forgive my license in putting you (anonymously) into my editorial!

You did well to give my name as a reference.

Your letter about your father gave me the idea that you ought to write a novel about your growing up—your letters about your parents have the intensity & sensitive awareness of Lawrence's *Sons & Lovers.* You have the Valley for beautiful background, as he had the environs of Nottingham. You seem to need a larger medium than the poems you've been writing. Why don't you tackle it?

Two years ago you were here for New Year's Eve. Tonight

will be quiet. I take Fay & my mother to an early movie, then call for them. And maybe we'll sit up by a log fire—maybe we'll go to bed before the witching hour. Who knows.

Put a new section of bookcase in my study—the first along the north wall. Of the collecting of books there is no end.

Onward into the 40's. What do they hold for us all?

Greetings to you & Edwa—
Larry

1941: POETRY AND PROSE

Sunday, Dec. [i.e., Jan.] 12, 1941
Selma
ALS, 2 p., 1 sheet

Dear Larry:—

We do not come south. The shape of events will not permit it.

Your suggestion of my doing a novel is interesting, but one of which I know myself incapable. Besides, my turning to prose at this time would be a confession of poetic failure, and I am not at that retreat yet.

You have said nothing for a long time of the Pickett work.

What's this on John Fiske?

I curse the circumstance that sent M.F. from Fisher when it did. The *Ghost* grew in intensity as it grew in length—those last pages are immense—a few dozen more like that would be invaluable.

The imagists scared me from *Paradise Lost* (remember Pound challenging Abercrombie to a duel for praising Milton?). But under pressure from a friend who has given me a finely designed, 2 vol, 1945 edition of the *Works,* I'm deep in the long and famous poem. And it deserves that fame. An immense and heroic thing. I have long felt that "Lycidas" is the greatest poem in the English language. Everything I aspire toward in poetry is directed toward that. I have also read the very great *Samson Agonistes.* Strangely enough I began with modern poetry, and only of recent years have gradually matured enough to read the classic sources. Spenser is marvelous. I take the *Fairy Queen* page after page. Play by play I read my excellent Tauchnitz edition of Shakespeare, and read the whole of *Tamburlaine* to Edwa one night as I modeled.

Edwa is gradually resuming work again. Don't say anything to Newell because it would affect his honesty when next she shows to him, but his cold reception set her back. She has the least confidence in herself of any person I have known; she can take very cheerfully criticism, but she is sensitive to the general attitude of the seeker, and if she senses either dislike or disinterestedness it throws her off. She simply gives up. It's so god damned easy for her to believe she's no good. Yet when she is working with confidence, her forms assume that invigorating spirit of power and health, and fine poetic feeling. Newell himself had only praise for the mood, the feeling, the inspirational qualities of what she had done. It was the execution that he objected to and found technically faulty. I feel she can master the last; I know she has a splendid sense for these sculptural forms.

The music she most enjoys is Bach. For Christmas she received the little album of two toccatas in D and G done by Schnabel on the piano. As for myself, I received Beethoven's *Eroica,* a symphony that I still stand up before God and man and declare in round terms to be the greatest ever written. It is so rarely played I have waited months to hear it on a program in which I could get good reception, and now that I have it, the Philharmonic offers it next Sunday! Did I tell you I am gradually thawing toward Brahms? I wonder if you heard Toscanini do Beethoven's *Missa Solemnis*? O Jesu what music! My tastes alter. My musical feeling solidifies and enrichens. Beethoven, Mozart, and Bach. I play my *Eroica* as often as I dare, fearing if I play it too much it will pall on me. In every chord rings the line from MacLeish in "Our history was grave, noble, and tragic."

Re: Milton: Two lines in Jeffers that have always stuck in my mind contain a figure that I encountered again today: "In the Giant's Ring" Jeffers says: "Jesus and Caesar out of the bricks of man's weakness, Washington out of the brittle bones of man's strength, built their memorials." Milton says: *Paradise Lost,* Line 425—"Nor founded on the brittle strength of bones."

There have been so many people here lately I feel now like seeking out the northern lights. Every week since before Christmas has brought a host of increasing friends. We like people, and after long periods of no company, we even seek them out, but lately it's been too much. I've had to work days and entertain nights, and it's a damned waste of time. Cal starts again and most will go back. I resent everything that interferes with my writing.

Bill

February 18, 1941
Los Angeles
ALS, 2 p.

Dear Bill—

I've owed you a letter for a long while. Have thought about you. Wondered what you are working on. Joyce is dead. A sad end he had, was driven, very poor. The two best obituaries: *Time*'s & Alfred Kazin's in *N.Y. Herald Tribune* "Books." A giant has left the literary world.

Fisher called my attention to an oriental proverb. The best destiny: to have genius & to remain obscure.

Have been reading *New Directions 1940* Annual. A review of the *Ghost,* written by F. himself [confidential], & his prose account of the death & burial of his father. As for the poetry included in the annual, it might have been written by one person, so stereotyped in the mold of surrealism is it. I fear that Laughlin is easily duped. He is due out here next month. Letter from Henry Miller in Atlanta. He is due this summer.

We are going east in June-July. You asked what I was doing with John Fiske. Writing a paper for the Bibliographical Society on the library of John Fiske—we have it at UCLA. Meeting in Boston in June. I have received a travel grant from the university. We are applying it on driving trip. Will combine my leave of absence with annual vacation. Hope to return via New York & Washington. Leave about June 10th. Be gone about one month.

Have you read all of the *Ghost?*

I have a 60-book Ritchie exhibit on at the library. I wish you could see it. Your book of course is included.

I have just finished judging the Western Books of 1940 Show, & am compiling a catalog for Stanford University Press to print.

Am not much of a hand at letters lately.

A good biography: R. C. Beatty's *Bayard Taylor*

Re-reading Norman Douglas's *Old Calabria*—

Frieda Lawrence is here for 2 months. Gawd, how we love that woman!

yrs. affectionately,
Larry

Feb. 24, 1941
Selma, Calif.
ALS, 2 p., 1 sheet

Dear Larry:—

I have just returned from the library where I read the *Nation*'s review of the *Ghost.* We can expect more of this sort of thing—the stuff Jeffers has been bucking these last ten years—criticism via the head *only,* the cold detached smug intellect peering out of its frosty depths, sure of itself, dead certain, passing judgment with that irrevocable doomsday damnation. Sons of bitches and poor disillusioned bastards! The poor lame crippled half-man fools! When will they learn you don't read poetry that way? When will they learn that you can't get at it that way? I can say only this: I have read the *Ghost in the Underblows* and I am willing to back everything I know about poetry, everything I *feel* about poetry, on the prediction that this work will take its place beside the major ones of these productive forty-one years of our century. If the *Ghost* is wrong then so am I. I've read it through and through. I browse in it constantly. I am dead sure.

I envy you your trip. God how I'd like to see New England!

I have never seen a *New Directions* annual, but will order it from the State Library.

The pipe work has about done me up of late—hard and heavy and long—come home all washed out, too tired to move. All that saves me are the rainy days when I can't work.

Immersed in Bach now. Edwa brought me around to him. We now have the Preludes and Fugues 44–48 of Fischer's performance of the last volume of *Well-tempered Clavier.* Are looking forward to the 35–44 volume; *Art of the Fugue,* eventually the *B Minor Mass* that magnificent Passacaglia and fugue in C minor—no need to wait for Beethoven! Have Stokowski's unsatisfactory romanticized transcription, but will never rest till I hear it for organ. The Suites are fine and the Brandenburg concertos. Bach I feel was the complete man—the whole man—the man who could attempt reality in its entirety, with an enormous faith, and not shrivel. He never would have written an "I am your son" poem—but then he never would have written a *Point Sur*—nor even a *Paradise Lost.*

Poor Joyce. There is some magnificent stuff in *Finnegans Wake*.

Three months my book has been at New Directions. I do not care if it is rejected. Much revision to do yet; much work. "The Masculine Dead" is better than when you saw it; but I still find things to work over. I'm writing new poems—laboriously—they won't shape up.

I listen to the "Invitation to Learning," and find it absorbing, though I don't always agree. Tate comes out entirely different than his cold detached written papers would indicate. I've admired some of his poetry chiefly the "Ode to the Confederate Dead," and some of his criticism, but shivered at his lack of warmth. Over the air his personality is much more human and my respect for him has increased vastly. Van Doren, I have felt, is a fine, sensitive individual—the kind there are never enough of. I'd like much to know him. Maybe we'll get down before long.

Bill

Feb. 25, 41
Selma
ALS, 1 p.

Dear Larry— forgot to get your letter off this morning and tonight my mss. came in by express. Laughlin says:

> Dear Mr. Everson
> I am very grateful to you for letting me read your manuscript of poems and wish that I did not have to return it to you.
> But, although I find things in your lines that I like, they do not set me on fire, as the saying goes, and, naturally, I never publish anything about which I'm not violently enthusiastic.
>
> Sincerely,

This is all right, but what beats me is that I sent the thing Nov. 26, 1940. Laughlin's letter is dated Dec. 4, 1940—about four days after he received the work. But it wasn't mailed until Feb. 19, almost 3 months, and then from Boston, not Norfolk. Screwy!

I'll not send it off again. Even if I cannot enjoy the distinction of the first part of Fisher's oriental proverb I can safely and quite easily attain its conclusion.

Bill

April 6, 1941
Selma
ALS, 3 p., 2 sheets

If my work permits we shall come to L.A. Thursday for a couple days. Edwa wants to purchase woodcarving tools. There is a possibility we cannot come. I shall phone you at the university.

Dear Larry:— By some miracle I have managed to escape through the dragon's teeth—though this is by no means indicative that I will not be sucked back into his maw when next he growls. What seems to have happened: after the draft was initiated, after the eloquent speeches, the soft-spoken reassurances, the outlines for the "new army" where the officers and men will be "friends," the "defense" army, where only the cream of the manpower would be used; after even the "liberal weeklies" came out for the army and for intervention (and this fact has become so intensified that articles in the *Nation* could be switched to *Liberty* without anyone's notice) after, I say, all the reassurances—the draft boards went ahead and classified in one great gulp the first 20%. I fell within that margin; but somehow all Fresno draft-boards did a very singular thing. They relegated all married men, regardless of their wives' economic status, to group III-A. In Dec. I received my papers, applied for conscientious objector exemption; and was, finally, in accord with the plans, also assigned to III-A. However, not much time passed before it became evident that if this procedure of husband-exemption were followed, the Fresno district would be unable to fill its quotas promptly enough, so the ruling was modified, and all married men with working wives are to be drafted. But present indications point to the fact that men already classified will not be reclassified until the rest of the list has been run through—this is better even than an original high drawing number! So I seem safe for a time. How long I am to remain safe I have no way of knowing.

Carothers came home this week on a short leave. Inducted four weeks ago: jobless, bewildered, thoroughly aimless, hating the whole procedure but lacking the stamina, the will, to resist, he drifted along and went in. He returns with the most disturbing information I have yet received. We all half-expect war—we expect it, yes, but we don't want to admit it; we clutch at our straws; we try to put it out of our minds. Carothers comes home with the information that the army is seething with it. Men are being inducted faster than they can be housed, faster than they can be clothed, faster even than they can be fed. The medical examination is a farce. A glance down your throat, a thump on your chest, and a quick look up your ass and you're done—one, two; heart, sound; can you hear me, Buddy? hearing O.K.; blood pressure, good enough; sure, sure, one two—next! Carothers is hard of hearing; has low blood pressure; a trace of T.B. In he went. A ganglia on the wrist was noted. After passing he came back and asked the doctor, casually: "Say, what is this?" "Hmm—ganglia—funny I never noticed that—by the way (turning to assistant) that is an exempting defect." Assistant: "The hell it is." Doc.: "Sure thing (producing list—'ganglia on wrist, etc., etc.')—better call over the sup." Superintendent called, examines object—"Harumph—well—harumph—we can't exempt a man for a little thing like that—harumph—pass him on in—!" There you are—the cream of the manpower. In camp things are in a mortal confusion. Not clothes enough. Every meal food is prematurely exhausted. Men rove over the tables searching for strays others have left. Enrollees with money go into town for a good steak. And the "new" army—built on the rotten old one—the same personnel, the same methods; the same furious awkward terrible costly haste of 1917! God almighty! You think of the pictures in *Life* magazine. I really believed that whatever could be said, this time the men would be well-fed and well-equipped—hell, the fat of the land goes to it—I think of *Life* magazine, its slick paper, its plush assurance, and its jingo! jingo! jingoism—and see beside that jingoism the sexy ads: the beautiful whores stretching languorously in silks, exposing their thighs, shaking their haircut over the come-on eyes—all in the name of America, of the Peet Soap Company; of Sweets of Sin perfume; of Figurine corsets—and the men, the thousands of them, the millions massing, massing, massing: and over it all the golden whores of American advertising—of America, America, that rotten sick-gutted slut! O Walt Whitman! Milton! Wordsworth!

I'm sick thinking about it: I'm sick through and through. I'm afraid. Tonight the Germans are in Yugoslavia, in Greece. I saw in a newsreel the Greeks, straggling through sparse Southern California [-like?] mountains; a-horse, a-foot, sometimes with their women; on a pack mule passing the camera there hung momentarily the white face of a blond child; scowling, sultry, and tense, a Norse face, caught there by God knows what throwback to God knows what ancestors—they are fighting their lives out; falling under the planes, falling under the heavy tanks; and the fair-limbed bodies of the German youth lie in the muck and rain and the shit of the mules—beyond one's pacifism (and all I have felt only intensifies that pacifistic conviction) beyond all one's pacifism proceeds this enormous human pattern, that cannot be ignored, that is so real, so intense, and so close. May we live through it: and may what follows the fearful collapse, the poverty, the degradation—may all that be less horrible than we expect.

Bill

April 8, 1941
Los Angeles
APS

Dear Bill—

Glad to hear you are coming south. Fay is not very well, so we can't offer much entertainment, but would like you to spend Thursday evening with us. Call me at the library when you get in town. Parrish exhibit will be on until Saturday.

Regards,
Larry

April 22, 1941
Selma
ALS, 4 p., 2 sheets

Dear Larry:—

Outside his chosen field a poet's sensibility is no more valid and his perceptions no more acute than any other sensitive person. In fact, as far as other media are concerned they are probably less so, for there is something about intense application to verbal response that colors a man's entire outlook. He tends to look at everything via the medium of words, and he tends to judge everything via the words of others, the reading matter of his past, rather than by any other criterion.

Therefore, when I stood with you before Parrish's paintings it was with the acute realization that here was something for which I certainly had no true basis of approach. I remembered the response of persons with no literary background to a finely wrought and well-turned poem—how they saw nothing at all or saw the wrong things; how the subtlety, the craft was lost upon them, so that they never really read the poem at all. And remembering that I wondered how much of these paintings I was really missing, and what subtleties there were manifested before my eyes that I was unaware of.

I did not wonder for long however because as I looked I forgot that I had no training and therefore no method of approach; I forgot that this was a complicated and difficult medium: I became absorbed in what I was seeing, and in being absorbed lost my inferiority complex and gave myself over to letting the quality of each picture as I stood before it do what it could to my consciousness. And rather than forgiving my critical sense I tuned it in on myself and tried to find out what it was about each picture that operated upon me as it did. I knew I was being stimulated and moved and I wanted to know why. That afternoon as we drove down to Long Beach and the next day as we drove through the Mojave I kept turning the things over in my mind and trying to come to some generalization that would let me know what had happened.

I think the impression that dominated all the others was the impression of integration. I have seen many paintings, watercolors especially, that had a quality which I referred to in my own vocabulary as impressionistic. It seemed to me that the painter was operating under the Romantic aesthetic of self-immersion, or self-effacement before the reality of his sensibilities. By allowing his being to be flooded with a particular scene, and by letting his sensibility short circuit through his eye to his hand directly he was attempting to get at the reality of what lay before him—and he did achieve a kind of stimulation. What I got out of Parrish was the feeling that everything about those melons was known: perceived, absorbed, and resolved. And that when he came to paint he placed them in their posed and logical place in the universe; with all their interrelationships balanced and adjusted; so that each painting as you stood before it gave off the sense of complete resolution. This seemed to me to be a matter of color as well as form. The colors and the forms seemed poised in an intricate and beautific [*sic*] relationship that left you feeling that here was one aspect of the universe that possessed above all things the quality of order.

When we were in San Francisco last June, we went to see the Picasso exhibit. We went through room after room; and before we were through, I could stand it no longer. I knew I was looking into the mouth of Hell itself and I had to get out. My whole sensibility was hammered by blow after blow, and all the blows were evil. It was a world in which there was no beauty—no sensory beauty, no lyricism, no poetry. There was only the abstract and terrifying organization of object against object. Later I came to believe that the man was the most lonely, god forsaken miserable utterly abandoned creature I had ever met—a man to be pitied, a man so terribly crippled of soul that he was forever beyond salvation.

Therefore it was with considerable surprise that I observed what I took to be the Picasso technique operating via an entirely different type of sensibility: these forms were drawn from a loving and aching sense of beauty (the religious pictures I did not care for so much because my poet's sensibility got in my way again and I saw neither angels nor human beings as I, a poet, would have seen them). There was affirmation of a most warm and expansive kind. And though many days have gone by now I can still see that Rooster: the living embodiment of all roosters, of all dawns, with his gigantic enormous head, his mouth open against that jagged and indestructible sun shouting life up out of the tides of darkness and sleep, triumphant: a thing of more intense affirmation I have never seen.

Bill

enclosing check for the Lincoln.

May 4, 1941
ALS, 1 p.

Dear Bill—

I trust you received the Lincoln from Szukalski. He was very glad to get the 5 dollars. I saw the print he was sending—a beauty. *New Directions* received. What do you think of it? McAlmon book I promised to send is out for awhile. I've changed my mind & would like back those copies of *Horizon,* if you still have them. I want to complete a file at the library. Am mailing you 3 numbers of *Partisan Review* to which I subscribed for a year. Interesting attack on MacLeish. Please return them when you've finished.

Most interesting letter about Parrish's painting. That roomful will always burn in my memory.

Am in the midst of writing paper on John Fiske. We leave for Boston on June 10th, to be gone about a month.

We enjoyed your last visit—& Fay her chance to become better acquainted with Edwa.

Greetings!
Larry

P.S. You ought to acknowledge that little book of poems R. Hoffman sent you.

14.iv.41
Bareacres
TLS, 1 p.

Dear Larry. . . . .

Thanks for letting us see this very interesting letter again. Tim is struck by Everson's liking the Rooster so much, because of all the pictures it is the one most directly influenced by Picasso. . . . in fact, the outlines of the bird are a copy, practically, of a small drawing in the book you have.

It interests me too, because several men who have been somewhat unnaturally preoccupied either with their own virility or their lack of it have been almost hypnotized by the Rooster. Would that be true with E?

Is there anything I can do to help either of you get ready for the Grand Tour? Please tell me.

I'm wondering if we'll see you before then. I know how busy you must be . . . . but we'll hope for the best . . . . . .

Love to you all . . . . .
M. F. K. [Fisher, now
Parrish]

May 28, 1941
Los Angeles
ALS, 2 p., 1 sheet

Dear Bill—

Today I sent you by express a package containing *Black Spring,* & the Symmes [Robert Duncan] magazines & correspondence. I appreciate your sending me this, particularly of course the Miller. Symmes I don't care for. A homo all right. Have to sew your britches on when he was around. You did well to break off with him. Of the two, Cooney is the better man.

You will notice a change in your copy of *Black Spring*! Strange that you should send it just at the time that Henry Miller was here. I asked him to autograph it for you, & have given him your address. He may not get to the central valley. Is going to Carmel and SF. I showed him your *San Joaquin*. He read the title poem & the one en face. Liked them. I want you to send him a copy & write to him; at once, so as to catch him: c/o William Roth, The Colt Press, San Francisco. Urge him to come down the valley; or go to S.F. to see him.

Here's a confession: I have been tremendously moved by Henry Miller. He and his books are one: he is a great writer & a great man. There hasn't been so marvelous a natural man since Thoreau & Whitman. Not only natural, but so perfectly integrated. Tom Wolfe & Lawrence had the great strain in them, but Miller goes beyond them. God almighty, Bill, you must not fail to meet him. My heart went out to the man—his courage, his wonderful devotion to his *demon,* & his simple kindness, & his eloquence. When he gets started he talks like he writes. God what a session we had here last night!

Ten years ago this autumn we met briefly in Dijon.

I can't write any more. I must write now in my journal. Have precious little time. We leave on the 9th or 10th.

I can't seem to find the 3 letters sent in your last package. Can I have returned them by mistake along with the Symmes stuff? If so, please forgive and send back! I'll re-read & answer in detail.

Send your book and letter at once to Miller. Please.

Yours,
Larry

June 4, 1941
Selma
ALS, 1 p.

Dear Larry:—

Your package followed your letter by a couple of days, so that I had not received *Black Spring* with its friendly autograph until after I had sent book and letter to Miller: consequently I felt self conscious about taking the initiative, and I'm afraid my letter must have contained circumlocutions that puzzled him. Your enthusiasm for the man is infecting; but it took no infection to make me see the worth of *Tropic of Cancer* and *Black Spring*.

Your books puzzle me—I mean the McAlmon and the Sitwell. If you're in Boston, how can I dispose of them? They're marked due the 6th—I can't even get them back in time for that. Did you stop them or what? Do I return them to your house? I'm worried about this.

Also, upon their covers are two identical ink spots, as if ink had been spilled and the books clasped together. Very unsightly. I want to establish innocence, not to escape any fine, which I would gladly pay as price for reading them, but to preserve my reputation as one careful with treasures.

My calendar tells me you leave Monday. I wish you all good luck and very much pleasure on this journey. I hope to have a small group of poems ready for your circumspection when you return. Please write before you leave, if only a card, relieving me of the above anxieties.

Bill

June 9, 1941
Los Angeles
APS

Dear Bill—

Disregard the date due in the books. When finished mail them to

Loan Desk, Univ. of Calif. Library, 405 Hilgard Ave., LA.

Forget the ink spots! Just boxing to leave. Will write from the East.

Yrs. Larry

June 17, 1941
Greenfield, Ind.
APS

Dear Mr. Everson,
Take inspiration. Strive and succeed.

Professor Powell

July 16 '41
Selma
ALS, 5 p., 3 sheets

Dear Larry:—

While you were away, we, too, vacationed. We loaded possessions into a trailer and started out for some unidentified spot on the northern California coast. Finally found the town of Elk, 150 miles north of S. F.—a half-deserted lumber town—and got a house over the cliffs and the sea for $3.00 for two weeks. Our first prolonged stay anywhere since we've been together, and really a great time. So profound a change in locale. Came back through S. F., tried to see Wm. Roth at the Colt Press, but he wasn't in.

Miller told me about Roth—even, I believe, wrote to Roth in my behalf. Miller stayed overnight here—slept on our living room floor with Gilbert and Margaret Neiman! I was somewhat disappointed in my expectations of Miller. I looked for an intense man—a man like the bust of him *Time* published, but to me he seemed soft, somehow—easy-going—almost old boyish. For the life of me I cannot connect him with his writing. If I learned tomorrow somebody had ghosted all that for him, nothing in me would be much affected. I don't intend this as an indictment. He seemed an honest, kind, thoroughly likeable individual, but not the one who would write: "so I tumbled her on the bed and threw a fuck into her." He wrote me a fine letter and evidently believes in me, which is very nice to know. You and he must have really hit it off. He spoke as highly in praise of you as a man could. He is, of course, a great writer, though a limited one, which makes me doubt you when you say he goes beyond either Lawrence and Wolfe—to say which does not incriminate the profound respect I have for much he has written.

On one point, Professor, I can't let you get by—since when have you ever felt impelled to slough a man off with—"as for John Holmes, I have never heard of him or his poetry." O devastating indictment! except for that unforgivable crack I liked your review of the records in Gateway to Music.

Do you know Tom Boggs, the anthologist? Couple of years ago he was scouting for material and dropped me a card. I sent him my book when it came out and he sent me his *Lyrics in Brief*—selections from classics and contemporaries. Last spring he asked me for something in a Compass anthology he was compiling for James A. Decker in Prairie City, Ill., but never used the poem I sent. Month or so ago I wrote asking him about publishing in N. Y., since he lives there and is around. In his reply, which wasn't encouraging, he mentioned Decker as the logical choice if one is to underwrite one's own book, since he has a good list of books by the younger poets and is well-known in the East. Then here comes in a letter from Boggs telling me Decker is bringing out an anthology similar to New Direction's 5 *Poets,* to be called *Seven Poets,* and asking me to come in. Each man to have 300 lines of verse, which as you see, is quite a selection. He urged airmail as Decker wanted it published in August. Well, we left for Elk the day before it arrived, and mail was held for a week. Finally getting it, I yet had only the carbon of my book ms. (which was at Duell, Sloan & Pearce in N.Y.—rejected since) to pick from. I picked best poems out of *San Joaquin* and the more suitable unpublished lyrics (Boggs listed others as Marshall Schacht, Robert Clairmont, E. L. Mayo, Lloyd Frankenberg, and himself—I tried to keep my selections confined to the more impersonal poems, since these boys are mostly in the detached modern school) and sent them off airmail special delivery. Time dragged by until today I received my poems back with a letter telling me he was sorry but the poems came in a week too late. Boggs professes to have a "genuine respect" for my work, but this I am inclined to doubt. In all his anthologies he has not confined himself to unpublished work but has selected from books; yet he has not taken from *San Joaquin.* Not only this but the fact that he waited till almost too late before asking me to come in shows he most certainly did not have me in mind. (I forgot to say that each poet was to contribute $15.00 for his share in the anthology. Please do not mention this. I was told in all confidence and would not have the leak through me. Decker is to appear as issuing the work at his own risk.) So it seems Boggs was caught short and turned to me as stop-gap. The anthology, according to this letter, will include Schacht, Mayo, Boggs, Clairmont, and Ciardi—Boggs says another one will come out in a few months—and implies I will be asked for that one—but, tactfully, nothing definite. I had it in my mind to haul off and blast the gentleman, but will bide my time. It is harder to break in [in] the east than I had thought. My book comes back time and again. I have enough egotism in me to feel that if Mr. Boggs ever condescends and out of the goodness of his infinite compassion allows me to slip in toward the back of the room and occupy one of the lower benches of nigger heaven, I have enough egotism, I say, to believe I will open his eyes. Boggs likes the neat, the deft, the well turned, and the precious. One of these days he is going to walk into a wind that will take his hat off—all right Everson, pull in your whiskers, you'll bust your vest at this rate.

Bill

Enclosed is a memo from Elk—with my regards!

Ward's superb little Blake selections on the occasion of the birth of Duncan, Thane of Hyperion Canyon, came in today. A veritable gem. I think it a gracious and charming custom to present these little memos as he does on special events. The man is a swell person.

This was intended for a post script, but I forgot to tell you of an amusing incident in S.F. I took a copy of *S. J.* up for Wm. Roth to see, and since he wasn't in decided to have booksellers there appraise it for me.

Paul Elder's was first. The man there looked at it, skimmed the pages, sniffed at it—I almost thought he was going to cautiously nibble it!—and then cleared his throat. He was afraid it wasn't the sort of thing they were in the market for. He might be ignorant, he said, but the name Everson was not of such weight to justify them rushing to snatch it up. I pointed out to him the merits of this particular book rested not so much on its author as on its imprint; I cited the Rounce and Coffin club selections and the Treasure Island exhibit. He shrugged. Ritchie of course did good work, but he wasn't a Grabhorn. They couldn't consider the book. It was the sort of thing that invariably showed up for a dollar a copy later on. Biting my tongue I subsided. When Edwa paid for the purchase with a check, the man must have read her signature with some embarrassment!

At Gelber, Lilienthal they were more polite, but unexcited. Supposed I could get the published price of writing when he saw it, but I at least thought he could see fine printing when stuck under his nose.

July 17, 1941
Los Angeles.
ALS, 2 p., 1 sheet

Dear Bill—

We arrived home safely a week ago. We were away a month to the day. A fine 6615 mile trip through this vast wonderful land that we inhabit. A week in Cambridge. A couple of days with Fisher in Northampton. A week in N.Y.

If you are still sending out *San Joaquin* mail one to the Poetry Room, Harvard College Library, Cambridge, Mass. A swell collection of contemporary poetry on open shelves; easy chairs & lamps. Same room houses Amy Lowell's books. It's where they make the recordings. Do you still get "On the Record" from Gateway to Music? In June I wrote a squib on the Harvard records.

I subscribed to Laughlin's Poet of the Month Series. Pretty thin, so far.

Took 2 books on the trip: *Ghost* & Rilke's *Duino Elegies* tr. by Leishman & Spender. They have something in common with the *Ghost*. In New York I bought a remaindered T. E.

Lawrence Letters for 1.49. Good. Human soul under terrific pressure, internal & external.

Now reading Matthiessen's *American Renaissance*. Good, but too wordy. Met Newton Arvin at Fisher's. Gentle, fine-drawn neurotic.

At Gotham Book Mart I can buy *Tropic of Cancer* for 6.00 less 20%. Let me know if you ever want a copy. Where, oh where are our *Capricorns??*

Look at the watermark on this paper. They want me to work there. If I can't get the head job here I'll probably go. This coming year will decide.

Are you ready to send me some of your recent poems? I am most eager to catch up with you.

How in hell are you?

I am Magnifico!

Larry

July 19, 1941
Selma
ALS, 3 p., 2 sheets

Dear Larry:—

Too bad our letters crossed, sort of tangles things. Your trip sounds wonderful. I received your quaint card from the Riley Memorial and was heartened into a stupendous burst of zeal! Your description of Harvard's Poetry Room makes it seem a good thing—I have wanted to find such a place as that here on the coast, but I doubt if one exists. The day we spent at the State Library helped but you can't browse; and I felt self-conscious asking for a book, keeping it only enough to see something of its nature, which was all I had time for, and then asking for another. Not only that, their modern poetry collection is pitifully inadequate. I have quit ordering books from there through our library, because for the past year practically everything I ordered they have not had. Discouraging. With just a bit more money I'd buy the books as they come out, but as it is I have to depend upon *Poetry* magazine for the Poetry Front. I'd give a lot to get ahold of Spender's *The Still Centre* before I buy it. Fresno library had MacNeice's *Poems* of 1937 which was attractively done, and which I read constantly. Bought the 1940 *Poems* by order, sight unseen, and practically never look at it—poems all jammed together, pulpy paper, type too large for page size etc. Strange. I'll have to buy the 1937 poems also I guess!

About Harvard Poetry Room, I'd be only too glad to send the book (I've sent none out that we talked of in Los Angeles—laziness). But would they accept it? Librarians, I fear, are like booksellers in that they are interested only in the "accepted." Advise me again with this in mind.

I, too, sent a subscription to the Poet of the Month—belatedly, so that I got them in a wad a couple of weeks ago. In his announcement Laughlin harped on the catholicism of the selections but that does not appear to be true so far. The man is interested only in extremes. The extreme of Romanticism—(Surrealism) or the ethic of classicism (Intellectualism). *New Directions Annual* is crammed with Surrealism and the Poet of the Month[s] are mostly dry-ball. Wheelwright I find rather like MacIntyre in the angle of his vision. One good poem in Larry Brown. The Donne was superb. Baker was god-awful. Williams boring. Miss Miles sent me a personal copy of her issue—a trade for the *S. J.* I sent her two years ago. She wrote me first before *S. J.* came out about *These Are the Ravens.* There are such terrific aesthetic gulfs between us we don't get on very well. Do you know her? She's UCLA graduate, I believe. Crippled. Young prof at FSC whom we know is close friend to her, and that's how it started. I get no joy from her poems.

I, too, took the *Ghost.* I had not touched it for a long time, my technical interests being elsewhere at the present. But at Elk I gave it a whole day again, and it is immense. That fact will stand.

Does the Spender-Leishman translation jibe with the MacIntyre? Newton Arvin I read in Zabel's *Literary Opinion*—with some disgust:

"It should be obvious that (American writers) unless they prefer a bleak or an elegant futility, can turn in but one direction, to the proletariat."

My sailor friend brought in all the Miller books and presented them to me. I am now reading *Capricorn*—so far, I solemnly believe, one of the world's great books. I'll send it down in a few days.

I hardly know what to say about the Harvard proposition. Better for you, but I'll hate to have you leave the coast. I really would hang that headman job if you can.

I've been dropping the necessary hints to get the Jeffers recordings for my birthday!

Ever since I quit work I've had fire working in my poems (except for Elk when I only got adjusted at the last) it is like opening up a vein of ore. You get an attitude and you explore it, as I did in *San Joaquin*. Then you mill around for a long time on incidental topics, which is not so good because there is little continuity in them and no prolonged drive. Then something happens in your life and out of that experience all your past comes up and synthesizes to meet it, and for awhile the surfaces and angles of it give you tremendous opportunity; you dig in and follow the thing out, facet by facet, and it keeps opening before you, all related and all busting from the central situation against which you have thrown your whole consciousness. It is a very big thing, and I thank God I've had the time to get what I have of it. We're making a deal for a ranch now and I've been thrown off for awhile, also the cannery starts next Wednesday, so this phase is about closed, but I have had a good grip on it, and I'm sending you the results. There are three poems in progress besides this; two post-Elk, and one pre-Elk, on Churchill and his speeches, started last spring. None of these I don't suppose are absolutely finished, but in the main they will stay as here given. It's quite a body isn't it? But not so much when considering it's everything I've done since "The Masculine Dead." The first was begun at the cannery last year. The next one's from Christmas up to now. Tell me what you think.

Bill

I was going to have Decker bring out my book, but if we can swing this ranch it'll drain us dry for a good five years. Boggs told me Decker could do a 48 pg. book for about 80 dollars. Which is not bad, considering the rising costs of printing—which is indeed damn good.

Capricorn is terrific. I am amazed, somewhat ashamed at my blindness that Miller was here in the flesh and I got nothing from it. Is something wrong with me? But everyone here who met him felt the same. I can't understand it. I think Miller's metaphysic is all shit—but after this book you can see why he holds it. I had forgotten most of *Cancer,* but here was the stuff again, twice as strong. Petronius is not in it with this man.

7-27-41
LA
ALS, 5 p., 4 sheets

Dear Bill—

Thanks for your two full letters, and the ltd. ed. from Elk. I shall treasure it among my bibelots! Newell was here when it came & liked it. He has been in Elk. I shall exhibit the opus to Ritchie. He'll be envious! I think your proposed Decker book good. 48 p. for $80 *is* cheap. Send *S. J.* to William A. Jackson, Harvard College Library, Cambridge, Mass., & mark package "for Poetry Room." If you want to drop him a note you might say that I noticed the book absent from the P. R. & asked you to send a copy. Did I tell you that Philip Horton will be custodian of the Room starting in Sept.? If I were to go to Harvard I would have general supervision of the Room, that is, with a custodian actually in the Room. Jackson now supervises, but is an Elizabethan & doesn't care for moderns.

Where is the ranch you are considering? You are fortunate in having the Miller books. By all means lend me *Capricorn.* When you send me express, direct to the University Library; there is no delivery here in the canyon & I have to pick up at the office.

Miller is in Hollywood, writing his American book. Zeitlin drives him to Carmel & back next week. They will see Jeffers. Miller has a way of relaxing & going along at a very low tension. Too bad he was that way when you saw him.

Josephine Miles is awful. I don't know her. I speak of her poetry. There's nothing behind it. She's a poetastress! Do you see the *Southern Review*? The Summer issue contains a superb omnibus review of poetry, by R. P. Blackmur. Thirty-six books were submitted; of these he reviewed eight & dismissed the rest. Conrad Aiken, Horace Gregory, J. P. Bishop, cummings, Baker, Winters, 5 young Am. poets, & Fisher! Yes, Fisher! The final 4 pages of 36-page review are devoted to the *Ghost.* "When he does pay attention to his craft, which happens on 30 or 40 pages of his 300, his craft rewards him with an extraordinarily rich-textured, deep-featured verse, & with an organization of imagery only surpassed in the great poets." "In the present state of my opinion, Books I, II, VIII, IX, X maintain the highest level & really constitute the effective part of the poem, but I am not anxious to argue the matter for I expect to be reading the poem for a long time & hope to find that the poem will gradually build its own judgement for me."

It is an extraordinarily sensitive, humble review—painstaking and painfully honest. I want you to read it. The same issue also contains a negative judgment of Jeffers, which quotes heavily from my book! If you haven't access to the *Southern Review,* I'll send you the library's copy. Let me know.

I am told that Allen Tate is doing the *Ghost* for *Partisan Review*—omnibus treatment. The John Hay juvenile notice in *Poetry;* the vicious paragraph in the *Nation;* Fisher's own review in New Directions; the *LA Times.* These are all the notices I've seen. Are there others that I've missed? We are getting out a postcard advertisement & I am collecting blurbs. Fisher once said that critics would either love or hate the book. Seems to be true. He will apply for a Guggenheim. The Blackmur notice, strict though it be, should help there. He plans another long poem, on a female Job. I am skeptical. The *Ghost* is a freak. It came & went. You saw clearly the gulf between it & "Death & Burial." Poor Fisher. Allen Tate is getting out a Princeton anthology. He asked Al to submit work done since the *Ghost.* Fisher has not written more than a line or two since 1931. He sent Tate a huge bundle of his college verse, to which he remains passionately attached—horrible imitative Greek stuff. Tate replied politely that he had decided after all to represent Fisher in the anthology by excerpts from the *Ghost*!

In spite of what Blackmur says about the poem being poor

in many parts, I believe that I would rather have erred in cutting too little than too much. As it was, I cut the poem about a quarter or more.

I've been a week back at work. Life is good. Busy.

I'd like to send you the first volume of the journal I kept in Europe. Oct. 1930 to March 1933. I am increasingly troubled by the need to write a book of my own covering some of those experiences. Rather than do a travel or literary book, I would write a study of several women I knew—an erotic gallery—& let all the rest of my life over there come in as incidental background. None of the women was alike. The material is in my journal & my imagination. The volume I would send, covers 4 of the 6.

I seek about for the proper form. First person? Keep to journal form? or straight narrative? Perhaps you can help me get launched. I do not want to write an unprintable book. The *fucking* words would be circumcised or circumscribed! Nor do I want to write for ordinary publication. Nor under my own name. Might issue the book privately printed to subscribers.

Or is it egotistical perversity? Should I burn all written records of my past? *No one has ever read my journals.* There is a second volume, 1933–1939; I am now into the third. Am too close to them to send them; even to you.

Yours,
Larry

7-27-41
[Los Angeles]
ALS, 4 p.

Bill,

Very good, & very bad. Like Jeffers', your abstract poems which go off the earth & have no natural figures, are not to my taste. His Self Criticism poems, Meditation on Saviors, & the rest of his self-preoccupied, neurotic poems, fine though they be for an understanding of his philosophy, are failures as separate poems.

I feel that instead of soaring, you should tunnel. Hug your valley. You once said that you planned to use *San Joaquin* in the way Whitman used *Leaves of Grass*—countless variations on a theme. Have you forgotten?

Your interest in abstractions doesn't make poetry. Stop using a telescope; use a microscope. I feel that you are heading the wrong way. Perhaps you will say that I am failing to understand your development in the way Edward Garnett parted with Lawrence after *Sons & Lovers.* Perhaps.

Don't be a luminous angel beating your wings in vain in the void, or whatever it was some ass called Shelley. Love your valley, but for God's sake don't go around on your hands & knees hammering the hollow weeds.

I believe you indulge yourself too much. Neuroticism. On the credit side, your poems show increasing ability to shape words. There is a sureness about your utterance. Very free from padding. No more MacLeishisms.

Jeffers is your worst enemy.

It would do you good to write a narrative poem, packed with detailed images.

Am I too hard?

I do not believe that you are retrogressing. Your verse gets better all the time. The trouble is you are hag-ridden—the creatures of abstract ideas. War, peace, heroism, abnegation. Forget them. I've said before that you take yourself too seriously. Sometime I'll show you the horrible stuff I cut out of the *Ghost.* Fisher in the robes of Aristotle. Walking around on words. Bullshit in heaps & piles.

God bless you, Bill. I hope this doesn't irritate you. These poems, when they are good, are fine. They should form a strong link in your work.

Send me the ones you are working on as soon as they are ready.

Yours
Larry

Mon. Aug. 3, 1941
Selma
ALS, 7 p., 6 sheets

Dear Larry:

Had I answered your letter when it arrived I would have written with more detail and concentration than I am able to at this time. The cannery is running at full blast and I have had to wait until today, which is my day of rest, in order to find any time at all for a reply. To give you an idea of what I have been doing I list my work hours this past week. Tues. 14-$^{3}/_{4}$ Wed. 13-$^{3}/_{4}$ Thurs. 16 Fri. 12-$^{1}/_{4}$ Sat. 13-$^{1}/_{2}$ Sun. 16. I have never had to work such hours for so prolonged a spell before. I am in charge of the syrup room this year, and have to accept responsibilities I gladly shirked before. Not only that, my daily work is more involved and I have no time to write poems on duty as previously—I have no time even to ponder the imponderables!

But even so, the influx of temperature readings and saccharometer reading was unable to smother out of my consciousness the various elements of your criticism and I have considered what you wrote many hours of those prolonged stretches. You have not, as you feared, irritated me, nor do I feel you were too hard. You were a bit rough, perhaps, but if you diagnosed the case correctly I think roughness was the required antidote. Nothing brings a skylark down to earth faster than to have "shit" flung in its face. And to have one's most inspired ravings so labeled certainly has a most sobering effect. If I can believe that your feeling, generally, is correct, or has an element of truth in it, I cannot yet believe it applies as far as you carry it. What I mean to say is that if I concede the failure of any given poem I am not prepared to concede the blanket dictum that I am on the wrong track. You refer constantly to my "soaring," when I do not feel that this is correct. That term is applied to work that depends upon an emotionality that has no foundation within the structure of the poem itself, or to work that jams more emotionality into the poem than its idea will bear. In every case (of these present poems) and chiefest in those very poems you most dislike, the "abstract" poems, the idea comes first and dominates the poem, rather than the associative material of poetry. If these poems fail it would seem to me far the opposite of soaring—pedestrianism—rather than far too much of it.

But your chiefest general criticism is, I take it, that "abstract" ideas do not kindle my imagination to its highest potential expression; that poems written out of such ideas do not have the sensuousness nor the freshness nor the richer appeal that more properly "lyric" poems possess; that by deserting the realm of nature, with all its possibilities of imagery and beauty I am cutting off my legs, so to speak. There is enough likelihood of such an event that I have to face it. I faced it knowingly when I made the choice and I am bound to heed your warning when I know it comes from your deepest feeling for, and insight into, the medium. I made my choice for one thing because I was personally thrown into a situation which as a man I could not accept, and which, as a poet and a man I could not help reacting to. I made the choice because I regard this craft with enough dignity and conviction to want to use it in the highest services of humanity: the upholding of the traditions of morality that are the bone and fiber of all we hold to. A statement you will regard as the same windy pomposity you objected to in the poems. I take myself seriously because I believe these things I feel to be true are not enough considered: that in a behaviorist world the absolutes of human relationships become ignored and forgotten; and every headstrong man plunges down the chutes of his personal desires. I do not think I am writing essays in cheap verse. I have tried to work the higher aspects of moral feeling into poetic expression:—to fuse the inherent stimulations of words and moral conviction into well-ordered units. Other men have done it. Wordsworth did it supremely well. From a technical point of view I have risked the absence of imagery in a concentration upon the ordering possibilities of this new free verse form. Look again at "One Born of This Time." If there is no luxuriant or sparkling imagery, see if instead there is not a gravity, a closeness of texture, and accumulating tension that never gets out of hand but follows up through the verses and flowers at least into something that cannot be detached and admired, no images, no outstanding lines, but a totality; the compressed weight of everything that went before. I feel it is a successful poem.

Did not you yourself in your prediction in the preface to *San Joaquin* qualify it with the words "if he can continue to expand his intellectual boundaries?"

As for my ideas themselves you do not agree with them, but they are at least tenable. If you believe we need more killing rather than less I assume you are ready to accept the personal consequences of such a belief. Do you really think that because an animal you killed in sport was an object of pity you were justified in your joy in the act of killing? Or do you bank on the possibility that all animals are so afflicted and you may thus indulge a primitive passion with equanimity? And because a notion you held about killing proved to be a literary notion and folded up at the first opportunity do you accuse me of the same instability? Is my poem so shallow and unconvincing, a poem that attempted to grasp all the terror of violence, and the spiritual pain of repentance, is it so shallow that you can pen in its margin a jocular invitation to nullify by repetitions all the personal consequences of that poem? You damn me as an idealist—do you suggest any other way than personal idealism by which humanity can realize its possibilities? I think there are none. Let me assure you that if I am a lily; that if the concepts of memory, pity of pain, the awareness of all the implications of dissolution—if these are lily virtues I am prepared to accept all their consequences and retire into any particular oblivion reserved for the species. I will continue to write out of my beliefs: to do otherwise is merely contemptible.

Which is not to say I do not recognize your warning. There is no reason why I should not so synthesize idea and poetic feeling into a far greater thing than either element alone. I understand your concern and I feel the sympathy you hold with all I try. Give me more time even yet. Most poets who turned out to be anything have written their greatest work before they attained my age. But give me time even yet. I see so clearly what needs to be done and all the time I am learning.

Blackmur's recognition of the existence of the *Ghost* is the greatest news of the summer. I was tremendously affected to learn of it, and I look forward to the complete review. I have followed Blackmur's criticism in the journals for about 5 or 6 years. I have read his book *The Double Agent* and unsuccessfully applied for the new one. Like all modern critics of that school, the intellectualist school stemming from Eliot, he has marked preferences, and biases, and blindnesses; but unlike most of them he brings to the reading of poetry so complete an absorption that everything he writes must be taken with respect. I think hardly any of the others approach him in that quality of earnest participation in what he approaches. He stands out in a school too much given to aloofness and superficiality. It is a great thing for all of us connected with the *Ghost* to have such a recognition as this. Even though the acceptance is by no means complete (and what modern has any of these men accepted without qualification?) at one blow the triviality of the *Nation* notice and the picayunishness of the *Poetry* review are annulled. We may rest easily now. The *Ghost* is launched. Do send the issue containing the review. I see *S. R.* in the State College Library, which is closed now. I should subscribe. No student of modern writing should be without it.

You say so much that is news to me; your letter was so meaty I won't try to comment on it all, but, know that I have overlooked none of it.

Capricorn gets thin in the middle phases. I was displeased with it and laid it aside. Some of the sexual passages seemed insincerely written—too glib somehow. I finished the book today and maybe it was my mood but it finished beautifully. An important, an immense book. I can't understand how I did it but I momentarily completely forgot my promise and lent the book to a friend. I'm sorry, but will send it down as soon as it returns. The copy I read today was the regular Paris edition the sailor left here to be bound. I would send it were it mine, but it is irreplaceable and I'd rather not let it out of the house. I'm sure you understand.

About your journal. I consider it an act of great trust that you offer to let me read this record of your life. I know how you feel, the hesitation that must be overcome before allowing anyone to see such a journal. If you do not change your mind, I should like to have you send it to me this Fall, when work is done and I can come to it with the leisure such a work requires. You mention again your need to write out of those experiences a creative work. I recall our conversation in your den, and recall your earlier work that you showed me. I can imagine the great hesitation with which you approach this thing; and yet also the great need that compels it. Considering it coldly, the difficulties to be overcome would be very large. Certainly it is true that only the masters seem to have been able to approach their past with the combination of candor and insight such a work requires. As I look at it, there is no question of should or shouldn't. If it doesn't compel itself, the notion is literary and will probably be a failure. If a man regards the elements of his past that have significance for him, and having an insight into the universal aspects of experience realizes the potential creative material of this experience, and possessing that combination of urgency and ability in such matters puts down his past as he remembers it in all its flavor and vitality, then you have material of value. You can't have a running series of names and references such as McAlmon's useless compendium and expect to get much. On the other hand you can't get too subjective and lose your focus. In the State Library I picked out the little book of Una Jeffers, and I swear the opening pages of that thing are a revelation on the misconception of what literary recollection should be. Lawrence and Brett is another case in point. These things are common enough; you can see them as clearly as I. Indeed, you seem to have detected some such traces in poems of mine! Let your own self tell you. It has to be authentic, but it has to be kept in focus. The earlier record you let me read lost focus occasionally, blurred. Its subjectivity did not always come across. I think therein lies the problem: to keep that subjectivity that is the very life and heart of the material always at the subtle balance between the welter of personal emotion and the communicability of literary expression. To see from the outside in. I think the emotion recollected in tranquility applies, with qualification, here.

As to the form in which to couch it, a delicate matter. Some critic said Wolfe should have written his stories in the first person but I do not think so. My own taste is always suspicious of any "I" too minutely describing its own experiences. The removal to the fictitious "he" seems to me a more satisfactory treatment. On the other hand, such a situation would open up entire realms of relationships having to do with the art of fiction you may not be willing to assume. Use "he" and you almost have to have plot. Use "I" and the reader takes it as he takes experience: in a steady stream. Perhaps at the last the best solution would be the fictitious "I" you used in your first record. That aspect of it seemed convincing enough. I think I should be inclined to favor, everything considered, a continuation of that policy. Does this seem pompous? Forgive me if I adopt the critic's platform.

One thing more: I should like to make a proposition, one which is usually implicit and has been with us, but which now I should like to bring out in the open as a frank proposal of policy:— Let us always be fair with one another—about our literary work I mean. It is so hard to do, so easy to hurt another's feelings that often a person does not say what he feels he should say. I ask you always to jump hard on elements of my work you do not like, as you have done with these recent poems, and I ask of you the permission to do likewise with anything you show me. On any other basis the friendship becomes constrained and unnatural. Certainly the cords of such a friendship as ours can weather even the delicate edges of such matters as these. I know what your answer will be.

Bill

August 10, 1941
Los Angeles
ALS, 2 p., 1 sheet

Dear Bill—

Yours is a very good answer. By all means do what you are compelled to do by your own necessity. I shall always respect your integrity, even though I don't like what you write. Of course there is & will be a policy of utmost honesty between us as to what we may send one another. The difference between us is that you regard yourself as consecrated to writing, & I don't regard myself as any more than an *amateur* of letters. I agree with you as to what you say about the texture of your verse having improved. Much freer of padding. Another difference between us is that you're an idealist, self-confessed, & I'm not. I don't believe anything can be done to better the human kind. I don't give a fart about mankind or its supposed progress. All I care about is a few individuals, dead & alive. You are however in great company. Your poem about that sticks in my mind. Those great who have stood out against the roiling pack. Am reading Herbert Gorman's *James Joyce.* Would you like me to send it up? Joyce—a wonderful example for you of a man who never compromised.

Here's a sad clipping. Please return. I wish you could have known him [Parrish]. The most gallant man I've ever known. I shall worship his memory as I did him in life. Since the exhibit he went slowly down. He spent everything on it. Thank God we were able to arrange it while he was still alive. And how glad I am that you saw it. Well, he got weaker & weaker. Couldn't walk without MF's support. Could paint only a little every day. And the pain from his "phantom leg" became something horrible. He was so full of morphine that the shots became almost useless. A living hell. Buerger's disease. Of course he knew of his death sentence, since going to Mayo's [Clinic] last year. And so the gunshot. I am sure it was with MF's consent. I have only talked with her on the phone. We are fearfully sad.

I am thinking about a memorial volume, to be in the form of a book on him as a painter, with reproductions of his best works. God what a triumph his last two years—It beats Van Gogh & Gauguin!

Mailed you *Southern Review.* Send *Capricorn* when available. Express to university. Thanks for your remarks on my project. I hope to send you the journal in the autumn, when you are free. Don't fall in the syrup pot & keep that saccharometer out of your ass.

Yours
Larry

Aug. 10, 1941
Selma
ALS, 1 p.

Dear Larry:—

It is Sunday, and ordinarily I shouldn't be home. (The radio is fiddling away with some Latin American crap. God how German music is gradually being sneaked off the air!) Last Tuesday an accident in the syrup room crippled me up. The hot water pot that supplies the cappers forms lime (you know how a tea-kettle gets) which in turn stops up the pipe-line. When this happens during the run it means the lime has to be cleaned or the whole plant stops. You can imagine the confusion. The trouble is usually handled by shutting off the water and blowing the line with steam. However, the steam blowout is downstairs and the water valve upstairs at the tank, so that close coordination is impossible. After alternate openings and shuttings to blow the lime without avail, we got a further order to stop the water for one more blowing. But before we could get the valve closed those down below in their hurry turned steam in the line which came up into the tank with great force spewing boiling water all about. I was very painfully burned upon the right arm, shoulders and face. Spent two days in the local hospital, coming home Thursday night, and will be off work I don't know how long. This is a blow, as the ranch is becoming more realizable, and we were driving for every penny. I haven't spoken to the company about compensation. By working day and night I had been making over $50 a week, most of which we were saving, having pared our living expenses down next to nothing.

This episode has been the most severe pain I have ever experienced, and has made a great impression on my mind. I recall nothing of the burning itself except the overwhelming realization that something terrific was happening to me, the confusion no doubt stemming from the fact that the water was flying all over the room, obscuring my glasses, (which luckily saved my eyes). I can remember screaming "I'm scalded! I'm scalded!" and flinging myself backward. I turned and crashed against a syrup tank (itself containing near-boiling syrup) and bruised my hip so that I am limping yet from it. I ran toward the door and was caught and held by the two fellows with me. I remember very distinctly one part of my brain realizing that I was then perfectly safe, out of reach of the boiling water, and yet unable to stop the purely animal driving of my legs! It was not, however, until I was down in the first aid room that the full realization of the pain came to me. These past few days have been something of an ordeal. My arm is most badly burnt: my face only incidentally, for which my vanity has reason to be thankful!

Sincerely
Bill

Mon. Aug. 11, 1941
Selma
ALS, 1 p.

Dear Larry:

Your letter today, which I find very full. Am low. One of those hard weeks behind me, and a cold settling in from the wetness of hosing out the syrup room. Everything is stalled: the ranch hangs fire; my ms. returned from Macmillan, lies in the express office. I haven't even had time to fetch it. Where will it go next? God help it, that poor miserable unwanted sheaf. If the ranch deal fails perhaps I can publish it. If the ranch goes through it will never see print, or not for years; we will have buried ourselves under an immense debt.

As for any new direction I feel now that my didactic strain is concluded: the war poems etc. I've said what I must, and though the Churchill poem if completed would have taken a proper place with them, my mind does not take to its problems now, and besides it's only a variant of the pacifistic poems. I shall try for broader problems, greater lyricism again, greater poetry and imagery. I am still concerned about mankind, still engulfed in finding a morality of conduct; for I know as long as any man suffers at another's hand that same fate is open for me. You cannot permit error in the parts and achieve perfection in the whole. Perfection is unattainable: the nature of things forbids it; but I believe in the essential perfectibility in the relationships of man. For I am a man, and I am good, that I believe without arrogance. The goodness in me is the goodness of humanity, the heritage of the human tradition, to which all are eligible. (I have crossed a line out.) And we that are good will survive, or rather our goodness will survive as long as there are men, for ours is the true tradition. But my poems now will be poems, with live limbs, I hope, and sound parts.

A terrible thing, Parrish's fate. Before such a thing a man stands shriveled. Your projected volume sounds a very sincere and worthy thing.

The Joyce I've read—I think I commented upon it at the time.

The *Southern Review* I read. Blackmur's review is a superb piece. Today I send *Capricorn.* I will not fall in any syrup pots and I will make sure the saccharometer remains in its rack. Yes.

You're a swell guy, Larry
Bill

Poor Cooney. Poor Cooney. The poor restless pitiful bastard.
One of the events of the week—of the year—was a letter from Gilbert Neiman, who was here with Miller. He was acknowledging the *San Joaquin* I gave him. I gave it on an impulse, not thinking he would really care for it, but he does.

8-21-41
LA
ALS, 1 p.

Dear Bill—

I am disturbed to hear of your burns, & your loss of employment. Take care of yourself, now & later. Where is the ranch you hope to get?

Capricorn arrived & I have now read it. A rich compost pile of a book. It lacks the youthful lyric quality of *Cancer*, but it's more dynamite. The Western Union office part is magnificent.

I'll return it in a few days.

Later I'll send you the Miller-Fraenkel Hamlet letters, volume 2. I got a review copy from the *LA Times*. Have never been able to pick up volume 1, published in 1939, out of print now. Do you know it?

Just time for a note.

Larry

Aug. 24, 1941
Selma, Calif.
ALS, 6 p. 3 sheets

Dear Larry:—

It is now 12:32 this Sunday noon, and I have just switched off the radio upon the completion of the address of Winston Churchill. As these speeches continue it becomes ever more apparent that that man is in many ways the greatest man in the world today. I am impressed. We have had in America great men—the greatest being I suppose Abraham Lincoln, and it seems clear that Lincoln's greatness resides chiefly in the fact that he was able at times to sum up in eloquent and impassioned speech an idealism of such profundity that the total effect can be nothing less than heroic. But for eloquence and for passion it is my belief that Churchill goes beyond him. I have not studied Lincoln's speeches, though it is indubitable that parts of them are unimpeachable, but the total effect of a Churchill speech is of such magnitude that I confess I have to account my reactions to them as among the highest literary experiences I have ever known. Raymond Gram Swing once referred to them as "Mr. Churchill's Shakespearean speeches." We look back upon the great moments of English history, particularly those moments when the literary and historical processes mingle in an unexpected high, with a kind of smothered excitement and yearning. We can find comfort in the fact that not fifteen minutes ago we were participating in one of those moments and that we will wear in our minds the psychological effects of that experience to the very grave.

I do not mean to say that I believe Churchill's speeches to be perfect examples of literature. They are spotted with unforgiveable lapses—so many millions "of German cannon fodder have bit the dust" struck me as bad. But the dominant effect is essentially a poetic effect, with a poet's insight into speech figures and speech rhythms.

For Churchill embodies in his language and in his attitude all that I have been attempting to muster in the poems I have written that have sprung from the world situation. A kind of unquestionable morality pervades them; and you have the feeling that the eloquence is bred *of* the morality, which is of course, the very essence of greatness in any form; the eloquence rising through the morality, compelled and dictated by it, as if all the finer aspects of the man's character, of the race's character, of the very fiber and texture of the English tradition were flowering into an utterance that is overwhelming. And to realize the eloquence is to realize that the eloquence is indistinguishable from the morality, which is a truth that strikes at the very root of the work that I last sent you, and to which you objected. I may have failed in that work, but what I was doing, the direction that I was going, these speeches of Churchill's seem to me to prove right: the greatness of them is beyond the eloquence, but is, as I said, indistinguishable from the morality. It is in that inextricable fusion that the supreme participation takes place. To that I attempt, and in the light of that the attempt must be judged.

It will be with considerable surprise that, in the light of all this hailing of the genius of Churchill you read the enclosed poem. The poem is not new. It was written, or conceived, last April, and has lain this time in various stages of composition, as you know my habit to be. I suppose it would be more appropriate for me to write a poem addressed to Hitler, who is certainly barbarism undisguised. I have not done that because it is not necessary. The man is so very black that anyone with a spark of decency can perceive it. It seemed to me more necessary to point out that however much of the *Right* Churchill can claim, he cannot, from my standpoint, claim *all* the Right, the whole Right. If I agree with all the morality of

Churchill, his indictment of Nazism, his appeal to the courage of his people, his stubbornness under ordeal, his courage, all these very great and heroic qualities, I do not and cannot agree with his methods of applying them. I do not believe the great danger to civilization to be the immediate threat by any one faction so much as I believe it to be in the concept of war itself: the concept that force, a military strength, can achieve any permanent good. A finer and more significant attitude is contained in Churchill's address itself, when, if I remember rightly, he appealed to the conquered Greeks to make the Nazis "in spite of their brutal triumph, feel that they are the moral outcasts of the world." Therein lies the great truth, the great concept. It can only get used by submission, which is a terrible thing to contemplate, but it holds the seeds of salvation. I do not expect it to be used, for I do not think the men of the world, the great masses, have the morality to accomplish it. The human is yet so much animal: the immediate effects of submission are so compelling, and the immediate alternative so attractive, that no one not disarmed will consider it. It is used as a last resort instead of a first resort, with the result that all these bloody ages, these brutal generations, merely repeat themselves. But even convinced of its inapplicability to humanity as it now stands does not deter me from advocating it, and standing by it whatever comes. We have only one obligation: not to [be a] traitor [to] the finer aspects of our beings. When we traitor those we traitor the race: we commit an act the consequences of which are of so much greater consequence than our own immediate fate that our action becomes momentous.

All these points are not brought out in the poem, and in that it is weak. I offer nothing opposed to Churchill's philosophy of military resistance but the vague concept of "love among men." This is the basic implication of course, and I hope it's an implication that gets across, but I am not ready or able at this time to make a detailed point within the poem itself. However, I do not think the work is quite completed. I had been working on it for an hour before Churchill began speaking, and laid it aside to hear him.

This poem, with the other two I enclose, are the three unfinished ones that I mentioned when I sent my ms. to you.

They are more recent, dating just before my cannery work, since which I had not written until I was burnt. Whatever money I lost, I yet have been able to write, which somewhat soothes me for my injury. I have completed these poems and started another in this last week. My arm is healed, and I should have worked at the cannery these last 3 days, but the doctor took his annual vacation this week, leaving specific orders with the nurse not to let me return to work before he could see me. I receive compensation after the seventh day of unemployment, 60% of 90% of my average, whatever that means.

This Churchill poem is the last war, or pacifistic poem I intend to write, as I have exploited the theme, and as the relaxation of tension in my own personal situation with the Draft Act has given me opportunity to turn my mind to kinder things. You understand that even though I still undertake what you call "abstract" poems I expect always to deal with personal angles as they come up, so that my work will have a greater variety and scope than if I confined myself to any one aspect. I picked up the 2nd volume of Amy Lowell's *John Keats* and have just finished it: the harrowing death, the terrific love affair. As far as the love affair goes my own period of separation from Edwa when we were newly in love had all the aspects of Keats' and Fanny Brawne's. I imagine that some of my letters must have been as hysterical if not so eloquent as his. It is amazing the way these things resolve themselves. If those two people—why speculate? Certain it is that Keats was far superior to Shelley. This reading has taken me to his poems, and I find I have broadened to the extent that I find them absolutely magnificent, something I could not have said a year ago. His poems will have a very beneficial effect upon my own mind and hence upon my verse I am sure. I simply know more about poetry after reading Keats. He wrote much tripe of course, but his great odes are towers.

Your letter arrived yesterday. The ranch is [a] half-mile south of here (toward town) on the road that skirts behind our present place. A 14-acre place with a nice-looking house. Small, the place, for a ranch, but especially good soil, and I hope it will work out. We will load ourselves beneath a terrific debt. $5,500, all borrowed! The prospect staggers me, but such a place is our only salvation. As it is now any quirk of fate might send us into the city, or across the country. With a piece of land we will be able to survive. I will send Miller's *Max* book. This is the sailor's, and irreplaceable. I break his trust by lending it, but I know what it will mean to you and I know how carefully you will watch it.

Bill

September 7, 1941
Los Angeles
ALS, 2 p., 1 sheet

Dear Bill—

Sunday evening. A big day. Henry Miller spent the morning here in my study. He smoked many cigarettes; between us we devoured a large bunch of grapes. He came to say good-bye. In a day or two—as soon as he sells his Buick—he leaves by train for San Francisco, thence to N.Y. via the northern route. We had two previous sessions in the past week. Lunches in the village. He would come walking into the Order Dept. at the Library, his bald head gleaming, his round face a great friendly smile, a few books under his arm. God, if the spinsters who work all around me only knew! The man is a great man. His life, his work, himself are one. I hate to see him leave! He gave me his *World of Sex*. Have you read it? If not, & if you can send me *Max*, I'll send them back together. I hope to get review copies of the Colt Press Greek book & Laughlin's *Wisdom of the Heart* when they appear. I am embarking on a comprehensive collecting of Miller's works, both in periodical and book form. He is apparently to be to me at this epoch of my life (I was 35 the 3rd!) something of what Jeffers & Lawrence were to me 10 years ago, decreasing in intensity between then & now. It's been nearly two weeks since your *fine letter & poem* on Churchill. The other two poems are good. I should like to keep them. There is a sureness & tightness about your lines that marks a real advance.

I wish I could write you oftener, & longer letters. I hope to see you around Christmas. Have saved 6 days of vacation &

plan to go to Berkeley. Pickett is on the verge of going to press [*sic*] & should be out at Christmas. [*sic*] I hope to see it completed when I am there. [*sic*] [The bracketed "sic" insertions are Powell's.]

We have been on the beach at Santa Monica every Saturday afternoon since return from east. Swimming & playing catch with bean bags.

Was *bowled over* the other night by Shostakovich's 1st symphony. Have been hearing it for 6 years or so, each time with increasing emotion. It's a great work. 21 years old when he wrote it!

I hope this finds you entirely recovered. Get that ranch. Miller spoke feelingly of his visit with you, of your transparent honesty, & of the ocean-like vineyards. I too remember my visit of 2 years ago & hope to see you in the bareness of winter. Greet Edwa & yourself.

Your affectionate
LC Powell

Mon. Sept. 24 1941
Selma
ALS, 8 p., 4 sheets

Dear Larry:—

If you have it at hand, I should like you to read Randall Jarrell's note to his poems in the New Directions volume *Five Young American Poets.* It has been some time since I read it, and I have lent the book out, so that I cannot immediately refer to it as I should like to do; but my mind has been turning upon these problems and it seems best to write of them now rather than wait until later. I mention this article because it seems to me to be a sort of culminating point—a conscious peak, or break, between two trends, a very definite mark in the poetic change which is being manifested all about us wherever we look today. The article seems significant to me because it is the summoning up, by an exponent of what appears to be a rising school, the qualities of the poetic body against which that school is making its revolution, and it does a good job, I think, in a very striking manner.

The dominant school of criticism today is what has been accurately called "neo-classicism," and I think that although the vast body of poetry being written is surely Romantic (as Jarrell points out, even the "classicists" write "romantic" poetry) yet the most serious of the new poets, the men most conscious of what they are about, who are not content to merely run in the groove and duplicate the attitudes so plentiful about them, the men who are striving to make their expression serve their intellectual tendencies, these men are doing all in their power to break the dominant molds of the day and return poetry to what they see as more healthful and vital channels. That they are not succeeding I do not doubt. I think the poetry of this *Five Young American Poets* volume is enough testimony to that. But with so much critical theorizing, and so much creative attempt being directed that way, the influence is very apt to be marked. Certainly any poet such as myself, who is not an intellectual, not a classicist, nor a neo-classicist, who has been fostered on what all these men are now beating against with all their strength, certainly such a one cannot ignore what will so much concern him. Because, for some time now, any book of merit published will be scrutinized by these men, and they are of enough weight that though they cannot kill a man off, they can isolate him, and make him appear as a belated outgrowth of something vanishing. They can ignore and injure, and they can possibly ruin.

I do not mean to say, as I have suggested, that I consider these people as enemies. A year ago I would have. But the year has brought me so far, and I have seen so many new possibilities in the language, and so much that is bad in sources I was following, that I tend to repudiate with them much of the recent past, though for my own part, not accepting all their methods and aims for the future. I find myself less and less sympathetic to such people as Lawrence and Wolfe, and in poetry, Jeffers. The aesthetic theory upon which they operated seems to me to be more and more limited. I mean the theory of writing "hot off the sensibility," the theory of sensuous reaction to the experience immediately transferred to the flow of language. You will recall about two years ago a letter of mine condemning Hardy. I attacked him for using a metaphysical (intellectual), or philosophical (abstract) language, to convey what seemed to me then that which should have been treated as Lawrence would have done—the sensuous or sensory reaction to nature. I no longer hold those opinions. And my work is tending more and more to compromise between the method of Hardy and the method of Lawrence. For me this is perhaps natural, I have been writing via the "sensory response" method for a good many years now, and there isn't much more I can do with it. Not only that, but my change is as much a change of philosophical attitude as it is a realization of the exploitation of a technique. Less and less, as I grow older, do I find my response to experience to be sensory—an immediate and consuming sensorial reaction. More and more as I mature am I becoming reflective and meditative—not in any sense of posturing as the learned thinker, for I am not that and hope never to acquire the more ludicrous aspects of such a character—but simply that I find less satisfaction in the sensorial experience *per se*. Where a sexual orgasm used to be a complete experience of itself, a total engulfment in the one overmastering sensation, the joy in that act is become less immediate and more detached. The facets of experience that *surround* the phenomena of sex, the pattern of daily life, the emergence through years of relationship of a spiritual love of a very high order, the recognizing of human traits and human characteristics in what was once almost completely biological: all these factors make the preliminary or associational characteristics of *sex* of increasing importance to me. This is for me no new thing—I have been aware of it for some time. But I use it here to illustrate what is happening throughout all my fields of experience to a greater degree, and it is happening in my poetry. It is not, however, happening enough. Although I can now find little pleasure to take in the poetry I have written between *San Joaquin* and through "The Masculine Dead" (which I see as the culminating and final manifestation of all those years of the sensorial method) even so my new poems contain too much of it to suit me. I feel as if the "making tides of energy" as Blackmur calls them, come from that same source of my mind, and it is as if my new method is a restraining order, or controlling force on what is basically unchanged. I make my best images, my best figures, out of the sensorial response, but I make my best organization, my best technical usage of speed-variation, rhythm, emphasis, etc., plus the ground work, the idea-content of my poems out of the emergent attitude. It seems to me that I have not yet achieved that welding of impulse and direction that will make the resolved and yet spontaneous poetry I am seeking.

Which brings me back to the neo-classicist movement and my own relationship to it. These men fail as poets, it seems to me, because they are so conscious of their historical position that they are afraid, literally, to move. They are suspicious of what to them must be called "lyricism," the flow of feeling, upon which all important literature of the last two or three decades has been based. Yet they cannot achieve effect without it. I think the authentic poet is possessed of a kind of fatal hardiness. He somehow fails to be frightened by all the literature behind him. He feels his response to language, and he accepts it, and he lands upon the particular literary situation with all the resources at his command. Poets rush in where literary historians such as Jarrell fear to tread: and it is only fair to add that they die by thousands. But they do rush in. And sometimes there comes one of great poetic sagacity, with talent and insight, and a knack of seeing what is good and what is bad or rather, what is *authentic* in language and what not authentic. He may not achieve it very often. Poets writing in times of great stress and change (and all Romanticisms have been born of such times) are doomed to a terrific amount of wastage—the ground pours out from under them, and material dies at their hands terribly—but they do see, the good ones, and all that they do which dies, bad as it is, is yet in the direction, in the attempt to achieve the authentic experience duplicated in the authentic language, and when they click as they do about six or seven times in a lifetime, then you have something. You have what Classicism and Romanticism (the formulization, the stylization of their loosely-classified tendencies) fall down before—a poetry that emerges beyond classification, and exists in the consciousness of the race. That is where I differ from the neo-classicists. I am willing to take the risks, the terrific risks of the mortality rate that is the Romantic method; because I know (and Jarrell admits) that romanticism is the only way to achieve effectiveness in literature until the dominant characteristics of life themselves outlive that tendency. I do not think the risks are as great as Jarrell puts them: for if you cannot realize poems more violent and explosive than those romanticisms have produced, you can realize poems more ordered, more sustained, more moulded, more resolved, fuller, closer, richer, the "lyricism" of romanticism (Blackmur's "making tides of energy"), served up in all that synthesis the language is capable of. That is why I am willing to stand between these modern factions and learn from the one while I draw from the other. It is the only way I see at this time.

* * *

Fri. Oct. 3—I'll get that *Max* down!

My work hangs on. Nights, mostly. Never have I worked so late in the year there. My nice autumn vacation has been plundered. The ranch deal fell through, but we are dickering for a less expensive place farther north. Perhaps.

Your last letter was very enjoyable; and we hope you can come through. It seems ages since you were here, and Fay has never been here has she? That will be fine. Edwa is maturing as a sculptor. She does fine work, what she does. I myself am very interested in the field and where I once was all vague before a piece now have dominant beliefs, reactions, and theories! Atkisson, my friend the Winters man, tears my poems apart, leaving me hopeless for half a week after each session. A marvelously fine fellow, personally. He gets his press soon. The *Silver Bough* came. I sent two of [the] best poems on request (via you, thanks). They were accepted a month ago, but today's mail returned them. They have folded. Have seen *Furioso* mag from Yale?

Bill

October twenty six
nineteen forty one
Selma Calif.
ALS, 2 p., 1 sheet

Dear Larry:—

I can't remember posting the letter, but since I can't find it, I must have. I can't even remember what was in it, so much time has gone by. It must be a couple of months since you wrote, and I'm sorry not to have answered sooner.

The peach pack shut down about the last of August, but the fig pack continued through September, and just into October: an unprecedented situation here. Work was mostly late. Towards the last we'd pack from about 6 in the evening to one or two o'clock. That gave me my days free, and I was doing good work writing. Edwa's school started about the 20th. Anyway, when the fig pack closed down the 3rd or 4th of October I decided to try the warehouse. I wanted my usual vacation as badly as ever, but we were close to getting a ranch then (we've been close to getting three now) and money seemed the thing. I have never before worked in the warehouse, in all my years at Libby's since 1927. I wanted to break my pipe-laying habit, which is really too hard work, and there is a possibility that the warehouse work will continue through the winter, though that seems unlikely. We work a five-day week and get 60¢ per hour. Three rainy days, now, which I'm used to having at home, I've had to work. I mention this because my best writing is done on rainy days. I haven't done much else but work. Little writing, which is infuriating. It takes so much time to live. Financially, we're better off than ever before. I was getting 70¢ in the syrup room and that counts up, though I suppose it is chicken-feed to the defense workers. My kid brother was through today. He superintends an assembly line at the big Lockheed plant in Burbank; 600 men under him. Draws down a cool $320 per month. When he started there 3 or 4 years ago they had 1200 men. They now have 50,000. That staggers me. What kind of an age do we live in? And what are we to think, we who try to wrest some sort of pattern out of the chaos, what are we to think to see these men, these terrifying modern men, drift through such a phenomenon as casual as I walk this vineyard. My brother, my kid brother, little Lloyd, Lloydie we used to call him, holding under his hands and shaping it—so much terror so much destruction! They know not what they do.

I have discarded most of the pacifist poems, though I may change back. That leaves about eight or nine for the past year's labor. I've a couple new ones to send soon, and a revision of "Though lying with woman" which is now perhaps my best poem. Do you remember how MacIntyre in his critique of *San Joaquin* told me to read Hopkins? I couldn't see it at that time. I was still after sensuous tonal modulations. I read him much now, and Donne. You'll notice in those last poems how the abrupt sounds, the th's, p's, g's are cropping up. I'm getting toughness. Hopkins carried that to its extreme. What I want to do is inject that element into my work without destroying the tonal background—a combination of expansion and resolution. There are certain elements in great poetry that Hopkins doesn't attempt. What I am trying is to mould the elements of great verse: the tonal fullness, the expansive completeness of music, and this new tough emphasis, this quality of aboutness. It's not new. Shakespeare did it the best of all. The more I find out about poetry the greater I see that man is.

This man Gilbert Neiman, down there, the man who came with Miller—do you know anything about him? He writes good letters, and he certainly likes my poetry. He translated Lorca's *Blood Wedding* for New Directions, but I've never seen it.

I'm ashamed not to have sent the *Max*. Edwa bound it up, but the end papers aren't in it yet. I promise to get it off. My whole concern in literature is away from the Lawrence-Miller-Jeffers school—the sensibility school.

Can you send your journal now? I've time now, nights. Don't take my shameful posturing about "honest" seriously, as if I meant to tear it to pieces just to display my arrogance. I don't know what got into me. For I know what a journal is. I know it's a personal record and I'll treat it as such. Please send it, Larry.

The year turns. Unusual prolonged autumn rains have soaked the ground. There is no dust. All the leaves yellow. Cool, now, nights, and our old wood stove feels fine. Ah me, another autumn. I'm racing toward 30, and life holds off. But I'm glad my work wasn't accepted for publication. There is much to be done. New techniques to iron out, new states of being to master. It takes so much time: and we have to waste so much in sheer grubbing. But that is what makes the states of being isn't it? Without resistance one would be nothing. There would be no need to make poems. To do all you can with what you have.

Edwa's sculpture library is getting along. Bought $42.00 worth in one bundle, mostly volumes of European carvers. What a superb thing sculpture is. Next to poetry and music it is tops. My own library comes along also. Have bought 5 *Young American Poets;* Spender's *The Still Centre;* Dylan Thomas' *The World I Breathe;* M. Moore's *Selected Poems;* Frankenberg's *The Red Kite* (remaindered, not good); have ordered Schwartz' *In Dreams Begin Responsibilities;* Auden's *On This Island;* Treece, 38 *Poems;* Eliot, *East Coker, Dry Salvages.* Tom Bogg's anthology has come out. He cut me out cold without a word, and I'm going to blast the son of a bitch.

Bill

30 October 1941
Los Angeles
ALS, 2 p., 1 sheet

Dear Bill—

You don't know how welcome your letter was! It's been a couple of months since I last heard from you. About once a year I suffer a complete physical collapse, & have to lie on my back for a couple of days, completely idle. No cold, no symptoms, other than a paralysis of body and will. Have just to lie quiet, & wait for the reservoir to fill up. October is always a wonderful month for me—exciting & abundant. This one was no exception, but I am paying for it now in two days of exhaustion. So you see how welcome was your letter!

The only reason I haven't sent the journal is that I've needed it for reference. Last weekend I wrote the first of what I envision as 5 studies of women, to be called "Quintette." God knows why I do it! It's hard to do when one is as settled in life as I am, to go back 10 years & live again in what Miller calls the Land of Fuck. And yet I have to do it. I feel compelled to round out & make a pattern of that part of my past. "Why is it these things will not pass for me, but stretch out hands, reach down, & demand recording?" So Fisher queried in the *Ghost*.

If you haven't already sent, don't send the *Max*. I have located a copy. Miller writes from New York. I've met Neiman only once, with Miller, & must confess I looked less at him than I did at his wife. Two weekends ago we spent at Hemet with MFK Parrish. Heard about his last days. A story of heroic courage to tear your very guts out. Gangrene was starting in his remaining leg; would have lost it in another week. Painting arm was going numb; could hold the brush only 10 minutes and then it would drop. Would have lost both arms, then would have lived on, a head, a torso & a powerful heart. Said this was not a dignified way for a man to live, so ordered everything, wrote a letter to the coroner, exonerating his wife; painted a *last* picture, a nude of his wife, his first & last portrait of her. Cleaned his brushes, destroyed the paintings he didn't want to survive him. Wrote with paint on his palette "Finis." Shot himself through the heart. O the courage it took to leave his beloved. Naturally she went through hell with him, & has been sometimes nearly out of her mind since. But she too is a wonderful human being.

I find myself lying awake at night thinking about it.

Good to hear of your activities. Greet Edwa & yourself.

Larry

He left me his clothes. We were the same size.

Nov. 14, 1941
Selma
ALS, 2 p., 1 sheet

Dear Larry:—

From your letter, I surmise my next to last one never arrived. Can't imagine what I did with it, as it has not shown up hereabouts, and we never throw such stuff away. What it contained I cannot remember, but it acknowledged receipt of your announcement of your possible visit, and urged it, which I now repeat and emphasize. It has been two years since you were here, and Fay has not been here, and we are looking forward to the both of you.

A ghastly thing you write, of Parrish. The imagination stops at such borders as that. What lies in those regions is incomprehensible to the normal mind. I mean, the being itself not afflicted. We stand outside and look in, like idiots staring.

My cannery work continues. The past week has been very hard. I have been trucking (hand truck) from the very fast labelling crew (these No. 2-1/2 size cans you see on the shelves) and every day has been bad. Through carelessness I neglected to purchase new shoes when my old ones wore out, and my feet broke down. My eyes, afflicted now with some chronic eyelid irritation which I have had 4 or 5 years, got worse and things were bad. I don't understand why it should be, but, although organically I am sound I am constantly pestered by annoying minor troubles. I am now, and have been for years, treating 4 different kinds of skin irritations. Then my eyes. My teeth have troubled me all my life. Now my feet. God damn it all. Job's boils indeed!

It looks as if the poems from the *San Joaquin* volume to "The Masculine Dead" will see print. A few days I should know and really a story it is. After things develop I shall relate.

No poetry gets written—that is the bad part. I get worried when I think of so much time going by, and nothing done. I'm simply too tired of nights. And also my poetic problem is more complex and hence more psychologically delicate:—I mean a greater emotional synthesis seems to be required, which is more rarely achieved. My literary problem is much greater than the more simple ones of *San Joaquin,* but if a corresponding heightening in quality can be gained, I shall regard it as ample compensation.

Have you seen *Invitation to Learning*? There are some good things in that book. Cairns comes out far better than on the air. I remembered the night on *Moll Flanders* as being particularly good and the reading affirms it. Only thing I can think of for comparison are the Goncourts' records of conversation with the greats, and these are superior—I mean the present discussions. Some very fine things. I benefited vastly from it.

You spoke of a recent unusual musical experience in the Russian composer's 1st symphony. Guess what my own has been—Mahler's song-cycle *Das Leid von der Erde.*

The year whirls. The autumn's rush over. This is the best of the year, right now, and I cannot enjoy it.

Bill

Has Tate's review of the *Ghost* appeared?

November 19—1941
Selma, Calif.
ALS, 10 p., 5 sheets

Dear Larry,

Milton in his blindness is reported to have practically killed his three daughters dictating *Paradise Lost,* but I hardly think that I in my blindness will enforce a like fate upon Edwa. At least she has consented to write this one letter for me (isn't this stupid?) for my eyes have given out completely yet there are things I should like to tell you. As for my eyes my left one is closed with an inflammation of the cornea and my right one seems unable to carry on by itself. I am not able to work this week but expect to be perfectly healed by next week.

The two letters I enclose are answers to your last ones. The first is a couple of months old and one I thought I had sent (Bill forgot to reckon with his wife's carelessness) it turned up in the pocket of the car and I send it without reading it or it would probably not get off at all. The second one I wrote some days ago and am only now getting around to mailing it, other than that they speak for themselves. The big news mentioned in the last one is this. The Sunday before Armistice Day Carothers who, as you know, has been in the army since March came walking through the vineyard with a bundle of hot Jazz under one arm, Schnabel's rendition of Bach's Italian

Concerto in F Major under the other and a six-dollar briar loaded with 30¢-an-ounce tobacco clamped in his jaws. After the music and the necessary exchange of information he declared he had a proposition to broach. He has been playing poker heavily ever since entering the army—indeed, ever since we have known him. Most of the records in this house were bought from his winnings—and this time he was well heeled. I had told him last June what Boggs had said concerning Decker as a publisher (Boggs's estimate you will remember was at that time for 80 dollars for a 48-page book) now Carothers wanted to finance "The Masculine Dead." He said he had 105 dollars loaned out in gambling debts, all cinches to pay the first of the month, not to mention the 25 or 30 on his person, and that he could think of no better way to spend it. He could not, he said, give it to his mother because he would have to explain how he made it and that would break the poor woman's heart. The only other recourse was to buy phonograph records. I urged him to do that. I told him printing costs had undoubtedly risen, that we would hardly be able to approach the price mentioned by Boggs in June but he insisted. I was sore put as to how to act but he was sincere enough and I guess I succumbed a little easier than I should have at any rate. I sent the "Masculine Dead" and all the poems between it and the *San Joaquin* volume to Decker for an estimate. Monday I received a reply from him. He wants very much to bring the volume out. He said prices would jump the middle of December but if we could proceed now he could bring the book out in a 300 volume [i.e., copy] edition for $85. That is surprisingly low and of course I accepted. Decker's method seems to me to be a very fair one. He charges only what it costs to print and depends on the sales for his margin. Many of the better younger poets are bringing their books out through him and he is in no way, I believe, to be confused or identified with the notorious "Vanity Press" racket. He publishes only books that he likes and he was enthusiastic about this one (I blush to write this—EE) to quote from his letter: "Let me say that I find the book most acceptable; I shall be proud to publish it under our imprint. I think that the title poem is what might be called an important poem; I think you need have no doubt as to its permanent value." And at the last,

"I will be anxious to hear from you; I want to do your book, for reasons entirely apart from financial considerations."

As to his judgement of the title poem you of course will demur but the father and son sequence will be there and all in all I am looking forward to the book's appearance. For I did sign the contract and the work will soon be under way. The contract, I guess, is a common one: I guarantee the work to be innocent. The publisher undertakes to publish the work "in such style as they deem best suited to its sale" in an edition of 300 copies at a catalogue price of not less than 1.50 nor more than 2.50, cloth style. I agree to underwrite publication. The publisher agrees to pay author a royalty of 60% on all copies sold not counting review copies. I get 50 free copies on publication. This last I do not intend to accept since Carothers is subsidizing the work (We're putting in only 30 ourselves), I owe it to him to sell all copies possible, hence I shall give none away as in *San Joaquin*. So that's the way it is. I don't know any other work in the world's past that saw the light purely from the good fortune of a poker player's hand! But that's the kind of fellow Carothers is. It may not seem like much money, not after Belt's backing of the *Ghost* and Ritchie's generosity with my book but Carothers comes from a family that has been on relief half of their lives. His father deserted his mother and left her to take care of the children herself and many a time they have known sharp need. Another person would be as close and grasping as they could be but Carothers even when making $20 a month as a student helper of a blind boy neglected his needs to buy records. There is that open-handed generosity about him that is amazing; when combined with his insight into poetry and music it makes him a really unique individual. He has stood by the "Dead" ever since it was written. He has enough faith in it now to make this gesture. You know of course what that means to me.

Decker seems to feel that with luck we can make this money back and I hope so too if only for Carothers' sake but I do not expect it.

The peculiar thing about the whole situation is that a letter arrived this morning from Wm. Roth of the Colt press asking to see the "Masculine Dead." I had sent him *San Joaquin* three months ago with a letter mentioning that I had a manuscript ready and asking if he would like to consider it for publication. Miller had advised me to this summer putting in a recommendation for me but after three months' wait without even an acknowledgement one naturally considered Roth to be uninterested. He is bringing out poems by Winters' group and I took it that his sympathies lay elsewhere. His letter came 2 days too late. So you can see it has been a rather full week so far. These things don't happen often. Not bringing your book out and going blind at the same time. Thanksgiving looms on the morrow, a day on which we have a little traditional feast, or have had heretofore. My favorite holiday in fact but tomorrow we will have to forego the usual festivities, things being as they are, but at any rate I hope this coming season will be a good one for you and am looking forward to seeing you here and I do not forget the imminent appearance of *Philosopher Pickett.*

Sincerely,
Bill

November 30, 1941
Los Angeles
ALS, 2 p., 1 sheet

Dear Bill—

I hope this finds your eyes recovered. Sounds bad. Thanks to Edwa for her very readable hand. Strange to read your thoughts in her writing! Presently unsure about seeing you Xmas. Plans now call for us to go to Avalon for a few days. Am looking forward to that. No crowds. Mild climate. Plan to walk and fish.

The plans for your Decker book sound very good. Carothers is [a] gentleman gambler. Sounds like a man after my own heart. I was a great crap shooter in high school & know the excitement of quick easy money. His putting it into records & books is a great gesture. So your book will be a creature of National Defense.

Whether or not I am enthusiastic over some of the individual poems, I heartily approve of your collecting the post-San

Joaquin work into a book & I look forward to its completion with real eagerness.

Miller writes from New York. Hope you read his book on Greece? Good. I wrote a squib about it for the local *Times.*

This autumn is a good one here in the canyon. The sycamores are putting on an extraordinary color show. Wonderful golden tones.

Listening to the NY Philharmonic & when it's over we are all going for a walk in the hills.

Take care of your ailments & beware of the one that gets us all: [drawing of skull & crossbones]

Larry

Dec. 18, 1941
Selma, Calif.
AL, 3 p., 2 sheets

Dear Larry:—

Shortly after my last letter, which was, you recall, dictated to Edwa, the Fresno specialist pronounced me cured and I returned to work in the warehouse. I worked a week, suffered a "relapse," and have been off since. The second "attack" was a bit the worse and held on longer, but I am now quite safe I think, though the dilation has not all passed.

Carothers came in the weekend before last (bringing me an imported Sasieni briar and bearing a Bach concerto!). He refuses to permit us to contribute to the "Dead," insisting that he wants to bear it all so that he may share in the "profits"! A strictly commercial enterprise, don't you know. He subsidizes the venture and, after it pays itself off, we share the gravy. Such an incredible idiot I never saw before. He knows as well as I it will never sell out. Peculiar fellow, a profound pacifist; but permitted himself to be inducted because he couldn't resist. Got in the clerical dept. so I suppose he's safe. Makes out court-martial reports. Lives in the same barracks with a young intellectual named Monroe who once read proof for Ritchie. The government is wasting money on fellows like

Carothers. Slip-shod, irresponsible, I don't understand what's kept him out of trouble. Writes superb letters (when he gets around to it) of camp life. A lost soul, really. Has practically ceased to read where once he read constantly. Lives only for poker and music.

Well, any comment now on the war is superfluous. Expect to be called up soon after the draft expansion, since Edwa is self-supporting. My pacifist's stand has been receiving some hard jolts lately. Friend, McKelvy, came down the other night and we got into it. Watkins is gone now, as I think I told you, and I have to sort of sustain myself. Not that I can't do it, but the pressure is increasing. The defense has so simplified its position it keeps pounding away on "We are right. We are right. There is no alternative we must fight." And they have a good case. A dominant Nazism would mean the destruction of just about everything most of us hold to. Or so it seems. The possibility has to be granted. It worries me that I should begin to have doubts now. When I went into this business I did so knowing that every possible situation had to be conceded *in advance* so that no matter [what] turn events took one would already have realized the reality of the situation and could meet it. I knew that unless I was prepared to be a pacifist under any situation there was no use being a pacifist at all. It makes me angry with myself that now emotional pressure from outside makes me question myself. Still, it's not the emotional pressure really—that only keeps me confronted with the basic problem, which is this: is civilization more endangered by total war or by the total domination of a ruthless terrible regime. I suppose the question will never be answered, for no people will ever bank on the less obvious alternative. And since it will never be answered I will always have doubts. But when I think, I know that the presence of doubts are not the signs of weakness; they are really only the signs that one is facing his problem. Weakness comes from yielding to doubts, and I have not done that yet. The trouble arises in the horror with which the enemy is constantly being described. That makes fear, naturally, and fear boosts doubt, so that after one of these radio pep talks that are constantly coming on, it's almost impossible not to doubt oneself. Did you hear the Anniversary of the Bill of Rights program? About the best program I've ever heard on the radio, I think. For the most part very effective. And of course they have a very good logical case. McKelvy came down right after that program: he has a fine mind, with great penetrating power, and when he got through with me I want to tell you I was pretty low. It hung on me like a black cloud for a day and a half. Then I got my balance again, as I always do, or at least always have, and I know I'm right. I'm a lot less hysterical about it than I was at first when it seemed to me imperial America was out to save good things mixed up in the bad. The good is being so emphasized now that the problem is simplified: are you willing to forfeit the obvious good things of the American way, for the dubious method of universal submission? That is a hard question. The facts are on their side, for all the good we know has come only by fighting for them: even the good of the pacifist, Christ, has been maintained by force of arms! The thing here is that no one has ever tried to make the goods rely on themselves alone. Not enough people believe it will work. The obvious thing is to reach for the sword, defend yourself, and then bring the good into being. That's what is said now: war is hell, yes, but only by war can we relieve ourselves of the possibility of war. But what always happens is no matter how hard you try to make a good peace after you've won, the sons of the men you killed hate you and rise up against you. I believe that the evils of Nazism are bred of the resistances to it. I don't mean to say that if Germany rules the world she will immediately become a softy and forgive it all. But we did that, after we beat Germany we felt guilty as hell. Only the bitter opposition of a certain group in power in France and England and here kept us from retracting most of our impositions. The hate went out of us. Might not it happen with the Germans?

So I go on—mulling these problems and many, many more aspects of these problems all day long. Back of it I have this bulwark: I cannot account for the world's action, but I can account for my own, and I have but one obligation: to conduct myself so that if everyone else did as I did there would be no trouble. But back flood the doubts—many and many, and the obligations.

What they will do to me I don't know. They may not even consider my grounds sufficient, in which case I have not heard what is being done when one still refuses. Heretofore, I believe, only bona-fide religious conscientious objectors were taken. One fellow I know, not a religious objector, they simply refused to classify. But now some provision will surely be made.

A nice article and a nice photo, Larry; by now you must have a bibliography of proportions!

1942: THE MASCULINE DEAD *AND* PHILOSOPHER PICKETT

January 2, 1942
Los Angeles
ALS, 2 p., 1 sheet

Dear Bill—

Back to work today after 8 days off. At the last minute we missed Catalina—boat service suspended. Bad weather kept us close to home. No trips farther than Bieler's in Altadena. And myself in a fruitful period, which I eagerly exploited. Now I am regretful at not having been able to come your way. We couldn't quite organize it. Takes effort & planning when children are involved. So the days have gone by, & the quiet cold nights holed up here in my study. Working on the European years. Two parts of five completed in first draft. Read back in your letters to your truly helpful notes on narrative of the college years. I think I am doing much better in this last work. Hard as hell to exhume the past; past loves, when you are happy in the present. Something Fay can hardly understand. Yet there is no help for it. I must do it. I must put it down, impose upon it a measure of order, extract from it all that was true & beautiful, make it live as long as our printing age shall live.

At the same time I have been carrying on several other projects. Cataloging everything printed by Ritchie, of which I have nearly all—some 200–300 pieces. Reading last proofs on the Pickett book. It's due the 20th of this month. And formulated & commenced a project to write a biography of my father.

Not to speak of reading Mac's *Faust,* Miller's *Wisdom* & Steinbeck's *Sea of Cortez.*

All in all a wonderful short vacation.

What do you do? What of the Decker book?

I think of you often.

How about the draft. Won't the condition of your eyes exempt you?

We are in a formidable anti-aircraft district, midway between the North American, Douglas & Lockheed plants.

Write.

Happy New Year [sic]
[*sic.*] to you both:

Larry

January 5, 1941 [i.e., 1942]
Selma
ALS, 2 p., 1 sheet

Dear Larry:—

Your letter today shames me. I felt guilty as hell for not writing, since this is your second. I have dug up this letter of some weeks ago; though it seems trite to me now, I will send it on. The doubts have vanished. I only worry about what will happen to me. Meanwhile, the days go on and no call.

My eyes are quite healed, and have been for days. I have been resting, however, to thoroughly gain my strength, so that a little cold will not set me back as heretofore. Today I went back to work at the pipe yard. The latest I have ever stayed away! It seemed intolerable, last night, to be going back there. But the actuality wasn't so bad as the anticipation. Only the getting up at 6:00 am when all is dark and icy cold, and the bitter cold of early morning is bad. Our wages have been raised from 40¢ to 50¢ per hour—far too low, of course, in relation. But then, they will always be so. I was quite welcome, as I have experience, where most of their men are new. I'm the best bander they have, which is a brag—but they tell me so to my face—and it makes me feel well that I can hold my own with practical men in a practical world. It's the same with syrup-making.

My poems go slowly. Am working on a couple new ones. Since I have discarded the pacifistic poems I have only about 10 pieces to show since "The Masculine Dead." But I'm very sure of those ten, and I know I haven't begun to tap the reservoir. Only things are so upset. But one thing this business has taught me: you can't write poems that will abide out of politics. One great lesson of the year 1941! Dorothy Norman of *Twice a Year* wrote me saying Miller recommended my work to her and that she would like to see some. I sent about seven, but said I wanted them all to be used or none—not in such flat terms, of course, but still that was the condition. They came back, of course. And I don't care. Really don't care. I never send off anymore. Never has magazine publication meant so little to me. Received the *Colossus* for Xmas, and have read a quarter. Superb! Really good, and I feel swell that Miller can keep on doing it! A real guy, that man, a real guy.

Drove to Berkeley New Year's eve, and spent a few days with the Watkins'. Rain all the way up, driving. A terrible trip, for one so little auto-wise as I. Buel is making warships—at $60.00 a week! My brother with Lockheed in Burbank has hundreds of men working under him and draws in over $300 per month. Root hogs! I refuse to be tempted. If I worked there, and they were bombed, and I were killed, I would die guilty. As it is, no matter what they do to me, I know I am innocent.

Berkeley was cold. We bought wood for Edwa's carving, and books. Such books we have now! I will hate to leave them. We left Saturday, missing the blackout. No loss.

Your letter was good. I feel your new work will be far superior to the journal you sent me.

The *Ghost* card is a good idea. Has Tate reviewed it? Any other new reviews of it?

Nothing on the Decker book.

Bill

Feb 7, 1942
Los Angeles
APS

Dear Bill—

What's become of you? Are you applying for Phelan fellowship? It's for poetry alone this year, & I think you'd have a good chance. I hope you are not in a draft snarl. Let me hear from you.

Larry

P.S. Heard Bruno Walter do Mozart's 39th!!

Feb. 22 1942
Selma
ALS, 1 p.

Dear Larry:—

It has been long since I have written you; and longer, save for your brief card, since I heard from you, so that there is probably much of interest that we both will have now forgotten. Certainly an examination of the immediate past reveals little I could count as momentous.

Josephine Miles wrote from Berkeley some time ago pointing out about the Phelan being exclusively for poets, and saying that if I competed Dr. Ben Lehman would write covering my entry. I remembered 1939, however, and declined. She wrote again a brief card urging me to reconsider; it arrived the same day as your own, and I decided to try. It took a telegram to get an entry there on time so late was it. I sent carbons (as she suggested) to her to give Dr. Lehman in his covering letter; and he wrote immediately the enclosed letter. Please return it.

Work goes on day after day and little writing gets done. The Draft board has let me alone. We are trying to buy land again, and think we can this time. Two adjoining pieces 8-½ acres and 6-½ acres closer in toward town, and are planning a house on them which I think I can build. These occupy much speculative thought; and if acquired will occupy more time, which I will begrudge, but which I will yield for the future enlargement on it I hope to attain. To work on the future these days is little more than an instinctive thing. With millions dying every week the world over, to entertain any certainty of continued existence is the sheerest sort of optimism. With this war loose in the world not a man nor woman nor child can count his future. I simply cannot encompass it. Where before I was angry and heroic and determined, I am now numbed by the realization of what goes on out there. I think I have spouted off to you a bit too much about this war: I know it has played too big a part in my few letters, but it rides my mind. I see so clearly in some respects; and so obscurely in others. There is so much of it beyond all of us; and we are carried beyond human relationships into metaphysical potentialities.

The mouthed terms Good and Evil, which are bandied about in philosophical discussions, are presented to us in all their starkness, and we find out how weak and futile we sounded when the Thing confronts us.

I received the card announcing *Philosopher Pickett*, but have not bought a copy as yet. I have heard not one word from Decker since mid-December, and am mystified as to his silence. His 1942 catalogue appeared listing my work. He describes it as being in Bodoni types, and selling at $2.00. I wrote him again at that time, but no word comes in. Write him for the catalogue. MacIntyre is bringing out a book with him also.

Carothers sent the string quartet version of Art of the Fugue (what a magnificent work) and Beethoven Trio Opus 97. There should be more to say, but I cannot remember it. I am sunk within myself most of the time; and it requires effort to break the spell.

Bill

Mar. 1, 1942
Selma
ALS, 2 p., 1 sheet

Dear Larry:—

When I went to work Thursday morning I left the house in a horrible mess—three days' dishes on the drain; the rugs filthy, clothes heaped about the living room, books, ms., records, piled upon them, the beds unmade, certainly as bad as our house ever gets, and the house of two people who both work out and who both begrudge every minute taken from their activity can get very bad. When I came in tired that evening about 5:00, I opened the door and the front room was straightened up a bit and I knew Edwa had got back before me. But there was a small grip on the floor and a case for carrying records, (phonograph records), and a man was in the kitchen with Edwa. Then Edwa said "Bill, this is Robert Duncan." I said "hello," and we shook hands; and I passed beyond them to put my lunch pail down in that vague trance-like feeling you always have when thrown unexpectedly into a strange situation—one half of your mind buzzing about sucking at the tubes of memory, past experience, while the other observes and records what is immediate. I took the man for the phonograph technician, since we were thinking about having one out and this fellow resembled one we have here. But then I knew that couldn't be, for this wasn't the man. The name meant nothing. He and Edwa went on talking over a cluttered table, having coffee. They were talking about modern art, about Miro, Arp, Klee; then as I came in the room again an allusion was made about poetry. My mind had all this time been crawling about like Jeffers' spider-in-its-web-image; and suddenly every thing came clear, of course, of course, for Robert Duncan was Robert Symmes, the poet, the editor of *The Experimental Review.* He had come in from the East to his parents in Bakersfield 3 days before and was now hitchhiking up to Berkeley. He had sent a letter, but it arrived after he did! In Selma he inquired where we lived and walked out here. No one home of course. A neighbor told him where Edwa taught and at noon took him out there. She didn't recognize him either, but they straightened it out. She had him take the car back home and then call for her at three. During that interval he did the dishes for us! After I got my clothes changed he began playing his records. Readings of poetry by Stein and Eliot. Abstract Cuban music of a surrealist twist. Modern abstract music by Stravinsky, Schoenberg. I watched him. Small-boned, dark haired, olive-skinned, an odd face. One eye a bit off, but only sometimes. Wore a Big Yank workshirt and a green jersey sweater with elbow-length sleeves. Grey pair of trousers with a large hole in the seat which he didn't discover until late that night and then kept his hand over. A curious odor about him. That night things weren't very free, but the next day I laid off work and things went better. Sometimes there was something womanish about him. When he got up to change the records he walked with that girlish sway characteristic of the homosexual. When talking about something of concern such as poetry or art or life—that is, when he is very intent, his eyes widen over the soft outline of his lower face rather unbelievably. They show much white then, and his countenance takes on a strange aspect of heightened awareness, almost of illumination. Out in the sun where his face naturally contrasts against the light he is another person, rather good looking and sophisticated in appearance. From his poems and letters, I expected a person definitely "odd." He is not. He talks very sanely, evenly, matter-of-factly—though incessantly. Generally his notions are quite sound. His tastes in poetry are sound, and in literature in general, apart from the natural divisions of taste, I would say very sound. His interest in abstract art and music I don't understand but he doesn't ride them: merely indicates them unobtrusively. He isn't mealymouthed about sexual issues, but he never made a pass at me! Friday we went over my poetry and he gave me very good criticism. What was strange was that the thing he criticized when merely evident in my poetry literally abides in his own. There never was, I am sure, a greater divergence between critical insight and creative practice in a writer. His critical views are the antithesis of his own poems, and that is really beyond me.

He stayed Thursday night, Fri., and most of Sat. We went up to Fresno then, and he hitched on up to Berkeley—or so I suppose. After he had gone it took me all last night to get back in the groove. A most unusual man (age 23). Really a most unusual man. One of the most unusual I ever met.

Bill

March 3, 1942
Los Angeles
ALS, 4 p.

Dear Bill—

Glad to have your letters. It is January 5 that I last heard from you, & I feared that you had gotten yourself hauled off to a c.o. camp. I wonder if you received the Fiske paper & the little Rounce & Coffin history, both of which I mailed you during the past 2 months? As I had not heard from you, I have been holding a copy of my Pickett book earmarked for you. So I am glad to hear that you have not bought one. Putting yours in the mail now. Also a Twain letter reprint, just to keep the chinks plugged in your Powell collection.

Have been busy so far this year, & probably will be for the balance. Did I tell you I've started a biography of my father? Finished "Quartet." Am tempted to send you the ms., which is in a ledger; but shall wait until I have typed & revised, in the one process I really can't tell what I have. I blow hot & cold—mostly the latter. But it's been a wonderful winter—to look forward through each day at the Library to the quiet evening at my desk. Nights are wonderfully peaceful here in the canyon. Everything's up in the air as far as my professional life is concerned. The war has held everything up.

The anti-aircraft uproar the other night was a fearful thing. I awoke about 3 a.m. Was it thunder? Unsure at first. And then I knew. It was gunfire. Jesus Xist, I was afraid! Waked Fay & we crept to the open window & there in the sky were fantastic orange trajectories. And the steady roar of many batteries firing. No planes heard. So back we crept & to sleep. Bad business. And worse to come.

Sorry your Decker book is held up. He announced Mac's last August; Even gave the pagination. But it didn't appear until two weeks ago. I'm doing a notice of it for the *LA Times.*

Thanks for sending Lehman's letter. Looks hopeful. He is highly influential up there. Miles ought to help too. I am glad you got in under the wire.

Quite a visit you had from Duncan-Symmes. In his drifting habits sounds a bit like Henry Miller.

Levin's book on Joyce is excellent. Don't miss it.

For the rest I have been reading a number of books on Burgundy—travel and history. Was started by the thing I was writing & found it hard to stop. I loved that land while I was there, & in retrospect even more so. Especially since France has undergone such a change. The nostalgia & the pity.

Greetings Wm.

Larry

Mar. 5, 1942
Selma, Calif.
ALS, 2 p., 1 sheet

Dear Larry

On reading your letter today I decided one of my letters must have become lost, for you say my last was Jan. 6, and I was certain I had written since then. But then when I looked in the file and saw your last letter was Jan. 2 I realized everything must have gone through. I thought I acknowledged the Fiske, if not I say now it is a well-written, well-rounded, competent and interesting account of one phase of one man's activity. The Rounce and Coffin Club Anniversary number was very well done and exhibits one of your finest literary traits—your wit. You use wit very effectively, giving your writing a pungency and natural ease that is absorbing. Your letters exhibit it also. One of the best aspects of your style.

The Pickett hasn't arrived, nor the Twain, but many thanks for the copy. I shall read it with great interest, and write then. Any reviews?

Also I look forward to the "Quartet" typescript; and note with interest and approval your projected biography of your father. I don't think I could write one of my own; I'm afraid my emotional cant would discolor even so packed and unbelievable a life as his.

The "air raid" must have been something! Nothing like that here yet, of course, but even the incessant ominous drone of our own planes gets me.

Two bad reports tonight—no more rubber [tires] (E's school is 4 miles off) and no more exemptions for farmers. We hope to own land before the month's out. Just think, I haven't once been called up for questioning! I can't understand it. How long will they let me alone? If I only knew.

Am looking forward to Levin's book on Joyce, but no such books as that get here. I'll buy it one of these months, but now every cent goes for the land.

And all my purpose. Me, a poet? Not now I'm not. Everything hangs, including my mind.

Finally a letter from Decker—no book till June, now. He says poetry sales are booming daily. Maybe Carothers will at least get his money back! If it sells out my half of profits will be enough to finance my next one.

Is Mac's book good: i.e., better than *Poems* or *Cafés?* How is the *Faust?* Is Mac still at U.C.?

Look at the stylistic qualities of this letter—shows what a state I'm in. Forgive. Said an Okie to me today with vast good humor: "God damn it, Bill, you stand there with one finger in your mouth and one in your ass, and every time some one speaks to you, you change hands!" Same man once said I was "just like a goat—had a hard head and a stinking ass." Beats me.

Last time Carothers was home (Dec. 7) brought this one

> There was a young lady named Gorse
> Who had an affair with a horse.
> Said she: "I used to like heifers,
> But Robinson Jeffers
> Convinced me that heifers were coarse. !!!

* * *

So, that's a-plenty
Bill

March 10, 1942
Los Angeles
ALS, 2 p.

Dear Bill—

Thanks for your letter. I hope the draft board continues to leave you alone. Would like to see you. If I get a couple of tires I'm on the trail of, maybe I can drive up for a brief visit later this spring.

Am in a fed-up period. Have lots I could & should do, but have neither interest or will for doing it. How dull!

Mac is still at U.C. His new book is mostly poems written between his 1936 volume & *Cafés & Cathedrals.* A sort of a potpourri; kaleidoscopic grabbag. I hope this spring to do a sort of introductory essay on his work. Reading the very fine

Southern Review Yeats issue (Don't miss it) led me to his *Letters on Poetry to Dorothy Wellesley*. Have you read it? Very moving book. Certainly a great man, a genuine consecrated poet. Reading about him makes me humble.

Have you read Jeffers' last book? Remarkable short poems in it. Perhaps like Yeats, he will go on getting hornier the older he grows. Shakespeare too. Read Lear. A riot of copulatory poetry.

Say, don't let *anything* keep you from being a poet.

Get that land.

Yrs.
Larry

April 19, 1942
Selma, Calif.
ALS, 9 p., 5 sheets

Dear Larry:

It is the knowledge of how hurt I would be were you to neglect any work of mine as long as I have neglected your Pickett that makes me so ashamed to be writing only now. I cannot insult you with an excuse: I have none: none except my own torpor, and my own egotism, with its disregard for the feelings of others. But I think what really lay behind it was my hesitation to come to grips with the book; if I had been enthusiastic about it I would have written immediately upon finishing it; but as I read I began to feel that it is the poorest of your major attempts, and the necessity of saying that, with the detail I felt was necessary to establish the point, kept me off. Weeks ran into months. Now I am compelled by the sheer pressure of guilt to face the issue. I'll try not to get pontifical, as I usually do when I adopt the role of critic. Be sure of my good intentions.

When a biographer exhumes the life of any obscure personage, and makes a literary work of it, the suspicious reader usually expects to find an attempt to make significant an insignificant life. Heaps of material are presented, every detail is scrutinized, and the result is usually a great tedious inflation. If I had expected any major defect in your book before I began reading it, it would have been such a one. As it turned out, the opposite is true. For, laying the book down, one has the feeling that the life of Pickett had enough interest of itself to support a volume of at least twice this length. I was not ready to quit reading about Pickett when I finished the book. I wanted to know more. The man's idealism, his high morality and his remarkable courage make a compelling account. A sort of Upton Sinclair (of whom my opinion has increased as I have become more aware of the importance of this type of reformer). It is upon this type of man that the democratic life really rests—not on my type certainly, who sludge in indifference and depend upon the Picketts to watch over us. Surely he is an important Californian; perhaps a great Californian: and you deserve all credit for perceiving that and bringing the man forward.

But so much lies yet to be done! I have the feeling that you never were really "in" this work, Larry. That feeling grows out of the whole atmosphere of the book. Whereas in the Jeffers work (first edition) if one fact comes out it is that you put yourself into it: blood, mind and sweat. The approach was intensive, thorough, painstaking. Every lead that came to you was explored and utilized. If the book has shortcomings it is of things you failed to see, which is an honest and natural shortcoming. But this work fails because of the least forgivable reasons: you did not work hard enough. I have no doubt that in view of your time and efforts that sounds like mockery—as the smug patron passes off the lean painter with—"you haven't suffered enough yet"—but I really believe it to be true. The work remains a sketch. We see the man only vaguely, in the outline of a life, and we want more.

It may be that no more is available. But one of the most disconcerting things about the presentation is that we seldom know whether a given generalization is actually obscure or whether you just never developed it. The work is like nothing so much as a condensation, of the *Reader's Digest* type, of a larger more extensive work—the kind that makes you wish you had gone down to the library and got the original in the first place. This criticism obtains chiefly in the opening chapters which deal with incidents and events, more than the later chapters which are more interpretive. If so little has been written about Pickett as you assume, then surely it is not too much to ask of you to list your sources point by point as they occur, and to quote them. In chapter 14 you quote George E. Barnes in *The California King* on an interesting point, concerning the Pickett-Stanford relationship. Couldn't you have quoted also your source that Pickett philosophized on shingles tacked up on trees in his Oregon days? Time and again I was aware, in reading, of this sort of lack of documentation; a deficiency I never expected to find in your work.

As I go back over the book I see that almost all the qualities that irritate me are in the opening chapters. The later passages that deal with Pickett's works and ideas are far more intensive. Whereas the style of the opening sections is more loose and discursive, sporting such clichés as "the *hated* Mormons" and glib mannerisms as "this retort vitriolic," and sometimes getting involved to such an extent as the following sentence: "The Church was unsuccessful in ousting Pickett, even though it went so far as to incite the Indians to attempt to murder him, and other land-hungry settlers then poured in and the missionaries' monopoly was broken."—(I complain about involved sentences and then get into this one!)—whereas, I say, the style of the opening sections is loose, that of the later passages becomes more dominant. Not only that, but you become more interpretive, bringing to bear your own powers of criticism. On page 64 I noted as I first read through: "good page—too rare!" but I had less cause to complain after that point than I had before.

But one of the really great lacks of the book is that not enough Pickett is quoted. It is too bad you couldn't have issued jointly a collected edition of his works. Short of that you should have quoted more extensively. Many a time I wanted Powell to let Pickett say more. Without Pickett's writings he is nothing: an incident or two would survive, as they have. What you have seen, and what makes your book significant, is that Pickett the reformer, the pamphleteer, the social critic—in short, the writer, was the important man, and that unquenchable courage, that idealism, and that absorbing egotism shines out of his style.

One more point: the death-scene is a fiasco. You had no business, Larry, after pages of detachment, to become emotionally involved in that death. The death was insignificant. It had no relation to your thesis because it was not immediately bred of the same forces that make up your thesis. The death was simply a termination. You make it a drama, an event. For incidental interest you could have quoted your sources: no harm: but to interpret your sources, to bring in "color," "atmosphere" and to weigh your style with such emphasis of impending consequence—no, you should not have done that. You must be careful of that.

* * *

I was interrupted at the word "style," came back later, and tacked on the next two lines, and was interrupted again. Coming back, colder than ever, I have decided to let well enough alone. Perhaps I have said too much already, such criticism does little good once a work is published and unchangeable. I am sorry I had to make this kind of report, and perhaps you will not think I have done justice. I have tried not to be arrogant, for I know that does no good either, but I have not wanted to pull punches merely because you are so close a friend of mine. Now that I look over the work and over my letter I worry as to whether or not what I said was as true as I indicate, or true to the extent of the point I have made of it. But that was my dominant impression.

On March 9, in the office of the Selma Branch of the Bank of America, I drafted a check for the sum of $500, which half paid for 8-1/2 acres of land, and which marked the beginning of the culmination of many years of aimless wishing and speculation. In these last months Edwa has been the spark, or the goad, that brought this thing to a head. Whereas I have tended to sit back and dream about how fine it would be to really own a farm, and then shudder at the thought of how wretched it must be to wade through all the personal contacts and worry involved, she has prodded and jerked me on, driven by a desire as deep as my own. Many a farm we looked at. Many a time our hopes rose, on seeing some secluded piece where we would like to settle, only to have these hopes leveled. The accessible places all turned out, under the scrutiny of hard-headed and shrewd farmer friends, to be not intrinsically good enough. The good ones came too high for us, now that the boom is on. Finally, just outside of Selma, we saw our chance. Two small pieces adjoined one another. If we could get them both, combine them, make one farm of them, would that not be enough? It would. The land was pronounced excellent—for fertility, etc. We inquired. Waited. Wrote letters to absentee owners. Things began to shape up. Then one day the owner of one piece came to town and the deal was settled. The other piece still hangs. We hope to make it though, and then, all we will have to do is work!

You will see [on the map enclosed] that this is not an ideal layout for a farm. The pieces are not compact, and the thing stretches out too long. But it is only by buying such odds and ends that we were able to get anything at all within our means. Most important, the land is good. That is the big thing. But it will take years of work, and I worry.

The big thing about this ground is that it is so involved in my past. As you know, our family house was right on the edge of town nearest the place, and my first forays out from the known lots and alleys and streets, into what was an enormous and mysterious natural terrain, took me into this sector. I couldn't have been over eight years old when I first set foot on that land. From that time until I grew up I passed over it constantly. I learned to hunt on it. I trapped squirrels in box traps on it. I slaughtered small and beautiful birds on it. I lay on that ground for hours with my first .22 until the squirrels came out, and without pity blew them to bits. That locality meant *Nature* for me for many a year. Not only that, but when the other aspect of my relation to Nature became evident, it was upon this land. The "Winter Plowing" in *These Are the Ravens,* was written after walking beside a farmer plowing that bare land of ours. "Muscat Pruning" too came from watching the pruners on those very vines. Those things have great meaning for me. I can go back in my mind—back and back, and pick out incident after incident that go to make up what I now am, that stemmed directly out of that land. Once settled there I can draw those forces about me and project my life out of them like a seed from soil. This will be a marvelous thing I have been able to do. How many a man has been able to achieve such a continuity? The pressure of events is too great to let it happen often. I consider myself lucky.

April 23

Should have got this off before but there were one or two things I wanted to add, then work opened up hard and I didn't get to it. Edwa and I have been going down to the farm after work and digging around the vines—shoveling, it's called. A regular spring cultural operation to clear out the weeds the plough can't get. These vines have been neglected for some years, having only been ploughed and cultivated a bit, so that much dirt has been piled up against the stumps and has hardened there. Not only that but the whole vineyard is over-run with Bermuda grass, especially around the stumps, and it is a back-breaking job. Putting in 9 hrs. pipe laying is enough for a man, but this week we've worked till dark every night and the place only about a quarter done. Edwa has been swell at it. Getting toughened up now. It's a great feeling to be working side by side in your own vineyard. Next step is to make it support us. After that we won't ask for anything further—except that the Gov. let us alone!

They have so far. Knowing draft status was being revised I hastened to announce to my board that I was now a farmer. Card came back "classification 3A continued." Heavy heavy hangs over thy head!

Today, working by the highway, we saw the troops go through in their trucks, hour after hour. Each truck loaded with men, their rifles over their knees. One man on each truck standing up, rifle at ready. Each truck towing a 6-inch cannon. Hour after hour. Watching it, you get the same feeling of irresistible power you get from a torrent. A tremendously attractive force, the great cumulative drive of it. All our crew wanted to be with them. They could hardly work for watching. Only I kept apart saying nothing, knowing how futile I would sound.

The [Lew] Ayres case was interesting. I got only radio reports, but the *Time* excerpt from his statement showed a fine man. I've never seen a picture of his.

Say, could you send me down the *Partisan Reviews* you've received since those two you sent a year ago? One of the best mags in the country. I can't afford to miss it yet I do.

I now have about 7 poems in various stages of completion, but none of them shape up. Beginning to treat the war objectively, as a human phenomenon; what I mean is, not my own attitude towards it, but to let the shadow of it fall through a poem.

Biggest thing I'm sorry about in this delay is what must seem like reluctance to see you in your first indication of coming down in years. Not so. Nothing could be finer. If you can still make it, do so. By all means, man, do so. There is much ground to cover.

Funny how a stand at one point keeps reverberating back in your life, forcing you to reevaluate all your practices. All my life my favorite food has been meat. Even now, the thought of a fine steak or a succulent roast or a superb chop makes me drool at the mouth. But for almost two months now I've eaten no meat. The slaughtering knife kept coming between my mouth and the morsel. Humanity's great secret of refinement is its ability to abstract an evil out of sight. The same process becomes its most heartless sin. The sin, in this case, is not that we kill to eat, for that is necessary, but that we lose sight of the implications of killing. The fat steer bawling in the pit, bawling in that split second before the blow falls and the great hooks seize his legs and hoist him dripping down the conveyor is taken for granted, is given no thought. He becomes only the beautiful steak, sizzling on the platter, flanked by the french fried potatoes and the marvelous sauce. And the men of good will, who in the time of his life had they met him would have slapped his flank with real affection, do not even see him. They forget that it is only by his terror and his bewilderment and the terrible violence of that falling blow that they are able to achieve the perfect elevation of an excellent meal. Therein lies the sin. More terrible and more sinful than that is the beautiful woman in the fur wrap. She walks in violence; enveloped in it, wearing a hundred agonies upon her shoulders, and is unaware. Only one man a generation sees that. How many Blakes have we? People still think him a bit cracked. But—

The wanton boy who kills the fly
Shall know the spider's enmity. . . .

I still wear leather—though how long I will be able to is problematical. That serves some function. For the other, I had only my appetite, and after I realized that, I could not continue for long.

Well, it grows late. There is much to say that my pen has not got around to. Write when you can, and I'll look forward to it. Come when you can, for you're overdue, and we must see each other again.

Bill

P.S. I enclose the Mariposa graveyard snaps I took. Thought you might like to have them, though you said not when I took them. They're yourn, feller.

April 28, 1942
Los Angeles
ALS, 8 p., 4 sheets

Dear Bill—

Your letter was welcome. I was afraid you were in trouble. I am glad to hear that you are not, and that the draft board keeps you in 3A. I have been increasingly dissatisfied with my status. Because of the war my professional advancement has come to a standstill. Eastern prospects do not materialize. I am writing to MacLeish to see if there is a Western office of his O.F.F. into which I could fit. In that case, I would get a leave from the university. Not being in any kind of a responsible position there, I feel almost a slacker!

Your reaction to Pickett is disappointing. Nevertheless I am glad you wrote as you did. Only I would rather have had it right after you had read the book. I am glad for your frankness, your honesty. And your negative opinion is of much more interest to me than generalized praise such as one receives.

Let me react a bit to your criticism. I find it extreme. You ask for too much. The fact that the book reads like a *Reader's*

Digest abridgement is because of the scarcity of material. To have made it longer would have been to pad it. Most of the reactions to date have been the opposite—that I was to be congratulated for not having blown up the material I had. The most severe, next to yours, was an historian, writing in the *Pacific Historical Review,* who questioned whether Pickett was worth as much space as I had given him!

On the contrary, you have found the philosopher sympathetic & scolded me for not giving more of him, for not having worked harder! I must confess that there is no more to give, & I do not know where to look for more. The book was finished exactly two years ago, & since then I have been constantly on the lookout, as have research librarians in key places; almost nothing new has come in. A few scraps, which I added to the proofs.

You fail to appreciate the amount of work I did. True I accomplished the entire project—conception, research & writing—in less than a year. But I organized my quest & systematically wrung all sources as dry as possible.

I am as conscious as you of the thinness of the first chapters. There were few facts to go on. *Pickett was young & obscure, & left almost no traces.* I could have padded here with descriptions of Oregon trail crossings, etc., but chose not to. You are correct in finding the book better as it progresses. That is because the sources became increasingly more abundant. I lament the fact that Pickett left no journal or autobiography.

Your call for more documentation puzzles me. There are over 100 documentary footnotes. You can't demand one for *every* statement in the book—that would appear ridiculous, & you would have been the first to score me for pedantry and scholarly fussiness. The fact that the book was judged adequately documented by the Editorial Committee of the University Press leads me to believe that you are asking too much, i.e., being extreme. I could well have put the source of Pickett's shingle philosophizing (it was Shuck's *Hist. of Bench & Bar*) which is the only example you give, but where is one to stop doing this?

I agree with you that it would have been desirable to issue a collected edition of his pamphlets & letters—& perhaps I can someday. But I would have to pay for the publication myself; no press would do it on their own. Lacking such, you feel that I should have quoted more from Pickett's writings. Perhaps I should. Throughout I was attempting to achieve as perfect a proportion as possible—largely shaped by the subconscious. I must say the book pleases me now in its proportions! I defend it stoutly. What most historians would have devoted a decade of research to, & 500 pages of repetitious over-elaboration, I did quickly but nonetheless surely and accurately. By your enthusiasm for Pickett, the knight sans peur et sans reproche, you are led into an excessive judgment of my book, demanding the impossible of it, not realizing that its length & proportions were largely dictated by the existence of a limited amount of material & my own artistic decision that this material be distributed & utilized as evenly as possible.

A word about your criticism of clichés. I intended at times their deliberate use, in a sort of echoing of the period & Pickett's own rhetoric, & with my pen in cheek. Such was the "retort vitriolic" cited by you.

I do not understand terming the death-scene a "fiasco," that I became "emotionally involved," & brought in "color" and "atmosphere." It is entirely factual. The paragraph at top of p. 130 is right out of the newspaper account (*Mariposa Gazette*), every word of it, tho not verbatim. My account is laconic, factual reporting. I purposely restrained myself from any elaboration or imaginative embroidering. I do not know how I could have treated it more simply. I suppose you are objecting to his drawing Mrs. Gallison's hands over his face, his pointing up & whispering "The Gate is Open." These were the facts as reported by the town's own newspaper. I gave the facts, without comment. I feel that you are stacking the deck against me!

One last point—you fail to find me heart & soul in the book as you did find me in the Jeffers. I admit the book is laconic & impersonal, intentionally so. A word as to its origin & purpose. When, three years ago this summer, I was mentioned as candidate for the UCLA librarianship, one of my closest friends on the faculty suggested that it would be good if I were to abandon work on contemporaries & in order to impress the more conventional faculty men, essay an historical piece of research. I agreed & cast about for a topic. Pickett appealed to me. I began to investigate him with the purpose only of writing an essay for the *California Historical Quarterly*. It grew, & Ward Ritchie saw my material & suggested I make a small booklet for him to publish immediately. I agreed. Then my faculty friend said, your candidacy will benefit from having the University press imprint on the book. I consulted Ward. He was good enough to relinquish his claim to the book. I finished it & submitted it to the Press Committee. They accepted it in the unprecedented time of 2 weeks. Then nearly 2 years passed before it appeared. It has had the proper effect on certain scholar-snobs on the campus. They have been impressed. Powell can do historical research. They ask how many years it took me to do the book. I am properly vague. To admit the truth—7 months—would be to lose face!

So there it is, a deliberate piece of special pleading for Powell's candidacy. Done fast in order to get it into print before my chief retired. In the hurry, I guess you're right, a lot of me got left out. But still it's a labor of love. Notice I chose Pickett & not just any old topic. I chose him because he excited my imagination. Three years ago he was all but forgotten forever. Now he lives. That he does not live enough to suit your demand causes me regret. I did the very best I could with all the material I could assemble from the forgotten files and corners. It is not just to say that I did not work hard enough. Next time you are here I will show you my file of materials, correspondence & notes. You will be impressed! I did not work long, but I worked with determined intensity, according to a deliberate plan of research, & toward a set goal. I know how much time & effort is wasted in so-called scholarly research. I wasted none.

I am sorry as hell that the book did not click with you. But no regrets. There's nothing to be done about it. Our friendship goes absolutely unchanged. I like you for your energetic opinions, & your bare-handed grip, even though it's around my neck this time!

May 2

The foregoing was written in a single burst the evening of the day your letter came. I put it aside, intending to add more.

Now, reading it over, I feel there is no more to add. My first impulse was to destroy it, for it cannot alter a conclusion to which you came some weeks ago. But I send it to you. It should enlarge your understanding of the book & of my ways of working, although I do not expect it to affect your basic conviction.

I am in a bad period now. Uncertainty as to the future keeps me from working whole heartedly on any of several projects I have started. My energy is good. I am not exhausted. Yet I cannot channel it effectively.

I read constantly. Travel. *Highway into Spain,* the account of a walking trip from Paris to Madrid circa 1927 by an Australian with a Texan as companion. I have a great hunger for the French countryside. Will I ever see it again?

Life races by. These are the best years of my life. I want to make the best use of them. The old Quaker Moralist in me.

The other night I was taking a bath at 10:30 before going to bed. Radio announced that records would play Smetana's *Quartet (From My Life).* I hurried dry & into pajamas & bathrobe & lay on top of bed alongside Fay, who had emerged earlier from a bath. And there in the dark room we heard the music, which I presently comprehend as a great and moving work of art. It was a most poignant and exalted end to a long day—an experience I shall long remember.

You have known such occasions, when everything unites to make the hearing of some music extraordinarily memorable.

Tomorrow is Sunday & we are having a library staff picnic at Tapir Park, in the Malibus 20 miles NW of here, in the country of *Sondelius* by Madeleine Ruthven. Fay & I are in charge of the food. I, chef, will cook hamburgers for two score unfucked females. Diable!

Greetings to you and Edwa. Congratulations on your land. I place it very well, thanks to your map & the references to *Ravens* poems. Have a month vacation coming up. Perhaps can come up on bus for a short visit, or if can get tires, will drive. Sometime this summer.

Don't wait so long to write.

Larry

June 3, 1942
Selma
ALS, 9 p., 5 sheets

Dear Larry:—

Well, man, perhaps my criticism was extreme. Certainly I know my tastes these last few months have been getting narrower and narrower—a bad sign. I find it harder to find pleasure in what I read. Work that once would have given me much joy, or at least work that I would once have viewed with sympathy and understanding I now lay aside. I find fault, tend to quibble over detail, picayunishly dabble with it. These are not good indications. But, going back through the Pickett I find my opinion unchanged as you expected, but beyond that I won't say any more. Reiteration would emphasize and I don't want to emphasize beyond what I've said. One thing only: I didn't ask for more accumulation of the scholastic machinery, only asked for more of the scholar's painstaking. I believe I conceded the scarcity of material; what I protested was that you did not permit the reader to share with you the excitement of grappling with the obscurity and the mystery surrounding that material. Your relating the motives behind the work, your reasons, and the subsequent limitations those reasons imposed on the composition, throw much light on it and affect the attitude to be taken toward it. They clear you of the charge that you failed in a major venture; for it turns out it was not a major venture; but they do not erase the charges incurred by legitimate criticism, any more than the explanation that I wrote the Wm. Herber poem carelessly and in haste for a specific purpose can clear it of the charges of legitimate criticism. Work shouldn't be done for those reasons; and I will not permit the citation of the Swan of Avon himself to shake me in that.

About a week ago I completed the longest session of enforced labor since we got married. Beginning last summer, I've worked practically uninterruptedly up till now, my only respites being for injury by burning and failure of my eyesight, which were really no respites at all. My poetry has suffered for it of course, but at that I've managed to get some of it out. I am working now on a fairly long poem (2 or 3 pages) which I want to use as the corner-post, or rear-foundation, to bring my present volume to a close. I have resurrected the better pacifistic poems, but between them and this poem lies an area of work not thoroughly resolved. I hope to round the work up before cannery time. You see I'm not counting on the Phelan this time!—though nothing is so irritating as the way that Award is being delayed—two months' overtime now.

We went to Berkeley two weeks ago, chiefly to get wood and stone-aggregate for Edwa, and because the Oakland Sculpture Exhibit, the only all-sculpture exhibit in the state—was on. Edwa is steadily maturing as an artist. Only one or two pieces in that show were the equal of her best pieces (that's no mere brag). We slipped two heads of hers unobtrusively into the local Fresno artists' show, and they burst like bombshells! Really great fun, our walking unknown about the formal reception that opened the event, with everyone wondering who the woman was! Brought us one good contact—Odorfer, a ceramist of national reputation, and who appears to be a real man personally. The heads bowled him over.

June now the month scheduled for "The M. Dead" to appear, I've written Decker. Every book in his catalogue has appeared except mine, and two evidently contracted since mine that are not in the catalogue. Perhaps I told you I insisted at first there was no hurry, that I would rather have him go slowly and make a better book, than throw it together. I think he has used that to cram in new work. Now the "Masculine Dead" will come out late, in a slack season, and be no better than it would have been. We live, and sometimes, bit by bit, painfully and at long last, we learn!

I have the new [W. R.] Rodgers book, *Awake,* which is making its sensational appearance. Read them, then compare them with the early Spender, from whom they derive. They can't stand up. Over-written, I believe, too great a reliance on the relish of words that Hopkins used. This, speaking of wind—

> that claps and batters
> The bent-backed and running roaring waters,
> That squats and squints and squeals evilly in trees,
> That follows and faces the fleeing leaves,
> That with hag hands hugs the hooked hawk down.

I have used this element more and more to toughen my poems, but this leans on it. And Hopkins made it really wonderful. Then, too, there is personified abstraction to excess:—

> Goodness is foreskinned and frisked by Evil,
> And Violence advances Reason's forces,
> Cruelty recruits Kindness, etc.

There is a kind of high and driving lyricism like Spender's great eloquence, but without Spender's wholeness and tonality. It's nearer Paul Engle, to whom he has not yet been compared, but to whom he will inevitably be. The long driving sentence, line over line, is what does it, and the use of double adjectives separated by "and," which occasionally has great power, as Jeffers uses it, but rapidly becomes depleting:

(Engle)

> The wild and dancing passion flower, the revealed and cringing human heart, the sunlit and dissolving lives of men, the vast and verge of space, our new and untried sails—

Time and again Engle uses it, and this, coupled with all the other methods of corrupting adjectives, from hyphenating them, to running them in strings of three and four, swamps the style. These things aren't bad in themselves, I've used them often, and before I knew better, too much—but to get back to Rodgers and the comparison:

Engle

> A vision of the universal heart,
> That recreates the living form of man
> In the unique and individual way
> That is the shape and spirit of that land.

(I could have found far far worse Engle than this. This shows better out of context than in it!)

Rodgers

> So War came,
> The *late and urgent* agent of Change, not

Of Chance. So will it always come to wake
The deepest sleepers. See how its sudden hands
Now *gather and grow* round us like quicksands
Here in these islands. O awake! awake!
And let us like the trapped intrepid man   fine figure [this phrase and the italicized words are Everson's comments]

* * *

Stooping, light fires of foresight that will *clean*
And clear the careless ground before us
Of all the *dry and tindery* increment
Of privilege.

This passage has been much quoted, surely for patriotic purposes, and it does have fine elements. But everybody seems to be taken in by the work completely. There are good poems in the volume, and in view of much work that gets praise, it deserves what it gets, but there is no new major voice here—not yet.

In Berkeley we looked up Duncan and had a session with him. The fellow fascinates me. I've never known such a person. Sparks fly off him!

Saw in S.F. the traveling show of Mexican art. Our painters can't touch them. That art talks, and talks big. I was marvelously uplifted.

A Poem

All night long in the high meadow
They shielded the city-light from their eyes under towering grass.
Weeds warded them:
Dock hung in his hair;
Mallow marred with its subtle stain her rumpled skirt.
Near midnight air chilled;
They drew about them his heavy coat—
(Soldier's gear brought to such usage!)—
And hoarded their heat.
Toward three they dozed,
All cramped and cold,
And went down in the dawn,
Limping under the early eyes,

Went their way,
Went out to the world,
To the War,
Bearing mallow, dock,
The odor of weed and the weed stain,
And the harsh print of the earth.

[later titled, "Weeds."]

I hope your own difficulties of situation and work straighten themselves out, or are already straightened. Our lives are being vastly changed all about us. There is so much we should speak of that doesn't get into our letters.

All the news now is of the big British raids. The desolation must be literally inconceivable. When it was "our" side that was taking it, it didn't seem so bad, like some natural catastrophe, sort of, that you accept because you cannot help it. But this, in which I, as an American, am participating, runs through me like guilt; and I know that I must stand judgement for that guilt, and expect calamity upon my head, as those people are now receiving calamity for the London raids. The Tokyo incident more so. I think of all the future wars—the real wars, the real wars, with Mr. Martin's monsters mere midgets,—oh, what's the use?

Say, has anything more come up about the *Ghost*? Has Tate reviewed it, or the *Partisan Review*, or the *Kenyon Review*? What is Laughlin's relation to it; I see he announces an unpublished portion of it in *N.D. 1941*. Was it work you had extracted from it, and is it good? Laughlin seems to think highly of it. I've read a story of Fisher's wife's in *Accent*. Not at all bad. I am interested in the *Ghost*, yet, and hope to keep track of all its comings and goings.

My father, at the age of 72, has married again. My sister told me two nights before the wedding what was coming off. That was too much for me. I wrote him a letter telling him I could not understand such a thing and that I didn't care to become further involved. I got back quite a letter myself. If the old fool was in his personal relationships as trenchant and solid as in his correspondence I should have no quarrel with him, and it makes me very puzzled and very interested about this aspect of the art of writing. For the old man wields a firm pen, and a firm pen should by all logic denote a firm mind; but I know for a fact, demonstrated by countless agonizing instances, that this man is a sentimentalist of the worst kind, that in practical instances he has no taste, absolutely no taste. I can't understand it. But once having made the break I am not anxious to mend it; and I haven't seen him for it must be 3 months now. I simply can't stand the man any longer, even thinking about him now, in this writing, I feel a slow flooding of resentment and anger against him. Not for marrying again—that was a foolish and stupid and inordinately weak thing to do—for I know all he wanted was someone to flatter and pamper him: no egotist such as he is can really enjoy being alone—but for other reasons. I still have dreams about him: dreams of parental rejection. For a long time they took the form of fear, and usually developed with my cowering before him. But for the last several years, and I have this sort of dream every month or so and sometimes oftener, I find that I am involved in some sort of action in which he opposes me but in which I reject him, or tell him off; the show-down, as it were. I have no idea how many elaborate situations have developed out of this pattern in my dreams. All this would be incomprehensible to him, for he does not remember all the violent scenes of the past; he does not remember all the emotional anguish he caused all of us; indeed, if he ever knew; and he thinks back upon his life with my mother as one of perfect bliss. But many's the time she's wept the night away, from his harshness. The violence of temperament is now gone out of him. The emotional nervous tension that kept him always on edge has faded. He was, in his prime, the most perfect example of the popular conception of a genius I've known. A highly creative person—he wrote music constantly then, and it came out of him in great obliterating floods that I am sure equaled in impetuosity and demand for release, the notorious Beethoven. But he was constantly tied down by two main things: the necessity to provide for his family, and the limitation of his intellect. Those blind him. In the first instance it meant deprivation of all his yearning for luxuries. In the second it meant he would never be more than a twentieth-rate musician. Of course he would never concede that; but then he hungered for fame, for acclaim, and his intellectual limitations never permitted him that. Consequently, I am sure his dominant emotional attitude was that that springs of being thwarted. The commonest trifles sent him, not into rages, for his every wish was obeyed, but into an explosion. One of us would be absorbed in some toy on the floor, and suddenly would come that terrifying rebuke. What was the worst was the unpredictability of it. You never knew when it would hit you. Glad we were that so many nights he would be gone, playing for dances. Yet that made him a stranger to us. All this, in my case, came to a head in the depression, when I couldn't find work, was literally too timid to hunt for work and yet hung around the house absorbed in poetry. That infuriated him. I am so tall, and he so short, 6 feet 4 on the one hand and 5 feet 4 on the other, that that too must have caused psychic disturbances. Not only that, I won my mother to my side, and that told on him—god, Larry, there's room here for all the Greek tragedies and the Elizabethan ones beside!

Anyway, this marriage I couldn't take. His wife was a friend of my mother's. I haven't seen her for years, but I went to her house constantly as a boy, and I was even then always filled with a vague uneasiness, a vague discomfiture. I wasn't going to get mixed up in that, and I'm well rid of it, but I wonder what will happen when we meet face-to-face on the streets.

He's a bit afraid of me of late, ever since my mother's funeral, and has had a tendency to shy clear of me. The whole family has. I think I've told you that my relationship with my mother wasn't very binding, but at any rate, an incident occurred at the funeral that has placed me in a special category in the family's eyes. That kind of thing, a funeral, I mean, is always trying enough. For a couple of days before it the whole atmosphere in which we moved was highly charged, and by the time the services began we were all on the breaking point. I, of course, realized the importance of the situation, even though no great grief was in me. I mean I saw that a major portion of my life was over, that, in fact, my past, all of it, was now thrown into a different light by this event. It severed years from me; erased the last hold I had on those years. I knew it was a momentary occasion, and I wanted the occasion to be worthy. As it was, the Order of the Eastern Star handled the services. Sisters of the Order read verses. A young minister, good enough as a man but no preacher, droned some stupid drivel. Minute after minute I sat there with my father sobbing and blubbering, not out of any great grief himself, for such an egotist never feels any great personal loss himself until *he* dies, but simply because he pitied himself and pictured himself alone in the world in his advancing age. At any rate, the paltriness of the services, the transparent grief of my father, the fake solemnity of the bought undertakers, the complete and unrelieved phoniness of this entire occasion (only my sister felt genuine grief) infuriated me. At the last, after the public had been ushered out, when we, the family and relatives, together with the hired attendants, were alone with the body, in that interval before the casket is taken to the hearse and conducted to the cemetery, something came over me. I felt a great sense of insufficiency, of lack, as if it were not right that this event should be allowed to pass. So meagerly saluted, and with the sense of lack came the desire to correct that lack. It was exactly as it is in writing a poem. An impulse comes over you that will find fulfillment in no other way than a deep personal utterance. I stepped in among them weeping about the coffin, and began to speak. I must have shouted. It was exactly like the first draft of a poem; what is needed is eloquence, and what comes out in those opening lines is chaos. I don't know what I said. I tried to say something about the magnitude of death; something adequate to the situation. All I remember out of my supreme agitation are their faces about me and their hands trying to hold me. The intense shock to them must have been terrific. All they could do was cry "Bill! Bill!" and try to hold me. I broke from them and went down the hall; the preacher followed me, beseeching me: I remember turning on him and cutting him short. Then Edwa was there, and she got me quieted down, and I went back and apologized, and the funeral went on. They were so scared, then, that I don't think the rest of the funeral really registered. Nobody wept any more: they forgot about mother and their own grief. They sort of went through with it in a stage of fearful suspension; holding their breath that I should not break out again, in public. I did not. The service got through. We went home and tried to cheer up. But even then they watched me, the family, the relatives, and the family friends. I felt their hushed, suspended numbness all about me. And they have never got over it.

I'm sorry about that. I'm sorry because I lost control of my judgement: and I'm not sure of myself anymore. I think I learned my lesson. I hope I have, I probably have not. But most of all I'm sorry because my ego, my personality, was asserted at a function that should have completely belonged to mother. And I have apologized to her, to my memory of her, many a time. It would have been so far decenter a thing to do to have hushed, kept my feelings about the service to myself (for it's true mother was then in her element, in her own conception of glory, there among her club members, in the long hall, with their tributes about her) and gone my way. I did not act out of reasons of personal diversion, certainly, but that was the effect of my act, and for that I'm sorry.

So, in a way, I think my father is almost afraid to confront me with his wife. He doesn't know what I'll do. He's afraid I'll make a public disturbance. Maybe I will. My letter to him was a rather bitter one. He referred to it to my sister as a "nasty" letter—

Well, I didn't intend to drag out all the family wash, Larry. But there are already stories around. You would have heard it, I suppose, anyway, before long. I'd rather have you have it straight.

I think people are beginning to think I'm a bit touched; especially since I don't eat meat. On the street they look at my long gait and my head of hair with either fear or amazement I don't know which.

I refused to buy bonds last week. Nothing from the draft board yet. I don't deserve it, but I'd like to hear from you—and see both of you if you can come. Edwa sends greetings.

Bill

P.S.: For a month half the town has been [half] closed to the Japanese and half open—U.S. 99, the official line, divides the town. Today comes the order that all the valley must be cleared. This evacuation plan is momentous for it means that no longer can citizenship protect one.

June 14, 1942
[Selma]
ALS, 2 p., 1 sheet

Dear Larry:—

I have just received a letter from Decker assuring me that the book will be published this month. He was very apologetic for his delay and grateful for my "patience," (he said anyone else in his experience would have sued him for fraud long ago!) and explained that he had been in rather tight circumstances, and had taken jobs ahead of mine to keep going. "I am forced to be, at times, a rank opportunist—printing this or that book first to rope in enough cash to print the next." So I guess he operates on a pretty slender margin—certainly the low requirement for printing costs indicates he depends only on his sales. And yet the announcement in *Poetry* a couple of months ago looked as if he were doing all right. Said absolutely no money would be required for future publication. Begged for material. Just before that his letter to me had said that sales had been increasing by leaps and bounds. I hope he can stick to his new policy. If this book sells it means he would probably handle my next one (it'll be done this summer) with no money requirement.

I suppose you read Humphries' article with the reference to Decker in the *Nation*. Somehow there was something arch and smug about his attitude that eats in my craw yet, even though I've had considerable respect for him heretofore; I assure you it's not wholly a defense-attitude with me either. If Decker had only a couple of scrubs on his list, and if it were apparent he was just another "vanity press" living off hopefuls, such asides might be in order. But poets have flocked to Decker, and the reason is sound. For here is a publisher that has organized his business so that the poet gets all the breaks possible. If poetry could support itself there wouldn't be any need of the Decker-type publisher and he wouldn't exist, except for "vanity" purposes. But poetry won't—and Decker is the one place where the publisher does take some risk—he asks only costs and both gamble on the profits. Sales being what they are, that's fair enough. That poets—young men working seriously with their craft—think so too is proved by his list. There is not another publisher in the country who can show a finer list of serious poets—not Laughlin himself with all his dough. For myself, I'm glad to be there; I don't wrinkle up my nose at the print jobs as does Humphries, because, in spite of their deficiencies, they are hand-made, they have the look about them of being done by men and not slapped out by huge machines. I have two or three Decker books now, Clark Mills' *The Migrants* and *A Suite for France,* Howard Nutt's *Special Laughter,* and the Englishman Henry Treece's *Towards a Personal Armageddon.* And though none of these books could in any way be called fine printing, none of them have that sparkling clarity and completed unification of conception of, say, *San Joaquin*—they are readable, they do have personality, they do have character. Beside such specimens as Engle's *American Song,* (most any of those Doubleday Doran atrocities) they breathe the living breath of real creativeness. I have not seen many books of earlier printing, but I've a friend in Berkeley who collects the books of his favorite classical authors, and those books—not the great earlier printings which are superb, but the standard editions of Dryden's time, poor as they are, have that same feeling of personal application. Their errors somehow are part of their total spirit. I am not meaning to say I prefer a Decker book to a Ritchie book—but I do prefer a Decker book to a Doran one. All this is behind what irritated me so much in the Humphries article. He should be well enough familiar with poetry publication to know that a man like Decker ought to be welcomed. In no other way can we escape the deadening, maddening lid of N.Y. commercial publishing. But Humphries, safe with his new Scribner imprint, is very satisfied.

Well, enough of this business. I only hope Decker can hold out. I know of no other place I'd rather appear. Certainly there's no danger of withering prematurely under the glare of limelight! Did I tell you Decker too was a C.O.? You find us in such unlikely places!

As you remember, in the contract Decker is to supply circulars and mail them—up to 500. I wonder if you could send me the addresses of any of the people who were interested in *San Joaquin.* For myself I don't care much, but I'd like at least to make back Carother's investment. I suppose most of those people were interested in the Ritchie imprint, but we could at least try them.

Sincerely,
Bill

Phelan went to somebody else.

June 22, 1942
Selma, Calif.
ALS, 2 p., 1 sheet

Dear Larry:—

Well, the Phelan award has been definitely settled. It went to Barbara Gibbs. Perhaps you'll remember her as one of Yvor Winters' Gyroscope Poets, the wife of J. V. Cunningham, whose poems the Colt Press has just issued. The judges were three women: Sara Bard Field, Josephine Miles, and Marie De La Welch. All this information came in the formal announcement this morning from Chretien, who also said I had been given an Honorable Mention, along with two others. My manuscript had come back long ago, about the 6th, and when no announcement came I figured a slip-up had been made and that I had not received the award. So I sent a note to Josephine Miles thanking her for sponsoring me, etc. Her card came back with these facts: she had been selected as a judge after she had written me; she had held out for me, but the other two were equally strong for another poet (she wasn't permitted to say who it was) and since that poet was also good that was the way the award went. She said the others were for me next. When you come that close your fate's in the hands of the Gods!

Gibbs's work is competent, in very strict form, and very intellectual, but somewhat dry. It hasn't (that which I've seen) much breadth to it. You'll recall Welch is the poet McWilliams wrote for the book about. Her work is also well turned (I haven't seen her last book) but somewhat slight. Sara Bard

Field's work you know, and Miles also. Miles is a good person. Her cards are swell.

The Solstice. Now the days will get shorter again. It always somehow saddens me to think about the Solstice—not saddens, maybe, sobers—the fact that even though the summer is just starting, and all the months of growth are ahead, already winter is on its way, inevitably. The days will get shorter.

I have read Brooks' *Opinions of Oliver Allston* (what the hell is his name, anyway) and was vastly uplifted by it. Certainly its premise is correct; though the petty treatment of Joyce is not. The first part of the book, the general subjects I thought were swell. Exactly what I feel about communism *v* socialism. My feeling for it has now tempered, but when I finished it I thought it was great. Read a bit of Mathiessen's *American Renaissance* before I had to return it. Swell on Whitman, the only one I really read. When I finished it I pronounced it as the best on Whitman I had read, but in a couple of days I had read also Mark Van Doren's *The Private Reader,* (another fine book, and one whose foreword I took to my heart) and the Whitman essay therein also was superb. Between these two works I got altogether a clearer picture of the Whitman situation. Glancing back through my letters to find a reference, I noticed you were reading Matthiessen just a year ago. You found him wordy. Your account of the tragic and harrowing death of Parrish stays with me. I have incorporated that situation as a kind of reference in a lyric I am writing.

I have not heard from Decker since I wrote you, but it's the 22nd, and no proofs yet, so I don't see how he can possibly make it this month.

How goes it all?
Bill

June 23

Received another card from Miles today (written before the announcement) saying she couldn't understand the delay; that they held their meeting in April. The letter from Chretien I received yesterday was dated *June* 3. Something funny.

There's no use in that. A person holds up his plans for an entire year waiting.

June 27, 1942
Los Angeles
ALS, 4 p., 2 sheets

Dear Bill—

You have fired three good letters at me during June, & I'm just getting around to answering. First of all, I'm sorry about the Phelan award. Strange they'd have 3 women poets as a jury; it's not surprising the award went to a woman! This morning at the library I put in a very satisfying exhibit, of the Poet of the Month series; I got Laughlin to send me several copies of each number so I could show inside & out. It makes a gay display.

I look forward to your Decker book. The only book of his I know is Mac's *Black Bull,* a bit of a stale gathering. I admire what Decker's doing more than Laughlin! On a separate page I'll give you some names for mailing list. [Eleven names were on the list.]

Your first letter about your mother's funeral & the townsfolk attitude toward you reminded me of nothing so much as Tom Wolfe. I've told you before I thought you ought to turn some of your fury into prose. The lyric is not a large enough vessel. It may dam up & destroy you. You've read Wolfe's books? I just read his last novel, *You Can't Go Home Again.* He had everything but a sense of form & proportion. Like an insane Beethoven. As a result his books leave you with a feeling of sadness at the lack which kept him from being a great artist.

You've got the sense of form & proportion. Shape yourself a large vessel & pour yourself into it.

I am still in a bad doldrums. The war has fucked up everything including LC Powell's plans. Many plums dangle just out of my reach. Everything's frozen. I keep telling myself to be patient & thankful that we have safe shelter & food. Vacation in August. Can make no plans that far ahead, but I do hope to be able to visit you.

Right now I am completing an ambitious bibliographical article in the field of history.

Fisher's *Ghost* has been shamefully ignored. Nothing to my knowledge since *Southern Review*. Nothing in *Partisan*. Do you want me to send you some issues of the latter? Fisher failed to get a Guggenheim.

The enclosed clipping (please return) tells the story of the worst blow I've had since Parrish's death. Rice was one of my best friends at the university. One of the finest men I've ever known. His wife worked in the library to enable him to complete his Ph.D., & resigned just this month, pregnant, preparatory to their setting up housekeeping at Occidental. His instinct told him not to take this trip, but Nelson urged him & paid all his expenses. Both had climbed the Grand Teton before. This time both fell to their death. Mrs. Rice fittingly left his body to be buried in the Teton park. Tomorrow we hold a memorial service at the university.

Last month I sat on Bill's Ph.D. committee, early this month I watched him graduate, tomorrow we eulogize him, dead. He was sandy-haired, blue-eyed, medium tall, lithe & strong, with a homely wide-mouthed face. Kind, energetic, modest. I loved the guy. Everything a young scholar should be. Future brilliant. Sudden reversal. Aristotelian tragedy in every sense. We have collected $500 for his wife. He had no insurance! I have been heartsick about it. Nearly every day for 3 years he would come by my desk & we would swap notes. I look for him. He comes no more.

Certain grandeur to his end. The thousand foot fall. He in all his young strength & triumph of attainment fallen. Did he cry out? Was there an agonized prelude of slipping? And did he cry to his beautiful blonde wife in whom he had planted seed? Good Christ, how she must miss him nights!

I can't write any more this letter.

Affectionate greetings as ever
Larry

June 30, 1942
Selma
AL, 3 p., 2 sheets

Dear Larry:

I was very glad to hear from you. Fact is, I was afraid I had alienated you with my long silences through the winter, which would have served me right; but which would have been one of those peculiar justices we all choke on. Those were hard days for me: every free moment I was either working on my poetry, or, more often, working up to working, or hoping to work—with greater ease my mind can turn to a broader scope.

I note what you say of my account of the funeral and of the resemblance to Wolfe. No higher compliment could be paid it; though I was not striving for any literary effects, simply setting down what transpired. I've read most of Wolfe: *Look Homeward Angel, Of Time and the River,* most of *You Can't Go Home Again,* a bit of *The Web and the Rock.* I know of no greater American writer. When he writes about England and Germany, as in the latter part of *You Can't Go Home Again,* his writing is beyond reproach. But it's a peculiar thing about my writing prose. Even when I am stimulated and impressed, as say, in a reading of Wolfe, I am strangely unmoved to attempt such myself. A corresponding poetic circumstance would set me off. Even a painting that impresses me prods me up so that I dabble around with paint till I throw up in disgust. When I first discovered music, there in '39, I yearned to write it: felt very badly when I found I couldn't. But prose? I can't figure it out, but I'm not moved toward it. Perhaps I'll try sometime, but I feel poetry amply takes care of my flow now. I think it is chiefly that I lack sustaining power: even the "Mas. Dead" was a series of lyrical sections.

I'm sorry about the discontentment and frustration that hangs over you. Something will surely break. No vacation till August? I'm working night and day through August, god damn it all.

Can't understand about the *Ghost.* I'd thought Blackmur's notice would have set off a flurry of excitement. Could you lend me some *P.R's?* I've seen none since Zabel's attack on MacLeish, and I'm rather famished for them.

Am deeply sorry about this tragedy: your friends appear to be dropping away. The sailor friend who brought in the Miller books from the Orient went down in the Atlantic last winter. Poor bastard: a Trotskyite who had set his life on the Revolution; I think of him in heaven saying with true Marxist detachment: "Yes. I was killed by the last throes of Capitalism." I have his Paris editions of Miller, and if you don't have *Capricorn* I could send you the pirated oriental edition.

It is now three o'clock of the afternoon of June 30th, and Mr. Decker has just nine hours remaining in which to fulfill his promise. Since I have not even received proof, I believe he is going to have to do some tall typesetting!

I wonder if you heard the Beethoven 9th over K.E.C.A. Sunday night. We listen to Philharmonia nightly, it comes in beautifully here.

I am beginning to make a name for myself around Berkeley. A young poet from there dropped by, George Leite, with his wife, and slept on the floor, as did Miller, Neiman, and later Duncan. He left a confirmed Everson enthusiast. Funny thing about poetic tastes. This Leite is a Jeffers man, but has had only the *Roan Stallion* volume. But he thinks *Roan Stallion* is tops! Then Van Doren, on "Invitation to Learning," once spoke of *The Tower Beyond Tragedy* as the one most critics consider tops. Duncan, I believe, prefers it. You like *Cawdor*. Frasier Taylor in *Poetry* points to *Give Your Heart to the Hawks*. While I, poor fool, find myself more and more obsessed with *At the Birth of an Age*. It beats me.

This fellow Leite is very young (21), but has a good talent, on what little of his I've seen.

Sept. 25, 1942
Libby's, Selma
ALS, 6 p.

Dear Larry:

I feel like a woman who has just delivered a twelve-months' infant, for not only is my sense of relief as great as hers, but my relief is also divided with horror, for this infant also is born dead—or, if not dead, a monstrosity. I'll not try to pursue so shaky an analogy and I apologize for ever attempting it, but the fact is that *The Masculine Dead* has arrived, but is so corrupted with typographical errors that I long to drop it down the drain as an abortion, or more properly, as after-birth. For not only are the typographical errors of such numbers and kind as to blight the aesthetic effect of the entire book, but the violence done to the text, the substitution of one word for another, the omission of entire lines, the omission of lines from one page and addition of those lines to another where they do not belong, an error in which the effect of both poems involved is ruined—these things are unendurable. How it happened I do not know. The errors were not in my typescript, for I checked my carbon. They are simply the result of haste and carelessness and it is all the more humiliating to me to remember that every other Decker book I've seen has been impeccably edited. I immediately wrote Decker an indignant letter, protesting such treatment and demanding he make out a sheet of errata to tab into all copies. I have not heard from him at this time, and I do not know what to do if he defies me, but if he does, he is fast on the road to ruin. He cannot cater to serious poets, treat them like this, and yet get by. I cannot make much trouble, but I can do a hell of a lot of talking, and that talk can hurt. I am so disappointed I hardly know what to do. I knew all the time that he was making a sucker of me by shunting me off, but I was willing to take it for the book's sake, in order that this very thing should not happen. The catalogue listed the book at $2.00. I do not know if he intends to maintain that price. If they were mine I would send you a copy immediately, but I have that obligation to Carothers, and I know you will understand. I could make the corrections in writing, or wait until the errata sheets arrive, or mail one later, or any way you wish.

Rummaging through my desk I found the enclosed fragment, and its date made me gasp. I simply cannot understand where the time has gone. I can concede the expanse of a month since you wrote—my mind accepts that—but *three!* And what excuses can I make? None, none, none. We used to exchange letters weekly!

But the summer has been pretty much hell. I've had hard work here at the cannery, cooped up with a god damned school teacher who kept me in mingled states of fury, contempt and tedium—"one of the low, on whom assurance sits"—and then too I've had the ranch as worry. We picked it ourselves, with one other, gleaning about 1250 trays from the five acres, and they're drying now; I watch the south-west with a more anxious eye than ever I did when I wrote "The Ruin"! But with luck we'll make it. Prices on raisins are high now. With luck we'll make it.

Or, provided the draft board lets me. Couple of weeks ago I got the 1st hint in a form pertaining to joint incomes. Last week another C.O. form to fill out. Today the dread sign:—a notice to appear the 30th for my physical exam. I'm a goner for sure, this time. I am not terrified as I once was, being somewhat older, and seeing my way a bit more clearly, but I am very sad about having to leave Edwa. In adolescence parting was a blind hell, being one long torment of sexual lack. Now, the loss is far greater, in a way I cannot say, but far far greater. I'm only half a man without her. I am unable to get a clear picture of what life will be like without her, as we are unable to picture how it would be to lose a leg. In my heart I know she is the finest woman that walks this green earth: and that lack will be the hardest.

I suppose you have been seeing H. Miller. A card from him told me he was in L.A. I'd like to see him again—one of the real ones, that man.

I see Dillon has left *Poetry* for the Army. Do you think I can ethically submit there again? After all, my quarrel was with him, not the magazine. The fact is, ever since my sundering I have been like Adam, on the outside looking in, hungry for the pastures of Paradise!

Gotham Book Mart is going to list *The Masculine Dead* in their next sheet.

A local boy, young fella interested in radio script writing, has a recording outfit and brought it out. I did the whole of *The Masculine Dead.* We used music as background: Bach's Passacaglia for the Prologue, and The Swan of Tuonela for the rest. I haven't heard them since, but if they turn out O.K. I'll send you a set. It was great fun, but you'd never recognize my voice. We managed the breaks very badly, and the cutting needle wore out. I had a hard time sustaining mood from record side to record side, there was so much confusion between. And I think possibly my interpretation was a little too pathetic, too "dramatic." I'm going to try to get him to do it again. Watkins was bumbling about the room with D. H. Lawrence on his mind, and the kid was all wrapped up in his gadget, giving me signs, etc. I made a bad burble in the Prologue, but I think the rest came off somewhat better.

Edwa for my birthday gave me a record of Jeffers reading from *The Tower Beyond Tragedy.* His voice is not as fine as I had expected, though I think the records deserve more than *Poetry* gave them. The chief stylistic defect of the poem—too many short subsidiary phrases—fucks up this record too. It tends to weary reader or listener.

One reason I'd like to make a good showing on any record is because I think a poet reading his work gives off "leads" as to the interpretation he himself meant when he wrote it. The Eliot records for instance, though somber and eloquent, tell their bit about the writer's attitude. "The Hollow Men"—a sentimental poem to my mind—is made bathetic by Eliot's lugubrious recording. That's why I want to be sure *The Masculine Dead* doesn't get read that way by me. It could so easily sound mawkish that great care must be exercised. When I read it alone I'm sure of it, but I think in the recording when I tried to read slowly and deliberately, my voice fell into a kind of chant that might not be the proper effect. It only now occurs to me that if my reading of my poem doesn't tell a tale about my attitude toward it, no other poet's necessarily does either!

Well, it's 2:00 in the morning—the morning of the 26th, and I've another 3 or 4 hrs. to work. I'm sorry as hell to have to write as I have about the book. At home I take down *San Joaquin,* and find again the wonder I have always known before its cohesion, its beauty, its taste, its *perfection.* That will never happen again. All around, *The Masc. Dead* is a pretty sorry piece of book-making.

Bill

Sept. 29, 1942
Selma, Calif.
ALS, 2 p., 1 sheet

Dear Larry:

I still have not got your letter off. Working all night and sleeping most of the day is such a demanding schedule. I can get nothing done. Yesterday I received an apologetic letter from Decker. He was at a loss to explain the errors; said he had entrusted the setting to his sister who had done innumerable books and was as careful as he himself, but he did not attempt to use this as an excuse, taking full blame. He willingly agreed to print the errata sheet, but requested that I list only the major errors, that I cut down the length of the errata sheet. He says:

> To list those minor errors does not help the poetry; they are errors which either do not affect the poetry (colon for semi-colon, etc.) or errors which the reader sees in reading and automatically blames the printer for, and corrects in his mind (up-side down letters etc.).
>
> I'm not trying to say that my wish to have you leave these unlisted is entirely unselfish; I know that the longer an errata slip, the more blame the printer gets. But I know this, too: a too-long errata inspires most reviewers to so many caustic and witty comments about the physical make-up of the book that they pay little or no attention to the poetry. I know; I've seen it happen, tho not with a book of mine. The point is simply that a long errata slip will not help either of us, and it will hurt both of us. I honestly wouldn't mind any panning of the printing, if it weren't for the fact that it will hurt the poetry directly, too. For I have a genuine interest in the poetry, and I want to see it get the right critical recognition.

I quote this at length because it throws me face to face with a problem about which I have here-to-fore been intractable. It asks me to sacrifice the highest merit of my poetry for the sake of a lesser expediency. The upside down letters I could readily concede, and even the misspelled words, when the word is intelligible. But the more important errors in punctuation are another matter; the interpretation of the text is at stake, and that should be all-important. Decker does not give my point of view complete justice here. And I doubt if I would concede to the argument of bad reviews of the book itself to the neglect of the poetry, which might be true enough, but which shouldn't be permitted to really affect the rightful presentation of the poetry.

I did, however, concede in the matter. An errata slip is such a hopeless make-shift that most people ignore them; they simply don't take the trouble to check back. Mostly, however, I'm warned about Decker. I still think he's the most important publisher in the U.S.—not for what he himself is, but for the need he's filling. The list of serious work pouring out of his press proves it. Everyone of his poets would probably prefer to publish elsewhere; but they can't. He's the one channel where serious work can appear *with some chance of adequate distribution.* Not the *one* channel, of course, but probably the one where the seriousness and the competency are the deciding factors. The big houses go by salability; the Laughlin's by the editor's preferences. I think it is important that Decker keeps going; and I know he can't survive many pannings. A few more and no poet is going to turn to him. A few more books like mine and he's through. It's the one point on which he can't compromise. I'm worried that he gets scotch and puts in cheap end papers, as in my book, when so very little more would have made so much greater a difference. It just isn't good business, good planning: those are the details that count with his type of customer. Frankly, I'm worried, I'd like to bring out subsequent books with him; but I doubt if he can go on like he has been, getting the kind of quips Humphries handed out in the *Nation,* and the kind of quips *The Masculine Dead* will undoubtedly receive. It's too bad.

I don't deserve it, but I'd give a nut—to steal your own fine phrase—to hear from you.

Bill

I have heard the records, and they stink. Please ignore the whole discussion.

October 4, 1942
Los Angeles
TLS, 2 p.

Dear Bill:

Sunday evening, family away for the day, I relishing one of my rare solitary times. Been typing all afternoon on that derned story of mine. Accustomed to typing so will swing into a letter to you, after refreshing myself with milk and grapes. Autumn, my favorite time of year, the canyon sycamores launching their colored argosies, the air warm and luminous as at no other time of year. Seems like we got to thinking about each other at the same time. When you were writing to me, I was mailing you that reprint of one of my "professional" articles. Am sorry to hear about the poor shape of your book. A pity you didn't get proofs. No money for books—having very hard time getting the four of us by on 150 per month—so suggest you get Decker to send me review copy for the *L.A. Times*, and I'll do a notice of it. Write him at once to do this; or if he has already mailed out copy to the editor I'll get it from him, if he's not given it out already. Am most anxious to see it. I'll have the library order a copy. Wish you would send me the records, even if you think they're bad. I have the three Jeffers recordings. Got a review set from Gateway to Music.

Had a wonderful evening here a couple of weeks ago. Friend in the speech department at the university read *Cawdor*. Cut it to about an hour and a half. Had about a dozen people in. Held them spellbound. We're going to have a reading a month; same fellow; *Loving Shepherdess* next time. Wish you could be here.

August was vacation. We had no choice but to stay home. A wonderful month though. Halcyon days. Did very little writing. Read a lot; travel, biographies; late poetry. [I] find that hardly any poem I can read through. Find my mind wandering. Respond only to a certain magical quality in verse. Hard to define.

Planned to devote my vacation to typing out my story. Instead didn't even touch it. Back to work in September and the urge hit me hard; but found I had to rewrite the whole thing again in longhand before typing. More time I have, like on vacation, less I do; put me in harness eight hours a day and I generate energy for a good sixteen-hour day. Marvelous to go through the paces at the library, padding efficiently around midst the herd of sterile females, secretly fabricating my world. I've figured it out, Bill, I'm a goddamned SCHIZOPHRENIC. So what.

Yes, I've seen Miller a bit. He's with the Neimans about two miles down the Glen. Neiman keeps grumbling about his delinquency in typescript; chaotic, badly organized. Hated it so he became incoherent. Doubleday of course didn't take it; too critical of the USA in these times. Miller works on continuation of *Capricorn.* He's badly discouraged by the war and all. Glands a bit exhausted. May decide to kill himself. Wouldn't surprise me. He's turned over to me for safekeeping a lot of typescripts, among others a huge one of letters he wrote to a New York friend, Emil, during the 20's and from the start of his 9-year stay in Paris. The first letters from Paris, when he was down and out, are particularly moving. Strange the way his and my paths have run parallel, diverged, then come together again. I might have lived more his reckless passionate life if I'd had more physical energy and less substantial family ties. As it is I've taken the safe respectable way. Any other, my physical nature being what it is, would have proved suicidal.

Ritchie is working at Douglas, editorial work in the preparation of operation manuals. Anderson runs the press. Work fell off so that there was not enough money for both. I don't see Ritchie much any more. His idea of amusements—badminton, games, etc.—and social aspirations cherished by his wife, are foreign to me. When we were young he was the serious celibate scholar, and I the cuntchasing jazzboy; now he amuses himself and I push a nocturnal pen in pursuit of some inevitable expression. I love the world, fucked up as it is, with increasing passion, and seek to attach myself to it in every way possible, to suck in a whole reservoir of other men's experiences, centuries of them.

Fisher I've not heard from for a year. Newell toils long hours in charge of plastics operations in a trailer factory, building units for the government. His wife does the sculpting. I've not seen him for several months. My old friend, Hal Bieler, M.D., I see every few weeks. Of all my old friends he has stayed the closest to me, because our tastes remain more or less constant in relation to each other.

I hope you don't get routed to a C.O. camp. I have a friend in one up in back of Placerville. Curious little homosexual chap, worked at the library for several years, got indiscreet in his room where he boarded; landlady reported him to university and he got canned. I got him a job with Zeitlin, where he stayed until they sent him off. Has bad asthma and could have been rejected on physical grounds, but wouldn't give them a chance. Said he was a C.O. from the beginning and stuck to it. Damned fool. Works hard up there cutting wood, with a bunch of Mennonites, and says he likes it. Do what you have to do, you mad goose, and don't get buggered bending over.

The world's completely fucked up. A mad world my masters. Pretty soon it will probably give the Powells a good whirl. All we get now is the pinch of small salary. Little enough to suffer.

Don't wait three months this time. Hope the rain holds off and you get your raisins in. I'd like to have been there when you were picking. I've got a terrible longing to go to Sequoia park and sit on my ass at the foot of the Grizzly Giant. See your stript vineyards too. See you and Edwa. As long as your love remains constant one to the other everything's all right. If you're thrust apart it will be anguish, but your art will thrive, see if it don't. God bless and keep you both.

Yours truly,
Larry
Professor Powell

SH:it

October 9, 1942
Los Angeles
ALS, 4 p.

Dear Bill—

I didn't expect you to send me your book. Therefore I was surprised & pleased. I have just come from reading it through, slowly, deliberately. It's a passionate book. Something in it that I haven't found for a long time—a breathing man, all of him, brain, cock & balls, not merely a trick brain ticking away à la mode. Many thanks for the experience.

The three poems—"Sides of a Mind," "From Bad Dreams" & "The Masculine Dead" are the book. I found them powerful, moving. The influence of Jeffers the least present. Did you arrange the order of the poems, or did Decker scramble them?

I won't say much about the inexcusably sloppy job he did on the book. I don't see how he has the nerve to take money for it. Do you want me to write him a letter? I share your indignation.

Add to your corrections "Betelgeuse" p. 6, "caressing" p. 37.

His section titles in *Mas. Dead* are set in the same size as the title & are thus confusing—should have been smaller & italicized. But I shan't point out the obvious.

Friday night and I'm dog-tired after a maddening week of library detail—all the tangled minutiae of an order dept. where our annual budget is $70,000 & the income averages 33,000 books & pamphlets in all languages. Constant tracking down of error, troubleshooting. I love it when I'm normal, but now I am tired & fighting off a cold—& inwardly sick at the world's frustration; I under the burning glass of delay. My life goes by; I should be at the head, not down the ladder. I was 36 on the 3rd of September.

I recall my piss & vinegar letter of last Sunday and smile a wry one. I want so much to finish my story & send it to you to read. It will be a couple of weeks yet. I have a desperate need to write something true & good, something simple & moving, that will be a testament.

Here I end up on myself. Such manners! All I meant was to write a heartfelt thank you for your book. The passion is in it, Bill; Decker couldn't suppress it! The book will make its way. Those three long poems are your testament & I find them good

& true, simple & moving. My heart leaps across the Tehachapis & beats on your fragile roof—hear it!

Larry

Oct. 12, 1942
Selma, Calif.
ALS, 2 p., 1 sheet

Dear Larry:—

A crowd of friends dropped by last night; stayed too long, talked too hard; drank too much; played too much jazz. I feel like hell this morning. One night of that makes me realize the superior position of the somewhat solitary life Edwa and I are living here together.

I was very glad to hear your reaction to the book; glad to know that the poems had a meaning for you. I sent the book to you when you suggested Decker mail a review copy: when the review copy arrives (or when you get it from the *Times*) send it in exchange. I'm getting sick of this damned commercial angle already. I hope you can do a review for the *Times*. I don't want you to praise it simply because we're friends; I know you wouldn't but I want you to know it's important with me that you don't. I'd rather have you in there hammering. What is important is that you get some space. Nothing is more discouraging than the brief Notices. But of course, that is out of your hands.

The arrangement of the poems is chronological and correct. Thanks for noting the two corrections—both my fault, not Decker's. If you spot any more, point them out. You're right about the headings in the *M. Dead*. I've groaned about that from the start. Also the large type of the dedication, when smaller type would have been more in order; also the poor design of title-page—etc., etc.!!

I'm looking forward to reading your story. It's been cropping up in your letters for a long time now, and I'm glad it's rounding off. I want to like it, Larry, I want an awfully lot to like it.

I note the enclosed circular on your Pickett talk, and share what must be your satisfaction that you can carry the testimonial both by way of pen and by way of mouth.

Your letter is indeed in different temper than the "piss & vinegar" one of last Sunday. The gall of your delay comes through it; the gall of being out of place in the middle of the ladder. The constipated machinery of bureaucracy hard dry shit.

I go back to the "piss and vinegar" now.

I share your feeling of Fall: my attraction to the season is I think because it is concerned with resolution, the resolving of all the summer projects; you can come to terms with autumn, whereas spring and summer are all motion. The poetry-reading evenings are a good thing, a fine thing; a too-rare thing. There are not enough people who can read well. Those who do, have too little an interest in poetry. I'm going to get another of the Jeffers records soon; one of the Lyrics; this *Tower Beyond Tragedy* one has too little good poetry in it.

The paragraph on Miller a rare bit, and I'm glad to know about him. I hope he comes out of it. We should rightfully expect many more things from Miller. A question that has long troubled me: how much of the *Cancer, Black Spring, Capricorn* trilogy is autobiographical and how much fiction? R. Duncan, who has had intimate sessions with Miller, implies most of the erotic adventures are fictional. The question is not as unimportant as it sounds. Obviously much of those documents are true; so much that they lend credence to what I otherwise couldn't believe.

The example of Ritchie and Newell I can understand but thoroughly deplore: thoroughly deplore. Of all objections to war I count this among the greatest: that under its bane the sensitive people of the earth, of their own volition, reject their rightful enterprise. I resist that to the very last.

Reclassification came in 4E. C.O. Didn't even interview me. Didn't even demand responses from my referents. I wrote a paper in 1940. Couple weeks ago when they re-submitted the form I submitted another, bringing my attitude up to date and reaffirming my stand. It was my best piece of prose writing, I think.

I think I'll go crazy in one of those God-Camps. Pray before meals, between meals, after meals; pray in the middle of the night I suppose. The 30 bucks a month angle beats me also. I don't see it that way.

Saturday night the High Command released a weather report. Edwa and I scurried down and put up the last couple hundred traps. No rain as yet, but it threatened. We're safe now.

I wish that wish to see the Grizzly Giant and our stript vineyards could have its way with you. Maybe we can get down. It's been years. We want to get away before the gas ration and the approaching, long-dreaded separation. I can't conceive of leaving her; my mind, my senses refuse to accept that situation. I catch myself thinking of it in a kind of consternation.

Bill

I return the clipping of last July. These things are terrible. *Poetry* came today. Note review of Mac's *Faust.* Still working at cannery. The last few crippling nights. This week will kill it. Thank God.
Before I go, I'll bind up a typescript of all poems since the *M.D.* so you may have them.

Nov. 4, 1942
Selma
APS

Dear Sir:—

My wife and I are contemplating an excursion to the Los Angeles area this coming weekend; if all goes well we should like to see you Saturday.

Sincerely,
Wm. O. Everson

Nov. 20, 1942
Los Angeles
APS

Dear Bill—

I hope to have the typescript ready to send you in a week. Keep me posted on your plans. We had a fine visit with you & Edwa—couldn't have been finer. Hope you have not forgotten the Miller books! Am enjoying Sherwood Anderson's memoirs, savoring them, a little every day.

Larry

Nov. 28, 1942
Selma:—
ALS, 2 p., 1 sheet

Dear Larry:—

It was indeed a fine night at your house. One of our very best; I was dumbfounded when we went up to the living room and regarded the time.

The whole weekend was fine; the trip a complete success. Sunday, as you probably know from Miller, we spent a couple of hours at his house. He was in excellent form, and we struck off well together. A really wonder-full man! Christ! He planted enough in my mind in 2 hrs. to keep me high for a week. I cherish my two visits with him.

I'm sorry about delaying his books: the fact is that when I came home I remembered they were only half-bound, and that stalled me. I promised *Black Spring,* but on remembrance, I'm fixed with a problem—the Shanghai edition is the one Miller autographed at your house, and I couldn't part with it; the Paris edition is so much more readable I hate to give it up. You understand. The *Capricorn* I send. Keep it closely, for the sailor may turn up yet, or his family demand his "books." I don't mean to attach any strings. It's yours, and God bless you! The *Max* has only a story or two not reprinted elsewhere. Send it back when you're finished.

Miller told us he hasn't even copies of his own books. I felt so astounded and sympathetic I almost committed these to him though I'd promised you! That's really a shame, but they're surely hard to come by. Bookseller in Fresno used to sell the sailor's cheap pirated editions for $15.00 a copy. I don't know what a Paris edition would fetch. Even they aren't well printed. Only the *Max* has lucid impression.

Last weekend Edwa and I went down to our ranch and gleaned what grapes we had missed, got 16 boxes, took them to the winery. Guess what we got? Over a dollar a box! We're putting all the ranch earnings right back into it—levelling, repairing, replanting, etc.

I've a scad of poems to send you when I can type them off. The errata sheets have finally arrived, though Decker even cut down on my revised list—one an important omission, too—the 1st one. The book is finally launched!—a year late.

Bill

I await and anticipate your typescript. I know what it means to you Larry, and I await it with expectancy. I enclose also a couple of proofs from my new book. It is coming very slowly; we have had a great deal of trouble mastering (sic) the merest technical problems. We simply cannot get even impression on the hard paper, though these pulps are better. Atkisson, a swell chap, really; I might say an extraordinary chap in many ways, is very painstaking and deliberate; though we can pull proofs all afternoon and never improve them, yet must we pull in the attempt none the less. Of the 32 pages we finished seven. That is not very rapid progress. I spent the afternoon over there today (29th) and only 2 pages emerged. With the gas rationing coming on I don't know what will come of the venture. Through an error I didn't order enough stock so the edition will be very small—under fifty.

Bill

Carothers came home over Thanksgiving. Christ I was glad to see him. Whereas Atkisson, when I show him poems, can find absolutely no sympathy for them, for neither their wholes nor their parts, nor their methods, nor their directions; I can always find deep sympathy and understanding from Carothers. It's not that he unreservedly commends everything I do, he does not; but he *understands* the attempts, he perceives the relationships; and even his criticisms are the greatest encouragement.

Fay's preserves were superb.

December 2, 1942
Los Angeles.
ALS, 2 p., 1 sheet

Dear Bill—

Your letter here today on the eve of my sending you the typescript. Inasmuch as I'm including a printed book, I'm sending the whole parcel "book rate." When you return it, please do so to me at the university: University of California Library, 405 Hilgard Ave. L.A.

The "Quartet" has gained a movement. It was originally planned in 5, then cut to 4, and finally ended up alongside the Dionnes [quintuplets]. I am stuck on neither the title nor the subindications. Perhaps the latter are artificial, affected? Perhaps just section numbers would be better? And a title "From My Life"? My whole effort has been to simplify, to underwrite, to avoid excessive emotion & statement. What else is there to say? Alas, I know not. Anyway, off it goes to you—its first reader—and God help us all!

Thanks for the errata slip. I'll paste it duly in. No copy yet from the *Times*.

I am delighted to hear that you make progress in printing your next book. Thanks for the proofs. They read well. I look forward to some typed ones. I wish I could print my story, just enough copies for my friends. Next I wish I could pay Ritchie to do it.

The typescript I send you is my only copy, so guard it. I still have the notebook ms., but it received much rewriting & expanding, etc.

Yes, Miller said he enjoyed your visit. Don't worry about his not having copies of his own books. He sells whatever he can lay hands on. He seems to prefer living hand-to-mouth by any means than working for a spell & saving up a stake. Whatever he does is all right with me, as long as he keeps on writing.

I'll look forward to the *Capricorn*. I understand about *Black Spring*.

I wish I could visit you. I have an "A" book [gas ration allowance] & ride to work with a librarian from San Fernando Valley. Have only Xmas & N.Y. off, worse luck.

Glad to hear you did so well with your crop.

Life is good. I think I'll tackle next the rewriting of Jo Meredith's "Personal Record"—the college years. [Jo Meredith is a pseudonym for Powell.] I see them with a different eye & write with a different (& I hope better) pen.

Greetings! Larry

Dec. 8, 1942
Los Angeles
TP

Dear Bill:

It was superb of you to transmit your enthusiasm by telephone. It was a pleasure to be roused. I cannot tell you how delighted I am that the piece has clicked with you. I felt you would have an intense reaction one way or another, but I feared it would be on the minus side. Hence my pleasure, delight, and general relief. I await a letter from you. The morning is gray and cold, but my blood circulates and keeps me warm. Greetings. L.

Dec. 8, 1942
Selma
ALS, 2 p., 1 sheet

Dear Larry:—

The cold and sober light of morning, a morning hooded and obscure in the clamp of a fog, brings with it the apprehension that my impetuous telephoning of last midnight, might not have been in the best form. The pattern of domesticity should be held in greater respect; and I fancy that fools, who might be tolerated in the breadth of day, are fixed upon with a steely eye when they drag one from his bed. My apologies to Fay, if I roused her—to your sons if I disturbed them, and to you, if I angered you, even momentarily. I have the excuse of sublime exaltation, and I did not feel it should be resisted.

Let me assure you that the morning clamped in its cold as it is, has not lessened my enthusiasm. You have done a magical thing. You have reached back through a decade and dragged a year of the past out of its grave. For the past is there, and it is alive. The landscapes live; the towns and the houses, the gardens, the streets; and the people live: all are restored and alive. And I, an American, a Californian, who has hardly crossed the borders of my state, am given once again to gaze beyond my confines to the heart of Europe, as I have done a few times before, in Lawrence, in the *Magic Mountain,* and in the travels of Wolfe. The *atmosphere* tingles. Only an acute and responsive imagination can do this; it is a quality that is primarily not literary at all; the literature is but the means; there is first the vibrant response to experience.

Without that, there can be skill, but the skill will be dead. The skill is here, indeed, but it is not dead. The skill is most certainly here. I am quite surprised at the surety with which a situation is handled. It is not a matter of deftness. The Sat Eve Postists can adroitly handle any conceivable situation. What I am trying to put my finger on, and it lies at the center of this work's success, is not the naked response itself, which can be intense but inarticulate, nor the surety of handling itself, which can be deft but dead; but rather that combination, that rare essentiality, wherein craft and response are so merged that neither one surmounts the other: that is the point where "writing" ends and "literature" begins. And its stamp is on every page.

Let this letter be entirely one of commendation. To not do that would be to cheat you, as you do not deserve, of the enthusiasm of two individuals (for Edwa too has read it; and seconds this judgement, and let me say she has a discernment in these matters the years have taught me to respect) who are happy and proud to be among the first of the many readers this book will certainly have. If a word, a twist of phrase, an observation here and there seem to me to be out of the spirit of the context, let me reserve them for a subsequent note, which I will enclose with the ms., and for light pencilings in the script itself. May I do this? The sheets will be returned very soon, not because I do not want them by me, but because you must bend your efforts to getting this thing into type. It should not be too small an edition.

With my great esteem—

Bill

The Ritchie flabbergasts me. A marvelous Christmas present, one I have desired for years. You are too good. And the catalogue—a storehouse! Do you want it returned? or may we keep it?

December 12, 1942
Los Angeles
ALS, 4 p., 2 sheets

Dear Bill—

I kept looking for your letter all week & finally it came today. What in hell happened to it? Run over by a steamroller?

I had hoped that you would like John Burgoyne's tale. I feared you might not. You do. Oh excellent!

Jesus Christ Mr Everson, is it that good? And Edwa thinks so too? Publish it? How can I? I don't think of it as being read by any but a few. I could not hawk it around on publishers' row, nor do I have the money to print it. But I'm essentially insouciant. What will be, will be.

I can't tell you how warm you have made my heart and brain. Your phone call was, I repeat, a superb gesture. I shall never forget it. And now your letter to confirm it.

I am eager to have your critical notes on the ms., and I know it will benefit from them. Pencilled notes on the ms. itself will be most acceptable. I want to eliminate false notes, words, phrases, etc. The thing must progress, modulate, develop with utmost simplicity & naturalness. You can help me here. I have had no help from anyone. I need it now. I have the feeling that I should fill in, enrich, smooth & polish the typescript & then have a final typing. My friend Catherine Wilson will type it for me.

In all of Henry Miller's work there is no sex tenderness, no rich & tender relationship between men & women. All is brutal. I do not say that he is wrong. Most relationships are as he writes. But I have gotten something from women he has apparently never gotten, & I wouldn't trade it for all the apples of Hesperus. Lawrence first called *Lady C.* "Tenderness." You know what I mean. You and Edwa have it. It is in your poetry, enriching it more than anything else.

Thank you for *Capricorn.* Sketching through it, the sex episodes stirred the paragraph above. Many thanks for this book. *Max* I returned by express, having read all of the contents one place or another. Thanks anyway for sending it.

I lent Miller *Masculine Dead* but have not seen him to get his reaction.

Newell was here last Saturday. We had a rare visit. I love him with all my heart. For 18 years we have been friends & our friendship endures. Nothing much else matters beside this affection between one's self & a few men & women. My life would stop without it. You have come into my life that way, William, as I tried to tell you the night you were here.

I am close to a good job here in Los Angeles. A library. I'll tell you if it comes.

I have done enough "scholarly" work to enable me to rest on my oars for awhile. Now I want to write my own heart's books & the devil drop a load of liquid shit on the hindmost. Now I want to go back 20 years & more. All of this has to be written in time left me after the day's work, but that's good. All through the day my subconscious toils for me.

Each noon while I eat my lunch I read a chapter in *Sea and Sardinia.* Have you read it? Years since I first read it. Affords a perfect little cross-section of pure Lawrence. God how the Sardinian hills & towns, inns & peasants come to life! Perfect command of his instrument, English prose. Vision & craft perfectly welded.

Enough for tonight. Will you send the typescript now & to the university? I am anxious to profit by your remarks.

Glad you like *Americans*. That red eagle of Szukalski's is one to put alongside Parrish's rooster!

Am toiling in the corner lot with crosscut saw & axe, getting in our winter pile of oak logs. To sit before a fire of one's own wood!

Again thanks for your response. It means *more* than I can say.

Larry

[Los Angeles]
[December 1942]

Bill—

Thanks for your lovely letter. I'll call you when we get in on Wed. & perhaps I can come by that evening.

Larry

Sun. Dec 13, 1942
Selma
ALS, 3 p., 2 sheets

Dear Larry:—

I have just finished the ms. and made my final notes. I told you I would get it right off in my earlier letter. I have not procrastinated, as in earlier instances, but I found that I could only read and notate a single episode a night, until tonight. Tonight I have gone through three; this has been because the quality of the work vastly improved as you progressed. You yourself made far less alterations in later pages.

As to my notes, consider them tentative and personal. I do not mean to be the sedulous critic weeding out little irregularities of style. When a thing popped into my head I put it down. I have not noted all the good things in the book. Sometimes when I thought an instance I felt uneasy about might be merely personal with me I said nothing. Take my remarks merely as pointers. If you see what I mean in any given instance and yet feel it should stand—let it. But then, of course, you would do that anyway. Who the hell am I that anyone should change his work for?

But let me say once again my extreme pleasure in reading the book. You have done a fine thing. Character is superbly handled. Every one of these women is unique with a quality of her own. And the thing is not a sex novel. Miller for instance, is masturbative, writing out of the sex itch, feeding his sex on the narration. In this, the sex is subordinate to the women, which is what it should be, and the women are subordinate to the totality of experience. The man here, the narrator, you, is a most marvelous guy, in his way, for he sees what counts in the totality of experience: he is aware that life is an extraordinary, a magical thing, and he does not deny it. Personally, I'm glad to know him; I'm glad to have read his book; and I know a bit more what it's all about than when I started.

* * *

To interject the wrong note in a letter such as this, but the truth is I received day before yesterday a form from the National Service Board of Religious Objectors in Washington. The form is to help properly locate religious objectors in satisfactory work. A manual enclosed said it took 3 to 4 weeks after receiving the form. Then 10 days. Then—in I go. So that's the way it is.

God (to quote one of your own phrases!) help us all!

Bill

P.S. I have to thank you again for Ritchie's *Americans*. In some ways I think it is the best designed book of modern poetry I've seen—the blackness of the type-face; red contrasting numerals on the distinctive quality of the paper, the magnificent title page—these things all total up to just about perfection. Yes, I think it's even better than *San Joaquin;* more masculine, bolder. Riding doesn't deserve it, and I'm jealous of her, the poetastress!—not that I am deserving of it! Let's see—who would that book suit? Donne.

Mon. morning—

Your card has just come. Did you get my soiled letter? I'll tell you about that. Wrote the letter last Tuesday morning. Tuesday night we took in a show, rare event for us, and I put the letter in my sweater-coat pocket. We were a bit late so I decided to post the letter afterward. Then forgot it. Wednesday morning, couldn't find it; thought I must have dropped it in the theatre. Went down midday, but the place was closed. Was worried. Had said about what I wanted to say, and then I could not get quite the same tune again. Show-time Wed. night went down again. Parked in exactly the same place I had Tues. night. Getting out, noticed a soiled square of paper on the pavement. Turned it over, it was your letter. A whole day's traffic before the busiest store in Selma had gone over it.

* * *

For months, well to be exact, since mid-September, not one word have I got from Decker. Then, Fri, in comes an envelope. It contained a mimeographed letter, stating that that communication was going to 500 people in an effort to sell books, that, frankly, his affairs were in desperate condition; that in the 3-odd years they'd been publishing they have grossed slightly less than $5,000. Out of that paid living expenses (wife, sister and he), and have published over 50 books of poetry.

"Our equipment is scant and well-worn, with the result that we have not always done the best of work. We are understaffed, with the result that we can't handle business details as promptly or as accurately as they should be handled," etc. etc. He has to sell five hundred dollars' worth of books by Dec. 24th. He lists a few books, mine not among them. Closes with an urgent appeal.

It looks like about the end. Too bad. Fucked away a whole year and the book not out for review yet. Now it won't be. Shit.

December 22, 1942
Beverly Glen
ALS, 2 p., 1 sheet

Dear Bill—

Typescript safely returned. Your notes are helpful. They couldn't be better. I have benefited from them all. Of course. Points of style, tone & taste. All just. I finally went blind to the whole thing. By the time it went off to you, I couldn't see it. It needed just the reading you gave it. Wonderfully sympathetic yet critical. I'm eternally grateful to you.

Of course I must rewrite the first episode & parts of the second. They did not benefit from a third rewrite which all the rest got. And then the first is always the hardest. Hard to focus & to keep a grip on. Once more over & I'll have it.

You did not answer my query about the title. Shall I keep it "Quintet," with the episodes marked? This is important. I must have your help here. I do not want a precious quality that might adhere to such a title & movements. I want simplicity, inevitability. Call it "From My Life"? An echo, of course, of the Smetana quartet & also a famous Goethe title—*Aus Meinem Leben.*

And yet the musical title & movements mean something—at least to me—in connection with the work. It is written for few parts, & on a small, compact scale. I could expand it into a long novel. But I don't want to. What I've sought is life's essence, the essence of young life, alive and aware. I have tried to do in a book what Beethoven did in his last quartets. Is it valid?

There are the recurrent few materials. Cafés, streets, railway stations & trains, perfumes—& women who are one & the same & yet not the same. They are anatomically the same & yet they are different. And the old people, sexually withered, in vignette. Just glimpsed, hobbling off. The gleaners, the old candymaker, pension keepers, the guide, the guard, etc. Just a handful of materials in the whole book, but packed & woven, dense & tight.

Tell me what you think.

How sorry I am to hear of Decker's plight and of your notice from Washington. Can I do anything to help?

I can't write any more. Night. 10 o'clock. Tired.
Am off for 4 days starting Thursday. Wish we could meet.

Merry Christmas to you
& Edwa.
Larry

Dec. 27, 1942
Selma, Calif.
ALS, 6 p.

Dear Larry:—

Your letter arrived yesterday, which leaves me two to dispose of; one, written in reply to my letter, the other in reply to my notes. To the first one:—

I'm very glad my reaction to the ms. uplifted you. I wanted it to, and to that end I reserved my adverse comments for the typescript itself. Too often the feeling of triumph and accomplishment is hedged in by a rift of reservation and qualification; the commentator is afraid to let himself go on his initial enthusiasm, wants to keep a loophole out in case his second sight comes out less; thinks always somewhat of himself, and never wholeheartedly of the other man. The writer is then thrown back on himself for his conviction, and something is lost. I went all-out on that letter because I felt you deserved it; my judgement does not carry much weight; but it is sincere, and, of course, I am very convinced of my own insight(!) which itself is conviction and adopts the tone of authority. I hope I did not do that. Any man, any unknown creative writer, who can bring off a piece of work that has the accomplishment of this one, shouldn't be denied his moment.

You say you feared I might not like the work, a just apprehension in view of my reaction to the Pickett, and perhaps two such extremes may seem to you to be the product of a willful and capricious attitude. My own protestations are of course insufficient to absolve me from the charge, but, surveying my mind, I do not feel that my position is contradictory; without wanting to bring the Pickett up for discussion again, it being of a special type and firmly in the past, I do think that the sense of insufficiency I felt there, and the sense of sufficiency I feel toward the more recent work, are both bred of a well-grounded attitude toward literature, subject of course to the vagaries of taste and unconscious prejudice.

You also ask, in evident surprise and delight "Is it that good?" and I assume you refer to my associating the ms. with the names of three stalwarts: Mann, Lawrence, and Wolfe. Edwa herself thought this coupling to be ill advised, and you will note that I used the reference in such a way as to be somewhat qualified. But you will note that I did use the references, and I did it deliberately.

What I said was that the feeling of Europe, the feeling that I cannot classify but which pervades, in my mind at least, the atmosphere of a few very moving pieces of writing dealing with the European environment, was present to a marked degree in your writing. In the opening pages of *The Magic Mountain* (and here I must confess and lament that my knowledge of that famous work stops there), as the protagonist deploys from the train and starts up toward the sanitorium, that feeling, if I remember rightly from a single reading several years ago, is evident. I have encountered it often in Lawrence, very markedly in the Alps denouement in *Women in Love,* and frequently in Wolfe, perhaps most in *Of Time and the River*. The feeling has to do with a sensuousness, a reaction to the environment, and I suppose that it is largely personal with me, certainly American, the raw-earth American feeling toward the antiquity, the moodiness, the humanitarianism, the culture of Europe. It is very evident in the "Quintet," and is the mark of a very poetic and thoroughly enchanting response, and it is evident to such a degree that it caused me to deliberately use the references that I did.

If the "Quintet" does not attain to the stature of the best writing of the men I mention (and do not forget the caliber of those men) it is because of something that is very hard to put the finger on, but that lies I think at the very point of division between a great work and a lesser one. The qualities of greatness that are evident in the "Quintet" are qualities that derive essentially from the nature of the attitude. It is the work of an amateur, as opposed to the work of a professional. I mean by that that it is the work of a man setting down, not necessarily his own experiences, but rather his own attitudes, his own intuitive responses to events, for reasons other than

Tues. Dec. 29.

Unfortunately, I was interrupted in that sentence by the arrival of a friend, and was forced to put the letter by. Rather than attempt to complete the sentence from a different mood, this abrupt break seems advisable.

I was trying to distinguish between the amateur and professional attitudes, and to get over it quickly, I'll say it something like this: in amateur writing what is being said conditions and creates the language; an amateur writes when he's moved and the quality of his writing is affected by the depth of his feeling. The professional has a great enough technical facility to handle the requirements of any situation, and does so. It's the difference between the creator and the craftsman, which doesn't deny the craftsman some occasional successes—but those are perhaps when he unconsciously becomes absorbed—oh hell, I guess there's considerable interplay.

To get to the "Quintet"—what keeps it out of the final level, as I was trying to say, is this: At the moments of greatest tension there is a softening, a relaxation, not conscious, but a lapse; an imperceptible failure to keep the objective. The words fail, somehow, to keep the correct correspondence between reader and writer. It isn't a damning defect. I doubt whether it's primarily a defect in craft at all, but perhaps of insight. This sounds far more condemnatory than I meant it to sound, my intention being simply to try to indicate at what point the difference lies. Does it mean more to say that there is a blurring at the moments of great tension; the situations become hazy because the words lose their edges.

Toscanini once said of Bruno Walter—"Where I suffer, Walter melts." If that is true it is not apparent throughout 95% of a work, but only at the point where the carbon becomes diamond. It is the greatest test of writing. I know myself I cannot attain it. I know in my heart there are situations that all I can do is insufficient to match. I know also I could never write the "Quintet" and bring it off as well as you have. It is like the music of Bruno Walter, ample, abundant, spacious, in taste, and fine. The Toscanini's are far between.

As to the notes, I'm glad they can help you. I know exactly how you feel, that "blindness" after so great an effort. In such times a man is wholly in the hands of his friends, and their responsibility is very great. I read a critical comment once on the relation between a writer and his friends, I'll try to find it sometime. It's an acute situation. I'm glad I can help, but you'd better not lean-all-out on those notes. My taste is vulnerable. I might have missed things: I might have been unjust. Be suspicious of me, Larry.

As to the title, I think the most original and perhaps the best way out is to retain the musical references. I've never seen that done. It fits well in the mood; "Quintet" is sparse and unpretentious. The subtitle—"from my life" may be added or not as you choose. It doesn't need it; but it's o.k. if you want it.

Thinking it over, one thing I'd like to discuss is the name of the protagonist. French name on American resident in France. My first reaction was that it was tricky, an attempt to ride in on the implications of a name. I was prepared to encounter instances wherein the confusion between the nationality and the name would affect various situations, and that would have completely justified its use. No one in the story notices it, however, and the reader remains uneasy as to its purpose. If you had actually had a French name (what the hell *is* your name, anyway) and had gone through 4 years in France uneventfully, I'd be prepared to retract immediately. But as it is, it isn't convincing to me. This may be personal with me, and hence inconsequential, but consider the matter.

It doesn't look as if Decker is going to issue any prospectuses, so the book won't get much airing. Whenever the occasion admits, or if any one happens to inquire, I've copies of the book here. If Decker is going to fold I'm not likely to see anything of what he might sell. Henry Miller wrote me a swell letter in regard to the book—really surprised me in taking such interest in the poems. My impulse was to send him a copy, for I know he has only enough to get by on, but the Carothers angle always cuts that sort of thing off. Kenny doesn't care, but the time's coming when another book is going to have to be got out, and I'd like to make some sort of showing. There's been a bit of response in Berkeley. Watkins took a bunch and is sort of peddling them around. Five or six copies already to friends there. It doesn't look as if Decker will get out the review copy to the *Times,* so if you want you can write the review anyway. If not, forget the whole business.

It's almost New Year's. I've just finished about the best year of writing I've ever put in. My work has been ample and far solider than before. So much of the earlier work depended upon a surface texture, but in this year's work I feel the poems have cores that support the texture and permit the peeling off of layers of effects. I feel very good about the way things are opening up for me. I can see always before me new modes manifesting themselves as I work through them, and I know that is the nature of the progression. The overhanging of the draft hasn't thrown me off. I can play cat and mouse as long as they choose! But I've had a tendency to neglect the farm in favor of the poetry, and I promised myself I wouldn't do that.

Well, let the new year be a good one, Larry. Get your new job or hang on to the old one. You say you don't want to hawk the "Quintet" on publisher's row—I think that's right, though it could stand up there. Come to think about it, most books we love don't seem as if they should come off publisher's row, but they do. Every writer despises the alley, but what can we do? Don't be in a hurry though—you're right in that. That book wasn't written for next week's dead-line.

Luck
Bill

P.S.: Edwa was given *This Is My Best.* Glancing through the pages I noticed the word Vézelay. It was Irwin Edman's piece, also about France. I read it, and felt how inadequate it was beside the "Quintet."—Maybe I'm making too much of a furor about that piece. Maybe it ain't that good. Maybe you'll go swell head. What?

1943: DRAFTEE AND DIRECTOR

January 3, 1943
Beverly Glen.
ALS, 4 p., 2 sheets

Dear Bill—

I have brooded the weekend over your 6 page letter. I of course understood that you meant that my work was comparable to Wolfe, Mann, Lawrence only in that it evoked the poetical essence of certain aspects of Europe. I know just what you mean by the slackness, lack of tension, that distinguishes a lesser work from a truly great one. I know all the virtues & faults of writing, but when it comes to my own work, I can do only what my essential & total nature permits me to do. I am working toward the day when I will be able to write something that is perfect. It will have to be something on a small scale. I know that the progress I have made in 9 years, as shown in the works of J. Meredith [pseudonym Powell planned to use] & J. Burgoyne, is promising. Give me ten more years and I'll do it. First I have to write my own story. Then perhaps I can write others'. I do not have a great deal of imaginative insight into other people's lives. But now I have more than once I had.

Your point about the protagonist's name is well raised. Burgoyne is an English version, I believe, of Bourgogne which is the French name for their own province of Burgundy. Thus John Burgoyne = Jean de Bourgogne or John of Burgundy. It's a sentimental pseudonym, to be sure. Burgoyne is not a common name in English, although in the paper the other night I noticed it in the column of vital statistics. You will recall General Burgoyne of Saratoga fame. I grant your point that in the story it would somewhere cause comment. I shall perhaps endeavor to introduce some explanatory conversation into one or more of the episodes. Or do you believe the choice is ill-advised & should be scrapped? If so, suggest alternatives, please.

You ask about my own name. Powell is pure Welsh. Clark is English. Lawrence is Norman-French. And that is precisely my ancestry, all three families traceable back to their emigration to the U.S. in the 17th century. I only know this because my mother's sister is an ardent genealogist. You will be interested to know that Fay is Norwegian on her mother's side, Wilkerson, hence Wilkie our youngest.

I have just got the ms. back from a local reader. What about his sole criticism? "Stop the Madeleine story where she leaves on the Blue Train. What follows, the Italian visit & Paris again, is another story. The idyllic poetry of the whole thing drops to commonplace at that part."

I am at a loss how to answer such a criticism. Is it valid? I do not feel that it is. A drop is precisely what I intended, not to the commonplace, but to the lower pitched poetry of denial. All of which is aimed to intensify that much more the final episode, as well as what came before.

I am *not* suspicious of your taste & judgement, as you advise me to be. I find them very close to my heart & brain.

I shall have to look up Edman on Vézelay. Must be in his *Philosopher's Holiday*. Do you recall the photograph of Vézelay in my mother's little book? It shows the ramparted grove of chestnuts in back of the cathedral. Pater wrote a poor essay on Vézelay. I am coming more & more to prefer Jack Burgoyne on the subject.

The raisins arrived Christmas morning. Many thanks! The box seems to be inexhaustible. We eat and eat, & still there are raisins.

We have had a rich and peaceful holiday time. I had 4 days off. Home all the time, except for a New Year jaunt to the Rose Bowl to see our Bruins play. Alas!

Reading two Huxley travel books: *Jesting Pilate* & *Beyond the Mexique Bay*. See Miller every few days. I was there the night he was writing to you & shared his enthusiasm. Somerset Maugham is now living farther down the Glen. What a canyon full!

Will you be able to finish your new book (the printing of it) before you go camping? I hope so. Send me some of your new poems, will you?

Happy New Year! (sic)
Larry

Jan. 8, 1943
Selma
ALS, 2 p., 1 sheet

Dear Larry:—

Glad to see your fine letterhead again. Thought you must have used it all up. My favorite letterhead, I think. Just the right firm masculine effect. Did you design it?

Brooded over my letter all weekend? Do not do that. What matters is the realization of the essential crystallization. You see that. You are striving toward that. In several instances you achieve it. Situations, I mean. The body of the work is high and sustained. Ten years, you? It will not take that long. Make no mistake about your achievement. You have come so far along, and you cannot lose that. From now on it's work, work. Mastery. Control. My ten years have taught me it's one long fight with yourself. Insight and control. Insight and control. The control means sweat, but by god it's the best labor in the world. You know that. And we cannot be cheated in our own hearts of our accomplishment. What we have done we have done, and we alone can measure the triumph over ourselves. What the world does with it is beyond our control. I suspect that's largely luck. But what we achieve within ourselves, the crystallization, that is not luck. Insight and effort. Insight and control. And it's all worth it.

No, do not change the man's name, if you can work in the little instances of interrogation it would cause the work to be enriched; the work will be enriched beyond the use of a straight "American" name. Those things make life what it is. That's the stuff a writer must exploit.

In regard to the Madeleine episode. Have you considered the device of putting a division, such as asterisks, after the train departure? This might indicate the termination of an emotional peak, reduce the shock of the reader, and psychologically prepare him for continuing the motif.

The local reader's comment is natural but shortsighted. The first feeling is that the episode should end there. But it later develops that the extended conclusion is actually what makes the episode what it is. It could end there quite naturally, but it would not be the same piece of work it is now. The sense of suspension, of waiting, of time passing, and then the crumbling of hope and the final acceptance of the loss. Certainly the local reader sees that this is the fullest realization that the episode affords. And he should see also how much the implications of the final episode depend upon this one. The psychological attitude with which the man enters that affair would not be so meaningful without this previous conclusion.

I do indeed remember your mother's sketch of Vézelay. It rang in my mind as I read the ms.

I do not hope to finish the book before I leave. Gas ration pinched us off. Sanger is 12 miles away. 24 miles a day on a bike takes too long. Atkisson says he will struggle along with it. I doubt if it ever comes off, knowing the man. The poems do not interest him, so there is not that stimulation. Or rather they interest him by their faults and excesses. But what I mean is he takes no joy in them.

I'll try to get some poems typed for you. I'd have before this but the typing is such drudgery.

Forgot to say that in November sent Dorothy Norman of *Twice A Year* the poem "One Born of This Time"—she liked it very much but wasn't sure about one or two points, and wanted me to explain. The implication was to revise. Pretty stupid stuff—misread the poem. I revised the conclusion and "explained" the rest. She may not want it. After 2½ years (since, that is, the *Poetry* episode) I am starting to submit to the magazines again.

Am doing farm work now on our place. Digging, pruning etc. In view of the imminence of departure probably won't work the pipe this winter. I'm lucky in that the pipe boss is also a C.O.

I await the event with equanimity, troubled only by worry for Edwa and the deep hollow unrealizable feeling of parting. But for my own self, I simply wait. The indignation, the bitterness, the horror, the fear, all have gone out of me. I am a pacifist now in the deepest and quietest sense, a sense something like serenity, a great and abiding spaciousness of soul that accepts what must come. I feel ten years older than when the war started, and look back on my antics with some embarrassment, though I realize it had to be before this itself could come.

Bill

I smile now at my railing against Decker about error. For I, even I, the infallible I,—I make them, too. No matter how closely I watch, the errors slip into the stick [while setting type] at my fingers' tips. "Ah me, I fondly dream!"

10:00 PM

I meant to get this off in today's mail, but it was not to be. I suppose you recall the HMV imported recordings in Gateway to Music's recent catalogue? Lo and behold, couple of days after Christmas in came a package from them. Gift from Carothers. Guess what? Landowska's harpsichord set of Bach's Goldberg Variations AND Schnabel's Beethoven—Diabelli Variations. This last is the most unutterable music man ever conceived. We were bowled over, as you can expect. A mere $40 worth of records. Trifling sum, what. All of them are superb. Last Christmas he gave us Art of the Fugue. He had me order the Limited Editions Club Casanova for a friend this Christmas. Christ, that man!

Broke down and gave Henry *Black Spring* and *Capricorn.* He needs them, badly, I believe. It's little enough to do for such a guy.

For a month (your ms. started it) I've been in a high state of musical reception. Listen to it by the hour. Wonderful, music. Nothing can quite match it. I've never outgrown the *Eroica.* It pulls me back and back. 1st movement especially. Every time I hear it I find myself down in front of the speaker like a gibbering idiot. Have just come from mass blood test—pre-army stuff. Thought of Lawrence's "The Nightmare." The old oppressive herd-revulsion got me in spite of myself—sheer romanticism, but for a solitary man it's hard—B.

Mon.—Jan. 11, 43
Selma.—
ALS, 1 p.

Larry:—

Really sorry not to have got this letter off, but stop-press news erupted in our midst and life has been a maelstrom of haste and violently conflicting emotions ever since. In the parlance of our imaginative underworld—this is the "the works." I go next Sunday—the 17th. The place—Waldport, Oregon. A Brethren camp. The map shows it as a tiny village 2/3 up the Oregon coast—on the ocean. That's all I know. My address will be, I am sure—Civilian Public Service Camp #56, Waldport, Oregon.

I won't have time to write Henry before I leave, so tell him.

God bless us all
Bill

Jan. 22, 1943
C.P.S. No. 56
Waldport, Ore.
ALS, 1 p.

Dear Larry:—

I haven't had much aptitude for writing since arrival, and haven't yet, so this won't be much. Had a hard trip up, missed a bus and was thrown off schedule, arriving late. Camp is good, as camps go—new, warm, and neat. The last C.C.C. camp to be built. The men (there are 150) are mostly deeply religious, and not too intelligent, but simple, unassuming, and reserved. Camp life is directed by the men themselves. A sprinkling of intellectuals throughout, but I haven't become acquainted very well. I'm not supposed to work till Monday, but they've run me in on a few camp jobs. We're right on the ocean, though it can't be seen from camp. No mail has come through. I haven't heard from you for a week or so before I left, and should really like a letter. My past life seems remote, my future seems blank. My spirits have been fairly high, but thinking about it now I'm beginning to feel sorry for myself, so I'll close. Tell Henry hello for me. The food is fine here, and everything even and moderate. Only I miss Edwa, and worry, worry. But that does no good.

So long
Bill

January 24, 1943
Beverly Glen
ALS, 4 p., 2 sheets

Dear Bill—

Greetings in your new abode! I am anxious to hear of your arrival & how you are faring. It is Sunday night & I am weary, after two days of digging out. A tremendous rainstorm; south-west gale brought over five inches here in the canyon. Roof leaked, creek overflowed into garage, trees blew down, etc. No serious damage. Wonderful benison after the long drought.

Miller was here a week ago today & took your new address.

Glad you like the letterhead. I found a few remaining sheets. Ward printed it to my general specification of "something bold & simple," along about 1937.

I was glad to get your full letter written soon before your departure & to have your additional notes on "Quintet." Your reaction to it was the needed spur which set me on the final revision. Just before the storm I completed a ms. rewrite & subsequent typing of the first two episodes—the ones that needed it most. Now I catch my breath before giving the next movements more or less the same treatment. Pruning, adding, seeking to crystallize, as you aptly put it, to heighten tensions & smooth modulations between tensions. You're right, it's the only labor in the world that really matters.

For these several weeks since your letters, I have worked nearly every night with sustained excitement carried safely throughout the day's work, husbanded & brought home to the quiet of my study—all this in a world spinning in blood. Yet I have to follow my own development, come what may. I think of Joyce in the last war—"silence, cunning & exile"—

I want to know if you will be able to write up there. Will you get leaves to come home? Can Edwa visit you? I think about you a great deal & pray that you will be able to turn the whole ordeal into something creative & great & good. I believe that you will.

Can I mail you any books? How about Rilke's *Wartime Letters* or George Lemaître's *From Cubism to Surrealism in French Literature*? The latter I have just finished—excellent. During my lunch hour I read an early Norman Douglas—*Siren Land,* an account of the Italian coast round about Naples & Capri.

Your Xmas haul of records sets my mouth to watering. I have heard the Goldberg album at Bieler's, but never the Beethoven Diabelli. Schnabel played on campus the other night—Schubert & Mozart—no Beethoven.

Enclose a letter of Newell's—please return—the Connell pictures are of Gordon's work—the piece I asked about is the one, I believe, of which you wrote the poem. I have a picture of it.

This letter started out with high hopes, but I am too weary to hold it on the road.

Only two thoughts that matter.

1. How are you?
2. I have just lived one of the finest six weeks of my life, toiling for the last (?) time at my book, under the pleasant spur of your superb criticism.

Larry

P.S. Am going to talk to some librarians next month on "Books I Have Liked"—It's going to be fun. If I write it out, I'll send you a copy.

[A later comment by Powell: this was the start of my career as a public speaker! 9/12/65—L.C.P.]

Thurs. Jan. 28, 1943
C.P.S. No. 56
ALS, 2 p., 1 sheet

Dear Larry:—

It is your letter, even more than Edwa's, that brings home to me the feeling that I am living in another world and another time than I was 10 days ago. The things you discuss and which so concerned me then I had almost forgotten in the absorption of meeting this new life. I am still a bit numb, though not so numb as when I wrote you the brief note a while back, of which I remember nothing, and which must have been bad. I too finished one of the best periods of my life, and can appreciate the bountiful feeling that yours has brought you, and am glad I was able to contribute to that bounty. I hope you can make it continue, I'm sure you can, for you are now experiencing I believe the prime ends of life, and will surely grow.

I can take my companions with less wonder and awe now; they are still fine, but the work program has set in, and men under the stress of labor are all toilers, and reduced more or less to the basic physical entity, which I have always known. The work is quite hard; we are crushing rock for a road, and heap fragments on a truck to be hauled to the crusher. The weather is cold, an icy wind has persisted, and rain falls. These factors would make any exposure uncomfortable, and handling the heavy and ragged stones with icy hands becomes a kind of drudgery. I look through the hours to the evenings in the warm barracks.

I have met several affinities. One, a Missourian with a great beard and a fine high-domed head [Glen Coffield], whose interest is writing but whose tastes can stand considerable refining, bunks across from me. Proximity has made him my closest acquaintance, but I still can't get completely next to him: an inherent uncrossable reserve holds me off.

Only person in camp whose literary tastes approximate mine is a young university man from the East [Harold Hackett]. He is also quite a Jeffers man, and deeply interested in modern poetry. He has a sound insight into these matters, though I cannot get him enthusiastic with anything of mine I have showed him.

There's also a half-assed sculptor [Larry Siemons], but, though I haven't seen anything of his work I have grave doubts about his talent.

One musicologist from L.A. [Robert Scott] whose musical tastes are acute and with whom I've had good moments. A musician himself, pianist, and exhibits the artificiality of the type in his mannerism. Sadly out of place on the rock-crusher, even ludicrous, and a shame to be put there.

I doubt if I'll do much writing up here. The work has so far proved too tiring. We work six days a week. I haven't explored the country hereabouts as yet, hoarding my free moments to spend over my board trying to come to grips with my uncompleted poems. I'm out of the psychological groove that germinated them, so that I cannot become immersed in them, but most of them were nearly done, so that I'm sure they will finish. Then I must wait on the problems this position engenders.

There is constant pacifistic discussion here, it crops up at all points, and is everywhere in the air. The War is remote, very remote, very little news is on our radios hereabouts. This tends to make an artificiality of feeling, for the only reason we are here is the War, and unless the war remains ever-present our situation loses meaning. The world situation and its realization is the one thing that can make our position tolerable. That lacking, it becomes just another job, and that should not be. At home, absorbed in the newscasts, the war was constantly present, overwhelming, immediate. It's absence here tends to make the discussions abstract and theoretical. I still doubt if many of the men have thought it clear through. Most of them are willing to endure whatever the government will impose upon them, and that is their chief central preoccupation: but the true test is whether or not they would be willing to endure what the Nazis would impose upon them, and that is another matter. I doubt if many of them have seen through to that. The Bible pacifists, the ones who are simply against war because it's against the Bible, are, in spite of their lovable qualities as persons, a bit pitiable from a conceptual standpoint. They miss so much, the universe is so much more terrible than they realize, and I cannot help but feel that the long age of death will find them sadly unprepared.

I'll look forward to your letters more than ever now. For

California, and home, and Edwa, Edwa, Edwa—they are all so very far away.

Bill

A good letter from Newell: I return it, with thanks.

Feb. 5, 1943
Los Angeles, Calif.
ALS, 2 p.

Dear Bill—

Your two letters, the second more reassuring than the first. Good to have the details of your environment. If you can remain master of this experience your life will be incredibly the richer. It is difficult for me to write to you where you are now. I do not want to offer you redundant sympathy, nor do I want to appear smugly wrapped in the blanket of my own content. I, librarian and secret nocturnal scribe! And yet I cannot present myself to you disguised. You know me too well. What I have been makes me what I am; & what I am I will be. So make allowances for me if I sound too other-worldly to you, you toiling, uprooted from your own land.

The draft seems to be reaching for L. Powell. By transferring to a job at Douglas or in my brother's sleeping-bag plant, I could get 3 B classification instead of my present, 3 A, which may be shifted to 1 A if Mr. McNutt has his way. But I don't want to leave the work I love; & perhaps I will sit tight & if drafted, later this year, go into the army with the hope of being put into library work after preliminary training is over. That would mean Fay would probably have to go to work. A dilemma both horns of which are giving me a simultaneous goosing.

Feb. 6, Sat. afternoon, at the Library

I'll finish this letter from here. Every 2 months my turn comes around to work the Sat. afternoon skeleton shift—a good time for meditation, as the place is nearly deserted, particularly the order dept. Up till now (4:30) I have been working on the talk I'm to give, next Saturday, on "Reading I've Liked." During lunch hour I read more in Rilke's letters.

We have a superb Rilke collection; mostly in German, it is true. Unfortunately we lack the volume of poems he wrote in French. He had an influence something like Lawrence's—a cult & all that. Something similar in their restless wanderings & the impact on them of the war.

Nearly every night I have been working on the "Quintet." Now it is almost "finished." What to do with it then, that is the problem! I am anxious to have it out of the way, finished to the best of my powers, so that I can take up something new.

Finished typing last night about nine-thirty & heard Beethoven's last quartet (op. 135) on the air. The nonchalant intensity, the easy mastery—what a marvel! To do something comparable—the greatest monument a man could hope for.

Greetings, sir!
Larry

[The next letter mentions the two mimeographed camp publications, *The Tide* and *The Untide*. The former was a bland, non-controversial sheet, begun in November 1942 and ending in July 1943; there were six issues in all. Bill Everson's poems are in issues 2–5 of 1943. There were twelve issues of *The Untide*, volume I, and three of volume II; these were dated from January 6 through September 5, 1943. Everson's "War Elegies" appeared in volume I. In May 1944, as newly appointed editor of *The Tide*, I satirized the earlier issues of *The Tide* in the manner of its rival, *The Untide*. There were no more issues of *The Tide*. But late in 1944, *The Untide* was revived by a group that turned it into a latter-day version of *The Tide*!—W.R.E.]

Feb. 21, 1943
Waldport
ALS, 2 p. 1 sheet

Dear Larry:—

Heap abuses upon me! Richly I deserve them. Time has poured on, your letter has been here a couple of weeks, and

I've never answered it. Somehow I cannot collect my thoughts, or synthesize a mood, that would produce a letter. I cannot yet settle down. The work consumes the day, and the nights are always full. I try to work my poetry, and a daily letter to Edwa engrosses, and then there's so much discussion, the camp teems with it. There's more activity here than I ever knew in college; everywhere you turn someone's up to their ears in it.

I had them send you a copy of the official camp news organ, *The Tide,* which ran an old poem of mine. *The Tide* is pretty stodgy stuff; sponsored by the Church and all, and somehow never gets much punch. A young rival [*The Untide*], which sprang up, and by virtue of its being a weekly, and copping the intellectual ferment of the camp, has about stolen the show. I am completely identified with this group. My poetry has gone over with them; they are all now close friends of mine; and I even helped get out the current issue. I'm enclosing the last couple copies, with the "War Elegies," which are going over very well.

The work has more or less resolved itself. I no longer find it so burdensome. The weather has cleared, and the outdoors is not so miserable. We are left up to our own initiative, there being no herding or driving. All that is to the good.

I am apprehensive about your own situation in relation to the draft. I hope all these things resolve themselves so that there is not the disruption of family that I am undergoing. To sunder man and wife, is, I am becoming more and more convinced, the greatest, and the most extensive, modern crime. In spite of all my running here and there, my surface activity, I am not living. That's why I cannot share your opinion that this will be a great period for me. At home, with Edwa, I was constantly synthesizing experience, breaking into the resistance of language, trying to relate language to experience in that particular way that characterizes the outstanding work. That was what was important, rather, I think, than the variety of experience itself. I have written here, but it is an exploitation of the new experience, rather than an exploitation of universal experience. It is all I can do for the time being, but I am not to be deluded into believing it is enough.

You mention the Rilke. I have never read enough of him. I was vastly stimulated by the Poet of the Month Rilke of last year. MacIntyre's Rilke I have never had long enough to know; nor have I ever seen the Norton translations, which are highly ranked. I intend to have all these before I am done, but they must wait.

Am greatly interested in Baudelaire. Ford's translations in Poet of the Month did it. Have worked at "The Voyage I" with a French dictionary, and help. I cannot get the music, but the conceptual element is incredible.

> They dream, as a conscript dreams of the cannon,
> Of vast sensualities—

I know the Opus 135 very well indeed—certainly a fitting conclusion for such a life. I'll try to get more off, sooner—

Bill

[Letter from Edwa]

Feb. 24, 1943
Selma, Calif.
APS

> Dear Fay & Larry,
> Thought I'd get a letter off to you but this card will have to do.
> Bill does not have the *Duino Elegies*. His only Rilke is that of the "Poet of the Month Series."
> Bill sent me your last letter; (I hope you don't mind?) & I do hope things work out better for you.
> Give my regards to Henry. I'm sure Bill would be grateful for any reading matter, poetry or prose.
>
> Edwa

Feb. 24, 1943
Beverly Glen
ALS, 2 p., 1 sheet

Dear Bill—

Thanks for the *Tide*. A whole page, with illustration, to "Clouds"! Some stuff—& I mean it! Good stuff. Why didn't you give 'em a new poem, instead of such an old one? Which is to say, I want to read what you've been writing. Don't talk to me of the drudgery of typing your own work. Two weeks ago I finished retyping—the second time—the ms. of "Quintet." I think I got it this time. I hope to send you a printed book for your next reading of it. I believe I have decided to send it to an eastern publisher—Alfred A. Knopf. He has printed similar length books, & as you know, is interested in love & Europe! I hope now, after a final polishing, to have it typed by a friend—& then off it goes. Shit, I say!

Nothing new to report. After finishing the book I was down for three days with a cold. Had a fine visit with Newell—he asked for your address. I have been reading Rilke like one mad—everything I can lay hands on, in three languages. It's been a marvelous experience. And all the time—night & day—I am turning over in my mind the material for my next book. I have not yet found the mold into which to cast it. Until I do, I cannot start. Perhaps it will come soon. My life has been so full & rich that I need the strictest discipline of form if I am to avoid confusion & incoherency.

Recent draft pronouncements gave me a bit of a scare. I decided though to stay where I am—& not be stampeded into so-called defence work—and let the army come & get me. Thus it stands.

I am preparing Aldous Huxley collection (Jake Zeitlin's) for exhibit in the library. After that, I hope to put on a two-poet show—Yeats & Rilke.

The other night before going to bed I read through your last book. I get more from it after each re-reading. How goes your life at camp? Any writing?

Wonderful rains here, after long drought. The canyon sycamores have burst into leaf. Yes, these are my best years, in spite of delay, discouragement & war.

Yours ever,
Larry

February 26, 1943
Beverly Glen
ALS, 2 p.

Dear Bill—

Copies of the *Untide* are good. I like the "War Elegies" Series. It pleases me to see you active in this way. Please send me all issues. I note the artist Kemper Nomland. Is he K. N. junior? I knew a local architect of the identical name—some years ago in fraternity work—he's a Columbia Phi Gam—is now about 50 years old. He couldn't be in a C.O. camp. Fay has seen plans by him in architectural magazines—liked them—& said if we ever build a house she would like Kemper Nomland for architect.

Glad to hear of your interest in Baudelaire. I have carried a copy of his *Fleurs* with me since 1930. I believe MacIntyre is translating him. I have not heard from Mac for a year, but just wrote to him.

Did I tell you I am planning two exhibits for the spring—the first is Jake Zeitlin's Aldous Huxley collection—Jake wants to print a catalog to accompany it. The other is "Two Poets: Yeats & Rilke"—drawn from our own holdings.

Last night I set down outline-notes for my next book. (How stuffy that sounds!) The college book. A reworking of "A Personal Record"—to be written probably without reference to the earlier ms. Now I've called my own bluff. I wonder if I'll be able to meet the challenge?

Yours
Larry

March 1, 1943
C.P.S. 56
ALS, 2 p. 1 sheet

Dear Larry:—

Your letter has just come in, crossing, perhaps, my own in the mails, and I hasten to pen a reply to save us the confusion of talking to each other always at cross purposes!

The *Tide* poem was amusing. My sole interests, as I believe I told you in my last letter, developed with the *Untide,* so that my work had appeared there before in the *Tide.* But the *Tide* editor looked me up, and asked to see some of my poems, and I showed him some in ms. He looked at them a moment, talking along, and finally said: "I wonder if you might have some that these fellows would understand." Which of course meant that he would understand! Finally he got back into the *San Joaquin* and hesitantly selected "Clouds," almost at random. *Untide* printed from *San Joaquin* first also, but that was because I was proceeding slowly and hadn't at that time shown any work in ms., preferring to consolidate my local position on the more impressive material of *Work In Print!* Now that's past. I'm well-known; principally as a poet, and enjoy a gratifying degree of respect. This is solely because I have impressed the few who count, who, in turn, impress those who can't tell but would like to. Outside 3 or 4 people, most of them simply don't know what the stuff's all about. The "War Elegies" sound impressive, the general title does, I mean, being about patriotism, but nothing seems to click with them. It's very amusing. The illustrations don't help them much, either!

Yesterday I gave a recital. It was fairly well attended, and well responded to, though everything that applies to the printed poems applies here too. But among the intelligentsia I am very well accepted, which, of course, pleases.

Of the 150 men here I have found one affinity; one near affinity, and a host of swell eggs. This is a most marvelous place to be cooped up in. And I suffer a deep sense of guilt that the situation is one I can enjoy while Edwa suffers in Selma. My work has been going along better than I expected. I am writing a series of poems out of the situation here, and I think they will be among my best. I suffer most the lack of privacy. You even shit in public, and that's going too far. Had I a place I could retreat to in the nights I could get far more done. The barracks are always abustle.

I am disturbed at the imminence of your draft situation, but I commend your decision not to stampede. Good man. Know that I understand your position, that I in no way harbor the slightest disrespect that you have not seen fit to accept the same recourses as myself. These things do not affect my friendships, my admirations, nor my trusts.

That you have decided to send on the "Quintet" to Knopf I heartily approve. It must be printed. I suspect it is only the prelude to a creative life.

O.K. I'll try to send some poems. You're going to be surprised. I should tell you—Carothers suffered a nervous breakdown and has [been] discharged from the service. It's quite a story.

Bill

My poems have even spread. Cascade Locks, Ore., (short residence of Lew Ayres), wants to use some of the Elegies.

[The preceding letter refers to the *Illiterati*, a mimeographed literary magazine published at the Cascade Locks Camp #21. Edited by Kermit Sheets and Kemper Nomland, Jr., it later was published at Waldport, when the editors transferred there. There were six issues in all, numbers 1–2 (1943) (mimeographed) from the Locks; #1 was banned by the Post Office and destroyed; #3 (1944) (mimeographed, but with printed cover and title page) from Waldport; #4 (1945) (printed) from Waldport; and #5 (1948) and #6 (1955) (both printed) from Pasadena, California. These last issues were done by Tom Polk Miller, Kemper Nomland, Jr., and me.—W.R.E.]

Mar. 3, 1943
C.P.S. camp 56
ALS, 1 p.

Dear Larry:—

Your letter yesterday, which so delightfully crossed up my purpose in a quick reply, preceded the Rilke today, which staggered me, and left me speechless and overwhelmed. It is one of the most important acquisitions to my library in recent years, for it will not only give me pleasure, but it will fill a need, and I have reason to believe there is much to be learned from it. I cannot thank you enough; I have longed to come to

Rilke for several years now, and only his unavailability has kept me from it. It is almost worth coming to C.P.S. to get such magnificent responses.

Kemper Nomland is indeed K. N. Junior. I felt sure he was your man's son when you mentioned it, for he is interested in architecture, and he has confirmed it. A slight, pug-nosed strawberry blond sort of guy, rather aloof and a bit of a snob. When I first came I noticed his pictures in his Dorm (as we call the barracks) and tried to get acquainted, but it was tough sledding. Then *Untide* had him do the "War Elegies." He came down from Cascade Locks in a group sent here till April to get the trees planted. Having sent *Untide* back to friends in Cascade Locks who were quite taken with the stuff, he warmed up. Oh, hell yes. Everything was hotsy-totsy. Know what I mean? Not a bad guy though. I'll be sorry to see him go back to Cascade Locks, certainly. He likes experimental art, which is good, but he can't quite swing it. I mean he lacks the conceptual insight and the spiritual depth to make it a vital thing. It's surface. I saw the Mexican exhibit in S.F. last year, and it was one of the profound experiences. For them, it [painting] was something great; for him, it is something like entertainment. Which is not to say he is not better than the usual traditional "artist"—he is at least intriguing.

I commend your new book exhibits, and note with pleasure your start on the new "Personal Record." I am penning out "Poems 1942" for you in the mornings before work. Again, believe me when I say that nothing could have pleased me more than the Rilke. I mean that.

Bill

March 7, 1943
Beverly Glen
ALS, 2 p.

Dear Bill—

Our letters indeed have been crossing us up. Can we get straightened out? Here I answer your last two. Elegy Number

3 at hand. They give me much pleasure, and I shall treasure the series. Do see that I miss none. How much time do you have to yourself? What hours do you work? Is there a camp library? Information please.

Glad you like the Rilke. I sent it to you in the belief that it would fill a need. I am just emerging from a veritable Rilke-jag. We have quite a collection in the library, & I have made 37 order cards for items we lack, both by and about him. There is really a formidable body of Rilke literature. Probably never again will he meet such a large particular need of mine. Between books for me & he plugged the gap. He & Beethoven—my old pal, L. Van B. His op. 135, which I bought at month's end. Budapest recording. A masterpiece, laconic & dazzling. I seem never to have heard it before. Reading Marliave's treatise on the quartets, which adds to my pleasure.

Also acquired an album by Villa-Lobos—a Festival of Brazilian Music. Have you heard it? Includes a beautiful evocation of Bach, for 8 celli, called Bachiana Brasileira—marvelous. Henry Miller dropped by yesterday (Sunday) and I played him this—also the Debussy quartet, which he had heard only once before. Miller continues his serene way; has gotten in some money & has no worries. I re-read his Greek book the other day & it gave me a damned good feeling.

I have not started on my next book, more than to make outline notes. I put it off. How long do you suppose I'll live? Postponements could prove fatal!!

Enjoyed G. Stein's little book on Picasso; most remarkable for its many reproductions. I think often of Parrish, the dead painter, & wear his clothes to work. I want to place his paintings intact in some museum. M.F. has them in storage, except for those on her & our walls.

A similarity between the last works of Beethoven & Rilke—the quartet & the elegies.

You'll remember my wanting to send you the first volume of my European journal & how instead I kept it throughout the writing of "Quintet." Sometime I'd like you to read the contemporary record. I suppose it would be better to wait until you are home. What do you think?

I'm fermenting inside. Hope I can bring off a good brew! Plant a tree for me.

Larry

P.S. Got a $25 a month raise from the legislature & are we fat! $180 now.

Mar. 15 1943
Waldport Ore.
ALS, 2 p. 1 sheet

Dear Larry:—

Just time for a quick one—Rilke's *Elegies* are marvelous—one of my most important literary experiences of all time!

Thanks for your letter, which I enjoyed greatly. I won't be able to supply much local information this time, but I'll at least get off the two *Untide*s. They're mostly of local interest, but perhaps something will come through—but remember the "Elegies" are to be bound up separately and disposed of that way—which pleases me.

Let me tell you how glad I am that you are creating—so many of my acquaintances have petered out in the creative line—rest on the indications of talent they never exploit (Carothers, Watkins, Curtin, Atkisson, and now up here my best friend Hackett) that to find a man busily engaged in spinning himself and his past out on a page is a matter for rejoicing. I would not, in myself, force any literary issue—re your period of gestation before beginning—but we all know ourselves best, and I can trust you to do the right thing in this.

I want very much to see that early typescript, but I don't think up here. I could not do it profitably, things being as they are, but remember the promise, and if things settle down I shall ask for it. You understand my present emotional situation.

No, I have no time to myself. Like a fish in a bowl. Even the toilets are side by side—but I have begun to train myself to dispose of that process on project, where I can have the privacy of a hollow stump. But even so, I write: drawing myself inside myself. I'm working on a series, I'm sure my best work to date. I hope to send some.

I've quit penning my poems but am typing instead, as I can. Bide with me a while yet.

Have never heard the Brazilian music. Will try to send you some snapshots of life here.

Bill

March 18, 1943
Beverly Glen
ALS, 4 p., 2 sheets

Dear Bill—

I mailed you a copy of Baudelaire the other day. Your recent remarks about him anent Ford's paraphrase in Poet of the Month were in my mind when I came across the *Fleurs* in a shipment of duplicates we were dispatching from the library, and so I culled it for you.

I knew the *Duino Elegies* would hit you hard. Day after tomorrow I put in the Rilke-Yeats books at the library. Also a MacLeish collection. He is speaking on campus Monday. It is Ritchie's collection—all of his books. R. has left Douglas to take a job as "production manager" with the local office of a great advertising company. I called on him yesterday to pick up the books. Streamlined office, big business associates, endless labor on a newspaper layout for—Purex! I doubt he ever returns to straight printing. He wants money, position in the community. His wife is partly responsible. I never felt so distant from him—whom I have known since kindergarten—as I did yesterday. Yet there is nothing to be done. He does what he must do. He is what he was, & will be what he is. He fulfills his necessary destiny. I am thankful to have shared in all he has done so far. But I cannot turn to him for sympathy and understanding, the way I once could, because our paths have diverged toward different goals. Our problems now are dissimilar.

He cannot be my idea of him—as poet (cf Peter Lum

Quince) [Ritchie's pseudonym] and artist. I do not sit in judgement on him.

Your letter & two *Untides* here today. A good little venture. The "Elegies" cumulate emotion. No. VI I had never read, I believe. Superb. The lines on the armies: 6–10. Give me a thrill like the worms rushing through their destinies in your last book. I'll look for the *Illiterati.* Will you send?

The past year & a half I have been writing has been a time of mounting tensions in my mind. More or less constant warfare in myself. Fay finds it hard to understand why I have to write & is not altogether happy that I draw, snail-like, into my shell at every opportunity. A sort of Jekyll-Hyde existence I lead, as I have written you. Library work 8 hours a day & then my nights. An excitement, though, about it all. *I am determined to realize my gifts to the utmost of my ability.* If in the end I prove a failure or, worse, a mediocrity, I hope I die without discovering it!

But now I *do* believe. A few days after writing you last I began the new book, & am now 30 pages into it. Safely into it, so that there can be no retreat and I feel relieved!

We have had good rains all February & March. Everything grows & blooms. The little creek flows even between storms.

I enclose the second *Flying Hiatus* [publication of the Rounce & Coffin Club]. Please wing it back!

Have not seen Newell for several weeks. I am nudging him back toward creative work. He is in a low period. Last time over I saw a fearful self-portrait he drew in pencil—a gaunt, haggard, crazed face. I didn't know whether to laugh or cry.

Jesus, what this war is doing to people aside from killing them! On the campus we have 400 army air cadets studying meteorology. I observe them closely & learn a good deal without saying a word. The tremendous regimentation, standardization going on. You, wise rebel!

Is there any censorship of mail at your camp, either incoming or outgoing—any spying?

I look forward to your new work.

Who is Hackett?

What happened to Carothers? A breakdown? Get him to will me the Casanova!

Have you had a haircut yet? Keep wearing in leonine. I

marveled when you were here last, and remembered wistfully the wonderful beard I wore in France.

Pax!
Larry

March 23, 1943
Waldport
ALS, 4 p., 2 sheets

Dear Larry:—

Yes, the Baudelaire came in, and I was tickled to get it. I have been wanting a complete edition of the poems, and although I cannot read the French I am going to get hold of a dictionary and work them out. Several fellows here, of course, can read the language, and already I have gone over some of them. That was a fine gift—one of the little things that make a day to day routine endurable.

The *Duino Elegies* grow on my mind. *Oh and there's Night, there's Night, when the wind full of cosmic space feeds on our faces.*—Those marvelous poems. Hackett's brother sent him the Norton translations almost the same day, so we've got a fair selection now.

I can understand your feeling of separateness from Ward, but I suppose I cannot really understand all that it is. These are strange things, and we can only accept them. Yet perhaps he will come back. I'm glad I knew him while he still had his grip, and *San Joaquin* will remain a testimonial to the man he was and can be.

I send on the current *Untide* though the poems were left out. We sat up till daylight Sat. night hammering out the Editorial here. It is mine and Hackett's. I am going to try to draw away from *Untide* for it seeps up valuable time and energy. Last month or so I've been helping out, though I don't claim the obvious corn it contains! The "Here on the Edge" in your issue was mine.

Glad you like "Elegy VI." The collection should be out soon. It will contain two that the editors feel they cannot run in

Untide—Eros and the Dunkards [i.e., the Brethren Church administration], you know.

The *Illiterati* is out of Cascade Locks Camp (old home of Lew Ayres), but I hope to pick up a few copies. Indeed I'll send.

I know well your feeling of conviction and purpose as you write, and it is the supreme reward: it will carry a man through a wretched life, and lift a good life to wonders: sometimes it is a dupe, and we never know when it is and it isn't. I've had the feeling over stuff that turned out to be sheer crud; but it doesn't dampen. Edwa and I had to thrash the problem out together from the start, but now that she sculpts she understands. Let us be of good faith. We have our function in the world, and as I see the soldiers, the factories, and read your account of the cadets at the stronghold of Culture and the Liberal Arts, I believe it is perhaps up to you and me and the other solitary workers in solitary rooms to preserve the conceptual attitude of the feeling man, the articulate man, these we know to be the supreme concerns, and each in our way, serve our purpose.

No, there's no censorship or spying, here. Everything's on the level. The director and all the staff are C.O.'s. Came up through "the ranks." We solve all problems mutually, and I have not seen one instance of coercion here. Compared to what an Army Camp must be, this is heaven. And outside my marriage and its obligations, I'd rather be here. I'll put it this way—separated from Edwa, I'd take this place, though we get but 2.50 per month.

Hackett is my best friend here. Born of missionary parents in Tokyo. Spent 15 years in Japan—speaks Jap, of course. The only man in camp really concerned critically in aesthetics, though Coffield, a ragged bearded recluse, has a great creative gift. Hackett is only 22—but a fine mind, and well trained in thinking. Graduate University of Minnesota. But has also an irritating sense of rebellion and irresponsibility.

As for Carothers, I don't know the total situation. I know he was discharged for disability. What he told me was that he collapsed one day, woke up in a psychopathic ward, three days later. A letter from a homo was found on him and he was accused of being one. Denied it; was not believed, and was discharged. There is more to it, but I don't know. Pressing

Edwa by mail she admitted that he had told her the complete situation, but had asked her not to tell me till later, and she in turn asked me not to insist. I trust them both implicitly in anything they say and have not demanded anything. But Edwa tells me the poor devil is in a bad way, shattered, despondent, a veritable wreck. When I saw him last, at Thanksgiving, he was in perfect spirits and health. The whole thing is beyond me. (But I don't believe he is a homo.)

Things rock along, I've neglected my poetry for a good ten days and hope to get into it again.

I have trouble with my haircuts. Edwa cuts them short every time. Here in camp, I came in with a good fine 3 months' growth—let it go another. The local barber sheared me down. Now I've got to let it get back to a decent length again. There are many beards here, and in all but one or two instances, they enhance the face. I tried to grow one, but after a week the itching drove me frantic, and I shaved. Most people were relieved. I shall try again, soon. My beard is heavy enough it should be fine.

Let me tell you about Edwa. She is living alone there in the little house, seeing no one but the school children and teachers. Ever since I left she has been going down to the vineyard after school and pruning. That completed (4 acres), she began to lay out and peg the bare 3 acres for planting, a meticulous job, incidentally, for everything has to be even and to line up. Yesterday's letter tells me she completed the planting of the grapevines alone working after school and by moonlight. Every farmer around there told her she couldn't do it. There's a woman. Since I left she's developed something of a heart ailment, though for the life of me I can't get anything out of her about it. All I can do is sit here and worry. Due to the work she's neglected her sculpting—when I left she was hewing out a fine female head, large, from one of the stone blocks you saw in the car last time we were in L.A. It should be her finest piece. I have a photo of one of her nudes pinned up on my locker, a superb reclining figure. She has an extraordinary creative talent locked within that hesitant soul of hers, but it's a job to get it released! Exploited the page and the time, so for now, adios.

Bill

I forgot to say Carothers went to Berkeley to get work. Forgive my hasty scrawling. I had them send on *The Tide*. We address the covers before they're bound, so I don't know what's in it yet, nor if your copy was fair. Thanks for *Hiatus*—nice going—and I return.

March 28, 1943
Beverly Glen
ALS, 4 p., 2 sheets

Dear Bill—

Thanks for your letter & the last issue. I missed your "Elegy" & look forward to reviewing the next issue. Here is a check for $5.00. Put me down for 50 copies of the collected issue advertised at 10¢ apiece. I want to give them away to people & some libraries. You will send your own to the Library of Congress? Please have them shipped flat & well packed—the 50 to me, that is. You are going to send out review copies?

My biggest experience since writing last has been to hear & meet MacLeish. I mailed you a copy of the campus paper which printed his Charter Day address in full. He's a spellbinder! Wonderful radiant personality—mixture of shyness & sophistication that bowled everyone over. And his voice—soft & flexible—read the poetic prose of his address with such compelling hypnotic effect that people sat entranced. A complete triumph. A huge ovation. He came over to the Library & spent some time looking at my exhibits of his books & those of Yeats & Rilke—and said, with truth, you have paid me the highest possible honor by including my books with those of Y. & R. A real spellbinder. Last night I led a faculty party in a discussion & reading of his work & tried to reveal the significance of his evolution from lyric poet to public figure. He has always been a restless man, abnormally sensitive to all kinds of influences which bedazzle his work & all his utterances. He has reached an audience now with his great rhetorical prose utterances such as he never could reach by his poetry. But—it is as a poet—the poet of *New Found Land*—that I like him best. And told him so. Much as I appreciate the stirring voice he has lent to my profession.

So much for Archie.

Your notes on your friends are interesting. Loyalty and devotion to one's friends. Little else matters. Edwa toils indeed. It's tremendous to think of her laboring solitary in the vineyard. Can you ever get leave? Or she visit you?

Sunday noon. Szigeti fiddles Brahms. Henry Miller here earlier. I have come in from cleaning up the yard. The canyon oaks are changing leaf. A high fog. Great rains have fallen. Everything lush. Roof leaky.

Am excited by a plan to translate François Mauriac's book of poems *Orages* into English. You will remember I used one from it in "Quintet"—"Phares"—I have that one & a few others from the book—which I transferred into my journal years ago in France. But since then I have never been able to locate a copy of *Orages*—Published in 1925. Our library is canvassing American libraries, to borrow it for me—& I will type its 74 pages.

My new book goes ahead. Five to eight pages a night. So far I have not paused to type & revise—I want to get the whole first part on pages before I go back. I plan four parts.

Well, Bill, my boy, Fay is calling me to lunch. I greet you on an empty stomach—shortly to be filled.

Larry

March 30, 1943
Waldport Ore.
ALS, 1 p.

Dear Larry:—

Well, I've finally fulfilled our long promise and am sending you the poems. This is 1942's work, an unusually good haul. I think they are better than the last ones you saw, but do not let my opinion deter you from a good blast! This situation has severed me from the trend that was in full swing when I came in. Cut it off. My emotional response is entirely different, and the direction of my thoughts. My new writing is different; and will have to work out in its new direction.

Some of the "War Elegies" should also fall in 1942's

work—nos. VII, VIII, IX being done then. Incidentally, they're about done. I enclose the last *Untide,* and will send the *War Elegies* when they are wrapped.

S'long
Bill

I think I told you nos. VIII & IX were not included in *Untide* as a matter of policy.

April 5, 43
Waldport
ALS, 1 p.

Dear Larry:—

A hasty, too hasty, reply to your letter and check of last week. The letter was good, the check amazing, and I am humbled and proud before the gesture. The *Untide* would not believe until I showed proof, and hardly then. I have not sent the 50 copies because we ran out of paper again, and had to suspend production until new stock comes in from Portland. We silk-screened 250 covers, and that will determine the extent of the first edition—but of course we can continue publication as long as orders come in! The thing is really quite nice—Nomland was just hitting his stride when the series came to an end, and his last designs I feel are quite good—exactly what is required. The cover is attractive and bright, also designed by Nomland, and is of itself good enough to sell the thing. Only thing wrong is a poor mimeograph, which wouldn't feed smoothly or straight.

With the drawing to a close of the planting season, the Cascade Locks boys have returned to their home camp. I really miss Nomland and his group. He's an active Socialist, and the whole group took a strong and trenchant stand on any debatable question.

Thanks for MacLeish's address—really one of his best things, infinitely superior to his recent poems. I agree on *New Found Land.* Do you know *Immortal Autumn*? But of course.

It must have been very interesting speaking with him; and you describe vividly.

Interesting project on Mauriac.

Your new work goes ahead—good.

Will get those copies off to you as soon as they are made. Have patience!

Bill

April 17, 1943
Beverly Glen
ALS, 4 p., 2 sheets

Dear Bill—

Two weeks since I wrote last. A week ago I came to the end of the first part of my new story—125 pages written in three weeks, hardly missed a night's work. This means to me more than it says, for in the past (even on the first draft of "Quintet") I was never able to work sustainedly on a story. I could not sustain my belief in its worth. Now I can, & I rejoice. Now I intend to type and revise Part I, before pressing on. I want to go back and see what I have; then will I know just where to go. The past week has seen us going out a couple of times. Can't play the hermit constantly and keep a wife!

Many things to acknowledge to you. The last two "Elegies," and *Tide,* & 2 letters. Forgive my unresponsiveness. The Pearl Harbor Elegy is one of the finest—the best war poem by anyone I have read so far. A very beautiful poem, Bill, daring & original. I am most anxious for my copies of the bound *Elegies* & hope the paper has arrived by this time.

This is Saturday night. A recording of *Carmen* on the radio—wonderful music—takes me back to one of my first nights in Paris, when I entered the Opéra Comique on a 12¢ ticket & sat way, way up top amidst corduroy-garbed workers, the air blue with smoke from their cigarettes.

This afternoon I took the kids to a baseball game on campus. A game I once played passing fair, & now love to watch.

I have been saving for last my words about your 1942 sheaf of poems. First of all, thanks for making the swell little booklet. My friend Bieler, to whom I read a few the other noon when we were eating lunch together in his car, would like to borrow it & have his secretary type him a copy. Okay with you?

It was with a great deal of excitement that I first read them through—mounting excitement, as I realized that you were indeed extending your intellectual boundaries as four years ago I hoped you would. Your growth, through the *Masculine Dead*, the *War Elegies* & these 1942 poems, is beautiful to see. You have not repeated yourself, & in these last poems you have almost entirely banished the shade of Jeffers who has haunted you so tenaciously. You have grown to manhood through the midst of a great world war. This fiery time is forging you, & you are enduring it successfully. I detect no weakness, only strength in your work. I can only faintly imagine the strain on you imposed by your pacifist stand, the pressure from without & within, & the going away from Edwa. You have come this far successfully, & now who knows how far you will go? If you are not careful, you are going to leave your thirties, having written some very great poetry. My faith & belief in you as poet (and man too, of course—how can they be separated?) has been immeasurably advanced by this last work of yours. It, almost as much as your recent months' letters, helps me in the struggle I am waging to triumph over my own inertia and the temptation to get by without developing my gifts to the utmost, come what may.

The first poem, for example—all your sorrow & joy is in it, & speaks to me.

The poems of sex are powerful and true—"lost in the latitudes of the bed." Number 4 best of all, perhaps—its last 6 lines are perfect. XI also fine. Five is a credo. I lack that power of sustained self analysis & disclosure. A marvelous Meditation on Birthdays. "And wrung on the rack of what mutations" is what I call Jefferese. Cast it forth.

I have pleaded with you before for titles to poems. They can provide a useful key to unlock poems. I like good titles to good poems.

XII I like. I can't comment anymore this time on individual poems. The ones about yourself move me the most; the ones about others, such as "The Janitor Knew," least. I'll try to write more another time, after more readings.

Many thanks!
Larry

April 22, 1943
Waldport
ALS, 2 p., 1 sheet

Dear Larry:—

I suppose there are fewer really rich and abundant satisfactions than receiving such a letter as this new one of yours. Its measured and earnest tone reinforces what you say more solidly than any lavish praise. A man should not get such assurance as that more than once every three or four years. It's all he needs.

You've picked the right poems, too, for the most part. I suppose "The Janitor Knew" is not so good. Those who have seen it all deem it so; I feel so myself. Not *bad* I don't think, but it just doesn't break through. I wrote it under the influence of Kafka's marvelous fragment, *The Castle*—that and seeing men on my jobs gradually being closed out without ever knowing what was up.

I suppose you've got one copy of the *Elegies*. The cover is done with silk-screen. We have an ex-sign painter here who is a whiz at cutting them. Kemper designed it. Today the paper came in. The company made a mistake and sent the wrong color last week. We were scared to death they were out of the tan, but it was merely a mistake. Incidentally, I think Kemper's drawings for the last 2 or 3 elegies are very good—exactly what they should be. He only got really going at the last. I guess I told you he's gone back to Cascade Locks. They have brought out the *Illiterati*—a somewhat pretentious bit of extravagance—and I'll try to get them to send you one.

Yes, it is quite all right that Bieler should make a copy of the ms. I'm enclosing one I missed—a small piece. You'll forgive me for taking out of its context a remark of a character of yours. I wrote the poem shortly after reading your "Quintet," and I tried to tie up the Old-New World relationship in a sexual situation. I hope it comes up to the others. It should be XII in the ms.

Incidentally, I saw a note in an L.A. paper about some sculpture by Hal Bieler. Is this our man?

I am glad that you have been able to extend your creativity into a cohesive flow. That should make for much better work. Edwa and I too have gone through the artist–wife difficulty. One of the most trying periods of our life, shortly after our marriage. I was working on the highly erotic "Seed" (long discarded you'll remember) and the constant absorption in the eroticism of that work, which was outside, and seemingly incompatible with, our own relationship, produced some very painful clashes. Edwa is an intensely possessive and jealous woman—though not so much of recent years. She now understands and does not object to eroticism in my work. (It is a real understanding, thank God, and not just a truculent truce.) Her own work in sculpture has vastly improved our relationship. Not since she has taken it up have we had the temperamental clashes as to what should come first in our lives. We simply understand one another now; and the problem, rather than being solved, actually vanished. It's a beautiful thing. But of course, as you say, there are times when the pen has to be laid aside in favor of the more immediately pressing problems.

Christ! Talking about her brings the whole thing, the whole unrecapturable past back to me. The great modern crime is the cleavage of man from woman. You can't live alone. It's not just a matter of your nuts. You have to have the all-pervasive abundance, the marvelous spiritual temper and grace of a woman. And it has to be available. One thing I know—the mailman can't deliver it to you on a piece of paper.

Well, I'll close. Our work goes on. We're done with tree-planting for the season. Doing road work—brushing of the sides. Exactly what I was doing 9 years ago in the C.C.C. "Recurrent episodes in the unchanging pattern."

We'll start tomorrow on the *Elegies*. Want to have yours to you inside next week.

Bill

P.S. I guess you're right about titles. They stump me, but I'll try to figure some out. I also enclose a proof of the title page Atkisson sent me from Sanger. He has done a fine thing, don't you think? The press-name is that of my own future press in Selma, as it is also the name of our future home. Here's *Untide* again. The jazz is mine. I do this stuff only to help get the thing on a more literary, less belligerent, level.

May 1, 1943
Waldport, Oreg.
APS

Dear Larry:—

I promised to have you the *Elegies* by this week. I'm sorry I haven't. The mimeograph has been occupied with *The Tide*. Then too, the *Untide* staff has sort of lost interest, being occupied with other things, and I can't keep going around jacking them up for my own project since time is so scarce here. I've just come out of a terrific situation. Had a chance at a maintenance job on a small station up north. One man job. Would have given me and Edwa all summer together up here. Thought I had it sewed up, and had built up terrific emotional steam (as you can understand) then lost it through favoritism. A crushing blow. Am just recovering.

Sorry about the delay.

Bill

May 15, 1943
Beverly Glen
ALS, 4 p., 3 sheets

Dear Bill—

At last the bundle of *Elegies* arrived! The single copy of the first issue came quite a while ago, and I have been expecting the others any day, when I would acknowledge all. The day has come. I like it immensely. The silk screen cover is a beauty, both in design & workmanship. And your foreword sounds the right note. All very good. Congratulations on having seen it through.

Pray answer some questions. Have you sent out review copies? Did you send to Library of Congress, or any other libraries? If not, I will do so out of my copies—to libraries, that is.

*Tide*s & *Untide*s duly received. Beautiful cover on the last *Tide*. Liked your jazz piece too. Say, it's been long since I've written! The title page proof from Broken Acres Press I like very much. Does it progress? Decker must be permanently on his ass. I ordered a copy of *M.D.* through the Westwood Bookstore 3 weeks ago & they have not yet received it. Also, the Library ordered a copy through our N.Y. agent, & the copy arrived with no errata slip. I believe Decker's taking money for that job was the act of a crook.

Bieler has returned your typescript, after making a copy. Yes, he's the one you saw the notice of. He took a prize in a Pasadena sculpture show. He's been doing it for a hobby the past 10 years. In your letter before last, you said you were enclosing a poem which sprang out of an incident in "Quintet"—but you failed to do so. Have another try, pal. Send!

"Quintet" sits. Henry Miller read it for the first time, in its final form. I must confess his enthusiasm almost bowled me over. He's re-reading it now & says he'll write me something about it. If he does, I'll immodestly send it on to you.

I have not yet come to sending it off. I shall though.

The new book has come to a pause after 125 pages. I have not touched it for a month, after nearly a month's steady effort. I have paused deliberately. I felt my grasp go slack. I need a hiatus to regain my hold on it. Any day now I will commence typing out the first part.

I did a little catalog of Zeitlin's Huxley collection, which he is having printed, to accompany an exhibition next month in the Library.

The future is unsettled. I don't know what lies ahead. This uncertainty affects me now & then, but most of the time I live fairly serenely from day to day.

I am glad to hear that you're going to do another mimeographed book up there. It's too bad that job didn't come through, so that Edwa could have been with you this summer. Any more projects?

The days lengthen. I wish we could have some kind of lasting peace.

Forgive me for having delayed so long in writing.

The *Elegies* make a rich pile here in the lamplight on my desk.

Send my love to Edwa. Courage to all.

Larry

May 19, 1943
Waldport
ALS, 1 p.

Dear Powell:—

I'm sending you under separate cover the 50 *Elegies*—at last! I presume you received the one copy I sent early. If so, hoard it, for it's the first edition. This thing is going to drive the bibliographers of the future frantic—it was conceived of first as inserts in *Untide;* then we decided to run off a few spare copies and bind them up. As each week rolled by we ran off our extras—never quite the same amount. Now that our stack and our energy have risen to the point of completing the issue, we found that all our stencils had been burned—all but XII; so that necessitated cutting new stencils. This we did, making corrections. But since no one poem ran out at the same time, any copy of the second issue may not be like any but a few others. That's why the first issue is, from a bibliological [bibliographical] standpoint, important!

We plan now to put out the "Poems 1942" the little group I sent you recently. We hope to get Nomland to illustrate them.

A fast one
Bill

July 17, 1943
Los Angeles
ALS, 2 p.

Dear Bill—

Are you all right? I've not heard from you since April or May & I wonder. Please account for yourself.

Nothing new to report here. Irons heating, but none ready to withdraw. Lots of work this spring at the library, & steady work at home on my story. It moves along & is perhaps more than half written, in first draft.

I have a superb letter from Henry Miller about "Quintet," which I want to send you. I hesitate to mail it until I hear of your whereabouts. Miller is in a funk & I've not seen much of him for a couple of months. He has been having an intense affair with a Greek girl at the university to whom I introduced him—& has done too much screwing. It has depleted his adrenal glands & lowered him into a near suicidal funk. I wish he could be helped.

What the hell is wrong with Decker? He doesn't respond to an order for your book placed with him months ago by a local bookstore. They've written him twice. Is he in the army? You ought to get the copies of your books & let Edwa fill orders from Selma.

What responses to *War Elegies*? I enclose a few. Don't return. Did you send out review copies?

I sent you a Huxley catalog. He spoke on campus at the opening of the exhibition, & I had the pleasure of introducing him to an audience of about 1000. A marvelous talk, gentle, skeptical, humane, on the "Influence of Books."

Am looking forward to vacation all of August. Perhaps we'll get away for the second week to a cabin on the shoulder of Mt. San Jacinto, over a mile up. Six miles from a camp. Sounds good.

Yours
Larry

Aug. 2, 1943
Waldport, Ore.
ALS, 5 p., 3 sheets

Dear Larry:—

Yes, I'm months overdue, and not a decent excuse. But I'll try to make a retrospective sketch. There's enough for chapters, some of the decisive moments of my life, but I can't set them down now. I'm out of tune with my pen, somehow, having written nothing for months, due to the engrossment and distraction of camp life. But I'll go back.

In April tree planting finished up. I went on road crew, then into the kitchen serving staff for the free time it would allow. My activities as head of the Workers Committee ate that up, however, and nothing much was accomplished. 1st of June I went out on the camp garden, to try to learn something that would be of benefit after CPS. I am still doing this work, very interested in it, and quite contented with my lot. Not only am I free from Forestry supervision, but have escaped the fire-fighting program, in which I have no interest. No sooner got on the farm however, when I caught a cold and my eyes went back, just as before. Laid me up in the hospital for 2 weeks, almost blind again. No pain this time, however. Edwa had been planning to come up after school was out, and I had been looking forward to it all winter. I had planned a reunion in Marshfield 85 miles south of here, and it looked as if my eyes might keep me from it, but I persuaded the infirmary attendant to let me go, and, equipped with a patch on my eye, I got away on a weekend pass the evening of June 12. I went down there under terrific tension. You can understand how I felt. Our last months together in Selma had seen our love raised to a level of maturity and intensification that none of the past could equal, and all that seen now through the emotional concentration of months of separation. At Marshfield I looked around the station with my one weak eye and saw that she was not there. I got over to the side of the room trying to collect my feelings, and took another look. A woman was running toward me. I didn't recognize her, but as she was coming directly toward me, I sensed something was up. The woman approached, smiling, and took me by the arm, starting to lead me toward the door. I pulled back puzzled, saying something about I was waiting for my wife. Then I recognized her clothes, they were Edwa's clothes, but this was not Edwa, surely this was not Edwa. Yet Edwa it was, so thin, so narrow, so unaccountably altered that I could not believe it. I could hardly touch her. She had the room already established, and we went there. I was in that state of numbed incredulity that the whole situation seemed fantastic. That night, as we went to bed, and I saw the thinness, the wasted, bony body, the long lean lines, (I have never tolerated thin women) and thought of the rich bodied and abundant woman I had left, it seemed like I had lost about everything I had. And I felt a keen pity for her, knowing the grinding toil on that farm it must have taken to have reduced her to this. She must have been about 150 when I left her, the perfection of womanly richness. She reached as low as 114, and was, when I saw her, about 118 or 120. I do not understand how her health stood up. That night I committed my first adultery, and the guilt lay on my heart, for no joy was in it, only the body in its starvation, begging its need.

In camp, she was an instantaneous success. For the first time in life she approached that criterion of physique that our foolish men, in their stupidity, have erected as a pattern for women. In Marshfield she was haggard from the ordeal of travelling, but with rest she bloomed out into a very attractive woman, and created quite a stir. My own group accepted her immediately. She laid hands on a chunk of myrtle-wood and began hewing a good sized head. I had arranged for a two week stay with the woman of a farm house adjoining camp, and I spent nights with her there, eating together at the camp mess hall. However, she had prepared for a longer stay, and we removed to an auto-court across the road, a little cottage facing the sea. It was nice there, a fireplace, warm and cozy, and the weeks went by, but we spent most of our time with the group in camp. As time went on, I began to recognize my wife again, though her weight went up only to 130, in spite of the enormous superb meals they serve here. Nevertheless, all was not right between us, the camp life never let us reestablish that community of feeling. We were quite casual, I suppose each holding off for the inevitable separation. I knew something was wrong, but attributed it to the punitive psychological situation.

I began to notice, however, that my best friend, Hackett, was avoiding me. This was not strange, for sometimes we get enough of each other, and stay apart. The last week, the sixth, Edwa and I were much closer together, under the imminence of separation again, but still not right, still something there. Then, that Friday night, two days before departure, pensive and troubled, she told me what had happened. She had fallen in love with Hackett.

Hackett had taken furlough in May, and as a matter of course, being in California, had looked her up. He had stayed there to assist in the irrigation, helping immensely, a life-saver, in fact, and had returned overflowing with her praises. He's a fine, a superb youth, and there was nothing underhanded in the affair. She did not fall in love with him until she was here in camp and the advances were all hers. As for him, I believe he fell in love with her in Selma, though such was our mutual admiration he could not bring himself to make an attempt, though he often warned me, in a jocular way, that if I ever turned out to be a shit-heel, he was going to start pitching. When the advances were purely hers, however, the moral situation changed, and he did not turn her away.

I had often speculated as to what one would do in such a situation. Of course, in the first disclosure, I could hardly believe it. I was worried about leaving her in Selma in January, for I know any man's presence has a 3 to 1 advantage on any other man's absence, but I had hardly expected such a development under my very nose. Hackett is only 22, while Edwa is 28. On the surface, here on paper, the thing seems ridiculous, and it seems to put her in a very bad light, but they have a great many things in common, and he is physically such a person as I cannot hope to compete with. At home, last January, no man on earth could have taken her away. Of that I'm convinced. But here, in the rapid exchange of group living, what qualities I have, qualities primarily of intensification, do not operate so well, and though I am as well respected here as I could hope to be, I can see how for a woman other qualities come into the ascendancy.

As it was, we talked it over, the three of us. In the first stunning sensation of disintegration, I gave them complete freedom. I could see her, in the grip of this yen for the man, being unable to resolve her situation because of a social block, and I've known enough of sexual frustration to know how bad that can be. Edwa, however, has some sense, and she is unwilling to forsake entirely what the past held for the uncertainties of that future. Hackett will make no move, he is leaving it up to her. By Saturday night and Sunday my personal plight had come home to me so poignantly that I told Edwa I could not give her up so easily, that I was going to do everything I could to bring her back to me. She left a week ago Sunday, heading for San Francisco, quite upset, hardly knowing which way to turn, and thoroughly wretched. For a good time I was in little better state. I have had several talks with Hackett, however, and my mind is vastly improved. I don't think he's too deeply emotionally involved. He has the objective critical mind, and is not swayed by his feelings. He states quite frankly that he feels he has the least to lose, and that if Edwa can come back to me that will be the happiest resolution. But he cannot break it off himself, saying that it is she who must choose, if any lesson at all is to be learned from the affair. For a while I was sure I had lost her. Now, I think I can get her back. I am to go down in September to harvest the grapes. We will have two weeks together, in our old home, our old emotional background, and I'm counting everything on that. Until then, I just wait.

Aug 3.

The affair is further complicated by the existence of Carothers. You will recall my telling you of Carothers' breakdown and subsequent discharge from the army. What really happened, I learned from Edwa, was this. He attempted suicide with sleeping tablets. He was unsuccessful. A letter from a homosexual was found on his person. He was accused of being a homosexual, and finally discharged. One reason among many for his attempted suicide: he also is in love with Edwa, and has been for a long time. All this she did not know until after his discharge and since my induction. She has no similar feeling toward him, though is very fond of him as a person. He realizes this, it only contributes to his own conviction that he is a complete failure. Not only that, he has a great feeling of friendship and trust for me, yet he's all fucked up emotionally when he finds himself resenting her coming up here to see me. A letter today from Edwa in Berkeley tells me he is more despondent than ever. She told me before leaving that she thought he would try suicide again.

So you see, it's a royal mess. A stinking royal mess. I blame much of it on the war, on conscription, on enforced separation. I know however that ultimately the responsibility resides upon the persons concerned. I cannot believe that I have lost, but from now on till the war's end, anything can happen. But I do not hold anything against Edwa. I know that she is sincere, a fine person. And I know that whatever she does, she will have had excellent reasons for doing it.

* * *

Well, so much for my own affairs. I'm glad your new story gets along. Good work.

Do send the Miller letter. I look forward to it.

Too bad about Henry. Somehow, I can't connect the suicidal impulse with the vitality of his writing. I'm sorry.

About Decker I don't know. I think he was going 4-E—a C.O. It seems strange he won't fill orders. Gotham Book Mart carries them, or preferably I could fill the order. But it's strange he won't. I've washed my hands of it, but I've been thinking about writing him.

You're on vacation now. Very good. I envy you.

The *Elegies* go along. We've sold or sent out 300 now, my biggest success. Responses have been swell. From CPS camps all over the country they came in. *Pacifica Views,* a CPS paper in Glendora, reviewed it, and that alone brought in a little flurry of orders. Your friend John Lee in Utah saw it and wrote me. Yes, review copies have gone out to the likely journals. I like the responses you sent me. Especially the dissenting voices, chiefly the one from "Earnest" of the Spanish Dept.

I'm afraid he errs, however. For instance he says: "I distrust people who pity because they are too often covering up self-pity and just plain scared." I could as well say: I distrust people who are "fearless," for they are too often only covering up self-fear, and equally scared. We are all scared, scared shitless, and neither my pity nor his pitilessness condemn either of us. He should have noticed, however, that the poems develop beyond the intensive introversion of the opening pieces, to a broader, wider attitude of acceptance and tolerance. He did not read either the foreword or the last poem closely. If I paint a too dramatic picture of my "tough-mindedness and adherence to truth" I cannot see how my present position indicates I am "too soft to face the 'howling fronts of revolution and hate.' " I did not dodge the draft, nor try to hide. And when I came here I assumed all the consequences that act entails. If I have not yet had to bear them, that does not invalidate my motive. Also, surely his judgement that I, II, & III are the best pieces is in error. I should say they were the worst. And though both Christ and I may be arrogant, neither he nor I are so much so as to annihilate those with whom we differ. Show me an arrogance to equal that of the man peering down the bomb sight to the heart of the city!

Yet it is good to get adverse reactions. Too many have been uncritically enthusiastic.

Incidentally, could you send *Capricorn* up for a while? The response to *Cancer* has been so enthusiastic, I should like to have the acquaintance broadened. I'll take good care of it.

There must be more to
write, but I'll close now

Bill

We have a press now, and are going to bring out "Poems 1942."

August 9, 1943
The Blackstone, Chicago
ALS, 4 p., 2 sheets

I was in Chicago 10 years ago this month,
on my way from Europe.
Dear Bill—

That's right—a secret mission! Here am I in Carl Sandburg's hog butchery, on my ass in velvet, eating & sleeping like the obscure solitary genius I am. Why, in God's name, why? Because Northwestern Univ., 15 miles up the lake, is looking for a head librarian, & paid my expenses to come back & be looked over. So I left Los Angeles a week ago tomorrow on Santa Fé's Super Chief & am returning tomorrow on that same beautiful diesel-drawn steel streamliner. After a few days in Evanston, I came downtown to this swank old hotel, where I live in solitary splendor. No one do I know in Chicago save wily Ben Abramson, master of the many-eyed Argus Book Shop, & with him I spent a good hour or two this afternoon, buying Eliot's *4 Quartets*, Miller-Fraenkel's *Hamlet* vol. 1 in the 2d enlarged edition & Van Wyck's *Jeffers* printed by Ritchie, of which I desired an additional copy.

Tomorrow I go to the Art Institute & see American water colors & French oils. At 5:30 my train leaves. Day after tomorrow I will be in Los Angeles at 9:15 in the morning.

It's been a marvelous vacation for me. I was yearning to be away from my family for a short spell; I got my desire, in a most unexpected way. How wonderful it is to be alone in city & on train, & to know that a woman waits for you to return!

You have been alone since January. How are you? I hope I find a letter from you on my homecoming. Up to the time I left, I had not heard from you since April or May. I want to hear from you.

I resigned my job before I left on vacation August 1st. A bridge burned. If I stay with U.C. they will have to give me a better job. Else I'll come back here. Or possibly, to avoid the draft, get a job driving a Greyhound bus for a year, until I'm 38. What do you think of that?

Have you seen David Daiches' omnibus poetry review in a recent *Nation?* He gives a couple of fine sentences (sic) to your *Masculine Dead* & *War Elegies.* I should have copied them for you, but saw the issue while being shown through the Northwestern library.

A beautiful building, in a grassy meadow on the edge of Lake Michigan—the most beautiful library I have ever seen. The job is tempting. They want me for what I am (my pseudonymous being excepted!) & not to be trammeled with routine—an asst. librarian to care for that.

This past year has been mounting steadily to a climax. Perhaps on my return I will find word on "Quintet," which I sent out for the first time on June 29th. Then what? God help me, I don't know.

A tug boat on the Lake whistles hoarsely. It is a hot nine o'clock evening. I sit on the bed with pillows at my back. My life spins in a vortex. Almost serenely I look down upon it, detached.

I long for music. When I get home I shall lie on the floor & listen to Beethoven's op. 127, & all will be well.

I think of you. If you have not written, write. I worry about your long silence. How is Edwa? Send her this.

I greet you both from my 12th-floor cubicle. Tomorrow at this hour I will be in a lower berth, racing willy-nilly, southwestwards—God speed us all.

Larry

August 20, 1943
Los Angeles 24
ALS, 4 p., 2 sheets

Dear Bill—

Your long letter was here when I returned from Chicago a week ago. I knew something was wrong—but had no inkling of what it actually was. I had almost written Edwa a month or so ago to find out if you had been transferred, etc. That would have been the wrong thing!

My heart goes out to you. I am glad you waited to write until you had arrived at a resting place. Your letter is good. You don't need anything I can give you. You understand the situation & I commend you for it. Edwa will probably come back to you a better, wiser woman. Give her all the rein. There's no other way. If she never comes back, remember always what you had together, & take yourself another woman when destiny brings one near. To her you will have a richer, stronger personality to offer. Thus you can't lose, come what may.

And all the while, know that I am your friend, offering you such affection & loyalty & understanding as I possess.

Was it the last time you sat in this study, in the winter, and we talked of the value of pre-marital experience both to the man & the woman? A sensitive, curious woman is never satisfied forever with a single man. But if he be a good man, her knowing another at a subsequent time, will return her to the first, full of a new appreciation of his worth.

I moralize. Forgive.

Although I wanted to write you as soon as I had read your letter, I found myself in a maelstrom, from which I have not yet emerged. Briefly, the campus is agog over my resignation—& there is a strong movement afoot to retain me here as successor to the head librarian who retires next June 30. If the appointment were guaranteed me, I would gladly lie low for the coming year. President Sproul asked for a couple of weeks to see what he could do for me. In the meantime, faculty friends & politicians phone, call & write at all hours. I am lying low, letting a couple of friends run things. Northwestern is pressing me for a decision. If they will not deal here, I shall go to Evanston—& a damned good job, too. Except that we don't want to move!

I toil at building a stone & concrete retaining wall along the stream that traverses our front yard. New work for me. Tonight my muscles ache.

I am delighted to hear of *War Elegies* success. Beware of a John G. Moore who wrote you. He is a literary racketeer. Tried once to blackmail the Jeffers. A scoundrel. Beware of any sort of dealing with him.

I will send you *Capricorn* when I get it back from Newell. Where is your nearest Railway Express agency office? I don't want to risk mailing the book.

I enclose Miller's beautiful letter on "Quintet"—and—and — a bitch of a one from Knopf, rejecting it. How simply wrong headed! How she missed the point! I am of course unable to write it or any book according to her formula. I am not discouraged—only irked.

Miller has come out of his funk—but is still in a bad mood over the Greek girl. I do not like to see him when he is mixed up with a woman. It makes him a bit insane! Surrealistic. Dangerous to an old married man like me!

For long I have been saving Elie Faure's *History of Art* for a vacation reading. Now I bought the 5-volume reprint edition @ 1.98 & am settling down in volume 1, ancient art. Do you know the work?

Write me again, soon, William my lad.

Yours ever
Larry

Aug. 29, 1943
Camp Angel
Waldport Ore.
ALS, 2 p., 1 sheet

Dear Larry:—

The letter out of Chicago really stopped me, first because it *was* from Chicago, and second because it gave me my first hint of this possibly drastic upheaval in your life, and third because it contains my first knowledge of the *New Republic*'s review.

Your recent letter brought the first instances up to date. Myself, I'm torn—just, I suppose as you are. I recognize the great possibilities at Northwestern, but I also hate to see you leave the Coast. In the end, I hope UCLA comes through. With you in Evanston, there will hardly be a reason for going to Los Angeles! Fellows here confirm your judgement of the beauty of Northwestern's library. Schillp, of that university's philosophy department, lectured here for three days last week. He told me the Library was the only liberal thing on the campus. "There has never been," he said, "an order for a single book from my department that was not purchased. I can't understand it." I wish you luck, Larry. And even though you go into that big job, something in the nature of a national figure, I know you'll be the same humble and considerate person, with your unpretentious ability to strike sympathetic responses from those about you. Good boy.

Christ, I hope you can duck the army till you're of age.

Well, my own situation hangs fire. Edwa is living in Berkeley with the Watkins', working at a department store. Thursday I leave on furlough, will pick her up there, and go on down to Selma to pick the grapes on our farm. Everything hinges on those few days. (I get 20 of them)—No, of course everything doesn't hinge on those few days. The forces go deeper than that, but all I'll know about them for a long time hinges on that. One side of my battle is temporarily won. Hackett, never an emotional person, is losing interest, due to her absence and the inferior moral position in which he finds himself. He can't see any kind of prospect as long as he's in CPS, and who knows how long that will be? So he's taking himself out of it. How Edwa will take all this I can't tell. She's an acutely sensitive person, with a basic inferiority complex that I've been working on ever since I recognized that it was there, and a wounding blow to her pride would be definitely bad for her. I've been considering her side of it for a long time, and sometimes even think a transfer would be best for her. At least she ought to be able to explore this new thing, to locate what it is within her, and learn to deal with it. As it is, the whole thing will be thwarted, and nobody any better off. If Hackett weren't so damned young and idealistic and puritanical he'd take her, give her a good lay, and send her back if the situation wouldn't permit anything else. We'd all three gain from it. As it is now he's pinching the thing off half-formed and I'm afraid there'll be a lot of loose ends and ragged edges getting under everyone's feet. I told him so, but it's no good. He's trying to "live by the rational approach" the damned fool.

Edwa has sent me the *N.R.* review. Very good.

Waldport has an express agency.

Yes, Miller's letter is beautiful. He brings to "Quintet" a whole quality that I could not, an appreciation for what its background and sources are that I can get only from the work itself, but that he can bring from life. Knopf's rejection is the usual stuff. Irritating. You can expect it. The bastards are caught in the toils of commercialism.

I'll watch your Mr. Moore closely. He's tried nothing so far—just a letter, with an order.

Yes Edwa has the Faure but I've not read it.

Well, I'll try to write from Selma, but things are going to be packed with work. There are the grapes to be picked and the young vines to be watered, and a mountain of work it will be. Jim Harman, a good friend here, is going down with me a few days to help. I'll need it.

I enclose a couple of photos. They were taken just before her departure. The group was taken in front of our cottage near camp. The other as we awaited the bus. All the group is behind the camera laughing at my refusal to grin at the lens, and Edwa laughs back at them.

So long
Bill

I've been working on the camp garden, and learning much that will help us later on our own semi-subsistence farm.

Will send *Capricorn* soon.

September 29, 1943
Beverly Glen
ALS, 6 p. 3 sheets

Dear Bill—

I guess your furlough is over & you're back at camp. I've put off answering your last letter in the day-to-day hope I'd have a final report to make. Now I have & I hasten it to you. I have been appointed head librarian at UCLA, commencing July 1, 1944. On January 1, 1944 I become head of the University's

William Andrews Clark Memorial Library (rare books & typography) which is down on West Adams Blvd., about 10 miles from the campus, on the Clark estate. After July 1 I'll have both it & the University library under me. How does it sound to you, pal? As good as it does to me? I hope so. Because I'm goddam well set-up, yes sir! What a two months! Northwestern wanted me badly & at the last moment, its President telephoned me an offer of $7500 plus all moving expenses. It was hard to turn down—but I did—& day before yesterday I signed the deal with Pres. Sproul. My salary at UCLA will be $6000—a cool thousand more than the incumbent has been receiving. It looks like I've arrived. I'm gladdest for Fay—for the respite from hard work it'll mean for her. Goddam this paper! It won't take ink.

For the next three months I'll probably go into a defense plant my brother is running; making life preservers & sleeping bags for the army. As a laborer @ 1.00 an hour. I want a change from libraries. I'll take the job if it doesn't entail being "frozen" in it.

It's been a hell of a strain for 2 months, but I've thrived on it. Never felt more brimful o' piss 'n vinegar. I was near you & Edwa two weeks ago. Made a quick round trip to Berkeley on the Owl. Wanted to stop over, but knew you'd be swamped with work, & besides had to get back close to campus for the denouement.

It's a rags-to-riches story that has the campus agog. Never before has anyone jumped from the bottom rank in a department (Librarian, junior grade) to the top spot in one lewd leap. The point is, the young men in the faculty are greatly encouraged. Powell has broken ground for them. Etc. Etc.

It means that I can put into practice much of my philosophy of books & people. Etc. Etc. For example, in the Clark Library I am going to commence a collection of western fine printing—Grabhorn, Ritchie, etc. And in the Univ. Lib. a collection of every book printed in Los Angeles. Etc. And poetry—man, poetry! Everything. I am going to make the library a throbbing heart. Dead books will live. Young men & women—students—& faculty—will enter a living atmosphere, not a mausoleum.

It means that I stay in the land I love, where my roots go deepest, the land whose hills & weather I know & love. And to live amidst my friends here & up the coast. Wow!

In Berkeley I crossed your hot spoor. In Creed's Bookstore near Sather Gate. Found the *Masculine Dead* salted through the stock, & bought a copy which they mailed to Hal Bieler. The bearded bookman spoke warmly of you & of Mac, to which I responded in kind.

The *Illiterati* came today, with your poems new & old. All good. I sent them a buck. Am tight pressed now, as my pay stopped August 31. Nomland did a remarkable job of design & illustration.

Tell me of your return to Selma with your wife. I hope for the best for you both.

Things have been rich for me. In spite of the fucking frustration, since my return from Evanston I have written 50 pages on my new book. Slowly it goes ahead. I have not sent out "Quintet" again. I shall when I get ready.

This past month at home I have finished my storm wall & poured a little concrete bridge—and re-roofed the house with 90 lb. paper. Mopped it down with boiling tar. Chewed the bold black stuff & stirred memories of boyhood.

I wrote to you of hearing Elgar's violin concerto (Menuhin) here in my study one night. How it moved me! Have you ever heard it? Of course, nothing can equal the solemn tympani opening of Beethoven's violin concerto. I write always to music. Ambition is to own a big automatic machine, that I can load with an evening's program & let her buck.

In the mad world I live my rich & secret life. I grieve, sorrow, rejoice, exalt—all things experience—& know I am keenly, vividly alive, in the prime years of my life—& that unless I channel my life in writing all the other triumphs are naught. Whether or not I publish doesn't matter now. To write is everything. I write.

Tell me of yourself. Report. Is the war's end in sight? How did you find your vineyard? Tell next to all.

1,000,000 greetings
Larry

Oct. 4, 1943
Waldport, Ore.
ALS, 6 p., 3 sheets

Dear Larry:—

The good news breaks. We were back in the hills brushing out an old logging railroad bed for a road when rain drove us in, drenched and shivering. A hot shower, dry clothes, a pipe full of tobacco, and your letter. Now with the rain smacking the roof I formulate this reply.

And I'm glad. Christ it's good you got this break. And the choice! My God, like pulling plums off of a pudding! Your enthusiasm literally bursts out of your letter, and Lord knows I share it. You're a great guy, Larry. Your plans sound swell: you'll make a great thing of that library.

I'd hate to have had to make such a choice. I can thoroughly understand how tempting the Northwestern offer must have been—yet I'm glad for your choice. I was afraid you'd get off there where I'd never see you. I think you did wisely. The cultural future of L.A. is limitless.

Sorry you couldn't have stopped off in Selma for an evening. Let's see, it's been a year since we were down.

Yes, I know Creed—through Watkins, who often watches store for him. Good man.

Glad too you keep writing. Yes, you must write, get it down, the living language. It's a great craft.

No, I do not know the Elgar, but here too we have music, some of the best music lovers I've known, formal record concerts once a week, with any number of sessions other than that. We have a sound camera here, projector, I mean, and have it fixed up to play records. It's really a fine reproducing medium, far better than ours at home.

[Jim] Harman and I left here after work on Sept. 2nd, and took a bus to Marshfield, getting an 85-mile jump on our furlough which did not start till next day. Next morning getting on a crowded bus I said "Why there's Theodore Dreiser," seeing a tall, heavy, stooped, slack-jawed, open-mouthed, white haired old man. Harman thought not. He had a younger woman with him, sort of tawny red-headed, carelessly dressed, amply proportioned, but still had her shape.

Wore a black dress and weird off-blue stockings. Every piss-stop down the coast I'd pass the old boy and become more and more convinced it was Dreiser. Finally at lunch in Gold Beach he went back to the crapper and we followed him in. He was taking a leak at the piss trough and Harman said:—"Are we correct in assuming that you are Theodore Dreiser?" He hunched there a moment, shaking his whang and replied: "That happens to be the case—yes." "We're a couple of young writers," I said, "coming down from a C.O. camp. We're interested in writing, and presume that to be sufficient to accost you like this—" or some such damned fool thing. A mistake, anyway, he hunched around, hobbled over the wash-basin and began washing his hands. "Well," he said, "that's interesting, I suppose, but so what?" Caught, I grinned like a cat in a slop pail and muttered a lame—"Nothing at all." He went on: "The country is full of writers. I know schools that have as high as 150 poets alone—and all trying to shock the world." He turned to go out. There was nothing more to say. Having rebuffed us, he softened a bit, permitted a friendlier gleam to enter his eye, and said in conclusion—"But I wish you luck." We thanked him and went out. His woman was anxiously awaiting him out on the street, casting frequent glances at the men's door.

The rest of the trip to S.F. which took that day and all that night, he avoided meeting our eyes in passing. Toward evening the woman, bored and weary, let a plump hand rest on his sparse hair, and stroked it. He permitted that, but when she let it drop around his neck he gave his head a sharp imperious shake, shot her a forbidding look—suddenly aware, I suppose, that he was known and under observation. She hastily withdrew. An odd relationship there.

Oh, well, even though he mistook us it's likely he'd have rebuffed us no matter what we'd said. I guess he's hounded.

We spent a day and night in Berkeley and San Francisco, renewing acquaintances, and went home on the streamliner. (Edwa had been in Berkeley since leaving camp, working in Oakland selling furs! I can hardly believe it, knowing her reticence, but she was quite a success—but then, she's a changed woman—nothing surprises me any more.) The vineyard had been uncared for since June, when Edwa left, and was overgrown with weeds, a disheartening sight. But the crop was fine—almost half again as much yield as last year, the price is much higher, and we should make a nice return if we can safely harvest them. The three of us picked for over a week, when Harman had to come back. Edwa and I continued. The picking took all my furlough. Harman's presence, (though he was "in on" the situation) prevented any intimacy between Edwa and me, but after he left, working beside her in the vineyard we carefully went over the whole problem. We were very close all that time, very tender in all our doings. Everything I am and have been with her draws her to me. I think of all of us rivals (and there have been more of us of late than I realized—even Harman felt himself slipping) she is drawn to me by the greatest number of facets. But gradually I learned, there in the vineyard, and over coffee, and in the bed of a night what it was. As far as her reaction to me is concerned, and she doubts if she would ever have realized this, had Hackett not come along, the one great lack is sexual. Not the technique of sex, but the natural sexual attraction. Hackett opened up whole continents of response, not by what he has done, but simply by what he is. I know what she means, for what he does to her, she does to me—a kindling, a fine, high, seminal awakening, coming up out of the base and making itself heard. You can't keep your hands off the person. *You* know it—hell, "Quintet" is full of it. So that's the way it is. Against that, I'm helpless. There's simply nothing I can do, for the deficiency is irremediable by conduct. Perceiving it, though I felt sad, lost, indeed, quite alone and forsaken, but perceiving it, and knowing the woman she is, and how honest and essentially good she is, for me to stand in the way would have been criminal. Before, I had thought—"This is surely just a passing thing. Why, hell, after what we've had together, am I not justified in believing we can have it again? The woman loves me, I'm sure of it—and what can Hackett offer?" So I'd kept in there trying, not forcing, but still trying. But after this trip, and what it had shown, I saw how wrong I'd been, and how much richer a life built upon such a natural thing could be for her—all else being equal.

But there's the rub—all else isn't equal. Hackett is young. He hates confinement. Though he was in love when she left, separation killed it. The moral situation he took to be against him. When Harman came back and told him how things were, (for Harman, too, had long conversations with her) how she felt that he, Hackett, was letting "logical" and moral reactions govern him, Hackett wrote her a crushing letter, a fierce and bitter thing, telling her he no longer loved her, that he was through. Harman persuaded him to burn it. Perhaps he's lost to her. He refuses to see her again. She's going to be deeply hurt, for now, only luck can save the situation for her. Could she see him, be with him again, I think he'd come around, but he's not going to let that happen. And if he doesn't, will I go in and try to make a life of it with her, knowing his presence in the world, and my own inadequacies? Yes, I will. There's more than enough for a life. And this thing has so deepened us, so broadened us, so *tested* us, that all we have ever been is brought up and illuminated by the light of this occurrence. She loves me very deeply, I believe she actually loves me more than she ever did, in a far finer way. I think she admires me more, respects me more. Certainly, I admire and respect her far, far more. But she is a person of such worth that I cannot claim her were she to go elsewhere. My luck is to have been her husband, and help make her what she is. That's small comfort, in the face of loss, but I'm proud.

While I'm writing, I want to bring the situation with my father up to date. A week before I left for camp, last January, I heard a car squeak outside. I looked out and it was the old man himself. He had sent both Edwa and me gifts that Christmas, with a nice little note, and I had been touched, thinking that perhaps the old egotistical wall had broken down and the poor old man was really hurt, so I'd written him in thanks, telling him I was sorry, sorry that the rift had come between us, and that the emotional tensions of the past were such that I could not go back. That brought him out. He entered the house and began on me. If I thought he was humbled and broken I was mistaken, the same old implacable arrogance, the terrific self-concentration, they were all there. Only his pride had been hurt. I saw that what I was, essentially, was very little to him—only his pride, his pride, and nothing much else, had been hurt. Before he left I told him I was leaving for CPS, a position I knew he regarded with contempt. He asked me to see him before I left, and I promised. I never kept it. The following week, for the first time in a year, the old tormenting dreams returned—those parental-rejection scenes boiling in my mind. I was planting vines in the day time, alone, and found myself cursing and shouting to empty space. I came directly to camp without seeing him.

Saturday, I received a letter from Edwa, from which I quote. "Mr. Manley [our grocer, a former Ku Klux Klanner, who was always friendly, but who is quite a gossip, and whom I was most distrustful of concerning my stand. He was nice on my furlough—shook hands—wished me luck—etc. to my surprise.] Mr. Manley got quite confidential with me the other day, and this is what I gather. Your 'stepmother' has had another attack," [I believe I told you of her mental lapses. These increased after her marriage to my father (which I can well imagine!) until on furlough I learned he had entered suit for divorce, then dropped it when she demanded half the property] I proceed—"worse and more permanent than the others. She has been taken to *St. Agnes* for a long stay, probably permanently. He spoke of your own difficulty with your father and said he nor no one else blamed you and that your father had been saying nasty things about you before and after you left. People haven't liked it, and from this loose talk of his plus his foolish marriage and more foolish divorce attempt he wouldn't get fifty votes if he were up for election today. That's too bad—for if he loses his job he'll blame your pacifism."

This will let you know how badly things have deteriorated. I'm sorry for him. I really am. But I wouldn't go back to him again.

Well, I've talked myself out. We're working on the church [Brethren headquarters] to make Santa Barbara a camp in creative arts. If it goes through, I'll surely see you. Again, congratulations on your phenomenal hurdle. A most marvelous leap—but no more than you deserve.

Bill

P.S. *Tropic* coming soon.

October 14, 1943
Beverly Glen
ALS, 4 p., 2 sheets

Dear Bill—

Enjoyed your airmail letter. Rain on the roof up there, eh? Dry as a fucked bone here. A threat of rain the other morning veered away inland. I near the end of my second week of toil. What am I? You want to know my title? Inspector in an Arctic Sleeping Bag Factory. Yessir. I inspect 50–60 of the blooming 7-foot down- & feather-filled bags every day, from 7 to 3:30, half hour for lunch. And drive 45 m. round trip to do it. Pay: $1.00 per hr. Nets me $52 for 48 hours. What a marvelous change! Joint employs about 200 men & women of all races & ages. Bed every night about 9; up at 5:30. Will be at it until the middle of December.

Had a nice card from Edwa & sent her one in return. I wish we could all get together for some talk. Your letter throws new light on your problem. This sexual magnetism that lures the faithful off the beam of routine is a thing that must be understood for what it is—powerful but evanescent. It's no good for two to build on. Enduring marriage is made with other adhesives. Yes, "Quintet" is full of the magic of touch—& the whole moral of the book is voiced by Madeleine in the 4th movement, & then put into practice by Jack in the 5th. The wonder is brief. If it comes to you without it being sought or forced, embrace it—then let go.

Every sensitive, normally-sexed person experiences it. The more experience before marriage, the better—because after marriage it is not compatible with serene life. In this time, while you & Edwa are apart, let her have all the rein. Take some yourself, if it presents itself. Let her go. Tell her to go. All in all, it is doubtful she'll find a man as wholly satisfying as you. Let her find it out. You can afford to gamble.

It seems to me that too many men around have been too much for her. I told her I'd like to talk with her. I would. You too. I hope you can get transferred to Santa Barbara. Then there's a chance for us to get together.

Don't be too "noble" toward your wife. She may well need a

straight to the jaw. Following the sexual magnet when it pulls her will bring her plenty trouble. This kid Hackett sounds fairly smart. Reading over your letter, I think you're the damned fool of the lot. "But after trying this trip, & what it had shown, I saw how wrong I'd been, & how much richer a life built upon such a natural thing could be for her." Come sir, let's not all be dupes. Wrong hell! Your & Edwa's foundations go deeper than any random magnetism she may encounter in her travels away from the native heath. Don't dupe yourself in this self-effacing role of nobility. If you need her, keep her. Kill, if necessary.

Do I get anywhere? I know that the basic themes between men & women are few, but that the variations on them are almost limitless. I know life for myself, as I have lived & observed it. But life for you & Edwa. That's another tune. Excuse please, if I whistle it sour.

Life is very short. I hate like hell to think mine probably more than half over. This week I have gotten back to work on the story for a while in the evening. First week squeezed all the juice out of me.

Your account of Dreiser is magnificent, simply magnificent! He is a disagreeable old bastard—"tough old mastodon," Jeffers called him. Your accosting him while he was shaking the dew from his dong is in the great American tradition. Could be a vignette from Dos Passos. Better though.

Before I'm through, I want to leave my testament. It will be on the other end from Tom Wolfe's. I play with Ravel, rather than Wagner.

I weaken. I doze. I creep to bed. I greet you.

Inspector Powell

P.S. Title of unwritten testament "Life in a Life Preserver Factory; or, Sleeping Bags I Have Known"

11–28-43
Beverly Glen
ALS, 1 p.

Dear Bill—

How are you? Is the Camp Angel Press at work on your new poems? [The Waldport camp was named when established for a U.S. congressman, Homer Angell. The C.O.s dropped the final "l."]

I have three more weeks to work in the plant. What a marvelous experience it's been! I could write a book about what it's doing for me.

Every night I type out a dozen pages of my story, then read a chapter in Enid Starkie's *Baudelaire*—a superb critical biography; and so to bed at 9:30, to sleep until 5:15. A very rich full life of mingled physical & mental exertion. You should see me whip a 250 lb. bale of Kapok!

Here is a squib for your Powell collection.

Sunday noon & listening to Glière's 3rd symphony.

I greet you!

Larry

Dec. 1, 1943
Waldport, Ore.
AL, 2 p., 1 sheet

Dear Larry:—

Glad to hear from you and sorry you had to jack me up—seeing as I owe you a letter. Time's been bowling along at its exceeding pace. We are planting trees again—have been for a month: the winter rains have set in, work is generally miserable and always a trial, we plant in such difficult terrain, that only the most strenuous activity can get one through the days. But I'm not complaining: I'm in marvelous health—perhaps the best of my life—I say this because [of] my incredible (for me) ability to recover. At home, a day in the fields left me stuporate. Here, I put in this monumental labor and have energy for evening. How it is I don't know, but I can now arrive at the top of a hill trembling with exhaustion and yet after a five minute blow be completely recovered. I'm really surprised. It must be the food!

But Lord knows the nights need energy. God, the things to be done. The press is finally ready. Paper holds us up. (I'm listening, in the music room, to Casals' recording of the Dvorak Concerto as I write—it's marvelous!) But we hope to have something to show before long—Coffield's new poems—*The Horned Moon*—to show we can do something besides Everson! After that the *Elegies* must go into reprint. I had got tired of them and wanted to get on with the "Poems 42." However, a letter came in 2 days ago from a Pacifist in N.Y. He wants to print a thousand copies for distribution here and in England. Held an *Untide* meeting and got in the worst controversy we've had. Some felt it would defeat the whole future of the Press to sell out our "star," just as we've got the press going. I think I'll do it here—creative reasons, the sense of mutual achievement etc. It's really put the drive in the bunch though. They've started a campaign suggesting the present *Elegies* as Christmas offerings. The stack of 600 is almost gone, now. I enclose our little ad to show our present typeface (Goudy 12 pt). We've just got Kennerly Italic 14 pt. for headings of Coffield's poems. The kid who owns the press is a real press man, but we don't quite know what the little thing will do.

My "Waldport Poems" (poems written here—a sort of CPS series) go forward slowly. The finest things I've done—though I always say that, don't I? Yet I hope it continues to be true!

Incidentally, you never mentioned the *Poetry* review. Did you see it? I wrote them a letter setting the man right as to my position.

Things at home are bad. Though the crop is all in (and nearly double last year's) Edwa is having to leave "the house in the vineyard, loosing its leaves on the autumn air." How we hate to leave that fine little house! It's become so much a part of me I cannot accept the fact that never again can I go back there. Edwa too. The poor woman is almost crazy with the pressure she's working under, she's starting to build a small house on our place!

Winter is cummen in,
Lhude sing Goddamn,
Raineth drop and staineth slop,
And how the wind doth ramm!
Sing: Goddamm.

EZ. Pound, that abortion
from the reeking rectum of
depravity!

The squib is swell—thanks.
Glad you've enjoyed heaving kapok!
And good [*sic*]

December 22, 1943
Beverly Glen
ALS, 4 p., 2 sheets

Dear Bill—

I greet you from the depths of the winter solstice! Shame for not mailing your letter of December, until weeks later! I had missed hearing from you, & your lines were welcome. Thanks too for the printed slips. I commend you for retaining the *Elegies* for your Press there, although I regret you had to pass up an opportunity to have 1000 copies printed & distributed. Still, literary loyalty is a rare good thing. You will be repaid for it. Your Goudy type is a pleasing one. Keep me stocked with whatever you do. When you can get around to it, I'd like to read your new poems. You are in the midst of a great experience. I am sorry to hear of Edwa's having to move. Greet her for me. Courage to both of you. I wish you both a better New Year.

I am enjoying a couple of weeks off before going to the University's W. A. Clark Library on the first. My three months as a working stiff are over. It was a vigorous, refreshing experience. I am glad I had it; I'm glad it's over.

Every day or night I have been typing & revising the ms. accumulated since last March—450 pages—which represents approximately half of the book I'm engaged upon. And last night, to the triumphant closing strains of that noblest of all symphonies—Brahms' First—I finished. Now I wonder how my new work, with its host of responsibilities, will affect the unwritten last half?

I am tempted to send you the typescript as far as it goes—but I think perhaps I prefer to wait until the book is completed. The whole effect is everything, and I want to be judged on it alone. I know you understand.

By the way, you have never acknowledged receipt of *Capricorn,* which I expressed to you several months ago.

The best book of the fall has been Enid Starkie's *Baudelaire*—a damned fine piece of biographical criticism. M.F.K. Parrish [i.e., Fisher] has published a beautiful book called *The Gastronomical Me*—mostly autobiographical. Read it if you get a chance. She has not yet used the story of her husband's painting—a book in itself.

We have had a glorious three-day rain. My new roof kept us dry! Damn it all, don't wait so long to write! Just got the new Busch recording of Beethoven op. 58, n. 1. Very grave & beautiful music.

You speak of a music room. Do you have a good machine? And many albums?

I had not seen the review in *Poetry* until you wrote. All these things I used to read from the library & so am behind since July. I phoned & had a girl drop by the issue. It made me terribly angry. What an ignorant smutch on the page! Bracketing your two works with Smith because you're both Californians—whatever that means—& then ignoring your Decker book & missing the whole point of the *Elegies*! My heart goes out to you, Bill. To have given your best & then have a ridiculous ass get hold of your work. I am glad you wrote them. I'll look for your letter, if they print it. The whole magazine is on a shockingly low level. And so is the whole state of American poetry, as you know better than I.

Have you seen Miller's letters in the *New Republic,* his picture in *Time,* etc.? I've only seen him a couple of times all fall & have not been yet to his exhibition. I saw him a few days [ago] & he said the manna was dropping all around. What do you think of Eliot's *Four Quartets?* I spent an evening in a Chicago hotel room, reading them—& I'm damned if I fancy some critics likening them to Beethoven's Quartets. God gave

Eliot a big brain & no balls. Too bad. Una reports Robin writing much & destroying most of it. No plan for a book. I'll wager he publishes nothing as long as the war lasts.

The city here is a horrible scene of obscene spending. I heard on the radio that in this area alone probably a million Christmas trees will go unsold. Keep planting, you rain-soaked bastard, & the entrepreneurs will chop 'em down come another Mary Xmas or two.

A burst here & there—but I'm really selfishly hoarding my words to spend on the 2d half that stretches before me, unwritten & fearsome.

Every affectionate wish to you & Edwa.

Larry

[The following letter was sent to Powell by Everson just for his information.]
[Copy]

Dec. 28, 1943
Waldport, Ore.
ALS, 3 p., 2 sheets

Dear Henry [Miller]:—

I know this is the wrong time to approach you, since "the manna is falling all around you," as *Time* and the good Powell tell me; but I at least want to approach you, and see perhaps if a blow cannot be struck for pacifism and the arts. Bluntly:—*will you come to Waldport and serve as director for a pacifist School of the Fine Arts?*

The background:

Last summer the Director of Brethren Service Committee of the Church of the Brethren (Dunkards—the people that are keeping us here) came through and a group of us cornered him and began talking up a School In Fine Arts. A school in cooperatives has already been tried in a Michigan camp and proved quite successful. A bunch of guys secure transfers to a given locality: BSC hires some leader in the field to run the show, and for a six months' period these fellows give all their time not given to forestry project work (62-½ hrs. per week) to developing their particular interest. These things are really not "schools." No classes. No formalization. The fellows just work together, developing their plans as they progress. To get on: this fellow was not too keen, but some of the other camps were interested and we all started pushing together. The Educational Director at headquarters (Elgin, Ill.) who is an enrollee and a damned fine one, got on too and the first thing we knew the thing was going across. Everybody thought of it for the camp at Santa Barbara, for obvious reasons. However, the director there is a conservative old man and it wouldn't take. Since a group of us here is already at work in the field, Waldport turned out to be second choice. Last week the Ed. Director from Elgin came through, put the finishing touches on it, and unless Selective Service objects, we'll have writers, artists, poets, sculptors, coming in (we hope) from over CPS to work here together. If we can get someone we can list as director, some man high in his field, we can make a far greater appeal to the men to come, and we can get the necessary push here to really make an active thing of it. That's why I'm writing to you.

I admit, on the face of it, it looks like a bore and a headache, especially to a creative man who has his own work and thinks this artist colony business is a lot of crap anyway (which it is as a rule, I admit—before CPS I wouldn't have looked twice at it—but—here I go—this is different!).

In the first place, we're pacifists—conscientious objectors, we're not dilettantes. We have the passionate conviction that if pacifism is going to do what it's got to do, it's going to have to grow up. American pacifism is in the hands of the Holy Joes, and until we can tie it up with the thinking people, the people of concern, we're merely going to appeal to the Bible boys. What we, as artists, want to do, is usurp, if we can, that whole range of response to aesthetic activity, that is being neglected now everywhere. We want to re-affirm the creative man—not for propaganda purposes, but because we know that what we as pacifists do as artists, regardless the mode, we'll speak more effectively than any tract we could write on our conviction and our purpose. Where else should the creative man assert himself more than here, among us, who refuse to howl up the furies? It seems to me we can really contribute, and we need the help and affirmation of you few people out there who have seen through the bloody scum, and have no use for it.

As for the practical details—I talked with the camp director last night and he assured me that if we could get some older more experienced man to come and stay here, though he did nothing of administration, or organization, but simply come and stay and act as a focal point and "consultant" his presence would be worth his while. Your days would be your own: the camp is mostly out on project, and you could carry on your own work. At night it would be mostly bull session and conversation. We have a press here now, and intend to put it to good use. You know our type pretty well—you met Nomland and Sheets this summer and they will be here. There are Holy Joes here, sure, the old conservatism, but there's tolerance here like I've never seen it elsewhere. You'll wonder about arrangements: I think it's something like this: transportation paid; room and board and about $80 per month—and the eats are swell. All this is tentative, of course, I haven't contacted BSC, but the group here are all for it; I'm pretty convinced that we can get the man we push for. Can you let me know your reaction? It would mean a hell of a lot to us, Henry, if you could say *yes*.

Sincerely
Bill

1944: ORGANIZERS BOTH

Jan. 8, 1944
Waldport, Ore.
ALS, 2 p., 1 sheet

Dear Larry:—

I don't have your letter by me, for I'm in the sick-room with a gut ache, but I want to pen off this letter anyway, and clear the deck.

First of all—Edwa arrived the 21 of December and leaves tomorrow—something like a 3-week stay. She has not been as happy here as she was last summer, for our group has more or less broken up, many have left camp, some are hardly on speaking terms with others! Not only that, Hackett gave her one continual rebuff, which didn't help her any. All in all, as I say, she has not had much of a time—partly my fault, trying to attend to camp business and keep up my marital obligations was not very successful.

We're organizing a Fine Arts School for Waldport, trying to get the artists from CPS to attend. I'm chairman of the Fine Arts Committee and most of the details fall to me.

We've gone in deep, [we] of the Untide [Press], and got a real press. Found an old monster in a storage house in Waldport. Paid $20 down and hauled it out here. Owe $40—God knows where we'll get it. But it's a real press. We can print 4 pages at once. We'll have some Coffieldiana out soon (printed on the little press—but well done). This is really a swell group of lyrics. I look forward to showing you our first printed opus.

Glad to hear you're well and hale. I envy your continuous life there. Civilian life is now so remote as to be something of another life. I do not see, after CPS, how I can go back to Selma and the isolate existence on the farm there. Yet I suppose I will, simply because of no other life to turn to. I'd like to fit into some pacifist commune somewhere. That was a good life, and a rich one, but, somehow, after the teachings of this life, somehow unsatisfactory. Above all, I want to continue the Untide Press, fit in the aesthetic-pacifist field, do all I can to tie those two—not using the propaganda technique, but simply emphasize by association. It should be done. We're going to have to undo a whole new Versailles, before long—

the world does I mean—don't get the idea I'm a crusader. But I want to have a position—a point of departure for what I do, that will relate to the larger problems of this time. I have that in pacifism. I do not intend to let it drop.

Well, forgive my tardiness in reply. You've been a swell correspondent—and I welcome the zest of your letters. I hope to Christ everything goes well with you, that you escape the draft, that you thrive and prosper, and above all, that your pen abounds with that creative flow. Nothing pleases me more, with every letter, than the assurance that your writing does go on. I expect you to improve. Your great resource is the richness, the emotional fullness of your perception. The rest is craft and labor and to be had.

Good luck to you. You're a swell guy.

Bill

The cards, both received here, are swell. Thanks to both you and Fay. And Edwa sends hers. Yes, I received *Capricorn,* it's been well-read, and I hope to get it back this week—Jan. 13, '44.

January 17, 1944
Clark Memorial Library
ALS, 4 p., 2 sheets

Dear Bill—

Glad to hear from you. If you haven't expressed *Capricorn* yet, send it to me at the above address, as there's no delivery up in the canyon. Letters as usual, however, to the home address.

I wish you could see this place. It's a gem, set in a 5-acre walled garden. I have 4 librarians, 3 gardeners & 1 janitor-bookbinder under me. A nice rehearsal for the bigger job to come in July. Then I'll have both libraries, with a deputy in charge here. Clark spent a million bucks on this building—all bronze & English oak, marble & travertine—in beautiful taste. I squat in my panelled office, my hoofs buried in an Oriental rug, & toss the flotsam & jetsam over my left shoulder into a $200 hand-carved oak waste-basket. We are endowed for a million & a half; about $20,000 of the income goes every year for book purchases. A wonderfully quiet restful place, about 12 miles downtown from the campus. Admission only by card. I look forward to the time when I can show you the place. Next year I'll try to spend a day a week here—a sort of idyllic retreat from the busy campus library.

But the real joy that's in my heart has nothing to do with all these material things; it's of the spirit. Finally to return to the University as somebody; to have authority & to be responsible only to the President—whose full confidence I have—this is what I cherish. I put in 5–1/2 years of penal servitude—& did not sour. Now I am sweet as a nut. I race through detail work like a mouse through cheese.

The other evening Newell came by the Library at 5 & we went down to one of the city's oldest restaurants, the Good Fellows Grotto, at 3d and Main, & had a leisurely fish dinner. He is on the verge of quitting his plastics work & becoming an artist again—& I am, as the jargon has it, aiding & abetting him. Newell is a man after my own heart. Knows when he's off the beam & strives to get back. Poor Ritchie, in contrast, grows more & more corrupt as an advertising executive.

Henry Miller came by yesterday for a chat. He is getting a New Miscellaneous volume ready for Laughlin, & leaves soon for Monterey, as guest of some Greek. Ben Abramson of the Argus is printing *Capricorn*—300 copies at $10.00.

I am pleased to hear of your new press & look forward to seeing Coffield's lyrics and yours! You are growing in this experience. I wish after the war is over you could establish a pacifist commune somewhere down here. You & I could stand seeing one another more often.

I find myself weakening & wanting to send you the typescript I have accumulated. Bieler & Newell are reading it now. The stuff doesn't breathe until it is read. It was your splendid encouragement & criticism that powered me through the final revision of "Quintet." I've worked almost a year now on this new book, without a person hearing or reading a word of it. You know, of course, what I mean.

Reading all I can lay hands on by Haniel Long, the Santa Fe man who founded the cooperative Writers Editions. His volume of poems *Atlantides*—a book on Whitman (best I have ever read) & a curious fable "Interlinear to Cabeza da Vaca." Ever read any of these? Savoring the last volume of Elie Faure, *The Spirit of the Forms.*

Bought the Busch recording of the 1st Razumovsky quartet.

I wish I could visit you. Perhaps in the late spring I might take to the road & vagabond my way up. I will have 2 weeks off before starting at the University library.

And how wonderful a few women can make life! Sometimes you never even talk with them, or see them up close. The mere sight of a girl, seen from an automobile, walking free-limbed on the sidewalk, bare-legged under the bare-limbed trees, wearing a gray skirt & a bright green jacket, blonde & bare-headed, & no sight of her face. Only the quick vision of a lovely body & carriage, how exciting to the imagination!

And going up into the hills for holly, breaking through the forest of dead mustard stalks & tall dry grasses. Say, a man & woman going into the hills for holly & becoming lovers for the first time, in the bedded dry grass under the berried toyon tree, up above the valley, secret, hidden, hot & ardent. Stories to write, Bill—I teem with them. And latterly it will not matter whether they actually happened to me or not. That is the freedom I am striving toward.

Affectionately,
Larry

January 25, 1944
Beverly Glen
ALS, 2 p.

Dear Bill—

Did I write you that Ben Abramson of the Argus Book Shop is issuing 300 copies of *Capricorn* @ 10.00? If you know of anyone who wants a copy, tell them to order now, as the edition will be oversubscribed many times. Address is 16 North Michigan Ave., Chicago. Henry also advises me that the Gotham Book Mart is selling a new monograph on him by the English poet, Nicholas Moore. I've not yet received my copy.

How do you like this paper? Clark had it especially made & watermarked in Holland, then Nash printed the name & address on it & the envelopes. I unearthed a nice little cache of 12,000 unprinted sheets, which I am going to have turned into gift acknowledgement forms, etc.

I wish you were here now to see the Clark Library. It's the most marvelous place I've ever inhabited.

As I told you, I am weakening, & want to send you the typescript I've accumulated. If you want me to send it, I wonder if you would do me a favor, after you have read it? Is there someone up there who would be interested in reading it? I mean someone tolerant, who doesn't know me from Adam, & who would express an honest opinion of the work on its own merits. Who is Coffield?

Of all the friends I have, you are the most detached in your ability to read & criticize what I write—& you have proved this repeatedly, to my genuine benefit. You will understand, of course, my added wish to get a completely "unfriendly" reaction!

My life seems to be getting richer every season. To what limit can this go? I want this richness for all my friends—for you & Edwa.

Yours ever,
Larry

Jan. 30, 1944
Waldport, Ore.
ALS, 1 p.

Dear Larry:—

Emerging from a mountain of work (Untide Press, Arts School, etc.). I hasten a reply to your fine letter on the unbelievable Holland paper.

Yes, you wrote concerning the Argus imprint of *Capricorn.* An opportunity, certainly, though I cannot take it now. But it does bring up a matter I cannot put off, though I had hoped to wait a bit before speaking of it. *Capricorn* has disappeared from my locker. I hope it will come back—I expect it will, in fact. I've kept it very close, been very careful about lending it, and administered caution at every loan. The reason I think it will come back is that both *Cancer* and *Black Spring*, more extensively read here, were not removed. I'm so sure of this that I had expected to wait longer before disclosing it to you, but the Argus issue makes it seem that it is only fair I tell you while you have an opportunity to replace. A thing like this is the most painful thing I have to do: I cannot remedy it. It's simply a fact, and, if it doesn't return, I can only give you the empty assuagement of a worded regret, I'm really sorry Larry. But I haven't given up yet.

Yes, do send on the new writing. I swear, yea, guarantee, absolute return. No, I can hardly do that, can I, not being God. But I do want to see it. And I will be exceptionally careful. I have one or two friends here who can be trusted for a fair, tolerant, and broad-minded judgement. I welcome, in fact, your permission to show it to them.

Sincerely,
Bill

Running into first local trouble. Local editor is after us for publishing. Even got Winchell to attack us over NBC. Editor quoted from "War Elegy No. II." We don't expect a witch hunt—yet.

February 3, 1944
Beverly Glen
ALS, 2 p.

Dear Bill—

Don't worry about the *Capricorn*. If it turns up, well & good; if it doesn't, then someone else will have it on his conscience. I have the Argus one ordered. Don't feel badly about it. After all, you gave me the book. It came to me in a generous act. That was the important thing. Possession isn't of any real importance. I believe that.

I'm sorry to hear they've been firing on you. Get yourself a good mink-hole & crouch low. No needless exposure. Mind!

The typescript of "First Symphony" heads north, as soon as I can get it wrapped & expressed. I am glad you have time & want to read it. Show it to your friends, who have hearts of an equal size to their brains. I really ought to work over the typescript & then retype it for you—but I simply haven't the time. Any time I have I want to put on writing the last half of the book. Always bear in mind that it is only half finished. Part 3 will be Europe—& not another version of "Quintet"! I still have a few tricks up my sleeve!!—and part 4 the return to Joy. The last is a story you've never heard, & by God, lad, it's almost indescribably rich & desperate. The book aims to grow in richness & complexity. Part 1 is simple post-adolescent, naive experience recounted in simple terms. Each part aims to grow progressively richer in awareness & emotion.

I will be very grateful for your aid. Your reading of "Quintet" in early draft gave me the necessary faith and force to rewrite & complete it. (Someday I want you to read the finished "Quintet.") I am paused now, & need a push. I hold back from commencing the last half. It looms before me confused & inchoate & I hesitate. I want so to render justice to experience, not to fumble & wander. Part 3 is the stumbling block. It will be in unconventional form—not straight narrative. Hell's fire! I babble!

I bought the Hyperion Press Maillol. I'll bet you & Edwa have it! Beautiful. Also the Thompson *Cyclopedia of Music & Musicians.* 1 vol. 2500 pages.

I wish I could talk with you.

Night. Rain falling. Landowska plays Bach. My heart brims. All day I mold my new job. Many, many angles. Calls for arch diplomacy every moment. Night comes & I am face-to-face with myself & my own problems as an artist. Above all I must be emotionally honest & a good craftsman. Those two things. Hard, hard, hard.

I know you will guard the typescript. I have no carbon. Only the original ms which was greatly rewritten in typing. Firm greetings.

Larry

Feb. 24, 1944
Berkeley, Calif.
APS

Dear Larry:—

Came home a week ago to "straighten up my affairs." We have sold all our household goods—the accumulation of years, and have put the farm on the block. It's Farewell to the San Joaquin. Now here at the Bay enjoying the last few days of my furlough. Ms. had not arrived when I left.

Sincerely,
Bill

February 24, 1944
Beverly Glen
ALS, 3 p., 2 sheets

Dear Bill:

A most wonderful thing has happened to me. For the past couple of years there has lived a few houses down canyon a strange emigré bookseller from London, one Dr. Jacob Schwartz, who once owned the Ulysses Book Shop in that city, & who now runs a private business from his house. About a year ago I was in his place, & he called me into their bedroom & showed me a framed wood-engraving which was hanging over the bed. White on black, it showed a man and a woman in sexual congress, the man kneeling, the woman also on her knees, facing him straddling his body & just easing down on his penis. Their arms are wrapped around each other, their heads together, his face against her shoulder, hers hidden behind his head. Only a few lines to portray this; the result a marvelous commingling of the virile & the tender. Schwartz explained. It was an original from a block engraved by Eric Gill, & given to Schwartz by Gill; and represented the artist's idea of an epitomizing illustration for *Lady Chatterley's Lover*.

Very few were printed & the block destroyed. It has never been published anywhere. I told Schwartz I thought it one of the most beautiful things I had ever seen.

A year or more passed. Last week I read Gill's autobiography & my memory was haunted by the *Lady Chatterley* print. A couple of days ago I heard that the Schwartzes had sold their house & were leaving the canyon. I dropped him a note & said if by any chance he was going to dispose of the print, please to give me first bid.

Last night he trudged up to my study door with the framed print in his hand. "I've lived with it ten years," he said, "& loved it very much; now I give it to you. Perhaps you can trade me something for it; not now, some day." And he walked off, leaving the wonderful couple on my desk.

My God, man! What else is there to say? It stands before me as I write. Schwartz was offered $200 cash for it by the man who bought his house, but my note had come a few hours earlier, & he wanted me to have it. How I want you & Edwa to see it! You will go quietly mad!

All the while I was reading Gill's autobiography, I kept thinking of you & wanting you to read it. Have you read it? If not, let me mail it up. Discount his Catholicism & you have a great & virile artist. It will speak to you. His self-portrait reminds me strongly of you. Ten or more years ago I first saw Gill's work in London. I was with "Deborah" & "Doreen," who is in my new book—the part yet unwritten.

I hope my typescript reached you in good order. Let me know when you can. I have been up to my ears in good hard work. Things at the library are clicking even better than I dreamed they would.

We are just through a 72-hour storm that dropped 7 inches. My roof & wall stood the test without flaw. We are going for the weekend to Hemet, to M.F.K. Parrish's. Over two years since we have been there.

Hope you are well & busy.

Yours
Larry

February 28, 1944
Los Angeles
ALS, 1 p.

Dear Bill—

Returned from weekend at Hemet to find your card of the 24th from Berkeley, stating that you had not received my ms. before you left Waldport. The question in my mind is, when did you leave camp on your furlough? I sent it by prepaid express on February 5th. I shudder to think something has gone wrong.

I hope you found it at the Waldport express office on your return. For God's sake, airmail me at once, yes or no! If it is no, I'll get the local office to trace.

It was a shock to hear you have liquidated in the San Joaquin. I had no inkling, except that I knew the load was too heavy for Edwa alone. Is she working in Berkeley?

How I wish you could have crossed the Tehachapis!

Write in supreme haste, I pray you! And to 2205 West Adams Blvd. LA 7.

Larry

3-2-44
[Waldport]
ALS, 1 p.

Dear Larry:—

Rest assured. Your panicky (understandably so) letter reached me today. The mss. was here on my return. Came in the day after I left (the 16th of Feb.). Watkins returned with me, and a heap of Art School correspondence lies at hand, so I have put aside reading it until I can really do it justice. I expect to do this the first of next week after Lee has returned—possibly before. It is a fine thick packet and I look forward to it. After the "Quintet" I am particularly anxious to see your development.

The furlough was a success. Established once more between Edwa and me some semblance of our old *rapport*.

Though I learned many things she had not told me, many important aspects of which I was completely ignorant. But I do feel much better about our chances.

The 4 days in Berkeley were swell. Edwa, whom I had hoped to bring back to camp, will stay on there, taking a course or two at Cal. I plan now to return there after the war and live for a while. I like it.

For now, so long
Bill

March 4, 1944
[Los Angeles]
APS

Dear Bill—

Am much relieved to learn that the ms. is safe. How do you like this card our Univ. Press designed for us?

Larry

March 12, 1944
Waldport, Oregon
ALS, 2 p., 1 sheet

Dear Larry:—

I suppose one of the tests of the validity of a work of art is whether or not [it] enriches your experience. The "First Symphony" does that. Having just laid it down, after having been over it most of the day, I have for it something of the excitement and the admiration that sent me, that night two years ago, to the telephone in Selma, rousing you from your bed in the dead of night, and letting my elation come to you straight. Tonight, the pen will have to do. I am four times as far away. But if the pen can say what I want it to say, that will be enough.

I am trying to figure out how it is you overcome your weaknesses. For I am going to tell you right out that the first half of this thing is, from the man who wrote "Quintet," unbelievably febrile. Little comes through. All of your work—the very best of it—is the work of an amateur. I use it in the best sense—a man writing to set down what is in him, as best he can, for what it is worth in the setting down. In your best work an unusual *richness* of response to experience lifts you bodily over dangerous defects of perception, over-emphasis, distortions, the emotion constantly getting in your way and blurring your eye. You overcome that. You even gain from it; gain by an intensity of purpose, an honesty that renders the experience whole and rich. But when, for one reason or another that I do not know, the experience was defective, then the writing becomes defective, becomes lame, crippled, sometimes even callow. I don't understand it. I hardly know what to say. Trudging along through it I kept saying to myself: "How can I ever tell him?" And yet, gradually, the writing richened, gained scope. Some of the distortion remained, as it did in "Quartet." The clichés kept cropping up. Yet the base of the material, the stuff of it was sound and good. The man fixed. He was no longer a puppet, jerked here and there by the whim of a college boy. He was a man. And that is enough to overcome all the defects and distortions, all the blurring of detail.

What else can I say? I decided not to pencil the sheets this time, though sometime my hand yearned for it—both to express anguish and admiration. Some things are wonderfully done. Your friends, for instance. Bart is well-done throughout—the only live person from the start. You have caught Ritchie perfectly. Thoroughly alive, both of them. Joy comes through, especially at the last, when your writing becomes more relaxed. Everything at first is made sterile by an attempt to grasp, to fasten, to secure; whereas at last it flows out from its own richness, and from the wealth of experience that must have gone behind it. The parting scene with MacIntyre is swell—that last drunken advice exceedingly well done. Bart's wedding night is superb. Again—all Bart is good, but, again, the last better than the first.

So that's the way I feel about it. I wouldn't have you try any other way; for the rewards are worth the losses. It's what you finally achieve, that counts. I feel good about the work, now that I've finished it. I really do. It has the ring of authenticity. I can't give you advice on how to improve it. "Quartet" I felt I could. For what I took to be flaws seemed like mere errors in a material essentially true from the start. How can I point out a correction in material that is not of itself true?

Am I blunt and brash? I haven't meant to be; for I was never more suspicious or distrustful of my own tastes than now. You're one of the best men I know, Larry. I think my truest friend. I know you've put your brain and your blood into this work; I have to tell you what I feel. I'm sorry it couldn't be all praise: but I can say the best praise: I feel bigger from your book, broader, I've lived. It's the real stuff. You've had a wonderfully rich life, because you know how to live.

With faith and
admiration
Bill

P.S. Most consistent literary defect, the inversion. Every page has it. Weed it out. A powerful device, but drugging. I'm giving the ms. to a friend to read as you asked. Return it in a few days.
P.S. I'm tired waiting on the other fellow, so I'll send this along. He has read it and is quite enthusiastic. I guess I'm wrong! Thinks we ought to try to print it, though that's impossible now. Was really impressed.

March 21, 1944
Beverly Glen
ALS, 5 p., 3 sheets

Dear Bill—

Evening of a long day early in spring! I am engaged in building my staff at the Clark & University libraries, filling men good & true. Many candidates. Letters to answer. Interviews to arrange. All work I love.

Your letter came yesterday at the vernal equinox. I had awaited it in fear & trembling. In the oak panelled quiet of my office, I read it, with the camphors in new leaf dancing outside the window—& I felt a boundless exaltation. I was aware of the faults you observed, but I could not be sure that my book would, as you say it did, enrich your experience. It is only half the book in second draft. I can overcome some of the faults by added work. And the total result will be not worse but better.

The problem of the first part—the Laura business—the experience was defective, the material that of an unawakened boy—I can't seem to fire it up. I am too far from it. Yet it is by contrast with the impoverished Laura experience that the fulfillment with Joy is meaningful. Newell found the identical fault you did. Do you believe the material of musician into poet is untrue? I am not sure where your line is drawn through the book. Is it Joy who brings the material to life?

I mean the progression of the ultimate four movements to be one from poverty & unawareness to richness & agonizing realization. The style as well as the subject becomes progressively rich & dense. I should have completed the book before giving it to you. I weakened!

But you encourage me. God almighty Bill, praise is not what I seek! I want understanding, tolerance, encouragement; the will to triumph in spite of my faults. All this you give me. And your letter was so goddamned honest & fine. I went to Newell's for lunch yesterday & read it to him—& he said it spoke for him. He's in the groove, doing a series of magnificent panels in wood. They are on the verge of buying a small ranch in the Malibus. How pleased he was to hear that you thought Bart the liveliest of them all! Of course he was—& is! And in the last half of the book, he & Richman will get up & walk, by Jesus they will! For by the time I get that far, my writing will be utterly relaxed & will, as you say it commences to do now in the story's latter part, flow from a rich reservoir of experience.

Encouragement to finish is what I needed. You have given it to me. There is no criticism I can't take. Never pull any punches on me. I wish you had marked some passages. That helped so much on "Quintet." I get blind. I note what you say about inversions. I shall weed them. I read Fowler on them in *Modern English Usage.* Should have done so earlier. Writing good English comes hard for me. I automatically write badly, & then have to pummel it into shape as best I can. I can spot bad writing instantly in everyone but myself! And to keep the emotion from blurring the perception: you should mark passages where you believe I fail to do so.

Your p.s. says your colleague is enthusiastic. Will he put anything down in writing? It's good of him to want to print it. That's furthest from my thoughts. It's only half written! I must finish it. "Quintet" should be printed first, if ever I decide to do it. I've not sent it out since Knopf knocked it. Knuts to him. I want you to read the final draft sometime.

The problem of what is true & untrue. Emelia Newell thought I falsified. But I am faced with material worked on by the subconscious through nearly 20 years. It is very hard to grasp experience & remold it in an artistic pattern after the passage of much time. You can't write things "just as they were." You simply can't even remember them in sequence! Art is the act of selecting & regrouping in a significant pattern the disparate elements of experience. Anguish. The pressure on me to drop all attempts. The constant struggle to keep the schizophrenic split from widening. My public days. My private nights. Yet what makes me a successful librarian is the same abundance of *elan vital* that drives me to "Quintet" & "First Symphony." I must leave a testament to the love I bear life. I must render back at least a symbol of what I have taken. Fisher's wonderful Ode to Art in the *Ghost.* "For Thee Earth I Make a Song."

I wish to God you were here or I there, & we could talk. I talk to Newell & to Bieler & write in my journal—but you alone of them have the critical sense.

I plan to go to Berkeley the first or second week of June. Any chance of your getting a furlough? Will Edwa be there then? I should like to see her.

Bought a copy of *San Joaquin* for the Clark Library. Dawson's $2.50.

What about your work? Is the Press printing your new poems? Please keep me up to date!

I am tired now. Grieg's Lyric Suite. Szigeti fiddling Bach's D Minor concerto.

Please write.

Affectionately
Larry

April 6, 1944
Waldport
ALS, 1 p.

Dear Larry:—

A quick one to acknowledge this lovely, wholly beautiful, superb drawing of the loving couple by Gill. It surpasses everything I have seen in its tenderness. How I envy you that print! Thanks many many times for sending me the reproduction. I shall always keep it.

Apologies for my silence. I promise a long and detailed letter this weekend, and the return of your ms. I have not been able to secure overhead time for the art school work these last two weeks, and things have picked up. Not only that but Edwa is here for a few days (leaving Sunday) and I have been concentrating most of my energy and mind on trying to straighten out our snarled relationship. Ah Christ!

Bill

April 10, 1944
Waldport, Ore.
ALS, 4 p., 2 sheets

Dear Larry

It's Monday night, and the long detailed letter I promised this weekend is not forthcoming. In a way, this is inexcusable. "First Symphony" deserves all the time and concentration I could afford it, now that you've asked for it, and to scant it, merely for trivial or secondary reasons, is hardly justifiable.

But I am ashamed about keeping it so long; and I feel I ought to get it back to you, and I have no assurance that further possession of it will bring the necessary impetus to tackle the job rightly. Edwa has been up here, left yesterday, our lives are quite upset, I've been immersed in our problems for days, weeks; the art school work piles about me, undone; I've been given no more time on overhead, and the evenings are demanding. These explain, but do not condone. As I say, "First Symphony" deserves the closest handling. But I'll try to answer your questions.

Your letter was swell. One of your best. I was very pleased that my own evaluation did not have a depressing effect upon you; that it encourages you, and stimulates you to write further.

Let me make a couple of generalities that have stuck in my mind over my thinking on this work. I have come to the conclusion that the writing of college life is one of the most difficult subjects to handle. Childhood is rich. I think almost anyone with a sense of the requirements of style can write effectively of childhood. Look what Steinbeck did with *The Red Pony*, or, better, Joyce in the opening chapters of *Portrait of the Artist*. You simply lapse into the state of wondrous regard for all detail and the mood flows. But the college age and the college life, from the point of view of the adult, is one of the most inexplicable, and I believe it can be said one of the most artificial of all the periods of development. The antics of the collegian appear inane; his enthusiasms unjustified, his reasoning callow, his whole thought process over-colored. The factors are true of any adolescence, but the collegian is complicated by the opening influence of intellectuality. He plunges into the realm of literature, ideas, art—and only partially grasps them. He likes everything for the wrong reasons. This is a generality, and I don't say it applies to your characters, but because their reactions are immature, it is doubly hard to make them completely meaningful to the adult, it requires the utmost detachment, sympathy, and perception to *understand* these tortured, shy, callow, often revolting youngsters. There are two stories I have recently read which point up the difference between writing of the two ages I should like you to read—they are the"Football Players," by

Wentzle Ruml, III, in the *Kenyon Review,* Winter, 1944, and "Of This Time, Of That Place," by Lionel Trilling, *Partisan Review,* Jan–Feb, 1943. But I think the problem is to make the *psychology* of the collegian evident, which a simple presentation of his action does not do.

This brings me back to the opening passages of the work, and I think a large part of the sterility is due to this fact: in the effort to write closely, straight, give the material forward without embellishment (generally a good motive for your type of writer, I believe), you have made it too sparse. I have the feeling there is too much dialogue without the enrichment of detail; and here the presentation of the psychology is attempted too much through the dialogue alone, which can be effective when the characters are conversationally subtle, but the collegians register only their blunt verbal reactions. Their *feelings* are what are important. Wolfe got through to that, but he could only draw their exaggerations. I should say that Harman was most impressed with these early dialogues.

April 11, 1944

(24 hr lapse—see what I mean?)

I discussed the preceding points with Harman and he does not agree. He feels that the early dialogues are effective precisely because they do not attempt to bolster with description, that they bring forth the character and situation, reveal the indeterminate nature of the relationship best by so doing. Well, I still don't think so, but I should temper my reaction with his. Generally speaking, I trust his judgement, and he's quite honest.

The problem of falsification. No. There is no requirement to abide by the past except for historical purposes. There is no such thing as falsification here. All art is "false." Our concern is not historical in these matters.

Transition from musician to poet. This general development was an actuality, as I recall. You've only altered the details. The thing here is, I believe, if there is a question of that transition, is that we are *told* of it, but are not *shown* it. In a way this is sound, for your focus is on the sexual relationship, and the extra activity sort of sketched in. On the other hand, the complication factor is the young poet's success. You get him to Europe on a scholarship, but we see little change in the man's psychology. Somehow we should be given something of the fellow's development as a writer. It's not necessary to quote, but I think we'd be better convinced if something of his concern as a poet does come through. As it is now, Farrand and the other prof stand around and pay him compliments, which is fine, but we'd rather be shown. If he weren't so successful it wouldn't be so important, but after all, achievements like that are significant, and we'd like to know what he *did* do. As I say, not so much his quotes, but his attitudes.

I can't draw a line through the book. I'll say generally it's around the meeting with Joy, perhaps after that affair gets going. But then Harman says there's no line—or rather that the line is natural. I don't know.

There should be more to say. Harman is typing out his remarks. I showed him your letter. He pointed to a line and said: "That, the man really does." I looked and read, "I must leave a testament to the love I bear life." And I concur.

As for me—things bowl along. We're not bringing out the unpublished poems, but are going to meet the demand to have the *Elegies* in print. I've added one that should have been included in the first series. Nomland designed it. If we can bring it off it will be one of the really *unique* books of the year.

Your finding *San Joaquin* surprises me. And at $2.50! Well!

I've about completed my "Waldport Poems" my CPS series. Will send soon.

And will write again soon. I've got a lot to get off my chest.

Bill

May get to Berkeley in June, but doubt it. Edwa's address 2209 Shattuck, Berkeley 4, Calif.

Almost tripled our money on the ranch.

April 15, 1944
Beverly Glen
ALS, 4 p., 2 sheets

Dear Bill—

Two letters from you this week. I knew you would love & cherish the Gill. Its coming to me is like a dream. I have wanted badly to hear from you. Your letters cheered me. Your spirit is good. We are both busy. The work lies ahead of me—whole continents of it. My practice is to give everything to the single thing I can do at a time. One by one I send them whipped & whimpering into my past.

Life has been marvelous & full for me since I wrote last. I have seen my closest friends down here—Newell & Bieler—at least once a week. Newell has finished another panel. Bieler is setting to music lyrics from John Russell McCarthy's last book *Enrico Considers*. The days have been halcyon. Nights of love and deep sleep.

At the vernal equinox a story came to birth in three successive night sessions—a story that had been working in me since last December. I send it to you herewith. I don't think I have anything more to say about it. It speaks for itself. You alone read it, then send it back, please, and keep its existence between us. It is the only time since our marriage that I have been moved this way—& God knows, I have been through the most poignant ecstasies. But—so help me God—I have it under control. The story proved a safety valve. It is the third & final draft I send you. I know you will be tender with it.

Thank God my feelings haven't dulled! I have never felt so alive as I have this spring. For about three years, from 1935 to 1938, my feelings died, & I thought I was finished. Too much fucking had done it. Have been coming back strong since 1938, when I got the job at UCLA—& met you!

I write this to Beethoven's op. 127—& on our new phonograph—a custom job from Gateway to Music—machine at one end of my study & loudspeaker, separate, on my desk. Record changer! Our first. Our old combination Victor upstairs we've had since 1929! The 1st & 3rd Razumovsky's move me deepest of all lately. Beethoven at his zenith. The violin concerto about that time. The *Eroica*. How I've lived with that man since 1930!

Thanks for your further remarks about "First Symphony." If you haven't sent the ms. yet, hold it & send back together with the enclosed story. And remember, all mss. to West Adams address, please! What you say about the difficulty of college material is true. I have purposely simplified, having stripped away the rallies, fraternities & other impediments—& Harman & I are in perfect agreement on that early part. It is meant to be lean & spare & rather unaware & unawakened. Sexual fulfillment brings awakening. The story is meant to grow richer & denser. I think perhaps, though, I can concede some to you & put a bit more meat on the bones of Part I. Try to at least. My mind has been full of this new story, & I have not thought at all of "First Symphony" since I wrote you nearly a month ago. So I have not minded your keeping it.

I have been busy with the Greek prose pastoral, "Daphnis & Chloe" by Longus, comparing the three English translations (Angel Daye, 1587, George Thornley, 1657, George Moore, 1923). The middle one is a masterpiece of English prose. I am assembling quite a collection of editions. Have you read *Daphnis & Chloe*?

I have struck up a friendship with the brother of a faculty wife—one Bill Maxwell, age 31, height 6′7″, weight 225—condition, a spastic paralytic. Seven years ago an auto accident injured his spine. For three years he lay completely paralyzed. Now he is gradually regaining some power. Can walk very slowly on crutches. Cannot yet unflex his fingers. Abdominal muscles limp & so cannot rise or sit without aid. Is so goddam big & heavy that he needs a derrick for a nurse. He was writing an M.A. on DHL at Berkeley, when Fate struck him down. Hell of a fine mind & character. Today he & the student who shaves him & drives him out twice a week, picked me up & we went over to the valley to call on a friend of his, who had the same kind of an accident 4 years ago & has been in bed, paralyzed from waist down, ever since. You see, there are stages in hell! And you & I know what a hair-line divides us from such a plight, from death itself.

Gone on now to op. 132.

Delighted to hear of the book plans for *War Elegies.* Send me the Waldport poems when you are ready.

I send you my affectionate greetings—

Larry

And thanks to Harman (who is he?) for reading the ms.

I have poured much into my journal these years. Someday I want you to read it. Now on vol. 4 of it.

April 18, 1944
Beverly Glen
ALS, 1 p.

Dear Bill—

I spent all day yesterday at the Quaker Whittier College, on an invitational survey of their library, then in the evening talked to their faculty on college library problems. A remarkable little nucleus of education. It was a full hard day, & I didn't get home here until 10 o'clock. Sunday I had spent in sawing & splitting logs. Today I returned to the Clark & found my typescript. So this is a note to acknowledge its safe receipt.

I must sit down & read it straight through, & hope that the experience will engender enthusiasm for completing the book. The story I sent you on Sunday filled my mind until it got written. Now I hope to be able to return to "First Symphony." I must not be deterred by knowledge of my shortcomings & weaknesses. I must triumph over them, as you say I do at the end. I must believe. I do believe. Without that belief, burning & ardent, nothing is done.

Has Harman any notes to send me? I thank you both!

Larry

April 19, 44
Waldport, Ore.
ALS, 1 p.

Dear Larry:—

Your story came today, I am on overhead, have had a bit of time, and have just completed it. I made occasional light pencilings as I went along and hope I didn't ruin a fair copy.

It's a pretty damned good tale. Nicely handled; carries the same pervasive charm that marks your work. If it had been dealing with realities, I'd have said it was swell. But somehow, as I penciled, I seem cheated. God damn it all! I think that is an immoral technique, foisting a dream off on a reader—as reality. Dreams, yes, but not dreams *as* actuality, then *poof!* down you go!

Too damned bad. Well, that's the way life is. Out there beyond your reach it shimmers.

Is that a permanent mar? I think it is. It builds up logically to that climax: it *should* have that climax. My god man, you've led us up page after page—feeding us crumbs. Remember the "cotton candy" they used to sell at the fairs? Take a big bite and get—nothing.

A sweet and charming tale—too bad it had such a finale. In life *and* on paper.

Bill

May 18, 1944
LA 7
ALS, 2 p., 1 sheet

Dear Bill—

Did you receive a story I mailed you over a month ago? It is of a nature that I don't want out of my hands for long, & I plan to bury it deep for posterity to unearth. So if you do have it on hand, pray speed it back to me soon at the above address.

I had a visit recently from George Leite & his wife. He left me the 2d number of *Circle* [which Leite edited]. Apart from your *Elegies* & Mac on Rilke, I do not think much of it. Miller on Nin smells of corruption. She is the type of female & writer that sets my teeth on edge.

Thanks for sending Coffield's *Horned Moon.* The poems do not move me to any particular emotion. As for the project itself, that of publishing original work in small handwork editions, I cannot commend it too highly. I look forward to seeing your *Elegies* in print. When? I'm sorry your "Poems 1942" is not being printed too. I was reading last night in the typescript you sent a year ago. What have you written in the past year? Is there anything you are ready to send me?

I shall be in Berkeley the first week in June. Any chance of your coming down? Thanks for sending Edwa's address. I hope to see her.

Hasty greetings
Larry

May 31, 1944
[L.A.]
ALS, 2 p., 1 sheet

Dear Bill—

I am a bit concerned at not having heard from you since my air mail request of two weeks ago for you please to return the story I sent you a couple of months ago.

I am leaving for Berkeley in the morning (San Joaquin Daylight) to be gone a week. If you haven't mailed the story yet, please hold it for a week; as I would not want it at the Library in my absence.

Last week I dropped Edwa a line to ask for her schedule, phone number, etc., so that I could get in touch with her & see if a meeting could be arranged. I have such a fearful number of university appointments to keep, as well as a side trip to Stanford, that I have tried to arrange things in advance.

I have not heard from her. Perhaps she is with you? In any case, I'll be at the Hotel Durant in Berkeley through next Tuesday night. Coming down on the Lark the following night.

I hope you are not ill, or that your silence means you have been plunged in good work.

Whatever, here's a greeting as ever!

Larry

June 1, 1944
[Waldport]
TLS, 1 p.

Dear Larry:

The day your story came I read it and wrote the enclosed reply. I wanted to set it down so that I would not fall into my old fallacy of never getting your stuff answered. However, what I had written did not seem adequate, so I set it aside. You are a busy man, really busy, with a whole institution to manage, and it must seem like pretty paltry stuff for me to make that excuse. I haven't treated you right. I have violated one of the best things life can hold—a deep friendship, not once, but several times. I would not have written like this had it been but once, for that is excusable, but I have done it too often. Forgive me.

Edwa arrived today. Which means you will miss her in Berkeley. She had only this month between semesters at the art school she is attending, so she came on up. She is looking much better. Life there agrees with her. I have not brought you up to date on our case, but I want to. It's strange. For me, anyway. The old certainties simply no longer exist. In one year I have changed from a metaphysical absolutist to a philosophical relativist. I think a good part of metaphysical absolutism comes from our emotional attitude toward purity, sexual purity, we want one woman for ourselves, always, safe, untouchable by anyone else. Our ego demands it, and when we have it we call it pure. That is a fallacy. An artifi [*sic*]

June 2

Shit. The crap that issues from my lips in lieu of words or ideas disgusts me. I am in low spirits. Christ how we wail for certitude! God how we moan! The truth? Shit. We bellow for the truth like a ham actor, and when we get it we fold like a dishrag. Miserable sons of bitches, all, and I the worst.
Well, enough. I return the ms., discreetly unread by any but me. It has the quality of an episode in a longer work, rather than the concision of a shorter piece. The qualities that make up your better work are there, but they are always qualities it takes time to reveal. I still think it would have been better to have had a conscious reverie than an unconscious dream. Thanks for sending it. Thanks for your tolerance, faith, earnestness. Thanks for all. I'll write again, picking up loose ends.

Bill

Received your letter to postpone and did so. Things are better now. Edwa leaves again in a week.

June 19, 1944
Beverly Glen
ALS, 3 p.

Dear Bill—

I was much relieved by your letter. I had begun to fear that you had fallen ill or been transferred or suffered a profound depression. And when I received no reply from Edwa to my note, I knew a fleeting fear that the two of you had united in a conspiracy of silence.

I am sorry to have missed her in Berkeley, but glad she was with you. I hope that life is good to the two of you—but frankly I feel that marriage without children can rarely be deep-rooted—& that there is no strong compulsion for fidelity. Please don't construe this as smugness. I know well how quickly life can don a new mask & how tenuous is anyone's hold on permanence.

I had a wonderful week in Berkeley. Up on the San Joaquin & back on the Owl. Took your name silently as we passed through Selma northbound. Valley very beautiful. Grain harvest in different stages. Peaches green on the trees. Very little automobile traffic.

Many university appointments in Berkeley. A trip to Stanford.

I am very glad to have the story back. Thanks for your remarks. I sent it to you as an emotional document rather than a literary exercise, although I realize that when the two are perfectly wedded the result is a greater or lesser masterpiece. When desire strikes a man he has two lightning rods to save him: his penis & his pen. In my case it was the latter—& since writing the story I have been serene. Would that life were always thus simple!

In two weeks I return to the University Library. At the Clark I'll have a young man assistant [H. Richard Archer], a Californian coming back via U. of Chicago. My spring has been increasingly busy. Good productive work. Very satisfying to be in a responsible post at last.

The Newells bought a 6-acre ranch in the Malibus, about 30 miles west of here. Just over the crest from the ocean, on the north slope looking down on the Seminole Hot Springs valley & over miles of tangled ranges to the Santa Susannas.

My reading this spring has been chiefly in material about 17th-century England—the strong field of interest at the Clark Library. I await your first visit. On your next furlough can't you & Edwa get this far?

I am writing this [on] a Sunday morning, propped up in bed, nursing a cold. There's not much fire in my pen. Have become a woodman. My boys & I have split & sawed a couple of cords of oak, cypress, deodar, black acacia & Monterey pine—all but the oak trimmings from the Clark estate. We have 8″ wedges, sledge, crosscut saw & axe. This will sound dilettante to you, from your piney shore & hours & days & weeks & months of toil! Forgive me!

Of course I have missed hearing from you—but I would not have you write unless really moved to do so. In friendship, as in love, there are times of outward fruitfulness & fallowness.

Lord make us all more worthy of our gifts & our friends! Are they printing your *Elegies*?

Yrs. ever
Larry

Aug. 9, 44
Waldport, Ore.
ALS, 4 p. 2 sheets

Dear Larry:—

The photograph I have pinned before my desk. It watches me, your countenance there, more resolute and purposeful than I knew it earlier, reminding me of my obligation to my craft and my friends. The face says: integrity, loyalty, resolve. Good. I accept its challenge.

Let me briefly recount: I took furlough last September, went home with Harman, harvested the grapes, trying to erect something of the old solidity. On returning, her [Edwa's] letters were frequent and full, I felt their participation and the sense of re-establishment. Then gradually they fell off. What came were moody, touched with indecision. The strain of school and harvesting (really a terrific job for a woman) were beginning to tell. She was giving up. When she arrived here in December she was in a state of apathy so far gone as to be dangerous. I should have said that Hackett's attention had subsided and he thoroughly rejected her. Once here, she met him again and got the rejection straight—a bitter, bad scene. That finished that. She was here three weeks, left in no better a state. I saw she must get out of there and wrote to her board of trustees asking a release. She had been absent as many days as she had taught and they let her go. Still, the letters did not come. She was simply incapable of making any move, least of all of resolving her affairs. Suddenly took furlough in February and went to Selma. We had lost the good house in the vineyard, the worst blow of all. Every place she moved circumstances forced her out. She moved five times that fall and winter. My father drove her out of the house when he learned she bought no war bonds. Once I was there she took heart. We arranged to sell the farm, sold all our stuff, a mad week, but it brought us together. Under this strong cooperative feeling the truth finally emerged: the Hackett incident was closed, that no longer worried her, but another—more prolonged and more deeply established—was there. Shortly after my induction Carothers was discharged, as I told you. He was in terrible shape, on the verge of another suicide: one reason, a bad case of prolonged impossible love—for her. As much out of pity as anything else she had taken him, but also as a rejection of me for my more or less "desertion"—refusal to take war work to avoid induction, one more instance, in her eyes, of my placing other values above our relationship. So the thing grew. What was done tentatively, solidified into an established relationship. When he left for S.F. she made frequent trips there, he back home also. They spent money like mad—they both had plenty—a fast round of entertainment, which was a release for her, an expansion, filling a need that I, home-loving and phlegmatic, never could. So, until Hackett. That affair erupted right in the middle of the Carothers thing. With Carothers she was under no real obsession; he is an excellent cocksman (though she is his only woman) and she had a real affection, but Hackett struck fire. His rejection swung her full back on Kenny. The Carothers appeal is this: he is finally one person less aggressive, less purposive, less strong than she, and being master of that situation gave her release. If I gave her security I also gave her repression, and with Kenny she could have her way. This is also, you understand, part of the sexual release. He absolutely abnegates himself, but he's always there, ready for her. This is her analyzation, not mine. He has an unusual potency. Gradually under the extended relationship, they become almost perfectly adjusted, more so than she and I had ever attained. I'm getting ahead of myself. When she told me all this in Selma it bowled me over, of course. I had been totally ignorant. On Kenny's return I had been made uneasy by the veiled references in her letters, but these were quieted. See Waldport poem Six, written at that time. I met Kenny in Berkeley and we talked it all over again. This was getting to be old stuff with me! In keeping with my previous policy I refused to interject myself between. You will, of course, call me fool, but I can only do this. I cannot act otherwise. It would violate all I have adhered to. Carothers, of course, guilt-stricken, could hardly face me. The poor guy is just too sensitive. I don't mean to derogate him. He's still one of the finest people I know, but lost, really. I told them if they needed each other to go ahead. I told her to solve her own problems, when she wanted me I would be waiting. I hold absolutely nothing against either of them. I know she needed him. She has grown, strengthened, gained assurance, self possession. For him, it's been a new lease on life. I came back to camp. She entered art school, began learning. The city was full of good and rich things. I came back to camp and tried to weather it as best I could. It was hard going. The knowledge of sexual inferiority gnawed like a canker. I was getting in bad shape. She came up for a week in April. It was hard establishing any rapport. She was really Carothers' wife, her sexual affiliation lay there, and I could sense that. But still she maintained they could have no permanency. He did not want to marry. He will not work, earning his living gambling. They live at night, sleep most of the day. A hectic life, and no solidity. She maintained she still thought in terms of me in the future. Playing both ends against the middle. I kept on for two reasons: first, I love the woman with all I am; second, I could see her side and realize the growth. In her position, I would want to do the same. She came down again in June, when you were in Berkeley. This was the best of any time since I left her a year and a half ago. The solidity did her good, gradually she came around. I felt her affection for the first time. But still she wanted to go back. Waldport is no home, no permanency: the city life is full. She maintained that though Carothers had taken her to heights, sexually, she had never thought possible, it was still in terms of life with me that she was thinking. I accepted this, realizing that the psychology of release had as much to do with those sexual heights as anything else. I knew I was no utter dolt in the business myself, having taken her a good way up those heights in my own right. But she still wanted to go back and complete her schooling (her sister is paying her way for a while, and that counts for something). We parted on excellent terms, and I was reassured. Once back there, however, her letters got scarce. Life was going like mad there. Analyzing the situation I came to this conclusion: if Carothers' strength lay in his weakness, then it was an affair that was basically, I felt, unsound. To let it extend was to risk her becoming so involved in that freedom that she would be unwilling to face the responsibilities of an equal relationship. Continued participation in that fast life also boded no good for the tranquility of domesticity. I had given her a year and a half to play around in. If we were going to reestablish ourselves, it was time to come to some terms. Also, I felt I should assert my position to maintain her respect, if nothing else. She always said that if I put my foot down she would return, though resenting me for it. I felt the time had come when I should risk that, if we were to survive together. I wrote asking her to set a date upon which I could expect her return. I had not heard from her for days. Her letter came, very upset, asking me not to force her back. Life was too full there, school work, cultural activity, etc. She listed her past week's activity. Budapest String Quartet, London String Quartet, two excellent movies: *Maltese Falcon, The Long Voyage Home,* and finally Louis Armstrong. The school continued to be a constantly engrossing thing. Of course Kenny mattered, mattered a great deal, but it was the totality of it all. If I had a permanent home to offer it would be different, etc. Would I not reconsider? That was two days ago. I consider it tantamount to a refusal and have been as low as I've ever been. I don't want her if she doesn't want to come. I'll not have her crawling back holding it against me. But neither can I endure longer this ever-present, eternal absorption in a mood of loss and rejection. I can't go on with it. I think she no longer needs me. I think she's found her feet. It may be that's really her kind of life. I know it isn't mine. So be it. I guess it's over.

This thin skeleton gives you the frame. It's only the bone, and doesn't do full justice to the ramifications, but I think you can get the direction. I no longer feel badly about Carothers' sexual supremacy, though for a long time that hit me in a place it was hard to take. I couldn't play that kind of a man to her: if I can't be equals, I don't want it, and I know equality in the bed means at least preliminary restraint. It means, rather, responsibility, and with Carothers she's relieved of that. In a way they're perfectly adjusted. Well, God bless 'em.

Adios
Bill

August 10, 1944
Beverly Glen
ALS, 3 p., 2 sheets

Dear Bill—

Your new book [*Waldport Poems*] broke your long silence—& a good break it is. My thanks to you for the inscribed copy. There is a warmth & richness about the format—the creamy Linweave paper, the brown illustrations, the unpinched, unmeager, wide-open title-page, the round roman type—that perfectly complements the restrained, almost austere poetry. The total effect is of courage & beauty—& I congratulate you & your co-workers in the venture.

The poems are certainly your most finished work. They are impressive. They carry weight & conviction. They are dignified, & very sad. Your forenote is excellent. The restraint shown in it & in the poems is fine. You have taken this experience like a man—& I am proud of you for having distilled this clear strong essence from the bitterest of experience. I seek to put myself imaginatively in your place, & I can hardly do it. Nor can I conceive of what your future writing will be. Are you writing now?

Here is $5.00. Please send 20 copies, well-packed to avoid crushing.

Let me know if you reprint. I detect a few misspellings.

I mailed you notice of Gregg Anderson's death. A blow to my heart. We had come to be close friends. I had a last letter from England, on the eve of the invasion. You can imagine what an even greater blow it was to Ritchie.

Since taking the new office July 1, my life has been solid

with satisfying work. The problems are mountainous. I have two fine young men, as right & left hands—one at the Clark, one as Head of Order Dept. in Univ. Lib.

Last weekend we visited M.F.K. Parrish at Hemet. Preparing a show for December at Occidental of Parrish's paintings. We brought back three loans for our home, & one for my office. The latter gray-blue hills, with a shell & red dahlia in immediate foreground.

Tomorrow we sneak off for the afternoon to visit the Newells on their 6-acre ranch, about 30 miles west of here, in the heart of the Malibus.

Since July, I started on the second half of my book. I hope I can re-infect myself with belief. Without it, I can write nothing. I wish I could talk with you.

I hope you will write soon. I miss hearing from you. I sent you a photograph taken by the University news service.

Yours ever
Larry

Aug. 14, 1944
Waldport
ALS, 2 p., 1 sheet

Dear Larry:—

Your letter replying to the *Waldport Poems* was very good, most welcome. I feel you saw to their essentiality, where many people say something like: "Isn't that apt!" I am most pleased at your response. I say again, I think you really see what I am getting at.

About the writing. Yes, I'm working on the "Waldport Poems: III Series." I am enclosing the ms. of "Series II." I think they speak for themselves. They're not quite done, some phrases must change. They were written last fall, between my grape-picking furlough and Christmas.

I'm also impressed with your reaction to the design and format. We put hours of labor on this thing: the solid blocks were especially hard to bring off. Linoleum blocks. I have learned a great deal about press-work and printing. We are now going to complete the printed edition of the *Elegies*.

This man Clayton James is the real thing. I want to say simply and earnestly that he is the greatest man I've ever met: not so much by what he does, though I feel he may be a great painter, but more by what he is. He and I have built up a profound relationship. We have built up, I feel, great meaning for each other. He has a wonderful wife: they have a cabin across the road. He has done some impressive oil paintings.

I'm sorry I didn't check your copy. As far as we know there are two misspellings, both on the next-to-the-last page. One was caught at about 200, the other at around 400. We never started slipsheeting until two color runs had been made, the W and the portrait, so that some of these offset. Please point out any other errors in spelling, etc.

I gave up my time on the Fine Arts job (the camp had granted us time for one man to work solely at that). I held it from about May to July. I'm still "Director," but have turned the work over to another man. We have 10 or 12 men here from all over CPS to participate in this project, and more coming. James is one. I'll have Dupré (my alternate) send our announcements.

I wonder if you know of Morris Graves, the young painter who impressed N.Y. with his debut there 3 or 4 years ago. This makes him sound like a salon painter. Nothing is further from the truth: almost a recluse, a very religious nature. He's here now, built a small camp near here, and paints. We go down in the evenings for long discussions around his fire. We're now showing a roomful of work he's done since arriving. Spent a year in the army (guardhouse) as a C.O. at Camp Roberts. [Reason for discharge:] 4-F (mental)! Carothers knew him there.

I'm a cook now in the kitchen. That's strange, is it not? Yet I like it.

I like the northwest, now. Living by the sea has been a very wonderful experience, keeping always this intensity near at hand. Nor, I think, have I fallen into Jeffersian attitudes because of it. I often think of my future in terms of the northwest, though that's so fucked up now I hardly know what to expect.

Have developed a fine friendship by mail with Ruth Suckow, and had it enhanced by a visit here from her. She was making a lecture tour. You know her, I believe. See Ferner Nuhn's write up of our work in the current *Fellowship*.

Bill

A friend, over my shoulder, pointing at the photo [of Powell]: "Why *that's* the man at the UCLA library!" Former student.

August 17, 1944
Beverly Glen
ALS, 3 p., 2 sheets

Dear Bill—

Write me either at home or the university library, rather than at the Clark, as I am over there only once a week now, on Wednesday. I got your letter there yesterday. I appreciate your bringing me up to date on your relationship with Edwa—& I only wish, as I did in my last letter, that we could talk together. Can you get a furlough in September? Why not spend it down here? I could arrange for you to have a cabin on the Newell's Malibu ranch, & in addition to activities here in the city, you could derive rest & comfort up there. I should like to see you have a complete change of scene from Waldport, Berkeley, Selma, etc.

You have taken a powerful beating from Edwa & your friends. I do not wonder that you feel low. Yet, as I read your letter, it all seemed inevitable. You never told me before that Edwa wanted you to take war work to escape induction. I always supposed she backed your pacificism 100%. Things are clearer now. I do not reproach you. Of course not. You were willing to sacrifice everything to your ideal. What woman would have followed you? I feel sorry as hell for you both. War casualties. Your home gone. It's tough, but you've got the guts to see it through. You're right. Don't force her back.

This will either make or break her. If when the war's over, you come together, you will be mighty strong, both of you. But now you have nothing to offer her, but a cold white ideal. You put yourself in a camp. You're going to have to see it through alone.

You know your own sexual power. No one has triumphed over you. Women are that way—the good ones—there comes a time when they crave another prick or two, to measure their husband's by. I know these things, by Jesus, the hard way—& have been "another prick" and a "husband prick"—& know that if you feel yourself inferior to another, & cry & whine, then you're done for. I've seen my friends Newell & Ritchie & Fisher, etc., through woman & wife trouble of various sorts—& have fucked & been fucked, in more than one sense, and I know this finally—that the dog must not return to its vomit. Strength & success lie in another direction. If you were strong enough to lock yourself in a camp, then you're strong enough to turn your back on Edwa until you can offer her a life together without a camp wall between you. If Carothers can't save himself, by himself, let him go under.

Bold words, pal, & I'll bet they come over you like misty shit. At this time no matter what I wrote would. So be it!

But I am your friend—yours to command—

Larry

August 21, 1944
Camp Angel
ALS, 2 p., 1 sheet

Dear Larry:—

Thanks for your letter today. There is considerable truth in it, I feel sure. I have learned enough by this time, however, to doubt the existence of any universal "truth," and especially any human "truth." There are cases and cases. You must remember my particular circumstances. You have known many women, and in retrospect the progression from one to another must seem like a wonderful unfolding. To close a door is for you the equivalent of opening another. I met Edwa when I was eighteen years old. She is the only woman I ever had. The only woman I have ever even taken out. My only "date" actually! Put in those terms the relationship must seem like a ridiculous piece of sentimentality, but there it is. To take such a step as I am taking is one absolutely unprecedented in my life. (No I exaggerate. Christ how the sense of a dramatic situation twists the telling of the truth. During eight years' courtship I broke with her several times, trying to go my own way, only to return, almost by chance. I am such a habit-forming person!) But surely you can see the enormous consequence for me. It preys on my mind. I love the woman.

But I have determined to keep my resolve. Not out of any sense of progression for myself, for I simply can't see any—there are no leads. But because I think she is living more fully now than she ever has before, and that she does not need me, that she is keeping me as her ace in the hole (pun!) against the future. I can't serve that function. And only when she makes it clear by some stringent and revealing act that I am of necessity to her sense of being, and that she is sure enough of it to sacrifice for it, do I intend to reestablish relationship with her. She has not yet comprehended the implications of the situation. My last letter, two or three weeks ago, was inconclusive, so as not to force or alarm her. A recent letter from her was almost casual. Pretty soon she will begin to question the silence. Let the silence speak.

Let me clear up the point about the war work. She never really raised it; I wouldn't let it rise. I simply made it clear from the start, in discussions with friends, etc., who suggested it, that it was something I couldn't do. It only came out in discussing what happened later that she indicated it was her sense that there were values for me over and above our relationship that undermined her faith in it. She is not a 100% pacifist, though she does not believe in the war. She is not 100% anything hypothetical. She is 100% woman, in that she deals with life as it manifests itself, on the basis of the immediate sensory situation: an attitude which I have admired in women ever since I became aware of it; and increasingly so in her in terms of this experience. My God how she's grown, how she's broadened! My simple regret is, speaking intellectually and apart from the innumerable emotional ties that so weave within the context, that it's only been after I leave her that the flowering develops. Like taking the cover off a plant. And a good part of my action may be seen as a very real and sincere desire not to put that cover on again. I have no question about my ability to progress. I do not doubt that I will take it and weather it and grow from it, as I have already grown from it, amazingly so, when I think of my former tight little mind, but Christ how difficult and painful it is to grow! And how reluctantly we move toward it!

Here, life barrels on, top-speed. My work in the kitchen, getting out two meals per day, is so compelling of thought and energy, that the days whizz.

September's a fire-season month. May get off in October, but hadn't thought what to do with it under this new development. You make a tempting offer. I'll see what works out.

And be of good cheer
Bill

August 26, 1944
Waldport
TLS, 1 p.

Dear Larry,
This is a kind of special communique. The Untide Press is faced again with the old story—finances. Our incoming sales make up enough to dribble by on, but before bringing out a book we have always had to borrow and scrape and pray to get by. In our last meeting we decided if each of us would ask several of his friends to donate what they could perhaps we might be able to build up a small reserve. It would have to be offered as a gift, for once sunk we have no means of reimbursement, other than sales, though we have hopes of some day clearing ourselves. What we can offer is the return in material up to the amount of investment. This applies to anything we do. We shall be very grateful for whatever assistance you can give us.

Sincerely,
Bill

Sept. 8, 44
[Waldport]
ALS, 1 p.

Dear Larry:—

Am sending on typescript of first European review. *Poetry Quarterly*—looks about like English equivalent of *American Quarterly*.

Been out two days and nights on a hot fire—careless smoker, as usual. My God how you work on those things. In kitchen again tomorrow. Sure, I can cook!

Bill

Did I tell you Laughlin wants to reprint *W.P.* in next *N.D. Annual?*

O yes. Miller has been cracking us about our dissatisfaction here—thinks we ought to love it or something. I wrote a reply that some here thought well enough to mimeo. Here tis:

August 28, 1944
Waldport
TLS, 2 p.

A FULSOME EXPRESSION

Dear Henry:

You've got us wrong. It's wonderful here. Surely you've jumped to conclusions. Why, we love it.

The great thing is: not having to be alone anymore. The simple sweet assurance that no matter when you raise your head your eyes will encounter some other brother's favored face. Mealtimes especially. Three times a day, punctually on the hour, we get to sit four abreast and face each other. The symmetry is very restful, helps the digestion along, and that's nice. When I think of how it will be if we ever got out and have to go back to a room of our own, maybe a whole hour's solitude, absolutely alone, it terrifies me. How did I ever stand it? And silence! I simply can't face the problem of not having some good brother reasonably extolling "What A Friend I Have In Jesus" down at the other end of the room, or the comforting clatter of a typewriter, or these wonderful radios that can run for hours and never once leave you to the desolation of your own resources. I remember when I invited you up here one of your reasons for declining was that you couldn't get on in groups. Henry, that's all in your head. I felt that way once, myself. It is hard at first, I admit, but I tell you the adaptability of the human constitution to endure is an amazing thing. Of course, CPS has a couple hundred psychiatric-case releases a year, but those are just the soft-brains without any idealism. They didn't try.

Then there's the matter of women. For six years I had accustomed myself to a bit of the tie that binds, every night or so. Christ, but I was carnal!! Compared to the spiritual amplifications of asceticism I must have been living a life of gross bestiality. Now all that's changed. We simply don't have to bother with it anymore. We have our spells, of course, time when you go about in a kind of diabolical rut. The hills become female. The dead snags strain their white phalluses at the heaving clouds. The semen pours down the canyons. The ocean pants in its vast erotic mumble, like Molly Bloom's orgasmic declaration in the night-mare of *Ulysses:* O! *Weeshwashtkissimapooisthnaphoohuck!* Even the forks of the little twigs acquire miniature cunts, and offer themselves for the ancient insertion. All this, however, is simply the temporal manifestation of the physical. Recognizing it, we can safely escape back to more ethereal preoccupations, and subdue the tyranny of the flesh in the all-pervasive quietude that remains the highest reward of meditation.

And this humdrum matter of money. Since there is none, it cannot taint us. We simply coast along in a kind of relaxed acceptance and take things as they come. Everything is handed to us. Only occasionally are we ever disturbed by the thought that out in the world, that grinding inhuman universe of give-and-take, someone, our wives, our families, our friends, or more often some total stranger whom we will never even know to thank, is sweating out his guts at some damnable job that we may luxuriate here in our somnambulistic reverie. Every once in a while your shoes wear out, or you need a new pair of pants, and you have to sit down and write that hardest of all letters to write: "Dear So-and-So: Can you spare me five dollars?" But most of the time this doesn't bother. After all, the Good Book says: *ask, and ye shall receive.* A wonderful teaching, that.

But best of all is the stimulating work we get to do. They let us work for fifty-one whole hours a week. We thrust manfully about the hills with axes and hoes (lovely tools, don't you think? I'll never forget the fine feel of a well-balanced grub-hoe). We sweat in the sunlight, or trudge through the rain (a hundred and four inches of it last year). A forestry foreman is always reassuringly close, with his little notebook. If he writes your name too many times, it means down the river to the Big House, but that's a minor matter. The rocks aren't really heavy, not when you love your work. And that wonderful feeling at coming in from a day well spent, so thoroughly exhausted you can do nothing but crawl upon these fabulously restful mattresses they provide for us.

And it gets better as it goes along. The weeks grow into months and the months into years, and the first thing you know you can't even remember how bad it was on the outside, in the old days. Just one long eternity of conscription. That's a beautiful word, Henry, the great word of the future. Not the least of our rewards is the knowledge that we're setting the precedent whereby many more men may enjoy the benefits of this amazing social reform. Just think of all the undesirables who are so unhappy out there in the world. Maladjusted. Just like us c.o.'s. But we have shown that the really humane thing to do is put us all to one side where we can form our own little worlds and be happy. Do you realize that we've done almost 25 million dollars worth of work for the government and not one penny given back in pay? That's a stimulating thing, Henry. Wait till the Jews and the Negroes and the Japs can be rescued and put to purpose. We're showing the way.

Yes, Henry, as you once said: "Why, you're *protected.*" That's exactly right. Protected from all the humdrum trivia that used to trouble our days. Protected from the freedom of movement, the necessity of pay, the bother of marriage, the worry of earning a living. There's a thick book of laws, conceived and executed in the infallible wisdom of the State, residing now in the superintendent's desk, which is our guarantee that these things need not concern us. Come on up and try it some time. You really can't make a fair test in less than a year, but you'll love it.

With best wishes,
Bill

* * *

[First European review.]

THIS IS THEIR LANGUAGE TOO

WILLIAM EVERSON, 10 *War Elegies* (Untide Press, Waldport, Ore.); ALAN SWALLOW, *XI Poems* (The Prairie Press, Muscatine, Iowa); *Meanjin Papers; Quarterly* (Brisbane, Queensland); *Quartos,* Nos. 2, 3, 4 (Runa Press, Dublin); FREDERICK MORTIMER CLAPP, *Against a Background of Fire* (Harpers, New York, $2.50).

The Gettysburg address was delivered in an accent very similar to that used by many an allied soldier when inviting a friend to join him in a pint. This thought springs to my protection whenever I hear a middle brow being condescending about 'colonials'. For a native texture is threaded through these poems as the caraway seeds are in Jewish bread. Beauty is revolutionary, communism is goodness, whatever the accent that cellophanes its expression.

Blessed are the humble for they inherit the review. Inside Cinderella's slipper I found the best verse. One only of these books, pamphlets and periodicals was not invited to the printing bench, but had to stay home and be duplicated and very nicely duplicated too. The sparrows and the hawks went to the feast, but the lark stayed home, he flies too high for the former and didn't wait for the latter. The 10 *War Elegies* of Mr. Everson are produced simply with great taste and cost the equivalent of our fivepence.

I shall certainly keep my copy, and hope that its author, far away on the lovely coast of Oregon, reads this review. These, it seems, are the first poems to be published, of a writer of deep culture and real ability. That quality of innocence which is a necessary ingredient to all real art is very present in William Everson's work. He writes:

'In the weak light
  Under high fractured cliffs,'

and concerns himself with the ordinary people along America's Pacific coast, who

'Went out of the world
Into the war.' [*sic*]

These are the opening lines of his eighth and, to me, best elegy:

'All night long in the high meadow
They shielded the city light from
Their eyes under towering glass [*sic*]
Weeds warded them;
Dock hung in his hair
Mallow marred with its subtle stain
Her rumpled skirt.'

Readers please note: the next time they see a 'drunken' American, or any other, soldier with a girl, in the doorway of a closed shop, that it is just possible, that ideas like these are beating in harmony with the rhythm of his blood as his hand moves toward her hair.

Oh, I know that I shall be accused of falling for the homespun get-up of this pamphlet with the beautiful cover, against the 'vellum' of Mr. Clapp's two-and-a-half dollars, two-hundred page, New York publisher. However, if these necessary limited quotations have wetted [*sic*] the appetite of any reader, he may most certainly borrow my copy, but he must first promise, on the Leaves of Grass of Walt Whitman, to return it.

* * *

—Paul Potts,
Poetry Quarterly, V. 6, No 2
The Grey Walls Press,
4 Vernon Place, London,
W. C. 1, England

September 9, 1944
Beverly Glen
ALS, 3 p., 2 sheets

Dear Bill—

You're four up on me! Letters, poems, & today No. 3 of the *Illiterati.* Thanks for all. It's Saturday afternoon & I sit here at my desk, the goldening sycamores & sunlit hill out the window, books & records piled around me, your letters spread out at my elbow. You will picture the setting, although nearly two years have passed since you were here.

My work seems to get increasingly heavy. Yesterday from 8:30 to 6:00 I was in my office, & not alone for more than a minute at a time. People-people-people—& many of them—& their problems & desires, of real interest. Then I come home & take a shower & have supper with my family. Afterwards I play new records (Franck violin sonata, Beethoven's op. 95, Beecham's *Carmen* suite), then work on letters & reports to hand over in the morning to my secretary for typing, etc. To bed at 10 or 10:30.

Night before last we called on Richard Aldington & his wife at their apt. in Hollywood, & discussed a forthcoming exhibition at the library of his collection of his own books. Do you know this versatile writer? I have been interested ever since I read his *Death of a Hero* in 1929. He is 52 now, with a young luscious wife & a 6 year [old] daughter.

Henry Miller's new book, *Sunday after the War,* came yesterday. I have been re-reading Rabelais & Whitman.

I like Series 2 of your "Waldport Poems." If you be not less strong than they, you will progress. I realize how different our experience has been, & expect you to filter all of my counsel in terms of the difference. I have suffered anguish through women, but as you rightly observe, have always opened a new door as the old one closed. My heart is with you in all you do.

With regard to your letter about friends for the Press, here is $5 for sustaining membership in the *Illiterati.* I cannot send more now. Hal Bieler said he will send money for copies of *Waldport Poems.*

Send a copy, with a strong letter of appeal, to Mrs. Kate Crane Gartz, 441 E. Mariposa, Altadena, Calif. She is a noted patron of socialists, pacifists, etc., including Upton Sinclair; & she liked very much your *Elegies,* given her by Bieler, I believe. She is the daughter of Crane Co., plumbing, & immensely wealthy.

We were at the Newell ranch last Saturday. He said he would write you to come next month. Come south, young man.

I remember Ruth Suckow & Ferner Nuhn from 10 years ago. Fine people.

Do you have any plans for after the war? I note your increasing devotion to the Northwest—one section of the USA I've never seen.

Yrs.
Larry

P.S. The *Illiterati* is superb!

September 19, 1944
Beverly Glen
ALS, 2 p., 1 sheet

Dear Bill—

Thanks for the additional copy of *Illiterati.* Also the English review. We either receive *Poetry Quarterly* at the Library or will. We receive an English, *Poetry Review,* I know.

Thanks too for your letter to Henry. Neatly done, pal. I just had a very bilious letter from Henry re the Porter bibliography. I've worked to bring order out of chaos. Fuck these young chaotic surrealists. What this world needs is beauty & order.

For example, K. Sheets in the *Illiterati.* A stinking offering to Miller. I am not amused.

Henry's trouble is that he's fucked out again. A female wrestler, June Lancaster, is said to be living with him. Same thing happened a year or so ago when he was here in the Glen—a Greek girl milked him dry. He has never practiced moderation. His genius certainly, but it will kill him before his time, I fear.

Have Budapest recording of the Harp Quartet, op. 74, & am walking on air.

Working like a bastard.

Yrs ever
Larry

So Laughlin wants to reprint *W.P.* in his annual! I remember the shabby way he treated your manuscript.

Nov. 18, 1944
Waldport
3 p., 2 sheets

Dear Larry:—

I was in Berkeley when your last letter arrived, and was forwarded and I had no time to answer then. I have neglected it till now. I went when fire season closed, and because Edwa begged me. It was our plan to go to some other place and see what could be seen. For one reason or another we stayed on in Berkeley the whole furlough: in some ways an error, in some ways not; it revealed some important things.

It revealed a great shift in attitude between E and C. I told you, I believe, of her dominant position. That no longer obtains. Having healed the man, she finds him her master! Where before, he was evasive before me, defensive, guilty, and rather weak, he is now assured and certain. He pities me a bit. Mingling together, I could see his unconscious usurpation of possession: the true mark of the husband. We did not talk of the matter together till my last two days. He was then surprised to learn she had asked me down, having thought I was there on my own. They withdrew after that for a pow-wow. I had the feeling of a casual acquaintance caught somehow in the snarls of a family quarrel.

From the emotional point of view, she practically shat on me. For having come at so urgent a plea I knew I was entitled to at least decency: as it was, she left the bed to go to him, would stay away all night, coming in at noon guilt-stricken. In the three weeks I was there, I had her only the last two nights, and those were mere tokens.

This was all the more astonishing to me, because her letters had under-emphasized Carothers' importance. She claimed the city-life, the dullness at Waldport. I was a kind of companion. This she said, also surprised her. It was my presence that brought out the attachment. She could not endure separation from him.

But the element of sexual superiority has vanished evidently. Now that the newness has been rubbed off—consolatory disclosure! Christ, how a man clings to his vanity in such matters!

And so I returned, actually, in worse position than when I left—though by letter she had half promised to return with me. You have marked me by now for a fool. I do not think so. I try constantly not to fall back into the conventional reactions, to react as I actually *feel,* not as we have been conditioned to feel by a world hypersensitive to sexual fidelity. It may be mere rationalization. It may be that the woman is not necessary to me, though at 32, having had none other, I can conceive of none. But somehow I loathe to play the hard hand. I have thought many times of divorce since my return. But against these remains our great respect for each other, her own admiration for me as a person, and I for her, though more, now, in regard to what she was, than what she is. Carothers has done her no good, but rather served to develop tendencies that may develop into weaknesses: i.e. she now supports herself at cards, or very nearly, as he does. I said C. has done her no good—wrong—he has shown her much that I never could, broadened her, enriched her in many realms. But I think the creativity has gone from the relationship. But now she loves him, and needs him. For she is not casual. She moves in a circle of men constantly on the make, and does not succumb. But this is, I am sure, lack of inclination. Were a man to take her eye, she would have him, I think, for she has no sense now of responsibility, nor of obligation, but her restraining factors would be rather judiciousness, and this is, I suppose, correct. But as I say, I think she is in danger, with Carothers, of becoming a weakling, of becoming a drifter, from one easy situation to another. Gambling, alcohol, even sex—all can become vices, if indulged in without discrimination. She has certain very great strengths of character, and I believe she counts on these, and an innate sense of modesty and even decorum, which should count as very great reserves in her favor. But she is also selfish, very much so, now especially, for she knows what I endure, and yet she wants no divorce, has faith in our survival, pleads that we continue. A most baffling situation. I have waded through several varieties of hell these several weeks, and don't know how much more I can carry.

As for camp life, generally, I'm becoming pretty conscription sick. Here, too, the creativity has gone. My mental state has not been good. But I have submerged myself in the Fine Arts Program, and carry on. That, and the Untide Press program, are a load. I long to have the leisure to write again, reflect, be indolent when I choose, enjoy ease and relaxation. My kitchen cooking is fascinating, but certainly demanding, and the press requires my every hour. Well—muddle through, muddle through, while the world grinds itself to pieces.

I am glad things have advanced so well for you. I long to see you again, and spend another of those memorable evenings in the dim comfortable rooms. We shall, surely.

Best wishes to Fay, and the two boys, who must be well up into the air by now,.for it has been 4 or 5 years since we saw them. (See how I still use the plural? Christ, I *am* the fool!)

Well, good luck, I'll try to write oftener. Many exciting things happen here, many fine developments from our activity. I salute you!

Bill

P.S. About the Miller blast. He sent me a most generous and gracious reply, and we are "*on*" again, so don't circulate it. I disagree about the Sheets' paper. Advised him to publish it, in fact. The kind of thing Henry himself would have done. Jabberwhorl, isn't it, in *Black Spring* and *The Cosmological Eye?* I hold no brief for *Illiterati* or Nomland however.

November 21, 1944
Beverly Glen
7 p., 4 sheets

Dear Bill—

It's been nearly three months since I'd heard from you, so I was very pleased to have your letter. I am sorry you didn't come south on your furlough, instead of hurting yourself in Berkeley. You can't go on this way forever. Sometime you've got to act in boldness, strength & courage. In that way you might bring Edwa to heel. Jesus, but I suffer with you, but I want to see you in the saddle again. I preach no conventional doctrine to you; it is merely primitive. You've got to be stronger than a woman to hold her. There is no other way. Beat the shit out of the jackal Carothers & take your woman back to your cave. And when you get her there, beat the shit out of her. This is what I told you in the beginning & what I tell you now. If you are not able to do it, then break it off. If she returns then, take her; if not, the devil take her. In any case, act as a man of strength, which you essentially are. Your world's in ruins & so's the greater world. Shore the ruins 'gainst your future. Or die. Goddamn you Bill, mind what I say!

My life flows on, brimful. The job is immensely satisfying. My two young men, Archer & Vosper, are excellent. I buy & hire & negotiate, & plan a $750,000 remodelling & completion of the building—& meet more & more good people, who are drawn to the library in search of learning.

Richard Aldington, for example. He appeared, for a Reader's card, & we have become acquainted. I borrowed his collection of his own books & have them now on display. Read him? *All Men Are Enemies?* He's 53 now, very bitter about this second war, a luscious young Scotch wife & 7-year-old daughter. Not a genius, but an immensely energetic, versatile, & honest craftsman.

A young millionaire [Orlando Weber], sort of Orson Welles, heir to Allied Chemical Co. fortune. Special student. Tutored all his life up to now. 25 years old. Brilliant. Renaissance man. Taken fancy to me & is pouring valuable books in to the Library as gifts. Today a marvelous uncut Bodoni *The Seasons*, 1794. He & I lunched with Guy Endore (*Werewolf of Paris*,

Casanova etc.), another Library Reader. More & more of these people, who know & love & make books. And my time is my own. I am responsible only to the President & have his complete confidence.

And every Wednesday I spend at the Clark Library, working out modern problems in the atmosphere of the 17th century. I want you to come down as soon as you can, Bill. I've got healing stuff for you. And so has Newell. The day after Thanksgiving I shall spend with him at their ranch. I haven't seen him for 6 weeks.

We've had a 4 inch November rain. Marvelous!

Have 8 of the 16 Beethoven quartets now.

We are looking for land to build on.

I am making slow but steady progress on Pt. 3 of my book. Only a few pages a week, but enough to keep it alive.

The other afternoon a woman came to my office, whom I loved in college, & we had not met for 15 years. It was very exciting. I shall tell you of it someday.

The enclosed leaflet is my latest production! It was printed by our Univ. Press, on their all-rag paper. The tail-piece is Clark's seal. Had the map drawn by a friend on campus.

I long to see you too, Bill. Life is getting very short. One's few friends are everything. I hope to make another Berkeley trip during the week between Xmas & New Year. Any chance of your coming down then?

Fay was pleased to have your greeting. She weighs about 120 pounds now, is 33 years old, & very lovely. Our relationship is more vital than ever. She is a woman, without a trace of masculinity. We are entirely opposite in temperament & yet alike in domestic habits, tastes, politics, etc. We enjoy intercourse about once a week; and about every fourth or fifth time it is magical beyond words. After fifteen years of it, off & on, more & less, it is very good to be able still to have it utterly magical. Don't think we haven't been through our hell. We have. You shall read my version of it when I come to write it.

I must bore you. Forgive.

Yes, the boys grow up.

My nephew David is en route from England. He is 17 & is coming to enlist in the navy. Born in South Africa, grew up in England & has been through Friends' school there. Is American, but has never been here. Is working his way on a freighter. Been a job getting it arranged. I am his guardian here. He will live with my mother until January, when he goes in. Wants to be a zoologist! I haven't seen him since London in 1933. Shades of Primrose Hill. A gun emplacement, my sister-in-law reports.

Now goddamn it, don't wait three months to write!

Yours
Larry

P.S. Are you reprinting *War Elegies*, as planned?
How has *Waldport Poems* gone?
Did you write Mrs. Gartz?

L.

December 22, 1944
Beverly Glen
ALS, 3 p., 2 sheets

Dear Bill—

I've returned from a week in Berkeley & found good things from you. First of all, let me tell you how excited I am by the printed *War Elegies*! It's a triumph—no less! How it glows & pulses with life! My congratulations to you & Nomland & the others who helped. I don't know what it sells for, but here's 5 bucks. Send me as many as you can.

Have I read V before? It's one of your best poems. I am very happy for you about this new book of yours. I cannot tell you how good the whole thing makes me feel. It's a magnificent affirmative act in this time of negative destruction.

Now if you can work toward a similar act in your emotional life—your relation with Edwa—you will be a whole man again.

My confidence, my faith in you as a man & a writer has never been higher.

I have just had a moving experience, about which I intended to write you on my return. It bears on your work. We drove up the Valley—first night in Tulare, on to Berkeley the next day. I don't recall having gone through the Valley in December. The orchards grey & shimmering, smoky from a distance; the scattered farms, the bright cottonwoods; & in the east the all-but-hidden mountains, rearing their white crowns.

Then in Berkeley, to cap it, I found copies of your *Ravens* & *San Joaquin* at my aunt's; and there, one evening, to the sound of pouring rain, I read them through again. Your poems moved me, as never before.

We drove home via 101. How different are the coastal valleys! The fields are beautiful now, ploughed, harrowed & disced.

Thanks too for *Compass.* Can you get me the numbers of volume 1? I note that one of them contains at least *material* about you. Your statements about the Fine Arts at Waldport are *fine!* Better yet are the pictures of you. Can you send me separate snapshots of you in your chair & at the Press? And any others.

I returned to find a mountain of matters to deal with. God, how the books are pouring in! My new order chief & I are buying like drunken helots. The Library is closed for a three-day weekend, & I will catch up with things. Am mailing you a magazine for your Powell collection!

Picked up Llewelyn Powys' novel *Apples Be Ripe* (1930) & found it very simple and moving. Ever read it, or his only other novel *Love & Death?*

I greet you, salute you, at year's end!

Larry

Dec. 30, 1944
Waldport
ALS, 2 p., 1 sheet

Dear Larry:—

I write from the tip of the year. It fades out in squalls and thunders. Right now the sky is clear, the moon full; the stainless stars sharp in their sky.

I was very pleased with the Christmas letter—it came on that good day—and your affirmation of *War Elegies.* Myself, I take little joy in it. Since the coming of James I have slowly altered my attitude toward art and illustration. Where once I was excited by the daring of Nomland's drawings, now I find them slick, glib, meaningless, insincere. It is too bad the book was not published when I could have enjoyed it.

I spent the summer in the kitchen, learning to cook, keeping in camp where my hand could be on Fine Arts activity. Two weeks ago I went once more on project, for the release from the pressure of preparing huge meals. It was a great transformation. I immediately set to work on the series of poems that will complete the cycle I have been working on since coming to Waldport almost two years ago. I have immersed in it to the extent of neglecting everything else, including my mail. But it is rich, working this last phase out of my system. I look forward to completing it.

Early in December I served warning on Edwa: unequivocal return or unequivocal separation. She came up; we spent a ghostly week together. Then she went back. I am announcing separation from her. She is dispirited and lifeless, somewhat occasioned by a serious development: a tumor on the wall of her heart, almost impossible to operate. Assistance will have to depend on slow treatment or none at all. One stinking, complex, unresolvable mess. I had to do what I did, hard as it is on her. I could take no more.

I think often of your "Quintet," the European quality of it, the sense of women, the quality of rich eroticism. I wish it were in print; it should be at hand.

Yes, [you] read Elegy V before. I remember sending it to you in a ms. in 1941 of poems you thought generally too introspective and self pitying. On this poem, next the lines: "nor let me scatter my strength in self-pity and fear" you had written the simple heartfelt and eloquent pronouncement: *amen*!!

I will try to find some back issues of *Compass.* They were published in other camps. I don't think I can get you the particular photos in the issue. Some others may be around though.

I should like very much to see you. The whole life back there seems so impossibly remote, I need to get some tangible reestablishment with you, shake your hand, drink your wine, pore over your books, hear your music.

You make your new job sound exciting. I hope your writing goes on. It should not be neglected. You are approaching a mastery of writing that must not be relaxed.

Clayton James is a great man. A terrific, natural, simple person. A man capable of enormous, sudden concentration. A religious man, batting his head out on the physical restrictions that keep him from God. His paintings are one prolonged search.

Good luck
Bill

P.S. Jim Harman has gone over the hill. He was growing crazy in camp; is partly crazy now, from reports that seep in: persecution complex. He is not clever and dishonest enough to avoid for long those governmental ferrets: it will be McNeil Island [Federal prison], I'm afraid. That's not much worse than CPS. I often contemplate walking out for the experience. There are many COs there now, several close friends I knew from here. Some have walked out, served sentence, been released on special parole, and are relatively free again. All in the short span I've been in camp. The war will drag through forty-five, forty-six, we'll be here till forty-seven. But that's little. The circumstances mean little any longer. Strange, how, when the past collapses, you lose your fears. Like being reborn. A whole new fresh vigorous life opens out. I'm happier now than I've been in months, but a bit melancholy tonight, writing from the year's end, thinking of all the year's ends I've known you. Since thirty-eight, it is. The year we were married. Goodbye to all that.

Do you have any word of Jeffers? Is he in Carmel and writing? Are the boys in the army?

1945: PRINTER AND PROMOTER

Jan 6, 1945
Waldport, Oreg.
APS

Dear Larry:—

I have been reading Rilke, the *Elegies* and Mac's volume which I bought last furlough. The *Ghost* is at my elbow. Your "Quintet" is in my mind, and I long for the nostalgia, the ancient imponderable atmosphere of Europe.

Bill

January 13, 1945
Beverly Glen
ALS, 6 p.

Dear Bill—

Saturday night. I returned from a day with the Newells at their mountain ranch to find your postal. Mail is bad. Took it 5 days to get here. Your year's end letter I had taken along to read to Gordon. He enjoyed it as much as I did. We read it sprawled on top of a tall steep lichen-covered sandstone outcropping. The rock was warm, the sky blue. Down below us the canyons threaded out, gray with the winter sycamores. That Malibu country is very beautiful in this mild season.

Newell is coming out of a profound physical slump. He & Emelia are having much trouble. Her ceramics pin business is supporting them. She has the whip-hand. He is her hired man & what energy he has goes for the farm chores. He is tempted to escape into the Merchant Marine for 6 months. I talk it over with both of them together, then with him alone. Poor Newell has always been disorganized. He cannot plan projects. He becomes enmeshed in more than he can handle. The more Emelia organizes his life the lower sinks his creative power. It's really a mess.

I had mailed him *War Elegies*, but it had not yet arrived. He will write you. He & Emelia had hoped you would come last October. When do you have another furlough? You must come down here.

I am very glad to hear of your break with Edwa, but sorry to hear of her physical condition. And glad to hear of your creative renewal after leaving the kitchen. I hope you will send me a typescript when you reach that point.

I too thought of you New Year's Eve. For the third year Fay & I were with our neighbors—"Gretchen" of the story & her husband. Up at their house this year, on the hill in back of us. She & Fay drank a bottle of Los Gatos sauterne, he talked endlessly of real-estate deals, while I, fires banked, stared tolerantly into the log-stuffed fireplace. It was serene.

Other food sustains me these days. Sweet forbidden fruit. Seventeen years ago I nibbled it. Night before last it fell, ripe, utterly ripe, into my hands, and I ate hungrily—& with unspeakable delight & satisfaction. Oh Bill my lad, what marvelous things life gives me! I cannot write this story now. It is not yet finished. But when I do, by God, 'twill be moving! To the music of Chausson's Quintet was closed a circle half-drawn seventeen years ago.

Your references to "Quintet" & to what I am working on are immensely encouraging. I have just emerged from a mad rush through Melville—& of all that I have read, that which is closest to my heart is his friendship with Hawthorne—& the immense encouragement H. gave M. while M. was writing *Moby-Dick.* The wonderful series of confessional letters Melville wrote to his country neighbor, Hawthorne, during & immediately after the creation of *Moby-Dick.* Then Melville's unwilling plunge into obscurity—the 20 years as customs inspector—& death at 72, nearly 40 years after *Moby-Dick.* Unspeakably sad.

I should like to privately print a few copies of "Quintet" for my friends. Maybe I will later, after my Library position is consolidated. I don't know. Now I am tempted to send you the final typescript, which you have never read. Shall I? It will probably be another year before I complete the final half of "First Symphony." In the meantime, I am working enough to keep it alive. I had a couple of bad experiences with "Quintet," when I gave it to people to read, in answer to repeated requests—& had it fall flat—& received the advice that it was a good outline for a long novel. Shit! Now it would take horses to get it away from me. And remember the letter from Knopf's bright young female reader?

You ask about Jeffers. I have heard that things go badly for him. Una drinks too much, & Robin lays unwanted hands on Carmel matrons. He was 58 on the 10th. Garth is in the army. I believe Donnan is 4-F—probably psycho-neurotic. Sorry to hear of Harman's trouble.

Last week I talked to a women's club on Jeffers & Steinbeck (for $25) & I hated doing it. I shall not do it again. All I want now is to read them. Very depressing to have to summarize them in 1 hour. Steinbeck's new book is too slick, too pat, too glib. Like the later Hemingway. The *Esquire* touch. Shit. We all go to Aldington's for tea tomorrow. He's a real man.

I hear that Henry Miller is married again! Ouch.

* * *

J'ai fait la magique étude
Du bonheur, quel nul n'élude.
O vive lui, chaque fois
Que chante le coq gaulois.

So long!
Larry

Tues. Feb. 26? 27? 1945
The Imperial Hotel
Portland 5, Oregon
ALS, 2 p. 1 sheet

Dear Larry:—

I write from a city of smoke and steel, in a bare room, alone. Part of my writing is to kill pain, for I had five teeth pulled a couple of hours ago, and numbness has worn off. A huge swarming town, thick with workers, and the first pretension of culture. Yet I am used to it, for Fresno is such a town.

It was here a month ago however that I saw the Robeson *Othello*, and my first ballet. And Schnabel comes in March.

The dentistry was exciting, for the first time in my life. We C.O.s go to a clinic, a dental college, where greenhorns work on us under supervision. The final product is highly reputable, but it takes twice as long. The instructor took one look in my mouth and said: "My God, you've spent half your life in a dentist's chair!" I have, damned near. As I say, he pulled 5. Two more to go next week. Wah!

I said it was exciting because 2 teeth broke off and the instructor had to take over. The class crowded around, all eyes converged down my gullet. I felt like a port-hole. At the last they used hammer and chisel.

In camp things go well, except that the local American Legion (a 10-member post) is gunning for us. Selective Service may tighten. We hope to keep the press.

Are almost done with the Jacob Sloan volume.

So long! Good luck. Good cheer.

Bill

Thanks for the Melville. A nice gift.

March 14, 1945
Los Angeles
APS

Dear Bill—

Thanks for your Portland letter. We too saw the Robeson *Othello*. Great! Enjoying the Mozart Divertimento (K. 563) for violin, viola, and cello. Carries me away. Working hard. Good rich results. Lots of fine marginalia. Luck to you!

Larry

3-26-45
Los Angeles
ALS, 2 p.

Bill—

Here's an extra copy for you of a good piece on Miller. It appeared in *Life & Letters Today* (London, June 1934).

Larry

Home address after July 1
1000 Manning Ave.
LA 24
It's a block or two due east of the campus.

April 23, 1945
Waldport, Ore.
ALS, 3 p.

Dear Larry:—

Christ what a furlough! My best. By far the best. After leaving you I looked up the poet, to find his lodging but nothing of him. The next day trekked out to Glendora, to learn of Roosevelt's death in circumstances entirely appropriate for me: a CPS camp. But that place disappointed me—a handful of tired radicals, almost inert. They seep away nightly to the city. Waldport is better. Geiger [editor of *Pacifica Views*] was on furlough, but I found him at Theosophy Hall, and had a rich evening to finish my stay in the Southland. Fashion note: When I got back home after my days with you I found a complete wardrobe awaiting me: the family disliked my shabbiness. They must have laid out fifty or sixty bucks. What can one say? They need the money more than I. They are so involved in it, worship it, dependent upon it. I wore the modish ensemble quite self-consciously from then on out. I balked at cutting my hair, and I cut a queer figure with my latest fashion and my prophetic head!

The fast train took me to Berkeley that Friday, once again over the blooming desert, the serene Tehachapis, the wonderful butt-busting San Joaquin. Broad ran the Kings, my own river. Level lay the Sacramento. I pulled into Berkeley about 9:00 that night and trudged up to my friend Watkins', though I could not resist skirting Edwa's place (dark it stood) and Kenny's (dark, dark and blind),—but our old Plymouth, that had carted me over so many miles, that I coaxed in the frosts and sheltered from the heat—it stood there before its new master's door. Quite patient.

I stayed at Watkins' the three days in Berkeley, but I saw Edwa. From the tales, I had expected a jade. She was little changed, however. For she is good yet: the woman is essentially untouched. She is caught in a context too big for her, but she is as she was—and not at all debased. For instance—she gambles only to kill time, and for the little money in it. There is no involvement there—she is not the true gamester. We talked quite simply. We kissed. We touched. She was good. But inside me nothing stirred, I walked away unmoved. A bit saddened to be unmoved. But so be it. In a way, she is quite pitiful. The doctors will not operate. They keep the tumor on the heart-wall down with medicines, but they predict death at any time. She has tried suicide twice, and behind her veiled, her not-at-all-dramatic asides, I got the feeling she would try it again. My God, Larry, is this not Hardyesque? To go through so botched, bitter, hacking, terrible a disruption and find at the last this final fatality. And surely there is something ironically appropriate in the nature of her infection: a tumor of the *heart!* Christ, how these things work themselves out.

After Berkeley, three days of it, I pulled east to the Mother Lode, where my friend Hamilton Tyler ("Mr. Milton and Mr. Eliot" in *Circle* magazine) owns a dairy. A good full two days. We covered many things. He plans to join us after the war.

Then north by bus, through the darkness over vast California, to home. To Waldport.

Now the sea thunders, the spring rains drip from the eaves, but my eye sees south to California.

Let me thank you now, and Fay and your mother, for the fine days. I was very happy to be with you.

The photostats of the luscious bridal-song came in Saturday. What are they, and from where? Surely a story is here.

Bill

May 8, 1945
Beverly Glen
ALS, 6 p., 3 sheets

Dear Bill—

"A Chronicle of Division" came several days ago. I read it through at once, sitting in the car while Fay marketed. And now in the evening quiet of my study, I have read it again. The first section appeared as *Waldport Poems.* The second you sent last summer or fall in typescript. The latter sections are new to me.

It is a most wonderful work. I thought, at first, that since *Look! We Have Come Through* I had not read such a moving chronicle of the suffering between man & woman. Tonight I think of Meredith's masterpiece, *Modern Love*—you know it, surely—I do not mean that you were influenced by either of the two; of course not. It is only that I search through the world's literature known to me for some equal to your "Chronicle." Only the two occur to me.

By God, you have achieved a most miraculous triumph over your personal tragedy. You have attained throughout a triumphant catharsis. Your letters to me through the past two years were sometimes screams of pain. I knew how low you were. It was terrible. I feared. In this work you sent me you have soared out of the depths.

I knew when you were here that you had regained the mastery of your heart. You were in good shape. I was happy. But I did not know at that time the true nature of your triumph. I could not know until your work came.

There is an anguished serenity about it—the diction is grave, lofty, noble—& even when you explode, as in IV of the last section, it is a perfectly controlled explosion. A wonderful change of tempo there.

I am very proud of your achievement. It is one of the finest & most moving ever attained by an artist. I say this & know it to be true.

I am sick to death of "modern" poetry. The curse of Eliot. The intellectual splinters. Surrealist shit. The poetasters. I have just finished Llewelyn Powys' *Letters*—a wonderful book—Six months before he died in December 1939 he wrote as follows to a friend—

> I was glad to get your letter & will try in as few words as possible to explain my attitude toward the art of letters. In the first place I am inclined to shy from such expressions as "the art of letters." I think if literature is to have lasting value it must be as close to life as fell [pelt or skin] to flesh. *Art for life's sake* would be a far sounder clue than art for art's sake. The greatest writers have always been first & foremost concerned with life—Lucretius who died of a love potion. Montaigne who would as lief play with his cat or talk to vineyard dressers as write one of his famous chapters, Shakespeare whose work is overflowing with snatches from his own life-experience, Keats whose poetry is always written with his life's blood. A writer's work should be a direct expression or flowering of his own life. It should be as close to his personal life as marrow to the bone. It should be an unstudied, a radiant & random reflection of his deepest thoughts & his deepest feelings. Man's peculiar prerogative is consciousness, & if there is any reward to be had out of his ephemeral days it comes from a heightened awareness of his existence during his scanted years.
>
> The present cry that the best literature is a mere product of the cunning of the cold intellect is but an empty store of words. Clever & artful poetry, clever & artful prose melts like hoar frost—the rudest proverb, the wildest verse from the oldest ballad lasts longer. Writing to be worth anything must have the thumb-mark of life upon it, heavy & spatulate. It must smell of sweat & be uplifted by what Shakespeare named so ruefully "the brutish sting." Really good writing has nothing to do with lamps. It uses a gray goose's feather for its mechanical expression, but its true inspiration is derived from the bed, the cradle, the crib, & the coffin. Its art is accidental, a mere fortuitous efflorescence of an ardor & spiritual passion that are part & parcel of a man's spiritual skin. Indeed it is not the brain that makes a great writer, it is the temper of his whole being in its approach to life as he finds it on the green earth under the golden sun. It has more to do with his codpiece than his sconce. Here are the words of Jonathan Swift—"For authors are to be used like lobsters, you must look for the best meat in the tail."

All of which is to say that I am immensely pleased that you are writing in this great tradition. The intense life-quality is what I seek in writers—Jeffers, Lawrence, Miller have it. When Miller writes of what he has lived, then he is great—when he spews forth, in the heavy & mystical German tradition, what he *thinks* about life—then I have no use for him. And the same holds for Lawrence. And anyone else. I am anti-intellectual.

Your first works were rooted in reality, & that is why I was drawn to them. Then when you wrote your first pacifist poems, I protested. Poetry & philosophy do not mix. The stuff was thin. Fine as the final *War Elegies* are, I prefer this "Chronicle," for it is rooted hard as a phallus in the rich soil of man-woman.

Section 3 is wonderful, poem 4 particularly. I am a simple bastard. I prefer fucking to philosophy. Now I am become inarticulate—

Your earlier letter was welcome. We were glad to hear of your safe return to Waldport. Your visit here was all too brief. How happy I was to see you in such good shape.

The Pessoa was loaned me by Richard Aldington. I photographed his copy. It was given him at Lisbon in 1930 by Simoes, a noted Portuguese writer, to whom Pessoa had presented it; with the hope that Aldington could interest English publishers. Nothing ever came of it. Aldington showed it me by chance. I seized upon it. We know nothing more of Pessoa.

The new *Circle* here today—scattered with monkey tricks, & yet I approve of the idea of little mags. Fisher's remarkable lyrics—almost the first poetry since the *Ghost*. Please write about the *Ghost* for *Circle*.

Nomland senior is to be our architect.

Forgive this rambling letter.

What plans for publishing the "Chronicle"? I want to review it.

I do not share all of Powys' thoughts, especially those about artlessness.

Newell in marvelous shape. Sorry to have missed you.

Yours ever
Larry

P.S. Your work has form, & style. It is Real, not Sur-Real. Above Reality lies a bleak realm of Sterility.

May 30, 45
Waldport
ALS, 2 p., 1 sheet

Dear Larry:—

Your comments, the long and plenteous letter on my "Chronicle," was a great boon to receive. I wanted to do that. I wanted to touch some element of humanity that could be made clear. The series is nothing more than a painful attempt to understand, and to understand one of the most common of experiences. It lies in that so much is left out. But in so far as it is honest, to that extent I think it is good.

None of the others I sent it to have taken it in the nature of a human document. I receive analysis of individual poems, etc. They will have to be judged at last in such ways, yes, but what you saw is something very needful to know as successful.

Your loyalty, man, is one of the best things I have ever had.

I have been going to Portland almost every week and am tired. I go again today. Nothing much gets done here, but my teeth are almost fixed.

We received our point-systems. 50 points for discharge. 1 point per month of service. 3 points for a wife. 13 points for a child.

I have 31 points.

So. Stick it out, man.

Though you have much truth in it, I don't agree about modern poetry. I think we are in an age of great minor verse. I have been looking through Williams' *New Poems 1944*. Almost every page has a kind of breakthrough in it. Excessive, chaotic, abstruse, perverted, broken, inverted—all these. But surely better, surely better by far, than the pontifical posturing of the Georgians, or the high-flown Victorians, or the dulcet Pre-Raphaelites. I love modern verse. I am glad to be alive, and of this company.

You saw the review in *Poetry*? And now in the *Nation*? The books are being noticed, but rarely with enthusiasm by the "better" critics. Such mags as *Circle* print meaningless praises (I believe, from the sloppiness of writing, Leite did that review).

Oh yes—Fisher's fine poems. Very good indeed.

Perhaps I'll try that *Ghost* piece.

Oh, yes—*Capricorn.*

Luck!
Bill

Wedding day—yesterday. 7 years! You saw us first on honeymoon. Recall?

6-23-45
Los Angeles
ALS, 2 p.

Dear Bill—

This is only a note to acknowledge a good letter from you & receipt of *Capricorn*—many thanks!

I have been working under unusually heavy pressure & now we are moving. Have a faculty home which we can rent for at least a year, until we can build. And are selling the house in the canyon. Feel a bit sad about it all, but it's the only thing to do.

Founder's Day at the Clark Library was an enormous success. 2000 attended.

I have never heard that you received the photograph sent by Railway Express. Hope you did!

My present dream of a vacation is to go over to Avalon on Catalina Island late in July or early in August.

Failing that, perhaps to San Francisco. And on to Waldport?

I'll write soon. Hope you are flourishing.

Larry

I have been reading many books by Arthur Symons (1854–1945). Know him?

July 14, 1945
Los Angeles 24
ALS, 2 p.

Dear Bill—

Fifteen years ago today—Bastille Day!—I sailed for France. A decade and a lustrum ago. Good God!

Your *Residual Years* came today. I like it very much, both content & format. It is a lovely piece of mimeographing—the red & black on the gray paper—beautiful; and I like your two simple drawings. All in all it is a beauty. Thank you!

It seems to me that I still have some credit with the Untide Press. If so, would you have 10 additional copies sent me? If that puts me into the red, let me know & I'll remit.

We've been here in our new home 2 weeks now, & are beginning to feel settled & rested. Moving is always exhausting & disturbing spiritually.

Picture me in a downstairs study, measuring 20′ × 20′, the walls nearly solid with books, & a waist-high corner fireplace, opening onto a walled garden. Our landlord, Westergaard, has gone to Copenhagen for a year, leaving his library here. It is the finest collection in these parts on the history of Northern Europe & Scandinavia, mostly in the Germanic languages. He cleared a section for me, & I have the cream of my books here; the rest are at my mother's & in my office.

In addition to moving, it has been heavy at the Library, with the end of the fiscal year, & the new budget to be tidied up. Vosper continues to be my right hand, Archer my left.

I hope to be in Berkeley the 2d week in August. Any chance of your being there then?

Write, Bill. Tell me how it goes with you. I promise a full letter in reply. In the meantime, these hasty, affectionate lines.

Larry

July 15, 45
Waldport
ALS, 3 p., 2 sheets

Dear Larry:—

Sunday morning. Outside, the sunlight, lambent and glossed, like varnish or shellac, spreads over all. Beyond the screen of firs that cuts it from the shore, the old ocean, with all its centuries heaped on its gray mounded back, roars and grinds. To the east, the hills, summer green. Above, the fleckless sky. Good.

On July 11, 1945, I came down from work and told them I could not go out anymore. It was a decision arrived at after many hours, many days, many weeks of thinking. When it was finally arrived at, it became almost an act of continuity: the effort to return no longer succumbed to the fear of punishment. I am staying in camp, going about my writing and printing. There is no local conflict. The director and I understand one another and I am welcome to stay. The Grand Jury does not re-convene until fall, so that I cannot be indicted before that time, and am assured of many weeks of good work. I feel easy in my mind, and look forward to prison, if and when it comes, with some interest.

Beyond that, my friend Tyler investigated the Russian River situation, was taken with it, and is now going there. I plan to join him. So another problem is settled. It is a country where vineyards and redwoods intermingle, it is said, and that won me.

I can't remember if I answered your last note, about moving, etc. If not, I am really myself somewhat saddened to see you leave the Glen. I have had only 3 or 4 occasions there, but they were all memorable.

A word from Edwa tells me the tumor has grown somewhat, but is beginning to separate, whatever that means, and the doctor is optimistic. Even better news is that she is going in with another woman on a kiln, the woman, an expert, and a friend of ours, a fine person, to handle the technical details, Edwa to finance and to learn. This makes me very happy. I hope it can re-kindle an interest in her life, and make emergent that quality it was my good fortune to know for many years.

Here, I am going back over my "Chronicle," in a process of

recreation and synthesis. There is much material I want to energize. I arise in the mornings, partake of a leisurely breakfast over the kitchen range (in the CCC this was a privilege accorded only the special friends of the cooks; here, it is accorded anyone). Then I return to my nook and write, till noon, usually, sometimes beyond, depending on my mood. In the afternoon I take up the presswork, it is the Patchen we are doing. The evenings go to sociability, or sometimes the pen.

But I cannot deny that, though my time here is the best possibly spent, my function here is really fulfilled, and I will not be happy until I leave. It is my strategy to stay, for there is a likelihood that if I do not leave camp I will not be molested by the police (one man stayed eight months, then left. No one has tried sitting it out). I may be able to last out the war, if that termination is not too distant, in which event it is wholly unlikely I would be prosecuted.

On the other hand, if the camp closes this winter I will go south, rather than follow the men elsewhere. Court action will then result.

Bill

August 2, 1945
LA 24
ALS, 2 p.

Dear Bill—

I have your letter telling of your decision not to go out for work any more. I hope you can sit it out. The war is nearing an end. For God's sake, don't get yourself a couple of years in prison just at the time you would have been discharged from camp. Be smart. A limber backbone will travel you farther than a ramrod stiff one. Be smart, now of all times.

I haven't received the 10 copies of *Residual Years.* If my credit is exhausted, send with bill. But send! Damn you.

The new *Illiterati* is stunning. Your poem one of the best. 15 years ago I was writing "poems" like Nomland's. Let's hope he outgrows such or improves. But the issue as a whole is good. Henry's piece not so good. I had read it before in typescript.

Like the rest of his American book it is inchoate. He should not write merely to write.

I note that you are going to settle on the Russian River. Sounds good, as does Edwa's improvement.

Fay & I are driving north on August 13. Will be at the Durant in Berkeley the rest of the week. Home via Carmel & plan to stop at Highlands Inn. I shall think of you there!

My work is going well. Everything's panning bright & rich. Am living down deep, both mind & body.

I wish you were here now. There's a hell of a lot I'd share with you. I think of you. Greetings, you rangy bastard!

Larry

Aug. 7, 1945
CPS 56 Waldport
ALS, 3 p., 2 sheets

Dear Larry:—

Glad to hear from you. I don't anticipate much trouble. I am, you remember, not a headlong or even adventurous person. This move was not political. I have issued no statement, in line with the usual CPS walk-out. I will probably go to jail—though the war's end in the next few months would probably save me—but I do not expect over a year's sentence (which is Harman's term, and everybody else's in Portland recently). That means nine months, with the traditional 1/3 off for "good time"—a mere trifle, it seems from this point in time (though that is probably illusory). Anyway, I can always apply for parole after 60 days—C.O. parole to a hospital, at $15 per month, or $50 per month after 6 months. I'm over the draft age, so it wouldn't be the old cat-and-mouse game the younger men go through. But as I say, I may not be picked up. One man sat here RTW [refuse to work] for 6 months, finally walked out. I got so damned involved in press work, etc., there was not time to write. I'm going to pull out of Untide; I've got to get back into the point of view of the writer, and keep it. Perhaps I'll have a small press for my own uses, but no publishing venture. Two years of that is enough.

In 2 or 3 weeks I'll have finished my "Poems: MCMXLII"—the little ms. I sent you 2 years ago and Bieler took a copy of. This is not an Untide publication, but a private one of my own. It's all done now but incidentals and cover. I'm just going to pass them around, more or less as I did *San Joaquin*. No fanfare. My present thought is to continue this practice. In the case of *San Joaquin* I have found it very convenient to have copies in strategically located libraries, so that people who write in can be referred there. As a librarian, I'd like your advice on which libraries to hit. Perhaps each State library, and the universities? Main city libraries? I guess it's just a matter of where you draw the line. There must be thousands of libraries if you wanted to go whole hog, which I don't. I'm doing an edition of 500. Perhaps one of your assistants could make me a list? Whatever you think.

I know you think I'm a damned fool for stepping out now. Maybe I am. I've held open in my mind the possibility of going back on project, but my days are so full here that that thought palls me. I guess it was time for me to make a move.

Aug. 8

I said above my move was not political. This is wrong. Any move that counters civil measure is political. Any move made in opposition to civil injustice is of political motivation. In my case the political relevance of my act was apparent for a long time: I simply did not follow it out. Only at the point where the personal bolstered the political did I act. In this sense my move was not political. It is hard for an outsider to understand the CPS walkout. From there it looks foolhardy, utopian, ineffectual. But here, an entirely different set of values obtains. The *temper* of society within the camp is pro-walkout. It is considered the most honorable move, the most logical move, the most effectual move, and the simplest one. Those who remain are the compromisers. We all understand *why* we remain, and have faced that problem and seen it through, and no one questions us, nor holds the choice against us. But in our discussions we all have to rationalize, to justify staying on purely personal grounds. While every other week some man leaves. He states his reasons and goes. And every time, your own position is thrown up, subtly but poignantly, against you. But still you hang on, out of many complex motives, until suddenly, one day, your personal reasons have caught up with your political ones, and you make the break. It is a curious thing. Wives have come here, anxious and alarmed at their husbands' letters. In two or three months they understand. Then they leave, and take the rap, and are satisfied. CPS is considered a pretty mangy compromise, and that works on a man. My own rationalization was the Press and its future. When that collapsed, it was very easy to go. You understand.

Fuck once for me at the Highland!

Bill

8-9-45
Los Angeles
ALS, 1 p.

Dear Bill—

Thanks for sending the 10 copies. Here's a $5 check to add wherever it'll do good.

Leaving for Berkeley in a couple of days. Will be at the Hotel Durant from August 14–18—then Carmel, we hope—

Larry

Aug. 23, 1945
Salinas
APS

Dear Bill—

Salinas last night. Carmel—the Jeffers—& Big Sur—Miller—today—Good sessions with MacIntyre in Berkeley—Hold everything now!

Larry

August 23, 1945
Los Angeles
ALS, 4 p., 2 sheets

Dear Bill—

Back from a glorious trip north I take up your letter of August 7 which I barely acknowledged before I left. I am very glad to hear that you are doing the *1942 Poems* yourself. Here are some key libraries that come to mind. [He listed 30.] You will doubtless want to add more—perhaps colleges & public libraries. I can mail you a library directory for the entire country, if you want it. May I have 10 copies of the book?

The great valley was in the prime of harvest—apricots gone, peaches & melons in & grapes coming. Faint signs of the Sierra through the enveloping haze. Everything changed since the December trip over the same road.

The biggest thing in Berkeley was my reunion with MacIntyre. We had not met for 5-½ years, nor had he written for several years. My appointment as Librarian coincided with his dismissal from the Univ., & he had brooded over this.

His house on the high slope of Grizzly Peak is much like the one overwhelmed by the La Crescenta flood. I saw him on three successive days. I went away laden with much of his work of recent years. He has done fine translations of the French symbolists. I am going to try to get him a job at Dijon Univ.! He wants to return to Europe. He is bitter at U.C., although he himself is much to blame for his trouble. Very fierce & proud, sad & bitter. 21 years I've known him—he changed the direction of my life. I owe him an immense debt.

We were unable to get lodgings in Carmel. Stayed in Salinas, then Santa Maria. Una Jeffers is fattening with age, Robin looks old & worn. He has just adapted the *Medea*. It will be produced in N.Y. this winter by the Theatre Guild. A new book will follow.

We found Miller in his redwood cabin high above the sea. Missed his wife. We hear that she types & orders the groceries. He needed such a person. He is in good shape.

On down the incredible coast, in & out of fog. The Jeffers country! At Piedras Blancas the wind had freshened & spindrift blew from the breakers. The castle shone on the sunlit hill. Driftwood littered the beaches. Miles of baled hay rotted in the fields. In the lee of San Simeon Cove a little fleet of fishing boats was anchored.

In Pismo we shared table with a beery lonesome sailor.

The war is over. When will you be free?

Yours ever
Larry

P.S. I'd like another 10 copies of *Residual Years,* please—

Aug. 31, 45
Waldport, Oregon
APS

Larry:—

A note before a sudden take-off to California on a dental-leave. I've sent *Poems 42* on. Esh [William Eshelman] will send the rest. Thanks for the library list, and would like the directory, if it isn't too big. Will write on return or en route.

Bill

Sept. 6, 1945
Los Angeles
APS

Dear Bill—

Poems 1942 received today. Mighty good! Note that more copies follow.

We're mailing you a copy of *American Library Directory.* Please return as soon as able—

Larry

Thurs. Sept. 6, 45
CPS No. 35
North Fork, Calif.
ALS, 3 p., 2 sheets

Dear Larry:—

I'm writing from a Mennonite camp in the Sierras East of Fresno. Clayt James and I are here to have our teeth fixed by a traveling CPS dentist. We came down by auto to Red Bluff, had a bad smash-up, sideswiped on the highway after dark, both cars ruined, but no one hurt—a miracle. Clayt, his wife Barbara and I were refused quarters in Red Bluff. (Clayt is bearded, they both dress relaxedly, and of course my haircut,—). Took a late train into Berkeley, were there a day at the Watkins', left Barbara; Clayt and I took Edwa's car Tuesday and came on down. Car trouble below Merced; barely limped into Fresno, spent a wonderful night sleeping in a stubble field under a full sky, my first in years after Oregon's fogs and forests, a great night there for me in my own San Joaquin, the vineyards, the fig orchards, and that enormous and clairvoyant sky.

Had the car repaired yesterday and came on up, expecting the worst: Mennonite camps are notorious throughout CPS for their strictness, authoritarianism, and piousness. We were both stunned to drive in and see a beautiful girl in pantaloons smoking a cigarette. She turned out to be one of the dentists' wives.

North Fork is the largest, and the most liberal, of the Mennonite camps, but compared to Waldport it's pretty bad—and strangely enough, more by camper opinion than by administrative direction. In most Mennonite camps the administration and the men see eye-to-eye = work, obey rules, and go to bed early. The dissenters are broken down or forced out. Here, the administration is ahead of the men. We can smoke, I have heard enough four-letter words to make me comfortable, and the lights don't go out at nine o'clock. The kitchen is bad: everything under lock and key, and poor meals. At Waldport we stroll in at will, any time night or day, and fix us up a snack. The religious set-up is pretty archaic here: they dim the lights at ten for devotion, hold long audible prayers at meals. This morning they all sang "Trust and obey, there is no other way—" and a visiting preacher blessed everybody at Great Length.

The dentists are good. They travel from camp to camp in a trailer. My work involves a few fillings and upper and lower partial plates, necessitated by the great elimination of teeth I went through in Portland. They'll do it in a couple of days. We go back through Berkeley again, through Guerneville, and on up the coast to Waldport.

Bill

P.S. On the books in Waldport, and on the records sent to Selective Service, I'm carried "Sick in Camp"!

September 9, 1945
Los Angeles
ALS, 2 p.

Dear Bill—

It was good to have your letter from the Mennonite Camp at North Fork. What a strange place! And your adventurous, hazard-fraught journey there. I can imagine how profoundly you were moved to sleep on the ground in your own land. Our timing was bad! We should have met in Berkeley!

Sometime next month I plan to take a long weekend & go with the family to Sequoia park. We have never been there.

Tomorrow is a university holiday & we visit the Newells in the Malibus. Today I have been loafing, reading the Ltd. Ed. Club Casanova—a great work.

The ten more *Poems 1942* came yesterday. I took a copy of it & *Residual Years* to Richard Hoffman, when I picked up the enclosed announcement. He is much interested in the work you have done up there.

A very good review of your *War Elegies* in *Poetry* this month. Nomland Sr. here today on our house & I showed it to him.

Came yesterday from England a book for which we at the Clark have long been searching: the 1657 edition of *Daphnis & Chloe,* translated by George Thornley. Cost $150 & worth it. Very rare. Wonderful cut of a printing press on the title page— At the Sign of the Rolling Press for Pictures.

Do you want to buy an early acorn hand press? Wilder Bentley in Berkeley has one for sale for $125. We considered it, but are not ready to put in a press at the Clark.

Why did you put the title & your name on widely separated pages? It seems to me an unfunctional eccentricity. A title page exists to provide information. Account please?

Larry

Sept. 24, 1945
Waldport______
ALS, 2 p., 1 sheet

Dear Larry:—

Back again to this place, and your letter, which came before me. I arrived, my mouth full of strange teeth, a bit sadder for it. I think of my real ones, that were taken away (9 of them) last spring in Portland. They were never good, but they served. Now some student practices on them, drilling away, stuffing with silver. Too bad. Well, a life alters. Every morning, fitting this strange device into place, I ponder the impermanence of matter, of our little lives, but regret its sentimentality, almost always. So—we progress.

It was a fine trip. Berkeley and the Bay were fine. The north country was fine. We stopped by Pond Farm at Guerneville where my friend Tyler is and where I plan to settle. But maybe not.

I was surprised at your reference to Wilder Bentley. A friend told me of him; I called up one Sunday and went over. We talked printing. I had brought along some of our things and he was surprised—pleasantly surprised, he said. He gave me many tips. I saw his presses, but he did not indicate any were for sale. The Acorn sounds good.

About the title-page of *Poems MCMXLII* your point is good, and of course, should generally be adhered to. When this book was designed, however, it was conceived of as going only to friends and acquaintances, who would know its origin. It was an extension of the epistolary motive—the name at the close of the letter. As it turned out, my purpose somewhat wavered and I included both names on the cover. The cover is the title page. I regret not acknowledging James's woodcut—it was done too late.

Sincerely
Bill

Latest demob. rumor from Wash: out by Spring.

October 6, 1945
Los Angeles
ALS, 1 p.

Dear Bill—

I was glad to get yours of Sept. 24 & to hear of your visit to Bentley. We are building an extraordinary collection of his things at the Clark. And also of the late Perry Stricker. Sorry you couldn't have been present at the R&C [Rounce & Coffin Club] memorial.

If you are interested in Bentley's Acorn, I suggest you write him that you are. There is no possibility of the Library's buying it, & he knows this.

The first rain came this morning. It's been bone dry since March or April, & last week we had a fearfully hot spell—low humidity made the 104° temerature bearable to me, but people did an unholy lot of grumbling.

I have been buying books (for the library & myself) in great quantities. And reading a few!

Just a line to say hello!

Larry

October 20, 1945
Los Angeles
ALS, 2 p.

Dear Bill—

I have not written since your letter of Sept. 24. We are just back from a fine journey—to Fallon, Nevada. Drove up the east side of the Sierra, stopping overnight both ways at Bishop. My first trip over this route. The mountains are superb, the way they soar straight up from the Valley, without benefit of foothills. The autumnal countryside is very lovely: yellow sage in various stages of bloom, & the cottonwood & poplar ranging from green to bright yellow & gold.

We went to get Fay's mother & aunt, on the latter's ranch. Have you ever been through the Fallon irrigation district? One of the earliest U.S. Reclamation projects. A dam across the Carson & Truckee rivers turned the trick. The desert bloomed! The ranch is right on the main canal. I had some good sundown walks along the banked path. The enormous clouded sky was breathtaking. It did me immense good to trudge across the fall landscape, everything gone yellow & brown, and wing-whistling flights of mallards overhead. It made me realize how much I lose, living here in the city.

Since returning home I have taken four or five additional days of vacation, spending most of the time here in my study, reading & writing.

Any late news on getting out?

I hope your mouth feels better.

Yrs as ever
Larry

Oct. 31, 1945
Waldport
ALS, 2 p., 1 sheet

Dear Larry:—

A fine letter, that last. The whole flavor of the desert in it. You are a rich man.

Discharges are being held up. The usual story: the Veterans protest, and Selective Service wheels like a weather-cock. It is strange. Not so much the policy of calculated deprivation, which is understandable, in view of our position, but SS had voluntarily set up and begun a system of discharge based on equality with the Forces. Yet they duck for cover at the first ripple.

As things stand now, well over a million men have been released from the Army. From CPS = 26: A few men over 38.

Latest report has it that all 3-year men are expected out by May first. That, then, is my date.

I'm having quite a time here, getting my sea-legs under me in regard to the woman question. They come into camp occasionally, looking things over, fine gals, generally, good looking and intelligent, attracted by Fine Arts and the guys here. Often, after they leave, I learn that caps had been set: the Everson myth is persuasive hereabouts, and I suppose a woman gravitates toward that kind of build-up. But only rarely have I actually been aware of it: the set-cap I mean.

The last one, though, I could see. A young Jewess, German, with a wide European background and a delightful brogue. She would invade the dorm, lie on my bed, and talk poetry, or art, or some such matter. It was very invigorating, sitting here, very self-contained, pulling my reserve around me, plucking it in like a cloak, letting out just enough to be more than civil, just enough to let it be known that there is warmth here, and that I liked her: she could see that. It was very good, very warming. She had a free and easy way about her, and a wide peasant build to her that takes my inclination. She was easy with men, too, with all of us here. She'd been around. I felt myself thawing out in that glacial region, the nuts!

But there wasn't enough to move on. I refuse to scrabble for it. I refuse to chase it. If it wants to come, let it come. But I'll not play this competitive game that always obtains hereabouts, one woman to a dozen men, and time too short, and the general lack of dignity of a piece pushed over on the beach.

But a good thing for me to understand that what I am is not alien to them all.

Edwa has been making very definite overtures for re-continuance after release, but I don't know, I'm thoroughly dead on that, inside, nothing kindles. I told her if something comes of it afterward, and we revive, and can touch the richness again, then very well. But not for the past's sake only.

And surely, nothing kindled when we met in September. I found myself watching her, feeling nothing, comparing her with other women, finding her constraint and bound-in quality, that I had to work so to release, too much. Well, we'll see.

This camp closes in December. I guess then to Cascade Locks. I cannot encompass it, after so long here. It seems wrong.

I wrote Bentley about that Acorn.

Bill

November 1, 1945
1000 Manning Ave. LA 24
ALS, 2 p.

Dear Bill—

I received a notice from *Compass* of 6 issues for $1.00. So here's a buck. Will you see that the Treasurer gets it? Just who publishes *Compass*?

It's been a long while since I've heard from you. Did I write upon our return from Nevada? I believe I did.

Hope your writing & printing go well.

Larry

P.S.: Ritchie's press is doing a little Christmas book for Fay & me. I'd like to use on the title page the vignette Buel did for *San Joaquin*. They can't find the cut, but need a slight reduction in size, so will make a new smaller one. Can you give me Buel's address, as I'd like to ask his permission to use his fine piece.

L

By the way, may I have also the author's permission?!

Nov. 3, 1945
Waldport, Ore.
ALS, 2 p., 1 sheet

NOVEMBER FIRST NINETEEN FORTY-FIVE

All day the wind,
Veering south and west,
The sea's quarter,
Strengthens to storm,
And brings the dropping dusk,
Hard on our houses,
And rain on it.

And I write this poem now to that lost girl my wife,
Whom I blunted in youth with my haste,
And learned too late to recover.
She sleeps in a far country,
She stirs in her own dream,
Moist and warm in her cover.

And I coax the liability of black ink on paper,
That holds no respite,
And con the riddle of error.

xxx

I recollect that it was ten years ago this month that *These Are the Ravens* was published; I had lately returned from Sunnyvale, that summer of work there in the cannery; and that it was ten years ago also the first poem in *San Joaquin* was written.

xxx

A letter today from Bentley. His hopes for foreign relief work with the Red Cross having fallen—denied because of asthma—he is not sure that he wants to sell the Acorn.

xxx

In San Francisco the last trip I had the good fortune to make the acquaintance of Kenneth Rexroth, an excellent person, spent a night there. We sat late, drinking wine, myself listening. He has proclaimed me the most consequential poet to emerge during the war!! Well, well! But really an excellent person. Let me commend to you his superb poem *The Phoenix and the Tortoise,* rather like the *Ghost,* I think.

XXX

I nurse a great dream now of acquiring a hand press, setting it up in a vineyard somewhere; and write my books, and print them, make them breathe from cover to cover, and see if it cannot be demonstrated that a life can be built of integrity and faith, devoted to the highest ideals of art and craft; of a degree of self-sufficiency, and not have to run howling to New York. I think the "Chronicle" could find a publisher there now, for I can show a substantial following developed under Untide, but I want to wait and see what I can work out myself. That would be simpler and better, and surely of greater worth.

Bill

Nov. 5, 45
Waldport, Oregon
APS

Dear Larry:—

I've turned the buck over to *Compass,* a magazine published separately from either *Illit.* or Untide [Press] by Martin Ponch and Lloyd Danziesen. I was about to mail you a copy. You remember the issue of last Fall with the Fine Arts article.

If it's all right with Buel it's all right with me. He should be pleased. Address: Route 1, Box 63A, Indio, California.

Haven't seen him since '42.

Good luck
Bill

November 10, 1945
Los Angeles
ALS, 4 p., 2 sheets

Dear Bill—

Thanks for Buel's address. And more for your letter. I cannot tell you how glad it makes me, to read of the return of spring to your balls! Ripeness is all. Good God yes! And you're a wise man to savor it slowly, & not snatch it on the run midst the wasteland of the beach. Bide your time. One day you will slip into it like a hot bath. I hope soon.

Summer came to an end for me, when she moved away. The last time was memorable. I shall tell you. Perhaps a story will come of it. I want very much to see you. I shall make a Berkeley trip, probably the week before Christmas. Any chance of your coming down then?

Yesterday I spoke with Pres. Sproul about my going abroad to buy for the University Libraries. Perhaps next spring or summer or fall. England, France, Switzerland. Your letter stirred something in me & I got out my "Quintet" & read it through, for the first time in a year or two. The few who have read it have either understood it perfectly or else missed it entirely, the latter saying that it is merely the outline for a novel. There's nothing I can say to that. It was meant to be to the novel what a string quartet is to a symphony—& after re-reading it, I feel more sure than ever that it is essentially right as it is. One or two passages perhaps need strengthening, enriching. My whole effort was to understate, to eliminate the padding of the average novel, to be eloquent & laconic at the same time. Chamber music in more than one sense!

Here's the point. May I send the typescript to you? I am curious as to how it will strike you now after your three years of Concentration. You have never read the final draft, written after your helpful criticism. Perhaps you will detect weak places, false notes, etc., & enable me to better it for a final typing.

My new work, of which you read the first half, inches forward. In the past year & a half I have written fewer than a hundred pages on the 3d part. But I have kept it alive, in spite of the pressure of my extrovert work—& I feel good in having done so. The influences on me to give up this "creative" writing are many, & I have to fight them off. In my heart creative work is all that matters in the world; those who do it are the true gods.

Do you know Scott Greer? At Henry Miller's request I have been mailing Greer books from the library, & he has sent me some of his poems. I like them. He & his wife are apparently fire-watchers in the mountains, via Bly, Oregon. I wonder if you are in correspondence with him?

I hope you will forgive me troubling you with my old work, but it is troubling me, & I wonder why it is that people either accept it implicitly or reject it utterly. It has made me goddamned timid about giving it to anyone to read. One seeks neither praise nor blame, but understanding. It has been your abundant gift of the latter that has often sustained me when I faltered.

Affectionately—
Larry

November 16, 1945
Los Angeles
ALS, 2 p., 1 sheet

Dear Bill—

Your letter was very welcome. Warmed the evening for me. Your good little poem "Nov. 1, 1945" and your meeting with Rexroth. I ordered his *Phoenix* for the library a year or so ago, but had never gotten my hands on it. Last night I brought it home. Very good indeed. I prefer the shorter poems to the title piece—on first reading. The dialectical or metaphysical passages in the *Phoenix* leave me unaroused. Here is a poet after my own heart. I like him! I like his classical paraphrases & translations. During the years, I have collected the Greek anthology in English & lately have gotten in a dozen or more editions, going back a century—& so am particularly happy to encounter Rexroth's versions—he's lusty. How can you beat a blend of nature, love & classics? Please give me his Bay

Region address. I'd like to write him & perhaps call when I'm North next month. Can you come down then? I'll probably be there the week before Xmas.

I approve of your dream of a vineyard & a press & you writing and printing your own books. Count me to help in any way I can. I have the utmost faith that you are heading for a rich & fruitful life as man & artist. Rexroth is right. Of course you are the most consequential poet to emerge during the war! But for me you emerged importantly years earlier, when one day I opened a letter from Fay Porter & your poems danced before me.

Man alive, this is Friday night & tomorrow morning I go to Newell's Malibu hideaway—& with me will be a girl of 23 summers, slim & copper-haired, here a month from England, where since she was 17 she has earned her living in the theater, as actress & designer—who is she? My niece—the daughter of my dead brother—Marcia Virginia Powell—and Bill my boy, she's fair & lovely, sensitive & intelligent—and in her delicate face lives the vivid memory of my brother, the moods, the expressions, the grimaces—all very moving, both in itself & for what it symbolizes. Think of me— I greet you!

Larry

November 18, 1945
Los Angeles
ALS, 4 p. 2 sheets

Dear Bill—

This Sunday morning I lay abed & re-read your "Chronicle of Division." I retrieved the typescript from Newell, who has had it for a month or two.

I want to tell you that it impressed even more than the first reading. It is a very moving erotic cycle. I like the way it is organized—tight & compact—& the way it progresses—with sure & solemn dignity, & rising emotion—until

> They touch,
> The swift tongues mate in the flowing mouths.

And the mad outcry of the next stanza. Oh this is very effective, just the way you've done it.

That you have made such a moving poem from your sorrow fills me with immense reverence for man-as-artist.

Two nights ago I wrote you, on the eve of going to Newells' with Marcia. We went yesterday, & Bill my lad, it was a day far exceeding my fondest hopes. It was one of the beautiful days of my life, showing her that tumbled mountain country on a late autumn day, persimmons & walnuts, sycamores & poplars colored leaved, the sunlight wan yet lambent. And finding Newell alone, his wife in town, riding high on a creative wave.

We sat by his fireplace & gazed out his front windows on an immense panorama of mountain & valley—& talked—God how we talked! I read them your last letter—& Gordon read from the *Ghost,* as of yore. Then we walked to his cabin studio & saw his newest work. The peacocks rattled on the roof, the Nubian goats made their noise, & we all felt so goddamned good & radiant! Back to the fire & drank hot tea. Talked & read. Talked of her theater work, during the 6 long years of the war.

We left at four o'clock & drove up to the crest & over, & down the ten miles of winding road to the ocean, reaching it at sunset. I parked & we watched the dark orange sun slide into low cloud on the sea horizon, then the fountaining light! And desultory words of love & marriage. Night fell on the channel & Catalina & us, as we sped along the shore road to Santa Monica.

She was a rare companion. I cannot tell you how exquisitely I felt everything yesterday. I longed for you to be with us. We talked of your vineyard & your press. We talked of you. Her first lover—6 years ago when she was 17—was an English C.O., a painter, 5 years older than she—& for 5 years they were in love. He did non-combatant work—firefighting & forestry—I wish we could come & visit you.

Tell me if you can come to Berkeley the week before Christmas?

This afternoon I went extrovert in a big way & took my family to a pro-football game—passes to the press-box—& then to Chinatown for supper.

William, I am completely beside myself, with my spirits'

riches keyed high about me. The other day the three of them were together—my dark wife, my fair holly idyll woman, & my copper thatched Marcia. Their sight, their mere presence so exalted me I nearly leaped from my skin. And before Xmas, en route north, I hope to visit the one I told you of when you were here in April. Look to the south, lad, that pillar on the horizon is Powell's pecker uplifted to the sky! Stuff this all in your heart, for Xist sake, & keep it there. And believe me, ever yrs.

Larry

Nov. 22, 1945
Feast Day
Waldport, Ore.
ALS, 4 p. 2 sheets

Dear Larry:—

So many rich offerings in so short an interval—I'm about whelmed under. All good. You lead a full life. Your letters show it. Then too, the season, autumn, we both favor it, I believe.

And now that it's Thanksgiving, my favorite day of the whole year, even as a child my favorite day, but during my marriage became a thing of such import, such lovely maturity, that excellent woman, her dignity and her grace, the shy reserve, and yet her wonderful capacity for the bed—it became a day of magical quality, and I can remember with distinction the five of them we had together.

But here, there is none of that. A braw day, the wind cold and gusting off the sea, threatening a cold rain, in a season that for a month has been cold and raw, wet, sudden petulant squalling storms, then the drizzle, with hardly a rare day in the lot. A fitting season for the termination of Waldport.

For the camp is to close by December 15, the men dispersed, hither and yon, the good fellowships of three years rudely dissevered. I go to government camp, having had my fill of the churches, and their dabbling in conscription. But which one, I don't know: Lapine, Ore; Mancos, Colorado; or Minersville, Calif. I await assignment.

As for the Press, the others may continue it. For myself, the relationship is over when we are physically separated.

And the camp is in uproar over the closure. Eleven have been on hunger strike for three days against the arbitrary wholesale assignments. Groups form and reform, argue, discuss, rage, protest. This morning's mail carried a terrific flood of letters out. The telegraph is busy. Even the director is resigning in protest. I haven't had a clear thought for days.

I think, in view of this, you had best not send the "Quintet" until I am settled elsewhere, but I'd like to see it again then. I am packing my books to send back. Going to G.C. pretty well stripped of my possessions, for I expect a February release.

Your proposed European trip sounds very fine, I'm glad for you.

No, I've never corresponded with Greer, though know many people who know him—Harman does, for one. Greer was in Portland, met the poet Wendell Anderson there, who brought him home to dinner. Greer and Mrs. Anderson fell in love, and are now married. Some friends disrespect Greer for his part—evidently Anderson is a pretty swell person, and had a fine marriage—but I know these things are too intricate for judgement. The amorality of love!

Rexroth lives at 692 Wisconsin St., San Francisco. I hope you can see him. But you both rate me too high—yet!

I wish I could be there in Berkeley, but my three months' work refusal cut off any future furlough.

I hear from Harman occasionally—in jail. He's having a hard time. Fell in love on his walk-out with a girl—also named Marcia. They were here for a while as man and wife. He hadn't been in jail a month before she had another man—also a walk-out. Didn't tell Jim. Just quit writing. The poor bastard almost went crazy trying to figure it out, begged me to tell him what the score was, if I knew. Finally did. Bad business. Son of a bitch, isn't it, the way these things work? Grit your teeth. Grind through. The only way.

Life has been very different here for me from the fine sensuous flavor, the "savor," as you say, that your letters breathe. Pulled tighter. Moral problem against moral problem: the terrible choices, the compulsion to act, the inability to act, the need and the fear; everything pulled to a stringency, a tension, and the inability to ever *know* which is right. And the nature of the place: immense, terrible, terribly beautiful, terribly remote, the forever sea, grinding, grinding, immense and beautiful and real, a great sense of terrible godliness, of reality beyond the human reality, so that I have become religious and somewhat ascetic by nature, pulled that way by the terror of the moral choices forever at hand, and the flashing face of non-human God. I see them already making the next war, the ferocity of that unbelievable Bomb, the nations beginning to go underground, and what can life hold but the comprehension of the great serene presence apart from and involved in the terrible turn of things. I expect little but that, from now on. It is great and remote, and to be come to only through pain and agony and spiritual travail. If there is any of the "savor," I shall be grateful for it: but the totalitarian world that we are shaping up, will permit little of that for the likes of me, or so I believe. But there are certain things no man can take away. And the multiplicity of a life, even its pain and its sorrow, and its immense contradictions, affords some insight into the majesty of things; to see; to touch; to apprehend. The smoke that drifts from the toppling wave: or the dawn spread-eagled on its bloody east: all are testament to that serene face, that eye, that looks and does not weep, at what we are.

I salute you, and smile to you across the intervention of space, and go out into the waiting darkness, the face, the night of time.

Bill

Nov. 24, 1945
Los Angeles
APS

Bill—

I am down to a single copy of your *Residual Years*. Do you have copies left? If so, please send me 10, together with bill. *Compass* not yet received.

L.

30 November 1945
Waldport
TPS

We are sending you today the following:
10 copies THE RESIDUAL YEARS (Everson) @ $.15 $1.60

The Untide Press
Tom Miller
by Tom Miller, in the absence
of Bill Eshelman

Bill [Everson]—Please pay this & apply the balance of the check to your work—

LCP

December 3, 1945
Los Angeles
ALS, 2 p.

Dear Bill—
Sheets & Eshelman called this afternoon. We had a couple of hours in my office. Vosper & Jake dropped in for awhile. A good session. Two good lads. Quite different from one another. I put in our bid again for the Fine Arts archives, against that of the Main Church [Brethren]. I suggested a token shipment to the Church, with the bulk of the stuff coming our way. Otherwise it's putting it all down an ultimate rat-hole. They will discuss it with the committee when they get back. Plug for us.

What pleased me most was to learn that you will be going to Cascade Locks. Sheets spoke highly of the place. Let me know when you are settled & I will send you "Quintet." Is there express service to there or a nearby point?

Your rich and melancholy letter has been read several times. My answer to it is the book I mailed you last week.

I am sorry we won't be meeting in Berkeley. Thanks for Rexroth's address. I shall be driving up alone. I plan to stop over in Tulare with my cousin—her husband is resident surgeon at the County Hospital; & has many a tale & gory to tell.

> The creative moment of a writer comes with the autumn. The winter is the time for reading, revision, preparation of the soil; the spring for thawing back to life; the summer is for the open air, for satiating the body with health & action, but from October to Christmas for the release of pent-up mental energy, the hard crown of the year. Cyril Connolly

A man who feels as we do! The autumn has been rich for me, but alas! people & many projects get most of my juice, & I don't have left as much as I should for my secret work.

Yes, I have cooled since I wrote you last, & now I simmer with the most tender & delicious nostalgia. If that's a mixed figure, then launch it up thy anal canal. In the name of Christ Cringle I greet you!

Larry

Dec. 7, 1945
Los Angeles
APS

Bill—

Am mailing you a book. Please return if you have it, as I have another use in mind.

LCP

12-9-45
Los Angeles
ALS, 1 p.

Dear Bill—
Please apply this to the printing of your "Chronicle."

Larry

The Night of the Eclipse Dec. 18, 45
Waldport
APS

Dear Larry:—
Both books arrived. I had neither and am glad to have both. *Glory of Life* quite fine. Not transferred yet, but await it any day. Wire from Edwa—"operation successful." Will write in greater detail. Many thanks.

Bill

12-24-45
Los Angeles
ALS, 1 p.

Dear Bill—
Please verify your existence & whereabouts.
Just back from a week's trip to Berkeley, by car, via Tulare & Santa Maria. How wonderful the Valley & coast in winter!
Greetings—& do write.

Larry

12–24-45
Los Angeles
ALS, 1 p.

Dear Bill—
Your card just came. Am much dismayed to learn that you are not at Cascade Locks! Sheets told me you would be there

after the 15th, so I have been sending items to you there. This morning an air mail letter with a small check in it.

Will they forward to you? I hope so!

Can't recall what other book I sent you, apart from *Glory of Life*. Was it *Apples Be Ripe*? Am slightly confused!

Merry Christmas.

Larry

Dec. 28, 1945
Cascade Locks
CPS No. 21
ALS, 2 p., 1 sheet

Dear Larry:—

Oktoberlied and your letter with your check were here when I arrived two days ago. Today your letter to Waldport, written in some alarm, was forwarded. I hasten to reassure you. Everything, I believe, came safely. I left Waldport on mid-afternoon of December 24, spent Christmas Eve and Day with my excellent friends Clayton and Barbara James at the home of Wilfred and Betty Lang in Portland. Lang too is a painter whom we met a year ago and have developed an affection for. Probably my most "normal" Christmas in CPS. James was convicted of "desertion" in the Federal Court in Portland and is out on bail pending a delayed sentence. We are all hoping for a suspended sentence or parole.

I came out the following day in a great storm, preceding all the other Waldport men, but me. I wanted to make a suitable place for the press. We got a terrific trailer-load of stuff up to Portland by another car on Christmas day (had built the trailer in the preceding weeks for this emergency) and a chap and I went back from here to Portland to pick it up. Brought it out at night up the Gorge in a howling storm, unloaded it yesterday, working like dogs. In fact my silence has been due to that: for the past week I've been through one long whirlwind of packing press material and my own books & things, of which I have four or five hundred pounds. Anyway, this is the first breather

I've had, and I'm still tired from my first day's project work today, which will account for this dog-trot style.

Let me thank you for the checks. I was amazed to receive the first one in Waldport, and deeply touched by your faith, and feel a great gratitude. I have put the money away separately, and will use it when the time comes to print the "Chronicle."

The second book you sent me was *The Unquiet Grave,* wrapped as a Christmas gift, and I would have waited till then to open it except for your having asked me whether I already had, in which case you would send it elsewhere. But, as I said, I did not have it, and look forward to reading it.

I had hoped for a long letter to you, but am too tired to go on. I'll write, probably after New Year's for over the three-day period we drive to Waldport to load and transport the press.

So long—
Bill

P.S. The *Oktoberlied* is a fine little piece, a most handsome Christmas card, and I smiled to see the Vine reestablished again [Buel's drawing].

Dec. 30, 1945
Los Angeles
APS

Dear Bill—

I have run out of presentation copies of *War Elegies, Waldport Poems* & *Poems 1942*. How is your stock? Would like 10 copies of each, if you have them.

LCP

1946: SEEKER AND SPEAKER

Jan. 4, 1946
Cascade Locks
AL, 1 p.

Dear Larry:—

I write from the sick-bay. When I wrote you last I was coming down with a cold, but fought it off, knowing the weekend, with this three-day respite, was the only chance to get the press. We left Sunday morning, drove down through Portland and along the Coast to Waldport. Nothing had been done by the fellows there about making the move ready, and we worked most of the night dismantling the press, tearing a section out of the building, and getting the press on the trailer. (Two wheel job. We made it ourselves a month or so ago.) The press vastly outweighed our predictions however, sat the bed right down on the axle, we started out Monday noon holding our breaths, the thin tires steaming under the strain. Got into Portland however New Year's Eve, spent that evening with my good friends the Langs (art work in *Illiterati* and *Compass*) and James's. Crippled out here New Year's Day. Helped my friend Bill Jadiker do some emergency work on his house (he had driven all the way) and that finished me. Came into the infirmary the 2nd and have been here since, now recovering, the flu still hanging on somewhat.

Jan. 6
out of the infirmary now

Jan. 6, 1946
The Locks
ALS, 4 p., 2 sheets

Dear Larry:—

Tonight I sit in the pressroom, or what will someday be a pressroom, alone, the rain on the roof, the litter about me of all the Untide books and equipment, and I nurse inside me a song for Waldport, a dirge, a lamentation, for would I were there, my heart is there, on the beach, where the breakers are grinding their immemorial wheels upon the sand.

You have only to walk into this kind of camp to realize what we had there, the thing we fashioned, and nourished, and brought to bear. For this is the society of manners, where people, penned out of their lives, fashion another, a kind of minor civilization, with emphasis on the social graces, and the social concerns, for they have little else. What there is of art here is the art of dilettante. What there is of music is the music of the Sunday afternoon concert-goer. And we will smile at one another and be cordial, and wear our women on our arm, for these, of course, are the things that count.

I say this camp is a year, is 2 years behind Waldport.
Even in politics: here it is the Liberal. At Waldport it was the Radical.

There were men there. And they saw to the heart of the pure creative substance, the rock, and they began cutting to it, and they hewed off layer after layer of incidentals, and they got to the heart of it, stripped it down, made it shine. They made it shine in painting, in music, in drama, and in writing, and nothing else really mattered, except when it came to another sphere—that of politics, and they made it shine too. When it got bad they walked out. But what was there was stripped. And it taught us. We called it the Fine Arts at Waldport. And it's dead. And the great years of my life lie there with it. And I'm proud. Proud of my part in it. Proud to be of those clean men. And to have done what I did, and built, not be satisfied with sitting on my ass. God bless it!

Well, another life. Another world. You can't go back. You create out of the inexplicable substance of experience, as it's loaded into your lap by the guy who operates the celestial garbage wagon. There are poems to be written. Books to be printed. And there's no weeping over the past, but let us at least salute it. *Waldport!*

I wander about here, like some taciturn outcast, who has seen better days, and knows they were better days, and is not satisfied with the fine favors, the welcomes, the cordiality, the good food, nor even the Columbia Gorge, which is quite a show, but let us not compare it with the sea. I have a great black hat, and a most *incredible* head of hair, and a long coat, and to these people I must seem rather like the ghost who came to dinner but would not eat. They are intimidated, and I am sorry for that, for I wish them no ill, but a man has seen better days, and he's not going to go grinning and scraping into the first hoytsy toytsy little bunch of slick dicks that open their arms. Well, I'll get on. Time will thaw me out. The other Waldport men who got here took to it easily enough. But give me a day or two to nurse the past, and let my loyalties wear, for I've seen better days, and by god I know it.

Bill

P.S. Out of *Waldport Poems.* Sending on *Poems 42* and *Elegies* tomorrow.

January 19, 1946
Los Angeles
ALS, 2 p.

O bad, your trouble—Newell's trouble—and now mine—She has revealed a love that is more glorious than anything on earth—I am shamed & humble & exalted beyond words. Ore pas nobis—

Dear Bill—

Your stirring lament for Waldport has given me repeated joy. God bless you, lad! My hat's off to you. You have drilled to rock & will have some wonderful intercourse on that enduring bed. I read your letter to Newell. He is in the hell of a long & cruel struggle with his wife, suffering agony & slowly dying as a creative man. I try to help him, but she is stronger than he & keeps his forces split. He is confused. Tragic.

I try to help—who need help, badly! I cannot write much to you. It would overwhelm me. I must not get started. Let me say only that the holly-gathering idyll—the honey-haired woman—has turned from dream to reality—& I am engaged in the deepest most soul shaking experience of my mature manhood. Bill, believe me, I am shaken, badly shaken. I may take a leave of a week or two & drive to see you. I may have to get away & try to get my feet on the bottom.

Our 4th New Year's Eve together—we two couples—& then & since then—18 days—the swift dissolving of 8 years' impersonality, of almost incredible mutual restraint—& the blending knowledge, in an increasingly naked series of incidents, that all along we have been hoping, dreaming the same thoughts—*& know & confess at last that we are desperately in love.* I with her she with me. And we have yet to kiss! We are afraid to.

Bill, this is the most desperate letter I have ever written you. For God's sake, tell me your friendship whatever happens.

Larry

Feb. 7, 1946
The Beaver
enroute
Berkeley to Portland
ALS, 2 p., 1 sheet

Dear Larry:—

It must seem almost an affront to you that I have not answered your letter before this, for it was written in great unrest, in great agitation of spirit, and though I do not have it by me now I recall its great cry, and its need. I did not write for I was in Berkeley, wound in the thread and tangle of my own involvement, totally unable to help you by any word I could write. Nor can I now, here in this speeding car, the young soldier asleep on my shoulder, and the couple ahead slumped in the long hypnotic kiss. For I know that the urgency that poured into your letter has had its resolution ere this; it could not have continued at such a pitch; and you have either taken the long plunge outward, or got your sea-legs under you again, and are weathering it through. I am not alarmed. For I know you to be too old a dog at this business not to keep one eye peeled on the bedroom door, and a quick shinny down the drain-pipe to the saving hedge.

Nor am I cynical in this. Your letter was clear enough that you were launched into no casual affair. But I know the stakes are extreme, and you were never rash. At any rate, fare well in it, and I await developments.

As for myself—I received a letter from Edwa that the operation was successful and that she had come home, after almost 2 months in the hospital, that she had suffered extreme pain, that she was in great despondency, and did not know the way out. I applied immediately for emergency furlough and fortunately got it. But arriving in Berkeley found I had misread certain qualities and was somewhat put aback. There was time enough to temper things a bit, and I return with the feeling of a clear advance, and look forward to release.

Great news is that I finally got a handpress, a big one, found in a printing equipment house in San Francisco. Not Wilder's. It was high. I paid $175 for it, and it has no tympan or frisket, but they are rare now, being in demand as proof presses, and I did not want to have to wait after demobilization. I was reluctant to take Wilder's, for he is one of the few hand-printers left, and though I think he wants to sell out, I should hate to see him drop it.

Goodnight for now, and keep your grip, and come through.

Bill

February 13, 1946
Los Angeles
ALS, 2 p., 1 sheet

Dear Bill—

Your train letter was very welcome. Thanks for it. You called the turn. Things couldn't have gone on indefinitely at that high tension. Your letter finds me riding at anchor in home port. Some voyage! Wow. Lasted exactly one month. Struck by a hurricane on February 1st. Damned near blew me under. You're right, I am an old sea dog, and I rode the son-of-a-bitch out. All the standard props of melodrama were present—heartbroken wife, murderous husband, etc.

What a gamble it was! My skin is sore, but whole. I had to choose in the showdown. No regrets for the choice I made. No regrets for the intensity I experienced. No regrets.

Our marriage, after 12 years, has weathered the only real storm we've encountered, and we have come together anew in a profounder intimacy than we ever dreamed was possible. It blew away all the drift & waste that had accumulated. Naked & clean. Very wonderful denouement of what seemed an impossible dilemma.

Thank God I was able to keep daily journal all through it—some 50 or 60 pages since New Year's Eve. Someday I'll write a masterpiece from them & the earlier ones—the holly idyll, etc.

I'll not try to write any more now. Perhaps when we meet next, if I can bear to read through them, we'll have a session over the journal pages. I feel stronger & better for what happened—sadder, wiser, more joyous & confident.

I am glad to hear of Edwa's coming through & that you are in process of coming together again. God keep us all, poor ignorant sinners. When are you discharged? Write soon.

Larry

2-15-46
Los Angeles
ALS, 1 p.

Dear Bill—

In my last letter I neglected to say how pleased I am to hear of your new press. Have you left it in S.F. [San Francisco] until you are demobbed? When will that be, do you know? Do you still have the Russian River plan?

My fond hope is someday to commission you to print a few copies of my "Quintet." Maybe years from now. Who knows? Would you do it? I would bear the cost.

Larry

Feb. 22, 1946
Cascade Locks
ALS, 8 p., 4 sheets

Dear Larry:—

The search for the handpress began last summer with your letter to me that Wilder Bentley had one for sale for $125.00. On my dental furlough in September I saw Wilder, spent a good afternoon with him, and saw the three or four presses that are there. These were the first handpresses I had ever examined. Wilder tried to dissuade me. Too slow, too much work for my purposes. I had told him I was a writer. When I showed him some of our work he was mildly surprised that it was as good as it was. But still he didn't think the handpress was the thing I wanted.

After I went down this trip we had another good afternoon. He had taken a job teaching in Stockton, but was home with a fever, and in bed. He said if I really had the bug he would sell me the Acorn, though he thought it was too large for my uses, and required too much work. He did not think I could find another handpress, but suggested I look anyway, and sent me down to the Westgate Press, who owned one, smaller, that would be better for me.

The Westgate Press had sold theirs a month before to some rich bitch over in Burlingame for $150.00. I had a good talk with the man there, asked him about the Acorn. He doubted that it was as good, by virtue of its design, as the standard handpresses, but had to admit Bentley's work had been superb on it. Bentley had previously told me of some particular peculiarities of his Acorn that I could expect trouble from; all of which sharpened my hopes of finding a different press. Whereas up to now I had been looking for a smaller press, I decided I would take a large standard one if I could find it, which, after the Westgate interview seemed highly unlikely. $150.00 for a smaller model showed the things were in demand. About the size, I remembered that the more size and power you have the better off you are, regardless of inconvenience; I had learned that with platen presses. Get a big form on and you never regret that awkward massiveness. Westgate sent me over to ATF in San Francisco, but I didn't get over there till my furlough was almost up. It seemed like a blind chance.

Instead, I spent my time in the Cal library digging up 19th-century printer's manuals, archaic old tomes, but engrossing, descriptive of current handpresses and techniques. I began to get a perspective on this business, got swept up in it. I had to have me a press.

Three days before I was to start back I finally got over to ATF. No go. They had seen nothing. The presses were in demand as proof presses, since none of the latter had been made during the war. Engravers were also buying them up. As I went out he mentioned I might try Ottsman's used printing supplies house on Sansome St. I didn't expect anything because I had tried those people in the East Bay without success, but I went over.

As I went in the door I saw it. It was a whopper. It had been resurrected from somewhere, cleaned up, painted a good grey. It stood there, seeming sparer than its kind, no cast iron ornamentation that period loved, lacked the Washington and Franklin medallions that gave this type its name in America. I took this to mean it was newer, perhaps early this century. Across its staple was cast the name of the manufacturer: R. Hoe & Co. New York and London. No. 5533. It was marked $175.00. I looked at it. Worked the rounce. Lowered the platen. Was it any good? How the hell was I to know? I'd never even seen one in operation. The high price chagrined me. There was no tympan attachment, but Ottsman said it was in the basement.

What to do? I went out and walked the streets. I wanted the press. I was taken with it. I wanted it badly, but I was afraid, I was so ignorant, so unsure, I knew myself easily swept away. I decided to go out to Rexroth's and spend the night, get up early, go over and see the Grabhorns and ask their advice. On the impulse I went into a phone booth and called them up, but it was late, and no one answered at their shop.

I spent a long night with Rexroth, talking many things, mostly about our personal lives, and hearing his advice concerning my tangled affair with Edwa, advice, mostly, that I have come to reject. But I did rise early, my mind made up about the press. I decided not to bother the Grabhorns who wouldn't be able to see the press anyway, and could only make general pronouncements, if at all. I went back to East Bay, looked up Edwa. I dug out an insurance policy that had been hanging about my neck and turned it in, then borrowed money from Edwa. She carried more than enough in her purse!

We drove back. Ottsman was gone, but his young employee was there and we went over the press carefully. It seemed quite sound, unworn, only the movement of the bed being impaired by rubbing on the too-thick strap that draws the bed under the platen. The tympan turned out to be thoroughly useless, a rickety wooden frame for proofing. I got him to agree to hold the press till July, which he did with some reluctance. That secured, I bought it, and left, in something of a cloud.

The next afternoon I went over to Bentley's to look at his presses to get some ideas on what type of tympan frames I should make. I stopped at the library to look in Simon's *Printing Explained,* the only modern work explaining the technique of handpress printing, which carries pen drawings of the Albion presses made in England. These illustrations are pretty clear, and I debated going back over to San Francisco to get specific measurements in order to construct tympan and frisket here in camp. I made rough sketches from those drawings.

Wilder I knew was in Stockton, but Ethel should be there. She was not, however. I entered the basement uninvited, and poked about there for an hour. These frames and friskets were so different from the English ones I got discouraged and decided I should wait till I got out. Back here in camp, however, I've talked with a friend who's a mechanic and he thinks we can make them from my sketches. I'm writing Ottsman for measurements on my press.

So came back, impatient to begin. Bought brayers [ink rollers] in Portland to practice hand-inking. Take the rollers off the clam-action, ink the form on the stone, lug it over to the press, pull a sheet, lug the form back to the stone, ink, repeat. A laborious process. But what a labor!

Now I await discharge in May. Less than three months.

About Edwa. Here in the Locks I was extremely dissatisfied, filled with unrest. I received a letter from her that she was back from the hospital in Santa Barbara, that she had suffered terribly, so much so that she would never have gone into it knowing that the tumor was malignant, and would recur, that she only awaited that eventuality, knowing she would never submit to another operation, that her life was empty. I answered that letter, asking about her relationship with Kenny, etc. Didn't wait for a reply. Asked for, and received, emergency furlough, surprised that my three month's refusal to work had not annulled the possibility. Climbed on a bus and went down. I went in high hopes, prepared to make concessions for a reunion. But arriving there I saw how mistaken I had been. There is no certainty that the tumor will return. She was weak yet, but not in really depressed spirits; she works at her kiln, earns her way at the card-table, and lives in a state of semi-matrimony with Carothers. (When I commented on the noisiness of room over the street-car tracks she remarked thoughtfully "Yes, it's bad, but I don't sleep here often." How revealing that phrase was, more potent, and of more import to me than any statistics of how much time she spent there!) Five hours before I arrived she had posted a letter (I received it by return mail five days later) in answer to mine, which, had I received in Cascade, I should never have come. For I went as much out of generosity as anything: there is a central lack of permanence or stability that one is constantly trying to fill, I mean one who once had a permanent marriage and no longer has, and that, I admit, brought me as much as anything. But as far as she herself was concerned I was emotionally out of it. The attraction was not that she was Edwa but that she was my ex-wife. I say I went out of generosity, and I believe it. The letter touched me. I felt great pity and sadness for her—for us both. I went down to restore. I expected a disconsolate woman.

But she was still deep with Kenny. Her letter told me she felt no other man could supply the sexual fulfillment he gave her. Which does not hurt me nor strike any longer at my pride, for I know those things are relative, and attested as much to the dissatisfaction of their total lives as to the man's individual prowess. For they are really fucked up, both of them, poor bewildered bastards, all. From the poker table to the cafe, to the concert hall, to the bed. They cling to each other like straws; blighted with a basic lack, shadowed by suicidal impulses.

Even so, Edwa was better than I'd ever seen her since induction. The killing of the cancer had brought a bloom back on her. And many times I was given to see glimpses of the woman I knew: the deep quietude, the essential gravity and inner richness. It sprang sparks out of me to see her move again; to see her at her kiln, throwing clay on the wheel, moulding it up between those sensitive hands, absorbed. It is in her self-absorption that she is great. Against the world she wears a mask, and I dislike it, for it is false, false as hell, and that's all anyone sees, and how they all misunderstand! But I know her better, and know the soft reflective glow that can illumine her whole being. *She* doesn't know it! But I do, and something in me breaks for the lost years, the good vineyard, and that woman again, laughing beside me in the vines, in the autumn harvest, the raisins fat on the trays and their odor rife in the air.

But, conversely, I anger her, as no one else does. She, relativist, rebels against my absolutism. The old psychological barrier I had erected so many years ago in my ignorant impetuous unseeing early youth, is still there. My unconcealable distaste for much of what she is doing, angers her. She does not want to totally give it up—it supplies too much that is within her, much that I cannot supply. Against that she rebels, and I can't help it.

Well, after my talk with Rexroth, who had advised and predicted reunion, I had a long talk with her, and told her what concessions I would make—the social ones, mainly—a greater concern for the appearances, and an attempt to participate in some of the urban activities that were necessary to her. She was touched, I believe. For she knew that there were things I could bring her more than anyone else, that Carothers never could touch, a creativity of life, an expression, a concentration of energy, that brought out the best in her own energy, an intensity brought upon more essential ends—all this she admitted, or, rather, herself pronounced. She wanted to return, but could not make that break—Carothers was too much with her yet. If I took that Sonoma farm would I let her come, and be with me again, and see if she could find herself with me again? I said yes. We left on that.

But back here again, in my withdrawal, do I want that? I don't know. I go back and back within myself, plumbing it out. Myself, I mean. Do I want, really, realignment? What is the nature of this lack, that is something apart from her as a person, this need of a relationship, that forms the vacuum that is the chief instability within me? Am I really prepared to make those commitments? There, I was. Back here, I doubt it. Always, I doubt. The great doubter! Nursing my hesitancies! You son of a bitch Everson! You miserable fucked up bastard! Can't you ever be clear and forthright, direct and concise? No. Always tempering everything out, softening it, modulating it, proceeding by half-steps and withdrawals, assimilating, rather than enforcing, no opinions, no directives, a great *perhaps*. Shit. Fah! I eat myself, and its taste is of gall.

Yet how wonderful, really to feel the great impermanence of experience, its wonderful soft modulated quality, to relate thing to thing, to assimilate, pull into the self, and try there, and accept or perhaps reject, and accept again, and see the relatedness of all things, all elements, the one with the other, in the great impermanent flux. Life becomes wholly wonderful and good, a fineness, a rich temperateness, so that all the excesses blend together, and finally emerges something rich and complex, muted and withdrawn. I love that. There are so many sides—the multi-faceted self. Which one will we follow?

I went up to Guerneville. Things had blown up there, and my friend Tyler has bought a wonderful 81-acre farm on a hill overlooking a valley near Sebastapol. It has an apple orchard, and fair sloping vineyard land, seven miles from the sea, glimpsible at times. He wants me to come, and build there in that redwood country. I was enchanted, and said I would, but now don't know, suspicious of "enterprises" after CPS, feeling basically I should build my own place, erect my press there, and make a self-contained life of it. I'll have to wait and see.

I have been studying lately, and would like to come down on a vacation to you this summer, to touch the great books of printing, and cover that field.

But I don't know.

Your letter was good. You have come through much, and are enriched, and carry a mine within you. I am glad for you.

About "Quintet," I don't know if I will be able to bring off that extended work by so laborious a means as the handpress. Perhaps I will become skilled enough. I can't tell.

But would you send on that rich work for me to read again now? I am better adjusted here, and ready for it, and look toward it.

Yours
Bill

February 26, 1946
Los Angeles
ALS, 2 p., 1 sheet

Dear Bill—

It's been a long while since I've had such a long rich letter from you. I rejoice that you are able to tap the deep well & let it flow.

The account of your handpress moved me very much. I shall read that part of your letter to Archer tomorrow, when I go to the Clark Library. Kemper Jr. was in to see me today, asking my advice about his & Eshelman's moving the Untide Press down here.

Even more moving was the episode of seeing Edwa again. I hardly know what to say, except that my heart is with you, whatever you do, wherever you go. Fare well!

By all means, plan to come down here sometime this summer. Most of June I'll be in the East on a library trip. July I'll be here. Part of August we'll be on a ranch in Colorado.

Today I sent you "Quintet" by 1st class registered mail. Please let me know of its safe receipt. I have only an unrevised earlier carbon copy. God knows how it will read to you since you've grown up!

Last weekend I transferred my entire Ritchie collection to the Clark Library.

Am a bit weary. Too much work on the woodpile & in bed. I'll be 40 this year. Whoa!

Yrs affectionately—
Larry

Mar 3, 1946
Cascade Locks
APS

Dear Larry:—
"Quintet" here. Came with your letter. Going into Portland this weekend. More to come.

Bill

March 12,1946
CPS 21 Cascade Locks
ALS, 3 p., 2 sheets

Dear Larry:—
All week "Quintet" sat on my shelf. I did not take it down. I was holding off, waiting for the mellow propitious moment, the amplitude of spirit that would mean the time had come to begin. It never showed. I sickened, took to bed with a slight fever. By week's end the unrest had thickened to guilt, and that worsened matters. Then, last night, the balance broke over. I took it down and began to read. A page or two and I was in, the mood spreading and rippling; all was well.

This will explain the delay. I apologize. Perhaps I can make it up with what will follow. For, Larry, your book will stand. It is a breathing book, and the breath you have blown into it is the breath of your life. That is the thing about it. It quickens and grows with the palpability of direct experience. It has the naivete of experience itself, a quality that our more astute gentlemen of the university quarterlies often refer to as "embarrassing." You go into it without shame, and reveal yourself, and stand forth as you feel, and you live. The reader at Knopf's was undoubtedly "embarrassed." This is the self-conscious age, and we mask our literature in a welter of abstractions, intellectualize it, and become ashamed, in time, of the simple and unabashed.

And the amazing thing to me is how you have done it. It is a wonderful thing to sense this clean revelation, the act of the touch emerging clear and undiluted, the body quivering in its expectancy, and the taste of that reality, loaded with anticipation, there on the mouth. We have plenty of sensualists in our writing. We can be hard-boiled about it. That's very well.

But the thing is, this is no sensualist's account. It is rather, to paraphrase Miller, the wisdom of the flesh. And it is brought about not wholly by the touch itself, but the whole vibrant breath of the life. The book evokes. I know of no work where this particular quality manifests itself. It's like Lawrence, but different. The MacLeish poem you quote, "Memory Green," has something of that in it. A ripe expectancy. A subtle sampling of the air, the nostrils aquiver in that deep tantalizing test. The atmosphere rings. The sounds drift in to the ear itself, not simply to the page of type to remain entrapped there. And over it all pervades the sense of Europe, with its ancient cultural ripeness, its deep fulfillment, and the young American, keyed to a pitch, on the verge of participation.

I am able to see this work better than I had before, and I think it comes through with something it did not have even then. It emerges as an act of great faith. Faith to oneself, to what one is. In this world of guilt, that act is of inestimable value. That act of truth is the most difficult feat facing any writer today. I believe that. And how many fizzle and shrivel away, in what is essentially an attempt at other-selfness, something one is not. The formula is to *remove* the self, to *project* the creative act. And it always fails. Or so rarely succeeds. But you, who somehow have always known how to live, have learned what few of the others have ever acquired, the simple testament of faith, and the revelation of the self.

So. Rest assured about this book. Never doubt it. It stands athwart our time. It is a book that many will laugh at, will even ridicule, as they ridiculed Lawrence. How droll! They will say, how utterly droll! But I tell you never doubt it. What emerges in that book is worth the tribe of them, ten times over. To ridicule that impulse is to ridicule life itself, as they constantly do. I understand this better than I ever did before, and it is in this context that "Quintet" stands greatest. I salute you!

By week's end I will have dispatched the book back by express, glad to have read it again. To touch and be touched. Like your very hand, Larry.

Bill

P.S. I remember the cut-out portion of the fourth episode. I think I favored that cutting, did I not? Now I don't know. For it seems as if the Paris episode that follows might be needful, a showing that the man had not yet learned Madeleine's wisdom, a wisdom taught him only at last in the Deborah episode. And somewhere lost I remember a poignant conclusion wherein the man places his hands on a cold table top and orders bread and milk; that was very good, a simple eloquent conclusion. I miss it.

(This kind of thing agonizes a writer, I know. Friends pleading for special inclusions etc. Your own sense will tell you, and what you end up with, I'll stand by.)

B.

March 19, 1946
Cascade Locks
APS

Dear Larry:—

The ms. did not go out over the weekend with the camp car as I expected and will be a little delayed. Letter from Bentley today telling me of his forthcoming exhibit of prints. He is going to keep his press, and I think was relieved that I found one.

Bill

Mar 29, 1946
Los Angeles
APS

Dear Bill—

Ms. received. Forgive my not acknowledging your heart-warming letter. Have been a bit low with a cold, but am beginning to recover. Will write next week, I hope. In the meantime, affectionate greetings!

Larry

April 6, 1946
Los Angeles
ALS, 3 p.

Dear Bill—

Just a line to let you know I'm okay! Suffered an inevitable reaction from the height of January & the depth of February. Very little impulse to write; not even journals or letters. Reading much. Enrollment to 10,000. Great pressure on Library. Love every aspect of my work—books & people, people & books. Rich & satisfying work. Immersed in it, as refuge from the cloying emotional reaction I'm experiencing.

Newell wants you to come to his ranch. He was going to write you. I hope he did.

Fay & I to Berkeley tomorrow on the coast Daylight, back Tuesday night on the Lark. I on business, she for the trip. I'm getting to be a regular commuter!

How are you, Bill?

Your letter is tremendous. I just re-read it for the first time since it came, nearly a month ago. God bless you for your perception and your faith. Coming at this very time, when if ever in my life I had occasion to doubt my own integrity, it meant more than I can tell you.

When I think now how I risked everything—job, family, my own life—for the ecstasy of touch & vibration, I shudder. I tight-roped a profound abyss. Here I am at the other side, still fearful & trembling. Yes, I have plunged into library work &

reading; & free daylight hours into sawing & splitting our next winter's wood. I have eucalyptus, orange, carob, avocado, oak—all hauled from the campus dump. Immense satisfaction.

I have every confidence in the future, when I digest this bellyfull of experience. I have had a profound lesson in human nature & behavior, which will profit both my life & my writing. Of this I am certain.

I do want to see you & read you the record of January.

Write!

yrs!
Larry

April 14, 1946
CPS 21, Cascade Locks
ALS, 5 p., 3 sheets

Dear Larry:—

It is Sunday afternoon: a pure day. I write from my little cabin back of camp, which I assumed 10 days ago when my friends, the Jadikers, were released. I am deeply at rest, for the most part. Here, a kind of preview I hope of what will obtain after release, I am building up the simple patterns of life by which I hope to exist: the ritualizing of the daily affairs of life, an attitude I learned from my friend Clayton James, who has great insight in these things. The Rising. The Dressing. The Laying of the Fire. The Preparation of the Food. These habits the self objectifies in its solitude, and makes significant. I finish my nightwatch duties at six (and the mornings are wonderful, a clear early light spilling westward down the Gorge and that resilient river, a riot of birds, no, a conversation of birds, interrogation and answer, call and reply, and off over the river a fight of ruffianly crows gabbling among themselves. Across the gorge the hulk of Wind Mountain, loose, a heap of rubble, long slides like aprons about it, and farther beyond it the huge snag-patches of the burns, where earlier fires have left only the forests of naked trunks, bleached white now, and from this distance whole areas like a kind of stubble, a grizzled quality, fascinating to me. I learned it well in the long days replanting those wastes at Waldport. They are very beautiful, though most people consider them the scenic bane). Then I blanket up my windows and retire, to rise about three in the afternoon; I now prepare a simple meal on my little stove (I no longer eat milk or eggs, as well as meat) usually of dried fruit and toast and coffee; light up my pipe; and prepare myself for the day. Here at this point a wonderful creative quality emerges. I am perfectly rested. I have eight hours of leisure before me, and, for the first time in three years, for the first time in my life, really, I am alone. I usually write. If not, I pick through the latest magazines and reviews, browsing here and there. (I have practically abandoned sustained reading, it is too engrossing, too consuming of the whole mind. I become the characters or the author, and have difficulty reestablishing myself.) At five-thirty I go down for my big meal at camp. Thereafter I either return to my cabin, or listen to some music, or, as of late, work with Eshelman finishing the Patchen (we have two more runs, then all the assembling). At ten my duties begin. I complete my first round in half an hour and my time is my own till two. After the two-o'clock round (these are fire-stoking rounds; I tend 25 stoves) I clean the kitchen, mop the floor, and prepare food for the cooks to assemble the project lunches. That done, it's time for me to prepare my breakfast. At five I make my final round and rouse up the cooks. At six I rouse up the waiters and go home. A light schedule, really. And the hours in the cabin, in the afternoons, as now the light slants eastward through the first and the leafing alders, (for spring is just arriving here) are magical.

I was a bit nervous at your silence following my letter, for I began to think I had hurt your feelings in some way, as one can, or had in some other way said something that made it difficult for you to reply. (Either blame or praise has this capacity I find.)

The "Quintet" was good to read. Jim Harman came by one night on his way from prison last month, we sat the night out. I gave him "Quintet" to read. You remember his letter on the other piece. He did not appear to like it as well as the previous one, though he had been up for two nights and was hardly himself under the impact of release. He spoke of such things as the woman's body—well-tuned instrument simile, which has been done so much before. I maintain that the general qualitative temper of the work raises it above such limitations. Jim is still, I think, following the structural aspects of literature, the Joycean objective, as, indeed, is the best, or rather, the most rigorous modern prose application. But it is becoming more and more apparent to me that that is a blind alley, which may be ok for the curbing of unruly creative energy, but has become a substitute for energy. The methodization of the sensibility! What your book does is simply and delightfully concern itself with the business of feeling. Most modern writing is done with the eye on the page, with words as surfaces, mirrorlike. But what you do, and herein lies your strength and weakness, is go through the page to the event, to the experience. One feels as if you are reliving the experience as well as rewriting it, an exposing of oneself to the experience and a dependence of the innermost self to evoke up the terminology. It is, I am convinced, the basic and fundamental way to write. Whatever one may construct the other way, there are whole areas of experience, and precisely the ones in which you deal, that can be rendered profoundly in no other way. This above is a simplification, of course. We both go back over, writing and rewriting. But the fundamental process comes first.

Yes, I received the excellent offer from Gordon [Newell]. It is a tempting one. If I knew more about the immediate situation I could understand more clearly what to do. I think mostly of the Bay region. Though I don't think I should go with the Tylers either in Sonoma county, as I once had planned. I am really pretty much up in the air about release. Wouldn't worry so much if I didn't have so much stuff that should be settled someplace. Oh well, something will work out. I am in such fine fettle I refuse to become burdened down with all these future concerns. I have been a worrier all my life and I'm going to try and break it.

Your letter trembles with a kind of amazement, the fearful, backward-bending gaze over the gulf just traversed. Good man; good man. I would say it whichever way you went. For the thing is to *know,* to look back, to see the consequence, and to emerge, as you have. Good man. I'll be down before long and get it all first hand. My heart's with you.

Bill

April 19, 1946
Cascade Locks
APS

Dear Larry:—

Dahlstrom Exhibit announcement received with thanks. Had thought to call my press the Equinox, after the seasons of balance and moderation, the equalizers, autumnal and vernal, the great suspension before the soar into summer and the plunge into fall. But I hear there is a commercial press in NY by that name. Can you confirm this? Three more weeks.

Bill

Jeffers' *Medea* is a masterpiece!

April 25, 1946
Los Angeles
ALS, 5 p.

Dear Bill—

Your card here today. Equinox Press would be a wonderful name. As you mention, there was a semi-commercial outfit in NY called the Equinox Cooperative Press. Apparently it has folded. They are not listed as having published any books in 1945, to date. If you want me to, I can find out for certain.

Yesterday I met Newell briefly at Dawson's Book Shop downtown. He is still eager for you to come & said he will write you again. Sheets came in last week for a visit.

I saw the Patchen book [*An Astonished Eye Looks Out of the*

Air] among the Rounce & Coffin entries. How about sending me a few copies with bill? It appears to be a beautiful tour de force of designer & printer—& quite unreadable. I have excellent eyes, but I would hesitate risking them on Patchen's pages. Spare the reader, lads, & remember that rubrication & embellishment & overprinting all make a book interesting to look at it, difficult to read. I have been increasingly suspicious of Patchen, of his surrealist-typographic hysteria.

Your idyllic letter came last week. Your routine appeals to me. You have stripped away the unessential. I know what you mean by the ritualizing of the daily routines. In my own way I have practiced it somewhat.

Christopher Isherwood called on me today at the Library to get some books. I liked him.

We saw the Aldingtons off to Jamaica. Shall miss them greatly.

I appreciate your further remarks about "Quintet." I cannot write other than I do. I have little or no mind, no power of analysis, no interest in complex characters or plots. The rich life of the body & the senses is what I hold to be sacred. No mysticism or claptrap or apology or fear, such as convulsed Lawrence, will I tie to the tail of my tale.

I don't want any audience in my lifetime. Miller is bitter about his audience. If he chose to, he would spend 4 hours a day replying to correspondents. The cranks & hysterics & lechers & sensualists are drawn to him. The mucky mass of Bern Porter's *Circle*. What shit he and Leite are shovelling about. I am sick to death of all this surrealist free expression. You & I know that one learns how to write first by living & then by offering the sacrifice of disciplined labor on the altar of one's life. So be it.

I am still in crisis. Hurt Fay so very deeply. I howl with reflected anguish. My responsibilities are many & mingled. My very strengths are my weakness.

I do want to see you. Do you think you will come down before I go east on June 3? I'll be away 19 days. My niece Marcia is living with us until she returns to England to be married.

Just read two very moving books about painting (novels) by

Max White—*Tiger Tiger* (1940) & *In the Blazing Light* (Goya) 1946. Just as you say, very little sustained reading these days. I demand increasingly a richness of experience & a depth of awareness & find it all too rarely.

Bonne nuit!
Larry

May 6, 1946
Cascade Locks
(Cabin)
ALS, 6 p., 3 sheets

Dear Larry:—

Wanted to answer your fine letter sooner but couldn't collect my wits. I have been going through one of those great revolutions when everything falls away, and is exposed, and has to be reformulated again. As I said, I rarely read a long work anymore, but someone put into my hands Wilhelm Reich's *The Function of the Orgasm* (not as clinical as it sounds by any means). I don't think I have ever had such a profound revelation before. My life jumped up at me, naked, suddenly revealed; and all the chaos, the inner agony, the painful search, all seen and understood. The great sexual violence is seen. The pounding drive. All, all exposed. This is the kind of thing that most men struggle with all their lives, those that have it, and never know. Now, in my thirty-third year, I have been shown. And I thank the fates.

May releases will be held back a bit by the moving up of some June men. I do not expect it before the 20th.

My mind is beginning to clutch right and left in a shiver of anticipatory fright. Three and a half years! And what years! How consequential! How full! But I found myself in them; and I have no regrets.

These last days, weeks, have been charged with energy. Here in the little cabin in the dogwood and maple, I brew my coffee and eat my bread. That great poem rushes out of me day after day. I double back on it constantly, picking it up, knitting it together. And the energy abides, flows out unabated. I don't know where it comes from. Look at this letter. I can hardly hold down the pen.

The Patchen was not done when we sent those copies. In December we salvaged some forty sheets from the wreckage and made up a few for Patchen. These you saw were of that group. The last tint-block of the book was printed short, so we overlapped the fold to hide it. Foolishly. For that threw the frontal pages off. The index for instance is jimmied. So now that we have got paper and finished printing we have re-folded all those mis-folded sheets, and are going to send the whole edition into Portland to be top-trimmed. The new copies when they are done will be better than those you saw. But not much. The book is a typographical atrocity, to my way of thinking. Well, maybe not an atrocity. I'm just down on it after all these months. You're right, really, it's a *tour-de-force,* and nothing else. But then that's all the poetry is, so why not? One thing: the tint block, done by a commercial press, was run far too dark. If it had been just the faint shadowy background it was supposed to be—almost undiscernible—things would have looked better. We learned a great deal from doing this book.

So we'll send copies when they're ready. You have money with us yet I believe.

Your letters constantly amaze me. I saw on my trip there something of your librarian's world, the world of executive responsibility. And yet your letters have never changed; they are as fresh and honest and unpretentious as always. And as frequent. How can you retain all that, and find the time, and remain your old self? It is a fine thing.

I do not expect to be down before June 3.

I have received many fine things from you in my years in CPS and I'm grateful. The Rilke you sent at first was one of the great events of my growth, and the little Baudelaire. Now comes the Wilde, and last of all the excellent little Marvell, in which you have managed to retain the feeling of "period" so well. This will be, I think, my favorite edition of this wonderful poem. (Amusing experience: In the *Explicator* someone analyzed the figure "iron gates of life" as a reference to the vagina.

I could not restrain writing and pointing out that if one is going to go in for anatomical puns, what happens to the second line above that one!)

If you could find out about the Equinox Press I would appreciate it. The name seems a natural, though now that it's been used seems a bit tarnished. Yet it conjured all I felt about my reaction to and reasons for the press.

Well, I poise for the great adventure. All life opens. The great forces unfold, reveal, and we see a way, and go toward it. Where the spirit calls, there we go. All my life I have been timid, hesitant, fearful. No more, I hope. Reich showed me why. Let those terrible chains fall away. Let me emerge to my fullest self. Who should fear, in so wonderful a world? The river below me, the great river of the Northwest, the Columbia, rolls to the sea. So let me, too, to my destination.

Bill

To My Ancient Enemy

(doleful stanzas in the Shropshire manner penned after reading *The Function of the Orgasm* by Wilhelm Reich)

Father, underneath the crust,
You breathe the old ancestral dust;
Accept the tribute and the tears
Of one who fought you thirty years;
Who crawled between you and your wife,
Ate your food and marred your life.
Though I made miserable your past,
Know now you have won out at last.
She for whom we rivals warred
You now can claim beneath the sward,
And may resume the full embrace
Undivided by my face.
When she died I broke the band,
Shunned your face and spurned your hand;
And yet when you encoffined lay
Was drawn eight hundred miles away.
Within your loins exhausted lie
The sons who never will defy.
The one who did must now acclaim
Your heritage, and wear your name.

Though you precede me to the grave
Be sure that I am still your slave
And flinch to hear your strident voice
Decree my portion and my choice.
Grin in the ground. You are not dead.
Your old commandment holds my head.
Only your body empty lies:
Your anger aches behind my eyes.

May 25, 1946
Los Angeles
ALS, 2 p.

Glad you like the Marvell!

Dear Bill—

Your fine letter of early this month has gone unanswered because I was laid up for 2 weeks with flu. A series of annoying colds during the spring climaxed in one bad one, & I found myself completely exhausted. The longest I have ever been laid up. The first week I managed to get around a bit, for we have had to find a house. Our landlord returns sooner than he planned, & so we have had to buy a small place, south of the Univ., near Culver City. Bad fortune.

I worried about this & at seeing my library work pile up. Next Sunday our second annual Founder's Day at Clark. Hell of a lot of preliminary work. And then the eastern trip to do. I leave a week from tomorrow.

My strength returned & I have had a good week back at work.

The great consolation while sick was in reading Casanova. I have the complete Machen translation, text & notes, in the 8-vol. Ltd. Ed. Club set, published in 1940. I have long been a Casanovist, but this is the first time I have read the complete English edition. Have been collecting editions of him at the Library, with the aid of Guy Endore, who has written the best book in English about Casanova.

What incomparable memoirs! Swarming with life. A veritable encyclopedia of life. If you have never read this complete edition, you have a tremendous experience ahead of you.

I shall look up Reich on the orgasm. We have the book, I know, for I remember signing a purchase order for it about a year ago. You impress me!

Try to let me hear from you before I leave, Monday, June 3.

Affectionately,
Larry

May 29,1946
Cascade Locks
ALS, 1 p.

Dear Larry:—

Have just come back from sailing on the Columbia, in a fine light boat made by some of the fellows here. My first sail. The river was wonderful, high swells under a brisk wind, the boat clipping along, taking them with a clean graceful lift. The Gorge, too, from the River, is superb, its great cliffs and buttes flushed with fading light. We came back in shadow, the sun down, but the walls still tinged above us. Very good. The boat leaves for good tomorrow.

On May 13 I participated in the nationwide C.O. Strike, and in retaliation our releases are being held. Two days ago the May releases came through, mine not among them. Rumors are that we will be held indefinitely. This camp closes within a month and I have no idea where I'll be sent. A bad break. I was almost out. I could smell it; taste it; feel it. Then pouf! The strike, the swift retaliation, and here I am. Months, maybe. So be it.

I have been pretty unstable the last few months, swinging rapidly from great emotional charges to glum depressions. Ever since demobilization began the camps have been a hell of a place to live—charged with unrest and uncertainty. We're pawns, all of us.

I've seen and looked through the L.E.C. Casanova, but never read it all: it's fascinating.

I met a fine girl in Portland the other day and I felt the bottom going out from under me again!

My plan, as I finally developed it was this: Go to Berkeley, find a place for the press, set it up temporarily, learn what I could from Bentley who has the summer free, study the lore at U.C. and maybe next winter or spring move out to the land. Now, that's all off. Bentley will probably leave the Bay and I'll have to fight out the problems myself.

Good luck East.
Bill

June 13, 1946
Cascade Locks
ALS, 7 p., 4 sheets

Dear Larry:—

You are in New York yet, but I write anyway.

Going through the camp library, the other day I chanced across Aldington's *Life for Life's Sake,* and I thought of you, and your occasional comments about seeing him in Los Angeles. Yesterday being restless and directionless I took it out and began to read it, chiefly as a commentary upon the teens, that period of literary revival that has always been of interest to me.

It is a pretty good book. I was intrigued by the childhood sketches and early London life. I find this very true of most contemporary autobiography. These books always begin with rich immediate responses to childhood and early manhood experiences, and then as they approach the day the pen is waking, get more general, more sketchy, more cautious, more modest, more—characterless. Aldington is not as severe an offender in this respect as some others, but it tends to apply. Generally speaking I liked the book—was certainly absorbed with it. I began it midafternoon yesterday and read right on through my whole nightwatch round last night, but being a slow reader and possessing tiring eyes I had to put the last two chapters off till this afternoon.

But it was sometime last night that I read the episode on the wine trip in Italy that I looked up from the page and said:

"Why, this is Powell!" And from then on I understood the man better and your friendship with him. The same lust for life is manifest: the glory in the great past and fullness of Europe; the treasure hunt of experience on the continent. Your pages tend to read alike, in that the evocative place-names flash up, the details of landscape, terrain, sky, foliage, sound. All the rich harmonious life that must have been Europe in what he calls The Great Armistice. Your account placed in the narrative form is more immediate and sensuous, but I would wager his own narrative work is like that.

In general he is a good writer, though he has momentary lapses (for me) and I like his attitudes, though I should have preferred a greater development of the ideational autobiography as well as the physical one. Maybe that comes out in other works. I didn't get much of a feeling about the development of mind, and by the last he was wheeling about Europe so rapidly, changing companions, etc., I had a hard time keeping up. It was like his earlier criticism of motor-rides. Things went too fast.

I liked his attitude toward other writers, not fawning on his gods, and pretty objective, though here again often the complexity of experience was brushed aside for the single commentary, the pen-stroke that tells just a bit, Aldington mocking behind his hand, as if he were thinking "I could say a hell of a lot more, but why get embroiled?"

But his great human virtues were paramount: honesty, courage, loyalty, directness. You felt a sense of intellectual integrity, the writer in the best sense of that word, the courage to stand behind the pen, not fawn for favor, and not afraid to speak. And a concern for the tradition of literature, the combination of scholar and writer that I find wholly admirable, though I cannot judge his success.

But I guess what I envy both you and him for the most is your capacity to enjoy. Not consistently, for I am largely satisfied with my life, and find it wonderful, but after reading your writing, and now after reading his, I am touched somewhat by that lack of the wonderful vibrancy of the living experience of enjoyment that has been less and less within me. I felt it for awhile in the first of marriage, when I found *Lady Chatterley,* and you, and tobacco, and wine, and the flowering of touch, and the tangibility of that wondrous woman who came to mean so much to me.

But the War stopped that—not immediately, but gradually, a kind of slow alteration from the exultation of *San Joaquin* (though it contained forebodings) to the rigor of *Poems MCMXLII* it became a grappling for the meaning of the self, and it went through many phases. The War forced choices I could not avoid, and such was my mind that I found it necessary to apply the consequences of one phase of my life to every other. The "Invocation" in *Poems MCMXLII,* which is my chief expression of this problem, follows most of the *War Elegies* as in my life the practice of vegetarianism followed my acceptance of pacifism.

I am not by nature an ascetic, but something in me constantly drives me that way. Through pacifism and vegetarianism I arrive at, of all things, anarchism. Not out of the sense of restriction that brought me to the others, the conception that what I can do is determined by what I cannot do, the whole "do unto others" belief, which all good men hold, driving me in a kind of intellectual rigorousness back to a narrower and narrower program of action, until sometimes I think I can hardly move.

But beside it goes this wild outpouring of expression which is really my only value to other men: the mysterious self that I cannot explain, that is not of the ME of logical procedure and consistency. I suspect constantly that I am very inconsistent, my logical mind betrayed by this upwelling self, unpredictable and largely untamed, to which I owe so much. And it is its revelation that carries me forward into ever expanding areas, so that as the regions the puritanical mind cut off for me in the physical sense decrease, the regions of the soul, shall I say, that the metaphysical mind proceeds into, forever enlarge. I find myself living more and more intensely. Richly, in one sense, but not the wonderful bodily richness I was moving into ten years ago; not the clear, untroubled enjoyment, like a good wine, the amplitude of sex, its rich abundance, its clean fragrance, its deep-rooted grace. I draw on these things of a fulsome past constantly, but extract them *toward* something else, toward an illumination, a blaze, a revelation I cannot understand, that is out there, toward which my life is converging, and which I never fully knew. It is not so much that I strive toward it, or yearn for it, but rather that I am moving steadily in that direction, from revelation to revelation, as if each disclosure is a confirmation, and an additional guarantee.

It is in relation to this that the Reich book was of such revolutionary consequence to me. It threw me momentarily back ten years, in a wild pagan rush of the senses; I felt again the rich rejoicing in the body's holding, its great capacity for pleasure and joy. The experience quelled the religious mysticism that had lately formed my mode of approach, by revealing the nature of what yearning was there. But I find that the month that has followed that reading, the complexity of emotion involved in the strike, my subsequent penalty, the crushing reversal of several anticipated months in camp, a wholly bewildering turn of events that left me intellectually dazed, followed by a slow picking up again, piece by piece, a synthesis, a clearer understanding of myself—all this has taken me back again, not to the religiousness but still an intense metaphysical awareness, a kind of understanding, that has been of inestimable value to me, and made the whole process one of the most significant of my life so far. This is about all I can say by way of explanation. I seize at it in poems: in two days I broached a series of ten that form a new direction and advance, after the three and a half years' burden of the "Chronicle." And I have just followed this with three to my friend Clayton James, who has seen fit to break with me in one of those great human events that are among our most poignant experiences. But everywhere the great feeling of consequence, discovery, and advance continues, and I follow it out.

Things generally look brighter. Yesterday word came from the Church agencies in Washington that probably our releases will come through in June, rather than the penalties first imposed—first of six, then of three months' withholding. I believe nothing as yet. I try to live in the day, not in the future, and find what I can as it unfolds. It is hard to do at this stage, but it has proved to be the only rewarding approach.

Somehow the Aldington book takes me back to C.F. MacIntyre, whom I met on my last trip South, and of whom I had wanted to write, but put off till a propitious moment—not now, but it must suffice.

I was quite surprised. I had expected a man of great stricture, intellectual rigorousness, severe thought, and brittle personality. The closeness of the writing of the Rilke notes, the severity of personal judgement, and the intellectual display of the 1938 *Poems* led me to such an expectation. I cannot for the life of me equate these works with the man I found. For here was great personal warmth, friendliness, and even naivete, and far from the sophisticated urbanity I expected, there was rather a bewildering crudity, or even coarseness, that I could not understand. I like the man, don't mistake me, nor was I offended by anything he said or did, but I was simply astounded between expectation and realization. What I liked most about him was his devotion to literature. He seemed a relic of a past when a literary man was a literary man and no social or political clap-trap mixed up in it. As the evening developed I perceived him as really a lost Romantic, what I thought would be strictures turned out to be merely opinions, and some of them incredibly wild. His personal judgements were delivered with an air of such ingenuous dogmatism that one immediately looked for the personal motivation behind it and found it easily enough. The man is terribly insecure. Every rejection he makes is a form of self-protection. He feels life slipping out from under him and his mark not yet made. Everything reverts back in time (and it is never very long) to his own accomplishments. His attacks on other translators, for instance, intended to be devastating, turn out to be merely ludicrous. He would say: "At least my translation is honest," and fling himself on notebook and volume to prove it. When we checked the dictionary for a word, and his rendition would turn out to be as clearly erroneous as his rival's, he would say with an honest but amazing blandness: "Hell, a man has to make a poem of it! I've got to be poetic!" Wonderful! We spent a long evening together. Halfway through a young soldier came in with a girl; some friend of Mac's, knew the family, etc. And caused a minor confusion in Mac to have a C.O. and an officer in the room at the same time. He was constantly incredulous about certain aspects of the C.O. stand. The adherence to principle on anything but literary matters seemed to have no meaning for him. All evening long he ducked and dodged and grasped at ideational straws to save himself. Everything was turned in some way to his advantage, a mode so necessary to him, so honestly necessary to him, I could not be offended.

But what energy! All evening long he was up and down, flinging himself from his chair, pouncing on a book for points, gulping down long breaths with a great groan, shaking his head fiercely as if he had got himself into a cul de sac he couldn't resolve and would scotch the whole problem with that great groaning shake of the head and a gulp of the ever-ready wine bottle.

My presence there was a great stimulus to him, I'm sure of it, for if there is anything I exude it is sympathy, and that man needs it. I hope wildly he will be a great success yet. I do. I want him to be fulfilled, that raw chaos in him swung into certainty, realized. He wants it so badly; needs it so much.

And how friendly he is, really, behind all the embittered rejection. There was not one poet, when the officer asked him, living today whom he could find wholehearted pleasure in. None he could admire; none he could respect. He attacked Rexroth on the ridiculous grounds that he lived off his wife. He attacked Miller I forget on what grounds, but his trip there was unsuccessful and he came away bitter. Over and over: rejection, rejection, rejection.

Yet help? My god he wants to help you if you show the least interest. He offered to lend me his only copy of his Baudelaire translations because I was interested. He wanted me to come back, to stay the night, to go over some other stuff the next day.

I left about three—I had to get back to the Watkins', and the next day I got involved in the mad chase for the handpress that took me right up till train time. I never got back, nor have written, but I mean to. And if I ever get down there and he's still about I'm going out again. He has more vitality than half the university put together, and I wouldn't have missed him. My friend.

And I meant to write of Scott Greer whom I've seen but that will have to wait.

Bill

June 15, 1946
Boston, Mass.
APS

Dear Bill—
I got your letter before leaving LA June 3. Have been in Wash., N.Y., Cambridge; & am leaving Boston in a few moments on night train to Buffalo, where the ALA conference meets. Will fly home June 20. I hope your release was not long delayed. I'll write from LA.

Larry

June 25, 1946
CPS 21
ALS, 3 p.

Dear Larry:—
My release has not come through but I can't say I have too much cause for regret. This is chiefly due to the creation of an extensive body of writing the past six weeks; and to the performance, in Portland, of a cycle of the Beethoven quartets, by the Budapest. Unfortunately I missed the first of the five programs, which contained the 3rd and 12th, but I have heard the subsequent three, and will go in tomorrow to hear the final one, in which the 9th (Razumovsky No. 3) and the great 14, in A sharp minor.

This whole experience has been of the utmost importance to me, and I cannot begin to describe my reaction. I had never heard a great quartet in action; I was blest with front row seats, and fair acquaintance with some of the numbers from phonograph records (14, 15 & 16 I know well from many hearings). But things emerged that I had never experienced before, and to participate in this kind of interaction, wherein the sound that had always issued mechanically from a phonograph, became the product and the activity of four sensitive and very much alive men, who are capable of exhilaration and honest sweat, is unforgettable. Not only that, to hear the quartets together, to seize their range and breadth of scope, is itself an experience of great value. And every concert is finished off with one of the great ones; last Wednesday it was the 15th, a wonder of complexity; Friday it was that magnificent No. 16, which for me is surely one of the great human statements; and Sunday it was No. 13, with the original finale: The Grosse Fugue. I had never heard this piece, and I do not believe I will ever forget it. Something obtained here of great rarity, and I am not sure that what went on was in the nature of art. The demands of the thing are so enormous that the medium of the quartet seems stretched beyond its limits to render it. The players had that aspect of men struggling against insuperable forces. Their rising to meet it took on the aspects of heroism—men pitted against gigantic elements. And the music encompassed them, encompassed us, all of us swept up in—not the torrent but rather the whirlwind. It was as if the universe were splitting at the seams, splitting with dissonance, that any minute we would be transformed, and our fates lay in the hands of these four heroically struggling men, and only they had the capacity to save us. I have not really got over it yet.

Most of the June releases are in but no strikers as yet. We expect them daily, but they hold off. Camp is scheduled to close the first, but one never does close on time.

Since the strike set-back I have written three series of poems—one long one of ten, two short ones of three each, and all of an advanced nature, moving into areas of thought and expression that are wholly new for me, and consequently difficult. But not uncertain. I feel my capacities are at their highest point now.

I got your card from Boston (I believe) and was pleased to hear from you. It must have been a fine jaunt.

Sincerely
Bill

Men with 24 months' service are at least eligible for release. I now have one of the longest records of any man left in CPS—41 months, exceeded only by one or two strikers in other camps with 42.

June 29, 1946
Los Angeles
ALS, 4 p., 2 sheets

Dear Bill—

I returned a week ago & found your rich letter about Aldington & Mac & yourself. I cannot tell you how glad it made me. The Aldingtons went to Jamaica a couple of months ago & I am getting fine letters from him. They will go next to Argentina, & eventually to France. Two years he was working in Hollywood & at the Library. I came to have real affection for him as a man, & great admiration as a writer. He works with enormous energy & efficiency at whatever he tackles. Read his two novels, *Death of a Hero* & *All Men Are Enemies*, in that order. Do you want me to send copies? Aldington is the most truly & widely cultured man I have ever met. The 2d war increased his bitterness. He hates mankind en masse.

Your remarks about MacIntyre are good & true. He is so insecure. He & Ezra Pound have a great deal in common! You can understand now why Ritchie, Newell, & I have been loyal to Mac, ever since we first sat in his class, September 1924. He needs more than anything to be freed from his erudition, to throw off all influences & write as Carlyle MacIntyre. Now & then, throughout his career, he has done this. I want to make a selection of these poems. Last Christmas when in Berkeley I had four good sessions with Mac. I was impressed by his capacity for devoted work. Did he show you the little colored drawings he has been doing? Did you see Newell's beautiful carved leaf on the mantel?

In the book I am working on I have tried to "capture" Mac. The La Crescenta cabin—remember? And back from Europe I now meet him again & comes the flood & wipes him out. Mac is terribly curious to know what I have written about him! I am holding out until the book is finished. God knows when that will be! Life is passing by so swiftly. How long am I to have?

My Eastern trip was entirely successful. I flew for the first time. Home from Chicago on the Constellation in 8 hours. Tremendous! Washington, New York, Cambridge, Buffalo.

Free from my office responsibilities & from my family. Good to do this now & then. In New York I bought for the Library over 100 unpublished D. H. Lawrence letters, mostly to Oriole of Florence, who published *Lady C.* These letters are written during the printing & after publication of the book. I hope to publish them in a book, together with an account of the reception & influence of *Lady C.* Together with *Ulysses* I believe it one of the most influential books of our time. On me, the most. These are marvelous letters.

Yesterday I talked to my staff for an hour about my trip. I have now to write a letter to the faculty. I shall be at the Library through July. We hope to move early in August, then drive the family to Fay's aunt's ranch in N.W. Colorado. We were there in 1940. Quaking aspen & trout stream country.

In September the Pacific Northwest Library assn. meets in Vancouver. I hope to fly up & back & in October fly to Washington for another professional meeting. Perhaps you will be in Berkeley or thereabouts in the autumn. That's when we might get together. I hope this finds you with knowledge of your release.

Affectionately
Larry

July 5, 1946
Minersville, Calif.
ALS, 2 p., 1 sheet

Dear Larry:—

Your letter today, forwarded from Cascade Locks, is the first one I have received at this new address. The day after I wrote the enclosed letter our papers arrived—but they were not releases, they were transfers, and to the notorious Minersville, "The Alcatraz of CPS." You will recall from the papers it was the order to transfer here issued to two men at Glendora that precipitated the strike there, which spread in time to the Locks and to me, and has now served the ironic purpose of depositing me here rather than them. By such strange machinations do we progress.

But it is not bad here. The slowdown strike, begun last year and still in force, has not been participated in by either we six from Cascade Locks, nor the nine sent here at the closing of Lapine, Ore. Most of the original strong men for whom this camp was created are now out—by one means or another. And save for a deliberate curtailment of food, which is irritating rather than actually injuring, things are not much different. I'm glad to be out from under the double-standard imposed by the church, and things are much more clear-cut. We know here exactly where we stand.

I am not slowdowning for various philosophical reasons, and because on arrival I was told word had come from Selective Service that I could re-apply for release on July 10—amounting to a 70 day penalty for my strike. After that, it should take about a month before the discharge finally comes through. This release was stipulated to be contingent upon a satisfactory performance of work, so I am cooperating sufficiently to get by. But not as I did at Waldport and the Locks. For three-and-a-half years I worked seriously and well for the government, and I'm through. From now on it gets only what it can squeeze out of me, and no more.

We're located in the Trinity National Forest northwest of Redding, on the east side of the coast range. We arrived here only July 1, and I haven't had time to do any exploring, but the country is thickly wooded, hilly, hot and dry. Nearby are the spectacular Trinity Alps, but out of sight of this camp.

It's good to get in California again, the heat and the clarity. I cannot believe that life in Oregon is over. It happened so quickly, the three-and-a-half years suddenly ended, gone down the great sluiceway into the past, and all dissolved. But not forgotten. The mark is on me. I am shaped by it, bent but bigger, and bad as they were I would not have traded a year of it. Surely this is the best attribute of a life: that one is happy in his past. As long as that continues, one remains whole and sane.

So complete has been the cleavage of this change that I cannot pick up the various threads of your letter, taken up, as it is, with the elements of which I wrote from Oregon. I will try to do that later, and say a bit more. I'm still in a vacuum here, unable to write, for the most part, unable to really think creatively, or make the necessary assimilation. But all that will come.

Bill

July 8, 1946
Los Angeles
ALS, 2 p., 1 sheet

I want to read your new poems.
Have you copies you can send?

Dear Bill—

A quick word of greeting to you, again on California soil. Welcome! Your two letters sang amidst the great pile of Monday morning mail. I leaned back & savored them, there in my office this morning, and paused to look to the wall where I've just hung two gorgeous eggplant paintings by Parrish. How long ago that exhibit seems! Do you remember seeing the eggplants? I believe we hung all three of them as a sort of vegetable triptych!

Saturday I went to the Newells' for the day & read Gordon some of your recent letters. They sold their Sur land & bought 160 more acres of mountain land nearly contiguous to their Malibu home. A wonderful North Slope of chaparral & trees & secret springs. Newell is in better shape; seems to have resolved his domestic discord.

Your account of the Beethoven cycle moved me. Several years ago we heard it at Occidental, & since then I have been collecting the recorded quartets, & now have all but four. I remember on your last visit to us in the Glen we played the 1st Razumovsky & the Harp. I do not hold that the last quartets are necessarily better than the middle ones. Certainly they are more mysterious, more curious, more exalted, but I care equally if not more for the lofty serenity of op. 59, N. 1. It's like the Archduke Trio. The night before my idyll was wrecked, I heard Schnabel play the Archduke, & she was at my side. That's the kind of serene climax we knew before desperation set in & screwed the strings till they screamed & snapped.

You've hit it perfectly in your last letter where you say that the best attribute of a life is that one be happy in his past. I think it wonderful that you have come through & are able to say that & to know it true for yourself. God knows it is for me too, but the war spared me. If you go to Berkeley on release, I'll try to schedule a trip north.

Cheers!
Larry

July 14, 1946
Minersville
ALS, 2 p., 1 sheet

Dear Larry:—

A good letter to mark the weekend. They had me on fire-standby and I couldn't leave camp—felt strangely confined, though there's not many places to go. I understand there's an old town site and a few graves a mile or so off, relic of the gold days. The country hereabouts is pock-marked with deserted mines. All the streams have been combed and combed. It's old gold country, and contains lore, but somehow all I feel about it I said in "Lines for the Last of a Gold Town," ten years ago.

In response to your query I borrowed a typewriter and typed up the final section of "Chronicle" for you. I wrote this at Cascade Locks, began it shortly after arriving there, and utilized some sea-scraps I had made just before leaving Waldport. It is a strange thing that it was only after leaving the sea that I felt I could come to terms with it in a poem. For three years I watched it, at first as an utter stranger, valley-man that I was, engrossed in it, but unable to arrive at any meaning in it for me, except in incidental flashes, as in some of the Waldport poems. But during my trouble with Edwa in 1944, under the influence of Clayton James and Morris Graves the painter, it became a thing of great solace. Somehow the answer lay out there in those great breakers, the tippage of it, the long heave, the champ. To strip and run out into that flashing has sheer exhilaration, the purest communion I have ever known.

But it was only last fall that I really got next to it. We worked on a site about 30 miles south of Camp Waldport, and every morning drove there, and every evening drove back, and that particular stretch of coast is the equal of any I've seen, including the Sur. But day after day I would watch it, from every angle as the road changed, in rain, in late sun and early, in fog, in dusk. And finally, after many weeks, I began to know it, to know what to expect of it. It was nothing I could put my finger on, but finally it did not seem remote any more, but mine, of me, of what I was, an intimacy, and for the first time it was like the Valley was for me, and I knew it.

This section draws from that.

It has been said that this section is too drastic a change in style and attitude to be part of the "Chronicle," and should be published separately. I should like your opinion on that. And on any details.

Are you still at Manning? I have sent my letters to the Library, not knowing where you were.

I read Fitzgerald's *The Great Gatsby* today, and liked it. All the way through I was uneasy, saying: this is not enough, there should be more here somehow, but he brought it to a close very well, and I laid it down content.

Bill

I applied for release the 10th. Let the clocks tick 'em off.

[July 24, 1946
Redding, Calif.]
APS

July Twenty Four
THIS IS IT!!

Bill

I'll write from Berkeley.

July 28, 1946
Berkeley 5
ALS, 2 p., 1 sheet

Dear Larry:—

It is Sunday. Nor can I tell you what it means to say that in these circumstances. For Sunday has not been Sunday for three-and-a-half years, save for the brevity of the furlough, but something else—a day of rest, and welcome, but not Sunday. For Sunday morning means coffee, coffee in thin cups over a late table; Sunday means Mozart and light in the room, the amplitude of spirit in its great abundance filling the room, imbued with the joy of living, the company of women, and the cigarettes over the many cups, and a poem hanging out there in the offing.

The last days at Minersville were crowded. Friday night a fire call came in from deep in the Trinity Forest, and we went, driving all night in the open truck, I plotting our course by the great circuit of the stars all night long. They gave us three hours' restless sleep after breakfast and Saturday afternoon we fought that fire, and mopped it up Sunday, and left Sunday night, and got back to camp near dawn Monday. Monday was ours; they gave us that; but Monday night lightning started another fire, and Tuesday we fought that. It was as I was getting off the truck Tuesday night that the government man came to me and told me. I stared at him in disbelief until it penetrated. Then I shouted JESUS CHRIST that must have been heard over in Humboldt County, and I ran.

That night they threw a little party down in a nearby cabin where a camper's wife stayed. I had helped them throw many a party for many an outgoing man, and now it was my turn; after all the months and the setbacks—now it was my turn.

So I left them, the next morning, going in to Redding on the government truck. I left them back there in that wilderness, with their congested lives, their baffled hopes, their enormous hunger, their multivarious needs. I had seen many a man go out that way and now it was my turn.

In five hours I was here with the Watkins in Berkeley. In three hours more I was sitting in on an exegesis of *Finnegans Wake,* with Robert Duncan presiding. Another life. Another time, what next, Lord?

To get the press out of hock; to get it set up and in operation; to begin the new integration.

Received your letter [missing from file] re Buffalo Library. No more *San Joaquin* but I'll send him *Ravens.*

When did you say you would next be here?

I go with Wilder today or tomorrow over to James Hart's to do some handprinting.

Bill

July 29 [i.e., 28], 1946
Sunday noon [Los Angeles]
ALS, 4 p.

Dear Bill—

Your joyous card came on the heels of your typescript. I shall write this note & await a Berkeley address from you. I read Pt. 5 through a couple of times & then last night I read clear through the 5 parts of the "Chronicle." I understand how one might feel that this latest part is a piece by itself. It is a withdrawn meditation that has no *obvious* link with what went before. I seem to remember comparing Pts. 1–4 with Meredith's *Modern Love;* Pt. 6 might be likened to one of the *Duino Elegies.* But I would reserve final judgement until I read Pt. 6 et seq. Then it may prove that this sombre threnody on an Oregon beach has a proper part in the whole. I found it very moving, &

mostly so when your gaze is outward, fastening on the gull on the wind's smoke or the sucked shell of the sandcrab, rather than when you turn inward & tend to obscure meaning by the over-use of long words of Latin origin. The "She" is not present to heighten & tighten the drama. Do you intend that the "Chronicle" keep growing, conditioned by events?

I am eager to hear of your arrival in Berkeley & of developments. We are not moved yet, but continue to write me at the Library. We hope to move within the next couple of weeks, & then to Colorado. I should like to come North via Big Sur in September.

Larry

Tuesday evening—July 30

Your Berkeley letter came this morning. A wonderful lyric cry. Go places now. There should be a long truce between wars. I feel surer than ever that you will pile up an increasingly rich store of poetry before your time comes to go beneath the blanket of earth. I cherish everything you have written. I carry it in my mind day & night. It has become part of me in the way Jeffers & Lawrence & Fisher & Miller & the middle-period MacLeish have. It is one of the rich threads in the beautiful tapestry of my life to this my 40th year.

Now you are free, & full of piss 'n vinegar. You don't need encouragement now. I merely want you to know that my belief in you as a man & writer & my friend has never been surer & stronger. You will write wonderful poems now from your new point of vantage in the world. Be God's secret spy. Rexroth's poet in skis. When a woman asked Renoir with what did he paint his pictures, he replied "With my penis, Madame, bien sure!" See that you root around with yours & then keep it stiff to write with. I have no fear that you will become an intellectual poet. Stay the poet of the entire body.

I was pleased to see the *Waldport Poems* in *New Directions IX.*

I greet you at the mid-point of a great career.

Hooray for Freedom.

Fuck all.

Larry

Treesbank
Rt 4, Box 426
Sebastopol, Calif.
Aug. 24, 1946
ALS, 1 p.

Dear Larry:—

Just a note to let you know where I am. I write in great haste between apple pickings. Arrived here about 10 days ago and set about making plans for the removal of my press to this wonderful Sonoma County farm. There is a great host of work to be done before I can begin, but things should move along.

Spent an idyllic three weeks in Berkeley. Went everywhere and saw everything. Worked with Wilder and Hart on the latter's handpress and got an inkling into what it's all about. Will write at greater length soon.

Bill

Bar Bell Ranch
Buford, Colorado
Aug. 26, 1946
APS

Dear Bill—

Our first visit here since 1940! Wonderful country—8000 ft.—on the White River. Am fishing & riding & loafing—Reading Wyndham Lewis's fine book on Villon. Going next to Fay's brother's ranch at Montrose, Colorado. Home in 2–3 weeks. Yippee!

LCP

Sept. 2, 1946
Montrose, Colo.
APS

We have moved south 200 miles from the White River & are visiting Fay's brother at Montrose. You ought to see me on an Arabian stallion—& not vice versa!

Larry

Ritchie is divorcing his wife.

September 7, 1946
3301 Kelton Ave.
Los Angeles 34
ALS, 2 p., 1 sheet

Dear Bill—

Back from our vacation trip to find your welcome letter. I want to hear more of your new location. Above is our new home address—3 miles directly south of Westwood Village, on the northern edge of Culver City—a small house on a little hill, with a steep terraced front yard & a wide view all around. A snug study.

I've been away from campus four weeks; the first week moving & then on our trip. I feel refreshed. We returned from Colorado via Mesa Verde & the Grand Canyon. Today I went to the Library & spent the morning working over accumulated mail & memoranda. We expect 15,000 students next week. Ouch!

I took on the trip D. B. Wyndham Lewis's book on Villon. It's a wonderful book. I recommend it to you, if you have not already read it. Also took Jacques LeClerc's modern translation of Rabelais. Good reading, but flat after Urquhart-Motteux. Like champagne that's lost its sparkle. Otherwise no reading. I fished for trout & rode horses & walked & sat.

I want to come north in a few weeks on university business & to see you. How are you fixed in your new place to see people? How far from Berkeley?

I was 40 on September 3d. God! Don't you have a birthday this month? Tell me.

Need to talk with you. Life is running out so fast, & I feel so acutely that I am not fulfilling my deepest potentialities. What are they? Self-delusion is so easy.

Affectionately
Larry

Sept. 18, 1946
Sebastopol
ALS, 2 p., 1 sheet

Dear Larry:

Today, after the many months, we assembled the press. That should make it a red-letter day on my all-time calendar. On the first of August Lee Watkins and I took my trailer over to San Francisco to Ed Ottsman's, on Sansome street, where the old monster had resided since my purchase of it last February. George Reeves of *Pacifica Views* and his brother-in-law came down and the four of us loaded it, piece by piece, and none of them light. We used the trailer we had made at Waldport to haul the Untide [Press] over the hump to Cascade Locks. Once loaded we brought it back to Berkeley and rolled trailer, press, and all into Lee's garage. I came up here in mid-August, helped immediately with the apple-harvest, and it wasn't till last Thursday I got back down to Berkeley. Ham [Tyler] brought the car down Friday, we hooked on and pulled her up here. Today we moved it into the old apple-dryer that is to make up my pressroom and living quarters, and put it together. It sits out there now, a monumental thing, the most beautiful and finest handpress within my limited experience. My fingers itch, but all the work of rebuilding the shed has yet to be done. We are making progress however, and by the rainy season things should be well lined out.

I stand on the threshold. I feel it. The consummation of a great dream. The country hereabouts is wonderful—a superb landscape, and beautiful region. We work with the apples, bringing them in to harvest. We build. All good labor—all good. My days have been too full to pick up pen, but now I'm moving out to my permanent quarters, with more relaxation—(I've been sleeping on a couch in the living room) and should be able to keep you better posted.

You say you're coming up. If you'll tell me when, I'll come into the city to meet you. Will you drive or by public conveyance? I look forward to seeing you again. There's much to tell, much to hear, and much to be done—

Bill

Sept. 19, 1946
Los Angeles
APS

Dear Bill—

I have extra copies of two books of poems by Lawrence Durrell—*A Private Country* & *Cities, Plains & People*. Have you read any of his work? I'll send you these books if you want them.

Larry

September 20, 1946
Los Angeles 34
ALS, 2 p.

Dear Bill—

On the eve of the equinox. Last year it brought wind & rain, but tonight is clear & warm, near the end of a hot dry week. Your letter today, telling of setting up the new press. Tell me whose place is Treesbank? You say you will come to the city to see me when I come north. Hell man, I want to come to see you in your press! I'll be driving, most likely, as I'll be going or coming via Big Sur, to pick up some archives from Henry.

Bern Porter [publisher of *Circle*] has turned over to the library his entire Miller collection—a rich haul. Will there be an extra cot in a corner of the press, or a hotel or auto court in nearby town? I do want to see your press & the country roundabout. And to have a long session or two free from interruption. Probably will be November before I can get away. My October trip will be south to La Jolla & Coronado to attend library meetings.

I sent you a card yesterday about Durrell's books. He & Rexroth are the only poets who have pleased me since God knows when.

This 10 × 10 study is cozy; windows on three sides. A new steel filing cabinet—something I have craved for years. Some tall dark oak bookshelves, not yet assembled. Netta Aldington's two portraits of Fay. My desk. My easy chair & straight work chair. We are increasingly happy in this little place. I look forward to a "season of teeming fruitfulness."

Unsubsiding waves of desire sweep over me. I think the only way I can calm down is to write the story. I don't know & won't until I do it. To have held an apple of Hesperides in hand & then to have put it away uneaten. Wild unreasonable regret. A fool at forty!

Larry

Sept. 23, 46
Treesbank
APS

Dear Larry:—

Your offer of the Durrell comes as a fine coincidence for we were about to order *Private Country*. Both Duncan and Ham know the work and speak highly of it, and I had been wanting to see it for some time now. The volumes will be warmly received and appreciated.

The work on the pressroom goes on—life here joyous and rich, with only an occasional war from family visits. Crown Oedipus king. He rules this world, believe me!

The equinoctial weather hereabouts quite warm—summer going out in its greatest blaze. Off there the sea, its light fogs once more emerging. All well, all good, all happy. Seeing you!

Bill

September 26, 1946
Los Angeles
ALS, 3 p.

Dear Bill—

I am glad my word reached you before you ordered Durrell's *Private Country*. His subsequent volume shows wonderful growth. I mail both to you. I am reading his prose book on Corfu, *Prospero's Cell*, but have alas no duplicate of it. I search for his other books. In the thousands of books which I handle each year so few, so very few of them hold magic for me. Durrell's do.

Good to see your poem in the new issue of *Circle*. Leite lifted the Durrell group from the Faber volume without so much as a credit line. He strikes me as a bit slippery.

Am eager for a letter from you.

Larry

later

P.S.

What is the magic that makes one book in ten thousand shine? Breadth of experience, depth of sympathy, height of awareness, power of expression—and character. If a writer possesses these things they are implicit in the smallest segment of his work—the page, the paragraph, the sentence; the stanza, the line, the word. I put this stick against each current little mag or book of verse or novel or autobiography that pauses beside my desk in its routine flow through the library to the stacks; against the *Circle!* Or music or painting. Any mode of creation. Very little measures anything at all.

I did this eight years ago when la belle Portère [Fay Porter] sent me a sheaf of your poems. I knew instantly that you had a destiny as a poet—& have believed it surely ever since. Do you now commence to print your "Chronicle"?

It is evening in my cell; nay, night. Rosh Hoshana & they play Hebrew music on the radio. Bloch, Wm. Walton, Schoenberg. I read a chapter in Durrell's *Prospero.* In Putnam's Rabelais. In the final volume of the Machen Casanova. At my hand is a rich letter from Richard Aldington in Paris. And your card, breathing serene content with your freedom. Apples be Ripe indeed! My cell measures 10 x 10. Small rooms discipline the mind. It pulses with the rich world's pulse. Corfu, the France of Rabelais & Aldington, Sebastopol, Calif! The mist arises the leaves fall, pour wine of seasons olden—and we will turn the gloomy days to golden, aye golden!

Strange that by this letter I send you word about two of my great maîtres—MacIntyre being the third. Please return the clippings.

Pax!
Larry

9–27-46
Sebastopol
ALS, 1 p.

Dear Larry:

It was not my thought to deflect you from my location! I merely thought to go in and accompany you out, but perhaps that would involve too much coordination. One of these times I'll draw a little map for you. It's easy enough to find.

I am on the farm of Hamilton and Mary Tyler. Ham is a friend from pre-war days, a Fresnan. He began as a scholar, doing a variorum edition of Lycidas, (as yet unpublished) and has since broadened out to other fields. You might have seen his essay on *Finnegans Wake* in *Circle,* the issue before this recent one. And, earlier, one on Eliot and Milton. He's writing a novel on Raleigh which I haven't seen yet, but God knows there's little enough time on a farm.

The work goes on. I hope to have my house habitable when you come. It's really a magnificent old structure, facing west across a valley to a soft ridge and a fine farm, sheltered from the south gales by a fine clump of redwood, looking over a good field. Built on the hillside as an old apple drier, I will live on the "ground floor" of one end, and operate the press on the floor level above.

Your disconsolate epigraph. Yes. The impossible choices. Unredeemable. The way not taken. Where lies fulfillment, when both are needful, and only one may be had? That is a thing we never know, eh? But be of good cheer; you richen, man, you ripen. More and more your letters savor of it. I think more than anyone I know you will not die empty. Rich-man; ripe-man.

I salute you
Bill

Oct. 14, 1946
Treesbank
ALS, 2 p., 1 sheet

Dear Larry:—

The Durrell books have been here a week or so. They make a fine autumnal gift for my 34th birthday. I like them, as books and as poems, favor particularly the *Cities, Plains & People,* with what I take to be its greater music, a more central rhythmic and emotional base, words grounded on a simpler center, not so concerned with purely verbal effects. Ham prefers *Private Country,* a long favorite of his. I shall read them many times.

Things rush on here. Just after receiving the books I went into Berkeley on a press-equipment expedition, stayed three or four days with Watkins. Edwa changed her attitude about the money [from their joint savings account], though I think reluctantly, but at her suggestion I took five hundred dollars and went about building up my workshop. This was a tremendously exciting thing for me. I have waited months, years. Now things draw to a focus.

Will use the Centaur types, which are manufactured in San Francisco, and hence readily available. Bought reglets and furniture, laid hands on a little paper, composing sticks, ink. The type has not yet come. But the press sits out there in its new room, monumental, a great thing to behold. South from its window the naked ridges dwindle away to the eye's failing, tawny, smoke shrouded.

Came back to find the open land on the farm burned off by fire, the redwood canyon cleaned out of its brush, but the great impervious trees unhurt. The fire broke loose again. We fought it in brush, and I took poison oak, am now swollen of arm!

A drunk had asked a farmer below us to take him home. On refusal, had threatened, left, set fire. Now he lies in jail. Society has triumphed! Justice is done! Are our burned acres, our spent labor, our swollen arms redeemed, now that he lies there? Pit unkindness against unkindness and the world grinds on.

Soon my house will be finished, and I can write again. After many hot days the sky now strains toward rain. Tonight will storm. The fields freshen. The year tips toward winter, the deepening fall, the autumn—

All things engender. The great cataract of life pitching forward, over the brink of time, forever and forever, I see life in transition extend its ever-unfolding veils, but not for nothing.

And you. There in your great complexity of life, like a king, with all the controls at your fingers. And your soft sensitivity in so many respects, your manfulness, your great ability to maintain your centralness of sensitivity and not grow hard, not bitter, not dead. You are fine, Larry. Fine and good.

Bill

October 16, 1946
La Jolla
ALS, 2 p.

Dear Bill—

Down here for a couple of days & nights to attend library conferences at the Scripps Institution of Oceanography & tomorrow at Coronado. Back home tomorrow night.

Night now & alone in a hotel room, number 1017, overlooking the ocean, the surf sound coming through the open window.

Have you been here? The ocean a deep dark blue. Cliffs of Sandstone. Brown hills. The celebrated Torrey pines. The town haunted by the walking dead—dowagers, retired industrialists, worse. All day long & not one woman to look twice at. Ah me!

Meeting over at four. At sunset a walk along the esplanade, the settling gulls, many planes overhead, a great sky cloudy sunset, the brown hills transmuted into gold.

Ah me Bill, I wish you were here now & we could settle down for a good long session of pure unadulterated bullshit.

My briefcase is hotch potch: The *NY Times Bk. Review,* the *Library Journal, College & Research Libraries* quarterly, dossiers on the meetings, package of dried black figs, & Durrell's *Corfu.* Wonderful book.

How did his poems hit you? Write, you lean lanky bastard.

I bought at Dawson's last week a fine edition of *The Tempest,* which snuggles next to *Prospero's Cell.* The Cambridge New Shakespeare, ed. by Quiller Couch & Dover Wilson—lovely little books designed by Bruce Rogers—I have just the one—but have ordered more from England.

Everson, what of the night? Powell sleeps. zzzz.

Larry

October 19, 1946
Los Angeles
ALS, 1 p.

Dear Bill—

Back from La Jolla to find your good letter. I hope you received one I wrote you from there, lacking your complete address.

With you I prefer Durrell's second book. To me it marks an impressive advance from *Private Country.* I'll try to find you a copy of his prose book on *Corfu*—a long prose poem—very fine. Am searching for his *Black Book,* which I have never read.

Three novels by Max White moved me to buy copies for myself: *Anna Becker* (1937), *Tiger Tiger* (1940), *In the Blazing Light* (1946). Ever read novels?

Pleased to hear of your purchases. What do you print first? I like Centaur. Hope to get away north about a month from now.

Yrs
Larry

November 2, 1946
Los Angeles 34
ALS, 1 p.

Dear Bill—

I am coming to Berkeley next week. Up on the night train, Sunday the 10th, back Wed. night. I shall have a car from the university garage & would like to come to your place Tuesday afternoon, spend the night & head back to Berkeley the next morning. Can you handle me overnight, or I can stay in Sebastopol, whichever is most convenient.

I'm certainly looking forward to a session with you. Thinking selfishly, I'd like to bring my journal along & relive last winter with you, if you would bear with me!

So let me hear from you, Bill, by return, if the above schedule is all right. And tell me how to get to your place from Berkeley.

Yrs.
Larry

Nov. 4, 1946
Treesbank
ALS, 2 p., 1 sheet

Dear Larry:—

I received both letters, the one from La Jolla, written in the night hours, from lonely hotel room no. 1017, overlooking the ocean, and the one following. I have never been to La Jolla; it chimes in my mind of the resort; and I am glad to be remembered in such places!

Well, I'm moved out into my own quarters at last. Though I've been sleeping here, only last week was a stove moved in, and I can really start to revolve in my own concentric swing again. There's a deal of patching to be done—hole plugging, crack-chinking etc: but I hope to have it shipshape for your visit. You'll sleep with me; and we'll have a breakfast of apple sauce, oatmeal mush, country eggs, wheatbread toasted, and piping coffee.

My type arrived. 18 pt. Centaur, and it's magnificent, a face of great strength and delicacy. Bruce Rogers designed it some thirty years ago, from the original face of Nicholas Jenson—but hell, you know all that. It's just that I'm becoming so engrossed in the love of this business one reference starts one off. I'm neglecting my other phases—have written hardly anything. But one can't go back once he gets in, but keeps pushing forward. I can't get books enough though. The library facilities in this county are most deplorable. (Can you lend me *Paragraphs on Printing* by Bruce Rogers and *Type Designs,* by A.F. Johnson, Grafton & Co., London 1934?)

You ask what I will print first. As I now see it, it will be the "Chronicle," though it's a pretty large work to begin on. But it stands first in line in my long-range program of writer-printer, and I should begin with it. I have encountered a central confusion that I can't quite resolve, or at least haven't, for the whole matter of publishing has suddenly been intensified by outside developments. You'll recall that *New Directions 9* contains the reprint of *The Waldport Poems.* Well, these have turned out to be about the most successful things in the book being highly praised in almost every review I've read. This is surprising, and I say it not out of modesty, but experience: the poems were either ignored or shrugged off in the original edition. But when brought out in the anthology, with a bona fide N.Y. publisher etc., etc.—you see? Anyway, Laughlin has been impressed, and wrote suggesting a "proper book" containing "Chronicle" and a liberal selection or composite of the earlier work. Of course, private and commercial publishing are not mutually exclusive, but the time element emerges.

Laughlin wants the book, and yet I want to do it here, this winter. I haven't discussed this with him; he's now in Europe, but expects to be on the coast this winter. All the San Francisco-Sonoma County group think I should get in print in N.Y., the sooner the better—especially Rexroth, who seems to have great influence with Laughlin, and who, in fact, is responsible for the New Directions reprint. He has done me much service in championing my work. To this add the additional confusion of what to include and exclude from a N.D. edition, and you have pay-off—everyone favoring different poems. I want to throw the whole thing up, many times. But I suppose it will gradually work itself out, as things always have.

Edwa was up a week ago, but a great many people were also. (We have a procession of guests here.) She is very beautiful, but hidden in reserve, wrapped in layer on layer of armour, impregnable. You would not know her. The gulf between us, the brutal years. I grope toward her but can't cross over, our present impulses sending us in opposite directions; she engrossed in her project of the kiln, I in my press. As for the others, all the good women of my age are married, and the youngsters are not mature. Besides, I haven't time! My work calls. So much to do in our time—as you, wrestling with mightier problems, and on a vaster scale, so well know. Bless you, Larry. It's all good.

Bill

November 19, 1946
Los Angeles
ALS, 4 p., 2 sheets

Dear Bill—

Safely home & back in harness. I got on the Owl in Berkeley & holed up in my bedroom, then opened my briefcase & pored over the inscriptions in your books. Neatly done, sir, and I thank you kindly! Had a wonderful night's sleep & woke at 6 somewhere in the Northern Antelope Valley. The desert was standing in rain. I got home to find 5 inches had fallen in Westwood! Our house proved snug & dry.

We are mailing you a package of books containing the Bruce Rogers & first 3 bound volumes of *Print* (loaned from the Library), and as presents from me to you: Fisher's *Ghost,* Mac's *Poems, Cafés & Cathedrals* & the *Brimming Cup.* You may keep the Library volumes until we have to call them in. No hurry. I found that we do not have Johnson's *Type Designs.* We are ordering from England. Be patient!

Tell Ham that we have only one of the books on his list: the Neve: and that is in the Clark & thus cannot be loaned. I'll try to borrow them for him from an eastern library.

I really cannot find words to tell you how deeply I enjoyed my visit to you. It stays with me like a bright autumn dream. Thank Ham & Mary again for me for their warm friendly hospitality. I was really touched. And I fell hard for Miss Tyler [the daughter]. She is incomparably the loveliest child I have seen in many a moon.

You are wonderfully fortunate, Bill, to be a part of that Treesbank idyll. Your every gesture there should prove a masterpiece.

Reading my notes to you gave me new insight into something I already knew from experience: that the raw stuff of experience, tumbled into a journal right after it happens, has no meaningful sequence, is banal, repetitious & cliché-ridden. You were very patient. The imagination has to sieve it fine & fire it in a new mold. That's what "Quintet" is. It came out of the rough ore of my journal. That's what must happen to this latter material, the most intrinsically rich I have ever mined. How & where I do not know, but I must not be impatient. I must forget it for awhile. I think I can now. I can see it clearly for what it is since reading to you.

When you get around to it, I'd like to have a copy of your woman poem.

Press ahead on printing the "Chronicle." Get your roof tight. Prune those trees, milk those cows. What a full rich life you're going to have.

Affectionately yrs.
Larry

December 2, 1946
Los Angeles
ALS, 1 p.

Dear Bill—

I have located a file of the *Experimental Review:* No. 1, spring 1940, No. 2, Jan. 1941, No. 3, Sept. 1941. Can you tell me or find out from Duncan whether this is all that was published?

Larry

Dec. 7, 1946
Berkeley, Calif.
ALS, 4 p., 2 sheets

Dear Larry:

The chain of events that has broken over me since I saw you will be too long to set down in any detail. I have wanted many times to write before this, but have not done so. You see by my letterhead that I am in Berkeley. I have been here almost two weeks. Mad weeks. But let me go back.

You left Treesbank on a Wednesday. The following Saturday she came on the place—almost as if she were blown in on the end of the fine first rain you brought with you. I knew her casually from the Berkeley group; had heard of her from Duncan for years. She paints and writes, and Edwa and I had bought a drawing of hers from Duncan years ago. She is an Italian girl, herself married, now divorced, about my own age. We watched each other across the table. That night there was jazz, and we danced, free improvisations, wonderful. Ham and Mary left the next day. She had come up with Hal's wife, Ricky, and they stayed on. The next night more dancing. As it broke up, I asked her if she would come to my shack. She looked at me out of her fine eyes and told me she could not, and touched my arm. The next day was rich, a watching, a hidden search for something between us. She left then, and in the days following I wrote this poem.

[The Sphinx]

All day my mind has fixed upon your face,
That drew me in the dance, yet was alone,
Saddened with a sorrow of its own;
And round that carven image wreathed a wraith,
As rain is wreathed across the graven stone.
Our years between us like twin rivers ran;
The dance you danced was on a nether shore;
Our bodies gestured but could do no more.
Like mutes we looked across that double span,
The years drew out their desultory roar.
Now in the dance's afterbeat I tread,
Stiff with constraint, and shuffle out its pace,
The sandy rivers merge about your face,
As round the monolith the rampant dead
Drain to their dim and unrevealing place.

That week word from Rexroth of a party in celebration of Lamantia's book. Sat. Nov. 23. I decided to go. To find out for myself. Well. She was there. I gave her the poem, asked to take her home. She said yes, that I could. We left early, (it was my first real literary party, and another story) and on the way home it began to kindle. She has a house near here on Ashby Avenue, lives with her sister- and brother-in-law, hers the upper story. But she asked me in, and we went up to that room, and that bed.

Since that time I have spent only one night away from there, and that for recuperation. I thought that I knew love, that I had been loved, but I did not really know. She gave herself to me in such [an] utter way. Always with Edwa I had to woo. With Mary my very touch kindles. She flames. She blazes under my hand, and I blaze. She draws out of me depths of potency I had no idea I possessed. The nights fall past us. We lie in the rare dawns and reduplicate the total love of the night. We find each other. Again and again we come back into each other, and are there revived, there blaze, there burn, there die and are reborn. She has a wonderful beauty of face, and beauty of soul. I find more and more of that in her—a great placidity of nature, a great temperateness of soul, a quietude of mind. And utter acceptance, utter enclosure. I am made new. I am. My disparate parts, scattered for many years by uncertainty, by self-doubt, by indecision, have been welded into a strong and masculine certitude that I never knew before. She is my woman. I possess her; in its complete and wholly meaningful sense. I possess her completely, and am hers, and have great surety in that knowledge, and am at one.

Well, the days go by. Soon I must leave and go back to Treesbank, to my press, to that life. I can hardly bear to leave her, but I must for the time. It will not be for long. I will let nothing come between us. For I have found a thing that I did not dream could be, and having at last been made whole, will not be divided again.

Today the Tylers came up. They brought me my sparse mail, with your letter about the *Experimental Review.* I think there were only the three issues. They might have counted that mimeographed *Ritual* as the first issue. I'm sure that those three titles you list are the only issued under that name. I'll ask Duncan.

Tylers said your books to me had been received and are safe. I look forward to seeing them.

From the heights of heaven, I salute you.

Bill

I go back to Treesbank, on Monday.

December 9,1946
Los Angeles
ALS, 2 p.

Dear Bill—

Your potent letter came this morning & nearly closed the library for the day. Tremendous! I cannot tell you how joyful I am for you.

I was not surprised though. I sensed you on the verge of a very rich period. I came away from Treesbank with that strong feeling. Everything there was rich. You couldn't miss in a setting like that—& with the richness of your own experience which you brought with you.

And so, I repeat, I am not surprised that a woman came to you on the tail of the storm.

Your wonderful poem to her.

O Bill, I am so happy for you! If ever a man deserved this experience, it is you. How well I know what it is to be healed by a woman's body! I have tried to write about it. My experience of last winter, incomplete. How glad I am that nothing prevented you from attaining complete fulfillment. So good. So very good.

I was at Newell's a week ago Saturday. He is painting some lovely pictures of men & women. No more abstracts. The luminous lambent human body, painted in warm tempera.

I spent a miserable weekend just past. Slowed down by rheumatism. Loafed & read. Happy with Fay, her comforting presence, but miserable from the unfulfillment. O perverse! Now only through writing it can I be fulfilled.

I send you the most formidable phallic salute!

Larry

12-13-46
Los Angeles
ALS, 2 p.

Dear Bill—

A little help on *Experimental Review,* please. Gotham Book Mart has sent what they describe as the first three numbers: the first is called *Ritual,* v. 1, N. 1, spring 1940 (& therein I see the name Mary Fabilli!). The second is called *Exp. Review* No. 2—Supplement, Jan. 1941—a half dozen page pamphlet. Question: is it a supplement to No. 2 or is it No. 2?

And finally, no. 3 in the orange covers, which I saw at Treesbank.

I'll appreciate your asking Duncan about this, or forwarding these pages to him & ask him to write me.

Thanks!

Larry

Dec. 13, 1946
Treesbank—
ALS, 5 p., 3 sheets

Dear Larry:—

Your good letter, your glad welcome: how good of you, to be so joyous at my own fortune. Myself I sing it to the sun. I float in it, upheld and buoyant. I am aloft.

I left Berkeley Monday with Jim Gallahan, a friend from camp, a proletarian, machinist, carpenter—he heard I had a press and thought he might be able to help me. A godsend. I needed the tympan and frisket fixed with hinges and we came up in his car, with Hal also, who had spent the weekend in the city. Well, it was hard to go. But when I arrived, I found that the typefounders had sent me the wrong fonts, in a large order recently: 16 on 18 pt. body instead of the 18 pt. Centaur I ordered. So. In I went with Jim. Called her up just after dark. What a reunion! We had looked forward to many bleak days and nights, and to find them vanquished so suddenly. We lay long abed, drinking in all that sweet rapture, fastened on one another. Finally the clock drove me out. In S.F. I adjusted my claim and came on up by bus. But that too was depressing.

Now, here at Treesbank, after four days, I know the end is in sight. I can't stay away. The whole quality of the place has altered, my heart is down there, with her. I cannot chance again on separation—lost one woman on it, will not risk another, a finer.

For she *is* finer. She is of a greater worth. Great as was our love, Edwa and I, but never like this. And after the injured years, the great hurt, the deep wounds. For though I poured out my passion to Edwa, in some deep and whole way it was not returned. Not that total compulsive spontaneous reciprocation that here obtains. Not that wholesale throwing aside of all defenses, shields, screens of the self, that utter exposure. For we do that. We strip our souls naked before each other—not by recounting our thoughts, by talking, but by that utter yielding, that throwing forward, that consummate and total giving outward—out of the self, out of its deep dungeons—throwing outward and into the other the whole nakedness of the soul. And to find it received, seized on, contained, enwrapped, loved—to see the face of that woman in her love of me is to have every scar and sore and wound and hurt of the heart wholly redeemed. I am healed. As purely and simply as that. All my old ghosts and devils sent flying, a huge rout of them scattered.

So it's good-bye Treesbank. And after all my work. No matter. First things first. The press venture is only postponed, not abandoned. I came back to give it a try, and it's no go. I'm not at ease here anymore. I long for that deep religiousness of intent we engender together. She is a wonderfully open and yet chaste woman: she brings to sex a kind of holiness, of attitude, not sanctimony, lord no, but as if it were in quality too fine to be tainted by any looseness, a sobriety and a gravity that are wholly wonderful, for it means, you see, that when she gives, she gives out of the very purity of the act, the gift and the counter-gift, and the final acceptance.

Larry, I'm almost beside myself. Not with madness but pure joy. I am serene inside for the first time in years. She wants children, badly—one of the reasons her other marriage failed. Very well, she shall have them. I fear nothing. Always before I feared. The thought of children terrified me. Now, I will not turn back from any natural requirement of life. I will not cut off my nose, any longer, to spite my face! My years in camp, through long hours of self analysis, considering the wreckage of my marriage, taught me that. The love of this woman confirms it. I go forward to meet whatever is required, with great joy, and serenity of soul.

So: first a divorce, then a new marriage, an operation, and the finding of a permanent place for my woman and my press. What an order! I've spent all my money on the press. I'll have to go to work and save. The thought staggers me, but tonight I have no fears. Time will tell all.

Sometimes I think I should hit for Nevada, take a temporary job, and get that divorce in the six weeks it takes, rather than the year it takes here. Know any ranchers over there, or any way of establishing residence? Mexico? etc. etc.?

Well. So much for that. I came back to find your great bounty of material. It had been opened and somewhat scattered by the others, (and found useful) and I missed the pleasure of opening and discovering that I love in packages—

but still, when I had it assembled, a very impressive haul. *The Ghost,* the MacIntyre books (that fine Ritchie item, a real charmer), the Bruce Rogers (which I read nightly). The magnificent *Print* collections. (Ever read Gregg Anderson's study of the Grabhorns? Probably the first time they've been really appraised by a man who was printer enough to do justice to their limitations and achievements. My opinion of Anderson soared.) I pore over them all. Thanks, thanks, many many thanks. You are a real and true friend.

Did I ever answer your first letter from your visit? I wanted to tell you I was dissatisfied with my inscription, that I had made two casual ones before I hit on the idea of relating each book to our mutual past. Too bad.

You must not discredit your journal because it seemed raw, for it is a naked and trembling account. In your exposure you get things a more judicious craftsmanship would have overlooked. That will come later. But as a personal journal, those accounts of yours are rare indeed. Don't lose 'em!

Ah love! love! love! love! love!

I burn with it!
Bill

Forgot to tell you I had resolved the question of the ND [New Directions] ms. Earlier, in desperation at the counter-purpose about what should be included I had thought one way out was to have a single person to make a selection—that would relieve me of the responsibility of appearing above a selected work—and approached Rexroth as a logical choice. However, he didn't think the work should be so presented, and anyway, only the first three volumes required editing. So on this last trip down we talked it over and arrived at a solution quite satisfactory to me: the book divided into 3 sections. No 1—"Chronicle of Division," entire. No 2—*Poems MCMXLII, Residual Years,* and *War Elegies* (the latter retitled and rearranged), entire, No 3—Rexroth's selections from *Masculine Dead, San Joaquin,* and *Ravens.* He's done a close and judicious job of selection—not the poems I would have, but his approach is consistent, and has thrown out most of the doubtful ones. I'm satisfied. Laughlin should be here any day. I typed up the ms. while in Berkeley, at Watkins. Wonderful thing: love all night and far into the day, in great wonder and languor at each other's presence, then arise, go to Watkins and type on my poems. They all seemed of a piece! All true, the true tone, the true creativity. I became proud of them! Ah me!

Dec. 16, 1946
Treesbank
ALS, 1 p.

Dear Larry:—

Your note today on *E.R.* The supplement you inquire about is not No. 2. No. 2 is a full-sized magazine the same proportions as the No. 3 you saw here. No. 2 appeared in Nov. 1940. Its contents: cover by Robert Symmes (Duncan. He's an adopted boy and changed back to his blood-name just after this). "Twelve Poems" by Sanders Russell. "Feast Day" by Wm. Everson. "The House of Incest," by Anaïs Nin. "Song" by Thomas Merton. "Toward the Shaman" by Robert Symmes. Drawing by Mary Fabilli. "Journal" by Aurora Bligh (Mary Fabilli. She's written in the Surrealist idiom under this pen name for *E. R., New Directions* 8 and *Circle*. No not *Circle*. Own name.) "The Sermon" by Lawrence Durrell, "Geography" by Harvey Breit, "Lies to the Young" by Breit, "Cathedral," by Virginia Admiral. "Sea Tower" by Jack Johnson, excerpts from Lao-Tse. Review of Patchen's *Albion* by Miller. Review of Miller's *Capricorn* by Symmes. Incidentals.

I have the supplement you mention but can't find it and can't remember what's in it. I believe it was the only supplement. So does Tyler.

Duncan is in Berkeley, but moving around and I've lost touch with him. I'll see him this week though. He's not a "faithful" correspondent—albeit a terrific one.

I go down in a couple of days. Better write me next at Watkins.

Bill

December 21, 1946
Los Angeles
ALS, 2 p.

Dear Bill—

Your lovely lyrical letter of the 13th, telling of the growth of your love, thrilled me deeply. Whatever you do now with her will be good, I am convinced of that. The idyll will change, no doubt, but into something rich & deep & not strange! O believe it!

I talked to Bieler. If you want him to, he will untie your tubes. He cannot guarantee success. I do not believe that he will charge you for the operation. He is a skillful surgeon. I want you two to meet. He has had a deep faith in your work from the beginning.

Hate to see you leave Treesbank. You can't take Mary with you, no?

Fay has an aunt in Fallon, Nevada, about 60 m. E. of Reno, but I doubt she would need any ranch help in winter. Want me to make an inquiry?

Good news about Rexroth & your book. I have great confidence in his selection. You couldn't have had a better editor. Glad that Laughlin did not do the picking. I have no liking for his taste.

Mailed you yesterday a little keepsake, done for her, my lost love—but will not dare to send it to her.

This is a good winter down here, cold & wet & foggy, for a change, after too many dry seasons. Solstice today.

Your letter & what has happened to you is very beautiful and wonderful. I rejoice for you with all my heart. Now you will write a book of love poems that will shine for lovers & warm them too, forever & ever, amen.

Larry

Sunday Dec. 29, 1946
Berkeley
ALS, 2 p.

Dear Larry:—

I am writing from Mary's house and do not have your last letter, brought down from Treesbank, by me; but the little *Daphnis & Chloe,* which is really a wonderful little keepsake, is here, and I'm reading it again. I am impelled to pick up this pen and this distressing ink, and write you again.

My address is 2918 Wheeler, as before. I came down from Treesbank on the Thursday before Christmas, and do not expect to go back, save on visits. The day before Christmas I began work at Creed's Book Store near the campus on Telegraph Ave.—a crowded dusty place stacked ceiling high with all manner of stuff, good, bad, and atrocious, and finished out the week. My work has been mostly alphabetizing the various sections which have been in huge disorder. I hope eventually to get in some binding and pick up that aspect of bookmaking while I have to stay in the city. I am going to try at the University of California Press, as I'd rather work there than any place else I know of.

From Treesbank I wrote Edwa about Mary and discussing the divorce. Day before yesterday I got a reply: the first part written immediately on receipt of my letter, and sad and rather anguished; the second part written days later and rather matter of fact. So I go ahead with the divorce. From here, I think: suffer out the year it takes in the California courts. What a barbarous practice!

But the nights are good. Long and rich. Have like a new life everywhere. As I walk these streets I see her face in every face.

Laughlin came to S.F. and left without seeing me. He and his wife were fighting: things very unsettled. Rexroth says to send the ms. on to him, but I haven't done it yet. I'm just a bit piqued by a man who tells me to hold a ms. for months till he can come out and see me, then leaves after two days without a word.

Best to you and Fay in the
New Year!

Bill

INDEX

All titles of books, poems, or other writings are listed under the writer's name. Topical discussions can be found under appropriate terms—art, music, conscientious objection, draft, war, and the like. Sub-entries are arranged chronologically.

The two correspondents are designated by WE for Everson, LCP for Powell. FAW stands for the Fine Arts at Waldport.

ABOUT THE AUTHORS

William Everson was born in Sacramento, California, and grew up in Selma, Fresno County. Here he came of age, launched his vocation as a poet, married, and planted a vineyard, substantially putting down roots. World War II shattered that dream. Drafted as a conscientious objector he spent three-and-a-half years planting trees in the wintertime and fighting fires in summer, besides heading a fine arts project after hours. Following the War he remarried, but soon converted to Catholicism, shortly entering the Dominican Order as a lay monk, receiving the name Brother Antoninus, the name under which he became well-known, reading his verse and performing to national audiences. After 13 years he left the Dominicans to remarry and accepted a post as Poet in Residence at the University of California, Santa Cruz. He has published some fifty titles of poetry, broadsides, and scholarship, and is a handpress printer of distinction. His honors include, among many, a Guggenheim Fellowship, a National Endowment of the Arts grant, and the Shelley Memorial Award. Bill Everson died in June 1994.

Lawrence Clark Powell, librarian, teacher, writer, and mentor, is pursuing his third career. Born in 1906, he celebrated 1991 with the publication of his four novels collected in one volume and gave the keynote address to the California Library Association. In the years between, after earning a doctorate at Dijon with a dissertation on Robinson Jeffers, he was elevated from a beginning position at the UCLA library to its director, headed also UCLA's rare book library donated by William Andrews Clark, and set the pace for the UCLA library to become a true partner to the University's much older library at Berkeley. The second career was to create one of the best library schools in the nation, recruiting an outstanding faculty and requiring that entering students show not only commitment to the profession, but zeal and enthusiasm. After early retirement in 1966, he moved to Arizona where he became in 1971 advisor to two presidents of the University, recruited a new librarian, and helped the library school there achieve accreditation. As mentor, his countless speeches, lectures, and writings drew many to the profession and confirmed others in their practice of it. He was president of the Bibliographical Society of America, received the Clarence Day Award and honorary membership from the American Library Association, and twice was a Guggenheim Fellow. When he retired from UCLA, the Regents of the University named the original library building the Powell Library.

ABOUT THE EDITOR

William R. Eshelman, is involved in writing and editing after a bifurcated career of practicing librarian and editor/publisher. Soon after obtaining his A.B. in 1943, he was drafted as a conscientious objector and sent to the Civilian Public Service Camp at Waldport, Oregon, where he met Everson. There he appeared in plays, wrote poetry, but mostly became a mainstay of the Untide Press, which published a series of chapbooks of poetry. After demobilization, he entered UCLA with the intention of earning a doctorate in literature, but was diverted to librarianship by Powell. With the M.A. from UCLA, he spent a year at Berkeley to obtain the B.L.S. and joined the library staff at what is now known as California State University at Los Angeles. After eight years in various positions he was put in charge of the library and developed a collegial form of administration. Six years later, in 1965, he was made University Librarian and Professor of Bibliography at Bucknell University in Lewisburg, Pennsylvania. There he revived a somnolent library, recruiting new staff, renovating the building, upgrading service to students, and forging ties to the faculty. An invitation to become editor of the *Wilson Library Bulletin,* one of two independent national journals in the field, drew him to New York City in 1968. After a decade, having produced one hundred issues for *WLB*'s 38,000 readers, he became president of The Scarecrow Press, publisher of books for libraries, where he oversaw the production of some 700 titles. He retired in 1986, founded a private press to produce chapbooks of poetry, and continues writing and editing.